W9-DCD-005

FOURTH EDITION

World Politics

Interests, Interactions, Institutions

FOURTH EDITION

World Politics

Interests, Interactions, Institutions

Jeffry A. Frieden
Harvard University

David A. Lake
University of California, San Diego

Kenneth A. Schultz
Stanford University

W. W. Norton & Company
New York • London

W. W. Norton & Company has been independent since its founding in 1923, when William Warder Norton and Mary D. Herter Norton first published lectures delivered at the People's Institute, the adult education division of New York City's Cooper Union. The firm soon expanded its program beyond the Institute, publishing books by celebrated academics from America and abroad. By midcentury, the two major pillars of Norton's publishing program — trade books and college texts — were firmly established. In the 1950s, the Norton family transferred control of the company to its employees, and today — with a staff of four hundred and a comparable number of trade, college, and professional titles published each year — W. W. Norton & Company stands as the largest and oldest publishing house owned wholly by its employees.

Copyright © 2019, 2016, 2013, 2010 by W. W. Norton & Company, Inc.

All rights reserved

Printed in Canada

Editor: Ann Shin

Associate Editors: Emily Stuart and Samantha Held

Project Editor: David Bradley

Editorial Assistant: Anna Olcott

Manuscript Editor: Stephanie Hiebert

Managing Editor, College: Marian Johnson

Managing Editor, College Digital Media: Kim Yi

Production Manager: Eric Pier-Hocking

Media Editor: Spencer Richardson-Jones

Associate Media Editor: Michael Jaoui

Media Project Editor: Marcus Van Harpen

Assistant Media Editor: Ariel Eaton

Ebook Production Manager: Mateus Manço Teixeira

Ebook Production Coordinator: Lizz Thabet

Marketing Manager, Political Science: Erin Brown

Design Director: Rubina Yeh

Photo Editor: Catherine Abelman

Permissions Manager: Megan Jackson Schindel

Composition: Graphic World

Manufacturing: Transcontinental Interglobe, Inc.

Permission to use copyrighted material is included on p. A-9

Library of Congress Cataloging-in-Publication Data

Names: Frieden, Jeffry A., author. | Lake, David A., 1956- author. | Schultz,
     Kenneth A., author.
Title: World politics : interests, interactions, institutions / Jeffry A.
     Frieden, Harvard University, David A. Lake, University of California, San
     Diego, Kenneth A. Schultz, Stanford University.
Description: Fourth edition. | New York : W.W. Norton & Company, [2019] |
     Includes bibliographical references and index.
Identifiers: LCCN 2018006585 | ISBN **9780393644494** (paperback)
Subjects: LCSH: International relations.
Classification: LCC JZ1242 .F748 2019 | DDC 327—dc23 LC record available at
     https://lccn.loc.gov/2018006585

W. W. Norton & Company, Inc., 500 Fifth Avenue, New York, NY 10110
wwnorton.com

W. W. Norton & Company Ltd., 15 Carlisle Street, London W1D 3BS

1 2 3 4 5 6 7 8 9 0

Contents in Brief

Contents

Part Two: War and Peace

Chapter 5: International Institutions and War   186

Chapter 6: Violence by Nonstate Actors: Civil War and Terrorism   236

Part Three: International Political Economy

Chapter 10: Development: Causes of the Wealth and Poverty of Nations

424

Part Four: Transnational Politics

Part Five: Looking Ahead

Preface

As this textbook has evolved over the course of four editions, we have been guided throughout by two principles that spurred our enthusiasm for the project and that, we believe, make this textbook special. First, this text is organized around substantive puzzles that draw scholars and students alike to the study of world politics. This is a field that grapples with some of the most interesting and important questions in political science: Why are there wars? Why do countries have a hard time cooperating to prevent genocides or global environmental problems? Why are some countries rich while others are poor? This book gives students the tools they need to start thinking analytically about the answers to such questions. Second, we have sought to bridge the gap between how scholars of international relations conduct their research and how they teach their students. The text draws from the insights and findings of contemporary international relations scholarship, and presents them in a way that is accessible to undergraduates who are just starting out in this field. Our ambition is to provide students with a "toolbox" of analytic concepts common to many theories of world politics that can be applied to a wide variety of topics. We hope to lay a solid foundation on which students can build their own understanding of the continually evolving world of international politics.

The core concepts in this toolbox are interests, interactions, and institutions. Chapter 2 presents the framework, and the remaining chapters apply it. The book is organized around the principle that problems in world politics can be analyzed using these key concepts:

- Who are the relevant actors and what are their interests?

- What is the nature of their interactions? What strategies can they be expected to pursue? When are their choices likely to bring about cooperation or conflict?

- How do institutions constrain and affect interactions? How might they impede or facilitate cooperation? When and how do institutions favor different actors and their interests?

Different problems and issues will emphasize interests, interactions, or institutions to varying degrees. There is no single model of world politics that applies equally to war, trade and international financial relations, and the struggles for improved human rights and a cleaner global environment. Nonetheless, any complete understanding must include all three concepts. Although we do not refer extensively to the traditional paradigms based on realism, liberalism, and constructivism in the book, we show briefly in the Introduction how each of these major "-isms" of international relations theory can be understood as a different set of assumptions about interests, interactions, and institutions in world politics.

Plan of the Book

This book has five parts. The first part (Chapters 1 and 2) introduces the broad patterns of conflict and cooperation in international history and lays out the text's framework. Part Two (Chapters 3 through 6) deals with the central puzzles in the study of war and political violence:

- Given the human and material costs of military conflict, why do countries sometimes wage war rather than resolve their disputes through negotiations? (Chapter 3)

- What if there are actors within a country who see war as beneficial and who expect to pay few or none of its costs? Do countries fight wars to satisfy influential domestic interests? (Chapter 4)

- Why is it so hard for the international community to prevent and punish acts of aggression among and within states? (Chapter 5)

- Why is so much political violence in the contemporary world conducted by or against nonstate actors, including rebel groups and terrorist organizations? Why do people sometimes use violence against their own governments or unarmed civilians? (Chapter 6)

Part Three (Chapters 7 through 10) discusses the main puzzles in international economic relations:

- Why are trade barriers so common despite the universal advice of economists? Why do trade policies vary so widely? (Chapter 7)

- Why is international finance so controversial? Why are international financial institutions like the International Monetary Fund so strong? (Chapter 8)

- Why do countries pursue different currency policies, from dollarizing or joining the euro, to letting their currency's value float freely? (Chapter 9)

- Why are some countries rich and some countries poor? (Chapter 10)

Part Four (Chapters 11 through 13) considers relatively new issues associated with global governance:

- How can the international community constrain a sovereign state's actions? When and why do states do what is "right"? (Chapter 11)

- Why do countries sometimes try to protect the human rights of people outside their borders? In light of widespread support for the principle of human rights, why has the movement to protect those rights not been more successful? (Chapter 12)

- Given that nearly everyone wants a cleaner and healthier environment, why is it so hard to cooperate internationally to protect the environment? (Chapter 13)

Part Five presents the concluding chapter (Chapter 14), which considers a variety of challenges to the international system in the coming decades, including the spread of weapons of mass destruction, the rising power of China, and a growing backlash against globalization.

Pedagogical Features: Applying the Concepts

Our approach to the study of international relations is problem-oriented. Each chapter begins with a puzzle about world politics: a question or set of questions that lack obvious answers. We then use the concepts of interests, interactions, and institutions — along with known empirical regularities, current research results, and illustrative cases — to "solve" the puzzle and lead students to a deeper understanding of world politics. Each chapter includes numerous pedagogical features intended to helps students learn — and apply — the concepts.

- **"Thinking Analytically"** sections at the start of each chapter preview how the concepts of interests, interactions, and institutions are used in the chapter's analysis.

- **"What Shaped Our World?"** boxes apply the interests, interactions, and institutions framework to explain historical events that continue to shape contemporary world politics and illustrate the analytic theme of the chapter.

- **"Controversy"** boxes probe ethical issues to stimulate classroom discussion and show how interests, interactions, and institutions can help us understand — if not necessarily resolve — the difficult normative trade-offs involved.

- **"How Do We Know?"** boxes survey published research findings and describe empirical facts or regularities that are important for understanding the larger puzzle discussed in the chapter.

- **"Study Tool Kit"** sections at the end of each chapter include key terms, further readings, and "Interests, Interactions, and Institutions in Context" sections that review key analytic insights in the chapter.

Innovative Online Resources for Students and Instructors

This Fourth Edition of *World Politics* is accompanied by an innovative formative assessment tool: InQuizitive. Developed by a team of *World Politics* users directed by Dustin Tingley (Harvard University) in close collaboration with the textbook authors, InQuizitive for *World Politics* helps students get the most out of their reading assignments. After students work through a few basic questions on key concepts and definitions, InQuizitive asks them to try their hand at applying the concepts from the text to alternative examples and cases. The result is deeper engagement with the text and a clear sense of how these concepts can be applied to real-world situations. See the back cover for more information.

An extensive set of additional materials for instructors and students supports this book's goal of making an analytical approach to world politics accessible to introductory-level students. The Coursepack, which you can upload into your campus's Learning Management System (LMS), offers chapter-based assignments, quizzes, and test banks, as well as assessments tied to "Controversy" analytical thinking questions and unique Bargaining Tutorials and Interactives. InQuizitive is also available with the coursepack; grades from InQuizitive can automatically populate the LMS gradebook, and sign-on is simple for your students. Speak with your Norton representative to set up InQuizitive in your LMS.

For instructors, Norton offers a Test Bank, an Interactive Instructor's Guide, and sets of lecture and art PowerPoint slides—all of which have been developed specifically to accompany *World Politics*.

Acknowledgments

We owe many debts in preparing this text. Roby Harrington at Norton brought us together and encouraged us to write this book. His vision, judgment, and steady editorial hand are reflected throughout. Ann Shin at Norton expertly guided the project from first draft to finished product and educated us in the art of writing and revising a textbook. The final form and content of this book reflect her efforts to keep three sometimes over-committed academics on track, on theme, and on time. We are grateful also to the rest of the Norton team that worked on this Fourth Edition, including associate editors Emily Stuart and Samantha Held, for their thoughtful editorial suggestions; David Bradley, for his work as project editor; and Stephanie Hiebert, for her thorough copyediting. Editorial assistant Anna Olcott helped keep the many pieces of the manuscript moving throughout the process, and production manager Eric Pier-Hocking kept a close eye on the quality of the printed book as all those pieces came together. Spencer Richardson-Jones, Michael Jaoui, and Ariel Eaton brought creativity and order to the development of the ancillary resources. We owe thanks to all of them.

We are enormously grateful to the many reviewers and class-testers who provided guidance and helpful comments at many different stages of this project. For their advice on the First Edition, we would like to thank

Rodwan Abouharb, *Louisiana State University*
Karen Adams, *University of Montana*
Todd Allee, *University of Illinois, Urbana-Champaign*
Juliann Allison, *University of California, Riverside*
Claire Apodaca, *Florida International University*
Alan Arwine, *Texas Tech University*
Robert Brown, *Temple University*
Renato Corbetta, *University of Alabama, Birmingham*
Andrew Cortell, *Lewis & Clark College*
Benjamin Fordham, *Binghamton University*

Giovanna Gismondi, *Ohio University*

Darren Hawkins, *Brigham Young University*

Paul Hensel, *Florida State University*

Uk Heo, *University of Wisconsin, Marathon*

Tobias Hofmann, *College of William & Mary*

Elizabeth Hurd, *Northwestern University*

Michael Kanner, *University of Colorado, Boulder*

Scott Kastner, *University of Maryland*

Jonathan Keller, *James Madison University*

Alan Kessler, *University of Texas*

Andy Konitzer, *Samford University*

David Leblang, *University of Virginia*

Ashley Leeds, *Rice University*

Lisa Martin, *University of Wisconsin*

Ronald Mitchell, *University of Oregon*

Will H. Moore, *Florida State University*

Layna Mosely, *University of North Carolina*

Robert Packer, *Pennsylvania State University*

Robert Pahre, *University of Illinois, Urbana-Champaign*

Glenn Palmer, *Pennsylvania State University*

Leanne Powner, *College of Wooster*

Tonya Putnam, *Columbia University*

Stephen Quackenbush, *University of Missouri*

John Quinn, *Truman State University*

Robert Rauchhaus, *University of California, Santa Barbara*

Chad Rector, *George Washington University*

Dan Reiter, *Emory University*

Stephen Saideman, *McGill University*

Idean Salehyan, *University of North Texas*

Todd Sechser, *University of Virginia*

Megan Shannon, *University of Mississippi*

Randolph Siverson, *University of California, Davis*

Oleg Smirnov, *Stony Brook University*

Mark Souva, *Florida State University*

Patricia Sullivan, *University of Georgia*

Hiroki Takeuchi, *Southern Methodist University*

Aleksandra Thurman, *University of Michigan*

Kelly Wurtz, *Trinity College*

For the Second Edition, we received helpful advice from the following reviewers:

David Andersen, *CSU Sacramento*

Philip Barker, *Austin College*

Marijke Breuning, *University of North Texas*

Tom Brister, *Wake Forest University*

Terry Chapman, *University of Texas at Austin*

John Conybeare, *University of Iowa*

Michaelene Cox, *Illinois State University*

Monti Datta, *University of Richmond*

David Dreyer, *Lenoir-Rhyne University*

Sean Ehrlich, *Florida State University*

Traci Fahimi, *Irvine Valley College*

David Grondin, *University of Ottawa*

Surupa Gupta, *University of Mary Washington*

Tamar Gutner, *American University*

Yoram Haftel, *University of Illinois at Chicago*

Phil Kelly, *Emporia State University*

Robert S. Kravchuk, *University of North Carolina-Charlotte*

Ashley Leeds, *Rice University*

Anika Leithner, *California Polytechnic State University*

Doug Lemke, *Pennsylvania State University*

Lisa Martin, *University of Wisconsin-Madison*

Molly Melin, *Loyola University Chicago*

Amanda Murdie, *Kansas State University*

Rusty Nichols, *Southwestern College*

Richard Nolan, *University of Florida*

Ausra Park, *Davidson College*

Mark Pollack, *Temple University*

Kathy Powers, *University of New Mexico*

Melanie Ram, *California State University, Fresno*

Dan Reiter, *Emory University*

Kirsten Rodine Hardy, *Northeastern University*

Stephen Saideman, *McGill University*

Chris Saladino, *Virginia Commonwealth University*

Susan Sell, *George Washington University*

Megan Shannon, *University of Mississippi*

Nicole Simonelli, *Purdue University*

Oleg Smirnov, *Stony Brook University*

Mark Souva, *Florida State University*

Allan Stam, *University of Michigan*

Richard Stoll, *Rice University*

Jelena Subotic, *Georgia State University*

Joel Trachtman, *Tufts University*

James Walsh, *University of North Carolina at Charlotte*

Jesse Wasson, *Rochester Institute of Technology*

Jeremy Youde, *University of Minnesota Duluth*

For their valuable suggestions for the Third Edition, we thank

Klint Alexander, *Vanderbilt University*

Sarah Bush, *Temple University*

Jennifer De Maio, *California State University, Northridge*

Erik Gartzke, *University of California, San Diego*

Amy Gurowitz, *University of California, Berkeley*

Marcus Holmes, *Fordham University*
Jesse Johnson, *Kansas State University*
Joon Kil, *Irvine Valley College*
Jenn Larson, *New York University*
Kyle M. Lascurettes, *Lewis & Clark College*
Brooke Miller, *Middle Georgia State College*
Paul Musgrave, *Georgetown University*
Simon Nicholson, *American University*
Dave Ohls, *American University, School of International Service*
Andy Owsiak, *University of Georgia*
Tonya Putnam, *Columbia University*
Ryan Salzman, *Northern Kentucky University*
Randolph Siverson, *University of California, Davis*
Adam Van Liere, *University of Wisconsin, La Crosse*
Byungwon Woo, *Oakland University*

For their advice on this Fourth Edition, we would like to thank
Michael Allen, *Boise State University*
Juliann Emmons Allison, *University of California, Riverside*
Thomas Ambrosio, *North Dakota State University*
Constantine Boussalis, *Trinity College Dublin*
Marissa Brookes, *University of California, Riverside*
Thomas Chadefaux, *Trinity College Dublin*
Stephen Chaudoin, *University of Illinois at Urbana-Champaign*
Olga Chyzh, *Iowa State University*
Jennifer Clemens, *University of Wisconsin, Milwaukee*
David Dreyer, *Lenoir-Rhyne University*
Imad El-Anis, *Nottingham Trent University*
Henry Esparza, *University of Texas, San Antonio*
Songying Fang, *Rice University*
Richard Frank, *Australian National University*
Arman Grigoryan, *Lehigh University*
Jillienne Haglund, *University of Kentucky*
Anjo G. Harryvan, *University of Groningen*
Jeff Kaplow, *College of William & Mary*
Barbara Koremenos, *University of Michigan*
Jenn Larson, *New York University*
Dirk Leuffen, *University of Konstanz*
Yonatan Lupu, *George Washington University*
Elizabeth Menninga, *University of Iowa*
Amanda Murdie, *University of Georgia*
João Nunes, *University of York*
Andrew Owsiak, *University of Georgia*
Lindsay Reid, *University of California, Davis*
Cynthia Roberts, *Hunter College*
Megan Shannon, *University of Colorado*

Carolyn Somerville, *Hunter College*
Feng Sun, *Troy University*
Taku Tamaki, *Loughborough University*
Daniel Thomas, *Leiden University*
Jakana Thomas, *Michigan State University*
Matt Wahlert, *Miami University*
Geoffrey Wallace, *University of Washington*
Neil Winn, *University of Leeds*

For research assistance, we thank Cynthia Mei Balloch, Eric Belz, Jeffrey Bengel, Charles Frentz, Lonjezo Hamisi, Oliver Kaplan, Aila Matanock, Brandon Merrell, Allison Myren, Alexander Noonan, Priya Rajdev, Rachel Schoner, and Stephanie Young. For this edition, Deborah Seligsohn assisted with the extensive revisions to Chapter 13 on the environment. We also thank Helena de Bres of Wellesley College for her thoughtful ideas and hard work on the "Controversy" boxes in the First Edition and David Singer of MIT for his work on the figures and boxes in the international political economy chapters in previous editions, some of which carry over into this Fourth Edition. Nancy Frieden graciously hosted an authors' meeting. Robert Trager of the University of California, Los Angeles, developed simulations and interactive bargaining models to accompany the text. Vasabjit Banerjee of Mississippi State University created content for the online Coursepack. Susan Sell of George Washington University revised the PowerPoint set that accompanies the book. Sean Ehrlich of Florida State University, Jillienne Haglund of the University of Kentucky, Steven Hall of Ball State University, Nina Kollars of Franklin & Marshall College, and Jakana Thomas of Michigan State University spent many hours working on the Test Bank for the Fourth Edition. James Igoe Walsh of the University of North Carolina at Charlotte brought his experience as a teacher to the Interactive Instructor's Guide for the Fourth Edition. Dustin Tingley of Harvard University and Lisa McKay helped develop the InQuizitive course that accompanies the book, which was executed by the talented author team of Celeste Beesley of Brigham Young University, Daniel Fuerstman of the State College of Florida, Steven Hall of Ball State University, and Lisa McKay. We are grateful for their contributions to the project.

Introduction

What Is World Politics and Why Do We Study It?

On May 1, 1921, a storm of violence broke out between Arabs and Jews living in Palestine.[1] Tensions between the communities were already high because Arabs resented the influx of Jewish migrants into the area and the encroachment of Jewish neighborhoods onto Arab-owned land. But the violence that began that day started from a misunderstanding. When a May Day demonstration by Jewish Marxists in Tel Aviv got out of control, police shot into the air to disperse the crowd. Arabs in nearby Jaffa interpreted the gunfire as the start of an attack and started killing Jews and smashing their shops. When Jews rushed out to confront them, a battle broke out.

In the midst of the violence, a rabbi named Ben-Zion Uziel donned his rabbinical robes, walked out between the two sides, and implored them to go back to their homes. The rabbi urged both sides to forswear war and instead focus on creating prosperity that all could enjoy: "We say to you that the land can bear all of us, can sustain all of us. Let us stop the battles among ourselves, for we are brothers."[2]

Chroniclers of this episode suggest that the appeal worked: the gunfire stopped, and the armed bands went home.[3] If so, the effect was at best temporary. The turmoil of 1921 continued for several days and spread to other parts of the country. Fighting between Arabs and Jews would begin anew only eight years later. In 1948, the state of Israel was created on that land, and that state has since seen frequent clashes with neighboring Arab states and with the stateless Palestinian people who once lived there. The Arab-Israeli conflict is one of the most intractable and dangerous rivalries in the world today. Still, as one scholar notes, "on that day in 1921, some men who otherwise would have died went home to enjoy life with their families."[4]

Though little more than a footnote in history, this anecdote illustrates what we study when we study world politics, and why we study it. The field of world politics — also called *international relations* — seeks to understand how the peoples and countries of the world get along. As the account suggests, international

---

1. For a discussion of the violence and its causes, see Mark Levine, *Overthrowing Geography: Jaffa, Tel Aviv, and the Struggle for Palestine 1880–1948* (Berkeley: University of California Press, 2005), 110–11.

2. Marc D. Angel, "The Grand Religious View of Rabbi Benzion Uziel," *Tradition* 30, no. 1 (1995): 47.

3. Abraham Joshua Heschel, *Israel: An Echo of Eternity* (New York: Farrar, Straus and Giroux, 1969), 175–78; Angel, "Grand Religious View," 47.

4. Arthur A. Stein, *Why Nations Cooperate* (Ithaca, NY: Cornell University Press, 1990), 210.

relations can span the continuum from open warfare to peaceful cooperation. Some countries fight wars against one another and, when they are not fighting, spend significant resources preparing to fight, while other countries have managed to live in peace for long periods. Sometimes countries engage in lucrative economic dealings, selling each other goods and services and investing in one another's economies. These interactions can make some people and nations very rich, while others stay mired in poverty.

Like the people in the anecdote, the countries of the world are also increasingly aware of the natural resources they share and depend on: the atmosphere, the water, the land. The common threat of environmental degradation creates a need for international cooperation; in some cases governments have responded to this need, and in other cases they have not. And, as the story of Rabbi Uziel suggests, small groups — even individuals — can sometimes make a difference, whether through the work of a mediator, the lobbying of human rights groups, or more ominously, the activities of terrorist organizations. Understanding this varied landscape of conflict and cooperation is the task of those who study world politics. Getting you started down this path is the task of this book.

Why study world politics? The nineteenth-century Scottish historian Thomas Carlyle once wrote of economics that it was not a happy science, but rather a "dreary, desolate, and, indeed, quite abject and distressing one; what we might call. . . . the dismal science."[5] Those who study world politics often think that Carlyle's criticism applies equally well to the field of international relations. The history of world politics, in fact, offers its fair share of distressing observations: international wars have claimed millions of lives, and civil wars and genocides have claimed millions more, and in most cases, outsiders who might have prevented these deaths have chosen not to get involved. Since 1945, international politics has taken place under the threat of nuclear war, which could destroy the planet, and fears about the potential use of these weapons have intensified as countries like North Korea and Iran and terrorist groups like Al Qaeda have actively sought to acquire them.

International economic relations have in some cases been harmonious and generated enormous wealth for some countries. Global income and living standards improved dramatically over the last century, making this the most prosperous time in world history. And yet, as one looks around the globe today, the inequality in living standards is also stark. About 10 percent of the world's population — more than 700 million people — live on less than two dollars a day, the international standard for extreme poverty.[6] Meanwhile, the richest 1 percent of the world's population owns 50 percent of total global wealth.[7] Concerns about the effects of

---

5. Carlyle used this phrase in an article defending slavery in the West Indies; see Thomas Carlyle, "Occasional Discourse on the Negro Question," *Fraser's Magazine* 40 (December 1848): 672.

6. For excellent data on the incidence of extreme poverty over time, see Max Roser and Esteban Ortiz-Ospina, "Global Extreme Poverty," *Our World in Data*, substantive revision March 27, 2017, https://ourworldindata.org/extreme-poverty.

7. Rupert Neate, "Richest 1% Own Half the World's Wealth, Study Finds," *Guardian*, November 14, 2017, www.theguardian.com/inequality/2017/nov/14/worlds-richest-wealth-credit-suisse.

globalization — the dramatic expansion of cross-border flows — have spurred resistance in both poor and rich countries, fueling the rise of nationalist and populist movements seeking to reverse this trend.

Countries have also struggled to act on common interests and values. While most states have signed treaties promising to protect the basic human rights of their citizens, many governments still kill, arrest, and torture their people, and outsiders usually do little to stop these violations. And despite the increasing awareness of threats to the global environment, international efforts to do something about them often fail.

Still, the picture is not entirely bleak. One can point to a number of examples in which the world has changed for the better. For hundreds of years, the continent of Europe experienced horrific warfare, culminating in the first half of the twentieth century in two world wars that claimed tens of millions of lives. Today, the countries of Europe are at peace, and a war between, say, Germany and France in the foreseeable future is inconceivable.

After World War II, many countries emerged economically shattered, or destitute after years of colonial rule, but some have experienced extraordinary prosperity in the decades since. For example, in the 1950s, South Korea had one of the world's poorest economies, with a per capita national income of about $1,000 a year. Today, South Korea boasts the fifteenth largest economy in the world, with a per capita national income of almost $35,000 a year.[8]

At the beginning of the twentieth century, only a handful of countries worldwide had political systems that guaranteed the civil rights of their citizens and gave people a say in their government through free and fair elections. By the beginning of the twenty-first century, more than half of the world's population lived in democratic countries. And despite the uneven track record of efforts to protect the global environment, cooperation in this area was virtually unknown a few decades ago. In recent years, the number of international environmental treaties and organizations has grown dramatically, as has awareness of the common challenges we face.

We study world politics because the bad things that happen in the world distress us and because the good things give us hope that, through understanding and effort, the world could be a better place.

Puzzles in Search of Explanations

This book is organized around what we consider to be the most compelling and pressing puzzles in the study of world politics. Puzzles are observations about the world that demand an explanation. In some cases they arise because the world

---

8. Gross domestic product (GDP) per capita is measured in 2011 dollars. Data are from the World Bank, https://data.worldbank.org/indicator/NY.GDP.PCAP.PP.KD?locations5KR (accessed 01/19/18); and Robert C. Feenstra, Robert Inklaar, and Marcel P. Timmer, "The Next Generation of the Penn World Table," *American Economic Review* 105 (2015): 3150–82, available for download at www.ggdc.net/pwt.

does not work in the way we might expect. Some things that happen seem like they should not, and some things that don't happen seem like they should.

War, for example, is a puzzling phenomenon. Given the enormous human and material costs that wars impose on the countries that fight them, one might wonder why countries do not settle their conflicts in other, more reasonable ways. The difficulty of achieving international cooperation to end genocides or to protect the environment presents another such puzzle: Given the widespread agreement that genocide is horrific and that the environment needs protecting, why is it so hard for countries to do something about these issues?

Other puzzles arise because of variations that need to be explained. Some countries today are enormously wealthy, with living standards more opulent than ever experienced in world history; in many other countries, people scrape by on meager incomes and suffer from malnutrition, poor health, and inadequate schooling. What accounts for these vastly different outcomes? The study of world politics is the effort to make sense of these puzzles.

Each chapter of this book poses one of these puzzles and then shows how we can build theories to make sense of it. A **theory** is a logically consistent set of statements that explains a phenomenon of interest. When we confront the puzzle "Why did this happen?" theories provide an answer. They specify the factors that play a role in causing the events we are trying to understand, and they show how these pieces fit together to make sense of the puzzle. A theory of war explains why wars happen and identifies the conditions that make war between countries more or less likely. A theory of trade explains why countries sometimes choose to trade with each other and identifies the factors that increase or decrease the amount of that trade. A theory of international environmental policy identifies the factors that foster or impede cooperation in this area.

theory

A logically consistent set of statements that explains a phenomenon of interest.

In addition to this primary role of explanation, theories help us to describe, predict, and prescribe. They help us to *describe* events by identifying which factors are important and which are not. Since it would be impossible to catalog all of the events that precede, say, the outbreak of a war, we need theories to filter the events that are worth including from those that are not. Theories help us to *predict* by offering a sense of how the world works, and how a change in one factor will lead to changes in behavior and outcomes. And theories may help *prescribe* policy responses by identifying what has to be changed to foster better outcomes. Once a good understanding has been established of why wars happen, it might be possible to take steps to prevent them. Knowing which factors help countries emerge from poverty makes it possible to advocate policies that have a chance of helping. Just as an understanding of how the human body works is important for curing diseases, developing theories of how the world works is the first step in the quest to make it better.

Theories also provide manageable explanations for complex phenomena. Given how complicated the world is, simplifying it in this way may seem like a misguided pursuit. Whereas the movement of a falling object may be characterized by mathematical equations dictated by the laws of physics, the decisions of individuals and groups are influenced by factors too numerous to list, let alone predict. Any theory, therefore, is doomed to oversimplify. But this is precisely the point of theorizing. We do not build theories because we believe the world is simple or mechanical. Rather, we build them because we know the world is extraordinarily complex, and the only way to understand important phenomena is to cut away some of the complexity and identify the most important factors. As a result, any general explanation will not be right in every single case.

Given this outlook, we generally aspire for probabilistic claims. A *probabilistic claim* is an argument about the factors that increase or decrease the likelihood that a particular outcome will occur. For example, while we cannot predict with certainty whether a given conflict will end in war or peace, we can identify conditions that increase or decrease the danger of war. Similarly, we use theories to identify factors that make trade protection, or international investment, or cooperation to protect human rights or the environment, more or less likely. Given the world's complexity, developing a compelling probabilistic argument is no small feat.

The Framework: Interests, Interactions, and Institutions

No single theory adequately answers all the puzzles posed in this book. Instead, we offer a framework — a way of thinking about world politics that will be useful in building theories to shed light on these puzzles. The framework rests on three core concepts: interests, interactions, and institutions.

interests

What actors want to achieve through political action; their preferences over the outcomes that might result from their political choices.

Interests are the goals that actors have, the outcomes they hope to obtain through political action. A state may have an interest in protecting its citizens or acquiring more territory; businesses generally have an interest in maximizing profits; an environmental activist has an interest in protecting the atmosphere, the oceans, or whales.

interactions

The ways in which the choices of two or more actors combine to produce political outcomes.

Interactions are the ways in which two or more actors' choices combine to produce political outcomes. The outcomes that we observe — wars, or trade and financial exchanges, or cooperation to protect human rights or the environment — reflect the choices of many actors, each looking out for their own interests, but also taking into account the interests and likely actions of others. War is the product of an interaction because it requires at least two sides: one side must attack, and the other must decide to resist. Similarly, efforts at international cooperation require multiple states to coordinate their policy choices toward a common goal.

institutions

Sets of rules (known and shared by the community) that structure interactions in specific ways.

Institutions are sets of rules, known and shared by the relevant community, that structure political interactions. Institutions define the "rules of the game," often embodied in formal treaties and laws or in organizations like the United Nations (UN). Institutions create procedures for making joint decisions, such as voting rules; they also lay out standards of acceptable behavior, and they often include provisions for monitoring compliance and punishing those who violate the rules.

Applying this framework to any particular puzzle is straightforward. We first think about who the relevant political actors are and what interests they may have. We think about the choices, or strategies, available to each actor; how those choices interact to produce outcomes; and how the strategic interaction influences what the actors actually decide to do. And we think about what institutions, if any, might exist to govern their behavior.

The framework is intentionally flexible, pragmatic, and open to a variety of assumptions about which interests, interactions, and institutions matter. A theory emerges when we identify the specific interests, interactions, and institutions that work together to account for the events, or pattern of events, we hope to explain.

In building explanations, we do not precommit to any single set of actors or interests as being the most important, regardless of the issue area. Sometimes it is useful to think about states as actors pursuing goals such as power, security, or territorial expansion. In other situations we get more leverage thinking about politicians concerned with holding on to their office, or businesses interested in maximizing profits, or labor unions interested in protecting their members' jobs, or groups of like-minded individuals with strong ideological interests in, say, protecting human rights or extending the dominion of a particular religion.

We cannot judge whether any particular assumption about actors and interests is right or wrong; rather, we judge whether that assumption is useful in explaining the puzzle. Indeed, assumptions are simplifying devices, which means that, strictly speaking, none captures the exact, entire truth. Since not all decisions are made by individuals, it is not precisely accurate to say that a state or an interest group or an institution is an actor; yet sometimes it is quite useful to assume precisely that. Similarly, ascribing interests to individuals — such as assuming that politicians care primarily about holding on to office — is a sweeping generalization that cannot be right 100 percent of the time, yet very powerful insights can be drawn from this assumption.

We focus on two broad types of interactions that arise, to one degree or another, in all aspects of politics: bargaining and cooperation. **Bargaining** describes situations in which two or more actors try to divide something they both want. States may bargain over the allocation of a disputed territory; finance ministers may bargain over how high or how low to set the exchange rate between their currencies; rich countries may bargain with poor countries over how much aid the former will give and what the recipients will do in return; governments may bargain over how much each will pay to alleviate some environmental harm.

Cooperation occurs when actors have common interests and need to act in a coordinated way to achieve those interests. Governments that want to stop one country from invading another may try to act collectively to impose military or economic sanctions on the aggressor. Governments that share an interest in preventing climate change or degradation of the ozone layer need to cooperate in restraining their countries' emissions of the offending pollutants. Individuals who want to lobby for a particular trade policy or an environmental regulation have to pool their time, money, and effort to achieve their common aim. In short, bargaining and cooperation are everywhere in political life.

bargaining

An interaction in which two or more actors must choose outcomes that make one better off at the expense of another. Bargaining is redistributive: it involves allocating a fixed sum of value between different actors.

cooperation

An interaction in which two or more actors adopt policies that make at least one actor better off relative to the status quo without making the others worse off.

The institutional setting can vary considerably, depending on the issues at stake. In some areas of world politics, there are well-established rules and mechanisms for enforcing those rules. International trade, for example, is governed by the World Trade Organization (WTO), which sets out rules that determine what kinds of trade policies member countries can and cannot have, and provides a dispute resolution mechanism that allows countries to challenge one another's policies.

Other areas of world politics have weaker institutions. As we will see in Chapter 5, the UN theoretically governs the use of military force by states, but in practice it has had a hard time enforcing these rules on its strongest members. As we will see in Chapter 12, an extensive body of international human rights law sets out standards for how governments should treat their citizens; unfortunately, noncompliance is common, and offenders are rarely punished.

We will also at times focus on institutions at the domestic level — that is, the rules that determine who governs within countries and how they make decisions. Domestic political institutions determine which actors have access to and influence on the policy-making process. In some cases, differences in domestic political institutions can have profound effects on world politics. In Chapter 4, for example, we will encounter a phenomenon known as the *democratic peace*, the observation that mature democratic states have rarely, if ever, engaged in a war against one another.

Levels of Analysis

The variety of actors and institutions that play a role in world politics means that we will see important interactions at three levels:

- At the *international level*, the representatives of states with different interests interact with one another, sometimes in the context of international institutions, such as the UN or WTO.

- At the *domestic level*, subnational actors with different interests — politicians, bureaucrats, business and labor groups, voters — interact within domestic institutions to determine the country's foreign policy choices.

- At the *transnational level*, groups whose members span borders — such as multinational corporations, transnational advocacy networks, and terrorist organizations — pursue their interests by trying to influence both domestic and international politics.

These levels are interconnected. The interests that states pursue at the international level often emerge from their domestic politics. For example, whether a country's representatives push for liberalizing trade agreements with other countries depends on whether the interests within that country that support freer trade prevail over those who oppose it. Similarly, the relative influence of actors within domestic politics may depend on international conditions. Leaders may be able to use militarized conflict with other states to enhance their hold on power at home. International institutions that promote trade liberalization enhance the power of domestic interests that benefit from trade. Finally, transnational actors operate at all levels. Transnational networks like Amnesty International or Greenpeace try to change national policies by lobbying governments or mobilizing public opinion within key countries, and they try to change international outcomes by working with (or against) international institutions.

Because of these interconnections, we do not automatically privilege one level of analysis over others. Although international relations scholarship has experienced vigorous debates over which level of analysis is the "right" or the "best" one,[9] we find that no single level is always superior to others in making sense of the puzzles. In some cases it is possible to build useful explanations from the bottom up, in a two-step process: (1) domestic interests, interactions, and institutions determine the interests that state representatives bring to the international level, and then (2) these interests combine in international interactions and institutions to determine the final outcome. Chapters 7–10, on international political economy, generally rely on this two-step logic.

In other cases, however, it is more useful to start elsewhere. In Chapters 3–6 we start the analysis of war on the international level. Given that states have conflicting interests over things like territory or one another's policies or regime composition, why does the bargaining interaction sometimes lead to war? Only after laying out this basic logic do we turn to some of the domestic factors that push states toward more or less belligerent policies. In Chapters 11–13, transnational actors play a central role, and we show how they pursue their goals by altering domestic interests and changing the prospects for international cooperation.

Integrating Insights from Realism, Liberalism, and Constructivism

In adopting a flexible framework based on interests, interactions, and institutions, we depart from the way the field of world politics is often organized. Many textbooks and courses on world politics emphasize the contrasts among three schools of thought: realism, liberalism, and constructivism. Unlike our framework, which holds few preconceptions about how the world works, these three "-isms" represent different worldviews about the nature of international politics. Much ink has been spilled over the years by proponents arguing for the superiority of their preferred approach.

We can understand the differences among realism, liberalism, and constructivism by mapping them into our framework (see Table A). Each school of thought is defined by a cluster of assumptions about which interests, interactions, and institutions are most important to understanding world politics.

Realism   Realist ideas can be found in the writings of Thucydides (ca. 460–400 B.C.E.), Niccolò Machiavelli (1469–1527), Thomas Hobbes (1588–1679), and Jean-Jacques Rousseau (1712–1778). Realism was most forcefully introduced to Americans by

---

9. For a classic statement of this debate, see J. David Singer, "The Levels-of-Analysis Problem in International Relations," *World Politics* 14, no. 1 (October 1961): 77–92.

TABLE A *Realism, Liberalism, and Constructivism*

	INTERESTS	INTERACTIONS	INSTITUTIONS
Realism	The state is the dominant actor. States seek security and/or power. States' interests are generally in conflict.	International politics is primarily about bargaining, in which coercion always remains a possibility.	The international system is anarchic, and institutions exert little independent effect. International institutions reflect the interests of powerful states.
Liberalism	Many types of actors are important, and no single interest dominates. Wealth is a common goal for many actors. Actors often have common interests, which can serve as the basis for cooperation.	International politics has an extensive scope for cooperation. Conflict is not inevitable but occurs when actors fail to recognize or act on common interests.	International institutions facilitate cooperation by setting out rules, providing information, and creating procedures for collective decision making. Democratic political institutions increase the scope for international politics to reflect the common interests of individuals.
Constructivism	Many types of actors are important. Actors' interests are influenced by culture, identity, and prevailing ideas. Actors' choices often reflect norms of appropriate behavior, rather than interests.	Interactions socialize actors to hold particular interests, but transformations can occur, caused by alternative understandings of those interests.	International institutions define identities and shape action through norms of just and appropriate behavior.

Hans Morgenthau, a German expatriate whose 1948 book *Politics among Nations* remains a classic statement of the realist approach.[10] Realism was given its modern and scientific guise by the contemporary scholar Kenneth Waltz.[11]

Realism starts with two key assumptions: that states are the dominant actors — indeed, some would say the only relevant actors — on the international stage, and that the institutional setting of world politics is characterized by anarchy. **Anarchy**, a term we will revisit in Chapter 2, refers in this context to the absence of a central authority in the international system — the fact that there is no world government ruling over states the way that countries have governments to rule over their citizens.

anarchy
The absence of a central authority with the ability to make and enforce laws that bind all actors.

---

10. Hans Morgenthau, *Politics among Nations: The Struggle for Power and Peace* (New York: Knopf). First published in 1948, this book has been released in many editions since then.

11. Kenneth N. Waltz, *Theory of International Politics* (Reading, MA: Addison-Wesley, 1979).

Realists assume that anarchy profoundly shapes the interests and interactions that matter in world politics. Because there is no central government and there is no international police force, states must live in constant fear of one another. With no external restraint on the use of military force, every state must, first and foremost, look out for its own survival and security. Hence, all states have an interest in security, and this interest dominates other possible interests because no other goal can be realized unless the state is secure.

In practice, the interest in security leads to an interest in acquiring power — primarily, military capabilities. By accumulating power and ensuring that potential enemies do not become more powerful, states can reduce their vulnerability to attack and conquest. Unfortunately, the quest for power inevitably brings states' interests into conflict with one another: when one state improves its military capabilities to enhance its own security, it typically undermines the security of its now comparatively weaker neighbors — a problem known as the "security dilemma." For realists, then, international politics is, as Hobbes described, the "state of nature": a war of "every man, against every man" in which life is "nasty, brutish, and short."[12]

Because states are concerned with security and power, nearly all interactions involve bargaining and coercion. Each state tries to get a bigger share for itself, one state's gain is another state's loss, and the threat of war looms over everything. Even when the potential gains from cooperation are large, realists argue, states worry more about the division of the benefits than about the overall gain. Each must fear that the state gaining the most will be able to exploit its gains for some future advantage. As a result, states may forgo mutually beneficial exchanges if they expect to be left at a disadvantage. Cooperation, realists conclude, is difficult and rare.

Finally, realists assert that because of the anarchic nature of the international system, international institutions are weak and exert little independent effect on world politics. Institutions like the UN and the WTO merely reflect the interests and power of the dominant countries, which had the most say in their creation and design. Although realists may recognize that institutions can matter at the margin, they conclude that rules are unlikely to be followed and that states will always bow to interests and power in the end.

In short, realism sees a rather bleak world of states jockeying for power under the shadow of war, and many of the unpleasant features of world politics mentioned earlier flow from this understanding. War is a permanent fixture of international relations because there is nothing to stop states from waging war when it is in their interests to do so. The risk of war can be managed by careful diplomacy and temporary alliances between states that face common threats, but neither domestic nor international institutions can deliver lasting peace.

Even the realm of international economic relations is colored by the struggle for power. Economists tell us that unfettered commerce makes all countries

---

12. These famous quotes are from Thomas Hobbes's *Leviathan*, originally published in 1651.

collectively better off, but realists understand that restrictions on trade and capital flows are often sensible measures to increase or preserve a state's relative power. Finally, cooperation is hard because states look out for themselves, and international institutions are generally too weak to compel desirable behaviors. As a result, realists are not surprised that many of the world's collective needs, such as the protection of human rights and the global environment, go unmet.

Liberalism

An equally venerable tradition, liberalism is rooted in the writings of philosophers John Locke (1632–1704) and Immanuel Kant (1724–1804), and economists Adam Smith (1723–1790) and David Ricardo (1772–1823). Contemporary advocates include Bruce Russett and John R. Oneal, who make the modern case for the pacifying effects of democracy, international commerce, and international law;[13] and Robert O. Keohane and Joseph S. Nye, whose work helped bring the study of international institutions to the fore.[14]

Analytically, liberalism is the school of thought that most closely resembles the approach taken in this book. Liberal theorists accept many different types of actors as important in world politics: individuals, firms, nongovernmental organizations, and states. Unlike realism, liberalism does not require that any one interest dominate all others. Instead, liberal theory, like the framework presented here, is quite flexible in ascribing goals to actors. While realism assumes that states' interests in security and power derive from external imperatives (the need to survive in an anarchic world), liberals are more likely to see governments' interests as coming from within (from the interplay of different domestic actors operating within domestic political institutions). Moreover, since wealth can be used to purchase the means to accommodate many different desires, liberals assume that, for many practical purposes, actors can be treated as if they wish to maximize wealth.

Liberals are generally optimistic about the possibilities for cooperation in world politics. Whereas realists see most situations as involving conflicting interests over relative power, liberals see many areas in which actors have common interests that can serve as the basis for cooperation. The costs of war mean that states have common interests in avoiding conflict. The potential for profitable exchanges creates a common interest in lowering barriers to allow the flow of goods and money across borders and in creating institutions to facilitate international transactions. The common interest in clean air and clean water creates a basis for cooperating to protect these shared resources. Although liberals acknowledge that world politics is often wracked by conflict, they do not believe that conflict is inevitable; rather, conflict arises when actors fail to recognize or act on common interests.

---

13. Bruce Russett and John R. Oneal, *Triangulating Peace: Democracy, Interdependence, and International Organizations* (New York: Norton, 2001).

14. Robert O. Keohane and Joseph S. Nye, *Power and Interdependence: World Politics in Transition* (New York: Longman); first published in 1977, this volume is now available in a third edition, published in 2000. Robert O. Keohane, *After Hegemony: Cooperation and Discord in the World Political Economy* (Princeton, NJ: Princeton University Press, 1984).

Whether actors can cooperate to further their common interests depends a great deal on institutions, both domestic and international. At the domestic level, liberals believe that democracy is the best way to ensure that governments' foreign policies reflect the underlying harmony of interests among individuals. In this view, which we will revisit in Chapter 4, conflict and war are the fault of selfish politicians, voracious militaries, and greedy interest groups, whose influence can be tamed only by empowering the people through democratic institutions. At the international level, the scope for cooperation gives rise to a demand for institutions. Liberals posit that international institutions facilitate cooperation by resolving a host of dilemmas that arise in strategic interactions and by making it easier for states to make collective decisions. In Chapter 2 we will consider these dilemmas and the ways in which institutions might resolve them.

Thus, while liberalism does not see a perfect world, it envisions a world in which progress is possible. The danger of war can be reduced by spreading democracy, strengthening global institutions, and fostering economic interdependence so that every country's welfare will be linked to that of others. Economic activity also has the potential to create great wealth, making it possible to lift countries and people out of poverty. And global challenges can give rise to international institutions that can make cooperation possible. While this optimistic view makes liberalism a more appealing theory than realism, theories must be judged by how closely they describe the world in which we actually live, not the world in which we would like to live.

Constructivism A relatively new approach, constructivism has roots in critical theory and sociology, and its most forceful proponents in world politics have been Peter J. Katzenstein, John G. Ruggie, and Alexander Wendt.[15] Like liberals, constructivists focus on a wide variety of actors and interests in world politics, and they believe that international institutions can be effective, even transformative. Constructivists depart from liberals, however, by de-emphasizing the material sources of interests (for example, wealth) and instead focusing on the role of nonmaterial factors, such as ideas, culture, and norms.

What actors want is not fixed and predetermined, but a function of their culture, prevailing ideas, and identity, or the conception of who they are. Whether states perceive common or conflicting interests depends not only on their relative military power or economic ties, but also on whether they share a common political or cultural identity (for example, "we are all democracies" or "we are all Western") or identify each other as foes ("you are not like us").

One prominent strand of constructivist thought emphasizes the role of norms, or standards of behavior defined in terms of rights and obligations (see Chapter 11). Whereas the other schools of thought assume that actors are purposive, selecting

---

15. Peter J. Katzenstein, ed., *The Culture of National Security: Norms and Identity in World Politics* (New York: Columbia University Press, 1996); John Gerard Ruggie, *Constructing the World Polity: Essays on International Institutionalization* (New York: Routledge, 1998); Alexander Wendt, *Social Theory of International Politics* (New York: Cambridge University Press, 1999).

among possible alternatives according to their anticipated effects, constructivists assume that social actors pursue what they believe is right and proper, as based on their conceptions of who they are and how they wish others to view them. So, for example, if a large number of countries decide that using a certain kind of weapon is barbaric, then states that wish to be seen as civilized may decide to forgo those weapons — even if using them would enhance their security. Thus, a desire to conform to certain standards of behavior can trump other interests.

Institutions, in turn, embody the rules appropriate for behavior, and thereby exert a profound effect on actions and observed outcomes. For example, once an international agreement or institution proscribes a behavior as illegal or illegitimate, states that care about how others view them will have incentive to conform. Thus, compliance with international institutions depends not only on their ability to monitor and enforce their terms, but also on the members' desire to be seen as compliant.

Because ideas about right or appropriate behaviors can change, constructivists see significant potential for change, even fundamental transformation, in world politics. The rough-and-tumble international system described by realists is not, according to this view, foreordained by the condition of anarchy. If actors come to understand their interests differently, their conception of appropriate behavior could change dramatically. More concretely, state behavior can be altered by the conscious efforts of activists to promote new norms, such as norms against the use of certain weapons (see Chapter 11), norms promoting intervention in genocidal conflicts (see Chapters 5 and 11), and norms favoring the protection of human rights (see Chapter 12). For this reason, constructivists place particular emphasis on the role of transnational actors, such as advocacy networks of human rights or environmental activists, who try to spread norms around the world.

All three approaches — realism, liberalism, constructivism — offer insights into important problems of world politics. Nonetheless, each tends to emphasize particular aspects of our framework at the expense of others, and all make strong assumptions about which interests, interactions, and institutions matter the most. As a result, each approach sacrifices explanatory power and flexibility for the sake of intellectual purity.

Not surprisingly, most international relations scholarship in recent years has moved away from arguments based on a single approach, instead borrowing insights from more than one. Indeed, as the field progresses, it has become harder to pigeonhole scholars and their work into any one category. For example, many contemporary scholars believe that coercive power plays a fundamental role in international politics (realism), but that power is often used in pursuit of goals that arise from the interplay of domestic interests (liberalism) and ideas (constructivism).[16] Hence, rather than trying to promote one school of thought over others, our goal is to answer important puzzles of international politics and, in the process, use the tools developed in this book to help us understand today's complex world.

---

16. See, for example, Jeffrey W. Legro and Andrew Moravcsik, "Is Anybody Still a Realist?" *International Security* 24, no. 2 (Autumn 1999): 5–55.

Thinking Analytically about World Politics

By the end of the course, you should not only know a lot about international politics, you should also know how to *think* about international politics. When bad or puzzling things happen, you should be able to ask: "Whose interests did that outcome serve? Why were the people or countries involved not able to cooperate to achieve something better? How might new institutions be created, or existing institutions reformed, so that this does not happen again?"

Ultimately, we study world politics because doing so lets us grapple with important and interesting questions about ourselves and our world. This book cannot provide definitive answers to all the questions. After all, while we are confident in our understanding of certain phenomena, for others our understanding is still evolving and our theories are tentative — perhaps waiting to be overturned by the next generation. Instead, this book seeks to equip you with the tools you need to develop your own understanding. In the "information age," in which facts (and assertions masquerading as facts) are cheap and plentiful, the most valuable skill is the ability to think critically and analytically about what shapes our world.

Study Tool Kit

Interests, Interactions, and Institutions in Context

- We can develop theories to explain behavior and outcomes in world politics by considering the interests of the main actors involved, the strategies available to them and how their choices interact to produce outcomes, and the institutions that govern their behavior.

- World politics reflects the interaction of a variety of actors — including states, politicians, business groups, terrorist organizations, transnational advocacy networks, and individuals — pursuing their interests.

- Most interactions involve either cooperation (which happens when actors with similar interests try to coordinate their behavior toward a common goal) or bargaining (which happens when actors with different interests try to get a favorable outcome at the expense of others).

- Institutions, both domestic and international, are the rules that can alter the costs and benefits of some strategies and determine how actors arrive at collective decisions.

- The main theoretical traditions in international relations — realism, liberalism, and constructivism — make different assumptions about which interests, interactions, and institutions are most important for building explanations.

Key Terms

theory, p. xxvii

interests, p. xxviii

interactions, p. xxviii

institutions, p. xxviii

bargaining, p. xxix

cooperation, p. xxix

anarchy, p. xxxii

For Further Reading

Finnemore, Martha. *The Purpose of Intervention: Changing Beliefs about the Use of Force.* **Cornell Studies in Security Affairs. Ithaca, NY: Cornell University Press, 2004.** Develops a constructivist argument that patterns of military intervention have changed over the last two centuries because of changing norms about the appropriate purposes for using force.

Katzenstein, Peter J., ed. *The Culture of National Security: Norms and Identity in World Politics.* **New Directions in World Politics. New York: Columbia University Press, 1996.** Presents a collection of essays showing how constructivism uses norms, culture, and identity to answer fundamental questions about international security.

Keohane, Robert O., and Joseph S. Nye. *Power and Interdependence.* **4th ed. Boston: Longman, 2012.** Presents a liberal argument that economic and political interdependence between states complicates the exercise of power in international relations.

Morgenthau, Hans J., Kenneth W. Thompson, and W. David Clinton. *Politics among Nations: The Struggle for Power and Peace.* **7th ed. Boston: McGraw-Hill Higher Education, 2006.** Presents an updated and abridged version of Morgenthau's classic statement of realist theory.

Russett, Bruce M., and John R. Oneal. *Triangulating Peace: Democracy, Interdependence, and International Organizations.* **New York: Norton, 2001.** Presents theory and evidence that three key pillars of liberalism — democracy, economic interdependence, and international institutions — can reduce the risk of war.

Waltz, Kenneth N. *Theory of International Politics.* **Long Grove, IL: Waveland Press, 2010.** Articulates a realist theory emphasizing the importance of power and anarchy in explaining recurring patterns of international politics.

FOURTH EDITION

World Politics

Interests, Interactions, Institutions

1

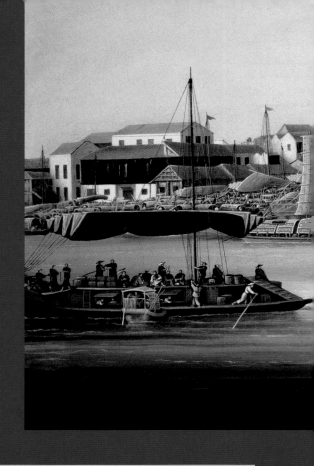

What Shaped Our World?
A Historical Introduction

THE PUZZLE *How has conflict among nations ebbed and flowed over the centuries? When and how have war or peace, prosperity or stagnation, prevailed?*

Above: During the nineteenth century, global trade grew at a rapid rate. While the increase in international trade was most pronounced in the advanced economies of Europe, many people in Asia also found themselves integrated into the global economy in new ways during this period. By the time of this painting, around 1840, Canton, China (present-day Guangzhou), had become a significant international trading port.

Most western Europeans and North Americans born around 1800 spent their adult lives in an atmosphere of peace and economic growth. So too did their children, and their children's children, and their children's children's children. Between the end of the Napoleonic Wars in 1815 and the start of World War I in 1914, peace and prosperity by and large reigned in western Europe and North America. There were periodic wars among the European great powers, but they were relatively short; there were brutal conflicts with the indigenous peoples of the Americas, but they were on sparsely inhabited frontiers; there was a bloody civil war in the United States, but it was confined to one country. There were occasional financial panics and recessions, but between 1815 and 1914 the advanced economies of western Europe and North America grew more than eightfold while output per person quadrupled.[1] This was the fastest growth in world history by a very long shot; it roughly equaled in a hundred years what had been achieved in the previous thousand.

---

1. Angus Maddison, *The World Economy: A Millennial Perspective* (Paris: OECD Publications, 2001).

Europeans and North Americans born around 1900 had a very different experience. While they were in their teens, the world plunged into a horrific, protracted war that wiped out the better part of a generation of young men. If those born around 1900 were fortunate enough to survive World War I, they and their children spent the next 10 years being subjected to postwar violence, economic uncertainty, fragile democracy, and ethnic conflict. Despite a brief recovery in the 1920s, in 1929 the world spiraled downward into economic depression, mass unemployment, dictatorship, trade wars, and eventually another global war. If they, and their children and their children's children, were again lucky and survived World War II, their world was then divided into two hostile camps—one led by the United States, the other by the Soviet Union. These two contending alliances carried on a cold war that included the deployment of enough nuclear weapons to annihilate life on earth several times over.

International relations profoundly affected these many generations of Europeans and North Americans—as they did, in different ways, generations of people in Africa, Asia, and Latin America. During the nineteenth century, the inhabitants of many poor countries found themselves absorbed into a world economy for the first time. Some prospered, others struggled. Latin Americans achieved independence from their colonial masters, while many areas of Africa and Asia were subjected to new colonial rule and domination by Europeans. The twentieth century brought industrialization and urbanization to much of the developing world and eventually saw the end of colonialism. For people north and south, east and west, global events beyond their control—great-power war, international financial crises, colonial expansion, the division of the world into warring camps—changed their lives profoundly, as they continue to change ours, and as they have changed lives for centuries.

Thinking Analytically about What Shaped Our World

Whether in the military realm or in the realm of international economics, the world's experiences range from deadly conflict to fruitful cooperation. At times, when national interests have clashed, countries have engaged in bitter armed battles over everything from territory to theology, and in equally bitter commercial conflicts over markets and money. At other times, the same countries have found common ground upon which to base harmonious interactions on everything from geopolitics to trade, investment, and finance.

What will the future bring for today's younger generation, those born around 2000? Will they experience general peace and prosperity, or war and deprivation? Will those born in the world's poor nations come closer to the living standards of the rich or fall further behind? Will governments cooperate or clash? Whose interests and which institutions will shape these interactions? These are the kinds of questions that the study of international politics hopes to illuminate. We do not aspire to predict the future, but we do seek to gain a fuller understanding of the past and present by providing guidelines for analyzing the choices available to people and governments and how they decide among those choices.

Much of the rest of this book provides and applies analytical tools for understanding international relations. This chapter sets the stage for what follows by reviewing the course of international political and economic relations in modern times, since about 1500. With this grounding, we move in subsequent chapters to providing theoretical principles with which to understand international relations and then to applying them to a wide variety of contemporary topics.

The Emergence of International Relations: The Mercantilist Era

The world as a meaningful political and economic unit emerged only after 1500. Before then, most major societies existed in practical or complete isolation from all but those on their immediate borders. To be sure, there was some trade among societies: China to Constantinople, Central Africa to North Africa, Constantinople to Europe. But this trade was extraordinarily difficult and expensive, and therefore it involved only the most valuable and easily transported goods.

All that changed after 1492, as wave upon wave of explorers, conquerors, traders, and settlers went forth from Europe's Atlantic nations. First Spain and Portugal, then England, France, and the Netherlands, sent soldiers and traders all over the New World, Africa, and Asia in search of possessions and profit. By 1700, the world was unquestionably controlled by western Europeans. They exercised direct rule over vast colonial possessions in the Western Hemisphere, India, Southeast Asia, and elsewhere, and their military might allowed them to assert their will on local rulers even where they did not establish colonial domain. European influence was rarely welcomed by local populations, and its effects were often disastrous for local societies. Nonetheless, western Europe's economic influence was global, and it dictated the character and direction of economic activity on every continent.

The centuries of European expansion after 1492 meant that world politics was dominated by European politics. In fact, the Europeans used their military prowess to control much of the rest of the world, with formal empires or without them. The European economies were the world center of economic activity. Important as developments outside Europe may have been for the people living there, the analysis of world politics after 1492 necessarily has Europe at its core. This would change only in the twentieth century, with the rise of militarily and economically important non-European powers: the United States, Japan, the Soviet Union, and eventually China.

For several hundred years beginning in the 1500s, however, it was the rulers of western Europe who held sway over the rest of the world. These governments, almost all of them absolute monarchies, had two main interests. First, they wanted to ensure their own political and military power. These interests led them to desire control over ever-greater territories and ever-greater resources. Second, the European governments wanted access to markets and resources in other parts of the world. European societies had thriving commercial classes, typically strongly allied with their respective monarchies, and each crown was hungry for revenue. There were rich natural treasures to be had abroad—precious metals, spices, tropical crops—and customers for the products of Europe's growing industries.

Western Europeans' economic and military interests were reflected in the colonial order they established, known as mercantilism. **Mercantilism** was a system by which imperial governments used military power to enrich themselves and their supporters, then used those riches to enhance their military power. Mercantilism's

mercantilism
An economic doctrine based on a belief that military power and economic influence complemented each other; applied especially to colonial empires in the sixteenth through eighteenth centuries. Mercantilist policies favored the mother country over its colonies and over its competitors.

principal mechanism was the establishment of monopolies that controlled trade and other economic activities, manipulating them to direct money into the coffers of the government and its business supporters.

Some mercantilist monopolies were held by a government itself, such as the Spanish crown's control over many of its colonies' gold and silver mines. Other mercantilist monopolies were granted by a government to private businesses, such as the Dutch East Indies Company and the Hudson's Bay Company. These private enterprises held exclusive rights to economic activities in vast areas of the colonial world.

The mercantilist powers' most important controls were those applied to trade. These controls typically served to manipulate the terms of trade, the prices paid for imports and received for exports. In the case of mercantilist policies, the goal was to turn the terms of trade against the colonies and in favor of the mother country—to reduce the prices that the mother country paid its colonists for what it bought and to raise the prices that the mother country charged its colonists for what it sold. One common way of achieving this effect was to require colonies to buy and sell certain goods only from and to the colonial power. In colonial Virginia, for example, farmers could sell their tobacco only to England—a restriction that artificially reduced demand for their tobacco and, therefore, its price. And Virginians could buy many manufactured goods only from England, which meant that the supply of manufactures was artificially reduced and their prices raised. Subjects received less for what they produced and paid more for what they consumed, but in return, they obtained the protection of a powerful empire. Supporters of mercantilism argued that it benefited both the empire, which became richer and more powerful, and its subjects, who were protected. Not all colonial subjects agreed, as "How Do We Know?" on page 7 explains.

The mercantilist powers' international political and economic interests were closely intertwined. For mercantilism's proponents, this was one of its great attractions. The English philosopher Thomas Hobbes wrote, "Wealth is power, and power is wealth." One of his fellow mercantilist thinkers drew out the connections: "Foreign trade produces riches, riches power, power preserves our trade and religion." And a French mercantilist was even more explicit: "Our colonies depend on our navy, our trade depends on our colonies, and our trade allows the state to maintain armies, increase the population, and provide for ever more glorious and useful functions."[2]

The British imposed mercantilist policies on their colonies in North America. For example, the tobacco being loaded onto these ships in the Virginia Colony could be exported only to Britain, where the American producers received a lower price for their crops than they would on world markets.

---

2. All cited in Jacob Viner, "Power versus Plenty as Objectives of Foreign Policy in the Seventeenth and Eighteenth Centuries," *World Politics* 1, no. 1 (October 1948): 15–16.

Mercantilism and the 13 Colonies

British colonialism in North America followed the patterns of mercantilism, the system adopted by European colonial powers after about 1500. How did mercantilism work? Whom did it help and hurt? Why did many colonies come to oppose it? Economic historian Robert Paul Thomas estimated the cost to the colonies of mercantilist economic restrictions in 1770, a representative year in the decade leading up to the outbreak of the American Revolution (Table A).

The most costly restriction was the "enumeration" of certain goods, which meant they could be exported only to Britain. This measure artificially increased the supply of the enumerated goods to the British market, which caused their price to drop, and it kept American producers from selling in markets with higher prices. There were also restrictions on what could be imported in the colonies, and certain goods were available only if they were bought from Britain—at a higher price than available elsewhere.

The principal cost to the 13 colonies was the lower price received for enumerated goods, especially the tobacco and rice that made up most of the colonies' exports. Thomas calculated that without enumeration, the colonists would have been able to sell their tobacco at a price 49 percent higher than what they actually received, and their rice for more than double. If prices had been higher, we can also assume that the colonists would have produced more of the goods, so the forgone production is factored in as well. In 1770, the total cost of these export controls, almost all due to tobacco and rice, was $2.4 million. Thomas further estimated that the restrictions on imports raised the price of goods that the colonists bought from abroad by more than one-third—a total burden of $560,000. Thomas then took into account rewards ("bounties") that the colonists earned for producing favored goods. The total net cost in 1770 was about $2.7 million, approximately $1.24 per person.

However, the 13 colonies received benefits from being in the British Empire. Most important was the protection of the British army and navy. Thomas calculated these benefits in two ways. First, he estimated the cost to the British government of stationing its troops in the region, along with how much American shippers would have had to pay for private insurance if they had not had the protection of the world's greatest navy. Second, Thomas calculated how much the American government spent to provide these services itself after independence. The lower of the two estimates was $1,775,000 in 1770. Subtracting the benefits from the costs, Thomas figured that the colonies' net burden from imperial rule in 1770 was about $885,000—or 42 cents per person, less than 0.5 percent of a colonist's average annual income. (When he calculated the average from 1763 to 1772, the net burden on the colonists was even lower: 26 cents per person per year.)

It hardly seems worth fighting a revolution over 42 cents a year. Even in today's money, the net burden (costs minus benefits) would come to about $200. It is important to note that the burden of mercantilism did not fall evenly on all colonists. The principal losers were the tobacco and rice planters of Virginia and South Carolina, as well as the merchants and craftsmen of New England. The former lost owing to export controls; the latter, owing to restrictions on shipping and manufacturing. Thus, it is perhaps not surprising that the principal supporters of independence were in these regions where the costs of colonialism were highest.

TABLE A   *Mercantilism: Costs and Benefits*

	1770	1763–72 (AVERAGE/YEAR)
Burdens		
Burden on colonial foreign commerce	$2,660,000	$2,255,000
Burden per capita	$1.24	$1.20
Benefits		
Benefit of British protection	$1,775,000	$1,775,000
Benefit per capita	$.82	$.94
Balance per capita	–$.42	–$.26

Source: Robert Paul Thomas, "A Quantitative Approach to the Study of the Effects of British Imperial Policy on Colonial Welfare," *Journal of Economic History* 25, no. 4 (December 1965).

As the European powers took control of ever-larger portions of the world, they also battled with one another over wealth and power. The struggle for supremacy in Europe was inextricably linked to the battle for possessions elsewhere, and the search for military advantage was closely tied to economic competition. International politics and markets were battlegrounds on which the major powers contended.

First the Spanish and Portuguese fought for predominance in the New World and elsewhere. After the Spaniards emerged victorious, they faced new contenders. Beginning in the 1560s, the Spanish possessions in the Netherlands revolted and eventually formed the new Dutch Republic. The British challenged Spain continually from the 1580s onward, defeating the Spanish Armada in 1588. Finally, in the Thirty Years' War (1618–48), the French, Dutch, and other allies sealed the decline of Spain. This war ended with the **Peace of Westphalia**, which stabilized the borders of the belligerents and attempted to resolve some of the religious conflicts that had complicated their relations. Because the peace treaties called on governments not to interfere in the internal affairs of other countries, some scholars regard this as the beginning of the modern system of states, which are expected to respect one another's **sovereignty** within their borders. Indeed, some analysts mark this treaty as the beginning of the modern system of sovereign states.

Once the anti-Spanish alliance had defeated Spain, its members turned on one another. The English and the Dutch fought each other in a series of wars, and both the wars and rapid English commercial growth meant that by the 1660s, the English had surpassed the Dutch as the world's leading trading and maritime power. This shift in power launched a 150-year conflict between England and its allies, on the one hand, and France and its allies, on the other. Anglo-French rivalry culminated with the Seven Years' War (1756–63, also called the French and Indian War in North America), which effectively ended the French presence in the New World and established British predominance. The French challenge to Britain resurged during the French Revolution, which began in 1789 and led to the Napoleonic Wars (1804–15). The British and their supporters finally defeated Napoleon at Waterloo in 1815, sealing British international **hegemony**.

For three centuries after 1492, world politics was dominated by the efforts of the principal European states to overpower one another and to control the non-European parts of the world (see "What Shaped Our World?" on p. 9). They pursued their economic and military interests by creating formal mercantilist colonial empires in some areas, by exercising less formal military and economic dominion elsewhere. Meanwhile, the principal European powers battled one another for their possessions and for global predominance. The rulers of western Europe fought on two fronts—to subdue the populations of their empires and to expand at the expense of other European rulers.

By the end of the Napoleonic Wars in 1815, however, both central organizing principles of the mercantilist era were being challenged. With the defeat of France by the anti-Napoleon coalition, conflict among the principal powers in Europe subsided and their security interests evolved. Meanwhile, the Industrial Revolution gathered force in Britain and in continental Europe, thus starting to alter the economic interests of the industrializing nations.

Peace of Westphalia

The settlement that ended the Thirty Years' War in 1648; often said to have created the modern state system because it included a general recognition of the principles of sovereignty and nonintervention.

sovereignty

The expectation that states have legal and political supremacy—or ultimate authority—within their territorial boundaries.

hegemony

The predominance of one nation-state over others.

Colonialists and the Colonized

Most of the Europeans who came to dominate the world after 1500 viewed Africa, Asia, and Latin America as full of primitive peoples who were centuries behind the civilizations of Europe. The reality was quite different. In 1500, as the first European colonial surge began, only one of the world's 10 largest cities was in Europe: the world's most populous city, Peking (now Beijing), was more than three times the size of Europe's largest city, Paris. When Spanish explorers arrived in Tenochtitlán, the capital city of the Aztecs—what is now Mexico City—they were amazed. One of the Spaniards wrote: "These great towns and temple-pyramids and buildings rising from the water, all made of stone, seemed like an enchanted vision."[a] The gap between Europe and the regions the Europeans colonized was often small; most of these regions had well-developed economies, social systems, and governments. How, then, did Europe come to rule the world so quickly and so completely?

Interests The causes of European imperialism remain hotly contested. At a minimum, European states were interested in securing access to the precious metals and trade of the lands they had newly "discovered." Rulers sponsoring the transoceanic expeditions wanted to enhance their own wealth and that of their merchants. They also wanted to strengthen their economies and societies against other European states, which they feared might gain riches abroad that would give them an advantage within Europe. These political interests overlapped with a religious motive, pushed by a still-powerful church and missionaries who sought new converts and strove to "uplift" supposedly primitive peoples to the standards of Christian civilization.

Interactions Imperialism was facilitated by industrialization in Europe, which quickly widened the wealth gap between it and the rest of the world: by 1870, income per person in the United Kingdom was five or six times what it was in Africa or Asia.[b] As the wealth gap grew, technological developments in transportation and communications gave

Spanish invaders in Tenochtitlán, 1520.

Europeans tremendous advantages: the steamship, the railroad, and the telegraph were crucial to imperial expansion. The Europeans' technological advantages meant that they largely controlled the result of their interactions with people elsewhere. Perhaps the most important European technological advances were related to the development of new weapons—such as long-distance artillery, accurate rifles, and the Maxim self-powered machine gun—that enabled relatively small numbers of Europeans to defeat large military forces in the rest of the world.

Institutions The institutional arrangements that resulted from these increasingly one-sided and violent interactions were colonial empires. Empire was an institution that transferred political authority from the local ruler to the imperialist home country. The European colonial powers typically ruled their colonies so as to further their own interests. Valuable resources were controlled by the colonialists, while the imperial powers usually gave the colonies only as much authority as was in the interests of the imperial center. Although local elites often retained some measure of autonomy, it existed only at the discretion of the imperial state. The lack of political rights and self-rule is what eventually gave rise to demands for independence, from the American Revolution of 1776 against the British, to the revolts against Spain and Portugal by Latin American states in the early eighteenth century, and finally to the collapse of nearly all remaining European empires after World War II.

---

a. Quoted in Michael E. Smith, *The Aztecs* (Oxford: Blackwell, 1996), 2.

b. Maddison, *World Economy: A Millennial Perspective*, 264.

The Pax Britannica

The century from 1815 to 1914 was remarkably different from those that preceded it and the one that followed. The major powers were far more interested than they had been in trading and investing worldwide, including with one another. Instead of imposing strict restraints on the movement of goods and money around the world, most governments welcomed ever-greater links among their economies. Their economic interactions became more cooperative as they pursued a common interest in global economic integration.

This cooperation contributed to the accelerated economic growth that much of the world experienced during this period (Figure 1.1). On the military front, global conflicts among the major powers gave way to generally peaceful ties among the countries of Europe (and, eventually, to North America and Japan). To be sure, Europeans continued to use military and economic means to tighten and expand their control over people in their colonies and other poor countries. But interactions among the industrialized nations were generally pacific, and the world economy became very tightly integrated.

Figure sources: Angus Maddison, *The World Economy: Historical Statistics* (Paris: OECD, 2003); 2010 data from www.ggdc.net/maddison/maddison-project/data/mpd_2013-01.xlsx (accessed 10/10/14).

*1990 international Geary-Khamis dollars (internationally comparable dollars of 1990).

The Hundred Years' Peace

Between 1815 and 1914, relations among the European powers—and such rising non-European powers as the United States and Japan—were far calmer than they had been for the previous 300 years. While powerful nations certainly continued

FIGURE 1.1 *Gross Domestic Product per Capita, 1500–2010**

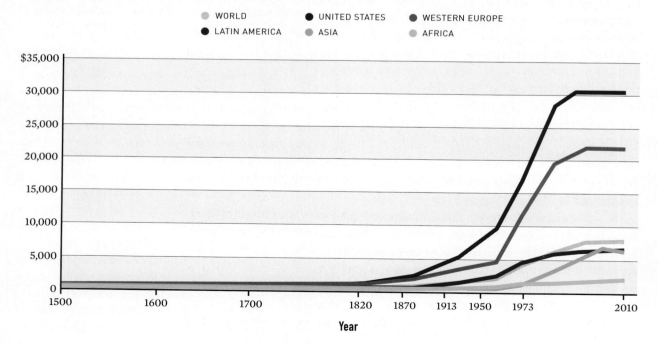

to care about their security interests, their relations became much more stable and cooperative.

Several sources contributed to the greater cooperation among European powers. The first was a common interest in protecting ruling regimes from new political pressures. The French Revolution and the ensuing wars had, among other things, pitted democratic revolutionaries against absolutist and autocratic governments, and the autocrats had won. Few European nations were at all democratic, and those that were democratic were very partially so: in 1830, barely 2 percent of the British population was permitted to vote, and even then the disproportionate allocation of seats meant that those city dwellers who could vote were unlikely to have much influence. All through the nineteenth century, however, movements for greater representation of the middle classes, farmers, and the working classes grew in strength. Sometimes rulers gave in to these demands. But throughout Europe there was a common fear of revolution—by democratic forces originally, and eventually by the growing socialist and communist movements.

The common interest of the European rulers in suppressing revolution helped overcome their political differences. The monarchies that ruled Prussia, Russia, and Austria, in fact, established a formal Holy Alliance in 1815 that was aimed largely at facing the revolutionary threat. Eventually, cooperation extended to most of Europe, in what came to be called the Concert of Europe, a system under which the major powers consulted one another on important diplomatic affairs. At the same time, the growing integration of the markets of the European powers gave them some common economic interests as well, as we will discuss in the next section.

In addition to the convergence of interests among the principal powers, their interactions were stabilized by the reality of British diplomatic, military, and economic predominance. In fact, the period is sometimes called the **Pax Britannica** (Latin for "British peace," by analogy with the Pax Romana that Rome was said to have created within its classical empire). British hegemony proved a stabilizing force among European nations. British military power was important—the British navy "ruled the waves" with few challengers—but the country's significance rested also on its role in affecting interactions among European countries that had long been in conflict. Britain tried to prevent the supremacy of any one country on the European continent, acting to maintain a balance of power. (As we will see in Chapter 5, countries may form alliances in an effort to balance the power of a stronger country.) If one country or coalition seemed too strong, Britain would ally itself with an opposing country or coalition. This rough balance, which was the general goal of British foreign policy throughout the century, helped deter military conflict among the European powers.

Conflicts among the powers were muted, and there were few periods of open military strife. The age of massive intra-European war appeared to be over. To be sure, the power balance did not always keep interactions peaceful, and European (and non-European) powers continued to compete with one another for military advantage and influence. The decline of one empire and the rise of another led to the century's biggest conflicts. The Ottoman Empire, which ruled much of the Middle East, North Africa, and southeastern Europe, weakened continually over the

Pax Britannica

"British Peace," a century-long period, beginning with Napoleon's defeat at Waterloo in 1815 and ending with the outbreak of World War I in 1914, during which Britain's economic and diplomatic influence contributed to economic openness and relative peace.

course of the nineteenth century. As the Ottoman state tottered, Russia attempted to expand its influence in the Middle East; and when other European countries sought to restrain Russia, the Crimean War (1853–56) and Russian defeat were the result. Meanwhile, Prussia gradually unified a new German empire under its control. The French tried to discourage this process, but Prussia's victory in the Franco-Prussian War (1870–71) settled the matter. The finalization of German unification indicated the arrival of a new power in Europe. Despite these conflicts, the century from 1815 to 1914 was one of relative peace among the world's principal diplomatic and military powers.

Free Trade

Just as the absolutist European rulers—monarchs or others—could agree on a common opposition to democratic and other revolutionaries, they could also agree on the desirability of ending the mercantilist economic controls of the earlier imperial period. To some extent, the reduction of barriers to trade among nations reflected the more peaceful nature of relations among the principal powers. But the reversal of mercantilism also came from changes in the economic interests of the major powers themselves.

British desires for more open trade first displaced mercantilist interests. In the late eighteenth century, British inventors and industrialists introduced a flurry of technological innovations that revolutionized production. Employers brought workers together in large factories to use new machinery, new energy sources, and new forms of organization. Power looms and mechanical spinners transformed the textile industry. Improvements in the use of water power, and eventually the development of steam power, made the machinery more powerful still. By the 1820s, British industry was producing cotton and other textiles, iron, chemicals, and machinery at an unprecedented rate and at extremely low prices.

The economic interests created by Britain's Industrial Revolution saw mercantilist barriers to trade as irrelevant or harmful. Allowing foreigners to sell their products freely to Britain promised several positive effects. British manufacturers could lower their costs directly by importing cheaper raw materials, and indirectly because cheaper imported food would allow factory owners to pay lower wages without reducing workers' standard of living. And if foreigners earned more by selling to Britain, they would be able to buy more British goods. For these reasons, Britain's manufacturing classes and regions developed a dislike of mercantilism and a desire for free trade.

The City of London, which had become the world's financial center, added its influence to that of other free-trade interests. After all, Britain's international bankers had a powerful reason to open up the British market to foreigners: the foreigners were their customers. American or Argentine access to the thriving British market would make it easier for the Americans and Argentines to pay their debts to London. Of course, there were supporters of mercantilism and of barriers to trade more generally. Foremost among them were British farmers, who were protected by the Corn Laws. These were taxes, or tariffs, on imported grain. For 20 years, protectionist British farmers squared off against industrialists and other city dwellers.

Eventually, over the course of the 1840s, Parliament repealed most of the previous British mercantile controls on foreign trade.

After Britain, the world's most important economy, discarded mercantilism, many of the nation's customers and suppliers followed suit. In 1860, France joined Great Britain in a sweeping commercial treaty that freed trade between them and subsequently drew most of the rest of Europe in this direction. As the German states moved toward unification in 1871, they created a free-trade area among themselves and then opened trade with the rest of the world. Many New World governments also reduced trade barriers, as did the remaining colonial possessions of the free-trading European powers.

Mercantilism was dead, and integration into world markets—trade liberalization—was the order of the day. Over the course of the 1800s, the trade of the advanced countries grew two to three times as fast as their economies. By the end of the century, trade was seven or eight times as large a share of the world's economy as it had been at the beginning of the century.[3]

The opening of world trade was encouraged by, and did itself encourage, major advances in transportation and communications. The railroad fundamentally changed the speed and cost of carrying cargo overland. The steamship revolutionized oceangoing shipping, reducing the Atlantic crossing from over a month in 1816 to less than a week in 1896. By the late 1800s, telegraphs, telephones, steamships, and railroads had replaced horses, carrier pigeons, couriers, and sails. The transportation revolution led to a 20-fold increase in the world's shipping capacity during the nineteenth century.[4]

The Gold Standard

The **gold standard** organized monetary relations in this global economic order. When a country's government went "on gold," it promised to exchange its currency for gold at a preestablished rate. The country's currency became equivalent to gold, interchangeable at a fixed rate with the money of any other gold-standard country. Britain had had a gold-backed currency since 1717. As international trade and investment grew, more countries were drawn away from silver and other monetary metals and toward gold, the traditional international medium of exchange. Great Britain's status as the global market leader attracted other countries to use the same monetary system.

By the 1870s, most of the industrial world had adopted the gold standard. With all major currencies directly convertible into gold at fixed rates, the industrial world essentially shared one international currency. The predictability of the gold standard facilitated world trade, lending, investment, migration, and payments (which we will examine in more detail in Chapter 9, on international monetary relations).

gold standard
The monetary system that prevailed between about 1870 and 1914, in which countries tied their currencies to gold at a legally fixed price.

---

3. Angus Maddison, *Monitoring the World Economy, 1820–1992* (Paris: Development Centre of the OECD, 1995), 38. For an excellent survey of the period, see Peter T. Marsh, *Bargaining on Europe: Britain and the First Common Market, 1860–1892* (New Haven, CT: Yale University Press, 1999).

4. Peter Mathias and Sidney Pollard, eds. *The Cambridge Economic History of Europe*, vol. 8, *The Industrial Economics: The Development of Economic and Social Policies* (Cambridge: Cambridge University Press, 1989), 56; and Maddison, *World Economy: A Millennial Perspective*, 95.

International trade, investment, and immigration grew dramatically. Citizens of rich countries invested huge portions of their savings abroad. In the 75 years before 1914, 50 million people left Europe for other continents, and another 50 million left their homelands in Asia to live elsewhere. Free trade, the gold standard, and the new technologies of transportation and communications linked world markets for goods, labor, and capital more tightly than ever before. In short, the world entered its first era of what we now call globalization.

Colonial Imperialism

However peaceful their diplomatic and economic relations may have been in Europe, the principal powers continued to use military force and economic controls on countries in the rest of the world. After a lull in the early part of the century, there was a burst of territorial expansion after 1870 that left most of Africa and Asia part of colonial empires.

The European powers, and eventually non-European powers such as the United States and Japan, were interested in the poor countries of Latin America, Africa, and Asia, for both security and economic reasons. The rich nations were interested in the resources and markets of the poor countries, in many cases wanting to secure them for themselves (rather than sharing them with others). The major powers also saw the rest of the world as a sort of chessboard on which they could fight battles among themselves in their quest for military supremacy. The European (and American and Japanese) presence in the rest of the world expanded, contracted, and adjusted in accordance with the changing goals of the major powers and changes in the interactions among them.

The colonies had been central to the mercantilist system, but as mercantilism declined, the economic interests in colonialism faded. For a hundred years after 1760, in fact, the European empires shrank dramatically. Many previous supporters of colonialism in the colonies began to favor independence, and many people in Europe (such as the father of modern economics, Adam Smith, along with other free traders in Britain) came to see the colonies as unnecessarily burdensome. Eventually, Britain, France, Spain, and Portugal lost almost all their New World colonies, and by 1850 the only major colonial possessions remaining were British India, the Dutch East Indies (now Indonesia), and French Algeria.[5]

In the 1870s, however, colonial expansion started anew. The new powers that arose inside and outside Europe—Germany, Italy, Japan, the United States—saw colonial possessions as a way of improving their military position. The established powers, especially Britain and France, did not want their newer rivals accumulating colonial power and wealth at their expense. At the same time, the growth of industry in the developed world increased the desire for overseas markets and resources. And there was an upsurge in nationalist sentiment, especially in such

---

5. Britain's Canadian and Australian possessions had obtained effective autonomy by the 1850s, although they were still formally colonies. Within the British Empire, certain colonial areas were given extensive grants of self-government; for all intents and purposes, by the late nineteenth century, Canada, Australia, and New Zealand acted as if they were independent.

newly important nations as Germany, Italy, and Japan, which spurred governments to satisfy nationalistic demands for expansion.

The result was a scramble for new colonies. From a few scattered outposts in Africa, Europeans quickly spread out to occupy and rule the entire continent, leaving only Ethiopia and Liberia independent by 1890. Britain consolidated and extended its control of South Asia, while it, France, the Netherlands, Germany, Japan, and the United States took over almost all the rest of Southeast and East Asia (Map 1.1). Within the space of a few decades, the industrialized nations had subjected most of the poor regions of the world to direct colonial control. The only major exceptions were Latin America, Persia (Iran), Siam (Thailand), and China, and even they had their sovereignty restricted by military and economic constraints imposed by the European nations, Japan, and the United States.

The Thirty Years' Crisis

A century of relative peace and prosperity in Europe ended with the most devastating military and economic conflicts in modern history. Generations of people in the advanced industrial world had their expectations of stability and security shattered by two terrible world wars and a catastrophic worldwide economic depression. The collapse of Europe's diplomatic balance led to three decades of global conflicts on the military, diplomatic, economic, and political fronts.

Tension in Europe

Contention among the principal powers had grown after 1900. One source of renewed conflict was the changing European power balance. On the one hand, the Ottoman, Austro-Hungarian, and Russian empires were weakening under the weight of socioeconomic stagnation, political instability, and ethnic conflict. On the other hand, new economic and political actors were joining the world stage: the United States, after decades of avoiding foreign entanglements, was becoming more engaged with the rest of the world both politically and economically, and Japan had become a serious international force, as reflected in its decisive victory in the Russo-Japanese War of 1904–5.

The most striking change in the European power balance was the rise of Germany. In 1870, the French and German populations and economies were of roughly similar size, and their economies were substantially smaller than Britain's, but by 1900, Germany's population and economy were the largest in Europe, larger even than those of Britain. This shift created frictions among European nations. The Germans, who had come late onto the world scene, felt that they had fallen behind in the race for colonies. Frustrated with its meager colonial possessions, Germany focused on Europe and appeared to have designs on neighboring lands with large German populations. These neighbors feared German expansionism and domination. For decades, the major European nations had had generally cooperative

MAP 1.1 *The Colonial Empires, 1914*

After 1870, European countries, Japan, and the United States
dramatically expanded their colonial possessions.
By 1914, almost all of Asia and Africa had been taken over
by the colonial powers. In the poorer regions of the world,
only Latin America, China, and a handful of countries in
Africa and Asia remained independent.

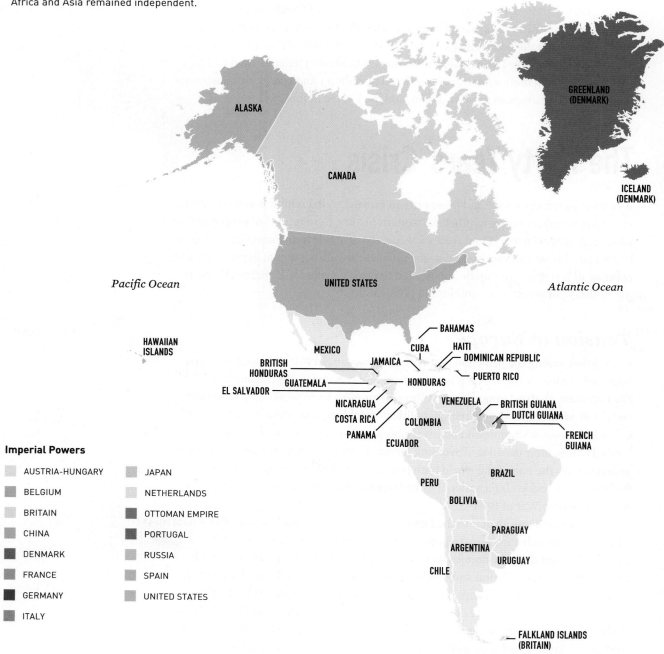

GREENLAND
(DENMARK)

ALASKA

ICELAND
(DENMARK)

CANADA

Pacific Ocean

UNITED STATES

Atlantic Ocean

HAWAIIAN
ISLANDS

BAHAMAS

MEXICO

CUBA

HAITI

BRITISH
HONDURAS

JAMAICA

DOMINICAN REPUBLIC

EL SALVADOR

GUATEMALA

HONDURAS

PUERTO RICO

NICARAGUA

VENEZUELA

BRITISH GUIANA

COSTA RICA

DUTCH GUIANA

COLOMBIA

PANAMA

ECUADOR

FRENCH
GUIANA

BRAZIL

PERU

BOLIVIA

PARAGUAY

ARGENTINA

URUGUAY

CHILE

FALKLAND ISLANDS
(BRITAIN)

Imperial Powers

- AUSTRIA-HUNGARY
- BELGIUM
- BRITAIN
- CHINA
- DENMARK
- FRANCE
- GERMANY
- ITALY
- JAPAN
- NETHERLANDS
- OTTOMAN EMPIRE
- PORTUGAL
- RUSSIA
- SPAIN
- UNITED STATES

Arctic Ocean

NORWAY SWEDEN

RUSSIAN EMPIRE

BRITAIN

IRELAND

NETH. DENMARK

BEL. GER.

FRANCE AUSTRIA-HUNGARY

MONGOLIA

KOREA JAPAN

SPAIN ITALY

PORTUGAL GREECE OTTOMAN EMPIRE AFGHANISTAN CHINA

FRENCH MOROCCO SPANISH MOROCCO PERSIA TIBET

CYRENAICA QATAR NEPAL

RIO DE ORO ALGERIA EGYPT TRUCIAL OMAN INDIA

GAMBIA OMAN BURMA TAIWAN Pacific Ocean

FRENCH WEST AFRICA ERITREA

SUDAN ADEN SIAM FRENCH INDOCHINA PHILIPPINES

GHANA FR. EQUATORIAL AFRICA FRENCH SOMALILAND

NIGERIA ETHIOPIA BRITISH SOMALILAND CEYLON MALAY STATES

LIBERIA TOGO CAMEROON ITALIAN SOMALILAND

SIERRA LEONE RIO MUNI UGANDA BRITISH EAST AFRICA DUTCH EAST INDIES GERMAN NEW GUINEA

FR. EQUATORIAL GUINEA BELGIAN CONGO GERMAN EAST AFRICA PAPUA

ANGOLA MOZAMBIQUE

PORTUGUESE GUINEA N. RHODESIA NYASALAND Indian Ocean

GER. SW. AFR. S. RHODESIA

BECHUANA-LAND MADAGASCAR AUSTRALIA

SWAZILAND

UNION OF SOUTH AFRICA BASUTOLAND

NEW ZEALAND

political and economic relations; now, the prospect of a challenge to the previous arrangements made governments wary and suspicious.

Eventually, Europe divided into two hostile camps. On the one side were the central and southern European powers of Germany, Austria-Hungary, and the Ottoman Empire; on the other were Britain and France to the west and Russia to the east. Crises, whether in Morocco or the Caribbean, the Balkans or Africa, aggravated tensions until war erupted in the summer of 1914. The Central powers—Germany, Austria-Hungary, the Ottoman Empire, and Bulgaria—were arrayed against the Allied powers: most of the rest of Europe (Map 1.2).

MAP 1.2 *Europe, 1914*

World War I and Its Effects

All participants expected the war to be short and decisive, but it turned out to be long and largely inconclusive—and extraordinarily bloody. Especially on the western front, in Belgium and northern France, huge armies settled into entrenched positions. Trench warfare was punctuated by attempts to break through enemy lines that typically led only to massive losses in dead, wounded, and captured troops on both sides. The first battle of the Marne, in September 1916, cost each side about a quarter million dead and wounded in a week. The entry of the United States in April 1917 on the side of the Allies, and the failure of German submarine warfare to cut Britain off from its supplies, guaranteed the defeat of the Central powers, but the victors had little to show for their success. The war was far longer and far costlier than anyone had imagined it would be; it took the lives of at least 15 million people, including about 7 million civilians.

Despite its immense cost, World War I did little to resolve the underlying political and military tensions that had unsettled Europe; indeed, it exacerbated them. The war utterly disrupted European politics both among and within nations. It led to the collapse of the four great empires of central, eastern, and southern Europe. In the territory from Finland to Yugoslavia, the Austro-Hungarian and Russian empires shattered into pieces, and central and eastern Europe suddenly had a dozen new "successor states." The Ottoman Empire, which before the war had stretched from the Persian Gulf to Libya, and from Albania to Yemen, was reduced to the far smaller country of Turkey. The German Empire lost what few colonies it had had, along with large portions of its European territory and population (Map 1.3).

In addition to changing the political map of Europe, the war fundamentally altered domestic social and economic conditions. For most of Europe, economic recovery was slow and partial; many central and eastern European countries went through debilitating bouts of hyperinflation, with prices rising by thousands or millions of percentages. In the most dramatic case, that of Germany, prices rose to a level *1 million million times*—that is, a trillion times—their immediate postwar level. The German mark, previously traded at 4.2 to the dollar, was eventually valued at 4,200,000,000,000—that is, 4.2 trillion—to the dollar. In the final months of the German hyperinflation, the central bank had to print so much currency that it used more than 30 dedicated paper mills, 29 plate manufacturers, and 132 printing plants.[6]

This terrible experience bankrupted much of the central European middle classes and helped alienate them from the new democratic systems. Along with farmers, the dissatisfied middle classes grew to be an important base for extreme right-wing movements, such as the Fascists in Italy and the Nazis in Germany. At the same time, the war and its aftermath increased the power and organization of European labor movements and the socialist parties they supported. In Russia, a radical socialist movement took power, and soon there were communist parties

---

6. Gerald D. Feldman, *The Great Disorder: Politics, Economics, and Society in the German Inflation, 1914–1924* (New York: Oxford University Press, 1993), 782–85.

MAP 1.3 *Europe after World War I, 1920*

everywhere, representing a revolutionary left-wing challenge to capitalism. The communists favored government ownership of the means of production rather than capitalist private property, and a planned economy rather than a market system. Politics was polarized and nationalist sentiments inflamed, promoting tensions among European nations.

While it further weakened the bases of peace in Europe, the war demonstrated the international economic and military predominance of the United States. The entry of the United States into the war in 1917, both with its millions of troops and with its billions of dollars in loans to the Allies, effectively guaranteed the Allied victory. President Woodrow Wilson guided the negotiations that led to the **Treaty of Versailles**, which ended the war. Economically, while the Europeans

Treaty of Versailles

The peace treaty between the Allies and Germany that formally ended World War I on June 28, 1919.

were engulfed in war, the United States rushed into the vacuum they left in the rest of the world and seized a dramatically increased share of global trade and investment. In fact, the United States became the principal source of war loans to the Allies, such that between 1914 and 1919, America changed from being the world's biggest debtor to its biggest lender. The European powers were dependent on the United States for financial, commercial, and diplomatic leadership to rebuild from the most destructive war the world had ever known.

After this flurry of involvement in European politics and economics, however, the United States drew back. President Wilson could not convince the U.S. Senate to approve American entry into the **League of Nations**. Ironically, this was an international institution created, largely along lines defined by Wilson at Versailles, to bring the world's nations together to increase cooperation and guarantee the peace. In 1920, the Republican Party swept the presidency and both houses of Congress on a platform opposed to Wilson's internationalism and committed to an isolationist foreign policy that would insulate the United States from the uncertainties of intra-European conflict.

League of Nations

A collective security organization founded in 1919 after World War I. The League ended in 1946 and was replaced by the United Nations.

Interwar Instability

Europe was left to its own devices, without even the semblance of the pre-1914 balance. The French and British were weak in victory, Germany was bitter in defeat, Russia was isolated in its communist experiment, and the Ottoman and Austro-Hungarian empires had dissolved into a series of small states beset by constant diplomatic and economic tensions. Economic conditions were unsettled, political systems were unstable, and diplomatic relations were tense when not downright hostile.

The French and Germans, in particular, continued to clash diplomatically over issues left unsettled on the battlefield. These included control of the border regions of Alsace, Lorraine, and the Saar—the former two of which went to France, the latter to Germany. Another issue was Germany's commitment not to militarize the Rhineland, a region of Germany bordering France. Germany objected to this restriction on its sovereignty, while France regarded the movement of troops into a border region as a threat.

French and German interests also conflicted over the so-called war debts–reparations tangle. The Treaty of Versailles imposed payments of reparations, a fine levied on the losers for having started the war. This demand created great resentment in Germany, especially given the country's troubled economic conditions. The French argued, among other things, that they needed reparations to pay their debts to the United States. They would, they said, reduce demands on Germany if the United States would forgive some or all of these war debts; after all, the European Allies had paid a high price in lives and property. But the Americans were in no mood to give away billions of dollars to further their involvement with Europe. And so, all throughout the 1920s and 1930s, the principals in World War I continued their battles in the diplomatic and economic realm.

After World War I ended, continuing tensions prevented cooperation on economic issues. Germany suffered hyperinflation that made its currency, the mark, virtually worthless. Here, children play with bundles of useless marks in the street.

The worst was yet to come: in 1929, the world spiraled downward toward further conflict. The global Great Depression that began in that year was more severe, lasted longer, and caused more hardship than any other economic downturn in modern history. Industrial production dropped by half in the United States, and by 1932, one-quarter of the country's workers were unemployed. In Germany, unemployment topped one-third of the labor force. No country was untouched.

The economic catastrophe deepened political polarization within nations, in many cases bringing extreme right-wing, highly nationalistic, often militaristic governments to power. By the late 1930s, the Nazis and their fascist allies controlled all of central, eastern, and southern Europe, as well as Japan. All these countries were hostile to the international economy and to the rich nations of western Europe and North America. In Latin America and in the colonial world, the collapse of the world economy drove nations to turn inward, strengthening the hand of nationalist and anticolonial forces.

World War II

Europe descended once again into war. World War II largely pitted the fascist governments that had turned against the global economy, on the one hand, against the democratic powers that remained committed to some form of international economic cooperation (along with the Soviet Union), on the other. In 1940, the three major fascist powers—Germany, Italy, and Japan—aimed at restoring and increasing their military might and territory, and in 1940 they established a formal alliance, the Axis. By invasion, coercion, and persuasion, they built a network of followers, protectorates, and colonies—Japan in East Asia, Italy and Germany in Europe and North Africa.

An expansionist Nazi Germany annexed Austria in 1938 and occupied Czechoslovakia in 1939. Also in 1939, Germany attacked Poland and quickly overpowered it, leading Britain and France to declare war on Germany in support of their Polish ally. But in May 1940, Germany invaded France, which it defeated and occupied within six weeks. The Axis powers thus controlled virtually all of Europe and Asia except for Britain and the Soviet Union; the democratic Allies were restricted to Britain, North America, Australia, and New Zealand. In June 1941, Germany invaded the Soviet Union, and soon German troops were on the outskirts of Moscow. In December, Japan—which had already occupied most of China and Indochina—attacked the American naval base at Pearl Harbor.

The United States had been supporting the British with supplies, but the Japanese attack on Pearl Harbor in 1941 overcame any lingering American reluctance to get involved in another world war. From then on, the war pitted the Axis against the three major Allies—the United States, Britain, and the Soviet Union. The bulk of the war in Europe was fought along the eastern front, between the Germans and the Soviets, where millions of troops faced each other over thousands of miles of territory. After an initial frenzied retreat, the Soviets battled back and turned the tide at Stalingrad in early 1943. Meanwhile, the British and Americans carried out operations in North Africa before invading Italy in 1943 and France in 1944, while American forces advanced against Japan in the Pacific. In May 1945, Germany surrendered unconditionally. In August, in an attempt to force a Japanese surrender, the United States dropped nuclear weapons on the cities of Hiroshima and Nagasaki; the Japanese surrendered several days later.

The human and economic costs of World War II were unimaginably large. About 110 million people served in the combined armed forces, of whom 25 million were killed. Approximately 30 million civilians were killed by the war directly, and this number does not include the 7 million or more people, mostly Jews, whom the Germans and their allies murdered in a planned genocide. Four-fifths of the dead were from Allied nations, including some 20 million from the Soviet Union (13 million military, 7 million civilian). Most of Europe and Japan were left in ruins.

The Cold War

The impact of World War II on international politics was profound. Unlike in 1918, the results of the war were conclusive, and they fundamentally altered international power relations. Germany, Japan, Italy, France, and Britain, which had defined great-power politics before the war, were effectively finished as world powers; the only two nations with the ability to project significant military power were the United States and the Soviet Union. The question that remained was how this two-power world would be ordered. On the one hand, the two principal wartime allies had cooperated in defeating the Axis powers. On the other hand, they represented fundamentally different socioeconomic systems and had divergent interests in the organization of the postwar world.

The Superpowers Emerge

At war's end, the United States, the Soviet Union, Great Britain, and France were united in victory. The Allies defined the terms of the peace, carved up Germany into zones of occupation, and divided Europe into spheres of influence. Many people, including in the United States, felt that the four principal victors could, should, and would cooperate under the auspices of the new United Nations (UN) to manage international relations peacefully.

But within months, conflicts grew between the United States and the Soviet Union. Perhaps disagreements were inevitable between a capitalist democracy and a communist one-party system. It may be that the two superpowers were driven toward discord by the very structure of their power relations, as they struggled for influence in Europe. Scholars continue to debate whether the source of the division was the inherently different economic or military interests of the two superpowers, or rather some failure in their attempts to interact productively.

By 1949, the two superpowers were consolidating control over their respective blocs. The United States drew together its new allies—including the defeated Axis nations—into a Western system. The Americans worked to solidify their coalition as a common military alliance (NATO) and as a collaborative economic order (the Bretton Woods System). The Soviet Union, for its part, now led a communist alliance that stretched from central Europe to the Pacific, because China, North Korea, and North Vietnam had joined. The international order divided into communist and capitalist parts, and the Cold War between them was the defining characteristic of international politics from the late 1940s until the late 1980s.

The Blocs Consolidate

The Cold War pitted the two superpowers against each other. Their military and economic interests were almost diametrically opposed. The United States favored market-based, capitalist economic activities, while the Soviet Union rejected markets and capitalism in favor of a centrally planned socialism. In the geopolitical sphere, the Soviets regarded a pro-American Western Europe as a threat to their western borders, and a pro-American Japan as a threat to the east; the Americans saw the Soviets and their communist allies as a military menace to their own European and Asian allies. In an atmosphere of trust and stability, it might have been possible for the two superpowers to work out an amicable understanding, but as it turned out, interactions between them quickly turned hostile and suspicious, and they devoted their efforts to fortifying themselves one against the other.

Each superpower went about building up its respective coalition. The United States provided $14 billion in Marshall Plan and other aid to Western Europe and Japan in order to speed postwar reconstruction. It also led the Western world in creating a system of military alliances in the North Atlantic, Southeast Asia, Latin America, and elsewhere. The most important of these, the **North Atlantic Treaty Organization (NATO)**, brought together North America and most of Western Europe in a collective military institution united against the Soviet Union and its allies (see Chapter 5 for more details on NATO and other military alliances).

The United States also guided its allies toward a newly integrated and strongly institutionalized Western economic order. The **Bretton Woods System**, so called because its founding documents were negotiated at the Bretton Woods resort in New Hampshire, included institutions intended to

North Atlantic Treaty Organization (NATO)
An alliance formed in 1949 among the United States, Canada, and most of the states of Western Europe in response to the threat posed by the Soviet Union. The alliance requires its members to consider an attack on any one of them as an attack on all.

Bretton Woods System
The economic order negotiated among allied nations at Bretton Woods, New Hampshire, in 1944, which led to a series of cooperative arrangements involving a commitment to relatively low barriers to international trade and investment.

encourage the freer movement of goods and capital around the world. In trade relations, the General Agreement on Tariffs and Trade (GATT) oversaw a substantial reduction in trade barriers.[7] In monetary affairs, the International Monetary Fund (IMF) supervised a restored but reformed gold-dollar standard, in which the U.S. dollar was tied to gold and all other currencies were tied to the dollar. The International Bank for Reconstruction and Development (also called the World Bank) worked to encourage a resumption of private investment, especially in the developing nations (these economic institutions are discussed in more detail in Part 3).

By the early 1960s, the Western world had rebuilt an integrated international economy—not a copy of the pre-1914 age of free trade and the gold standard, but something new. The commitment to economic integration was now combined with social welfare programs such as unemployment insurance and the widespread public provision of health care, pensions, housing, and other social benefits. This extensive social safety net helped cushion workers from the harshest effects of global competition, and the Bretton Woods System thus represented a compromise between economic integration and national commitments to social reform and the welfare state.

The Soviet Union also consolidated its bloc. It created a military alliance with its European allies, the **Warsaw Pact**. It strengthened military ties with the communist government that took power in China in 1949. In the economic realm, the Soviet bloc developed a socialist variant of economic integration in which different nations specialized in different products. This economic cooperation was overseen by an institution called the Council for Mutual Economic Assistance, which brought together the communist nations and some of their supporters in the developing world. The Cold War, indeed, extended to competition over the support of many newly independent countries in Africa, Asia, and the Caribbean. Eventually, there was a rough division of the world between countries that tended to ally with the United States and those that tended to ally with the Soviet Union (Map 1.4).

The defining feature of military relations between the two superpowers was the development of nuclear weapons. By 1954, both the United States and the Soviet Union had atomic and hydrogen bombs, possessing a destructive power far beyond anything previously possible. With the development of long-distance bombers and missiles, eventually both superpowers had the ability to destroy each other (and their allies) many times over. The potent American and Soviet weapon stockpiles led to a real fear that war between the two superpowers might be unimaginably devastating and might threaten all humanity.

However, the roughly equal arsenals of nuclear weapons created something of a standoff: each side's destructive capacity was sufficient to deter an attack on its homeland or its close allies. Since neither the United States nor the Soviet Union

Warsaw Pact

A military alliance formed in 1955 to bring together the Soviet Union and its Cold War allies in Eastern Europe and elsewhere; dissolved on March 31, 1991, as the Cold War ended.

---

7. The original institution was to be the International Trade Organization, but it encountered opposition in the United States. As a result, an "interim" institution, the GATT, was established.

MAP 1.4　*The Cold War and Its Alliances, 1980*

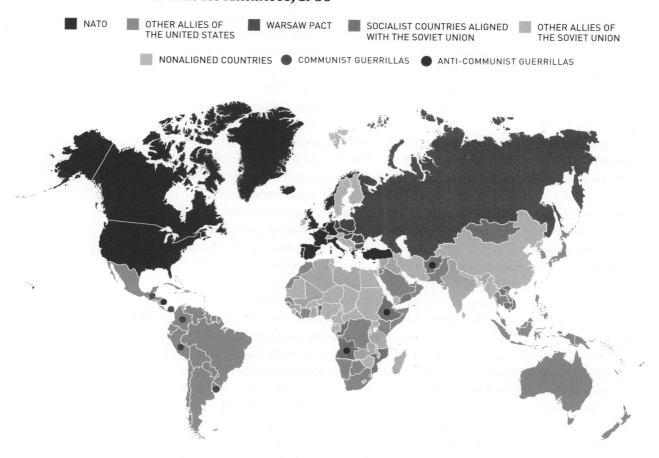

could really hope to conquer the other or its principal friends, their competition was limited to other regions of the globe.

Indeed, despite the absence of direct warfare between the superpowers, the Cold War was by no means a peaceful time for people in much of the world. On several occasions, crises between the two came to the brink of war, such as the 1949 Berlin airlift and the 1962 Cuban missile crisis. In the aftermath of the German surrender, Germany was divided into four zones, controlled respectively by the Americans, British, French, and Soviets. The country's traditional capital, Berlin, which was located deep inside the Soviet zone, was also divided in four. Over time, the Western allies worked together in their zones, but there was constant friction between them and the Soviets. In June 1948, the Soviet Union blockaded land and rail routes into Berlin from the Western zones. This action cut West Berlin off from supplies of everything from food to coal. The Soviets clearly expected the Western allies to either withdraw or give in to several Soviet demands about the occupation. But the allies quickly organized a massive airlift that lasted nearly a year and involved almost 300,000 flights, providing millions of tons of supplies to the residents of West Berlin. In May 1949, the Soviets finally backed down and once again permitted transport between the Western occupation zones and West Berlin. However, the level of tension between East and West remained high. It was only heightened in 1961, when the East Germans built a wall between East and West Berlin, cutting the city in half.

Perhaps the most dramatic confrontation of the Cold War took place soon after the Berlin Wall went up, several thousand miles away, in Cuba. In 1959, a left-wing nationalist movement headed by Fidel Castro succeeded in ousting pro-American dictator Fulgencio Batista. Over the next several years, the new revolutionary government of Cuba moved quickly leftward and allied itself with the Soviet Union. An American-sponsored invasion in April 1961 failed, but the Cuban government was deeply fearful of American attempts to undermine it. Meanwhile, the Soviet government under Nikita Khrushchev was concerned that it was losing the nuclear arms race to the United States. In the summer of 1962, the Soviets secretly began installing nuclear missiles in Cuba; these were intended both to help protect the pro-Soviet Cuban government and, more important, to help even out the nuclear balance by putting Soviet missiles within easy striking distance of the United States.

In October 1962, American spy planes spotted the missile installations, which the U.S. government regarded as a clear and present danger to American national security. American ships encircled the island, prepared to prevent Soviet naval vessels from reaching it, and plans for an American invasion were developed, even though many of the participants realized that such an action might lead to a nuclear war between the two sides. For about a week, the U.S. and Soviet governments bargained over the missiles in an atmosphere of extraordinary tension and widespread expectation that war would break out. Finally, the two sides agreed to a deal: the Soviets would dismantle their missiles in Cuba if the United States withdrew its nuclear missiles from Turkey.[8]

In addition to the threat of war between the two nations, each superpower routinely used military force to prevent other countries from falling into the sphere of its rival. The United States had its military and intelligence services undermine governments that were communist or seen as likely to come under communist influence: Iran in 1953, Guatemala in 1954, the Congo and Cuba in 1961, the Dominican Republic in 1962, Chile in 1971, and Nicaragua from 1979 to 1988. The Soviet Union similarly used military power to extend or preserve its own influence. Its forces invaded Hungary in 1956 and Czechoslovakia in 1968, when these allies seemed likely to leave the Soviet orbit. The Soviet Union also invaded Afghanistan in 1979, leading to a decade-long war that sapped the Soviets' military might.

---

8. The literature on the crisis is enormous; for an example, see Michael Dobbs, *One Minute to Midnight: Kennedy, Khrushchev, and Castro on the Brink of Nuclear War* (New York: Knopf, 2008). The tense showdown during the crisis is an example of brinkmanship, which we will discuss in Chapter 3.

In the colonial and postcolonial world, especially, the two superpowers constantly jockeyed for influence. Wars in Korea and Vietnam were the most obvious instances. In both cases, the Soviets supported one side of a civil conflict while the Americans supported another side. The United States and some of its allies sent troops to both South Korea and South Vietnam; the Soviet Union and some of its allies sent supplies to both North Korea and North Vietnam. The same sort of "proxy war" was fought in many regions and over many decades. Much of the developing world became a Cold War battleground between pro-American and pro-Soviet forces.

Decolonization

The involvement of the two superpowers in the affairs of Africa, Asia, and Latin America was part of a broader emergence of these regions to a prominent place in world politics. This was a relatively new phenomenon in the modern era: between 1914 and the mid-1950s, the developing world was largely at the margins of world politics. Europe, North America, and Japan were preoccupied with two world wars, the Great Depression, postwar reconstruction, and the Cold War. Under these conditions, relations with the colonies and the independent developing nations were of less importance. The economic implications were particularly striking. For decades, Africa, Asia, and Latin America had supported themselves by exporting agricultural products and raw materials to the industrial world and importing manufactured products. But for much of the time between 1914 and 1955, the rich nations were unwilling or unable to continue normal trade relations; they were absorbed in war, devastated by economic crisis, or rebuilding after war.

The developing world thus was forced to rely less on its economic ties with the industrial nations and more on its own markets and products. While in the early stages it was external events—depression and war—that cut the developing world off, eventually governments encouraged the process. Many countries, and even some colonies, undertook substantial efforts at industrial development, providing at home what had previously been imported from Europe or North America. For example, by the early 1960s Brazil's industries supplied 99 percent of the country's consumer goods, 91 percent of its intermediate inputs (such as steel and chemicals), and 87 percent of its capital goods (such as machinery and equipment).[9] At that point the Brazilian economy, which was roughly the size of the Dutch economy, was close to self-sufficient in manufactured goods.

This economic turn inward was accompanied by an upsurge in nationalist sentiment. In Latin America, China, and Turkey, this trend brought to power governments that were unfavorable—even hostile—to foreign trade, foreign investment, and foreign finance. In many colonies, the rise in nationalism fed into dissatisfaction with continued colonial rule.

After World War II ended, the colonial clamor for greater autonomy, and even independence, increased. The European empires had been weakened by

---

9. Werner Baer, *The Brazilian Economy: Growth and Development*, 3rd ed. (New York: Praeger, 1989), 70.

the war, and their ability to sustain colonialism by force had diminished. Meanwhile, the nationalist movements had grown in strength and resolve, and they demanded autonomy and even independence more insistently. Many in the developing world looked to the experience of the United States and the Latin American republics, which had gained their independence in the late eighteenth and early nineteenth centuries. Now **decolonization** was on the agenda again, as another group of colonial subjects fought to leave the colonial empires. In some instances, such as British India, the colonial powers gave in to these demands, albeit reluctantly, recognizing that they had little alternative. But in other instances, such as British Kenya, French Algeria, and the Dutch East Indies (Indonesia), independence came only after violent conflict between the colonialists and the colonized.

Pressure on the colonial powers did not come only from the nationalist independence movements. In many instances, the United States encouraged its European allies to release their subjects. American anticolonialism had moral sources but also more material origins. For example, American businesses welcomed a decolonization that would allow them fuller access to the markets of the developing world. And in the context of the Cold War, the United States was particularly concerned that colonialism would undermine American influence in the developing world. With so much of the world under European colonial control, it was hard for the United States to make a case for the evils of Soviet domination. The Americans feared that colonialism would push independence-minded Africans and Asians toward the communists in their search for allies.

decolonization

The process of shedding colonial possessions, especially during the rapid end of the European empires in Africa, Asia, and the Caribbean between the 1940s and the 1960s.

During the Cold War, both superpowers sought the support of newly independent African countries. This Soviet poster calls for "Death to Colonialism!" and the liberation of Antoine Gizenga, a political prisoner in the Congo.

Developments within the colonies, within the imperial nations, and in international politics brought the end of colonialism more quickly than anyone had imagined possible. Within a few years of the end of World War II, almost all of colonial Asia and the Middle East were independent; North Africa gained its independence over the course of the 1950s, and by 1965 almost all of Africa was free. Colonialism was finished, and the world was made up of sovereign states.

The Rise of the Third World

Many of the newly independent nations of Africa, Asia, and the Caribbean resisted involvement in the battle between the American and Soviet blocs. They concentrated on problems in the relationship between the rich industrialized nations and the poor developing countries—the divide between North and South rather than East and West. In the late 1950s and early 1960s, leaders of such countries as India, Egypt, Ghana, and the Philippines came together to form a nonaligned movement of nations that professed independence from both blocs. These members of the third world, so called to distinguish them from the capitalist first and communist second worlds, aimed to redress perceived inequities in their relationship with the advanced industrial world, especially in the nature of their economic ties.

Most third-world attempts to reform the international economy were ineffectual, as they lacked the power to make their points any more than rhetorically. But in 1973, the success of the major oil-producing developing nations in manipulating world oil markets and dramatically increasing oil prices sparked hope for more balance in North-South economic relations. The developing nations had raw materials that the industrialized world wanted, and if they could organize themselves as effectively as had the members of the Organization of the Petroleum Exporting Countries (OPEC), they might be able to extract more resources from the rich nations. Some producers of raw materials followed OPEC in organizing cartels to try to raise prices (copper, bauxite, and bananas, for example), with mixed success. But the third world also agitated more generally for what it called the New International Economic Order, which would be more favorable to developing nations.

The Cold War Thaws

Even as the developing world organized itself in ways that did not fit the East-West dimension, by the mid-1960s the two superpower alliances were themselves beginning to show signs of strain. France withdrew from NATO, and the United States got bogged down in a war in Vietnam that was unpopular both abroad and at home. The Soviet Union lost its most important ally when China broke with the rest of the Soviet bloc, while dissatisfaction in Eastern Europe and at home put pressure on the Soviet government to provide greater political and economic freedoms.

Although conflict persisted in relations between the United States and the Soviet Union, in the 1970s both sides warily attempted a relaxation of tensions. The two blocs built more political, economic, and cultural ties, and they negotiated a series of agreements to limit the arms race between them. This reduction in hostility, or détente, was set back by continued competition in the third world and Europe, but the threat of armed conflict seemed to recede.

The Age of Globalization

The relaxation of U.S.-Soviet tensions reduced the threat of superpower war. But the postwar patterns of international political and economic relations were soon disrupted by two decades of upheavals. Even as the world economy became more globalized, states faced new diplomatic and security challenges.

The Cold War Ends

In 1979, relations between the United States and the Soviet Union, which had been improving for over 15 years, took a turn toward much greater hostility. In December of that year, Soviet troops entered Afghanistan to support a fragile pro-Soviet government. The United States and its allies responded vigorously to this first direct use of Soviet troops outside of the Warsaw Pact, imposing trade sanctions, financing Afghan insurgents, and boycotting the 1980 Olympic Games in Moscow. Soviet troops were soon engaged in a guerrilla war that many observers compared to the American experience in Vietnam.

In 1981, Ronald Reagan, committed to a strongly anti-Soviet stance, took office as U.S. president. The Reagan administration substantially increased military

The fall of the Berlin Wall in 1989 provided a powerful symbol of the end of the Cold War. During the Cold War, the Berlin Wall divided West Berlin from Communist East Berlin.

spending, especially spending connected to the U.S.-Soviet rivalry. In reaction, the Soviets attempted to increase their own military spending.

The renewed tension put great strains both on international relations and on the Soviet economic and political order. The Soviet economy was falling increasingly behind that of the West, and the faltering Soviet system was finding it more difficult to keep up militarily. Upon taking power in the Soviet Union in 1985, however, Mikhail Gorbachev moved quickly to improve relations with the United States and to encourage greater political openness (*glasnost*) and economic reconstruction (*perestroika*) in the troubled Soviet system. In 1988, the Soviets relaxed their control over their Eastern European allies; in 1989, Soviet troops withdrew from Afghanistan, the Berlin Wall came down, and communists began loosening their grip on governments all over central and eastern Europe. By 1991, the Soviet Union had dissolved into 15 new, independent, non-communist countries, and the communist governments of the Soviet Union's European allies were out of power. The Cold War was over, and only one superpower was left standing.

Worldwide Economic Developments

It was not just the world of East-West diplomacy that changed greatly in the 1970s and 1980s. After the OPEC oil shocks of 1973–74, the industrialized capitalist world entered a decade of recession, high unemployment, and high inflation. In the early 1980s, austerity measures to cut government spending and restrain wages helped bring inflation under control, but many economies remained stagnant. The developing nations too ran into trouble as a global debt crisis erupted in 1982 and drove many heavily indebted poor nations into crisis. As mentioned earlier, economic growth in the Soviet bloc slowed dramatically, and social unrest exploded into open protest.

Over the course of the 1980s, supporters and opponents of increasing the role of market forces in economic activity faced off in developed, developing, and communist countries. In almost all instances, the crisis eventually led to a turn toward the market. The fact that international trade, finance, and investment were at very high levels probably increased the attractiveness of this evolution, since it held out the promise of access to lucrative global economic opportunities.

In the West, cross-border trade and investment increased very substantially. Regional trade agreements (RTAs) were strengthened. The European Union, first created as the European Coal and Steel Community by Belgium, France, West Germany, Italy, the Netherlands, and Luxembourg in 1951, grew to include almost all of western Europe by 1995 (only Norway, Iceland, and Switzerland refrained from joining), removed all barriers to the movement of goods and capital among member states in 1991, and eventually replaced most of their national currencies, such as the French franc and the German mark, with a common currency, the euro, in 1999. The United States, Canada, and Mexico created the North American Free Trade Agreement (NAFTA) in 1994, which similarly removed many economic

FIGURE 1.2 *Regional Trade Agreements (RTAs), 1948–2017*

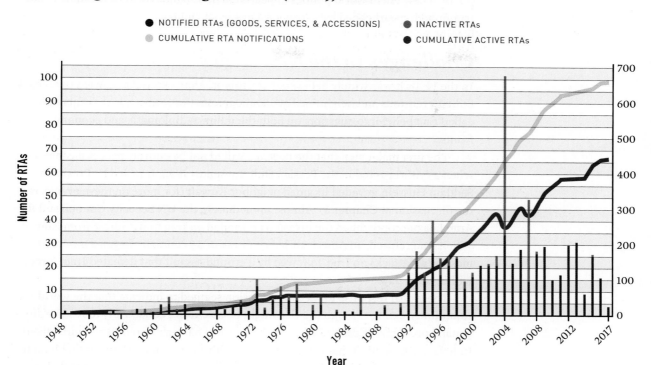

● NOTIFIED RTAs (GOODS, SERVICES, & ACCESSIONS)   ● INACTIVE RTAs
● CUMULATIVE RTA NOTIFICATIONS   ● CUMULATIVE ACTIVE RTAs

Figure source: World Trade Organization, www.wto.org/english/tratop_e/region_e/regfac_e.htm (accessed 11/27/17).

barriers among those three countries. Figure 1.2 provides an overview of RTAs established during the 1948–2017 period.

Most developing countries responded to the difficulties of the 1980s by removing previous barriers to international economic involvement, welcoming foreign trade and investment. The watchword of the period since about 1990 has been *globalization*, with a level of international economic integration that had not been seen since 1914.

The most stunning changes took place in the communist world. China and Vietnam embraced capitalist economic reform in the early 1980s but maintained their one-party systems. Attempts to reform the Soviet system and maintain communist control failed, and the Soviet Union broke up into 15 separate independent states. Some of them, along with many of the former communist-run countries of central and eastern Europe, joined the European Union, and some also adopted the euro. Russia, however, remained somewhat aloof from Europe, preferring to try to build ties with some of the other former component parts of the Soviet Union.

Despite differences among regions and countries, by the turn of the millennium the world economy was far more globalized than it had been since the 1920s. Every major country seemed committed to substantial involvement in world

trade, investment, and finance. With the Cold War over and globalization trium-
phant, a new era in world politics appeared to be at hand. Western capitalism had
triumphed, spearheaded by a strong American-led alliance.

Challenges to the New Order

In the 1990s it was widely believed that the world had entered a new era of relaxed
military tensions and heightened economic integration. Subsequent events have
called that belief into question, on both the military-diplomatic and economic
fronts.

The first major sign that the new age would not be entirely peaceful came
when a crisis erupted in the Persian Gulf. In August 1990, Iraq, led by President
Saddam Hussein, invaded its small neighbor Kuwait (for more on these events, see
the discussion in Chapter 3). Almost immediately, the UN Security Council and the
Arab League condemned the invasion and called on Iraq to withdraw from Kuwait.
When Iraq refused, an American-led coalition of 34 countries began a month of
massive air attacks on Iraq, followed by a ground assault that defeated Iraqi forces
within three days.

The global response to the Iraqi invasion seemed to indicate that the world
community, acting through the UN, might be able to act collectively to resolve diplomatic problems of general concern. The record has turned out to be more mixed.
In 1992, a UN mission that went to Somalia with the intent of ensuring that humanitarian supplies would reach the civilian population as the country descended into
a state of lawlessness was a qualified success. A year later, another UN mission, sent
to Rwanda to try to mediate a resolution of that country's civil war, was unable to
halt a horrific genocide in which the Rwandan government orchestrated the murder of as many as a million Rwandan citizens, most of them from the minority Tutsi
ethnic group. Despite a mixed record, UN involvement in these and other conflicts
fostered the hope of further international collaboration to resolve difficult diplomatic and military problems.

The terror attacks of September 11, 2001, made shockingly clear that military
conflicts would continue, and alerted the world to a new kind of international
threat. On that day, 19 members of the Islamic extremist network Al Qaeda hijacked
four passenger airplanes from Boston, New York, and Washington, D.C. The terrorists flew two of the planes into the World Trade Center in New York City and one
into the Pentagon outside Washington; the fourth crashed in rural Pennsylvania.
Some 3,000 people were killed in the attacks. Within a month, the United States
and its NATO allies launched an invasion of Afghanistan, whose extremist government harbored Al Qaeda's leader Osama bin Laden and refused to hand him over
to American authorities. The regime fell quickly, but conflict continued between
Islamic extremists and the new American-backed government. The Security Council eventually provided a UN force to help enforce peace in the country in the face
of a continued extremist insurgency.

The growth of a new period of military and diplomatic tension was highlighted in the following years as the major powers debated how to deal with the

Iraqi government of Saddam Hussein, which had flouted previous UN decisions. As we will see in Chapters 2 and 5, some policy makers wanted the UN to formulate a common response, but the United States was dissatisfied with the speed and character of UN actions, and it and the United Kingdom organized an independent "coalition of the willing," which launched an invasion and occupation of Iraq in March 2003.

The second Iraq war began a period of turmoil in the Middle and Near East. The war in Iraq dragged on for years, continuing even after American and other coalition troops left the country. Meanwhile, a series of anti-authoritarian uprisings that began in Tunisia in 2010 soon spread throughout North Africa and much of the rest of the Muslim world, launching a decade of political unrest in the region. In Syria, opposition to the regime turned into outright civil war and eventually grew into a region-wide conflict that appeared to pit, variously, Sunnis against Shiites, Kurds against Arabs, Islamists against secularists, and extremists against moderates. The Middle and Near Eastern conflicts eventually drew in nations from outside the region and spilled over into neighboring regions. NATO forces provided military support for the rebels that overthrew Libyan leader Mu'ammar Qaddafi in 2011. The United States and most of its allies supported some of the insurgents in Syria, while Russia and Iran backed the regime.

In the midst of this unrest, a movement that appeared even more extreme than Al Qaeda emerged in 2014, calling itself the Islamic State of Iraq and Syria

The recent influx of refugees and migrants into Europe, triggered by unrest in the Middle East, has emboldened nationalist groups in many European countries. Riding a wave of anti-immigrant sentiment, the Alternative for Germany political party won seats in the lower house of the German legislature after the 2017 elections, making it the first far-right party to do so since World War II.

(ISIS), commonly known as simply the Islamic State (IS), and declared a worldwide caliphate. It quickly seized substantial territory in Iraq and Syria, built alliances with other Islamic extremists, and sponsored or endorsed a barrage of terrorist attacks in Western countries.

The rise of IS and the brutality of the civil war in Syria, along with difficult economic and political conditions throughout the region, drove millions of refugees and migrants out of their native lands. The result was a crisis in Europe as unprecedented numbers of people from the Middle East and North Africa sought refuge. While some Europeans welcomed the refugees, others saw them as an unwanted immigrant burden.

Conflicts brewed elsewhere in Asia. An economically and politically resurgent China confronted several of its neighbors, especially Japan and Vietnam, over long-standing territorial disputes. North Korea joined the nuclear club and set about expanding its arsenal and ballistic missile capabilities, despite nearly universal condemnation and sanctions.

Even as they took different sides in the Middle Eastern conflicts, Russia and the West separately found themselves locked in the most serious disagreement since the end of the Cold War. In February 2014, the pro-Russian government of Ukraine was forced out of office by popular demonstrations and was replaced by a pro-European coalition. The Russian government responded by annexing the Crimean Peninsula, a largely Russian-speaking region that had been ceded to Ukraine under Soviet rule in the 1950s. Soon after, Russian-backed separatists in the largely Russian-speaking eastern Ukraine launched military operations that created separatist enclaves on Ukrainian territory. The West imposed escalating economic sanctions against Russia, but the war continued as antagonism grew between Russia on the one hand, and Europe and the United States on the other.

Challenges to the post–Cold War diplomatic order were followed by serious challenges to its economic order as well. Enthusiasm for economic globalization began to wane in the first decades of the 2000s. This trend was accelerated by the global financial crisis that began in 2008 and turned into the deepest economic decline since the 1930s.

As the crisis dragged on, skepticism grew about economic integration: globalization no longer seemed appealing to many people. In the European Union, the backlash against globalization largely took the form of left-wing opposition to the austerity measures provoked by the crisis, and right-wing hostility to the European Union. In the United Kingdom, voters shocked the world by choosing, in a June 2016 referendum, to have their country leave the European Union—the first time a member state left the union. In the United States, strong antiglobalization sentiment emerged among both Democrats and Republicans, and Republican Donald Trump won the presidency in 2016 after a campaign that was more hostile to international trade, international investment, and immigration than any major-party candidate had been since the 1930s.

As what came to be called "nationalist populism" of both the left and the right grew, previous commitments to international economic cooperation were called into question. It appeared that just as international diplomatic affairs were taking a more combative turn, international economic relations were also heading toward more troubled waters. Major questions remain on both diplomatic and economic fronts about how world politics might evolve over the coming decades.

What Will Shape Our World in the Future?

Today, the two overriding questions in international affairs have to do with the United States' role in world politics, and with the future of globalization. On the military and diplomatic front, the United States remains predominant: its military spending is almost equal to that of the ten next-largest spenders combined. However, other powers are on the horizon. Meanwhile, questions have been raised about how strong and durable the long-standing ties between the United States and its allies may be. Economically, the world remains more tightly linked than it has been since 1914, but in many quarters, hostility to globalization appears to be strong and growing. There remain important uncertainties about both the security and the economic dimensions of world politics. To understand where the world is likely to head, we need to identify the interests of the major actors in contemporary world politics, and to analyze how these interests interact as they work themselves out on the world stage.

America's Role in the World

The United States is likely to play a dominant part in the international political order for the foreseeable future. Nonetheless, relations between the United States, on the one hand, and its traditional allies in Europe and Asia, on the other, have been strained by the Trump administration's embrace of a less globalist, more unilateralist attitude toward international politics. American relations with Russia remain antagonistic, and there are many sources of tension between the United States and China. One important set of questions thus has to do with America's interests: What security and economic goals will the United States pursue? Will it remain committed to multilateral military and diplomatic cooperation, within the institutional framework built after World War II (NATO and the United Nations, for example)? These questions appear unanswered within the United States and will have a powerful impact on the rest of the world.

The second set of questions has to do with the ways other major countries interact with the United States in the international arena. Depending on how the United States defines its interests, how will such other countries (or groups of countries) as the European Union, Russia, and China react? Will they focus on attempting to collaborate with the United States in pursuit of any common goals that remain, or will they attempt to challenge the United States' position in particular regions or issue areas? And how will the West deal with the continuing challenges from Islamic extremists whose influence in the Muslim world seems to remain strong and whose resources—including military might—appear substantial?

Globalization

The future of globalization similarly appears in question. The world's major nations no longer seem to agree on the desirability of further international economic integration.

Skepticism about globalization was undoubtedly spurred by the economic crisis that began in 2008 (for details, see Chapter 8). That crisis led to major upheavals in global financial markets, a serious drop in world trade, and costly debt crises in a succession of countries.

Although the general structure of international economic institutions and interactions survived the crisis and its aftermath, the crisis raised questions about the extent to which countries are interested in closer integration with the global economy. While most governments continue to profess an interest in economic openness, ongoing disputes may indicate that these interests are not so clear-cut. The Trump administration evinces grave doubts about the way the United States' international trade and investment ties have developed, and appears uninterested in any expansion of trade agreements. Russia shows little interest in opening its borders more fully to international trade, finance, and investment. Some developing countries, similarly, appear to be pulling away from the world economy as economic openness proves less effective, and more costly, than anticipated. Almost every member of the European Union has a political movement that is skeptical about European integration—or downright opposed to it. The United Kingdom voted to leave the EU. Did enthusiasm for international economic engagement peak in the 1990s? Are countries (and regional groupings such as the European Union) now more concerned with their own affairs than with global cooperation?

There is also growing concern that international economic trends may pose a threat to social and environmental goals. Certainly, rapid growth in the developing world challenges the planet's ability to support more industry, more cities, more automobiles—more of the features of modern life that billions of poor people hope for but that may not be compatible with environmental sustainability. Is there enough interest among governments to deal with the problem? Is there an ability to work together to address the issues?

Looking Ahead

What will the lives of today's generation, those born around 2000, be like in the future? Will there be serious military threats, and will these threats come from conflicts among the major powers—the United States, Europe, Russia, China—or from religiously motivated terrorists? Will the industrialized world collaborate in diplomatic affairs, or will it splinter into contending blocs? For those born in the poor nations of Asia, Africa, and Latin America, will the next 50 years bring prosperity and a hope of catching up with the West, or will poverty persist and spread?

Will the international economic order remain open and relations among the major economic centers remain collaborative, or will countries and regions turn toward self-sufficiency?

Our best hope for understanding the future of world politics is to develop analytical tools that accurately reflect the basic forces at play. This brief overview of the historical processes and events that created today's world shows how the interests of people and countries affect the way they interact with one another, as well as how their interactions influence and are influenced by the institutions of international politics. The chapters that follow suggest ways of thinking about the interests, interactions, and institutions that have shaped the world we live in and that will continue to shape it for us, our children, and our children's children.

Study Tool Kit

Interests, Interactions, and Institutions in Context

- Conflict and cooperation among nations have ebbed and flowed over time. Individual countries have also varied in their own relations with other nations. Explaining the ebbs and flows, and the differences among countries, is the principal purpose of the study of international relations.

- Our explanations focus on understanding how the interests of the world's countries, and of the people in them, lead the world's nations to interact with one another, and to what effect.

- We also study the kinds of international institutions that arise from and mediate these interactions.

Key Terms

mercantilism, p. 5

Peace of Westphalia, p. 8

sovereignty, p. 8

hegemony, p. 8

Pax Britannica, p. 11

gold standard, p. 13

Treaty of Versailles, p. 20

League of Nations, p. 21

North Atlantic Treaty Organization (NATO), p. 24

Bretton Woods System, p. 24

Warsaw Pact, p. 25

decolonization, p. 29

For Further Reading

Burbank, Jane, and Frederick Cooper. *Empires in World History: Power and the Politics of Difference.* **Princeton, NJ: Princeton University Press, 2011.** Surveys the role of empires and imperialism from Roman times to the present.

Carr, E. H. *The Twenty Years' Crisis, 1919–1939.* **New York: Harper & Row, 1964.** Originally published in 1939, serves as a classic analysis of how and why the world collapsed into conflict during the decades after World War I.

Findlay, Ronald, and Kevin O'Rourke. *Power and Plenty: Trade, War, and the World Economy in the Second Millennium.* **Princeton, NJ: Princeton University Press, 2007.** Surveys the interrelated development of international trade and international power politics since early medieval times.

Frieden, Jeffry A. *Global Capitalism: Its Fall and Rise in the Twentieth Century.* **New York: Norton, 2006.** Presents an overview of the development of the modern world economy from the 1890s to the present.

Gordon, Paul, Gordon Craig, and Alexander George. *Force and Statecraft: Diplomatic Challenges of Our Time,* **5th ed. Oxford: Oxford University Press, 2013.** Gives an overview of modern diplomatic history, with an analysis of basic concepts in diplomacy.

Williamson, Jeffrey G. *Trade and Poverty: When the Third World Fell Behind.* **Cambridge, MA: MIT Press, 2011.** Analyzes the history of economic growth and development, and how trade affected the development process of non-European regions of the world.

2

Understanding Interests, Interactions, and Institutions

THE PUZZLE *What explains the patterns of world politics? Why do interests, interactions, and institutions matter in international relations?*

Above: Iraqi Special Operations Forces patrol Mosul, Iraq, in 2017, amid the destruction sustained during the Islamic State's occupation of the city. Iraq regained control of Mosul in the summer of 2017, after nearly a year of fighting IS insurgents. After U.S. forces withdrew from Iraq at the end of 2011, sectarian rule and continuing violence created the political opening for IS to challenge the regime in Baghdad.

On March 19, 2003, the United States launched a preventive war against Iraq, beginning one of the longest and most inconclusive wars in U.S. history. U.S. forces first withdrew in 2011, but only three years later, by the summer of 2014, U.S. troops were back in Iraq to prop up the failing state and help battle a new insurgency led by the terrorist group the Islamic State (IS).[1] By 2017, Iraqi forces—trained and assisted by U.S. troops—were finally making inroads against IS, recapturing the city of Mosul in July. With IS fighters dispersing internationally, and the civil war that has been raging in neighboring Syria since 2011 continuing to roil the region, the future of the war in Iraq remains uncertain.

Tensions between the United States and Iraq had been high since 1990, when Iraq invaded Kuwait—its small, oil-rich neighbor—and the United States led a multinational coalition to war in early 1991 to restore sovereignty to Kuwait. As a condition of the cease-fire that ended that

war, Iraq agreed to eliminate its programs to develop nuclear, chemical, and biological weapons and to permit United Nations (UN) inspectors to monitor its compliance. For most of the next decade, the Iraqi government attempted to undermine the inspections regime and its economic sanctions. In 2002, the administration of U.S. president George W. Bush argued that Iraq's weapons of mass destruction (WMD) programs were rapidly reaching fruition. Concerned that Iraq might use its new weapons to act aggressively in the region, the Bush administration decided to remove Iraq's dictator, Saddam Hussein, from power—by force if necessary. Bush may also have been seeking to assert American power to demonstrate a new, more forceful foreign policy, to secure supplies of oil from the Persian Gulf, and to transform the Middle East by building an effective democracy in an important country.

The United States turned to the UN Security Council to support its policy of regime change in Iraq, but it faced determined opposition from France, Russia, and China, each of which can veto any substantive resolution within the Security Council. Although these states shared concerns about the Iraqi regime and its suspected weapons

---

1. The full Arabic name is *al-Dawlah al-Islamiyah fil Iraq wa al-Sham.* Variants include "Daesh," an acronym of the Arabic name, the "Islamic State of Iraq and Syria" (ISIS), and the "Islamic State of Iraq and the Levant" (ISIL), based on an alternative translation of the Arabic.

programs, they were reluctant to endorse military action. Though the United States failed to obtain authorization from the Security Council for the war, it claimed sufficient authority under past UN resolutions on Iraq and under the right of self-defense in the UN Charter. After Hussein rejected an ultimatum to step down, the United States led a "coalition of the willing" to a rapid military victory in 2003.

To the surprise of many, the United States did not find the stockpiles of chemical and biological weapons it had claimed existed. This embarrassment helped turn sentiment at home against the war. The Bush administration also did not consider adequately the extent to which Hussein had brutalized Iraqi society and gutted any social institutions not loyal to the regime, nor did it anticipate the damage that the decade of sanctions had wreaked on Iraq's social and physical infrastructure. Planning on a rapid turnover of political power to Iraqi exiles and other insurgent groups, the Bush administration soon found itself leading a "failed state" and embroiled in a broad-based insurgency. With a surge in U.S. forces beginning in early 2007 and a new counterinsurgency strategy, the United States eventually tamped down the violence, but tensions between the Shiite majority and the Sunni minority remained high, and the Kurds established essentially an autonomous enclave in the north of the country. U.S. forces finally left Iraq in December 2011, thus ending what was, at the time, the second-longest war in U.S. history.

By 2014, however, IS had seized large sections of territory in northern and northwestern Iraq. The international community also responded to the escalation of violence. By the fall of that year, President Barack Obama had sent 3,000 American military troops back to Iraq and authorized a series of air strikes against IS forces. These efforts, however, were not sufficient to stem the IS tide that swept across northern Iraq and Syria, necessitating an expanding role and number of U.S. troops. The administration of President Donald Trump has stopped disclosing current troop levels to maintain the "element of surprise," and a pending reduction in forces was announced in February 2018, but estimates are that the United States now has 5,200 soldiers in Iraq.[2]

The Iraq War and its aftermath lead us to consider several questions. Why did the United States seek regime change in Iraq in 2003? Was the U.S. government motivated by concerns about American security, an economic interest in Middle East oil, the president's own political fortunes, or something else? Why did Saddam Hussein resist demands to cooperate fully with weapons inspectors and, later, to step down from power peacefully? The invasion shattered his country and led to his eventual execution in 2006. Certainly Hussein would have been better off accepting the U.S. ultimatum and slinking into a comfortable retirement in exile. Why did the Bush administration attempt to pursue its policy through the UN, and why did it eventually abandon those efforts? Would the war in Iraq have unfolded differently if it had been carried out under the auspices of the UN?

2. Mohammed Tawfeeq, "US will reduce troop levels in Iraq, Baghdad says," CNN.com, February 6, 2018, https://www.cnn.com/2018/02/06/middleeast/american-troops-iraq-intl/index.html.

Thinking Analytically about Interests, Interactions, and Institutions

We study international relations in order to gain insight into such questions of conflict and cooperation. We seek to understand why states and their leaders make certain choices and why we observe certain outcomes. To help in our task, this chapter takes a closer look at three core concepts that enable us to think analytically about world politics: interests, interactions, and institutions.

Interests are the fundamental building blocks of politics. Explanations of international political events begin by specifying the relevant actors (such as the United States, Saddam Hussein, or IS) and their interests (such as power or security). As actors pursue their interests, they interact with other actors; the nature of these *interactions* affects the outcomes and whether actors can get what they want. *Institutions* (such as the UN) may also influence the outcomes of interactions by providing rules that facilitate cooperation. This framework can be used to analyze and understand not only the Iraq War, but also the puzzles described in the chapters that follow and, equally important, others that will arise in the future.

Interests: What Do Actors Want from Politics?

Interests are what actors want to achieve through political action. For example, in international relations we often assume that states have an interest in security—that is, in preventing attacks on their territories and citizens. This interest prompts states to take steps to confront potential enemies and to protect friends whose security is linked to their own. In the showdown with Iraq, an interest in security might explain the U.S. government's desire to remove a regime that threatened American allies in the region and was suspected of developing WMD. As the primary motivations behind actors' choices, interests are the fundamental building blocks of any political analysis.[3]

More precisely, interests are the preferences of actors over the possible outcomes that might result from their political choices. Interests determine how actors rank the desirability of different outcomes, from most to least preferred. An actor motivated by an interest in money prefers outcomes that give it more money over those that give it less. A state interested in security prefers outcomes that strengthen it and weaken its adversaries over outcomes that have the opposite effect. For example, given the United States' general interest in security, it might prefer a democratic Iraq that is friendly toward American allies and encourages the democratization of other states in the Middle East (Map 2.1). If this best outcome were to prove impossible, the United States' second-best result might be a pro-Western dictator in Iraq. This outcome would be preferable to an anti-American Islamist government, which, in turn, would be preferable to widespread instability and chaos in Iraq and the region more generally. Between each of these broad alternatives, of course, are many intermediate outcomes that can be similarly rank-ordered.

Interests can be many and varied, depending on the specific policy or event under examination. In identifying the interests of an actor, analysts sometimes draw on prior theories of human nature or behavior; at other times, they rely on the statements or actions of the actors themselves; and at other times still, they simply assume that actors have a particular interest. At the most general level, analysts often group interests into three categories: power or security, economic or material welfare, and ideological goals.

In the first category, all political actors are understood to require a degree of security as a prerequisite to all other goals or, at an extreme, to desire power and the ability to dominate others either as part of human nature or as essential to survival in a competitive international environment. In the second category, political actors

interests

What actors want to achieve through political action; their preferences over the outcomes that might result from their political choices.

---

3. For a more extensive treatment of the theoretical and methodological issues in studying interests, see Jeffry A. Frieden, "Actors and Preferences in International Relations," in *Strategic Choice and International Relations*, ed. David A. Lake and Robert Powell, 39–76 (Princeton, NJ: Princeton University Press, 1999).

MAP 2.1 *The Middle East*

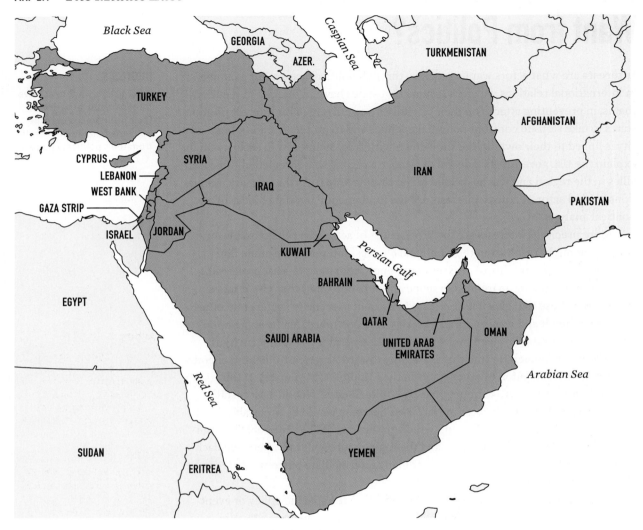

are presumed to desire a higher standard of living or quality of life, defined largely in terms of greater income, more consumable goods and services, or more leisure time (less work). This second set of interests is not incompatible with the first if we think of economic welfare as the long-term goal and security or power as a means to this end. Finally, political actors may also desire moral, religious, or other ideological goals, including democracy, human equality and dignity, the glory of a particular god, and so on. In this category, ideas often play a key role in shaping what actors want or believe to be good and desirable, including even what it means to be secure or wealthy. Again, there is not necessarily a conflict between these interests and others, as power or wealth may be a means toward ideological ends.

Scholars have long debated whether one conception of interest is more universal, true, or useful than others. Indeed, the three sets of general interests roughly divide the three schools of realism, liberalism, and constructivism identified in this book's Introduction. In turn, various debates over what the interests of actors *should be* are often tied to debates over what policies should be pursued in specific contexts. For example, the Iraq War tapped into a long-standing debate in the United States over whether foreign policy should be narrowly defined to meet security threats or should also seek to undermine repressive regimes and promote the spread of democracy.

Our approach in this book is agnostic; that is, we do not assume that one set of interests is always better in helping unravel puzzles of world politics. Rather, for some puzzles it may be sufficient to specify a general interest in security, increased international trade, or protecting the environment. For other puzzles, it may be necessary to move beyond general assumptions and specify interests over narrow sets of outcomes—say, between deploying 100,000 versus 200,000 troops or between negotiating a multilateral international environmental treaty versus following a unilateral policy. Whichever level of detail is relevant depends on the purpose of the analysis, the questions being asked, and the puzzle under consideration.

Actors and Interests

Many different types of actors participate in international relations. In the story of the Iraq War, we have already encountered *states* (the United States and Iraq), *governments* (the Bush administration and the regime of Saddam Hussein), *groups* within countries (the Sunni and Shiite religious groups in Iraq), and *international organizations* (the UN Security Council).

Individuals are always the most basic political actors, as they cannot be divided into smaller political units. And in some cases, particular individuals, such as Bush and Hussein, are crucial actors in their own right. But it is often convenient to group individuals into larger categories of people who share common interests (the Sunnis in Iraq, for instance) or who somehow combine their conflicting desires into a joint or collective interest (the election of a government, for example). We call both individuals and these composite groups of individuals **actors**.

Of these composite actors, one that has particular prominence in international relations is the state. A **state** is a central authority that has the ability to make and enforce laws, rules, and decisions within its territory. Most countries are governed by states, though some may experience a breakdown of central authority and become what are sometimes called failed states.[4] The concept of sovereignty is a key part of the definition of the state. **Sovereignty** refers to the expectation that states have legal and political supremacy within their boundaries. To say that states are sovereign means that they have ultimate authority over their own policies and political processes, such as the maintenance of domestic order and the provision of governance (see "What Shaped Our World?" on p. 48). In theory, state sovereignty is often assumed to be a defining feature of the modern international system, creating a condition of **anarchy** in which there is no legal authority higher than or above the state to make and enforce laws that bind international actors.

actors
The basic unit for the analysis of international politics; can be either individuals or groups of people with common interests.

state
A central authority with the ability to make and enforce laws, rules, and decisions within a specified territory.

sovereignty
The expectation that states have legal and political supremacy—or ultimate authority—within their territorial boundaries.

anarchy
The absence of a central authority with the ability to make and enforce laws that bind all actors.

---

4. On failed states and state building, see Timothy Sisk, *Statebuilding: War and Conflict in the Modern World* (Malden, MA: Polity, 2013).

The Rise of the State

We currently live in a world of nearly 200 states. States are some of the most important actors in world politics. How did an international system of states come to be?

Interests All political systems involve a relationship between the rulers and the ruled. The rulers aim to satisfy their interests in wealth and power, whereas the ruled hope to obtain physical security, basic needs, and public amenities such as education and roads. Thus, the rulers and the ruled make an exchange: the rulers are supposed to provide the goods that their citizens want, and the ruled provide military manpower, money (usually in the form of taxes), and perhaps other kinds of services. The nature of the bargain is not always fair, and one of the core dilemmas of politics is how to structure the relationship so that the rulers actually act in the interests of the ruled.

Institutions The modern state is just one, relatively recent, way of organizing politics. Sociologist Max Weber (1864–1920) defined the state as "a human community that (successfully) claims the monopoly of the legitimate use of physical force within a given territory." This means that states are territorially bounded political units in which a central governing authority is the only actor that can legitimately use force, both against its own citizens and against other states.

Yet things were not always this way. In 1000 C.E., Europe was fractured into an uncounted number of political units, all enmeshed in often crosscutting lines of authority. Under feudalism, kings granted landholdings to the aristocracy, who in turn owed obligations to the king, including supplying military manpower. Nobles in one realm could acquire lands in another, thereby owing obligations to two or more kings. There were also self-governing "free cities," which owed allegiance to no king. The Catholic Church wielded political authority through entities like the Holy Roman Empire (962–1806). Prior to the emergence of the state, many rulers shared and competed for authority over any particular area.

Over time, an informal international institution emerged to ensure the state's exclusive control within its boundaries: sovereignty. Sovereignty is composed of four core elements: (1) the sovereign possesses ultimate authority over the people and territory of a given realm, (2) other states and religious bodies are excluded from exercising political authority over a sovereign people or territory, (3) sovereignty is indivisible, and (4) all sovereign units are formally equal or have the same legal status. The core principles of sovereignty are often violated in practice, but the concept has a profound impact on world politics.

Interactions How did a system of sovereign states come about? One prominent argument comes from Charles Tilly, who contended that "states make wars, and wars make the state." As they bargained and fought over territory and wealth, small units either merged or were absorbed by larger ones. Polities that managed to raise money and manpower effectively outcompeted those that did not.

The institution of sovereignty also emerged out of competitive interactions. The Thirty Years' War (1618–48) was a bloody, Europe-wide affair that stemmed in part from emerging states' efforts to meddle in one another's internal affairs. The Peace of Westphalia, which ended that conflict, enshrined (even if it did not invent) the concept of sovereignty as a way to constrain this destructive behavior.

As we will see in later chapters, new actors and interactions have challenged the nature of sovereignty. Although the future remains uncertain, what is clear is that states as political units will continue to evolve.

The signing of the Peace of Westphalia.

When discussing states as actors, we may use the concept of the *state* in two different ways that are important to distinguish. Scholars sometimes assume that states are motivated by an interest in security—that is, safety from external and internal threats—and in accumulating power as a means to ensure security. These goals are said to be **national interests**, or interests that belong to the state itself. In this usage, the states-as-actors assumption sees international politics as driven by states' quest for security and power.

Alternatively, the states-as-actors concept serves as convenient shorthand for sets of national leaders acting in the name of their countries. This use of the term reflects the fact that many actions in international politics are taken by individuals who represent the state: political leaders, diplomats, members of the armed forces, or others acting in an official capacity. Hence, we often lapse into language like "the United States threatened Iraq," when in fact it was certain representatives of the United States who threatened representatives of Iraq. When using the concept of the state as a shorthand for a set of composite interests, we can make no prior assumption about where the interests pursued by those agents originate. Sometimes the state's representatives act on behalf of a particular domestic interest group—for example, when negotiating a trade agreement that is in the interest of exporting industries. Alternatively, state leaders might act to further their own personal or political agendas. In such cases, the interests that matter are those of the interest group or politician, but when those interests play out at the international level, they are pursued by people acting in the name of the state.

As this discussion suggests, there is no fixed or permanent set of actors in international relations. Like interests, actors are an analytical concept that is imposed on explanations by observers seeking to understand why events happen in a certain way. Selecting the set of individuals who are identified as the actors in any explanation is a choice we make to help account for observed outcomes. There is no right or wrong way to specify the actors in any event or set of events. As with interests, we judge different conceptualizations of actors only by whether they are useful in helping us understand world politics.

For example, the Iraq War was itself conditioned by the prior Persian Gulf War of 1991, which in turn was influenced by the end of the Cold War, and specifically by the Soviet Union's decision not to try to counter the expansion of U.S. power in the Persian Gulf. The Persian Gulf War was influenced by the Iran-Iraq War of 1980–88, which left Iraq deeply in debt to its neighbors. One might include all of these actors in a complete explanation of the war. But as an initial point of departure, we might prefer a simpler formulation that focuses on the relationship between President Bush and Saddam Hussein as the "key" actors in the run-up to the 2003 war. Even in this more narrow focus, however, we need to decide how to think about President Bush as an actor. We know that Bush made the decision to invade Iraq, but how should we interpret his choice?

We could think of Bush as the head of a state seeking to further the state's interest in security or access to a key natural resource; in this case, the state is the actor whose interests are driving choices. We could also understand him as a politician pursuing his personal interest in getting reelected to the presidency; in this case, the

national interests
Interests attributed to the state itself, usually security and power.

individual politician is the actor whose political interests are driving the choices. We might also focus on the interests of groups that helped support Bush's reelection bid, such as oil companies or defense contractors that benefited from the administration's more aggressive stance toward Iraq. Alternatively, we could think of Bush as an individual motivated by personal ideology about democracy. For any given policy choice, it may be difficult to know for sure which interests are being pursued; indeed, a single decision may further more than one interest. In these cases, we judge any assumption about actors by how useful it is in explaining the overall pattern of events we observe.

Thus, any analysis starts with the question, Who are the actors, and what are their interests? But, as noted above, the analyst must consider how much "history," or background, is necessary and who the key actors are in any explanation. This is very much a subjective decision by the analyst. In general, we prefer explanations that are simpler over those that are more complex, but how simple a good explanation must be is never defined in the abstract. Moreover, as we will see in the rest of this chapter, this question of which actors and their interests to include cannot be answered by itself, but requires attention to the interactions and institutions in which those actors are embedded. All three concepts—interests, interactions, and institutions—are necessary for a sufficient explanation of any particular event.

Table 2.1 lists key categories of actors in world politics, the interests commonly ascribed to these actors by analysts, and specific examples. The list, of course, is not

TABLE 2.1 *Key Categories of Actors and Interests in World Politics*

ACTOR	COMMONLY ASCRIBED INTERESTS	EXAMPLES
States	Security, power, wealth, ideology	United States, Canada, China, Switzerland, India, Uruguay
Politicians	Reelection/retention of office, ideology, policy goals	President of the United States, prime minister of Great Britain, Speaker of the U.S. House of Representatives
Firms, industries, or business associations	Wealth, profit	General Motors, Sony, the pharmaceutical industry, National Association of Manufacturers, Business Roundtable
Classes or factors of production	Material well-being, wealth	Capital, labor, land, human capital
Bureaucracies	Budget maximization, influence, policy preferences; often summarized by the adage of "where you stand depends on where you sit"	Department of Defense, Department of Commerce, National Security Council, Ministry of Foreign Affairs
International organizations	As composites of states, they reflect the interests of member states according to their voting power. As organizations, they are assumed to be similar to domestic bureaucracies.	United Nations, International Monetary Fund, Universal Postal Union, Organisation for Economic Co-operation and Development
Nongovernmental organizations, often transnational or international in scope and membership	Moral, ideological, or policy goals; human rights, the environment, religion	Red Cross, Amnesty International, Greenpeace, the Catholic Church

exhaustive. Any of the actors can be broken down into smaller sets of individuals for explanatory purposes. But we will encounter these actors again and again throughout this book. In the following chapters, we specify different sets of actors and their interests as needed to explain the puzzles being addressed.

Interactions: Why Can't Actors Always Get What They Want?

Actors make choices in order to further their interests. Yet political outcomes depend not just on the choices of one actor, but on the choices of others as well. The United States might have preferred that Saddam Hussein step down peacefully, but the Iraqi dictator refused to yield, and it ultimately took a war to drive him from power. Interests are essential in analyzing any event in international relations because they represent how actors rank alternative outcomes. But to account for outcomes, we must examine the choices of all the relevant actors and how those choices interact to produce a particular result. As we use the term here, **interactions** are the ways in which the choices of two or more actors combine to produce political outcomes.

When outcomes result from an interaction, actors have to anticipate the likely choices of others and take those choices into account when making their own decisions. In March 2003, Saddam Hussein's interests in his personal well-being might have led to the following ordering of possible outcomes: (1) stay in power and continue present policies, (2) go into exile in a friendly state, (3) fight and lose a war with the United States. Hussein's only chance at getting his best possible outcome required that he resist U.S. demands to step down. But to resist risked bringing about his worst possible outcome: war.

Whether resisting would lead to Hussein's best or worst outcome depended on what the United States would do in response. Would Bush carry out his threat to attack, or would he back down? Whether it made sense for Hussein to resist or step down depended crucially on the answer to this question. If he expected Bush to back down, then resisting U.S. demands would get him his best outcome; if Hussein expected Bush to carry out his threat, then resistance would lead to his worst outcome, and it would be better to step down. Hence, in making his choice, Hussein had to consider not only what he himself wanted, but also what he expected Bush to do. In this case, there is evidence suggesting that Hussein expected opposition on the part of other states, especially Russia and France, to prevent Bush from carrying out his threat—an erroneous expectation that led him to resist.[5] When combined with Bush's determination to invade, this choice ensured a war.

Had Hussein been certain that Bush would act as he did, bringing about Hussein's eventual execution, he might have chosen differently, even though his

interactions

The ways in which the choices of two or more actors combine to produce political outcomes.

---

5. Kevin Woods, Lacey James, and Williamson Murray, "Saddam's Delusions: The View from Inside," *Foreign Affairs* 75 (May–June 2006): 2–26.

After being captured by U.S. forces in 2003, Saddam Hussein was tried and convicted on charges of war crimes and crimes against humanity. How can we understand Hussein's decision to risk war with a much more powerful country?

underlying interests would have been the same. We call such situations *strategic* interactions because each actor's strategy, or plan of action, depends on the anticipated strategy of others. Many of the most intriguing puzzles of international politics derive from such interactions.

We make two assumptions in studying interactions. First, we assume that actors behave with the intention of producing a desired result. That is, actors are assumed to choose among available options with due regard for their consequences and with the aim of bringing about outcomes they prefer. Second, in cases of strategic interaction, we assume that actors adopt strategies according to what they believe to be the interests and likely actions of others. That is, actors develop strategies that they believe are a best response to the anticipated strategies of others. In the preceding example, if Hussein believed that Bush would back down from his threat, the best response was to resist American demands; if he believed that Bush would carry out his threat, then the best response was to step down, even though doing so would have meant accepting his second-best outcome. A best-response strategy is the actor's plan to do as well as possible in light of the interests and likely strategies of the other relevant actors. Together, these assumptions link interests to choices and, through the interaction of choices, to outcomes.

Formulating a strategy as a best response, of course, does not guarantee that the actor will obtain its most preferred or even a desirable outcome. Sometimes the choices made by others leave actors facing a highly unwelcome outcome, one that may leave them far worse off than the status quo. If one state chooses to initiate a war, for instance, the other state must respond by either giving in to its demands or fighting back, and both options may leave the second state worse off than before the attack. Saddam Hussein was clearly better off before the U.S. attack in March 2003, but once the fighting began, the prewar status quo was no longer an option. A strategy is a plan to do as well as possible, given one's expectations about the interests and actions of others. It is not a guarantee of obtaining one's most preferred result.

Understanding the outcomes produced by the often complex interplay of the strategies of two or more actors can be difficult. A specialized form of theory, called game theory, has been invented to study strategic interactions. We offer a brief introduction to game theory in the "Special Topic" appendix to this chapter (p. 82), focusing on relatively simple games to communicate the core ideas behind strategic interaction.

Cooperation and Bargaining

Interactions can take various forms, but most can be grouped into two broad categories: cooperation and bargaining. Political interactions usually involve both forms in varying degrees.

Interactions are cooperative when actors have a shared interest in achieving an outcome and must work together to do so. **Cooperation** occurs when two or more actors adopt policies that make at least one actor better off without making any other actor worse off. Opportunities for cooperation arise all the time in social and political life. For example, when a group of friends wants to throw a party, they may find that none of them can spare the time or money to do so alone. But if they all contribute a little, they can each enjoy the benefits of throwing the party. The members of a community all benefit if there are good roads to drive on and clean water to drink, but again, most likely no individual alone is able to provide these. If they all agree to pay taxes to a central agency that will provide roads and water, then they can all be better off. A group of firms may share an interest in lobbying Congress for trade protection from foreign imports. By pooling their resources and acting together, they may be more effective at getting their way than they would be on their own. In the international system, states may have opportunities to cooperate to defend one another from attack, to further a shared interest in free trade or stable monetary relations, to protect the global environment, or to uphold human rights.

We will look more closely at each of these types of situations in the following chapters. In the case of Iraq, numerous states in the international community loathed or feared Saddam Hussein's regime, and they may have seen his removal as preferable to the status quo. Some of these chose to cooperate in a military effort to oust Hussein's regime. Foremost among them were the United States and Great Britain, both contributing significant military forces and other resources in the expectation that joint action would make them better off relative to either maintaining the status quo or acting alone.

Cooperation is defined from the perspectives of the two or more actors who are interacting. Even though their cooperation may benefit those actors, it may hurt other parties. The friends agreeing to throw a party together may disrupt their neighbors by making noise late into the night. Firms that cooperate to lobby Congress for trade protection may impose higher prices on consumers. The countries

cooperation

An interaction in which two or more actors adopt policies that make at least one actor better off relative to the status quo without making others worse off.

that cooperated to oust Saddam Hussein clearly made the dictator worse off. Indeed, cooperation is not always an unmitigated good; its benefits exist only for those who adjust their policies to bring about an outcome they prefer.

Figure 2.1 depicts in simple terms the problem of cooperation between two actors. Imagine that two actors can enact policies that have the potential to increase their overall income or welfare. The income of the actors is plotted along two dimensions, with Actor A's income increasing along the horizontal axis and Actor B's income increasing along the vertical axis. Since the concept is easier to illustrate with a divisible good like money, we use dollars in the example, but welfare is the more general concept, which includes not only income but other desired goods or outcomes. All points within the graph represent possible outcomes produced by different combinations of policies chosen by the two actors.

Assume that by cooperating, the two actors can make as much as $1,000, a limit determined in this case by the available technology and resources. This limit is depicted by the downward-sloping line in Figure 2.1, which shows all the different ways $1,000 can be divided between the two actors. The point at which the line touches the horizontal axis depicts a situation in which Actor A gets $1,000 and Actor B gets nothing, the point at which the line touches the vertical axis depicts a situation in which Actor B gets all the money, and every point in between represents different divisions of the maximum feasible income. For example, if the two actors cooperate to make the maximum income in such a way that State A gets $600, then

---

FIGURE 2.1 *Cooperation*

In this world, there is $1,000 worth of a good that can be captured by State A and State B. In the status quo, State A gets $200 and State B gets $200. Through cooperation, both states can improve their outcomes by capturing and sharing the remaining $600. The green-shaded triangle—defined by the points *q*, *a*, and *b*—outlines all possible superior outcomes.

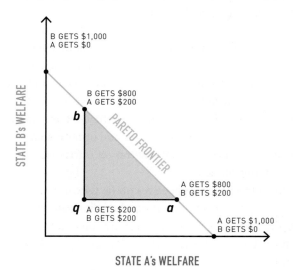

State B gets $400; if State A gets $200, then State B gets $800. This line representing the possible divisions of the maximum feasible benefit is called the *Pareto frontier*, after the Italian economist Vilfredo Pareto (1848–1923), who developed these ideas.

However, the actors may have chosen policies that do not result in the maximum possible benefit. Let's assume that past policy combinations have produced an outcome referred to as the status quo (*q*). As *q* is depicted in Figure 2.1, the actors are not doing as well as they could, with each making $200, for a total of $400 rather than $1,000. This means that they could potentially benefit by changing their policies to get closer to the Pareto frontier line and thus to the maximum feasible income. Any policy combination that leads to an outcome in the shaded area *qba* would make both actors better off than they are under the status quo. Moving outward from *q*, into the shaded area, represents cooperation, or an improvement in the welfare of at least one actor.

We can see that policies along the line segment between *q* and *a* improve A's welfare at no loss to B, while policies along the line segment between *q* and *b* improve B's welfare at no loss to A. Any movement into the shaded area defined by points *q*, *b*, and *a* represents an improvement in the welfare of both actors, and any policy combination on the Pareto frontier between *b* and *a* makes the actors as well off as possible, given available resources and technology. Cooperation consists of mutual policy adjustments that move actors toward or onto the Pareto frontier, increasing the welfare of some or all partners without diminishing the welfare of any one actor. Because it makes at least one party better off than otherwise, we refer to cooperation as a *positive-sum game*.

Whereas cooperative interactions involve the potential for mutual gain, **bargaining** describes an interaction in which actors must choose outcomes that make one better off at the expense of another. For example, two states may want the same piece of territory. Bargaining describes the process by which they come to divide the territory. They may negotiate, impose sanctions on one another, or fight. All these tactics are different forms of bargaining. Given the nature of the situation, the more territory one side gets, the less the other gets.

Bargaining is illustrated in Figure 2.2. When actors bargain, they move along the Pareto frontier, as represented by the green arrow. On the frontier line, any improvement in A's welfare comes strictly at the expense of B's welfare. For this reason, bargaining is sometimes called a *zero-sum game*, because the gains for one side perfectly match the losses of the other. For example, if Actor A gains 100 percent of a contested piece of territory under a given bargain, that means Actor B gets 0 percent of the territory; if Actor A gives up 20 percent of the territory through bargaining, Actor B gains that 20 percent of the territory. Bargaining is purely redistributive; that is, rather than creating additional value, as in the case of cooperation, it only allocates a fixed sum of value between different actors.

We typically represent war as a bargaining interaction. In the case of the Iraq War, the United States and Iraq were not cooperating, but bargaining over the latter's WMD programs and, ultimately, its regime. We will take a closer look at bargaining in war in Chapter 3.

bargaining
An interaction in which two or more actors must choose outcomes that make one better off at the expense of another. Bargaining is redistributive: it involves allocating a fixed sum of value between different actors.

FIGURE 2.2 *Bargaining*

State A and State B are bargaining over the division of $1,000. Each point along the line is a possible division. For every $1 that State A gains, State B loses $1, and vice versa.

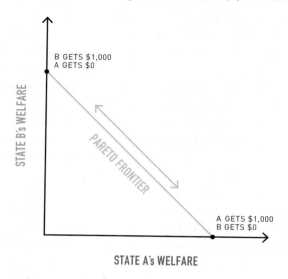

The horizontal bar below is a different representation of the same concept as the diagonal line above. The bar represents a good that States A and B both want. The more State A gets, the less State B gets (possible deal 1); the more State B gets, the less State A gets (possible deal 2).

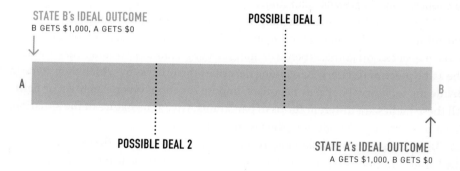

Most interactions in international relations combine elements of both cooperation and bargaining (Figure 2.3). Although both states may gain by moving to the frontier, A prefers bargains that leave it closer to *a*, whereas B prefers bargains that leave it closer to *b*. Movement toward the frontier makes at least one actor better off, but where on the frontier they end up makes an important difference. For example, even as the United States, Britain, and other states had interests in cooperating to defeat Iraq, they bargained over how much each would contribute to the effort. In many interactions, actors are cooperating and bargaining simultaneously, and the outcomes of both interactions are linked. Successful cooperation generates gains

FIGURE 2.3 *Cooperation and Bargaining*

Through cooperation, State A and State B can improve their joint outcome from the starting point—the status quo—to capture an additional $600. But they have to bargain over exactly how that $600 will be divided between them.

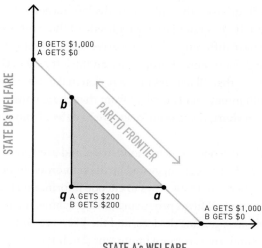

worth bargaining over. And if the actors cannot reach a bargain over the division of gains, they may end up failing to cooperate.[6]

Cooperation and bargaining can succeed or fail for many reasons. Just because actors might benefit from cooperation does not mean they will actually change their policies to realize the possible gains. And even though bargaining might seem doomed to fail—after all, why would one actor agree to reduce its welfare?—actors often do succeed in redistributing valuable goods between themselves. We now turn to some of the primary factors that influence the success or failure of cooperation and, later, of bargaining.

When Can Actors Cooperate?

If cooperation makes actors better off, why do they sometimes fail to cooperate? By far the most important factor is each actor's interests. Even when actors have a collective interest in cooperating, situations exist in which their individual interests lead them to "defect"—that is, to adopt an uncooperative strategy that undermines the collective goal. How strong the incentives are to defect goes a long way toward determining the prospects for cooperation.[7]

---

6. On bargaining and cooperating simultaneously, see James D. Fearon, "Bargaining, Enforcement, and International Cooperation," *International Organization* 52 (1998): 269–305.

7. On the general forms of cooperation reviewed here, see Arthur A. Stein, "Coordination and Collaboration Regimes in an Anarchic World," *International Organization* 36 (1982): 299–324; Duncan Snidal, "Coordination versus Prisoner's Dilemma: Implications for International Cooperation and Regimes," *American Political Science Review* 79 (December 1985): 923–42; and Lisa L. Martin, "Interests, Power, and Multilateralism," *International Organization* 46 (1992): 765–92.

coordination

A type of cooperative interaction in which actors benefit from all making the same choices and subsequently have no incentive not to comply.

collaboration

A type of cooperative interaction in which actors gain from working together but nonetheless have incentives not to comply with any agreement.

Consider the easiest kind of cooperative interaction, what we call a problem of **coordination**. This kind of situation arises when actors need only coordinate their actions with one another, and once their actions are coordinated, none receive any benefit from defecting. A classic example is deciding which side of the road cars should drive on. Drivers have a shared interest in avoiding crashes, so they are always better off if all drive on the right or on the left, rather than some driving on each side of the road. It does not matter which side of the road is selected; indeed, different countries have different rules: cars drive on the right side of the road in the United States and continental Europe, and on the left side in Great Britain and Japan. What matters is that all drivers in the region make the same choice. Moreover, no driver would intentionally deviate from that choice, since doing so would be very dangerous. In short, there is no incentive to defect from the coordinated arrangement.

In the international economy, firms, industries, and even governments face coordination problems all the time, as suggested by the numerous agreements on international standards. There are many ways to encode information to be sent over the Internet, for instance, but all firms producing devices connected to the Internet—computers, smartphones, gaming devices, and the like—are better off coordinating on a single format. Similarly, it is more important that international airline pilots speak a single language so as to communicate effectively with one another and with air traffic controllers worldwide than that they choose any given specific language. In coordination situations, cooperation is self-sustaining because once coordination is achieved, no one can benefit by unilaterally defecting.

A more serious barrier to cooperation arises if the actors have an individual incentive to defect from cooperation, even though cooperation could make everyone better off. Cooperative interactions in which actors have a unilateral incentive to defect are called problems of **collaboration**. This kind of problem is often illustrated by a simple game called the Prisoner's Dilemma. Imagine that two criminals have been detained by the police. The district attorney does not have enough evidence to convict them on felony charges but can convict each suspect for a misdemeanor. She confines the prisoners separately and presents each with the following offer: "If neither of you is willing to testify, I will charge both of you with a misdemeanor and sentence you each to one year in prison. If you defect on your accomplice by providing evidence against him, I will let you go free and will put him in prison for ten years. However, he has been offered the same deal. If he provides evidence against you, you'll be the one behind bars. Finally, if you both squeal on one another, you'll each be charged with a felony, but your sentences will be reduced to five years in exchange for testifying."

Collectively, the prisoners would do best by cooperating with each other and refusing to testify; they would, together, serve a total of only two years behind bars. However, the prisoners are motivated not by the collective outcome but rather by the desire to shorten their own individual sentences. Thus, they have an incentive to rat out the other. Each prisoner reasons as follows: "Suppose my partner stays quiet. In that case, I should defect on him so that I will be released immediately rather than remain quiet and spend a year behind bars. On the other hand, suppose that my accomplice plans to defect on me. In that case, I should also defect on him, because giving testimony will reduce my sentence to five years rather than the ten I will face if I stay quiet."

Because both prisoners reason the same way, both will end up providing evidence against the other and both will be imprisoned for five years. This outcome, of course, is worse for each of them than the outcome they could achieve if they cooperated with one another and remained silent; the dilemma is that each individual's incentive to defect against the other undermines their collective interest in cooperation. For a more formal and complete discussion of this dilemma, see the "Special Topic" appendix to this chapter (p. 82), a discussion of game theory that includes the Prisoner's Dilemma.

Although the dilemma of fictional prisoners may seem remote from the subject matter of this book, analogous situations often arise in international relations. Consider the nuclear arms race between the United States and the Soviet Union during the Cold War. Both countries built costly nuclear weapons at a furious pace, such that by the late 1980s the United States had about 23,000 nuclear weapons, while the Soviet Union had about 42,000 (Figure 2.4).

Figure source: Hans M. Kristensen and Robert S. Norris, "Global Nuclear Weapons Inventories, 1945–2013," *Bulletin of the Atomic Scientists* 69 (2013): 75–81. Updated through 2017 through the *Bulletin of the Atomic Scientists*' Nuclear Notebook series, available at http://explore.tandfonline.com/page/pgas/rbul-nuclear-notebooks (accessed 07/15/17).

One might ask, Why not agree to stop building when the United States had 2,300 warheads and the Soviet Union had 4,200? Stopping at that point would have kept the same ratio of forces but at much lower cost. Both states might have been better off with such an agreement. The problem, however, is that each state had an incentive to cheat on such a deal in order to attain (or maintain) superiority over the other. If one stopped building, the other would be tempted to keep

FIGURE 2.4 *U.S. and USSR/Russian Strategic Nuclear Weapons Inventories, 1945–2017*

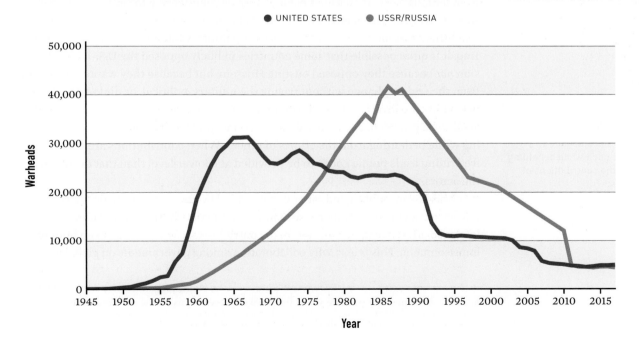

● UNITED STATES   ● USSR/RUSSIA

going. Therefore, each feared that its own restraint in building weapons would be exploited, leaving it vulnerable. Given these incentives and fears, the best strategy for each state was to go on amassing weapons. As a result, both countries ended up worse off than if they could have cooperated to limit their arms competition.[8]

A specific type of collaboration problem arises in providing **public goods**, which are products such as national defense, clean air and water, and the eradication of communicable diseases. Public goods are defined by two qualities. First, if the good is provided to one person, others cannot be excluded from enjoying it as well (formally, the good is *nonexcludable*). If one person in a country is protected from foreign invasion, for instance, all other citizens are also protected. Second, if one person consumes or benefits from the public good, the quantity available to others is not diminished (formally, the good is *nonrival in consumption*). Again using an example from national defense, one person's enjoyment of protection from foreign invasion does not diminish the quantity of security available to others. Many global environmental issues, such as ozone depletion and climate change, are also public goods (as we will discuss in more detail in Chapter 13).

Public goods are contrasted with purely private goods, which are products that only one person can possess and consume. Your sandwich for lunch is a private good: if it's available to you, it is not automatically available to all others, and if you eat it, it is not available to be eaten by any others.

Efforts to produce public goods always face **collective action problems**, which we will encounter many times in this book. Given that actors can enjoy public goods whether or not they contribute to the provision of those goods, each acts with the expectation that others will pay to produce the good while it gets to enjoy the good for free. That is, each actor aims to benefit from the contributions of others without bearing the costs itself. For example, individuals would prefer to benefit from national security without paying taxes or volunteering for military service. Alternatively, all states might want a genocide to be stopped, but each would prefer that others assume the risks of the necessary military intervention. In the case of Iraq, it is quite possible that some countries publicly opposed the U.S.-led invasion *not* because they opposed ousting Hussein, but because they wanted to benefit from the regime change without paying the military, political, or diplomatic costs of backing the invasion. In such situations, even though everyone wants the public good to be provided, each individual has an incentive to **free ride** by not contributing while benefiting from the efforts of others. When contributions are voluntary, free riding leads public goods to be provided at a lower level than that desired by the actors.

This is why public goods are often provided by governments, which have the power to tax citizens or otherwise mandate their contributions. Free riding is no longer so attractive if, say, the failure to contribute taxes can lead to steep fines or imprisonment. This is also why collaboration among governments on global issues

public goods
Products that are nonexcludable and nonrival in consumption, such as national defense.

collective action problems
Obstacles to cooperation that occur when actors have incentives to collaborate but each acts with the expectation that others will pay the costs of cooperation.

free ride
To fail to contribute to a public good while benefiting from the contributions of others.

---

8. In fact, the United States and the Soviet Union did sign several arms control agreements, which may have prevented the arms race from being even worse. It was not until the collapse of the Soviet Union in 1991 that serious reductions in nuclear armaments took place.

can prove so difficult, as there is no international authority that can mandate their contributions to global public goods.

As this discussion suggests, some of the problems associated with cooperation are addressed by institutions, which might be able to alter actors' incentives so that their individual interests line up with the collective interest. The role of institutions in promoting cooperation is discussed later in this chapter. Even in the absence of institutions, though, we can identify several factors that facilitate cooperation.

Numbers and Relative Sizes of Actors
It is easier for a small number of actors to cooperate and, if necessary, to monitor each other's behavior than for a larger number of actors to do so. Two actors can communicate more readily and observe each other's actions better than a thousand actors can. Thus, the smaller the number of actors, the more likely they are to cooperate successfully. As we will see in Chapter 7, firms can organize more easily to lobby their governments for trade protection than can consumers, who are typically more numerous. Environmental agreements are easier to monitor and enforce—thus, more likely to be agreed upon—among small groups of countries.

The United States' disproportionately large role in cooperative organizations such as the North Atlantic Treaty Organization (NATO) gives the country an advantage in renegotiating existing agreements to its benefit. At a May 2017 NATO meeting, U.S. president Donald Trump voiced his skepticism that the other NATO members were pulling their weight in terms of defense spending and sought to secure a better "deal" for the United States.

In the case of public goods, moreover, some groups may have a single member or a small coalition of members willing to pay for the entire public good. This could happen if these members receive benefits from the public good sufficient to offset the entire costs of providing it. In such *privileged groups*, the single member or small coalition of members provides the public good despite free riding by others.[9]

As we will see in Chapter 5, international efforts to enforce agreements in civil conflicts generally require that a very powerful state, such as the United States, be motivated to conduct a peacekeeping operation largely on its own. Similarly, success in limiting ozone emissions (see Chapter 13) stemmed in part from the disproportionately large role of the United States, Russia, and Japan in the industries responsible for the emissions. Some analysts attribute the economic openness of the international economy in the mid-nineteenth and mid-twentieth centuries to public goods like the international monetary regime provided unilaterally by Britain and the United States, which were the largest powers in those eras, respectively.

---

9. On privileged groups, see Mancur Olson, *The Logic of Collective Action: Public Goods and the Theory of Groups* (Cambridge, MA: Harvard University Press, 1965).

Iteration, Linkage, and Strategies of Reciprocal Punishment

Cooperation is more likely when actors have opportunities to cooperate over time and across issues. The incentive to defect or free ride in any given interaction can be overcome if actors expect to be involved in multiple, repeated interactions with the same partners.[10] In this situation—commonly known as **iteration**—actors can prevent one another from cheating by threatening to withhold cooperation in the future. Even when an actor has incentives to defect in the current interaction, knowing that the other actor will refuse to cooperate with it in the future can offset those temptations. Thus, "good behavior" can be induced today by the fear of losing the benefits of cooperation tomorrow. The threat of reciprocal punishment can be a powerful tool for enforcing cooperation even when actors are tempted to cheat.[11] You are more likely to leave a generous tip for the waiter at a local restaurant you think you will frequent in the future—lest you get poor service on another visit—than you are in a restaurant you don't expect ever to visit again.

Countries are less likely to cheat on a trade agreement with a country they trade with more often and expect to trade with again in the future (see Chapter 7). In one particularly telling example, a system of "live and let live" emerged during the trench warfare of World War I. After an initial period of rapid gains, troops on both sides of the war bogged down in fixed trenches within rifle range of one another. Despite incentives to kill the enemy whenever possible, lest he kill you, many areas along the trenches developed a form of restrained cooperation in which, even in the absence of any communication, the troops stationed there in practice did not fire upon one another. Occasional failures of cooperation, when shooting began for some reason, were punished by two-for-one or three-for-one retaliation by the other side. This response usually led back to restraint and renewed cooperation. What made cooperation possible even in this most unlikely of circumstances was the long-term deployment of troops in the same area, creating iteration and reciprocity in action.

Closely related to iteration is the concept of **linkage**, which ties cooperation on one policy dimension to cooperation on other dimensions. Whereas iteration enables victims to punish cheaters by withholding the gains from future cooperation, linkage enables victims to retaliate by withholding cooperation on other issues. Defection on military affairs, for instance, might be punished by withdrawing cooperation on economic matters. One of the reasons the United States and Great Britain have been able to sustain their "special relationship" of deep cooperation, including on Iraq, is that they are bound together on so many different issues. The failure of cooperation on one dimension puts cooperation on other issues at risk and reinforces cooperation on all.

iteration

Repeated interactions with the same partners.

linkage

The linking of cooperation on one issue to interactions on a second issue.

---

10. On iteration and international cooperation, see Robert Axelrod, *The Evolution of Cooperation* (New York: Basic Books, 1984). The trench warfare example mentioned in the following text is described in Chapter 4.

11. For the expectation of future punishment to induce current cooperation, however, actors must value the future enough that future gains matter. Everyone discounts the future; that is, they value it somewhat less than the present. A dollar today is worth more to us than a dollar next year, and much more than a dollar received in 20 years. The more actors discount the future, the less likely the threat of future punishment will encourage them to cooperate today. Conversely, the more actors value the future, the more likely the threat of future punishment will encourage cooperation now.

Information One final factor that affects the likelihood of cooperation is the availability of information. In some cases, it is easy to observe whether a partner has cooperated or defected, such as when cooperation entails a public act like participating in a military operation. In other cases, however, cooperative and uncooperative acts may be hard to observe or distinguish from one another. If cooperation involves reducing armaments, for example, the fact that states can build weapons in secret means that defection may go unobserved.

When actors lack information about the actions taken by another party, cooperation may fail because of uncertainty and misperception.[12] A state might defect under the mistaken belief that it can get away with it, or because it doubts other parties will abide by its terms. Alternatively, cooperation might unravel if cooperative acts are mistaken for defection. Suppose one party mistakenly believes that the other has defected and cuts off cooperation as punishment; the other party, which has been cooperating all along, then perceives the first actor's punishment as a new defection and cuts off cooperation in retaliation. Simple misperceptions can lead to hostile punishments and the breakdown of cooperation, even though all actors thought they were acting cooperatively.[13]

In the years leading up to the Iraq War, Saddam Hussein really had dismantled his WMD programs as required by the UN, but he was reluctant to reveal this information because he wanted to use the possibility of such weapons to deter domestic insurgents and other regional powers, especially Iran.[14] Had Iraq's disarmament been more easily confirmed, the main rationale for the war would have been eliminated.

Who Wins and Who Loses in Bargaining?

Whereas cooperation has the potential to make actors collectively better off, bargaining creates winners and losers: each actor's gains come at the expense of someone else. When two or more actors desire the same good—for example, a sum of money or a piece of territory—it is impossible for all of them to get their best possible outcome at the same time. Why, then, are bargains ever reached? Why do actors consent to losses? What determines who wins and who loses?

Considering these questions introduces a core concept in international politics: power. In the standard definition, which we owe to the political scientist Robert Dahl, **power** is the ability of Actor A to get Actor B to do something that B would otherwise not do.[15] In the context of bargaining, power is most usefully seen as the ability to get the other side to make concessions and to avoid having to make

power
The ability of Actor A to get Actor B to do something that B would otherwise not do; the ability to get the other side to make concessions and to avoid having to make concessions oneself.

---

12. On the consequences of misperception, see Robert Jervis, *Perception and Misperception in International Relations* (Princeton, NJ: Princeton University Press, 1976).

13. George W. Downs, David M. Rocke, and Randolph M. Siverson, "Arms Race and Cooperation," in *Cooperation under Anarchy*, ed. Kenneth Oye, 118–46 (Princeton, NJ: Princeton University Press, 1986).

14. This is the conclusion reached by the Iraq Survey Group, which examined Iraq's WMD program after the regime fell. See U.S. Central Intelligence Agency, "Comprehensive Report of the Special Advisor to the DCI on Iraq's WMD," September 30, 2004, https://www.cia.gov/library/reports/general-reports-1/iraq_wmd_2004/ (accessed 11/21/17).

15. Robert A. Dahl, "The Concept of Power," *Systems Research and Behavioral Science* 2, no. 3 (July 1957): 201–15.

concessions oneself. The more power an actor has, the more it can expect to get from others in the final outcome of bargaining.

Power is one of the most frequently used yet ambiguous terms in the study of international relations. Sometimes it is understood as an end in itself—an interest, as we have defined that concept—and sometimes as a means toward other ends. Other times it is conceived as a structure or constraint created by past interactions that limit the choices currently available to actors. Their large economies, past investments in military forces, and large stockpiles of nuclear weapons, for instance, gave the United States and Soviet Union enormous political advantages over other countries during the Cold War, deterring other states from even contemplating challenging the core interests of either superpower.

Our focus here, in the context of explaining bargaining outcomes, is what is sometimes called compulsory power, or the ability of one actor to compel another to act in certain ways.[16] Understood in this way, the outcome of any bargaining interaction is fundamentally influenced by what would happen in the event that no bargain was reached. The outcome that occurs when no bargain is achieved is often called the *reversion outcome*. In some cases, the reversion outcome is the same as the status quo. For example, if a car buyer and a prospective seller cannot agree on a price, then the seller is left with his car and the buyer keeps her money. What is lost is a chance to make a potentially profitable deal.

When actors bargain over the terms of cooperation, a failure to agree can prevent the collective benefits from being enjoyed. For example, if states contemplating intervention in a civil war or negotiating an environmental treaty cannot agree on how to divide the costs, then the civil conflict will rage on or the environmental harm will continue. In other cases, the consequences of disagreement are more severe: the reversion outcome may be a war or some other kind of conflict, such as economic sanctions, that leaves one or even both actors worse off than they were before the dispute began.

The actor that would be more satisfied with the reversion outcome generally has less incentive to make concessions in order to reach a successful bargain. Conversely, the actor that would be less satisfied with the reversion outcome becomes desperate to reach an agreement and thus offers relatively bigger concessions in the hopes of inducing the more satisfied actor to agree. In short, bargaining power belongs to those actors who would be most satisfied with, or most willing to endure, the reversion outcome. In the car-buying example, if the seller needs money and is anxious to sell the car quickly, a more patient buyer can extract a better deal.

Internationally, in negotiations over global climate change, the United States has been less willing to go along with other countries, in part, because the expected costs of climate change to the United States are lower. Given its geography and economic resources, the United States is better equipped than many other states to weather the effects of a warming planet and rising sea levels. As a result, the United

---

16. See Michael Barnett and Raymond Duvall, eds., *Power in Global Governance* (New York: Cambridge University Press, 2005).

States has, so far, successfully shifted the burden of cutting greenhouse gas emissions onto others. This helps explain the continuing unwillingness of the United States to adhere to international environmental agreements, including the Paris Agreement that finally brought the developing countries into the international environmental regime and thus addressed some of its prior objections (see Chapter 13).

In the case of Iraq, the United States had a great stake in rebuilding that country and ending the violence that killed thousands of U.S. troops. Despite its enormous power in most respects, the United States had a hard time convincing other countries, which were less directly hurt by the status quo, to share the costs of Iraq's reconstruction. Those most in need of agreement are likely to get worse bargains than those who can better tolerate the reversion outcome.

Because bargaining outcomes are determined largely by how each actor evaluates the reversion outcome, power derives from the ability to make the reversion outcome better for oneself and/or worse for the other side. To shift the reversion outcome in their favor, actors have three basic ways of exercising power: coercion, outside options, and agenda setting.

Coercion The most obvious strategy for exercising power is coercion. **Coercion** is the threat or imposition of costs on other actors to reduce the value of the reversion outcome (no agreement) and change their behavior. Thus, states can use their ability to impose costs on others to demand a more favorable bargain than they would otherwise receive. The demand of the United States that Saddam Hussein step down or be removed by force is an example of coercive bargaining that left the Iraqi dictator worse off than before the threat was made. The target, of course, can itself try to impose costs on the challenger. What matters is the net ability to impose costs on the other—that is, the difference between the coercion employed by one side and that employed by the other. If the costs each side can impose on the other are equal, neither party has power. The reversion outcome for both parties will be worse than the status quo and both will be more desperate to reach agreement, but neither will have any greater power over the other. The ability of one actor to impose greater costs on another actor than that other actor can impose on the first is what creates power through coercion.

Means of international coercion include military force and economic sanctions. The ability to impose costs on others and to defend against others' efforts to impose costs on oneself derives in large part from material capabilities—the physical resources that enable an actor to inflict harm and/or withstand the infliction of harm. In coercive interactions among states, these capabilities are often measured in terms of military resources—such as the number of military personnel or level of military spending—as well as measures of economic strength, since economic resources can be converted into military power. The balance of such capabilities among states is a strong predictor (though not the only one) of who wins and who loses in warfare.[17] Similarly, the size of a country's economy has an impact on its

coercion

A strategy of imposing or threatening to impose costs on other actors in order to induce a change in their behavior.

---

17. See, for example, Dan Reiter and Allan C. Stam, *Democracies at War* (Princeton, NJ: Princeton University Press, 2002).

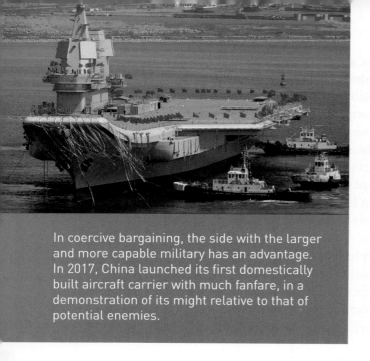

In coercive bargaining, the side with the larger and more capable military has an advantage. In 2017, China launched its first domestically built aircraft carrier with much fanfare, in a demonstration of its might relative to that of potential enemies.

ability to impose and/or withstand economic sanctions, which cut off a country's access to international trade.

Although material capabilities such as guns and money are important components of power, we will see in Chapter 3 that other factors can also be sources of power in coercive bargaining. Since the use of force is costly and risky, an actor's willingness to absorb costs and take risks can also generate an advantage. The economist Thomas Schelling famously described international crises as competitions in risk taking likely to be "won" by the side that blinks second (see the game of Chicken described in the "Special Topic" appendix to this chapter, on pp. 84–85).[18]

This helps explain why weak states can at times defeat great powers. When France tried to reassert colonial control over Vietnam after World War II, the leader of the Vietnamese resistance, Ho Chi Minh, warned the French that their superior military power would not matter: "You will kill 10 of our men, and we will kill 1 of yours, and in the end it will be you who tire of it."[19] The Vietnamese leader's optimism sprang from the belief that his people were more willing than the French to bear the costs of war. His power stemmed not from military capabilities but from what we will refer to in Chapter 3 as resolve.

Outside Options

outside options
The alternatives to bargaining with a specific actor.

Outside Options Actors can also get a better deal when they have attractive **outside options**, or alternatives to reaching a bargain with a particular partner that are more attractive than the status quo. In this case, the reversion outcome is the next-best alternative for the party with the outside option. An actor with an attractive alternative can walk away from the bargaining table more easily than an actor without such an option.

The actor with the better outside option can use its leverage, the threat to leave negotiations, to get a better deal. For example, even though the United States might have preferred to work through the UN to remove Saddam Hussein from power in Iraq in 2003, the U.S. government felt that it had an attractive outside option: acting unilaterally. U.S. military capabilities meant that even though the United States might benefit from international support, it did not feel that such support was necessary to prevail. Thus, while other countries on the Security Council tried to influence U.S. policy in the dispute, their bargaining power was greatly diminished by the fact that the United States felt it could "go it alone."

Like coercion, however, the relative attractiveness of each actor's outside option is what matters. Both actors may have alternatives, but the one with the

---

18. Thomas C. Schelling, *The Strategy of Conflict* (Cambridge, MA: Harvard University Press, 1960).

19. This quotation is often cited, and the exact wording sometimes varies. The original source is Jean Sainteny, *L'histoire d'une paix manquée: Indochine, 1945–47* (Paris: Amiot-Dumont, 1953), 231.

more attractive outside option can more credibly threaten to walk away and, therefore, can get the better deal. In competitive economic markets with many buyers and sellers, for instance, little power is exercised by any given actor, since every buyer and seller has equally attractive outside options. In the case of the UN, again, the United States had an ability to act unilaterally that was not available to the Security Council, which had only the very unattractive alternatives of fielding a military force of its own to stop the United States from invading Iraq or perhaps imposing sanctions on the United States for ignoring the council's wishes. The Security Council could not, therefore, exercise any significant power over the United States.

Agenda Setting
Similarly, actors might gain leverage in bargaining through **agenda setting**. Whereas an outside option is exercised after bargaining fails, agenda setting consists of actions taken before or during bargaining that make the reversion outcome more favorable for one party. A party that can act first to set the agenda transforms the choices available to others. For example, by sponsoring legislative proposals, calling public attention to issues, and cajoling individual legislators, the president of the United States has important agenda-setting power in Congress. Faced with a presidential proposal or a presidentially inspired public outcry, legislators often have little choice but to respond to the president's initiative; they do not necessarily have to agree with the president's proposal, but they must respond to an issue they might otherwise have preferred to avoid.[20]

agenda setting
Actions taken before or during bargaining that make the reversion outcome more favorable for one party.

The same agenda-setting power exists between countries. When the United States deregulated its airline industry to capitalize on its market position and benefit its domestic consumers, other countries were forced to deregulate their industries as well in order to remain competitive, often over the opposition of their national air carriers. In the Iraq War, the United States exercised its agenda-setting power both by bringing the inspection issue before the UN Security Council and by unilaterally initiating a war against Iraq, to which other countries were then forced to respond.

Even though bargaining creates winners and losers, bargains can be made as long as they give all parties more than (or at least as much as) they can expect to get in the reversion outcome. In other words, actors consent to painful concessions when the consequences of not agreeing are even more painful. As we will see in Chapter 3, the fact that bargains exist that all sides prefer over war does not guarantee that those bargains will always be reached. A host of problems can prevent actors from finding or agreeing to mutually beneficial deals. For example, uncertainty about how each side evaluates its prospects in a war can make it hard to know which bargains are preferable to war. There may also be situations in which states cannot credibly promise to abide by an agreement that has already been made. Bargaining may also be complicated if the good being bargained over is hard to divide. (Since this is a broad topic, we leave fuller consideration of these issues for Chapter 3.)

20. John W. Kingdon, *Agendas, Alternatives, and Public Policies*, 2nd ed. (New York: HarperCollins, 1995).

In sum, both interests and interactions matter in politics. Political outcomes depend on the choices of two or more actors. Since political outcomes are contingent on the choices of multiple actors, any given actor does not always or even most of the time get its most preferred interest. Indeed, in bargaining, an actor may be worse off afterward than if it had never entered the interaction. Interactions are often quite complex, but they are critical to understanding how interests are transformed into outcomes—often in paradoxical ways.

Institutions: Do Rules Matter in World Politics?

institutions

Sets of rules (known and shared by the community) that structure interactions in specific ways.

Institutions play a major role in social and political life, domestically and internationally. We typically define **institutions** as sets of rules, known and shared by the relevant community, that structure interactions in specific ways. Many political institutions are embodied in laws or organizations. The U.S. Congress has rules that determine who gets elected to it and how it passes laws. Additional rules determine how Congress deals with other American political institutions, such as the presidency and the courts. The UN is an institution in which states make collective decisions about military actions or economic sanctions; the UN has rules that determine which states have a say over these matters and how their votes are counted. International economic institutions include the International Monetary Fund (IMF), the World Trade Organization (WTO), and the World Bank. Other institutions are more informal and exist only as shared understandings of principles and norms. These informal institutions, such as the widespread international norm against slavery, can also be important (see Chapter 11).

Institutions vary in their goals and rules, but they generally serve to facilitate cooperation among their members.[21] As discussed in the previous section, even when actors have common interests, certain factors may make cooperation more difficult. Cooperation can flounder if the problems identified earlier—incentives to defect, large numbers of actors, nonrepeated interactions, and imperfect information—are not successfully resolved. Institutions can provide solutions to these problems. Indeed, it is precisely to facilitate cooperation that actors first create and subsequently comply with the rules embodied in institutions.

How Do Institutions Affect Cooperation?

In much of political and social life, the primary way that institutions promote cooperation is through enforcement, or the imposing of punishments on actors who fail to cooperate. Imagine, for example, that the prisoners in the Prisoner's Dilemma

---

21. See Robert O. Keohane, *After Hegemony: Cooperation and Discord in the World Political Economy* (Princeton, NJ: Princeton University Press, 1984).

game described earlier were both members of an organized crime group, and it was understood that members who rat each other out would find themselves at the bottom of a river wearing cement shoes. In that case, the prisoners would no longer have an individual incentive to defect on each other; the external enforcement by the organization would change the way they rank-ordered the possible outcomes, and cooperation between them now would make sense both individually and collectively.

Similarly, governments provide public goods by compelling individuals to pay for them in the form of taxes; the threat of fines or jail time for failing to pay weakens the incentive to free ride on the contributions of others. Cooperation among private actors within a country may also be enforced by institutions. For example, a sales contract between a customer and a firm can be enforced by courts, whose rulings are backed by the police powers of the state. In short, when institutions have means of imposing punishments for defection, they can effectively enforce cooperation.

Institutions at the international level generally lack the capacity to impose punishments on states. The international system is characterized by anarchy, as explained earlier. Whereas most countries are governed by a state—a central authority with the ability to make and enforce laws within its boundaries—there is no such central authority at the global level. Some people think the UN is a world government, but as we will see in Chapters 5 and 11, this is not the case. Even poor, weak states have more enforcement power over their citizens than the UN has over actors in the international system. It cannot tax its members, raise its own military, or field its own police force.

The condition of anarchy means that international institutions do not generally enforce cooperation among their members. Instead, cooperation at the international level has to be self-enforcing; that is, the members have to police themselves and assume responsibility for punishing defectors. The fact that countries are largely dependent on self-help does not mean that international institutions are useless, but it does shape our understanding of the role they play. In general, international institutions, even informal ones, facilitate cooperation by making self-enforcement easier. They do so in at least four ways: by setting standards of behavior, verifying compliance, reducing the costs of joint decision making, and resolving disputes. Different institutions may emphasize one or another of these tasks, but all are important.

Setting Standards of Behavior
Clear standards of behavior reduce ambiguity and enhance cooperation. For example, parents who tell a teenager, "Don't stay out too late or else," invite continuing conflict. What does "too late" mean? "Or else" is also ambiguous. If the parent grounds the teenager for a week, is this "unfair," as the aggrieved youth will likely claim, or "letting her off easy," as the parent will likely retort? The costs of such a conflict could be avoided with a clear statement: "Be home by midnight, or you'll be grounded for a week." The teenager might still choose to stay out later, but the standard for evaluating lateness and the consequences would no longer be in dispute.

International institutions set standards of behavior in similar ways. The North American Free Trade Agreement (NAFTA) among the United States, Mexico, and Canada contains 22 chapters and 7 annexes of detailed rules governing trade and investment among the three countries, as well as exceptions to general rules for particular practices and industries. Arms control agreements between the United States and the Soviet Union during the Cold War often ran to hundreds of pages, detailing precise numbers for different types of weapons systems and limits on their capabilities. Following the 1991 Persian Gulf War, the UN Security Council passed Resolution 661, prohibiting Iraq from possessing or developing all chemical, biological, and nuclear weapons and any ballistic missile with a range greater than 150 kilometers. It also banned all facilities for the development, support, or manufacture of such weapons, their precursors, or their subcomponents. This resolution defined carefully which weapons Iraq was and was not allowed to possess.

Clear standards of behavior enable others to determine whether an actor is violating an agreement. The aggrieved parties can call violators to account and, if the violations are not corrected, can withdraw from cooperation entirely or impose sanctions. Clear standards are especially important for international agreements, which must be enforced by participants (as opposed to third parties, as in domestic affairs). Without an authoritative third-party enforcement mechanism, such as the courts or the police, there is a real potential for disputes to escalate on account of incomplete or inaccurate information. By accurately identifying violations and violators, international institutions can help defuse potentially costly cycles of reciprocal punishments set off by misperceived violations.

Clear standards of behavior cannot eliminate all disputes. Rules can never address all possible circumstances, and there may well be ambiguous situations that those looking to evade the rules can exploit. Saddam Hussein skirted his obligations under UN Security Council Resolution 661 and played on divisions among the permanent members of the Security Council to avoid complying with restrictions, especially in reporting and inspections. But the resolution was nonetheless important in setting the standard against which his behavior was ultimately judged. Although disputes occur, clear standards help support cooperation by identifying violations and allowing enforcement procedures to function.

Verifying Compliance

In addition to standards against which actors can judge compliance, institutions often provide ways to acquire information on compliance. President Ronald Reagan famously said about arms control agreements with the Soviet Union, "Trust, but verify"—a rough translation of an old Russian proverb.

In many international institutions, self-reporting is common practice: countries are required to submit reports documenting their compliance. Such a procedure might appear weak, but it allows other parties of the agreement to inspect the self-reporting of others, assess those reports against their private knowledge of others' compliance, and publicize and criticize any inconsistencies. Discrepancies between self-reports and later-verified accounts open the country to further disrepute and possible sanctions. In the fall of 2002, for example, the United States asked the UN Security Council to demand of Iraq a detailed accounting of its WMD programs, and then the United States highlighted inconsistencies not only within the hundreds of thousands of pages of documents but also among the documents, past inspection reports, and its own intelligence estimates.

At the other extreme, some international agreements permit on-site inspections. The International Atomic Energy Agency (IAEA), for instance, inspects declared nuclear material facilities in over 70 countries under the Treaty on the Non-Proliferation of Nuclear Weapons (NPT). This treaty, adopted in 1968, prohibits most countries from diverting fissionable material from civilian nuclear reactors for use in making nuclear weapons. The IAEA inspectors help to monitor compliance with this prohibition. UN Security Council Resolution 661 also provided for the IAEA to lead inspection teams in Iraq to search for possible nuclear weapons and development sites. As an example of highly intrusive inspections, drilling down deeply in what used to be considered the domestic affairs of states, the international monitoring of elections in newly democratizing countries has recently become an international norm (see "How Do We Know?" on p. 72).

Regularly inspecting nuclear power facilities to promote safe and peaceful use of nuclear technology is one way that international institutions verify compliance with standards. Here, International Atomic Energy Agency officials examine uranium enrichment in Iran.

Finally, institutions protect the ability of countries to verify compliance independently. Rules specifying the status of embassies and the treatment of embassy personnel allow for diplomatic representation of one country on the territory of another, but they also permit embassy officials on-site access to collect information and track developments in the foreign state. Similarly, the Treaty on Open Skies, signed in 1992 and ratified by the United States and 34 other countries, formally permits states to use "national technical means," including satellites and high-flying spy planes, to observe developments on the ground below in foreign territories. Such tools were important in verifying the arms control agreements between the United States and the Soviet Union during the Cold War. The treaty, which was negotiated just as the Cold War was ending, formally acknowledged and ratified what had been long-standing practice. National technical means were important—even if misleading and incomplete—in monitoring Iraq's WMD programs in the 1990s.

Reducing the Costs of Joint Decision Making
Institutions make it easier for actors to make decisions collectively. Recall the example of the "rules of the road" from the discussion of coordination earlier in this chapter. In a society where the side-of-the-road rule had not been established, each driver would have to negotiate with each oncoming car over who would drive on the left and who would drive on the right. Stops would be frequent, and crashes would be inevitable. The time lost in travel as a result of negotiating these individual encounters, as well as the crashes,

The International Diffusion of Election Monitoring

Before 1962, no national election was ever monitored by international observers. Today, nearly 80 percent of all elections are observed by a variety of organizations, including other national governments, international organizations, and private entities. This growing trend is illustrated in Figure A. International election monitoring challenges the norm of international sovereignty, which, in principle, gives states wide latitude in how they choose their governments. Incumbent governments must invite international monitors, and most now do so seemingly voluntarily. How did this new international institution of election monitoring get established?

In original research, Susan Hyde theorizes that election monitoring grew from the need for "true" democrats to signal their commitment to free and fair elections in the face of international skepticism and from the desire of established democratic states to promote new democracies. Hyde begins from the supposition that some leaders—like the first U.S. president, George Washington, who intentionally stepped down after two terms in office to set a precedent of limited executive rule—are sincere in their commitment to democracy. Other leaders, she argues, are pseudo-democrats who will cheat to obtain or remain in office. In elections in countries that have reestablished democracy after periods of authoritarian rule or that have recently gained independence, true democrats must find some way of identifying themselves to voters at home and supporters abroad as sincerely committed to democracy. Inviting observers to monitor the election and certify the result as "free and fair" is one way of doing this. Thus, the first leaders to invite international monitors were trying to distinguish themselves from the potentially larger set of leaders who were not necessarily committed to democracy. It was in the interests of these true democrats to invite election monitors, and as Figure A demonstrates, few early cases of monitoring were criticized for significant electoral fraud. True democrats do not cheat.

As the practice of monitoring began to spread, established democracies in North America and Europe started to reward leaders that both invited monitors and held honest elections. Greater foreign aid was one of a range of benefits provided. This change in their interactions with donor states reinforced the desire of true democrats to invite election monitors. Yet this same interaction prompted some pseudo-democrats also to invite international election monitors in the hopes that (1) their cheating would go undetected and (2) they could receive the benefits provided by the international community as well. In short, the pseudo-democrats had an interest in mimicking the behavior of true democrats. The result of this now broader set of interactions, however, was to spread the institution of election monitoring to nearly all countries. At present, any new democracy that does not invite election monitors is immediately suspected of engaging in election fraud.

Ironically, as the practice of election monitoring spread, more and more cases of electoral fraud were discovered. Pseudo-democrats both invite monitors and cheat, and their efforts to manipulate elections are sometimes uncovered. Hyde finds that true democrats respond by inviting larger and more professional observer missions, further institutionalizing the practice of election monitoring. In turn, pseudo-democrats once again copy their true democratic cousins and invite larger missions as well. The effect has been to expand and institutionalize the practice of election monitoring. Whether or not total electoral fraud has decreased as a result of this uptick in monitoring remains an open question that is very difficult to answer.

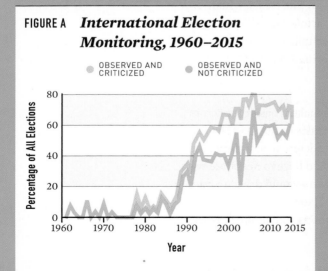

FIGURE A *International Election Monitoring, 1960–2015*

OBSERVED AND CRITICIZED   OBSERVED AND NOT CRITICIZED

Percentage of All Elections

80
60
40
20
0

1960 1970 1980 1990 2000 2010 2015

Year

Source: Susan D. Hyde, *The Pseudo-Democrat's Dilemma: Why Election Observation Became an International Norm* (Ithaca, NY: Cornell University Press, 2011).

would be the costs of joint decision making. Given the huge costs, societies establish institutions—rules of the road—to routinize decision making, avoid conflicts, and reduce the costs of driving. Smoother traffic flow and faster commutes are the benefits of the institution.

Domestic political institutions similarly operate to reduce the costs of joint decision making. Imagine that a society needed to decide collectively on all matters of policy in the absence of any agreed-upon rules. Every time someone wanted to propose a new policy, he or she would have to get all citizens to figure out how they would decide. Should the policy be enacted by popular referendum? If so, who could vote? Would it pass by a simple majority (50 percent plus one vote), by a supermajority (greater than 50 percent, usually two-thirds), or by unanimous consent? Alternatively, would policy be decided by a subgroup of society? Would this subgroup be a representative body, only the most highly affected individuals, or a single individual? What powers would this subgroup have? Would it be able not only to establish the policy, but also to tax others if necessary to implement the policy?

The list of possible decision-making rules and the alternatives to be considered for each policy are virtually endless. In the absence of some agreed-upon rules on collective decision making, the costs of any policy initiative would be enormous. These might be so large, in fact, that no policy would ever generate sufficient benefits to offset the costs of enacting that policy. Nothing would ever get done. For this reason, societies create political institutions—rules of the political game—that define how joint political decisions will be made. These institutions are useful because they reduce the costs of joint decision making.

International institutions serve to reduce the costs of joint decision making among nations in the same way. The UN was created as a permanent forum where countries could come together to deliberate and attempt to resolve disagreements. Since its founding, the UN and its associated agencies have undertaken 69 peace-keeping operations, fought the Korean War, authorized the 1991 Persian Gulf War, rewritten the law of the sea, managed refugee problems worldwide, fed people displaced by conflict or famine, helped eliminate smallpox globally, and undertaken a host of other activities. A relatively clear set of rules determines which issues get referred to the General Assembly and which to the Security Council, and each body has specific voting rules. These rules reduce the costs of joint decision making among member states just as they do in other social settings. A large number of other international institutions help reduce the costs of joint decision making on a broad range of issues.

Resolving Disputes International institutions also facilitate cooperation by providing mechanisms for resolving disputes. When parties disagree about whether one or more of them have violated an agreement or how to interpret the terms of an agreement, it can be helpful to have determined in advance how to handle such differences. Domestically, disputes are routinely referred to courts for authoritative resolution; in fact, courts are the default forum for dispute resolution, unless the parties to an agreement have specifically consented to other provisions, such as arbitration. Most international agreements, however, do not contain explicit dispute resolution procedures, and each party may seek to interpret the agreement according to its own interests and be limited only by its desire for a reputation as a "good partner."

Nonetheless, many international economic transactions regularly delegate dispute resolution to national courts—for instance, agreeing in advance that disputes will be decided according to the laws of the state of New York—or to one of many international arbitration boards. In a limited number of cases, states will create new dispute settlement procedures as part of an agreement, as in the WTO and regional economic blocs such as NAFTA. By creating mechanisms to resolve disputes, actors increase their expectations that others will uphold their commitments, prevent retaliation from escalating out of control, resolve ambiguities in their agreements, and enable mutually beneficial cooperation. Note that the dispute resolution body itself does not have to enforce the rules by punishing violators. Rather, by interpreting rules when they are ambiguous or subject to conflicting interpretations, dispute settlement bodies help identify violator and victim, permit actors to employ self-help sanctions more efficiently, and potentially keep disputes from escalating.

In sum, institutions facilitate international cooperation in important ways. International institutions do not, however, directly enforce cooperation, except in extremely rare cases when they are empowered to punish defectors directly. Rather, despite a well-developed infrastructure of institutions, international politics remains largely a realm of self-help in which states alone must choose whether and how to penalize those who fail to cooperate. What international institutions do, however, is make compliance more likely by clarifying the terms of cooperation, providing information, and lowering the costs of joint decision making—including the costs of deciding when to punish states that choose not to follow the rules.

Whom Do Institutions Benefit?

Institutions may help states cooperate, and in that sense they can make all their members better off. But institutions rarely benefit everyone equally. Institutions are themselves a product of the cooperation and bargaining that brought them into being. They reflect past political bargains, with the winners getting to write the rules or, at least, having a disproportionate say over the rules. As a result, rules are never neutral; instead, they embody the bargaining strength of the actors at the time the rules were written or amended. Thus, all institutions contain what we describe as a policy bias.[22]

Institutions bias outcomes in many ways. In the United States, for instance, citizens' interests are represented at the national level through different electoral institutions. These institutions themselves are a reflection of bargaining within the constitutional convention of 1787. The more populous states at the time sought a

---

22. For a review of the effects of institutions, including policy bias, see Ronald Rogowski, "Institutions as Constraints on Strategic Choice," in Lake and Powell, *Strategic Choice*, 115–36.

legislature in which representatives were allocated by population, which would give them a larger voice. The less populous states, knowing they would be routinely outvoted, wanted some form of guaranteed representation. The result was a compromise, with seats in the House of Representatives being determined by population and seats in the Senate being reserved two for each state. The larger states were forced to compromise by the unwillingness of the smaller states to agree to the Constitution without this provision.

These rules matter. Since they are elected by and responsive to different subsets of the national population, it is hardly surprising that the majority of the House of Representatives, the majority of the Senate, and the president—with the largest constituency—often differ in their interests. Indeed, the framers of the Constitution explicitly intended to create competing branches of government with different constituencies and policy preferences. Institutions that represent many smaller constituencies are likely to produce policies that favor particular groups in society through large, omnibus "log rolls" that contain something for everyone. Institutions that represent larger constituencies are more likely to enact policies that benefit society as a whole. For this reason, Congress is often thought to be more beholden to "special interests," whereas the president is expected to act more in the national interest.

One manifestation of this difference is that members of the House of Representatives are typically more responsive to industries in their districts that compete with foreign imports, and thus they are more protectionist in trade policy. The president, on the other hand, is more likely to support freer trade, which promotes the interests of consumers as a whole. President Trump, however, is more protectionist, at least in his rhetoric, than the Republican majority in the House or Senate. Nonetheless, as a general rule, presidents have been more supportive of free trade than Congress has.

International institutions differ widely in their rules and in their policy bias. Many institutions, including the General Assembly of the UN, have a one country–one vote rule. China, with a population of over 1.3 billion, has the same official weight as Tuvalu, whose population is under 11,000. This rule gives each citizen of Tuvalu the same voice in the General Assembly as about 125,000 Chinese. The Security Council, by contrast, has voting rules that privilege five particular states—the United States, Great Britain, France, Russia, and China—by giving them a veto over any action the council might take. This means that even if a majority of states on the Security Council, or around the world, want the UN to enact a particular policy, it can be blocked by any one of these five states.

Why these particular states? They were the five major victors of World War II, and hence they were in a position to write the rules when the UN was created in the aftermath of that war. The privileged position of these states helps explain why French and Russian opposition to the U.S.-led invasion of Iraq was so consequential: without their support, the Security Council could not authorize the use of force.

Other organizations have weighted voting rules, which give the largest contributors the most influence. In the IMF, for example, the United States contributes

The European Union and the United States each have enough votes within the IMF to veto any major decision by the organization. Many critics charge that the IMF, as a result, is biased in its policies toward the interests of the developed countries.

about 17 percent of the fund's resources, and consequently it gets 17 percent of the votes on the organization's Board of Governors—by far the largest vote share of any individual country. The weights have been periodically renegotiated to reflect changes in the contributions and bargaining power of states, but the United States and the European Union still retain large enough shares of the votes to each block any important decision within the organization.

Still other institutions operate by unanimous consent, permitting any member to veto an action. In its early decades, the Council of Ministers of the European Economic Community (later the European Community, now the European Union) used a unanimity rule. As the policy-making demands of deeper economic integration became more intense, the council made a historic decision to adopt a qualified majority voting rule in the Single European Act signed in 1986. This was understood to be a major transfer of power away from member states, who could previously veto any initiative they found objectionable, and to the European Community as a whole. As in domestic institutions, rules matter in international institutions.

Because institutions matter and bias policy in consequential ways, states struggle over their rules. Institutions are both the shapers of politics (by facilitating cooperation) and the products of political action. Given the relative consistency in the basic institutions of government in the United States and many other countries, we often attribute a "taken for granted" or natural quality to political institutions. But it is important to understand that all institutions reflect particular policy biases and, as a result, are always the object of continuing political debate and struggle.

Why Follow the Rules?

Why do actors follow rules? If they have incentives to defect from rules and ignore institutions, why do they not always do so? If the rules are biased against them, why would they go along with them anyway? These have been key questions for many scholars of international relations. Some analysts argue that states ignore institutions whenever those institutions do not serve their interests, so the institutions we see merely reflect the current bargaining strength of states and do not affect policy.[23] Others argue that if institutions did not matter, states would not devote so much energy to writing the extensive rules we observe. In this view, rates of compliance in international politics are surprisingly high. Indeed, although this finding remains contested, international lawyers argue that when states do violate international

---

23. For a skeptical view of international institutions, see John J. Mearsheimer, "The False Promise of International Institutions," *International Security* 19 (1994): 5–49.

rules, the reason is more often a lack of capacity to live up to their obligations than an attempt to seize an advantage over others.[24]

Actors comply with institutions for two reasons. First, since many problems in international relations combine both cooperation and bargaining, actors may agree to comply with rules for the broader cooperation they facilitate, even though the outcome of those particular rules is biased against them. In these situations, the value of the cooperation created by the institution outweighs the costs of a relatively disadvantageous bargain. States observe the rules of the WTO not just because other countries might be authorized to punish them for violations, but also because the wider system of free trade that the WTO supports and promotes is of great benefit to them. They fear that defiance of its mandates would place at risk the whole system of trade rules and the gains from trade.

Thus, even the United States, the world's largest trader, complies with the findings of the WTO dispute settlement process. In 1995, the small country of Costa Rica brought suit against the United States in the WTO, for instance, for restrictions on cotton and synthetic-fiber underwear exported from that country. The United States tried to defend its restrictions as necessary to prevent serious damage to its domestic industry, but it was repeatedly found to be in violation of WTO rules. Washington eventually complied, to the protests of domestic producers, even though retaliation from Costa Rica itself would have been but a minor irritant. Similarly, countries abide by the NPT not just because the inspections of the IAEA may reveal cheating that could then be referred to the UN Security Council for possible sanctioning, but also because the restraints on all countries make the world a safer place. In such cases, the prospect of continued, mutually beneficial cooperation restrains the short-run temptation for countries to ignore rules they do not like.

The second reason actors comply with institutions is that they are already in place and often cheaper to use, even if they are biased, than are the costs of creating a brand-new institution that might more fully reflect the actors' interests. Creating new institutions is not easy. As we've discussed, actors must agree on the members, voting rules, and many other procedures that the institution comprises. Since those rules will affect the cooperation and bargains reached, actors will struggle over which rules should be adopted. In the negotiations that eventually led to the end of the Vietnam War, the parties spent more than six months just wrangling over the shape of the table at which they would sit.

The time and effort spent negotiating new rules can be considerable. In the case of an existing institution, the costs of creating a set of rules have already been paid. The costs of any new institution, however better suited to the matter now under discussion, would have to be paid anew. If the policy bias of an institution is small enough, actors may choose to work within the existing rules rather than create new ones from scratch. If the policy bias is too large, actors will choose to

---

24. See Abram Chayes and Antonia Handler Chayes, "On Compliance," *International Organization* 47, no. 2 (1993): 175–205. This view is criticized in George W. Downs, David M. Rocke, and Peter N. Barsoom, "Is the Good News about Compliance Good News about Cooperation?" *International Organization* 50, no. 3 (1996): 397–406.

disband the institution, ignore it, or reform it.[25] In many circumstances, however, they recognize that maintaining the institution, though far from ideal, is less costly than creating a new one.

The benefits of an established forum and set of rules for joint decision making are substantial. Indeed, the United States continues to work through the UN, even though the other member states have failed to approve policies it supports. Despite failing to get UN approval for its invasion of Iraq, by 2006 the United States was once again working vigorously through the Security Council to condemn Iran's past violation of IAEA safeguards and to prevent that country's progress toward acquiring a nuclear weapon. In this case, the cooperation of all major powers was required for effective sanctions to force Iran to the bargaining table and to the successful conclusion of the Joint Comprehensive Plan of Action halting its nuclear program, signed in 2015 and in effect beginning January 2016. The Iran agreement remains controversial, and President Trump has said that he may not certify Iran's compliance in the future. The UN remains the most effective forum for negotiating a common position with other states. Even though the United States has not always gotten its way in the past, the institution remains sufficiently valuable that the United States often prefers to work within rather than outside its rules or to create yet another organization.

Institutions are the rules of the political game. Valued and respected for the cooperation they facilitate, institutions are not, however, a panacea for problems of international cooperation. When the temptation to defect becomes too large, or the fear of being taken advantage of grows too severe, countries will violate the rules—just as actors within countries choose at times to disobey the law. Yet institutions do make international cooperation more likely, and countries that desire cooperation follow the rules more often than we might otherwise expect.

Conclusion: Explaining World Politics

This chapter has outlined the basic concepts of interests, interactions, and institutions that serve throughout the book to unravel a variety of puzzles of international politics.

To illustrate how this analytical framework can be used in concrete ways, we return to the example that opened this chapter. In the Iraq War of 2003, the interests of the United States and Iraq were diametrically opposed, thus throwing the two countries into an interaction of pure bargaining. The United States wanted, at a minimum, to eliminate Iraq's ability to deploy weapons of mass destruction and, at

---

25. Joseph Jupille, Walter Mattle, and Duncan Snidal, *Institutional Choice and Global Commerce* (New York: Cambridge University Press, 2013).

a maximum, to eliminate the regime of Saddam Hussein. The maximum demand of the United States was rooted in a belief that even though Hussein might be successfully contained today, he could not be trusted not to develop or use WMD in the future.

These interests were reinforced by (1) the personal interests of the U.S. president and others in his administration to stand tough in international politics and promote democracy abroad, especially in the Middle East; (2) the desire for stable and cheap oil from Middle East suppliers; and (3) a general sense of insecurity on the part of many Americans after the terrorist attacks of 9/11. This confluence of interests combined to justify taking a hard-line stance against Iraq's purported weapons programs. The Iraqi ruler, in turn, wanted to remain in power and perhaps build Iraq into a regional power. Given these opposing interests, the United States and Iraq were bargaining over the extent of international controls on the latter's weapons programs and the nature of its government. With its coercive power and ability to set the agenda by increasing pressure on Iraq and, ultimately, initiating war, the United States was unwilling to accept anything less than Iraq's complete capitulation.

As we will see more fully in Chapter 3, war is a bargaining failure in which the parties are unable to reach an agreement on acceptable terms. In this case, the United States and Iraq were unable to devise a set of institutions, or to use existing ones, that would set agreed-upon standards for Iraq's weapons programs or effectively monitor and enforce the restrictions desired by the United States. In retrospect, it also became clear that the United States suffered from a serious lack of information—not only about Iraq's weapons program and military capabilities but also about the costs of rebuilding the country and ensuring internal political stability after the war. Despite facing almost certain defeat, in turn, Saddam Hussein gambled that he would be no worse off after the war than if he voluntarily relinquished power and went into exile. In either case, he would lose his office and likely be killed either in battle or in retribution for his crimes against the Iraqi people—as he eventually was in December 2006. He had little to lose by choosing to stand and fight. He also misjudged the United States' willingness to fight a war to remove him from power.

The great tragedy of the 2003 Iraq War is that the previous inspection and disarmament efforts after the 1991 Gulf War, conducted through the UN, had effectively disarmed Iraq. The inspection regime—an international institution—had worked. But for a variety of reasons, Iraq could not allow the UN open access to all possible weapons sites. For Saddam Hussein to admit that he did not have stockpiles of WMD might have emboldened domestic insurgents and other regional powers, especially Iran. In turn, the United States, after a decade of failed Iraqi promises and thwarted inspections, did not believe it could trust Hussein to honor any agreement. As a result, there was no way Iraq could credibly demonstrate to the United States that it had, in fact, dismantled its weapons programs. The United States discovered the truth for itself only after it had begun what turned out to be a long and costly war.

Study Tool Kit

Interests, Interactions, and Institutions in Context

- Interests are the fundamental building blocks of politics. Explanations of international political events begin by specifying the relevant actors and their interests.

- Cooperation is a type of interaction involving two or more actors working together to achieve a preferred outcome. Successful cooperation depends on the number and relative sizes of actors involved, the number of interactions among the actors, and the accuracy of the information they possess.

- Bargaining is a type of interaction involving the distribution of a fixed value: if one actor gets "more," someone else necessarily gets "less." In bargaining, outcomes depend on what will happen in the event that no agreement is reached. Actors derive power from their ability to make the consequences of no agreement less attractive for the other side.

- Institutions are sets of rules. Actors comply with institutions because they facilitate cooperation and lower the cost of joint decision making in the pursuit of valued goals.

- Institutions also bias policy outcomes. Rules restrain what actors can and cannot do, and thus they make some outcomes more or less likely. Actors struggle over institutions in efforts to shift policy toward outcomes they prefer.

Key Terms

For Further Reading

Avant, Deborah D., Martha Finnemore, and Susan K. Sell, eds. *Who Governs the Globe?* New York: Cambridge University Press, 2010. Explores new patterns of governance within the otherwise anarchic international system.

Bueno de Mesquita, Bruce, Alastair Smith, Randolph M. Siverson, and James D. Morrow. *The Logic of Political Survival*. Cambridge, MA: MIT Press, 2003. Integrates interests, interactions, and institutions to explain a wide range of behaviors in domestic and international politics.

Enloe, Cynthia. *Bananas, Beaches, and Bases: Making Feminist Sense of International Politics*. 2nd ed. Berkeley: University of California Press, 2014. Updated edition of a path-breaking feminist analysis of international politics.

Gordon, Michael R., and Bernard E. Trainor. *The Endgame: The Inside Story of the Struggle for Iraq, from George W. Bush to Barack Obama*. New York: Vintage, 2013. Still the definitive history and analysis of the Iraq War.

Jamal, Amaney A. *Of Empires and Citizens: Pro-American Democracy or No Democracy at All?* Princeton, NJ: Princeton University Press, 2012. Important study of the U.S. role in contemporary Middle Eastern politics.

Keohane, Robert O. *After Hegemony: Cooperation and Discord in the World Political Economy*. Princeton, NJ: Princeton University Press, 1984. Classic statement on the role and importance of international institutions.

Kydd, Andrew H. *International Relations Theory: The Game Theoretic Approach*. New York: Cambridge University Press, 2015. Introduction to game theory with applications to world politics.

Lake, David A., and Robert Powell, eds. *Strategic Choice and International Relations*. Princeton, NJ: Princeton University Press, 1999. Examines interests, interactions, and institutions in detail within the context of international relations theory.

Milner, Helen V., and Dustin Tingley. *Sailing the Water's Edge: The Domestic Politics of American Foreign Policy*. Princeton, NJ: Princeton University Press, 2015. Explores how the interactions of the president, Congress, interest groups, bureaucracies, and the public have influenced U.S. foreign policy since 1945.

A Primer on Game Theory

Game theory is a tool for analyzing strategic interactions. Over the last 50 years, it has been developed and applied broadly in nearly all the social sciences, as well as in biology and other physical sciences—and it is even making inroads in the humanities. Among its earliest and most useful applications was international politics. We provide here a brief overview of game theory to introduce strategic thinking and illustrate concepts discussed in the text.

Imagine two actors, Actor 1 (A1) and Actor 2 (A2), with only two choices, which we call cooperation (C) and defection (D). Since each actor has two choices, there are four possible outcomes to this "game": both might cooperate (CC), both might defect (DD), A1 might cooperate while A2 defects (CD), and A1 might defect while A2 cooperates (DC). The mapping of choices into outcomes is best depicted using a 2 x 2 matrix, as shown in Figure A.1.[a] As defined in the chapter text, the actors' interests determine how they rank the four possible outcomes from best (4) to worst (1), with higher "payoffs" representing more preferred outcomes. A1's payoffs are given first in each cell; A2's are given second.

Both actors choose simultaneously without knowledge of the other's choices but with knowledge of their own preferences and those of the other actor.[b] The outcome we observe is a function of the interaction—that is, the choices of both actors. Each actor can choose only C or D, but their payoffs differ across the four possible outcomes. Suppose A1 chooses C and ranks CC (mutual cooperation) over CD; in choosing C, A1 only partially controls which outcome arises. Having chosen C, A1's actual payoff depends crucially on whether A2 chooses C (creating CC) or D (creating CD). This scenario highlights a key point: that *strategic interaction depends on the choices of all relevant actors*, and it is most important in explaining situations in which outcomes are contingent on the choices of all parties.

In such a setting, purposive actors—that is, actors who seek their highest expected payoff—choose strategies, or plans of action, that are a best response to the anticipated actions of the other. Sometimes it makes sense for an actor to make the same choice (C or D) regardless of what the opponent does; in these cases, the actor is said to have a *dominant strategy*. In other cases, each player's best choice depends on what the opponent does. For example, a best response might be to cooperate when the other side cooperates and defect when the other side defects.

Since each player is trying to play a best response, and since each expects the other to play a best response, the outcome of the game is given by two strategies,

---

a. The same games can be represented in extensive form as a "game tree." Both are common in the larger literature.

b. In some of the games discussed here, the outcome does not depend on the assumption that the actors move simultaneously.

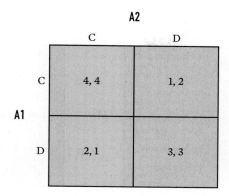

FIGURE A.1 *A Game Matrix*

each of which is a best response to the other. An outcome that arises from each side choosing best-response strategies is called an *equilibrium*. An equilibrium outcome is stable because the actors have no incentive to alter their choices; since, in equilibrium, both are playing their best responses, by definition they cannot do better by changing their choices. In the game illustrations that follow, the equilibrium (or *equilibria*, when there is more than one) is denoted by an asterisk (*) in the appropriate cell.

The Prisoner's Dilemma

As described in the text (pp. 58–59), the Prisoner's Dilemma is a commonly cited game in international relations because it captures problems of collaboration, such as arms races and public goods provision. Reread the full text on pages 58–59, and keep in mind that each prisoner can either *cooperate with his accomplice* and refuse to provide evidence to the district attorney or *defect on his accomplice* by ratting him out. Therefore, four different outcomes are possible for each player, ranked as follows:

- **Best outcome (ranked 4):** The prisoner defects while his partner cooperates (DC), meaning that he is freed immediately, while his partner is jailed for 10 years.

- **Second-best outcome (3):** The prisoner and his partner both cooperate (CC), and therefore each spends only 1 year in prison.

- **Third-best outcome (2):** The prisoner and his partner both defect (DD), and each is imprisoned for 5 years.

- **Worst outcome (1):** The prisoner cooperates while his partner defects (CD), meaning that he goes to prison for 10 years while his partner goes free.

In short, each prisoner has identical interests and ranks the four possible outcomes as DC > CC > DD > CD (the "greater than" symbol should be read in each case

FIGURE A.2 *The Prisoner's Dilemma*

<table>
<tr><td></td><td colspan="3" align="center">A2</td></tr>
<tr><td></td><td></td><td align="center">C</td><td align="center">D</td></tr>
<tr><td rowspan="2">A1</td><td>C</td><td>Both prisoners get out and split the loot.</td><td>A1 goes to jail; A2 goes free and keeps all the loot.</td></tr>
<tr><td>D</td><td>A1 goes free and keeps all the loot; A2 goes to jail.</td><td>Both go to jail and split the loot later.</td></tr>
</table>

<table>
<tr><td></td><td colspan="3" align="center">A2</td></tr>
<tr><td></td><td></td><td align="center">C</td><td align="center">D</td></tr>
<tr><td rowspan="2">A1</td><td>C</td><td align="center">3, 3</td><td align="center">1, 4</td></tr>
<tr><td>D</td><td align="center">4, 1</td><td align="center">2, 2*</td></tr>
</table>

as meaning that the first outcome is "preferred over" the second), as depicted in Figure A.2.

What each prisoner should do is unclear at this point, but here is where the techniques of game theory help. As close examination of the matrix reveals, each criminal's dominant strategy is to defect, regardless of his partner's actions. If his partner cooperates (that is, stays quiet), he is better off defecting (that is, talking to the district attorney) (DC > CC). If his partner defects, he is also better off defecting (DD > CD). The equilibrium that results from each prisoner playing his best response is DD, or mutual defection. The paradox, or dilemma, arises because both criminals would be better off if they remained silent and got released relatively quickly than if they both provided evidence and went to jail (CC > DD). But despite knowing this, each still has incentives to defect in order to get off easy (DC) or at least safeguard against his partner's defection (DD). The only actor who wins in this contrived situation is the district attorney, who sends both criminals to jail.

Although it is a considerable simplification, many analysts have used the Prisoner's Dilemma to capture the essential strategic dilemma at the core of the collective action problem. Each individual prefers free riding while others contribute to the public good of, say, national defense, over contributing if everyone else does and receiving the good, over not contributing if no one else does, and finally over contributing if no one else contributes (DC > CC > DD > CD). As with the prisoners, each individual has a dominant strategy of not contributing (that is, defecting); thus, the public good of national defense is not provided voluntarily. The dilemma is solved only by the imposition of taxes by an authoritative state.

Chicken

The game of Chicken represents a second strategic dilemma. The animating story here is the game played by teenagers in the 1950s (and perhaps today by teenagers not yet familiar with game theory!). Two drivers speed down the middle of the road toward one another. The first to turn aside, the "chicken," earns the derision

FIGURE A.3 *Chicken*

	A2	
	C	**D**
A1 **C**	Both drivers swerve; neither is humiliated or harmed.	A1 is "chicken"; A2 "wins."
D	A1 "wins"; A2 is "chicken."	Both drivers are killed in a serious wreck.

	A2	
	C	**D**
A1 **C**	3, 3	2, 4*
D	4, 2*	1, 1

of his or her peers. The other driver wins. If both swerve simultaneously, neither is humiliated. If neither turns aside, both risk death in a serious wreck. If turning aside is understood as cooperation and continuing down the middle of the road as defection, the actors' interests are DC > CC > CD > DD, as shown in Figure A.3 (note that this is the same preference ordering as in the Prisoner's Dilemma, except for the reversal of the last two outcomes).

Lacking a dominant strategy, the key to one's strategy in Chicken is to do the opposite of what you think the other driver is likely to do. If you think your opponent will stand tough (D), you should turn aside (C). If you think your opponent will turn aside (C), you should stand tough (D). Two equilibria exist (DC and CD). The winner is the driver who by bluster, swagger, or past reputation convinces the other that she is more willing to risk a crash.

Chicken is often taken as a metaphor for coercive bargaining (see p. 66 in the text). Nuclear crises are usually thought of as Chicken games. Both sides want to avoid nuclear disaster (DD), but each has incentives to stand tough and get the other to back down (DC). The state willing to take the greatest risk of nuclear war is therefore likely to force the other to capitulate. The danger, of course, is that if both sides are willing to run high risks of nuclear war to win, small mistakes in judgment or calculation can have horrific consequences.

The Stag Hunt

A final game, which is often taken as a metaphor for problems of coordination in international relations (see p. 58 in the chapter text), is the Stag Hunt. This is one of a larger class of what are known as assurance games.[c] The motivating parable was told by political philosopher Jean-Jacques Rousseau. Only by working together can

---

c. Another common assurance game is Battle of the Sexes. In this game, a couple wants to spend the evening together, but one partner wants to attend a sporting event and the other a movie. The worst outcome for each is to spend the evening alone. Interested readers should model this game and describe its dynamics in terms similar to those for the Stag Hunt and the other games in this appendix.

two hunters kill a stag and feed their families well. One must flush the deer from the forest, and the other must be ready to fire his arrow as the animal emerges. In the midst of the hunt, a lone rabbit wanders by. Each hunter now faces a decision: he could capture the rabbit alone, but to do so he must abandon the stag, ensuring that it will get away.

A rabbit is good sustenance but not as fine as the hunter's expected share of the stag. In this game, both hunters are best off cooperating (CC) and sharing the stag. The next-best outcome is to get a rabbit while the other tries for the stag (DC); however, if both go for the rabbit (DD), they then split the rabbit. The worst outcome for each hunter is to spend time and energy hunting the stag while the other hunts the rabbit (CD), leaving him and his family with nothing. Thus, each hunter's interests create the ranking CC > DC > DD > CD, as depicted in Figure A.4.

Despite the clear superiority of mutual cooperation, a coordination dilemma arises. If each hunter expects that the other will cooperate and help bring down the stag, each is best off cooperating in the hunt. But if each expects that the other will be tempted to defect and grab the rabbit, thereby letting the stag get away, he will also defect and try to grab the rabbit. Lacking a dominant strategy, each can do no better than what he expects the other to do—creating two equilibria (CC and DD).

The Stag Hunt resembles the problem of setting international standards (see p. 69 in the chapter text). If a firm expects all others to use one format (C) for encoding DVDs, it should also use that format; if it expects others to use a different format (D), even if that format is inferior, it should use the second format as well. The worst outcome is for it to manufacture a product using the opposite format, leaving it with no compatible users. The Stag Hunt also captures situations in which the primary barrier to cooperation is not an individual incentive to defect but a lack of trust. If we define trust in this context as an expectation that the partner will cooperate, then trust leads to mutual cooperation while a lack of trust leads to mutual defection. (By contrast, in the Prisoner's Dilemma it never makes sense to

FIGURE A.4 *The Stag Hunt*

		A2				A2	
		C	D			C	D
A1	C	Both hunters split the stag.	A1 goes hungry; A2 eats the rabbit.	A1	C	4, 4*	1, 3
	D	A1 eats the rabbit; A2 goes hungry.	Both hunters split the rabbit.		D	3, 1	2, 2*

trust an accomplice, and if one accomplice expects the other accomplice to cooperate, the best response is to defect.)

As this brief survey suggests, game theory helps clarify the core dilemmas in certain types of strategic situations. Many games are far more complex than the examples described here, with more possible actions than "cooperate" or "defect," information asymmetries, random chance, and many more devices to capture elements of real-world strategic situations. The games presented here are more like metaphors than accurate representations of actual situations in international relations. But they illustrate how thinking systematically about strategic interaction helps us understand why actors cannot always get what they want—and, in fact, often get rather disappointing outcomes, even though all actors might prefer other results. In both the Prisoner's Dilemma and the Stag Hunt, for instance, all actors prefer CC over DD, and this mutual preference is known in advance. Nonetheless, in the Prisoner's Dilemma mutual defection is the equilibrium result, and in the Stag Hunt it is one of two expected outcomes. In all three games, outcomes are the result of the choices not of one actor, but of all.

3

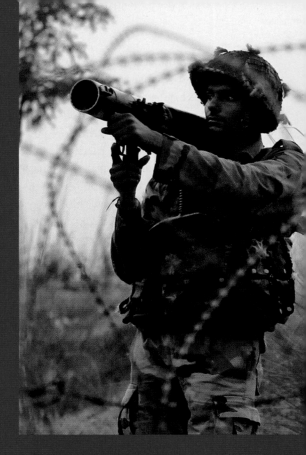

Why Are There Wars?

THE PUZZLE *War is an extremely costly way for states to settle their disputes. Given the human and material costs of military conflict, why do states sometimes wage war rather than resolving their disputes through negotiations?*

Above: States may go to war over territory that they consider integral to their nation. Indian soldiers (above) and Pakistani soldiers are stationed along the heavily militarized Line of Control that divides the contested territory of Kashmir between the two countries, and troops occasionally exchange cross-border fire. Could tensions over the Kashmir region lead to war?

In August 1914, the major countries of Europe embarked on a war the likes of which the world had never before seen. Convinced that the war would be over by Christmas, European leaders sent a generation of young men into a fight that would last four years and claim more than 15 million lives. The fighting was so intense that in one battle the British army lost 20,000 soldiers in a single day, as wave after wave of attacking infantrymen were cut down by German machine guns. At the time, it was called the Great War. Those who could never imagine another such horrific event dubbed it the "war to end all wars." Today, we know this event as the First World War, or World War I, because 20 years later the countries of Europe were at it once again. World War II (1939–45) claimed 30–50 million lives.

There is no puzzle in the study of international politics more pressing and important than the question of why states go to war. It is the most tragic and costly phenomenon that we observe in social and political life. The costs of war can be counted on a number of dimensions. The most obvious cost is the loss of human life. By one estimate, wars among states in the twentieth century led to 40 million deaths directly from combat, plus tens of millions

more deaths owing to war-related hardships.[1] In addition, wars have left untold millions injured, displaced from their homes and countries, impoverished, and diseased.

War has economic and material costs as well. Between 2001 and 2017, the United States spent $1.8 trillion fighting wars in Iraq and Afghanistan.[2] Large sums of money are also spent every year to prepare for the possibility of war. In 2016, military expenditures by all countries amounted to about $1.7 trillion—a sum that represented about $227 per person.[3] Wars can also disrupt the international economy. Conflicts in the oil-rich Middle East, including the Iran-Iraq War (1980–88),

1. Bethany Ann Lacina and Nils Petter Gleditsch, "Monitoring Trends in Global Combat: A New Dataset of Battle Deaths," *European Journal of Population* 21 (2005): 145–66.

2. Neta C. Crawford, "U.S. Budgetary Costs of Wars through 2016," Watson Institute for International and Public Affairs, Boston University, September 2016, http://watson.brown.edu/costsofwar/files/cow/imce/papers/2016/Costs%20of%20War%20through%202016%20FINAL%20final%20v2.pdf.

3. Nan Tian, Aude Fleurant, Pieter D. Wezeman, and Siemon T. Wezeman, "Trends in World Military Expenditure, 2016," Stockholm International Peace Research Institute, April 24, 2017, https://www.sipri.org/sites/default/files/Trends-world-military-expenditure-2016.pdf.

the Persian Gulf War (1990–91), and the Iraq War (2003–10), contributed to spikes in world oil prices (see Figure 4.1 on p. 91). In short, as U.S. Civil War general William Sherman famously declared, "War is hell."

But if everyone recognizes that war is hell, why do wars happen? The very costs that make the puzzle of war so pressing also make the phenomenon so puzzling. Given the enormous costs associated with war, why would states sometimes choose this course?

At first glance, the answer might seem straightforward: states fight wars because they have conflicting interests over important issues. Often, two states desire the same piece of territory. Nazi Germany wanted to expand into central Europe; World War II started when the Poles, who did not want to give up their territory, fought back. In 1980, Iraq invaded Iran, in part, to seize the latter's southern oil fields, leading to the Iran-Iraq War. Alternatively, one state might object to the policies or ideology of another. World War I grew out of Austria-Hungary's demand that Serbia end nationalist agitation that threatened to tear the multiethnic empire apart. The war between the United States and Afghanistan in 2001 occurred because the United States wanted Afghanistan to hand over Osama bin Laden and dismantle terrorist training camps on its territory, something that the Afghans refused to do. Clearly, part of the explanation for any war requires that we identify the conflicting interests that motivated the combatants.

Although such explanations are correct, they are also incomplete. By identifying the object or issue over which a war was fought, they neglect the key question of why war was the strategy that states resorted to in order to resolve their dispute. In each case, the conflicts were disastrously costly to at least one and, in some cases, all the states involved. In addition to the millions of dead mentioned earlier, World War I led to the ouster of three of the leaders who brought their countries into the war, and it hastened the breakup of the Austro-Hungarian, Russian, and Ottoman empires. World War II brought about the defeat and occupation of its main instigators, Germany and Japan. The Nazi leader Adolf Hitler committed suicide, and his Italian ally, Benito Mussolini, was hung by his own people. Iran and Iraq fought to a stalemate for eight years, causing 1–2 million casualties and leaving Iraq on the brink of economic collapse. The Afghan government's refusal to hand over bin Laden led to its removal from power. Given these grave consequences, it makes sense to wonder whether all participants would have been better off if they could have come to a settlement that would have enabled them to avoid the costs of war. Explaining war thus requires us to explain why the participants failed to reach such an agreement.

Thinking Analytically about Why Wars Happen

Most disputes between states are settled without the parties resorting to war. Although wars tend to capture our attention, it is important to remember that war is an exceedingly rare phenomenon; most countries are at peace with each other most of the time. Figure 3.1 shows the number of states involved in interstate wars in each year from 1820 to 2017, expressed as a percentage of the total number of states in existence at the time. As the figure indicates, war is a recurrent feature of international politics in the sense that it fluctuates in frequency but never disappears completely. Yet war is the exception rather than the rule: in most years, the percentage of states involved in war is quite low. All this peace cannot be explained by an absence of issues to fight over.

Hence, when seeking to explain war, we need to ask not only, "What are they fighting over?" but also "Why are they fighting?"[4] In terms of the framework laid out in Chapter 2, answering the first question requires that we understand how states' interests can give rise to conflicts over things like territory, policies, and the composition or character of each other's government. The answer to the second question lies in the strategic interactions that determine whether or how these conflicts are resolved. As we saw, the international system lacks institutions—such as legislatures, courts, or international police forces—that can resolve conflicts between states through legal, judicial, or electoral mechanisms. As a result, interstate conflicts have to be settled through bargaining. Understanding why wars occur requires that we identify the factors that sometimes prevent states from settling their conflicts through peaceful bargains that would permit them to avoid the costs of war.

---

4. The theory of war developed in this chapter relies extensively on James D. Fearon, "Rationalist Explanations for War," *International Organization* 49 (Summer 1995): 379–414.

FIGURE 3.1 **The Percentage of States Involved in Interstate War per Year, 1820–2017**

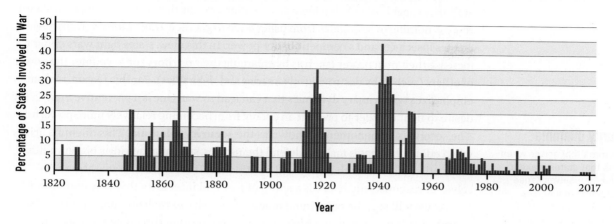

What Is the Purpose of War?

A **war** is an event involving the organized use of military force by at least two parties that reaches a minimum threshold of severity.[5] All the components of this definition are important. The requirement that force be *organized* rules out spontaneous, disorganized violence, such as large-scale rioting. The requirement that force be used by *at least two parties* distinguishes war from mass killings perpetrated by a government against some group that does not fight back. The *minimum threshold*—scholars often require that a war cause at least 1,000 battle deaths—excludes cases in which military force is used at low levels, such as brief skirmishes or minor clashes. If the main adversaries in the conflict are states, then we refer to the event as an **interstate war**; if the main parties to the conflict are actors within a state—such as a government fighting a rebel group—then the event is a **civil war**.[6] In this chapter, the discussion focuses on understanding interstate wars. Chapter 6 covers conflicts involving nonstate actors, including civil wars.

Given that scholars have been trying to understand war for millennia, the number of theories and explanations that have been proposed over the years is naturally quite large, and the bargaining model that we lay out in this chapter is only one approach. At least three other broad schools of thought have been influential in modern scholarship. While these approaches contribute important insights, they also have gaps that are filled by the bargaining approach.

Figure source: Meredith Reid Sarkees and Frank Wayman, *Resort to War: 1816–2007* (Washington, DC: CQ Press, 2010). Updated to 2017 by author.

war

An event involving the organized use of military force by at least two parties that reaches a minimum threshold of severity.

interstate war

A war in which the main participants are states.

civil war

A war in which the main participants are within the same state, such as the government and a rebel group.

---

5. See, for example, J. David Singer and Melvin Small, *The Wages of War, 1816–1965: A Statistical Handbook* (New York: Wiley, 1972).

6. There are also cases that have elements of both kinds of wars. In the Vietnam War, South Vietnam, with the support of the United States, fought a civil war against a communist insurgency while at the same time fighting an interstate war against communist North Vietnam, which was supporting the rebellion. See Chapter 6 for more on the international dimensions of civil wars.

The first, described in this book's Introduction as realism, argues that war is the inevitable result of international anarchy (pp. xxxi–xxxiv). The absence of a central authority capable of policing interstate relations means that wars can happen because there is nothing to stop states from using force to get their way.[7] Moreover, anarchy creates insecurity and a competition for power. In this view, states fight wars either to increase their own power (such as by enlarging their territory) or to counter the power of others (such as by destroying adversaries and their allies). For this reason, realism emphasizes two primary dynamics that can lead to war. One is a preventive motive: the desire to fight in order to prevent an enemy from becoming relatively more powerful.[8] The second is a phenomenon known as the **security dilemma**. This dilemma arises when efforts that states make to defend themselves, such as acquiring a bigger military, make other states fear that they will be attacked. If threatened states arm themselves in response, the result is a spiral of fear and insecurity that may end in war.[9]

As we will see, the bargaining model of war shares realism's presumption that anarchy leads to a world in which military force is often threatened or used to further state interests, and conflicts are addressed through bargaining rather than institutions like courts. The bargaining model also anticipates prevention and the fear of attack as two of several mechanisms that can lead to war. The main departure from realism is in recognizing that the use of military power imposes costs on states, so even if threatening force is useful to get a better deal, states are generally better off if they do not have to actually use force—creating the puzzle that is at the heart of this chapter.

A second alternative approach emphasizes the role of misperceptions or mistakes. Starting from the observation that the costs of war often far exceed any potential benefits, scholars in this tradition conclude that wars must occur because decision makers inaccurately estimate their chances of winning or the costs that will have to be paid. When European leaders sent their armies to war in August 1914, most were convinced that the troops would be home by Christmas—a prediction that turned out to be off by four years. Both sides also expected to win the war, meaning that at least one side was being overly optimistic. This kind of argument rests either on research in cognitive psychology showing that people are bad at weighing risks and often fall prey to wishful thinking, or on organizational approaches that emphasize how the ideology and interests of political and military elites can lead to incorrect and overly optimistic assessments of war.[10]

A concern about such theories is that while perceptual pitfalls are universal, war is quite rare, and these theories have a hard time explaining why wars happen

7. Kenneth N. Waltz, *Theory of International Politics* (Long Grove, IL: Waveland Press, Inc.).

8. See, for example, Dale C. Copeland, *The Origins of Major War* (Ithaca, NY: Cornell University Press, 2000); and Stephen Van Evera, *Causes of War* (Ithaca, NY: Cornell University Press, 2001).

9. Robert Jervis, "Cooperation under the Security Dilemma," *World Politics* 30 (January 1978): 167–214.

10. The classic work applying cognitive psychology to international relations is Robert Jervis, *Perception and Misperception in International Politics* (Princeton, NJ: Princeton University Press, 1976). For an argument that military ideologies can lead to incorrect and overly optimistic assessments, see Stephen Van Evera, "The Cult of the Offensive and the Origins of the First World War," *International Security* 9, no. 1 (Summer 1984): 58–107. The effect of military biases may depend on domestic institutions that influence how much civilians control the military; this argument is taken up in Chapter 4.

security dilemma

A dilemma that arises when efforts that states make to defend themselves cause other states to feel less secure; can lead to arms races and war because of the fear of being attacked.

at some points in time but not others. As we will see, uncertainty about the likely outcome and costs of war plays an important role in the approach developed here, but we emphasize not the psychological or organizational origins of potential mistakes, but rather the difficulties of gathering the necessary information in the strategic context of bargaining.

Finally, a long tradition of scholarship argues that wars are fought not because they serve the interests of states, but because they serve the interests of influential groups within the state, such as corporations, arms merchants, and the military.[11] In this view, the puzzle of war has an easy answer: Wars are fought in spite of their costs because those costs do not fall on the actors who call the shots. Although this chapter introduces the bargaining model by treating states as the main actors, without internal politics, we will see in Chapter 4 that the potential role of domestic interests can be incorporated quite easily.

Interests at War: What Do States Fight Over?

At the root of every war lies a conflict over something that states value. The purpose of warfare is not to fight but rather to obtain, through fighting or the threat of fighting, something the state wants. Hence, we should think about the problem of war as a problem of bargaining over objects or issues that are of value to more than one state. Using the framework developed in Chapter 2, we focus on situations in which states' interests conflict, giving rise to a strategic interaction that involves bargaining over the distribution of whatever is in dispute. The analysis thus starts by assuming that there is an object of value—what we will sometimes refer to as a "good"—and that each state prefers more of the good over less.

What kinds of goods do states fight over? *Territory* has historically been the most common source of trouble. Indeed, a study of 155 wars over the last three centuries found that over half (83) involved conflicts over territory—more than any other single issue.[12] States come into conflict if more than one wants the same piece of territory. There are a number of reasons why a piece of territory may be valuable to more than one state. First, it might contribute to the wealth of the state, particularly if it contains valuable resources such as oil, natural gas, or minerals. Iran and Iraq fought a lengthy war, from 1980 to 1988, in part because Iraq coveted Iran's southern oil fields. Territory can also be economically valuable simply by adding to the industrial or agricultural resources at the state's disposal.

A second reason that territory can cause conflict between two states is its military or strategic value. For example, the Golan Heights, on the border between Israel and Syria, has a commanding position over northern Israel from which it is possible to launch devastating attacks on the towns below. Israel seized the Golan Heights from Syria in the 1967 Six Day War, and this territory has been a source of conflict between the two states ever since.

---

11. See citations to this literature in Chapter 4.

12. Kalevi J. Holsti, *Peace and War: Armed Conflicts and International Order, 1648–1989* (Cambridge: Cambridge University Press, 1991).

MAP 3.1 *Territorial Claims in the Kashmir Region*

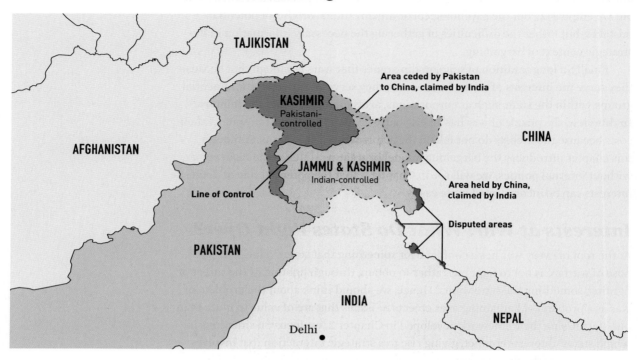

Map note: The Line of Control, which originated as a cease-fire line after the First Kashmir War (1947–48), divides the region into Indian- and Pakistani-administered areas.

Finally, a piece of territory might be valuable for ethnic, cultural, or historical reasons. The long-standing conflict between Israel and its Arab neighbors stems from the latter's resistance to the creation of a Jewish state on a land where many Arabs lived. In this case, the dispute goes beyond simply the location of a border, as some Arab states have refused to recognize Israel's right to exist.[13]

Similarly, the long-running conflict between India and Pakistan is driven by the fact that both have historical and ethnic claims to the region of Kashmir. When the two countries gained their independence from Britain in 1947, India pressured Kashmir's Hindu leader to join with India, which is predominantly Hindu. However, because the people of Kashmir, like the people of Pakistan, are predominantly Muslim, Pakistan has claimed the territory on the basis of religious ties. Map 3.1 illustrates the current boundaries of the disputed area, which are further complicated by China's claims to neighboring portions of Tibet. In territorial disputes, states threaten or use military force to compel concessions and/or to seize and hold disputed land.

Wars can also arise out of conflicts over states' *policies.* Such conflicts come about when one state enacts a policy that benefits it but harms the interests of another. The conflict that led to the Iraq War centered on Iraq's alleged pursuit of weapons of mass destruction (WMD), which the United States saw as threatening

---

13. Egypt recognized Israel in 1979, and Jordan did likewise in 1994.

to its broader interests in the region. Ongoing U.S. conflicts with North Korea and Iran have similar sources. Conflict between Russia and Ukraine that started in 2014 revolved around the latter's decision to pursue closer economic ties to the West and policies that were alleged to harm the interests of ethnic Russians living there. A state's mistreatment of its own citizens can also spark international conflict. For example, the United States and its allies waged war against Serbia in 1999 for its repressive treatment of civilians in the Kosovo region. Similarly, the United States launched cruise missiles against Syria in 2017 after the government used chemical weapons against its own people.

When states have policy disputes, war, or the threat of war, may be a mechanism for compelling policy change. In the case of Kosovo, two months of bombing by the United States and its allies led the Serb government to end its military campaign against the Kosovars; in the case of Syria, U.S. threats led to a deal in which that regime gave up its chemical arsenal. Alternatively, war may be used to replace the offending regime with a friendlier one that will pursue different policies. This was the U.S. plan in Iraq and Afghanistan, though the effort to install more pliant regimes in those countries embroiled American forces in civil wars that lasted much longer than the initial operations to oust the former, hostile regimes (see Chapter 6).

The possibility of using military force to change regimes suggests a third kind of conflict between states: conflicts over *regime type*, or the composition of another country's government. In its conflict with Ukraine, Russia sought reforms of the Ukrainian political system that would give the Russian minority there greater

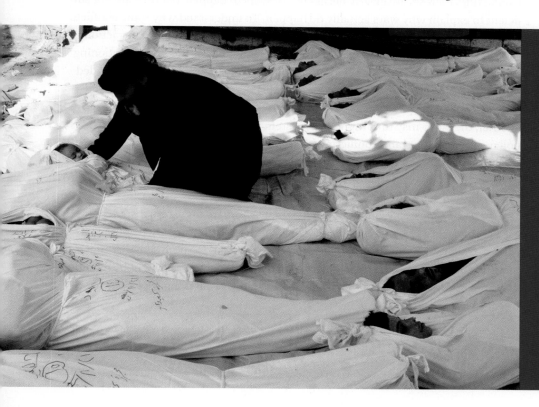

States sometimes make threats or use military force to influence the policies of foreign governments. The Syrian government attacked rebel-held villages with chemical weapons in August 2013 (pictured here), and April 2017. After the second attack, the United States carried out an air strike on a Syrian air base that it believed to be the source.

autonomy and influence. During the Cold War, the United States saw communist regimes as natural allies of the Soviet Union, and hence it sought to prevent the establishment of such regimes. U.S. involvement in the Vietnam War was driven by the desire to protect the pro-American South Vietnamese government from internal and external enemies bent on overthrowing it. During this period, both superpowers intervened regularly in other states to prop up friendly governments or to remove unfriendly ones. The role of outside powers in civil wars, such as in Vietnam, will be addressed in Chapter 6.

As this last example suggests, conflicts over territory, policy, and/or regime may spring from deeper conflicts that give rise to concerns about relative power. The specific conflict that started World War II was a territorial dispute between Germany and Poland over a small strip of territory that lay between them. However, Britain and France were concerned that a victory over Poland would further strengthen and embolden Germany, making it a more formidable foe in their ongoing struggle for influence and territory in Europe. Hence, the German-Polish territorial dispute impinged on the interests of other states because of its potential impact on their relative power vis-à-vis Germany. The Cold War rivalry between the United States and the Soviet Union similarly imbued many local conflicts with global importance because of their perceived impact on the relative strength of the superpowers.

Bargaining and War

Conflicting interests are clearly necessary for wars to happen, but they are not sufficient to explain why wars actually do happen. To understand why some conflicts become wars and others do not, we have to think about the strategic interactions that states engage in when they seek to settle their disputes. In a well-functioning domestic political system, the kinds of disputes that lead to wars are often settled through institutional mechanisms. Property disputes can be resolved by courts backed by effective police powers. If one person engages in actions that harm another, the latter may turn to the legal system to solve the problem. Within states, policy disagreements and conflicting ideas over who should govern can be settled by elections. As noted in Chapter 2, however, the international system lacks reliable legal, judicial, and electoral institutions. For this reason, states must generally try to settle conflicts with one another through bargaining.[14]

Bargaining describes interactions in which actors try to resolve disputes over the allocation of a good. They may bargain over the distribution of a disputed territory to determine whether there is a division acceptable to both sides. Or they may bargain over each other's policies so that objectionable ones might be modified or eliminated. Although we often think of bargaining as entailing compromise or

---

14. Although some interstate disputes have been adjudicated through institutions like the International Court of Justice (ICJ), these institutions lack strong enforcement mechanisms to guarantee compliance with their rulings, and disputants often engage in bargaining after an ICJ ruling to determine whether and how its terms will be implemented. Hence, these rulings are a part of, rather than a substitute for, the bargaining process. See, for example, Cole Paulson, "Compliance with Final Judgments of the International Court of Justice since 1987," *American Journal of International Law* 98 (2004): 434–61.

give-and-take, the bargaining process does not always imply that differences will be split. Indeed, in many cases, states assume all-or-nothing bargaining positions. For example, when President Bush demanded in October 2001 that the Afghan government hand over Al Qaeda leaders responsible for the 9/11 terrorist attacks, he declared that "these demands are not open to negotiation or discussion."[15]

A crisis occurs when at least one state seeks to influence the outcome of bargaining by threatening to use military force in the event that it does not get what it wants. At this point, we enter the domain of coercive bargaining, in which the consequences of not reaching an agreement can involve the use of force, including war. We sometimes refer to bargaining under the threat of war as **crisis bargaining** or **coercive diplomacy**. In all such interactions, at least one state sends the message "Satisfy my demands, or else"—where the "or else" involves imposing costs on the other side through military action.

In some cases, this message takes the form of an explicit ultimatum, such as Bush's March 2003 pronouncement that Iraqi leader Saddam Hussein had 48 hours to leave the country or face an invasion. In other cases, the threat is conveyed implicitly, through menacing actions such as mobilization of troops or military maneuvers. The Russian military incursion into Ukraine in August 2014 was preceded by the massing of troops on the border and military exercises, but not by an explicit ultimatum or set of demands (at least not publicly). Whether explicit or implicit, the purpose of such actions is clear: they seek to wrest concessions from the other side by making the alternative seem unacceptably costly.

The costs and likely outcome of a war determine which deals each side will consider acceptable in crisis bargaining. We can generally assume that the best possible outcome for a state in a crisis is to get the entire good without having to fight. If the other side gives in, the state gets its most preferred settlement of the underlying issue and avoids paying the costs associated with war. It is quite likely, though, that a state would also accept something less than its most preferred settlement, given that the alternative of fighting is costly.

For example, imagine a conflict over a piece of territory worth $100 million. Assume a state believes that in the event of a war, it is certain to win the territory; however, the costs of war, if put in monetary terms, would amount to $30 million. In that case, the expected value of going to war for that state is $100 million – $30 million = $70 million. Hence, the state should be willing to accept any deal that gives it at least $70 million worth of the territory. Since a state has the option to wage war if it determines that doing so is in its interests, the state will accept a bargain only if that bargain gives it at least as much as it can expect to get from war. And for any deal to prevent a war, it must satisfy all sides in this way: each state must decide that it prefers the deal over fighting a war. Hence, in our simple example, war can be averted only if the other state is willing to settle for the remaining $30 million worth of territory or less.

15. Elizabeth Bumiller, "Bush Pledges Attack on Afghanistan Unless It Surrenders bin Laden Now," *New York Times*, September 21, 2001, A1.

crisis bargaining

A bargaining interaction in which at least one actor threatens to use force in the event that its demands are not met.

coercive diplomacy

The use of threats to advance specific demands in a bargaining interaction.

The discussion at the outset of this chapter implies a very simple proposition: Because war is costly, a settlement that all sides prefer over war generally exists.[16] The graphic on pages 100–101 illustrates the simple idea behind this proposition. Assume that two states—call them State A and State B—have conflicting interests over the division of a particular good, represented by the green bar in each diagram on the left-hand page. To make this concrete, think of this good as a piece of territory, as in the example on the right-hand page. Any line dividing the bar, such as the dotted line labeled *Possible deal* in panel 1, represents a possible division of the good, such as a border drawn through the territory. State A receives the share of the good to the left of that line, and State B receives the share of the good to the right. Since both states prefer more of the good over less, State A wants to get a deal as far to the right as possible, and State B wants to get a deal as far to the left as possible. Put another way, State A's most preferred outcome, or ideal point, is at the far right of the bar, which would mean State A gets all the good, and State B's ideal point is on the far left, which would mean State B gets all the good. (Hence, this horizontal bar is identical to the diagonal line used to illustrate bargaining in Figure 2.2 on p. 56).

Now consider what happens if the two states go to war. Moving to panel 2, the line labeled *War outcome* indicates the actual, or expected, outcome of a violent conflict. In the case of a conflict over territory, we can think of this line as indicating how much territory each state would control after a war. The farther that line is to the right, the better State A is expected to fare in the event of war; the farther it is to the left, the better State B is expected to fare.

Crucially, fighting entails costs. These costs diminish the value of the expected war outcome to each state. As shown in panel 3, the value of war to each state is the share of the good it expects to win, minus the costs it expects to incur. Notice that the value of war to State A (which corresponds to the portion of the bar to the left of the dotted red line) is smaller than the share of the good that it expects to get from war (the portion of the bar to the left of the *War outcome* line). Indeed, as the figure is constructed, State A expects to win more of the good in a war than it would get from the possible deal in the first panel, but once the costs of war are taken into account, the possible deal is actually preferable to war.

To understand how the costs affect the value of war for each state, we have to think about those costs as they relate to the value of the good. Looking at the corresponding example on the right-hand page of the graphic, imagine that State A expects to win 70 percent of the territory, at the cost of 5,000 lives. State A's war value hinges on how much State A values those lost lives relative to the value of the territory. If State A thinks that losing those soldiers is equivalent to losing 30 percent of the territory, then its value for war is 70 − 30 = 40 percent of the value of the territory. State B would make a similar calculation. For both states, the costs of war would effectively go up if either the number of lives lost went up or the value attached to the territory went down.

As panel 4 shows, State A prefers any deal over war that gives it more than its value for war (deals that fall to the right of the dotted red line). Deals in this range

---

16. See Fearon, "Rationalist Explanations for War."

give State A more than it expects to get through war, once the costs are taken into account. Similarly, State B prefers any deal over war that gives it more than its value for war (deals that fall to the left of the dotted blue line). Notice that the set of deals that State A prefers to war overlaps with the set of deals that State B prefers to war, creating a region called the **bargaining range**. Any division of the good in this bargaining range gives both states more than they expect to get from fighting a war. As this exercise demonstrates, the fact that war imposes costs on both sides means that such a range of deals always exists. Hence, in theory, there are bargains that both sides would prefer over war.

Although the preceding exercise treated the good in dispute as a piece of territory, the general framework and insight can be applied to any kind of issue over which states have conflicting interests. For example, consider the conflict between North Korea and the United States over the former's nuclear program. In this case, the United States' ideal outcome, which we could put at one end of the bar, is for North Korea to disarm completely and become a democratic state. North Korea's ideal outcome, which would be located at the opposite end of the bar, would be for the United States to accept North Korea's status as a nuclear power and recognize its existing regime.

In between are various compromise alternatives that neither considers ideal, including the current status quo, in which North Korea has a small number of nuclear devices but the United States refuses to recognize its right to them. This point is close to North Korea's ideal point. Another point on the bar, closer to the U.S. ideal point than to the status quo, would be for North Korea to freeze its nuclear program and admit international inspectors. Though the substantive meaning of any location on the bar depends on the exact issue in dispute, the basic argument for the existence of a bargaining range holds across issues. (See "Controversy" on p. 104 for an extended discussion of negotiations between the United States and North Korea.)

This simple model is useful not because it is right in the sense that it correctly describes the complexity of real-world bargaining interactions, but rather because it forces us to think about all the ways in which bargaining could go wrong. Understanding why wars happen even though a peaceful bargain theoretically exists for virtually any conflict is the main purpose of this chapter.

Compellence and Deterrence: Varieties of Coercive Bargaining

The model is also useful for thinking about the conditions under which states might have an interest in initiating a crisis in the first place. The pre-crisis distribution, or status quo, can be represented as a line dividing the bar. Where the status quo is located relative to the states' values for war determines which state, if any, might have an interest in changing the status quo through a threat of force. If a state is already getting from the status quo at least as much as it expects to get through war, then it generally cannot gain by threatening war to change the status quo. However, if a state expects to get more through war than it has in the status quo, then it has an interest in making a challenge.

bargaining range
The set of deals that both parties in a bargaining interaction prefer over the reversion outcome. When the reversion outcome is war, the bargaining range is the set of deals that both sides prefer over war.

The Model: Bargaining and War

1. A possible deal: Two states, A and B, have conflicting interests over a good (represented by the green bar). Both states want as much of the good as possible. The dotted line represents the distribution of the good based on *one* possible deal. Any deal determines A's and B's shares.

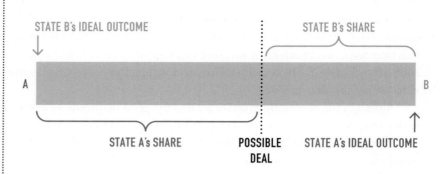

2. The expected outcome of war: As they bargain, each state evaluates how much it can expect to get as a result of war. The dotted line shows the expected outcome of war. Here, A would get more by going to war than by accepting the above deal.

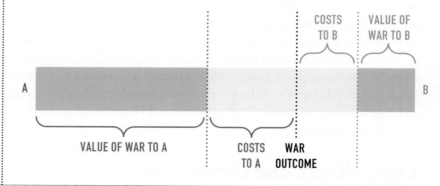

3. Costs of war: However, war also involves costs, and these costs must be subtracted from what each state hopes to gain. So, although war would give A more of the good than it would get under the deal in panel 1, the costs incurred reduce the value of war to A.

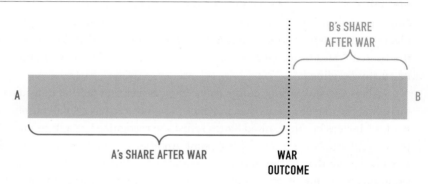

4. The bargaining range: Each state prefers any deal that gives it more than its expected value of war, once costs are subtracted. Because war inflicts costs on both sides, there is a range of possible deals that both sides would prefer over war.

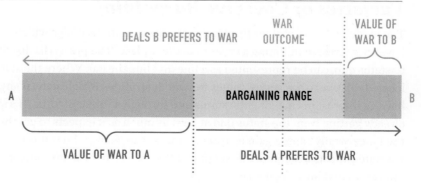

An Example: Bargaining over Territory

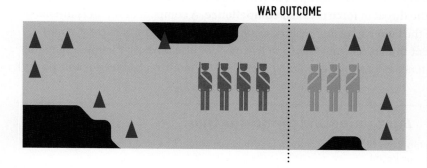

POSSIBLE DEAL

1. A conflict over territory:
Imagine two states have a conflict of interest over a piece of territory. State A would like to have the whole territory, as would State B. A deal is proposed to divide the territory at the dotted line.

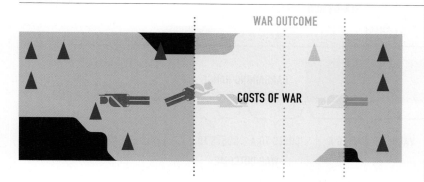

WAR OUTCOME

2. The expected outcome of war:
Based on the strength of their respective armies and other resources, a war over the territory is expected to result in State A winning the portion of the territory to the left of the dotted line.

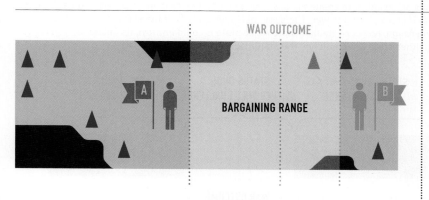

WAR OUTCOME

COSTS OF WAR

3. Costs of war:
Each side also considers the costs of war. Imagine that State A values the territory it would win as a result of war at $100 million but values the costs of war (both financial and human) at $30 million. These costs would reduce the value of war to A by 30 percent.

WAR OUTCOME

BARGAINING RANGE

4. The bargaining range:
Each side should prefer any deal that gives it more territory than what it expects from war, once the costs of war are subtracted from the territory it wins. Any border drawn through the shaded range divides the territory into shares that both sides prefer over war.

The top panel of Figure 3.2 depicts such a situation: in the status quo, State A's share of the good is less than the value of war to A, even when the costs of war are taken into account. This does not mean that there will be a war, since, after all, a bargaining range still exists. But in this situation, the dissatisfied state can profit by threatening war in order to get a better deal. As the lower panel in Figure 3.2 shows, this logic divides the bar into three segments. If the status quo is to the left of the red dotted line indicating State A's value for war, then State A has an interest in threatening war to try to get a better outcome. Similarly, if the status quo is to the right of the blue dotted line indicating State B's value for war, then State B prefers war over the status quo and thus has an interest in sparking a crisis. Finally, if the status quo is in the bargaining range, then both prefer the current situation over war, and neither can expect to gain by waging war.

We often classify threats according to whether they are intended to preserve or change the existing relationship between states. An effort to change the status quo through the threat of force is called **compellence**. A compellent threat is intended to coerce the target state into making a concession or changing a current policy. Compellent threats take the form of "Give me *y*, or else" (where *y* is something that the threatener values) or "Stop doing *x*, or else" (where *x* is an objectionable policy).

compellence

An effort to change the status quo through the threat of force.

FIGURE 3.2 *Bargaining and the Status Quo*

Here, the status quo clearly gives State A less than war would (the value of war equals the war outcome minus costs).

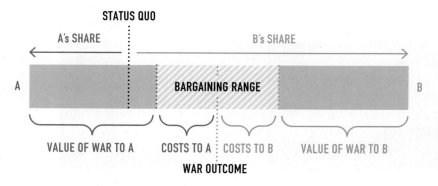

State A has an incentive to challenge any status quo that gives it less than war would, because it could do better by going to war. The same holds for State B. If the status quo is within the bargaining range, however, neither State A nor State B could improve its outcome by going to war, so neither state will challenge the status quo.

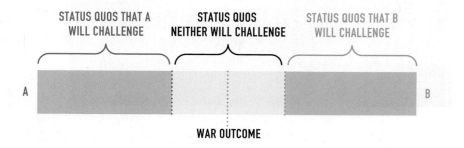

The U.S. demand that Afghanistan hand over Osama bin Laden and stop harboring the Al Qaeda terrorist network after the 9/11 attacks is an example of compellence.

Deterrence, by contrast, is used to preserve the status quo by threatening the other side with unacceptable costs if it seeks to alter the current relationship. A deterrent threat takes the form of "Don't do *x*, or else" (where *x* is some possible future action that the threatener finds objectionable). The most common deterrent threat is one that all states make implicitly all the time: "Don't attack me, or I'll fight back." The effort to deter attacks on one's own country is referred to as *general deterrence*, and it is an activity that states are constantly engaged in. Another form of deterrence occurs when a state seeks to protect a friend. In this case, the deterrent message takes the form of "Don't attack my ally *x*, or else." This kind of threat is generally referred to as *extended deterrence* because in this case the threatener attempts to extend protection to another state. Extended deterrence is crucial in the context of alliances, a subject that we will consider in Chapter 5.

In a 2012 speech to the United Nations, Israeli prime minister Benjamin Netanyahu declared that Israel would not permit Iran to reach the final stage of acquiring a nuclear weapon. He argued that a credible threat of military action was needed to deter Iran from crossing that "red line."

In general, crises may involve a combination of deterrent and compellent threats. When one side tries to compel another, the target may issue deterrent threats, or some third state may issue a deterrent threat on the target's behalf. Crises often involve such threats and counterthreats, as each side tries to improve its bargaining position by bringing to bear its capability to harm the other. In many cases, threats alone will succeed in bringing about an outcome that both sides find acceptable. Indeed, the most effective threats never need to be carried out, since they coerce the target into making the desired concessions or refraining from objectionable actions. When this contest of threats fails to generate an outcome that both sides prefer over fighting is when we observe the descent into war. This brings us back to the core puzzle: Given the costs associated with war, why does crisis bargaining sometimes fail to achieve a peaceful solution? The following sections elaborate several possible answers.

deterrence
An effort to preserve the status quo through the threat of force.

Do Wars Happen by Mistake? War from Incomplete Information

In July 1990, Iraq was engaged in coercive diplomacy with its small neighbor to the south, Kuwait. Two years earlier, Iraq had emerged from a disastrous, eight-year war with Iran, and Iraqi leader Saddam Hussein desperately needed to rebuild his

Can We Negotiate with North Korea?

North Korea has one of the most oppressive regimes on the planet. It has been governed by a dictatorship since 1948, passed down across three generations. The regime, now led by Kim Jong-Un, has murdered, tortured, and starved its people into submission. It has sealed them off from the outside world, denying virtually all contact with relatives in South Korea and with other foreigners. In foreign affairs, North Korea has waged war on its southern neighbor, spewed threats at others in the region, sold missile technology to other "rogue" regimes, and kidnapped Japanese citizens.

North Korea has also spent the last three decades developing nuclear weapons. In 2006 it test-detonated a nuclear device, and the country is now believed to have somewhere between 20 and 60 warheads. In 2017, North Korea tested a ballistic missile capable of hitting not just its immediate neighbors, but also anywhere in the United States. As a result, the United States and other countries have sought to persuade the regime to end its nuclear program and give up its weapons.

Applying the Concepts

Although bargaining provides a way for states to settle disputes and avoid the costs of war, the question of whether to negotiate with North Korea over its nuclear ambitions has been fraught with controversy. Disagreements revolve around whether the **interests** motivating North Korea's quest for these weapons make negotiations viable and whether, with its autocratic domestic **institutions**, North Korea is likely to live up to any agreement it signs. There is also disagreement about the role that military force should play in this **interaction**.

The argument against negotiating hinges on the view that North Korea neither wants a deal nor can be trusted to honor one. From this perspective, the regime's interest in nuclear weapons stems from a desire to reunify the Korean peninsula by force. Nuclear weapons are useful because they would deter the United States and Japan from coming to South Korea's aid in the event of war. Thus, negotiations are unlikely to succeed, and they serve only

to give North Korea time to advance its program. In addition, North Korea's closed, highly autocratic regime presents a key impediment, since it can easily cheat. Because it can advance its nuclear program in secrecy, away from the prying eyes of satellites and inspectors, it could break a deal without being detected.

Doubts about negotiating are also based on a series of broken agreements between the United States and North Korea over the last three decades. After nearing the brink of war in 1994, the United States and North Korea signed the Agreed Framework, under which North Korea pledged to freeze construction and operation of all nuclear reactors. In return, the United States promised oil, two proliferation-resistant nuclear reactors, and to work toward a normalization of trade and diplomatic relations, which have been suspended since the Korean War (1950–53).

While this agreement froze North Korea's plutonium production, the deal collapsed in 2002 after the United States accused North Korea of circumventing the agreement by engaging in uranium enrichment. Subsequent deals in 2007 and 2011 also unraveled within a year or two of signing. The end result of decades of negotiation is a nuclear-armed adversary. In light of this situation, some argue, the ultimate goal of U.S. policy should be to change the regime, not to negotiate with it.

The alternative argument is that North Korea's interest in nuclear weapons stems not from ambition, but from fear: the regime is built on suspicion of outsiders and worries about being overthrown. This insecurity is not unreasonable, since the United States has, in both rhetoric and practice, shown its willingness to oust hostile dictators. In

U.S. State Department officials return from a diplomatic mission in North Korea with boxes of information on the country's nuclear operations.

North Korean dictator Kim Jong-Un controls the country's military and nuclear arsenal.

2003 the United States invaded Iraq and removed Saddam Hussein on the basis of inflated claims about that country's WMD capabilities; in 2011 the United States and its allies intervened in a civil war against Libyan leader Mu'ammar Qaddafi, who had earlier agreed to give up his nuclear and chemical weapons programs. Watching these events could have easily convinced Kim that the possession of nuclear weapons would guard against a similar fate.

In this view, negotiations might work, but only if Washington can credibly commit not to seek regime change if North Korea lowers its defenses. Such a commitment would involve economic assistance to help bolster the regime and promote development. In past negotiations, North Korea also sought security guarantees, including a formal promise that the United States would not attack it and a reduction of the U.S. military presence in South Korea and Japan. Whether a comprehensive deal along these lines could have worked when North Korea's program was in its infancy, now that Kim actually has a nuclear arsenal and means of delivery it is unclear what concessions would convince him to give them up.

In early 2018, U.S. president Donald Trump signaled his willingness to hold direct talks with the North Korean leader. At the time of this writing, it was unclear whether such negotiations would take place or what would come out of them. Although a meeting between the heads of state would be unprecedented, failed talks or an agreement that soon collapses would not.

If a lasting deal is not reached, the question becomes, What role will the threat of military force play in this interaction? Key advisers to Trump have argued that, given North Korea's aggressive intentions and barbaric regime, the United States cannot tolerate that country's capability to hit the United States with a nuclear weapon. In this view, the United States and its allies have to apply maximum pressure to induce disarmament, including either a limited military strike to convince Kim of the costs of defiance or a broader attack designed to eliminate his arsenal.

Those who believe that the regime is motivated by fear worry that such a strategy is both unnecessary and counterproductive. If Kim is interested in his own survival, then the threat of retaliation by the United States can deter North Korea from using nuclear weapons. If so, there is no urgency to eliminate the program by force—a prospect that carries enormous risks and costs.

An attempt to disarm North Korea by force might fail to destroy its arsenal, creating the risk of a nuclear attack on South Korea, Japan, or the United States. Even if North Korea did not use its nuclear weapons, its enormous conventional capabilities, including thousands of artillery pieces within range of Seoul, could inflict horrendous losses on South Korea and the U.S. troops stationed there. The United States would likely prevail in a war, but at a cost that could run to hundreds of thousands of lives. Ultimately, the price of war may mean that there is no alternative but for the two sides to talk about a way to manage this dangerous rivalry.

Thinking Analytically

1. How might Kim Jong-Un respond to a limited military strike by the United States? How do different assumptions about his interests lead to different expectations about his response?

2. Should countries that value human rights negotiate with regimes that brutalize their own people? What are the costs and benefits of engaging a regime like North Korea?

shattered economy. Given that Iraq was sitting on oil deposits containing an estimated 112 billion barrels of oil, it was not hard to imagine where money for reconstruction would come from. But Hussein was not content simply to pump and sell Iraq's own oil, and he quickly turned his gun sights on Kuwait.

Kuwait's 95 billion barrels of recoverable oil reserves made a tempting target, and moreover, Hussein felt that his neighbor was standing in the way of his plans for economic recovery. For one thing, Kuwait was pumping more oil than it had previously agreed to. This extra supply meant that the price of oil was lower than it would otherwise be, depriving Iraq of needed revenue. Iraq also charged that Kuwait was stealing oil from oil fields that straddled the countries' shared border. Finally, Kuwait had lent Iraq substantial sums of money during the war, and Saddam Hussein hoped to get this debt forgiven. When Kuwait refused these demands, Iraq flexed its military muscle. Beginning in mid-July, Iraq started moving its forces closer to the border with Kuwait, at one point moving an entire division per day. By the end of the month, 100,000 Iraqi troops, supported by thousands of tanks, were in position near the border.

With the help of spy satellites, American officials watched the buildup, and they passed on their intelligence to the Kuwaitis. Despite their concern, most officials in the U.S. government did not anticipate that Iraq would invade, nor did the Kuwaitis bow to Hussein's demands. To many observers, the Iraqi moves looked like an effort to intimidate, not a prelude to invasion. According to reporter Bob Woodward's account, "Everything Saddam had to do to prepare for an invasion was exactly what he also had to do if his intention was simply to scare the Kuwaitis. There was no way to distinguish the two."[17] On August 2, with Kuwait still holding out, Hussein revealed that he had not simply been bluffing: Iraqi forces swept into Kuwait and fully occupied the country in a matter of hours.

In retrospect, it is clear that Iraq was willing and able to wage war against Kuwait if its demands were not met. At the time, however, key decision makers in Kuwait and Washington were not sure of Hussein's intentions. Would he really risk the wrath of the world by gobbling up his small neighbor? Would he be willing to put his military and his country through another war so soon after the previous one? The invasion of Kuwait happened in part because, unsure of the answers to these questions, the Kuwaitis decided that calling Hussein's bluff was preferable to giving in to his demands. When it became apparent that the threat was not, in fact, a bluff, war was already upon them.

This episode illustrates one reason that bargaining can fail to resolve disputes and avert war. When states have poor and incomplete information about each other's willingness and ability to wage war, two mistakes are possible, both of which can lead to war. First, a state confronted by demands may mistakenly yield too little or not at all—just as Kuwait failed to budge in the face of Hussein's threats. In these cases, bargaining can break down because at least one state feels that it can achieve more through fighting (in this case, Iraq) than the other is willing to offer in the

17. Bob Woodward, *The Commanders* (New York: Pocket Star Books, 1991), 200.

negotiations (Kuwait). The second, related danger is that a state may demand too much (Iraq in this example) under the mistaken belief that the other side will cave in (Kuwait, and its protector, the United States). In this event, the state may not realize its mistake until war is already upon it. In either case, even though there might be a settlement of the issue that both sides would prefer to war, uncertainty about each other's willingness to wage war can prevent such a settlement from being reached.

Where does this uncertainty come from? Recall that the main issue in crisis bargaining is how each state evaluates its prospects in a war. How likely is it that the state will be able to win the war? What will the human, financial, and political costs be? These assessments are important because each state's value for war determines what bargains it prefers over fighting. If one state is uncertain of how much its adversary values war, then it is also uncertain of how much it must concede in order to prevent a war. This uncertainty will arise whenever a state lacks information about any of the myriad factors that determine its adversary's evaluation of war.

A poker analogy is useful here. In poker, the fact that at least some cards are hidden from view means that each player knows more about the strength of her own hand than do her opponents. The hidden cards are what might be called private information: important facts that are known only to the player who observes those cards. Because no player sees all the cards, the game is played under a condition known as **incomplete information**. All players lack information about their opponents' hands and have private access to information about their own hands.

Incomplete information arises in crisis bargaining when states cannot readily observe or measure the key political and military factors that determine their adversaries' expected value for war. The hidden cards in this context can be many and varied, and we typically differentiate between two broad classes of unknowns: capabilities and resolve. *Capabilities* are the state's physical ability to prevail in war: the number of troops it can mobilize, the number and quality of its armaments, the economic resources it has to sustain the war effort. We might also include in this list the quality of the country's military leadership and military strategies. In addition, since third parties sometimes join wars on one or both sides, any uncertainty about what those third parties will do can lead to uncertainty about the capabilities that each side will bring to bear in the event of war (see Chapter 5).

Resolve, a more abstract concept, refers to a state's willingness to bear the costs of fighting and how much the state values the object of the dispute relative to those costs. How many people is the country willing to lose in order to obtain, say, a given piece of territory? How much is it willing to pay in blood and money in order to win policy concessions or change another country's regime? Resolve not only determines whether a state is willing to fight, but also how much of the state's potential capabilities would actually be mobilized in the event of war. We frequently make the distinction between *total wars* (in which states mobilize their entire military and economic resources) and *limited wars* (in which states fight with something less than their full potential, often because their aims are limited or of relatively low value).

incomplete information

A situation in which actors in a strategic interaction lack information about other actors' interests and/or capabilities.

resolve

The willingness of an actor to endure costs in order to acquire a particular good.

In September 2016, Russia initiated massive military drills, showcasing the country's ships, cruise missiles, and antiaircraft system, off the coast of Crimea. How much of a country's capabilities it is willing to mobilize for war can be a source of uncertainty in bargaining.

How a state evaluates the stakes of conflict determines where on this continuum its effort will be. World War II, for example, was seen as a war of national survival, and during the height of the war (1943–45) the United States spent about 37 percent of its gross domestic product (GDP) on defense, and other belligerents spent half of their GDP or more. By contrast, total U.S. defense spending in 2008, in the midst of wars in Iraq and Afghanistan, amounted to about 4 percent of GDP, and only a portion of that paid for those wars. Resolve is obviously a difficult quality to measure, as it hinges on a variety of political, ideological, and psychological factors. Indeed, it may be difficult for a leader to accurately assess his or her own country's resolve, much less the resolve of its adversary.

How could such uncertainty lead to war? When states have incomplete information about the capabilities and/or resolve of their opponents, bargaining over goods that they both desire may fail to achieve peaceful settlements. A central dynamic of bargaining under this kind of uncertainty is a phenomenon known as a **risk-return trade-off**: essentially, there is a trade-off between trying to get a good deal and trying to minimize the possibility that war will break out.

At one extreme, a state can generally ensure peace by capitulating to all of its adversary's demands. "Peace at any price" might not be a very attractive outcome, however. Kuwait, for example, could have given in to all of Iraq's demands and would likely have avoided war. At the other extreme, a state can hold firm and yield nothing to its adversary. This strategy promises a good deal if it works, but doing so runs a risk that the adversary will decide to fight rather than settle for nothing—as Iraq did when Kuwait refused to give in. Between these extremes, a state will generally find that it can reduce the risk of war only by making more generous offers, moving farther from its ideal outcome. Put another way, a state can improve the bargaining outcome for itself only by embracing a higher risk of war. Although war is costly and regrettable in retrospect, bargaining strategies that entail a risk of war can be perfectly rational, given the uncertainty that states face.

risk-return trade-off

In crisis bargaining, the trade-off between trying to get a better deal and trying to avoid a war.

Incentives to Misrepresent and the Problem of Credibility

Given that incomplete information can lead to war, why can't states simply tell each other how capable and resolved they are and thereby avoid war? Actually, a large part of what goes on in a crisis consists precisely of such efforts at communication. Crises are generally characterized by diplomatic exchanges, threats and counter-threats, mobilization of forces, movement of troops, and positioning of weaponry. These actions, in part, have a military purpose: one cannot wage war, after all, without first mobilizing the necessary forces and putting them in place. But these actions also have a political purpose: they are the language of coercive diplomacy, the vocabulary that states use to convince one another that they are willing to back their bargaining positions with the threat of force.

The problem that arises in this context is that, as much as states may have an interest in communicating their hidden information, they may not always be able to do so effectively. A crucial question that arises in crisis bargaining is whether the messages a state sends have **credibility**. A credible threat is a threat that the target believes will be carried out. We say a threat lacks credibility if its target has reason to doubt that the threat will be carried out. The credibility of a threat refers not only to the belief that the threatener will start a war; the target also has to believe that the threatener is willing to fight long enough and hard enough that giving in to its demands is a better option. In the case of the U.S. war against Afghanistan, the Taliban government probably had little doubt that President Bush would implement his threat to invade, but it may have doubted that the United States would be willing and able to bear the costs of a long war. In other words, the threat to start a war was credible, but the threat to remove Taliban leaders from power was, in their eyes, not.

Note that the credibility of the threat refers to the target's beliefs, not the actual intentions of the state issuing the threat. A state may fully intend to carry through on a threat, but it may have a hard time convincing its adversaries. Saddam Hussein genuinely intended to invade Kuwait if his demands were not met; observers in the United States and Kuwait, however, did not see the threat conveyed by his mobilization as credible. Similarly, a state may have no intention of carrying out its threat, but the target may mistakenly believe otherwise. In such cases, the bluff can succeed.

Why is credibility hard to achieve? There are two interrelated reasons. First, carrying through on threats is costly. A state may say that it will wage war if its demands are not met, but the costs of war might be such that it would not make sense to fulfill this threat if called on to do so. This concern about credibility was particularly pronounced during the Cold War between the United States and the Soviet Union. With both sides in possession of large arsenals of nuclear weapons, it was well understood that war could quickly escalate into total annihilation. Given this situation, officials in the United States worried about how they could deter the Soviet Union from attacking Western Europe. Would the United States really risk New York to save London or Paris? If the Soviets believed the answer to

credibility

Believability. A credible threat is a threat that the recipient believes will be carried out. A credible commitment is a commitment or promise that the recipient believes will be honored.

this question was no, then the U.S. commitment to defend Western Europe would lack credibility. It was precisely these kinds of concerns that led Great Britain and France to develop their own nuclear capabilities in order to deter the Soviets; after all, it was much more credible that France would risk Paris to save Paris.

Even without the prospect of nuclear annihilation, threats may lack credibility because their targets appreciate the costs of carrying them out. In the midst of the crisis between Iraq and Kuwait in 1990, the United States announced joint naval exercises with the United Arab Emirates. On the same day, the State Department spokesperson issued an extended deterrent threat by reaffirming the U.S. commitment to protect its friends in the Persian Gulf. Iraq's response was contemptuous. Hussein called the U.S. ambassador to his office the next day and told her that he was not scared by American threats. After all, he reportedly said, "Yours is a society which cannot accept 10,000 dead in one battle."[18] Thus, the U.S. deterrent threat had little credibility in Hussein's eyes because he believed that the United States would be unwilling to bear the costs of war.

The second reason that credibility is hard to achieve stems from the conflicting interests at the heart of the bargaining interaction. Even though states have a common interest in avoiding war, each also wants the best possible deal for itself, so they have incentives to hide or misrepresent their information.

In some cases, this incentive means that states will conceal information about their true strength. After Iraq invaded Kuwait, the United States massed a large force in Saudi Arabia and threatened war unless Iraq retreated. It was widely assumed that if war came, U.S. forces would attack Iraqi positions in Kuwait head-on. Such a strategy would have provided the most direct route to the objective, but there were clear costs involved: the Iraqi forces in Kuwait were dug in behind strong defenses, including trenches filled with oil that could be lit on fire as soon as U.S. troops tried to cross.

Saddam Hussein's resistance to U.S. pressure stemmed in part from his belief that his defenses would make the liberation of Kuwait very costly. In fact, war planners in the United States decided early on that they would not attack directly at the strength of the Iraqi positions. Instead, they secretly shifted the bulk of the U.S. force into the desert west of the Kuwaiti border. The military plan called for a "left hook": U.S. tanks would enter Iraq on the western flank of Iraqi forces in Kuwait and then swoop around behind them, thereby outflanking the enemy's fortifications. This tactical decision meant that the United States expected to incur lower casualties than Iraq expected to be able to inflict.[19]

Theoretically, if the United States could have communicated these expectations to Iraq, its threat would have been more credible and perhaps Hussein would have decided to back down. But it is easy to see why the United States could not say to

---

18. A transcript of this meeting was published in the *New York Times*, on September 22, 1990. Hussein may also have been encouraged to ignore U.S. threats because American ambassador April Glaspie seemed to indicate that the United States had no strong interest in the outcome of the Iraq-Kuwait dispute.

19. For a discussion of Persian Gulf War strategy, see Lawrence Freedman and Efraim Karsh, "How Kuwait Was Won: Strategy in the Gulf War," *International Security* 16 (Autumn 1991): 5–41.

Hussein: "You think that war will be too costly for us, but you are mistaken. Rather than attack your forces head-on, we will go around them on the western flank." Had the United States sent such a message, Iraq could have taken measures to counter the tactic, such as by repositioning its forces to the west. Hence, any bargaining advantage that the United States might have reaped by revealing its strength would have been nullified. In the strategic context of the crisis, it made sense for the United States to hide its strongest cards.

In other cases, states misrepresent in order to hide their weakest cards. Anyone who has played poker knows that it sometimes makes sense to bluff—that is, to act as if one has a strong hand in the hopes that others will fold. A similar incentive exists in international crises. In this context, a bluff is a threat to use force that the sender does not intend to carry out. In a crisis, a successful bluff could reap large rewards. In 1936, Germany marched its military forces into a region on its border with France known as the Rhineland—a region that, by the 1919 treaty that ended World War I, Germany was required to keep demilitarized. Hitler sent his forces in anyway, daring the Western powers to stop him. Though alarmed by this move, both France and Great Britain chose not to risk a full-scale war over the issue, and the remilitarization of the Rhineland took place unopposed. Interestingly, there is good reason to believe that Hitler's move was a bluff. Although this point is somewhat controversial, there is evidence that German troops were under orders to retreat if confronted.[20] If so, then one of the key moments in the lead-up to World War II was a well-executed bluff.

This observation raises a dilemma: How can states credibly convey their information in order to diminish the risk of war due to uncertainty? Given a strategic environment that sometimes rewards misrepresentation, how can a genuine threat be made believable?

Communicating Resolve: The Language of Coercion

To help us answer these questions, another example will be helpful. On June 25, 1950, without any warning, North Korea invaded South Korea. The Korean peninsula had been split in two after World War II, divided at the 38th parallel between the communist North and the non-communist and pro-Western South. North Korea's attack was a bold attempt to reunify the country under communist rule, and the United States quickly joined the South in repelling the attack. After three months, the U.S. efforts were largely successful, and North Korean forces began to retreat to their side of the 38th parallel. At this point, the United States decided to press the attack, cross into North Korea, and topple the communist regime there.

This possibility raised grave concerns in neighboring China, which had only the previous year been taken over by a communist government. On October 3,

---

20. James Thomas Emmerson, *The Rhineland Crisis, 7 March 1936* (Ames: Iowa State University Press, 1977), 98–100.

1950, Chinese diplomats conveyed a message through the Indian ambassador that a move across the 38th parallel would trigger Chinese intervention.[21] Nonetheless, the threat went unheeded. The U.S. operation had been planned and authorized under the assumption that the Chinese would not intervene, and the October 3 warning did nothing to change any minds.[22] U.S. forces crossed into North Korea on October 7 and advanced rapidly. In response, 600,000 Chinese troops poured into the Korean peninsula, leading to three more years of fighting and a costly stalemate.

Why was the Chinese threat dismissed, in the words of Secretary of State Dean Acheson, as "a Chinese Communist bluff"? An October 4 memorandum describes Acheson's rationale:

> The Secretary pointed out that the Chinese Communists were themselves taking no risk in as much as their private talks to the Indian Ambassador could be disavowed. . . . if they wanted to take part in the "poker game" they would have to put more on the table than they had up to the present.[23]

Acheson's reasoning for downplaying the Chinese threat is instructive. The Chinese government was making an extended deterrent threat: "Don't invade North Korea, or we will intervene to defend it." From the U.S. perspective, it was possible that China would actually make good on this threat, but it was also possible that China was simply trying to bluff the United States into staying out of North Korea. Regardless of which possibility was true, the message conveyed through the Indian ambassador was cheap and easy to send. There was nothing in the message or the way it was sent that would give American decision makers reasons to think that China was not simply bluffing. Unless the Chinese were willing to pay some costs—"to put more on the table"—there was little reason to take their threat seriously.

This example suggests a more general insight: For threats to be credible, they have to be costly in such a way that the sender would make the threat only if it really intended to carry the threat out. Consider the problem that the United States faced in October 1950 in these, admittedly oversimplified, terms:

> *It is possible that the Chinese government is resolved to intervene if we attack North Korea, and it is possible that it is not so resolved. How can we know if we are facing a "resolute" China or an "irresolute" China? What would we look for to distinguish these two "types" of adversaries? The answer is this: We would want to look for actions that a resolute China would be willing to take but an irresolute China would be unwilling (or, at least, less likely) to take. If we see such actions, then we are more*

---

21. The United States did not recognize the People's Republic of China as a legitimate government, so the two countries did not have direct diplomatic contacts.

22. See, for example, William Stueck, *Rethinking the Korean War* (Princeton, NJ: Princeton University Press, 2002), chap. 4.

23. U.S. Department of State, *Foreign Relations of the United States, 1950*, vol. 7, *Korea* (Washington, DC: U.S. Government Printing Office, 1976), 868–69.

likely to be facing a resolute China, and we have to take its threat seriously. If we do not see such actions, then there may be reason to doubt China's resolve.

The message that the Chinese actually sent did not have much credibility because an irresolute China could just as easily have made the same claim.

What kinds of actions can help an opponent distinguish whether its adversary is resolved? In general, the literature has identified three mechanisms that states use to make their threats credible: brinksmanship, tying hands, and paying for power.

Brinksmanship: The "Slippery Slope"

Some of the earliest scholarship on the question of how to make threats credible took place in the 1950s, when policy makers and academics were preoccupied by the credibility of threats in the nuclear age. If everyone understood that nuclear war would bring total annihilation to each side, then under what conditions could threats between nuclear powers ever be credible? Since no state would ever intentionally "pull the trigger" and bring about Armageddon, the threat to do so was not credible. This observation raised the question of whether nuclear weapons had any utility at all in the emerging Cold War between the United States and the Soviet Union.

The most important insight into this issue came from Thomas Schelling, an early theorist of the strategy of crisis bargaining. In Schelling's view, although it was understood that no state would intentionally bring about its own destruction by starting a total nuclear war, these weapons could nonetheless be wielded for diplomatic effect through a strategy known as **brinksmanship**. The basic idea was that states could signal their resolve in the crisis by approaching the "brink" of war through provocative actions. Schelling describes this concept:

> The brink is not, in this view, the sharp edge of a cliff where one can stand firmly, look down, and decide whether or not to plunge. The brink is a curved slope that one can stand on with some risk of slipping, the slope gets steeper and the risk of slipping greater as one moves toward the chasm.[24]

The costs of war are such that, if faced with a simple choice of whether to jump or not, no sane decision maker would jump. But rational leaders might decide to step out onto the "slippery slope" and thereby increase the risk that war would start inadvertently. Schelling famously referred to such an act as a "threat that leaves something to chance."[25] The willingness to take such a chance separates resolute from irresolute adversaries. After all, the less the state values the good in dispute, and the more it fears a war over that issue, the less willing it will be to step onto the slope and embrace a risk of war.

In a brinksmanship crisis, each side bids up the risk of war—moving further and further down the slippery slope—until either one side decides to give in or they fall together into the precipice (as in the game of Chicken discussed in the

brinksmanship
A strategy in which adversaries take actions that increase the risk of accidental war, with the hope that the other will "blink" (lose its nerve) first and make concessions.

---

24. Thomas C. Schelling, *The Strategy of Conflict* (Cambridge, MA: Harvard University Press, 1960), 199.
25. Schelling, *Strategy of Conflict*, 187.

Leaders may use brinksmanship to make the threat of nuclear war credible. In the 1962 Cuban missile crisis, American president John F. Kennedy took steps toward nuclear war—for example, putting missile crews on alert—in order to pressure the Soviets to dismantle nuclear missile sites in Cuba.

"Special Topic" appendix to Chapter 2, on pp. 84–85). Exactly how a war might start "inadvertently" is not always clear; fortunately, in the case of nuclear war, we do not know the answer to that question. Absent a computer glitch, it still takes a human hand to pull the trigger.

The general idea was that as tensions rose in an international crisis, the risk of accidents would increase. A limited skirmish between forces could inadvertently escalate if a nervous local commander thought his position was about to be overrun and decided to launch his tactical nuclear weapons in order not to lose them to the enemy. Or, in the midst of a tense crisis, a flock of geese might be mistaken on the radar for incoming bombers (as actually happened in the 1950s), leading to a decision to launch rather than risk being disarmed by a first strike (which, fortunately, did not happen in this incident). Alternatively, the tension of a nerve-wracking crisis might cause leaders to give in to passion and fury and lose their cool, rational heads. In any event, it was precisely the willingness to court this risk that would credibly separate the genuinely resolved opponents from the bluffers.

Tying Hands   A second way in which states can send credible signals of their willingness to fight is by making threats in ways that would make backing down difficult. For example, after Iraq invaded Kuwait in August 1990, President Bush repeatedly and publicly stated that the conquest "will not stand." He made this commitment first on August 5, 1990, and reiterated it throughout the crisis, including during his State of the Union address on January 29, 1991. These words were also matched by deeds, particularly the deployment of over 500,000 U.S. troops to the region and an extensive diplomatic effort to build international consensus for an attack. Unlike the case with the Chinese threat, which Acheson felt could be disavowed, Bush was clearly on record as asserting that the policy of his administration was to reverse the Iraqi invasion.

By taking such clear, public statements and actions, Bush put his reputation, and that of the country, on the line. It was not unreasonable to expect that in doing so, he had made it quite costly to retreat from this position—to decide, in the face of Iraqi resistance, that the invasion would be allowed to stand after all. Doing so would have been embarrassing for him as a leader and for the country as a whole. It would have called into question the credibility of future U.S. threats, and Bush could expect his political opponents to use such a retreat against him at the next election.

The general insight here is that under some conditions, threats can generate what are known as **audience costs**—that is, negative repercussions that arise if the leader does not follow through on the threat.[26] Two audiences might impose these costs. The first is the international audience—other states that might doubt future threats made by the president or by the country. Such international audience costs could be felt through an inability to convince future adversaries of one's resolve. For example, one of the reasons that U.S. decision makers were skeptical of the Chinese threat to intervene in the Korean War was that it came in the wake of a series of unfulfilled threats over a different issue: Taiwan. As early as March 1949, the Chinese communist government began issuing threats to "liberate" Taiwan from the Nationalist Chinese forces that had fled there. These threats, repeated several times over the course of the next year and a half, combined with China's failure to carry them out, led some analysts in the United States to discount the threats over Korea as similarly empty bluster.[27] International-audience costs might also arise if allies come to doubt the trustworthiness of the country's threats, which may lead them to seek other protectors (see Chapter 5).

A second audience that might punish a leader for backing down from a threat is in the leader's own country: voters and political opponents who might seek to reprimand a president who has tarnished the country's honor and reputation by making empty threats. For example, in 2012 U.S. president Barack Obama declared that any use of chemical weapons by the Syrian regime against its people would cross a "red line" and compel a forceful response. His subsequent decision not to strike Syria after it used the banned weapons the following year was widely criticized by domestic opponents and used to foster the perception that Obama was weak on foreign policy.

In either event, if threats expose state leaders to audience costs, they can have the effect of "tying their hands." This phrase comes from a famous scene in Homer's *Odyssey* in which the main character, Odysseus, asks to have his hands tied to the mast of his ship as they sailed past the sirens. The call of the sirens was so beautiful that sailors who heard it were bewitched into steering their ship into the rocks.

audience costs
Negative repercussions for failing to follow through on a threat or to honor a commitment.

---

26. James D. Fearon, "Domestic Political Audiences and the Escalation of International Disputes," *American Political Science Review* 88 (September 1994): 577–92. For recent arguments that audience costs do not play a major role in crises, see Marc Trachtenberg, "Audience Costs: An Historical Analysis," *Security Studies* 21 (2012): 3–42; and Jack Snyder and Erica D. Borghard, "The Cost of Empty Threats: A Penny, Not a Pound," *American Political Science Review* 105 (August 2011): 437–56.

27. Anne Sartori, *Deterrence by Diplomacy* (Princeton, NJ: Princeton University Press, 2005), 33–39.

By tying his hands to the mast, Odysseus hoped to experience the sirens' call without succumbing to this enchantment. State leaders in a crisis tie their hands for similar reasons: because threats are costly to carry out, they know that they might choose not to follow through if faced with that decision. By exposing themselves to audience costs, they blunt the temptation to back down from their threats and thereby tie their own hands.

In the process of tying their hands, of course, state leaders also send a powerful message to their opponents: "I cannot back down; hence, my threat is completely credible." As with acts of brinksmanship, engaging in actions that incur audience costs separates the resolute from the irresolute. Those most likely to back down from a threat are less willing to take steps that will make backing down costly.

Paying for Power A final mechanism that states use to signal their resolve in a crisis involves taking costly steps to increase their capabilities, such as by mobilizing and deploying a large military force, increasing military manpower, and/or spending large sums of money. For example, during a 1961 crisis between the United States and the Soviet Union over Berlin, President Kennedy asked Congress to increase the army's strength by 350,000 troops, with much of the growth coming from an increase in the number of people drafted and a call-up of reserve forces. This last step was particularly costly, in a political sense, because reservists are people who have finished their military service and have families and regular jobs. As a result, calling up 150,000 reservists led to political resistance. There was also a concrete monetary cost to these actions.

As already noted, military mobilizations play an important role in crises because they give the states the material capabilities needed to back up their threats. The most credible threat is not going to be effective unless the action threatened is very costly to the adversary. Thus, one purpose of military mobilization is to put force behind diplomatic maneuvers. At the same time, costly actions of this sort can also affect the opponent's estimate of the state's resolve, through several mechanisms.[28] First, by increasing the state's military capabilities, these actions may decrease the costs associated with carrying out the threat. Since the costs of carrying out a threat are what call credibility into question in the first place, visible steps taken to reduce those costs can make it more believable that the threatener will do what it says. Second, the willingness to pay the costs associated with these actions can signal that this issue is one that the threatening state cares a great deal about. By calling up the reserves, Kennedy was trying to send the message that he cared so much about the fate of Berlin that he was willing to pay the political costs associated with this action.

We started this section by noting that a condition of incomplete information is dangerous because states might miscalculate in bargaining, such as by mistakenly resisting threats that turn out to be genuine. Such mistakes played a role in the Iraqi invasion of Kuwait in 1990 and in the onset of war between the United States and China in 1950. Brinksmanship, tying hands, and paying for power are strategies for

---

28. Branislav Slantchev, *Military Threats: The Costs of Coercion and the Price of Peace* (Cambridge: Cambridge University Press, 2011).

communicating a willingness to fight; they are mechanisms that help states figure out which threats are genuine and which are not. Interestingly, though, these cures for incomplete information entail risks that can be just as dangerous as the underlying problem they address.

This danger is clearest in the case of brinksmanship strategies, through which states bid up the risk of accidental war in order to prove their resolve. The hope in doing so is that the adversary will blink, and thus war will be averted. But there is no guarantee that the states will not lose control and fall into the precipice. Ironically, then, to avoid a war driven by uncertainty, states have to embrace some risk of accidental war. Hand-tying strategies can have similar risks. Although actions that raise the costs of backing down can convince the other side to give in, there is also a risk that both sides will tie their hands in a contest of threats and counterthreats. Both sides can then become locked into intransigent and incompatible bargaining positions from which it is too costly to retreat. Once each side has eliminated its ability to compromise, war may be inevitable—even if the initial uncertainty that led to the crisis has been removed. Finally, while military mobilizations might persuade the adversary to yield, they can also provoke the other side to strike first—a possibility that we will revisit shortly.

In the case of the Persian Gulf War, it is quite possible that President Bush's hand-tying actions between August 1990 and January 1991 eventually convinced Saddam Hussein that the United States was willing to fight, in spite of his original belief to the contrary. He may have resisted nonetheless because his own pattern of defiance and counterthreats in those months had served to tie his own hands as well. Hussein may have feared domestic repercussions for a retreat in the face of American threats, or he may have been concerned that such a retreat would embolden Iraq's neighbor and long-standing enemy, Iran. By January 15, 1991, neither side was willing to compromise, and the U.S.-led war to liberate Kuwait began. We thus see that incomplete information can cause war both directly, through miscalculation, and indirectly, by forcing states to communicate their resolve in ways that can foreclose successful bargaining.

This discussion generates several predictions about the conditions that make war more or less likely. In general, the harder it is for states to learn about each other's capabilities and resolve, the more severe the problem of incomplete information will be. When states are relatively opaque, in the sense that it is hard for outsiders to observe their military capabilities or their political decision-making processes, there is likely to be greater scope for uncertainties of this kind to arise and bedevil the quest for negotiated settlements. The strategic situation might also influence the degree of uncertainty that states face. For example, as the number of states that might potentially get involved in a particular crisis increases, the number and importance of the "hidden cards" grows dramatically: in the event of a war, who will join and who will not? Finally, this discussion sensitizes us to the question of whether states can find ways to signal their intentions in a credible manner. Problems of incomplete information are more likely to be overcome when states can find costly ways to signal their intentions and thereby convince their adversaries to make concessions.

Can an Adversary Be Trusted to Honor a Deal? War from Commitment Problems

Incomplete information provides one compelling answer to the puzzle of war: uncertainty about capabilities or resolve can make it difficult for states to agree on a settlement that all sides prefer over war. The ability to identify such a settlement, however, does not always guarantee that war will be avoided. What happens if the states do not trust one another to abide by that settlement in the future?

In this section we develop a second set of explanations for why bargaining may fail. The causes of war considered here all arise from a common underlying challenge: the difficulty that states can have making credible promises *not* to use force to revise the settlement at a later date. In this context, credibility has the same meaning as before, but we use it here to describe not a threat to use force but rather a promise not to. A credible commitment to abide by a deal is a commitment by one state assuring the other side that it will not threaten force to revise the terms of the deal. A commitment problem arises when a state cannot make such a promise in a credible manner.

The Prisoner's Dilemma introduced in Chapter 2 is a quintessential example of such a problem. Although the prisoners in this game would like to commit to cooperating with each other, their incentives are such that a commitment to do so is not credible: when given the choice, they will prefer to defect. Commitment problems are particularly common in the absence of any enforcement mechanism, such as a court, that can hold people to their commitments. In the international system, external enforcement of commitments can be difficult to arrange (though not impossible, as we will see in the concluding section of this chapter). Next we consider three ways in which an inability to make credible commitments to a bargain might undermine the search for a peaceful settlement of international disputes.[29]

Bargaining over Goods That Are a Source of Future Bargaining Power

The clearest place to see the role of commitment problems is in disputes over goods that can serve as a source of future bargaining power. The best examples of such goods are strategically important pieces of territory and weapons programs. States bargain over territory all the time, but in some cases the piece of territory in question has military significance, perhaps because it contains high ground from which one could launch an effective attack or islands that sit astride strategically

---

29. The ideas are introduced in Fearon, "Rationalist Explanations for War," and are further elaborated in Robert Powell, "War as a Commitment Problem," *International Organization* 60 (2006): 169–203.

important sea routes. For example, China and Japan have in recent years been locked in dispute over eight uninhabited islands in the East China Sea, known as the Senkaku to Japan and the Diaoyu to China. Not only are the surrounding waters rich in fish and in oil and gas deposits, but the islands are also close to strategically important sea routes that are vital for naval movements in the region. As a result, control over the islands potentially impacts the countries' relative military power.

Bargaining over weapons programs has a similar quality. In recent years, the United States has sought to pressure several states—including Iraq (prior to 2003), Libya, Iran, and North Korea—into abandoning the development of WMD. These efforts have met with varying levels of success. Libya agreed to dismantle its weapons programs in December 2003. North Korea agreed several times to freeze its nuclear program, but these deals unraveled, and North Korea effectively entered the nuclear club in 2006. In 2015, the United States and its partners reached a deal with Iran to freeze its nuclear program for at least a decade. As with strategically important territory, a deal on this matter does not simply resolve a dispute; it also directly affects the military capabilities of the participants. A country that agrees to give up a weapons program makes itself weaker by doing so.

Territory with military-strategic value can be hard to bargain over because control over the good affects the states' relative military power. The uninhabited Senkaku/Diaoyu Islands have been a source of conflict between Japan and China partly because they sit astride strategically important sea routes.

The difficulty in bargaining over such objects is that a state will be reluctant to render itself more vulnerable to attack without credible promises that the other side will not exploit that vulnerability in the future. The state may be able to avoid war now by making concessions, but doing so entails a risk that its adversary, made stronger by the deal, will then press new claims. Unless there is some way for the other side to credibly commit *not* to use its newfound power, a threatened state may decide that it would rather fight today than face a future in which it is considerably weaker. Thus, even if there is some deal that is preferable to war now, if this deal will lead to a change in capabilities that can be exploited later, the state that would be rendered weaker may decide to forgo that deal and gamble on a war.

This strategic dilemma has presented an important obstacle in U.S. efforts to convince countries like North Korea and Iran to give up their nuclear programs peacefully. It is important to remember that the United States had hostile relations with these countries prior to their seeking nuclear weapons. As we already saw, the United States fought a war against North Korea from 1950 to 1953. That war ended with a cease-fire but not a peace treaty, and ever since, more than 30,000 U.S. troops have been stationed in South Korea. U.S. hostility toward the North is driven not only by the lingering issue of Korea's division but also by the nature of its regime, which is one of the most repressive systems in the world. Similarly, hostility between the United States and Iran dates back to the 1979 revolution, which toppled Iran's pro-American leader and installed an Islamic fundamentalist government.

To the extent that these states see their nuclear programs as a counterweight against American (and, in the case of Iran, also Israeli) power, they would be reluctant to give up those programs if by doing so, they rendered themselves more vulnerable to U.S. demands on other issues. The experience of Libya is instructive in this respect. As noted earlier, Libya agreed in December 2003 to end its chemical and nuclear weapons programs and to submit to international inspections. In return, the United States and Britain promised to normalize relations with the country and not to press for fundamental changes in the regime of Libyan leader Mu'ammar Qaddafi—even though he ran a brutal dictatorship. In March 2011, however, Qaddafi faced a rebellion against his rule, and his attacks on civilians triggered military action by the United States, Britain, and other European countries. Qaddafi was ousted and then killed by rebel forces seven months later.

Whether or not this intervention would have been deterred if Libya had continued its weapons programs, the lesson was clear: a promise by the United States to forswear regime change is not necessarily a credible or lasting guarantee. The success of any effort to end these programs peacefully requires the United States to find a way to commit credibly not to exploit the power shift brought about by disarmament.

Prevention: War in Response to Changing Power

A second, related problem arises if the balance of military capabilities is anticipated to change because of factors external to the bargaining process. A common source of this kind of power shift is different rates of economic growth. As noted in Chapter 1, uneven economic development has led to the relative rise and decline of states over time. The growth of Germany's power in the late nineteenth and early twentieth centuries had a dramatic impact on that country's ability to challenge its neighbors. Similarly, as we will discuss in Chapter 14, China's impressive economic growth since 1980 has greatly increased its influence in international politics. If a state is growing much more rapidly than its adversary, then the military capabilities that it can bring to bear in future disputes will be greater than those it can bring to bear today. A second important source of large shifts in military capabilities is the development and acquisition of new technologies, such as nuclear weapons. The acquisition of nuclear weapons can cause an abrupt and profound shift in a state's capacity to impose costs on its adversaries.

Regardless of their exact source, anticipated changes in military capabilities can present an insurmountable dilemma in crisis bargaining. To see this, we revisit the bargaining model introduced earlier. Figure 3.3 illustrates what happens to the bargaining interaction when the power of one state, in this case State A, is expected to increase. In the top panel, the expected outcome of the war is initially close to State B's ideal point (or the far left of the bar, where State B would get all of the

FIGURE 3.3 *Bargaining and Shifting Power*

Initial power distribution: Today, State B is more powerful than State A, so fighting a war favors State B, as indicated by the fact that the war outcome is close to State B's ideal point.

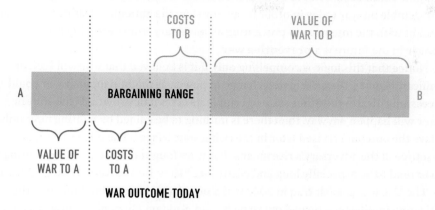

WAR OUTCOME TODAY

Future power distribution: Tomorrow, after State A's power increases, fighting a war will favor State A, as indicated by the fact that the war outcome is now close to State A's ideal point. The best possible deal that State B can get after the power shift is indicated by the red dotted line. Because this deal gives State B less than it can expect to get from war today (the blue dotted line in the top panel), State B has an incentive to wage war now in order to prevent the power shift.

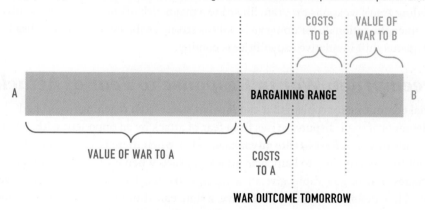

WAR OUTCOME TOMORROW

good). Let's assume, however, that State A's power is expected to grow, so that, at some time in the future, the new war outcome will be closer to State A's ideal point (or the far right of the bar), as in the lower panel.

In the initial period, the states can agree to some distribution inside the bargaining range. But both sides can anticipate that, in the future, State A will no longer be satisfied with this deal and will demand a new deal in the new bargaining range. As this example is constructed, State B prefers the war outcome it could obtain under the initial power distribution (labeled in blue in the top panel of Figure 3.3) over any outcome that falls in the future bargaining range. Even the best deal that State B can hope to get in the future (the red dotted line in the lower panel), gives State B less than it expects to get from war today. Hence, State B would rather fight a war now than face worse terms in the future.

preventive war

A war fought with the intention of preventing an adversary from becoming stronger in the future. Preventive wars arise because a state whose power is increasing cannot commit not to exploit that power in future bargaining interactions.

Thus, even if the states can locate a deal that they prefer over war today, the state that is getting stronger will face a strong temptation to use its future power to try to revise the deal later. Unless there is some way for the growing state to make a credible commitment not to do that, then its adversary may decide that it is better to gamble on war today in order to stop or slow the anticipated shift. A war that is fought with the intention of preventing an adversary from becoming relatively stronger in the future is a **preventive war**.

Notice that this logic is compelling only if it is believed that war will halt, or significantly delay, the anticipated change in power, as might happen if war could successfully disarm the other state or cripple its economic growth. If the shift in power will happen anyway, then there is nothing to be gained by fighting now, only to have the outcome revised later in the rising state's favor. The need to destroy the source of the adversary's rise means that wars fought in the context of shifting power tend to be especially long and costly (see "How Do We Know?" on p. 124).

The U.S. war against Iraq in 2003 had a preventive logic, even if much of the motivating intelligence turned out to be flawed. Saddam Hussein's regime was believed to have some minimal capability—and a demonstrated intention—to develop WMD. The preventive argument for attacking was that it would be easier to oust Hussein before he had fully developed these capabilities than to do so after he had succeeded in deploying them in his arsenal. Of course, the uncertainties surrounding Iraq's weapons program illustrate a major risk of engaging in preventive war, since the rationale for doing so is only as strong as the evidence that a disadvantageous shift in relative capabilities is coming.

Preemption: War in Response to Fear of Attack

A final commitment problem that can prevent states from reaching negotiated settlements of their disputes arises from fear of attack by an opponent with a first-strike advantage. A **first-strike advantage** exists when there is a considerable benefit to being the first to launch an attack. It arises when military technology, strategies, and/or geography give an advantage to offensive actions over defensive ones. When defense is relatively effective, a state can afford to wait to see whether its opponent is going to attack because a first strike can be defeated or absorbed. When offense is relatively effective, a first strike is potentially devastating, and fear of attack creates incentives to abandon the bargaining table and rush to the battlefield.[30]

first-strike advantage

The situation that arises when military technology, military strategies, and/or geography give a significant advantage to whichever state attacks first in a war.

For example, if one state could launch its nuclear missiles and destroy all of its adversary's missiles on the ground before they could be launched, then that state would enjoy a first-strike advantage. A state that can land a disarming blow may be tempted to do so, and a state that is vulnerable to such a blow may feel a "use it or lose it" imperative to strike first rather than be disarmed.

---

30. There is a considerable literature on the "offense-defense balance" and its effect on the likelihood of war; see, for example, Keir Lieber, "Grasping the Technological Peace: The Offense-Defense Balance and International Security," *International Security* 25 (Summer 2000): 71–104. A related literature emphasizes that what matters is not the actual offense-defense balance but rather the balance that is perceived by military and political leaders; see Van Evera, "Cult of the Offensive."

First-strike advantages can create a potentially insurmountable commitment problem: unless each state can credibly promise the other not to attack first, there is a danger that bargaining will break down as each side hurries to get in the first blow. Each side may be confident that if it manages to strike first, it can do better in war than if it accepts the deal currently on offer. Indeed, there may be no deal that both sides prefer over a war that they start.

An example of this situation is depicted in Figure 3.4. Here, we assume that there are two different war outcomes, depending on which state lands the first blow. The expected outcome of a war started by State A is depicted in the top panel, and the expected outcome of a war started by State B is depicted in the lower panel. The first-strike advantage is captured by the assumption that each side expects to do better in a war that it starts than in a war started by the adversary (that is, the war outcome in the top panel is closer to State A's ideal point than the war outcome

---

FIGURE 3.4 *Bargaining and First-Strike Advantages*

State A attacks first: State A enjoys a significant advantage in war if it attacks first, and the war outcome will be close to its ideal point.

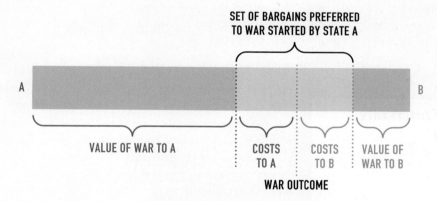

State B attacks first: Here, the war outcome heavily favors State B. Because the bargaining ranges in the top and lower panels do not overlap, there is no deal that both sides prefer over a war that they initiate.

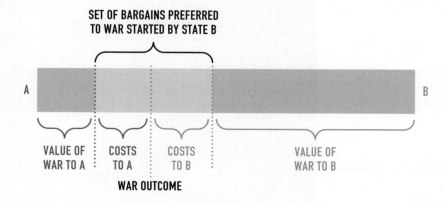

Bargaining and the Duration of War

The duration of interstate wars varies a good deal. Figure A shows the distribution of war durations for 125 interstate wars over the last two centuries. About 10 wars have lasted three years or more, and they account for most of the combat deaths from wars in this period. However, most wars are relatively brief.

What determines how long a war will last? A number of factors might explain why some wars are longer than others, including the power of the adversaries and what they are fighting over. But, at a more general level, how long a war lasts is related to the strategic problem that caused the war in the first place. Once the adversaries go to war, the incentive to reach a deal that spares each side the costs of fighting does not disappear. Indeed, relatively few wars are fought until one of the states is completely occupied or unable to mount further operations; most end with some kind of bargain. This observation raises a puzzle: How does war make it possible for states to reach a settlement when they could not do so beforehand?

In a recent book, Alex Weisiger argues that if bargaining fails because of incomplete information about relative capabilities and resolve, then war can bring about a deal by revealing the hidden information.[a] As states compete on the battlefield, features that were hard to observe beforehand—the power of each state, the effectiveness of military technologies and strategies, the willingness of the populace to bear the burdens of war—become observable. In this case, war lasts as long as is necessary for uncertainties to be resolved.

Alternatively, if the war came about because of a commitment problem, then the war can end only when the source of that problem is removed. A preventive war fought in response to the rising power of an opponent can end when either the declining power is unable to keep fighting or the rising power is crippled to the point that its rise has been forestalled.

To test these propositions, Weisiger collected data on 103 cases of interstate war since 1816 and estimated the effect of different factors on how long each war lasted. He found that one of the strongest predictors of long and severe wars was whether the war was preceded by a large shift in the adversaries' relative military capabilities, as measured not only by the size of their militaries, but also by their population size and level of economic development. In particular, the typical duration of a war preceded by a large power shift is three times that of war preceded by little or no such shift. Thus, as expected, the longest wars tend to be those fought between declining and rising states, when preventive motivations loom largest. On the other hand, among wars that were not preceded by a shift in power—and were therefore more likely to be rooted in an information problem—those that experienced relatively frequent and intense battles tended to end more quickly. This finding is consistent with the idea that battles serve to resolve uncertainty, permitting the adversaries to find a settlement that both prefer over continued bloodshed.

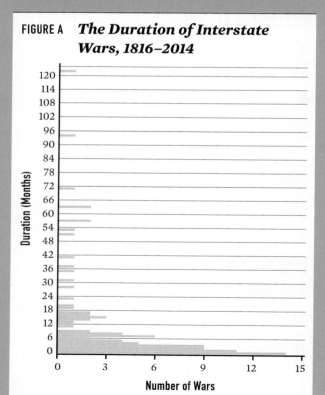

FIGURE A *The Duration of Interstate Wars, 1816–2014*

Source: Meredith Reid Sarkees and Frank Wayman, *Resort to War: 1816–2007* (Washington, DC: Congressional Quarterly Press, 2010).

---

a. Alex Weisiger, *Logics of War: Explanations for Limited and Unlimited Conflicts* (Ithaca, NY: Cornell University Press, 2013). For another important study along these lines, see Branislav Slantchev, "How Initiators End Their Wars: The Duration of Warfare and the Terms of Peace," *American Political Science Review* 48 (September 2004): 813–29.

in the lower panel, and the opposite is true for State B). As a result, although there is a set of deals that both states prefer over a war started by either State A or State B, no deal is preferable to *both* of these possible wars. A deal within the lower bargaining range would satisfy State B but give State A less than it expects to get by attacking first (the area labeled in red in the top panel). Similarly, a deal within the upper bargaining range would satisfy State A but give State B less than it expects to get by striking first (the area labeled in blue in the lower panel).

Under these conditions, neither state will make concessions to the other at the bargaining table; instead, both will likely rush to the exits, each trying to beat the other to the punch. Negotiations in this context may be seen as nothing more than a ploy to delay the other side from mobilizing. A war that arises in this way is a **preemptive war**.[31]

The 1967 Six Day War between Israel and four Arab states (Egypt, Syria, Jordan, and Iraq) is a classic case of a war that started this way. In May 1967, Egypt responded to border skirmishes between Israel and Syria by massing troops on the Israeli border and imposing a partial blockade. On June 5, fearing that war was likely, Israel launched a surprise, preemptive attack on the Egyptian air force, destroying 300 aircraft while they were still on the ground. With Egypt's main offensive threat crippled, the ensuing war lasted six days and left Israel in control of large swaths of formerly Arab-held territory.

This dynamic forms an important component of what we referred to earlier as the security dilemma. When military technology favors offensive action, a state that builds arms, even out of purely defensive motives, inevitably makes other states worry about a possible attack. If threatened states arm in response, the original state will, in turn, feel less secure, feeding a self-reinforcing cycle of fear. In addition to causing arms races and hampering international cooperation, the commitment problem created by this fear fuels a risk of war.

Both preemption and prevention arise from the difficulty states can have in making credible commitments not to use their military power. The difference between the two concepts revolves around timing. Preemption is a response to an imminent threat when there is an existing first-strike advantage. Prevention is a response to anticipated changes in the distribution of power that might result in an increased threat sometime in the future. (For a discussion of how such considerations contributed to the outbreak of World War I, see "What Shaped Our World?" on p. 126.)

We have seen, then, that even if states can locate a deal that both prefer over war at the moment, concerns about their willingness to abide by the deal in the future can cause bargaining failure and war. Although these concerns can arise for different reasons, all the paths to war discussed in this section have at their root a common commitment problem: the difficulty of committing not to use one's power to one's advantage in the future.

preemptive war
A war fought with the anticipation that an attack by the other side is imminent.

---

31. It should be emphasized that this example assumes a very large first-strike advantage relative to the costs of war, so it is possible that this kind of situation arises only rarely. For a historical overview of preemptive war, which finds that very few wars start this way, see Dan Reiter, "Exploding the Powder Keg Myth: Preemptive Wars Almost Never Happen," *International Security* 20, no. 2 (Autumn 1995): 5–34.

Prevention and Preemption in World War I

World War I redrew the maps of Europe, the Middle East, and Africa. It decimated a generation of young people, and the postwar settlement contributed to World War II 20 years later, as well as to more recent conflicts.

For all its far-reaching consequences, the First World War had relatively modest origins. On June 28, 1914, Archduke Franz Ferdinand, heir to the throne of the Austro-Hungarian Empire, was assassinated during a visit to neighboring Serbia. How could this event lead to a war that would ultimately involve 32 states fighting on three continents?

Interests Europe in 1914 was rife with conflicting interests. Germany's growing power brought it into competition with Britain and provoked fear in its neighbors. France hoped to reclaim territory from Germany, which in turn had designs on territory in Russia and overseas. Austria-Hungary and Russia were competing for influence in the Balkan region. The Ottoman Empire was in decline, and outsiders sought to expand at its expense.

Institutions States with compatible interests often form alliances, institutions that help them to cooperate militarily (see Chapter 5). By 1914, the major powers were divided into two hostile camps: Germany, Austria-Hungary, and Italy formed the Triple Alliance against Great Britain, France, and Russia in the Triple Entente. This alliance system meant that any conflict had the potential to expand throughout Europe. It also posed a problem for German military planners, who knew that, in the event of a war, they would face foes to the east and west.

Interactions In this combustible atmosphere, the assassination of the archduke by Serb terrorists created a dangerous spark. Austria-Hungary had a substantial Serb minority, and agitation by Serb nationalists threatened to tear the multiethnic empire apart. Austria-Hungary sought to compel Serbia to end its support for these militants and threatened war. This threat brought a deterrent response from the Russians. Germany then promised to protect the Austrians. Though, in principle, the conflict could have been defused by a negotiated bargain, preventive and preemptive considerations loomed large.

Although German leaders did not relish a war with Russia, they feared Russia's growing power. In the decades prior to the war, Russia had made great economic strides, building its heavy industries and railroad network. Germany's leaders watched these developments with concern and came to believe that they had a short "window of opportunity" in which to prevent future Russian domination.

In contemplating war with Russia, however, there was a significant obstacle: France. To deal with the possibility of a two-front war, the Germans came up with an audacious solution. The Schlieffen Plan took advantage of the fact that Russia's vast size made its military machine very slow. After the Russians started mobilizing, it would take six weeks before their forces could join the fight. The Germans hoped to exploit this delay to invade and quickly defeat France. German troops could then be shifted to the east, in time to meet the Russian advance.

Planners believed that the strategic situation gave an advantage to whoever struck first. By acting quickly, Germany could seize key bridges and tunnels in Belgium, roll onward into Paris, and then turn their attention to Russia. If they waited, the Belgians could fortify or destroy the bridges, causing the German army to bog down in the west, while the Russian "steamroller" bore down from the east. Under these conditions, negotiations threatened an intolerable delay. Preemptive incentives also meant that military mobilizations were not a useful instrument of crisis diplomacy. When the Russians mobilized on July 30, they hoped that signaling their resolve would lead the Austrians to reduce their demands. Instead, Russia's mobilization spurred the adversaries to the battlefield.

By August 3, Europe was at war. When the Russian army mobilized, Germany invaded Belgium and France. Great Britain joined the fray. Other states were tempted by one side or the other to pile on, and the battlefield expanded across and beyond Europe.

In addition to shedding light on the general problem of war, this discussion generates a number of predictions about the conditions under which war is more or less likely to occur. First, war is more likely to occur when the good in dispute is a source of power to those who possess it. For example, it is harder to strike bargains over strategically important territory than over territory that is valuable for economic reasons.[32] Second, preventive incentives arise when there are relatively rapid and dramatic changes in the military balance between two countries. Hence, war is more likely when such changes are anticipated or under way. Finally, bargaining failures are more common when the military-strategic situation creates substantial advantages for striking first. These advantages generally arise from the nature of military technology, which sometimes imparts large advantages to the actor who goes on the offensive first—although, as we saw in the case of World War I, particular military strategies can also create pressure to act preemptively.

Is Compromise Always Possible? War from Indivisibility

Finally, we consider a third kind of problem that can prevent states from reaching mutually beneficial settlements of their disputes because the disputed good cannot be divided. A good is divisible if there are ways to split it into smaller shares; an **indivisible good** cannot be divided without destroying its value. Imagine, for example, the difference between having 100 pennies and having one dollar bill. Although the amount of money available is the same in both cases, the pennies can be divided up between two people in many different ways, while the dollar bill cannot be split without ruining it. When the good in question is indivisible, compromise solutions are impossible to reach, and the bargaining becomes "all or nothing."

It is easy to see how indivisible goods could create an insurmountable obstacle in crisis bargaining. Consider a situation in which each state would prefer to fight a war rather than get none of the good. Even though there might be deals that both sides prefer over war—such as, say, a 50-50 split—an inability to divide the good into the necessary shares renders such a deal unattainable. In an all-or-nothing bargaining situation, one state must get nothing. And if both states prefer war over getting nothing, then war becomes inevitable.

Although the logic of indivisibility is quite clear, what is less clear is whether or how often indivisibility is actually a problem in international politics. What goods are truly indivisible? A key point is that indivisibility is not a physical property of a good, but rather the way in which that good is valued. This point is made most dramatically by the biblical story in which King Solomon, confronted by two women claiming to be the mother of the same baby, decides that the only fair solution in

indivisible good
A good that cannot be divided without diminishing its value.

---

32. Paul K. Huth, *Standing Your Ground* (Ann Arbor: University of Michigan Press, 1996).

In Jerusalem, the Dome of the Rock, one of Islam's holiest shrines, sits on top of the Temple Mount, the site of the Jewish temple until 70 C.E. The concentration of holy sites in Jerusalem complicates negotiations between Israelis and Palestinians over whether and how to divide or share the city, which both sides claim as their capital.

the face of these incompatible claims is to cut the baby in half. This solution seems odd not because it cannot be physically implemented, but because the process of doing so would kill the baby. (Fortunately, in King Solomon's case, the decision did not have to be carried out, since one woman insisted that she would rather let the other woman have her child than see it killed—whereupon Solomon decided that this woman must be the true mother.) Similarly, in a dispute over a valuable painting, one could slice the painting in two, but doing so would destroy the object's value.

Hence, when we say that a good cannot be divided, we generally do not mean this literally. Rather, we mean that the good loses much, if not all, of its value when it is divided.[33] This can be the case with core values that cannot be compromised or with divisible goods that are closely linked to such core values.

A commonly cited example of an indivisible good in international relations is the city of Jerusalem.[34] It is a city that contains some of the holiest sites of Christianity, Islam, and Judaism and has historical, cultural, and religious significance unlike any other piece of territory in the world. As a result, the status of Jerusalem is a major stumbling block in efforts to bring about peace in the Middle East.

For many Jews, Jerusalem is the focal point of the desire—sometimes symbolic, sometimes literal—to return to the promised land of Zion. Every year at Passover, Jews all over the world utter the words "Next year in Jerusalem," underscoring the role of that city in forging a connection between the land of Israel and the Jewish identity. The centrality of this city has been given political expression as well: a Basic Law passed by Israel in 1980 declares that "Jerusalem, complete and united, is the capital of Israel."

For Muslims, East Jerusalem, or Al-Quds, is the third-holiest city (after Mecca and Medina in Saudi Arabia) and the site of the Dome of the Rock, where the prophet Mohammed is believed to have ascended to Paradise.

Palestinians claim East Jerusalem, which Israel annexed after the 1967 Six Day War, as the capital of an eventual Palestinian state. This claim clearly clashes with the Israeli position that the city is indivisible and the capital of the Jewish state. Moreover, the holiest sites for both faiths sit literally on top of one another. The Dome of the Rock and Al-Aqsa Mosque were built (1,300 years ago) directly on the Temple Mount—the site of the original Jewish temple—whose Western Wall is an

---

33. H. Peyton Young, "Dividing the Indivisible," *American Behavioral Scientist* 38, no. 6 (1995): 904–20.

34. See, for example, Cecilia Albin, "Negotiating Indivisible Goods: The Case of Jerusalem," *Jerusalem Journal of International Relations* 13, no. 1 (1991): 45–76.

important place of worship for Jews. The question of whether or how to divide the city, and how to ensure that people of all faiths have access to their holy sites, is one that has so far defied resolution.

It is important, however, not to place undue emphasis on indivisibility as a source of bargaining failures. First, some of the difficulty of dealing with indivisible goods arises not from indivisibility per se, but from weak enforcement mechanisms. King Solomon's quandary is one that divorcing parents routinely face when each wants custody of their children. These disputes are settled not by dividing the children physically, but by dividing the time they spend with each parent. This kind of alternating possession would generally fail in international politics, however, because a state would not trust its adversary to hand over the good when the time came to do so. In child-custody cases, the deal is enforced by courts and police, which are generally lacking in the international context. Thus, the main obstacle to striking such a deal lies not in the nature of the good, but in the difficulty of making a credible commitment to share that good over time.[35]

A second reason to be skeptical of claims of indivisibility is that states may have strategic incentives to claim that they cannot compromise on a particular issue, even if they actually could. Recall that one of the strategies that states employ in crisis bargaining is to tie their hands through public pronouncements from which it would be costly to back down. It is quite possible that claims of indivisibility—such as the Israeli Basic Law pronouncing Jerusalem the capital of Israel—have a strategic quality: they represent an effort to tie the government's hands so that it will find compromise difficult, if not impossible. The hope in making such claims is that the other side will realize that it has no choice but to give in entirely. In this sense, objects may take on the appearance of indivisibility in the course of the bargaining process through the public positions that states take.[36]

The point of this discussion is not to suggest that indivisible goods do not exist in international politics. Rather, it is to suggest that we be appropriately skeptical when the participants in a dispute claim that the good in question is indivisible and hence no compromise is possible. Such a claim may reflect a bargaining position adopted for strategic reasons rather than a true description of the fundamental nature of the good in question.

In any event, there may be ways to allocate apparently indivisible goods that do not involve physical division. One possible mechanism is shared control. It has been proposed, for example, that Israelis and Palestinians jointly control certain portions of Jerusalem to ensure that all people have access to the sacred sites. Indeed, this already happens to some degree at the Temple Mount: though the site falls under Israeli sovereignty, the area on top, including the Dome of the Rock and the Al-Aqsa Mosque, is administered by Islamic authorities.

---

35. See Powell, "War as a Commitment Problem," for a discussion of how indivisibility leads to commitment problems.

36. See Stacie E. Goddard, "Uncommon Ground: Indivisible Territory and the Politics of Legitimacy," *International Organization* 60 (2006): 35–68.

A second mechanism for dealing with indivisible goods is compensation on another issue. Although a rare painting cannot be physically divided, a dispute over it can be resolved by having one party compensate the other in exchange for the good. In this case, the object is made divisible by adding a new dimension to the deal: rather than arguing about who gets the painting, the issue becomes how much money one is willing to pay the other to get it. Since money is generally divisible, adding this new dimension creates the possibility for compromise where none previously existed. Hence, disputants may be able to find a second issue dimension on which the loser in the main issue can be compensated. The strategy of making one dispute easier to solve by bringing in a second issue is known as linkage, as we saw in Chapter 2.

Has War Become Obsolete?

War arises from a variety of factors that can prevent states from reaching peaceful settlements of their disputes. Of course, the reason we study war is not just to understand why it happens, but also to identify factors that might reduce or eliminate its occurrence. On this front, there is some room for optimism. One striking observation from Figure 3.1 is that the incidence of interstate war seems to have dropped since 1950. Moreover, there has not been a war between two great powers since the Korean War ended in 1953—the longest such streak in modern history.[37]

The apparent decline in interstate war over the last six decades has been the subject of considerable attention among political scientists.[38] However, we must approach this trend carefully. As Figure 3.1 shows, earlier periods in history experienced dips in the frequency of war that turned out to be temporary. And as this book was going to press in 2018, numerous crises involving the United States, Russia, China, North Korea, and Iran were threatening to escalate. Depending on what happens in the world, a section on the obsolescence of war might not be appropriate for the next edition of this book, a few years from now. Still, the observation that the past six decades have seen a decline in interstate war is striking and important enough to motivate the following questions: Have there been changes in world politics that could explain a decline in the incidence of interstate war since World War II? To what extent can the framework offered in this chapter guide our thinking about this development?

The logic developed in this chapter has three main components: (1) war becomes possible when states have conflicting interests over a contentious issue, (2) the costs of war ensure that there exists a peaceful deal that both states prefer

---

37. Scholars typically identify the following states as great powers in the post–World War II period: the United States, the Soviet Union/Russia, Great Britain, France, China (after 1950), Germany (after 1991), and Japan (after 1991).

38. See, for example, John E. Mueller, *Retreat from Doomsday: The Obsolescence of Major War* (New York: Basic Books, 1989); Joshua S. Goldstein, *Winning the War on War: The Decline of Armed Conflict Worldwide* (New York: Dutton, 2011); Steven Pinker, *The Better Angels of Our Nature: Why Violence Has Declined* (New York: Viking, 2011). For a skeptical view, see Tanisha M. Fazal, "Dead Wrong? Battle Deaths, Military Medicine, and Exaggerated Reports of War's Demise," *International Security* 39 (Summer 2014): 95–125; and Bear F. Braumoeller, "Systemic Trends in War and Peace." In The Causes of Peace: What We Now Know–Nobel Symposium 161, edited by Olav Njølstad. (Oslo, Norway: The Norwegian Nobel Institute, 2017.)

over fighting, but (3) bargaining may fail because of information or commitment problems or because of an inability to divide the good at stake. It follows that a decline in war could arise from (1) changing interests that lead to a decrease in the value of goods that have historically driven conflict, (2) an increase in the costs of war that leads to changing interactions, or (3) the growth of institutions that help states solve the information or commitment problems associated with uncertainty and changing power, or the problem of the indivisibility of a good. There is reason to think that all three of these factors have changed in ways that have made war less likely overall.

Changing Interests: Declining Conflict over Territory

A striking feature of world politics since 1945 is the declining role of territory in driving interstate conflicts. Not only has there been a drop in the frequency of interstate wars over territory, but there have also been fewer instances of successful conquest or annexation of territory since World War II.[39] Explanations for this observation abound, but any understanding has to start with changes in the value of possessing territory in the modern era. Whereas control of territory and population was historically an important source of state power, technological changes have weakened this link. In an age of nuclear weapons, precision-guided missiles, and increasing reliance on unmanned aerial vehicles (popularly known as *drones*), military power no longer depends on how large an army a state can field. Moreover, the growth of international trade and investment (see Chapters 7 and 8) means that it is generally easier to acquire resources through markets than through conquest.[40] At the same time, the spread of nationalism has made it harder for foreign states to control conquered populations, thereby raising the costs of taking territory. Thus, some of the interests that drove states to contest territory have become less potent.

The interests of key states also changed after World War II. Whereas previously the rival territorial ambitions of the European great powers had cast that continent into frequent warfare, leadership of the international system after 1945 passed to two states—the United States and the Soviet Union—with little interest in further territorial expansion. The United States had satisfied all of its ambitions by the early twentieth century, with the end of westward expansion against the Native American tribes and the final settlement of the Canadian boundary in 1902. The Soviet Union used its military success in World War II to restore its dominance over lands that it had historically controlled. Thus, the most powerful states in the system had an interest in stabilizing the territorial order rather than changing it. The United States, in particular, played a role in advancing and defending a norm of "territorial integrity"—the idea that borders should not be changed through

---

39. See, for example, Mark W. Zacher, "The Territorial Integrity Norm: International Boundaries and the Use of Force," *International Organization* 55, no. 2 (2001): 215–50; Tanisha M. Fazal, *State Death: The Politics and Geography of Conquest, Occupation, and Annexation* (Princeton, NJ: Princeton University Press, 2007); and Gary Goertz, Paul F. Diehl, and Alexandru Balas, *The Puzzle of Peace: The Evolution of Peace in the International System* (New York: Oxford University Press, 2016).

40. Stephen G. Brooks, *Producing Security: Multinational Corporations, Globalization, and the Changing Calculus of Conflict* (Princeton, NJ: Princeton University Press, 2007).

force—a norm that became enshrined in international institutions like the United Nations (for more on the role of norms, see Chapter 11).[41]

Many newly decolonized countries also embraced this norm, even though their borders often made little sense, having been drawn in European capitals by imperial powers with scant knowledge of local conditions. Leaders in these new states decided that it was generally in their interests to respect the inherited borders and consolidate power within them, rather than open up a Pandora's box by calling all of the colonial borders into question.[42] In sum, changes in the international system after 1945 reduced states' interest in fighting over territory—reducing the value of territory as a good—which has historically been a major cause of interstate war.

Changing Interactions: The Rising Costs of War

One of the main disincentives for engaging in war is the human, economic, material, and psychological costs it imposes. Indeed, the costs of war generally ensure that states can do better by finding a negotiated settlement of their disputes. As war becomes less attractive, states are more willing to make compromises in order to avoid it. In addition, increasing the costs of war increases the range of status quo distributions that neither state has an incentive to challenge (see Figure 3.2).

At least two major developments since 1945 have increased the expected costs of war. One is the advent of nuclear weapons, which gave states the ability to completely obliterate each other. As a result, the expected costs of a war that involve nuclear exchange are so large that they swamp the value of whatever good is at stake. The threat of "mutually assured destruction" in the event of war engenders caution among nuclear-armed states, reducing the attractiveness of taking risks in a crisis. Indeed, it is striking that despite five decades of intense hostility between the United States and the Soviet Union during the Cold War, the two superpowers never waged war directly against one another. Although there are many theories about the cause of this so-called long peace, both states' possession of nuclear weapons certainly played a stabilizing role.[43] We will return to this topic in Chapter 14, when we consider the implications of the spread of nuclear weapons.

The second major development since 1945 is the explosive growth of international trade and financial transactions (see Figure 14.2 on p. 589). Scholars have long thought that, as countries became more economically interdependent, the costs of war between them would grow. The more two countries value one another as trading partners, the more incentive they have to avoid conflicts that could disrupt those

---

41. Zacher, "Territorial Integrity Norm"; Fazal, *State Death*, 47–52.

42. Jeffrey Ira Herbst, *States and Power in Africa: Comparative Lessons in Authority and Control* (Princeton, NJ: Princeton University Press, 2014).

43. See, for example, John Lewis Gaddis, "The Long Peace: Elements of Stability in the Postwar International System," *International Security* 10 (Spring 1986): 99–142.

profitable exchanges.[44] Whether this theory is right has been a subject of vigorous academic debate.[45]

Part of the challenge is that while it is plausible that increased trade makes countries less likely to fight one another, the reverse could also be true: peaceful relations create the conditions for greater interdependence through trade. So, although countries that trade more do fight less, figuring out how much of that relationship is due to trade causing peace—rather than peace causing trade—is difficult. On balance, though, most scholars consider growing commercial and financial interdependence since 1945 as a contributor to peaceful relations, particularly among the advanced industrial countries.[46]

Although recent decades have been relatively free of interstate war, disputes among nuclear-armed states, such as China, persist. The high expected costs of nuclear war have contributed to peace among these states, since the threat of "mutually assured destruction" makes them cautious to escalate conflicts.

Changing Institutions: Democracy and International Organizations

Finally, the decline in interstate conflict may be due to the growth of institutions that have helped states overcome information and commitment problems that can cause bargaining to fail. Two kinds of institutions could play a role in this regard: domestic and international.

On the domestic front, the major trend since World War II has been the expansion in the number of countries that have democratic political systems (see Figure 4.6 on p. 170). This development is striking when paired with the observation that there are few, if any, clear cases of war between democratic states. This means that the spread of democratic institutions might account for some of the overall decline in interstate war in the past six decades. Why democracy might have this effect is the subject of a larger discussion in the next chapter, but prominent explanations center on three factors that are relevant to the discussion here. First, democracy may make the leaders of states more sensitive to the costs of war. Second, democracy may make states more transparent to outsiders, thereby reducing uncertainty about their capabilities and resolve. Third, democratic states may bargain with one another differently than they do with other states, avoiding threats and emphasizing compromise.

The post-1945 world has also seen a dramatic expansion in the number and activity of international organizations (see Figure 14.1 on p. 587). This period witnessed the emergence and growing assertiveness of the United Nations, as well as the

---

44. For a good discussion of some of the intellectual origins of this view, see Michael W. Doyle, *Ways of War and Peace: Realism, Liberalism, and Socialism* (New York: Norton, 1997), chap. 7.

45. For a recent review, see Erik Gartzke and Jiakun Jack Zhang, "Trade and War," in *The Oxford Handbook of the Political Economy of International Trade*, ed. Lisa L. Martin (Oxford: Oxford University Press, 2015), www.oxfordhandbooks.com/view/10.1093/oxfordhb/9780199981755.001.0001/oxfordhb-9780199981755-e-27.

46. See, for example, Håvard Hegre, John R. Oneal, and Bruce Russett, "Trade Does Promote Peace: New Simultaneous Estimates of the Reciprocal Effects of Trade and Conflict," *Journal of Peace Research* 47 (November 2010): 763–74.

development of numerous regional organizations devoted to promoting peace and security.[47] A fuller examination of the role and track record of these organizations will come in Chapter 5, but we can anticipate some of the ways these institutions may have improved states' abilities to solve informational and commitment problems.

First, international organizations may enhance transparency by providing neutral observers of a state's military activities. The International Atomic Energy Agency (IAEA), for example, conducts inspections of members' nuclear energy programs in order to determine whether nuclear fuel has been diverted to produce weapons. Similarly, the United Nations often provides monitors to help observe whether parties to a conflict are fulfilling pledges to withdraw troops or disarm, thereby reducing uncertainty among adversaries about what the other side is up to.[48]

International organizations may also make it easier to resolve commitment problems. As discussed earlier, a promise not to use one's power to one's advantage is a very difficult commitment to make in a credible fashion, largely because states cannot generally rely on repeated interaction to hold one another to such a promise. Repeated interaction can help make promises credible if the prospect of future dealings leads a state to forgo the temptation to break a promise today because it fears retaliation by the other state tomorrow. Under conditions of shifting power, however, the state that is becoming more powerful has less to fear from the other side's retaliation. Furthermore, if a state can use its increased power to destroy the other state, then there may be no "shadow of the future" to stay the growing state's hand. The same holds in situations involving first-strike advantages: the temptation to deliver a crippling blow is hard to blunt if the other side's retaliatory capability will be rendered ineffective in the process.

Because adversaries generally cannot solve this commitment problem on their own, any solutions are most likely to come from third parties—that is, a state or group of states, including international organizations, that are not directly involved in the bargaining game between the opponents. In some cases, such outsiders may be able to help build credibility for the opposing states' commitments not to exploit power or first-strike advantages. Third parties can play this role by monitoring and enforcing agreements, by providing security guarantees to one or both sides, and sometimes by interposing their forces directly between two potential combatants—all roles that the United Nations performs, as we will see in Chapter 5.

In sum, changes in interests, interactions, and institutions since 1945 have contributed to conditions that make peace more likely in international disputes. It is too strong to declare war obsolete or a thing of the past. But even incremental reductions in the risk of war are reason for optimism and opportunities for greater understanding of this phenomenon.

---

47. Goldstein, *Winning the War on War*.

48. See, for example, Virginia Page Fortna, *Peace Time: Cease-Fire Agreements and the Durability of Peace* (Princeton, NJ: Princeton University Press, 2004).

Conclusion: Why War?

We started this chapter with a puzzle: Why do states fight wars in spite of the enormous costs associated with fighting? The answer involves two ingredients: a conflict in states' interests, and some factor or factors that prevent states from reaching a peaceful solution to that conflict. States' underlying interests in power, security, wealth, and/or national identities can give rise to disputes over territories, policies, and the composition of one another's governments. In the absence of authoritative institutions that resolve interstate disputes, states engage in a bargaining interaction over these issues, sometimes invoking the threat of military force to enhance their leverage. War occurs when features of this strategic interaction prevent states from reaching a settlement that both prefer over war, with all its uncertainties and costs.

Three kinds of problems can prevent states from settling their disputes in ways that enable them to avoid the costs of war: incomplete information, difficulty in committing to honor a deal, and goods that are hard to divide. Since these obstacles occur in different degrees and in different combinations from one crisis to the next, there is no single answer to the puzzle at the heart of this chapter. Instead, the discussion has sought to identify and explore a set of mechanisms that can stymie the effort to resolve disputes peacefully. Having done so, we are in a better position to understand and interpret behavior and outcomes in international crises. The concepts introduced here highlight some of the key factors that determine whether a dispute can be settled without resorting to war.

In particular, we need to pay attention to (1) what the adversaries in a dispute believe about one another's willingness and ability to wage war and how uncertain those beliefs are; (2) how each side seeks to communicate its resolve, whether those efforts are credible, and to what extent they either entail a danger of accidental war or "lock in" incompatible bargaining positions; (3) whether the good in the dispute is a source of future bargaining power; (4) whether the distribution of power between the adversaries is expected to change as a result of different economic growth rates or technological progress; (5) whether the military technologies and strategies of the adversaries generate sizable first-strike advantages; and (6) whether the good in question is indivisible because of its close connection to core values, such as religious identity.

In spite of the many things that can go wrong and prevent a peaceful solution, it is important to remember this point: Wars are rare and appear to have become rarer over time. Even though information is often incomplete, credible commitments are difficult to make, and core values are hard to compromise, most states most of the time are at peace with one another. The costs of war mean that not every disagreement is worth fighting over or even threatening to fight over. Hence, the very costs that make war hell also ensure that war is not the most common way that states settle their disputes.

Study Tool Kit

Interests, Interactions, and Institutions in Context

- States may have conflicting interests over goods like territory, policies, or the composition of one another's governments. However, because war is costly, a peaceful settlement that all sides would prefer over war generally exists. War occurs when the bargaining interaction fails to reach such a deal.

- In the bargaining interaction, states may be unable to reach negotiated settlements when they are uncertain about one another's willingness and ability to wage war.

- Even if states can find a mutually acceptable bargain, peace can break down if they cannot credibly commit to abide by the terms of the agreement.

- Bargaining may also fail if the disputed good is hard to divide, which makes compromise agreements impossible to reach.

- The apparent decline in interstate war since 1945 coincides with a decrease in states' interest in territorial conquest, an increase in the costs of war due to nuclear weapons and economic interdependence that leads to a change in interactions between states, and the spread of domestic and international institutions that help resolve information and commitment problems.

Key Terms

war, p. 91

interstate war, p. 91

civil war, p. 91

security dilemma, p. 92

crisis bargaining, p. 97

coercive diplomacy, p. 97

bargaining range, p. 99

compellence, p. 102

deterrence, p. 103

incomplete information, p. 107

resolve, p. 107

risk-return trade-off, p. 108

credibility, p. 109

brinksmanship, p. 113

audience costs, p. 115

preventive war, p. 122

first-strike advantage, p. 122

preemptive war, p. 125

indivisible good, p. 127

For Further Reading

Blainey, Geoffrey. *The Causes of War.* **3rd ed. New York: Free Press, 1988.** Presents a historical examination of war informed by bargaining theory.

Fazal, Tanisha M. *State Death: The Politics and Geography of Conquest, Occupation, and Annexatio***n. Princeton: Princeton University Press, 2011.** Examines how changing norms of territorial conquest affect the survival of states.

Fearon, James D. "Rationalist Explanations for War." *International Organization* **49 (Summer 1995): 379–414.** Serves as the seminal statement of the theory of war developed in this chapter.

Goddard, Stacie E. *Indivisible Territory and the Politics of Legitimacy: Jerusalem and Northern Ireland.* **Cambridge: Cambridge University Press, 2009.** Argues that territories can become indivisible because of the way states try to legitimize their claims.

McManus, Roseanne W. *Statements of Resolve: Achieving Coercive Credibility in International Conflict.* **Cambridge: Cambridge University Press, 2017.** Examines the conditions under which leaders can convey resolve through public threats and statements.

Pinker, Steven. *The Better Angels of Our Nature: Why Violence Has Declined.* **New York: Viking, 2011.** Offers a sociologist's perspective on why interstate war has declined along with other forms of violence.

Reiter, Dan. "Exploring the Bargaining Model of War." *Perspectives on Politics* **1 (2003): 27–43.** Evaluates the argument that war is a product, as well as a continuation, of interstate bargaining.

Schelling, Thomas C. *Arms and Influence.* **New Haven, CT: Yale University Press, 1966.** Serves as an accessible introduction to the strategic problems that arise in coercive interactions, including problems of credibility and commitment.

Van Evera, Stephen. *Causes of War.* **Ithaca, NY: Cornell University Press, 2001.** Explores how power shifts and first-strike advantages contributed to major wars throughout history.

Weisiger, Alex. *Logics of War: Explanations for Limited and Unlimited Conflicts.* **Ithaca, NY: Cornell University Press, 2013.** Uses insights from the bargaining model of war to understand why some wars last much longer than others.

4

Domestic Politics and War

THE PUZZLE *War is costly for states, but what if there are actors within the state—such as politicians, businesses, or the military—who see war as beneficial and who expect to pay few or none of its costs? Do states fight wars to satisfy influential domestic interests?*

Above: In democratic systems, voters can influence foreign policy by removing (or threatening to remove) leaders who make unpopular decisions. In 2014, thousands of protesters in London let their government know how they felt about renewing military engagement in Iraq.

On March 30, 1982, thousands of demonstrators marched in the streets of Buenos Aires, the capital of Argentina, denouncing the country's military government for its harsh economic policies and oppressive rule. Riot police used tear gas, rubber bullets, and water cannons to break up the protests, and over 2,000 people were arrested. A week later, the streets of Buenos Aires filled with demonstrators once more, but this time the demonstrations voiced enthusiastic support for the military regime, as many of those who had earlier called for the government's ouster now joined in the outpouring of praise. What changed in the course of a week? On April 2, Argentine naval forces invaded a small group of islands 300 miles off the Argentine coast that were the subject of a long-standing dispute between Argentina and Britain. Is there any connection between these events? Did the Argentine government provoke a war with Britain in order to revive its popularity with its people?

In 1954, representatives of the United Fruit Company went to Washington, D.C., to voice concerns about the leader of Guatemala, a man named Jacobo Arbenz. Arbenz had pushed a land reform program that led to the seizure of almost 400,000 acres belonging to the American company. Arbenz offered to compensate United Fruit to the tune of $1.2 million, the value of the land that the company claimed for tax purposes. The U.S. government insisted on behalf of United Fruit that the company be paid almost $16 million. In June of that year, rebels armed and trained by the U.S. Central Intelligence Agency (CIA) invaded Guatemala. Fearing a full-scale American invasion, parts of the Guatemalan military revolted, Arbenz resigned from office and fled the country, and a pro-American leader was installed. The operation cost the CIA just under $3 million.[1] Did the United States overthrow a foreign leader to benefit a single company at the expense of American taxpayers?

Our first look at the puzzle of war in Chapter 3 considered this problem from the perspective of states. We assumed two states in conflict over a particular good, such as a piece of territory, and trying to arrive at a settlement that would avoid the costs of war. This kind of analysis is very common in international relations scholarship, where

---

1. U.S. Central Intelligence Agency, "CIA's Role in the Overthrow of Arbenz," Job 79-01025A, Box 153, Folder 3, www.state.gov/r/pa/ ho/frus/ike/guat/20181.htm (accessed 11/07/07).

it is often referred to as the *unitary state assumption*: the treatment of states as coherent actors with a set of interests that belong to the state. While this assumption can be a useful starting place for analysis, we must remember that states are legal and political constructs, not beings capable of taking actions. The choices and actions of states are made by people. Decisions about waging war are made by a state's political leaders. Military plans are drawn up by military officials and carried out by soldiers.

Others within the country may also be able to influence foreign policy choices, even if they have no direct say over them. There may be interest groups such as business or ethnic lobbies that influence decision making through their organizational and financial resources. In democratic systems, voters influence policy decisions because of their ability to remove leaders who make unpopular choices. Looking inside the state reveals new actors with varied interests, as well as variation across states in the political institutions that determine who affects decision making.

How does our understanding of the causes of war change when we look inside the state and consider the interests, interactions, and institutions within it? In Chapter 3, we argued that to understand why wars happen, we need to understand why states at times cannot solve their conflicts peacefully, in a way that avoids the costs associated with fighting. This argument rested on the assumption that war is costly to those engaged in the interaction. These costs create a bargaining range, or a set of deals that both states prefer over fighting. The assumption that war is costly makes sense when we think of the state as a unitary actor, but once we look inside the state, it is clear that the costs and benefits of war are not distributed equally within the country.

Different actors within the state may place more or less value on the issue in dispute. A disputed territory might represent a source of livelihood, profit, or national pride to some, a tract of worthless land to others. The persecution of a minority group in a foreign country might arouse outrage in some, perhaps owing to ethnic attachment to the victims, while others greet it with indifference. Most Americans in 1954 had little or no stake in the land reform policies of the Guatemalan government; to the United Fruit Company, however, millions of dollars' worth of land were at risk.

The costs of war are also distributed unevenly. Some people, such as those who might be drafted to serve in the military, can expect to pay very high and direct costs from war. Others may see the costs of war in economic terms, if the need to finance the conflict leads to higher taxes. In contrast, there are some groups within a country that may profit from war financially or professionally: arms manufacturers benefit from increased purchases of their products; for military officers, combat experience leads to opportunities for medals and promotions; and for unpopular governments, such as the Argentine junta in 1982, war can build support domestically and solidify their hold on power.

These observations raise a number of questions: To what extent is war rooted not in the information and commitment problems discussed in Chapter 3, but rather in the interests of domestic actors who see personal benefit and little or no cost to war? Do wars serve the national interest or the narrow interests of office-hungry politicians, multinational companies, and/or a "military-industrial complex" composed of glory-seeking militaries and profit-seeking arms merchants? How do domestic institutions, such as democracy, influence a government's decisions and the likelihood of war between states?

Thinking Analytically about Domestic Politics and War

To answer the questions posed here, we must consider the different interests that domestic actors have in terms of war and peace. Simply identifying these interests is not enough, however, since not all actors within the state have equal say over foreign policy choices and hence not all interests are represented equally. Which domestic interests drive foreign policy choices depends on two factors: the strategic interactions between actors, which determine which individuals and groups can exert effective influence and which cannot; and the institutions within the state, which determine how different actors have access to the decision-making process. Further, we have to recall that war is not the choice of a single state, but rather an outcome of the interaction between or among multiple states. Hence, as we consider domestic influences on foreign policy, we need to examine how these factors shape bargaining at the international level.

Whose Interests Count in Matters of War and Peace?

In the previous chapter, we observed that international disputes generally arise over territory, policies, and the characteristics of countries' domestic regimes. Why these conflicts of interest arise in the first place is a complicated question with no single answer. One view, referred to in this book's Introduction as realism, is that states' interests are largely, if not entirely, dictated by external factors. States want to preserve their sovereignty and territorial integrity. To do so, they need power—primarily, military power. Hence, they seek opportunities to expand their own power and/or to diminish the power of those that threaten them. In this view, states' interests are fixed, determined largely by their material resources and geographic position, and they are not shaped by domestic factors.

Although this argument is sometimes useful in understanding sources of conflict in the world, it is also overly simplistic. The interactions among states at the international level can be fundamentally affected by interactions among actors at the domestic level.[2] Look inside any country, and there are a large number of individuals and groups motivated by a variety of different interests: workers who want a job and secure income, companies that want to increase their profits, organizations that want to further a cause they care about or extend the reach of their ideology or religion, and politicians who want to wield political power for personal or ideological ends. The interaction of these interests within the context of domestic political institutions can fundamentally affect the interests that the national government pursues and the choices it makes when dealing with other countries.

National versus Particularistic Interests

In considering the kinds of domestic interests that can influence foreign policy, it is useful to distinguish between general interests and narrow or particularistic interests. A general interest is something that most, if not all, actors within the country share. For example, virtually everyone has an interest in the country's physical security and economic well-being. If most people within the state share a common religious or ethnic identity, then the state's foreign policy interests likely reflect those identities. It makes sense to refer to such interests as national interests, or interests that are so widely shared that they can be attributed to the state as a whole. Narrow or particularistic interests are those held by only a relatively small number of actors within the country, such as a particular business, an ethnic minority group, or individuals within government.

To make this distinction concrete, consider the case of oil. The United States has long professed, and acted on, an interest in ensuring a steady supply of oil,

---

2. Robert D. Putnam, "Diplomacy and Domestic Politics: The Logic of Two-Level Games," *International Organization* 42 (1988): 427–60.

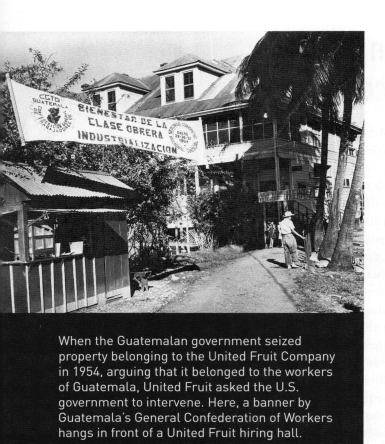

When the Guatemalan government seized property belonging to the United Fruit Company in 1954, arguing that it belonged to the workers of Guatemala, United Fruit asked the U.S. government to intervene. Here, a banner by Guatemala's General Confederation of Workers hangs in front of a United Fruit hiring hall.

particularly from the oil-rich countries in the Middle East. In 1943, President Franklin Roosevelt declared that the defense of Saudi Arabia was vital to the defense of the United States, and an American company, the Arabian-American Oil Company (Aramco), became the main player in developing and exploiting the oil fields there. The commitment to defend Saudi Arabia was reinforced on a number of occasions. In 1979, the Soviet Union invaded Afghanistan, putting Soviet forces on the doorstep of the Middle East and American allies in the Persian Gulf. President Jimmy Carter responded by articulating what became known as the Carter Doctrine: "Any attempt by an outside force to gain control of the Persian Gulf region will be regarded as an assault on the vital interests of the United States of America, and such an assault will be repelled by any means necessary, including military force." And the need to preserve stability and American influence in this region was cited to justify both the 1991 Persian Gulf War and the 2003 Iraq War.[3]

Why has the United States had such a consistent interest in oil and the Middle East? A national interest–based argument hinges on the observation that oil is vital to U.S. power because a modern military of tanks and airplanes consumes large quantities of fuel. It is no coincidence that Roosevelt's concern for Saudi Arabia arose during World War II, at a time when American war planners were worried about running out of gas. The Cold War that followed did nothing to alleviate concerns about maintaining access to this strategically valuable material that was crucial to the economic and military might of the United States and its allies. In this view, the U.S. interest in oil stems from a national interest in ensuring its military power and security.

An alternative argument, also based on general interests, revolves around the U.S. economy's dependence on stable and plentiful oil supplies. The U.S. economy runs on oil—to fuel cars, to transport goods around the country, to heat homes and power businesses. Shocks to the price of oil can thus have substantial effects on the economic welfare of U.S. citizens, influencing inflation, unemployment, and disposable income. As Figure 4.1 shows, the price of oil over time has been highly sensitive to events in the Middle East, with major spikes occurring during times of war and revolution. Such dramatic price increases can affect people in a variety of ways, sparking inflation and unemployment and eating into consumers' pocketbooks.

---

3. For a comprehensive history of the role of oil in international politics, see Daniel Yergin, *The Prize: The Epic Quest for Oil, Money, and Power* (New York: Free Press, 1991).

FIGURE 4.1 **The Price of Oil, 1960–2018**

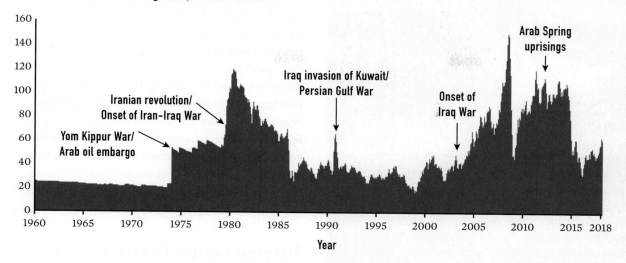

Figure source: Federal Reserve Bank of St. Louis, Spot Crude Oil Price: West Texas Intermediate (WTI) [WTISPLC], retrieved from FRED, Federal Reserve Bank of St. Louis; https://fred.stlouisfed.org/series/WTISPLC, March 19, 2018.

* In 2017 U.S. dollars.

Hence, American citizens have a general interest in ensuring stability in the Middle East in order to prevent oil price shocks that would hurt the economy.

Set against these views of the United States' national interest is one that sees the pursuit of oil as benefiting a small group of businesses: oil companies. After World War II, U.S. companies like Aramco played a direct role in pumping and selling Middle Eastern oil, making huge profits. Since the 1960s and 1970s, producer countries have generally nationalized their oil industries, meaning that oil companies have to negotiate deals with these governments. U.S. firms like ExxonMobil profit from their participation in the exploration, drilling, refining, and marketing of oil, but their access to these activities depends on the willingness of foreign governments to do business with them. It is possible, then, that U.S. foreign policy toward the Middle East is driven by these companies' desire to expand and protect their profits.

In this view, firms use their influence over policy makers to ensure that the United States defends friendly regimes (like that of Saudi Arabia) and undermines hostile regimes (like that of Iraq under Saddam Hussein) that are bad for business. Because these policies can impose costs on American soldiers and taxpayers, this view sees U.S. foreign policy in the Middle East as benefiting a narrow set of interests within the country at the expense of everyone else.

As this discussion suggests, the distinction between national and particularistic interests is easy to make in the abstract but harder to observe in practice. While oil clearly influences U.S. policy in the Middle East, it is difficult to say with confidence whether the general or narrow interests are more important. Nonetheless, the distinction is crucial for thinking about what causes war. Recall from Chapter 2 that an actor is a group of individuals with similar interests. To the extent that groups or individuals within the state have different interests over the outcomes of international bargaining, the analytical utility of assuming that the state is an actor diminishes—and we have to start looking within the state for new actors.

In 1973 and 1979, conflicts in the Middle East led to gasoline shortages in the United States, and some stations ran out of gas entirely. The dependence of the U.S. economy on gasoline means that American consumers have an economic interest in the stability of the oil-rich Middle East.

This quest is important because the analysis of war presented in Chapter 3 assumed that war is a costly outcome for the actors engaged in international bargaining. These costs ensure the existence of deals that all sides prefer over war, and they underpin an understanding of war that focuses on the information, commitment, and divisibility problems that can prevent such deals from being reached. If, however, the benefits of war are enjoyed by a different set of actors from those that pay the costs, then this view may need to be revised. Does war arise not because of obstacles to the bargaining interaction, but because war furthers the interests of particular actors within the country?

Interactions, Institutions, and Influence

When we drop the unitary actor assumption and look within states, an enormous number of individuals and groups, with a variety of interests, come into focus. Which actors matter, and which interests are likely to influence foreign policy decisions? The answer lies in institutions and interactions. Recall from Chapter 2 that institutions are sets of rules and decision-making procedures.

Within each country, domestic institutions help determine who runs the government, how decisions are made, and how disputes are resolved. In a monarchy, for example, the ruler is determined through a system of succession often based on birth order. In other systems, the leader is the person who commands the greatest support within the military and therefore can repress challengers with force. In democratic political systems, leaders are selected through regular elections in which winners are decided by the amount of popular support they can muster. Domestic institutions also determine how much power an individual leader has to make decisions. In some political systems, rulers can dictate the state's policies on their own or with the support of a relatively small number of key actors. In other systems, the institutions of government may distribute decision-making power among more than one body, such as a president and a legislature.

By shaping how leaders obtain power and make decisions, domestic institutions determine which actors' interests are taken into account. Leaders whose hold on power is unchallenged may not have to consider the interests of anyone else, and they can act on the basis of their personal interests or whims. More commonly, a ruler may only have to worry about maintaining the loyalty of the military by catering to that organization's interests.

In democratic political institutions, by contrast, the need to win elections forces leaders to think about how the voting public will respond to their policy choices. It also makes them dependent on organized groups that are willing to donate money and time to election campaigns. Although voters and organized interest groups are not literally in the room when decisions are made, democratic institutions force those who *are* in the room to take those actors' interests into account. Thus, institutions determine which actors and interests have a (figurative) seat at the table.

Some domestic actors may also have strategic advantages that magnify their influence. In Chapter 2 we introduced a strategic dilemma known as the collective action problem. This problem arises when a group of individuals with common interests seeks to act collectively to further that interest. As we saw, such efforts can fall short if each individual prefers to free ride on the efforts of others. One implication of this insight is that relatively small groups can be more effective at cooperating to further common interests than large groups are. Indeed, small groups of highly motivated and informed individuals are better able to organize and coordinate their activities and prevent others from free riding. By contrast, large, dispersed groups in which each individual has only a small stake in or knowledge about the policy decision are generally very hard to organize. For example, whereas United Fruit stood to lose millions of dollars of property in Guatemala, the intervention cost each U.S. taxpayer only a few pennies. Had taxpayers been opposed to having their money spent this way, they would have had a hard time cooperating, since no individual had any incentive to spend time and money on such an effort. To the extent that a group's political influence depends on the ability of its members to cooperate, this strategic problem favors the few over the many. Thus, a relatively narrow interest group can successfully demand a policy that benefits that group at the expense of everyone else.

Appreciating the role of institutions and interactions, we can organize a discussion of domestic interests around four different kinds of actors, depicted in Figure 4.2.

FIGURE 4.2 *Key Domestic Actors in Foreign Policy*

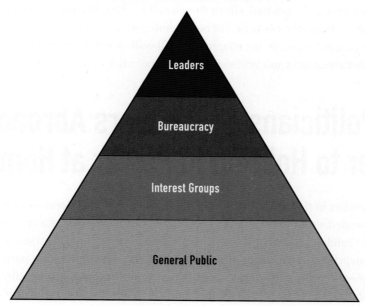

The first type consists of the leaders who make foreign policy decisions. State leaders decide when to make threats, what demands to issue, and ultimately, whether to wage war. These individuals matter the most because, by whatever rules of politics operate in their country, they have the authority to make these decisions. The next type comprises organized groups that have sufficient resources and information to influence the decisions made by the political leaders. Two such groups are of particular relevance: bureaucratic actors and interest groups.

The state apparatus is made up of a variety of different organizations collectively known as the **bureaucracy**. These organizations—which include the military, diplomatic corps, and intelligence agencies—may wield considerable influence because of their institutional resources and knowledge. The military in particular, by virtue of its coercive power, organizational discipline, and expertise in war fighting, can shape decisions about the use of force both through its role in implementation and through its influence over political leaders.

Interest groups are groups of individuals with common interests that organize in order to push for policies that benefit their members. Of particular importance in the present context are economic interest groups, such as companies or groups of companies, and ethnic lobbies comprising people with similar policy interests owing to their common ethnic background. In later chapters, when we turn to issues like human rights (Chapter 12) and the environment (Chapter 13), interest groups that organize around other principles will come to the fore.

The final type of actor to consider is the most numerous but rarely the most powerful: the general public. As already suggested, the influence of ordinary citizens varies considerably with domestic institutions. In democratic countries, free and fair elections provide individuals with a low-cost way to participate in deciding who governs. In other kinds of countries, it is harder for individual citizens to have much influence, since political leaders do not depend on their support. As long as the regime can count on the repressive power of the police and military, general-public interests can be ignored. Given this situation, the question of how the general public matters is largely a question of how democracy matters.

As we proceed through this chapter, we will walk down the pyramid in Figure 4.2 and consider arguments and evidence about the behavior of actors at each level.

bureaucracy

The collection of organizations—including the military, diplomatic corps, and intelligence agencies—that carry out most tasks of governance within the state.

interest groups

Groups of individuals with common interests that organize to influence public policy in a manner that benefits their members.

Do Politicians Spark Wars Abroad in Order to Hold On to Power at Home?

As noted earlier in this chapter, Argentina sparked a war with Great Britain in 1982 when it invaded a set of nearby islands that had been in dispute for a century and a half: the "Falkland Islands" to the British, the "Malvinas" to Argentines. This war was surprising in a number of respects. First, the islands were not particularly valuable pieces of territory. At the time of the war, the islands had a population of less than 2,000, and their primary source of income was sheep farming. Indeed, just prior to the war, Britain had taken steps to weaken its hold over the islands. In 1981, Britain readied plans to withdraw the last of its naval vessels in the region and passed an act that stripped the islanders of full British citizenship.

Second, the war was surprising because of the imbalance in military power between the two states. Though separated from the islands by a larger distance, Britain had a far superior naval force. After Argentina invaded and occupied the Falklands on April 2, 1982, it took only 74 days for British forces to retake the islands. There were 255 dead on the British side, 635 on the Argentine side. So why did Argentina pick a fight with such a formidable foe, and why did Britain react so strongly to defend its right to islands that seemed to be of diminishing importance?

A large part of the answer to this puzzle lies not in international considerations, but in the domestic political interests of the countries' governments. At the time, leaders in both countries had pressing domestic problems to which military conflict may have seemed the perfect solution. The Argentine government—a group of military officers known as a junta—had seized power in 1976, and its rule had become increasingly repressive and unpopular over time. In the early 1980s, Argentina suffered a severe economic downturn, which led to civil unrest and splits within the ruling group. Facing a dire threat to its rule, the junta leader, General Leopoldo Galtieri, decided that an attack on the Malvinas might help solve its problem.

Knowing that most Argentines resented British control of the islands, Galtieri hoped that a bold move to seize the islands would stir up nationalist sentiment, distract people from their economic hardships, and give the military government a popular achievement that would bolster its prestige and legitimacy. Indeed, the invasion of the Malvinas had precisely this effect. Hence, Galtieri was seeking more than just territory when he seized the islands; he was also looking to solidify his hold on power.[4]

On the British side, Prime Minister Margaret Thatcher also had to worry about her political survival. Like Argentina, Britain in 1982 was in the midst of a severe recession. With unemployment soaring, Thatcher's popularity dropped precipitously. In February 1982, the month before the invasion, only 29 percent of Britons said that they approved of the job she was doing. Thatcher's firm response to the Falkland Islands crisis caused her poll numbers to soar. By May, with British operations to retake the Falklands under way, Thatcher's approval rating jumped to 44 percent. By the end of the war, her approval stood at 51 percent. The British prime minister rode this wave of popularity to electoral victory a year later. Hence, Thatcher's unexpectedly strong response to the Argentine invasion not only restored British control over the Falklands, but also revived her political fortunes.[5]

---

4. Jack Levy and Lily Vakily, "External Scapegoating in Authoritarian Regimes: Argentina in the Falklands/Malvinas Case," in *The Internationalization of Communal Strife*, ed. Manus Midlarski, 118–46 (London: Routledge, 1992).

5. Approval figures are from David Butler and Gareth Butler, eds., *British Political Fact 1900–1994*, 7th ed. (London: Macmillan, 1994), 256. There is some controversy over how much the Falklands War contributed to the Conservative victory in 1983. See Harold D. Clarke, William Mishler, and Paul Whiteley, "Recapturing the Falklands: Models of Conservative Popularity, 1979–83," *British Journal of Political Science* 20, no 1. (January 1990): 63–81.

British prime minister Margaret Thatcher, here visiting troops in the Falkland Islands, benefited politically from the Falklands War. Before the war, poor economic conditions in Britain had helped bring Thatcher's public approval rating down to just 29 percent. Once the war began, the British public rallied behind their leader, sending her approval rating up to 51 percent.

What Do Leaders Want?

The leaders of states are not solely, if at all, statesmen or stateswomen looking out for the best interests of the nation; they are also individuals with many varied interests of their own. Some may have very strong ideological beliefs that increase their willingness to pay costs or run risks in foreign policy. It is hard to understand World War II, for example, without reference to German leader Adolf Hitler's extreme ideology, which motivated him to seek out *Lebensraum* ("living space") for the German people by attacking Poland and then the Soviet Union.[6] Even in the absence of such extreme motivations, different leaders may come into office with different ideas or prior life experiences that shape how they think about foreign policy, including the desirability of using military force (see "How Do We Know?" on p. 149).[7]

State leaders may also have more prosaic personal motivations. As the story of the Falklands War reminds us, leaders are also politicians, people who benefit from holding political office. Being in office confers all manner of benefits: the ego boost of having power, opportunities to enrich oneself and one's friends, the ability to shape policy in desired ways. As a result, politicians think a lot about how to obtain office and, once in power, how to secure their hold on it. This means that political leaders make choices with an eye toward how those choices will influence their chances of staying in power.

How could these motivations affect leaders' decisions about war and peace? At the most general level, the desire to stay in power means that leaders have to be responsive to the interests of those who control their political fate, whether voters, organized interest groups, the military, or other groups. As a result, the assumption that political leaders want to remain in office plays a key role in almost every aspect of this chapter, since it helps account for the influence of special interest groups that can provide resources useful for maintaining power; it contributes to an understanding of the role of the military, whose support is often necessary for a government to stay in power; and it is a necessary element in arguments about the effects of accountability in democratic political systems. In short, leaders' desire to hold office explains how the interests of actors within the country can matter at the level of policy making.

6. There is a debate among historians about how much of Hitler's foreign policy is explained by his personal ideology. For a balanced view, which ultimately concludes that ideology played an important role, see Allan Bullock, "Hitler and the Origins of the Second World War," in *The Origins of the Second World War: A. J. P. Taylor and His Critics*, ed. William Roger Louis, 117–45 (New York: Wiley, 1972).

7. See, for example, Elizabeth N. Saunders, *Leaders at War* (Ithaca, NY: Cornell University Press, 2011); and Michael C. Horowitz, Allan C. Stam, and Cali M. Ellis, *Why Leaders Fight* (New York: Cambridge University Press, 2015).

Are Women Leaders More Peaceful than Men?

A remarkable global trend in recent decades has been the increasing number of countries led by women. While history provides examples of queens and empresses, female heads of state have been rare in the modern era, with the numbers taking off only since the 1980s (see Figure A). The figures are still low in absolute terms—in 2018, only 13 of the 193 countries in the world had a woman chief executive—but the recent growth is part of a broader trend that has also seen increased representation of women in legislatures and militaries. What impact does the gender of the leader have on a state's foreign policy?

A wealth of research on the general population shows that, on average, women are less aggressive than men and more likely to seek compromise solutions to disputes. Survey data show that women are less likely than men, particularly in Western countries, to support the use of military force. Evidence also suggests that states with more gender equality domestically, including more women in the legislature, use less violence in international crises and spend less on their militaries.[a]

So, does having a female leader make a state less likely to wage war? To answer this question, Michael Horowitz, Allan Stam, and Cali Ellis collected information on all heads of state from 1875 to 2004. They then examined whether leaders' propensity to threaten or use military force against other states depends on a variety of personal characteristics. The authors found that, on average, gender has little effect on dispute behavior, and if anything, women are more conflict-prone than men. While 30 percent of male leaders initiated at least one militarized conflict during their tenure, 36 percent of female leaders did.[b] This finding replicates earlier work, focused on democratic countries, indicating that female presidents and prime ministers engage in more conflictual behavior internationally than men do.[c]

What might explain this result? One explanation is that, even if there are differences across men and women in the general population, those differences do not hold among the subset of individuals who become heads of state. The process of leader selection may penalize women who are seen as insufficiently "tough." Particularly when voters are concerned about foreign threats, women candidates face a disadvantage, forcing them to compensate by acting in a manner that runs counter to the gender stereotype.[d]

A second explanation hinges on the beliefs and behavior of other states when confronting a female leader. Military conflict is the outcome of a strategic interaction between at least two states, not the choice of a single individual. If adversaries expect female leaders to be more dovish, then they will make greater demands on them, thus increasing the risk of conflict. Women may also need to use greater levels of force to persuade opponents of their resolve.[e]

Overall, then, while the literature suggests that increasing gender equality has a number of beneficial effects, the rising prevalence of female heads of state does not necessarily portend a more peaceful world.

---

a. For a review of findings on gender effects on international relations, see Dan Reiter, "The Positivist Study of Gender and International Relations," *Journal of Conflict Resolution* 59 (2015): 1301–26.

b. Michael C. Horowitz, Allan C. Stam, and Cali M. Ellis, *Why Leaders Fight* (New York: Cambridge University Press, 2015), 158–77.

c. Michael T. Koch and Sarah A. Fulton, "In the Defense of Women: Gender, Office Holding, and National Security Policy in Established Democracies," *Journal of Politics* 73 (2001): 1–16; see also Mary Caprioli and Mark A. Boyer, "Gender, Violence, and International Crisis," *Journal of Conflict Resolution* 45 (2001): 503–18.

d. See, for example, Jennifer L. Lawless, "Women, War, and Winning Elections: Gender Stereotyping in the Post-September 11th Era," *Political Research Quarterly* 57 (2004): 479–90.

e. Caprioli and Boyer, "Gender, Violence, and International Crisis," 508.

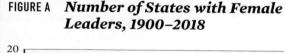

FIGURE A ***Number of States with Female Leaders, 1900–2018***

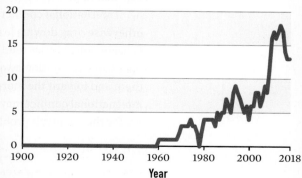

Year

Source: Archigos: A Database of Political Leaders, version 4.1; Henk E. Goemans, Kristian Skrede Gleditsch, and Giacomo Chiozza, "Introducing *Archigos*: A Data Set of Political Leaders," *Journal of Peace Research* 49 (2009): 269–83. Updated to 2018 by Curtis Bell, *The Rulers, Elections, and Irregular Governance Dataset (REIGN)* (Broomfield, CO: OEF Research, 2018). Available at oefresearch.org.

But an interest in holding on to power does not turn political leaders into mere instruments of other actors. Strategic politicians can use their control of policy to shape their political environment, rather than just respond to it. In the case of war and peace, a common argument is that leaders sometimes use force abroad not to further any national interest, but rather to enhance their hold on power at home.

The Rally Effect and the Diversionary Incentive

The idea that leaders can further their own political interests by fighting a war flows from the rally-'round-the-flag effect, or rally effect for short. The term **rally effect** refers to people's tendency to become more supportive of their country's government when it experiences dramatic international events, such as wars. This effect is most apparent in countries in which public opinion polling regularly measures the level of support for a leader.

Often, approval ratings jump up at the onset of a war or some other international crisis, as in the case of Thatcher's approval ratings at the outset of the Falklands War. The most dramatic rally event ever recorded followed the terrorist attacks of September 11, 2001, which caused President George W. Bush's approval rating to jump immediately from 51 to 86 percent, eventually reaching as high as 90 percent. Even in countries without opinion polls and approval ratings, we see cases in which the start of war caused an upsurge of national unity and support for the government. As we noted at the outset of this chapter, in 1982, Argentina's military government reversed a tide of public discontent by invading the Falkland Islands.

Why do people rally around the flag at times of international crisis? There are a number of explanations. Social psychologists have shown that members of a group often feel greater attachment and loyalty to the group when they experience conflict with outsiders.[8] Hence, international conflict can cause an upwelling of patriotism, and the leader derives increased support as the protector of the group's interests. At the same time, political opponents may decide to dampen their criticism of the government at a time of national crisis, and the government may use the emergency to crack down on dissent. This means that the government dominates the political discourse and can frame the public's evaluation of its policies without fear that opposing voices will split public opinion.[9]

International conflict can also create a diversion from problems that might otherwise drag down a leader's popularity, such as economic troubles or scandals. Foreign policy crises tend to drive other issues out of the news headlines, redirecting people's attention away from the domestic issues that divide and disappoint them and toward the more unifying challenge of meeting a foreign threat. Finally, international conflict may give embattled leaders an opportunity to blame foreigners for the country's problems—a phenomenon known as scapegoating.

8. See, for example, Lewis A. Coser, *The Functions of Social Conflict* (New York: Free Press, 1956). The pioneering work of the rally effect in the United States is John E. Mueller, *War, Presidents, and Public Opinion* (New York: Wiley, 1973).

9. Richard A. Brody and Catherine R. Shapiro, "A Reconsideration of the Rally Phenomenon in Public Opinion," in *Political Behavior Annual*, ed. S. Long, 77–102 (Boulder, CO: Westview Press, 1989).

rally effect

The tendency for people to become more supportive of their country's government in response to dramatic international events, such as crises or wars.

Just a few days before invading the Falkland Islands, the Argentine government faced massive protests and calls for the overthrow of the ruling junta. Rioters confronted police, and thousands were arrested. The war with Britain provided the Argentine junta a (temporary) reprieve from these problems by shifting the public's attention away from domestic issues.

The existence of rally effects suggests that political leaders may at times face a **diversionary incentive**: a temptation to spark an international crisis in order to rally public support at home. This idea was popularized in the 1997 movie *Wag the Dog*, in which a scandal-plagued national leader hires a movie director to produce news footage of a fake war in order to boost his approval ratings. The logic, however, long precedes Hollywood. In William Shakespeare's *Henry IV, Part II*, a dying King Henry advises his son, Prince Hal, that to prevent plots against him he needs to "busy giddy minds / With foreign quarrels." This advice echoes in the words of a Russian minister who, during a 1904 dispute with Japan, reportedly told the tsar, "What this country needs is a short, victorious war to stem the tide of revolution."[10] Whether the tsar found this argument persuasive or not, Russia and Japan declared war on each other on February 10, 1904.

The danger posed by the rally effect should be clear from the discussion in Chapter 3. There, it was assumed that a state's first-best outcome in a crisis is to get its way without having to fight. Fighting, after all, imposes costs that the state should prefer to avoid. A diversionary temptation could alter the balance of costs and benefits. If those who control the state's foreign policy think that using force abroad would greatly improve their chances of staying in power, then they may prefer war over a negotiated settlement, even one that gives them most of what they want.

diversionary incentive
The incentive that state leaders have to start international crises in order to rally public support at home.

---

10. This quotation is attributed to Russian interior minister Vladimir Plehve. However, the authenticity of the quotation is unclear, and it has been suggested that it was attributed to Plehve only later by his political enemies.

These benefits may be particularly tempting to leaders who are insecure domestically because of discontent with their policies or hard economic times. Such a leader may decide that doing nothing would mean losing office, so waging war and invoking the rally effect may be an appealing gamble. This phenomenon has been called gambling for resurrection: taking a risky action, such as starting a war, when the alternative is certain to be very bad.

A sports analogy is useful here. Hockey teams trailing in the final minutes of a game sometimes pull their goalie in order to replace him with an additional attacker. Doing so increases the chances that they can even the score, but it also makes it easier for the other team to score against their undefended net. The gamble makes sense because a loss is a loss regardless of whether a team loses by one goal or by many. Consequently, the downside risk of pulling the goalie is small compared to the upside potential of tying the game. Political leaders who are certain they will lose office because of poor economic conditions, such as the Argentine junta in 1982, might similarly see a large upside to starting a war and gambling that the outcome will be positive.

Do Leaders "Wag the Dog"?

Do leaders routinely gamble for resurrection by starting wars abroad at times of political need? Given the intuitive nature of this argument, it may come as a surprise to learn that scholars have found little consistent support for the hypothesis that leaders systematically resort to force when they are in trouble domestically. Numerous studies have sought to determine whether the likelihood that a state will get involved in military conflict increases when the leader is unpopular, the country is in a recession, or citizens face high unemployment or inflation, or, in the case of democratic countries, when a well-timed rally shortly before an election could be particularly useful. Although some studies have shown such effects, the results have been neither consistent nor particularly strong. Rather than a straightforward relationship between, say, economic problems and international conflict, effects tend to depend on a number of factors; that is, some kinds of governments may be sensitive to certain kinds of economic conditions at some times.[11]

In addition, some research suggests that the relationship between international conflict and leaders' political security is the opposite of what diversionary theory suggests: international conflict is more likely to be initiated by leaders whose hold on office is relatively strong.[12] For example, in democratic systems, leaders are more likely to start wars right *after* elections, not right before them as diversionary theory would suggest. A democratic leader is most secure just after an election, since the next election is, at that point, several years away.[13]

---

11. See, for example, Philip Arena and Glenn Palmer, "Politics or the Economy? Domestic Correlates of Dispute Involvement in Developed Democracies," *International Studies Quarterly* 53 (December 2009): 955–75; and Sara McLaughlin Mitchell and Brandon C. Prins, "Rivalry and Diversionary Uses of Force," *Journal of Conflict Resolution* 48 (December 2004): 937–61.

12. See Giacomo Chiozza and H. E. Goemans, "Peace through Insecurity: Tenure and International Conflict," *Journal of Conflict Resolution* 47 (August 2003): 443–67.

13. Kurt Taylor Gaubatz, "Election Cycles and War," *Journal of Conflict Resolution* 35, no. 2 (June 1991): 212–44.

This is not to say that diversionary incentives never play a role in particular cases; in fact, historians cite many examples in which such logic contributed to the onset of war. What these results do suggest, however, is that leaders do not *systematically* use international conflict for diversionary purposes or to gamble for resurrection. In other words, even if diversionary incentives have contributed to war in some cases, they account for only a portion of the conflict behavior we observe.

Why might this be the case? If sparking international conflict serves leaders' political interests, why do we not see stronger evidence of this effect? One possible answer is that most political leaders are not as cynical as we assume and they would not actually start a war simply to maintain their hold on power. Although we cannot rule out this possibility, there are other conceivable explanations for why even cynical leaders might not start a war to further their own political interests.

The first explanation is that the domestic political benefits of war relative to peace have to be large—perhaps unrealistically large—in order to eliminate the possibility of a peaceful bargain. Recall the simple bargaining framework we illustrated in the previous chapter, now depicted in Figure 4.3. As shown in the top panel, the size of the bargaining range is determined by the sum of the war costs to both sides. Now imagine that the leader of State A expects to reap political benefits from waging war. This benefit increases the value of war to the leader as indicated in the

---

FIGURE 4.3 *Rally Effects and the Bargaining Range*

The top panel shows the expected outcome of a war between State A and State B, as well as the resulting bargaining range. The lower panel shows how the bargaining range shrinks if the leader of State A expects political benefits, in the form of a rally, as a result of war. This benefit increases the value of war to A, offsetting some or all of its costs, but as long as the benefit does not exceed the costs of war to *both* states, a bargaining range still exists.

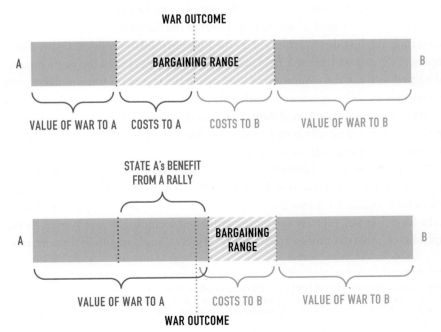

lower panel. This added benefit shrinks the bargaining range, but even if this benefit is greater than the costs to State A—so that the leader sees a net benefit rather than a net cost to war—a bargaining range could still exist, as shown.

The size of this new bargaining range is given by the sum of the net costs (the total costs to both states minus the additional political benefit). Only if this benefit exceeds the sum of the war costs to both states does the bargaining range vanish, making war inevitable. Hence, even if the leader of one state expected large political benefits from waging war, these benefits would be sufficient to cause war only if they outweighed the war costs to *both* sides. This condition becomes more likely if the leaders of both states expect political benefits from war, as was the case in the Falklands War. Notice also that the political benefits from war mean that State A can demand a better deal from State B than it otherwise could. Knowing this, potential targets might avoid picking fights with politically vulnerable leaders, thereby depriving them of the opportunity to use force opportunistically.[14] These observations remind us that war is the product of an interaction between at least two actors and not the choice of a single actor.

The Political Costs of War

A second reason why diversionary effects might be weak is that war can impose domestic political costs in addition to promising benefits. This is evident from the Falklands case as well. While Thatcher rode her postwar wave of support to a resounding electoral victory in Britain, the Argentine junta that lost the war met a very different fate. Following Argentina's defeat, angry protesters once again filled the streets. Galtieri and other members of the junta resigned or were stripped of their posts, and several went to prison.

The story of the Russo-Japanese War has a similar ending. Far from the short, victorious war the Russians hoped for, the war actually lasted almost two years, and the Russians suffered a humiliating defeat at the hands of the Japanese. Rather than stemming the tide of revolution, as the Russian minister reportedly predicted, successive defeats on the battlefield increased unhappiness with the tsar's regime and helped usher in the revolution of 1905, when the tsar was forced to make political concessions to his opponents. Full-scale revolution would hit Russia in 1917, in the midst of yet more battlefield defeats in World War I. Indeed, the initial surge of patriotism that generally accompanies the onset of war can quickly give way to discontent and rebellion if the war goes badly.

One way to see the relationship between the costs of war and its domestic political repercussions is to consider how public support for war changes as the costs mount. Figure 4.4 shows the relationship between public support and battle deaths for major U.S. military operations since and including World War II. As the graph shows, most operations started with very high levels of public support, but

---

14. See, for example, Benjamin O. Fordham, "Strategic Conflict Avoidance and the Diversionary Use of Force," *Journal of Politics* 67 (February 2005): 132–53; and Brett Ashley Leeds and David R. Davis, "Domestic Political Vulnerability and International Disputes," *Journal of Conflict Resolution* 41 (December 1997): 814–34.

FIGURE 4.4 *U.S. Battle Deaths and Public Support for War*

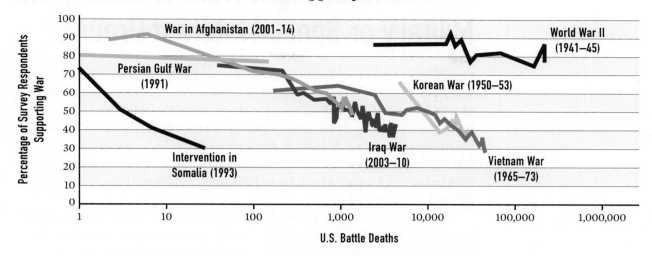

this support generally fell off as the number of U.S. battle deaths mounted. The only wars that remained popular throughout were World War II—a war of national survival that followed the Japanese attack on the U.S. homeland—and the Persian Gulf War, which caused relatively few deaths on the American side.

Moreover, in cases in which support for the war collapsed, the presidents' approval ratings also suffered. During the Korean War, President Truman saw his approval rating fall to as low as 22 percent, and he declined to run for reelection in 1952. The unpopularity of the Vietnam War similarly doomed the presidency of Lyndon Johnson, who dropped his bid for reelection in March 1968. The Iraq War dragged down President Bush's approval ratings, causing his Republican Party to lose control of Congress in 2006 and contributing to the election of Democrat Barack Obama in 2008. More generally, research has shown that leaders who fight losing or costly wars are more likely to be removed from office than those who win wars.[15]

The evidence suggests that in terms of their political interests, leaders should see war not as a pure opportunity, but as a gamble—and one that has a downside risk. Hence, in thinking about how reelection incentives influence the way leaders think about war and peace, we need to set the costs of losing a war against the potential benefits of the rally effect. These costs may explain why we do not see strong or systematic evidence that politically insecure politicians engage in diversionary conflict.

In light of this observation, it is worth recalling that the scandal-plagued leader in the movie *Wag the Dog* does not start an actual war; instead, he hires a movie producer to stage a fake war for public consumption. The attraction of doing this is clear: when you script the war yourself, you can make sure the right side wins. In the real world, war is a risky gamble—not just for the state, but also for the political interests of its leaders.

Figure sources: Numbers for World War II, Korea, Vietnam, the Gulf War, and Somalia come from Eric V. Larson, *Casualties and Consensus* (Santa Monica, CA: RAND, 1996). Other poll numbers come from Gallup, http://www.gallup.com/file/poll/183590/Mistake_Going_into_Iraq_and_Afghanistan_150612.pdf (accessed 11/22/17). Casualty figures for Iraq and Afghanistan are from www.icasualties.org (accessed 01/20/15).

---

15. See, for example, Hein Goemans, *War and Punishment* (Princeton, NJ: Princeton University Press, 2001).

Do Countries Fight Wars to Satisfy the Military or Special Interest Groups?

From 1898 to 1902, Great Britain engaged in a costly and divisive war with the Boer states in South Africa. The Boer War, which lasted three years and claimed about 50,000 lives, was a climactic episode of a larger process in which the European states carved up and colonized the continent of Africa, as described in Chapter 1. To the British economist J. A. Hobson, this scramble for colonies and the bloody wars that it gave rise to presented a puzzle. Why had Britain expended so many young lives and so much money to acquire and defend an empire in Africa, as well as in Asia and the Americas?

The answer that Hobson arrived at was unsettling. He calculated that although imperialism did not benefit the British nation as a whole, it was extremely profitable for a few small groups within the country. The primary beneficiaries, he argued, were rich people with the ability to invest overseas. With colonial possessions came many opportunities for profitable investments. Wealthy people could invest in railroads, mines, and other properties and receive very high rates of return. They could lend money to colonial governments at favorable interest rates. In pushing for colonial possessions, Hobson argued, financial interests found allies in powerful places: military leaders seeking glory and larger budgets, and arms manufacturers seeking profits. In his view, these groups used their power and influence to force British governments to pursue a policy that benefited them at the expense of the greater good.[16]

Hobson's theory of imperialism is not without critics, but the general thesis—that wars are fought to benefit military and business interests—is a familiar one. It echoes famously in the words of U.S. president Dwight Eisenhower, who warned of the influence of a **military-industrial complex**, an alliance of military leaders and arms manufacturers that presumably have an interest in an aggressive foreign policy.

In this section we consider the influence of the military and interest groups with respect to questions of war and peace. As we will see, there are times when these actors might be expected to have hawkish interests, because they anticipate benefits from war and/or pay few of the costs. These two sets of actors also have strategic advantages that they can exploit in their interaction with political leaders and others within the country. That said, we will see that the primary effect of hawkish actors is not to cause wars per se—by eliminating the bargaining range—but rather to expand the scope of the state's ambitions and to increase the conditions under which the state would consider fighting a war. Hence, hawkish domestic interests do not lead directly to the breakdown of bargaining, but they do create more opportunities for such failures to occur.

military-industrial complex

An alliance between military leaders and the industries that benefit from international conflict, such as arms manufacturers.

---

16. J. A. Hobson, *Imperialism: A Study* (London: James Nisbet, 1902).

Bureaucratic Politics and the Military

Although the ultimate decision to wage war may lie in the hands of a few individuals, the actual machinery of government that deals with matters of war and peace is much larger and more complex. The leader of a modern state sits atop a large bureaucratic apparatus: a collection of organizations that manage many of the details of governance. Wars are planned and implemented by the state's military—usually a massive organization with thousands and, in some cases, millions of individuals. Negotiations with other countries are conducted by a host of diplomats around the world, typically overseen by a ministry of foreign affairs (known in the United States as the State Department). Information about other countries' military capabilities and intentions are collected and analyzed by intelligence organizations, like the United States' CIA, Britain's MI6 (Military Intelligence, Section 6), or Russia's SVR (Foreign Intelligence Service). Given all the tasks that governments have to perform and all the individuals that are needed to carry out those tasks, such organizations are a necessary part of any modern state.

This observation opens up the possibility that decisions about war and peace are shaped not only by state leaders, but also by the interests of the bureaucratic organizations involved in the decision-making process.[17] While such organizations care about what is best for the country, they may also care about the resources that they control and the influence that they themselves wield. They generally seek bigger budgets, more input on policy making, and opportunities for personal promotion. As a result, they may press for policies that boost their own status or fit their own worldview.

For example, prior to the 2003 Iraq War there were serious disagreements within the U.S. government between the Defense Department and the State Department. Civilian leaders at the Pentagon generally expected war to be easy, while those at the State Department were more cautious and emphasized the need for international diplomacy. There were also disagreements over which agency should take the lead role in rebuilding Iraq politically and economically in the aftermath of the conflict. These debates reflect a common aphorism about bureaucratic politics that "where you stand depends on where you sit"—that is, the leaders of bureaucratic agencies often take policy stands that reflect their own organizations' needs. In the end, the Defense Department won these scuffles.[18]

As this example suggests, the military is usually the most influential bureaucratic actor in matters of war and peace. Up to now, our discussion has treated the military as an instrument of the state—a tool that states use to increase their leverage in international bargaining. What happens when we think about the military as an actor in its own right?

There is a compelling—although, as we will see, incomplete—argument to be made that the more influence the military has over foreign policy decision making,

---

17. The classic investigation of bureaucratic politics is Graham Allison and Philip Zelikow, *Essence of Decision: Explaining the Cuban Missile Crisis*, 2nd ed. (New York: Longman, 1999).
18. See, for example, Bob Woodward, *Plan of Attack* (New York: Simon & Schuster, 2004).

the more aggressive the state will be. This argument rests on the assumption that members of the military have ideological, organizational, and professional interests in policies that make war more likely. Ideologically, leaders in the armed forces may be predisposed to seeing military solutions to foreign policy problems, overestimating the effectiveness of force relative to other alternatives. As an organization, the military can demand larger budgets and more personnel when the state is frequently engaged in international conflict than when it is at peace. And professionally, military officers find that combat experience is crucial to being promoted to the highest ranks. All these considerations suggest that the military sees benefits to war that other actors may not.

Perhaps the most dramatic example of how military influence can lead to aggressive foreign policy is the case of Japan in the 1930s. During this period, Japan pursued a relentless campaign of expansion against its neighbors, ultimately bringing the country into war with China, France, Britain, the Netherlands, and the United States. This aggressive turn in foreign policy coincided with a creeping takeover by the military, which undermined the democratic system that had been developing in the country.

In 1931, elements of the Japanese military provoked a war with China and seized a region known as Manchuria, which military leaders prized for its coal and iron. A year later, the prime minister of Japan was assassinated by a group of naval officers—an event that ushered in the end of civilian control of Japanese politics. The Japanese military became the main instigator of that country's expansionist policies. This case is an extreme example, but there is broader evidence to suggest that countries in which civilian leadership has weak control of the military are more likely to initiate militarized conflicts.[19] (See "What Shaped Our World?" on p. 159 for another example.)

Nevertheless, it is important not to automatically equate the military with militarism. One study examined the advice that military leaders gave U.S. decision makers in about 20 key crises during the Cold War, comparing how aggressive the officers were relative to the president's civilian advisers. The study found that military advisers were no more likely than civilians to advocate the use of force in a crisis; rather, the main difference between the two groups was over the level of force that should be used in the event of an operation, with military advisers consistently preferring larger deployments. The author concluded that the "stereotype of a belligerent chorus of generals and admirals intimidating a pacific civilian establishment is not supported by the evidence."[20]

Similarly, a study of elite opinion in the United States shows that military leaders are inclined to advocate the use of force in a narrower set of cases than

---

19. Todd S. Sechser, "Are Soldiers Less War-Prone than Statesmen?" *Journal of Conflict Resolution* 48, no. 5 (2004): 746–74. The idea that civilians can lose control of the military also plays a large role in explanations of World War I. See Stephen Van Evera, "The Cult of the Offensive and the Origins of the First World War," *International Security* 9, no. 1 (Summer 1984): 58–107; and Samuel R. Williamson Jr. and Russel Van Wyk, *July 1914: Soldiers, Statesmen, and the Coming of the Great War* (Boston: Bedford/ St. Martin's, 2003).

20. Richard K. Betts, *Soldiers, Statesmen, and Cold War Crises* (New York: Columbia University Press, 1991), 4.

The Kargil War and Military Influence in War

One of the more dangerous episodes in modern history started rather quietly in April 1999, when Pakistani military forces secretly infiltrated across the Line of Control (LoC) that separates the Pakistani- and Indian-controlled areas of the disputed Kashmir region. When the incursion was discovered, India mobilized to repel the attack. Over the next several weeks, the two countries fought a war in the high mountains near the town of Kargil. This was neither the first nor the bloodiest war between the two countries, but it was the first that took place under the specter of nuclear war. Only a year earlier, the two countries had openly tested nuclear devices. It was also a rare example of war between two democratic countries. How can we explain this episode?

Interests At the root of the conflict is a long-standing territorial dispute over the region of Kashmir, which both India and Pakistan claim on historical and religious grounds (see Map 3.1 on p. 94). But even while both states want to possess the entire region, actors within each country place different values on it and are willing to pay different costs to obtain it. In particular, the military in Pakistan has generally been more willing than the country's civilian leaders to run a risk of war with India.

Interactions The conflict over Kashmir has led to repeated episodes of bargaining in which force has been threatened and used, including full-scale wars in 1947, 1965, and 1971. Even so, only weeks before the Kargil War broke out, the countries' leaders had met to affirm their desire for a peaceful resolution. The infiltration of Pakistani forces across the LoC thus represented an unexpected escalation, designed to bolster Pakistan's bargaining power. Once India responded, the subsequent fighting took place in the shadow of deterrent threats. Pakistan put its nuclear forces on alert and threatened to use every weapon in its arsenal if India invaded; India responded by putting its own missiles on alert. With the risks so high and foreign pressure mounting, Pakistan had little choice but to pull its forces back behind the LoC. So why did Pakistan initiate such a dangerous gamble?

Institutions The answer lies in the country's domestic political institutions. Even though Pakistan has a democratically elected government, its military is very powerful and has on several occasions ousted civilian leaders that it did not like. Indeed, shortly after the Kargil War, the prime minister, Nawaz Sharif, was deposed and replaced by the army's chief of staff, General Pervez Musharraf. The danger of removal by the military has led to weak civilian control and oversight of that organization.

Although there are many unknowns about Pakistan's decision making in the lead-up to the war, there is good reason to believe that the military command manipulated Sharif into starting a conflict he did not fully understand.[a] When India accused Pakistan of crossing the LoC in May 1999, Sharif claimed that the invaders were local Kashmiri insurgents operating on their own initiative. Sharif and others claim that when he was briefed on the plan to support the insurgency, he was not told that Pakistani military forces would cross the LoC in large numbers. In addition, U.S. officials reportedly believed that the move to put Pakistani nuclear forces on alert during the war was done without Sharif's knowledge.

As this episode suggests, military organizations may sometimes be willing to run greater risks than are the civilian authorities whom they are supposed to serve. When the military wields enormous influence and civilian control is weak, this behavior can have dangerous consequences for the country, its neighbors, and the world.

---

a. This discussion is based on Owen Bennett Jones, *Pakistan: Eye of the Storm* (New Haven, CT: Yale University Press, 2003), 87–109.

are civilian leaders without any military experience.[21] Indeed, by all accounts, U.S. military officers were much more reluctant to go to war against Iraq in 2003 than was the civilian leadership at the Pentagon and White House. Many top commanders thought that war with Iraq would be costly and that conducting it successfully would require larger commitments of manpower and money than the civilian leadership was willing to make.[22] Such observations suggest that, in some contexts at least, the military's interests push in a conservative direction—more appreciative of the limits of what can be achieved through force and more sensitive to the human costs of war, which are, after all, borne by its personnel.

Interest Groups: Economic and Ethnic Lobbies

The possibility that special interest groups can influence foreign policy in a manner that furthers their particular interests is familiar to most people. In the wake of the 2003 U.S. invasion of Iraq, Vice President Richard Cheney's former company, Halliburton, was awarded contracts worth billions of dollars to rebuild Iraq's infrastructure and supply American troops. By the end of 2006, the company's stock was worth four times its value when the war started. Considering also that President Bush himself had once been an oil industry executive, some observers speculated that the Iraq War was fought at the behest of oil companies interested in Iraq's oil and of military contractors interested in taxpayer dollars.

Such charges are not new. U.S. interventions in Latin American countries have often been ascribed to the influence of American businesses whose properties in those countries were at risk. The previously mentioned case of Guatemala, where United Fruit feared a major loss at the hands of an unfriendly government, was by no means unique. The United States also intervened in Cuba (1961), the Dominican Republic (1965), and Chile (1973)—all places where American investors had substantial assets.

Although economic actors such as companies and industries figure most prominently in such stories, not all interest groups organize around economic motives. Interest groups that organize around ethnic ties are another influence on foreign policy. For example, governments may respond to pressure from politically powerful ethnic groups to intervene in neighbors' civil wars on behalf of ethnic kin who live across the border.[23]

In the United States, two particularly influential groups stand out. One is the pro-Israel lobby: a collection of individuals and groups who want the U.S. government to support and defend the state of Israel—a stance that often brings the United States into conflict with Israel's adversaries in the region. The main lobbying arm of

---

21. See Peter D. Feaver and Christopher Gelpi, *Choosing Your Battles: American Civil-Military Relations and the Use of Force* (Princeton, NJ: Princeton University Press, 2004).

22. See, for example, Michael R. Gordon and Bernard E. Trainor, *Cobra II: The Inside Story of the Invasion and Occupation of Iraq* (New York: Pantheon, 2006).

23. Stephen M. Saideman, *The Ties that Divide: Ethnic Politics, Foreign Policy, and International Conflict* (New York: Columbia University Press, 2001).

this group is the American Israel Public Affairs Committee (AIPAC), which is considered one of the most effective lobbying groups in Washington.[24]

The second standout is the anti-Castro lobby—groups that represent Cuban Americans opposed to the communist regime in Cuba. A large number of Cubans fled after Fidel Castro took over in 1959 and seized their property. Cuban American groups have lobbied the U.S. government to take strong actions to contain and undermine the Castro regime, including supporting a failed invasion by exiles in 1961 and imposing a strict economic embargo on the country. In 2014, President Barack Obama announced that he would restore some diplomatic and economic ties with Cuba, arguing that more than five decades of isolation had failed to change the regime. Nonetheless, the effort to lift the embargo faced resistance from the Cuban American lobby and its supporters in the U.S. Congress, and President Donald Trump took steps to reverse the opening after he came into office in 2017.

Why do interest groups care about the state's foreign policy? In cases like the pro-Israel and anti-Castro lobbies, group members are motivated by ethnic attachment or ideological interests to support or oppose a particular country or regime. In the case of economic actors, preferences over foreign policy arise whenever an actor's income depends on events in other countries or on the relationship between countries. A multinational company like United Fruit may have production facilities in numerous countries. If those countries experience political instability that threatens to disrupt the company's business, or if they have unfriendly regimes that might confiscate the company's property, then the company might lobby for some form of intervention to protect its interests.

Similarly, an investor that owns stock in a foreign company or a bank that has lent money to a foreign government might lobby its own government to use military force to ensure the return on its investment or the repayment of its loan. Such lobbying could lead to intervention against unstable or unfriendly regimes. In the extreme case that Hobson considered, economic actors with international investments might even lobby their governments to extend direct imperial control over other countries. Although establishing and maintaining such control was costly, imperialism made it safer to invest overseas, since there was less danger that investments would be wiped out by instability or hostile governments. A smaller set of economic actors, primarily those that make and sell military armaments, also have a direct interest in their country's foreign policy, since a belligerent foreign policy keeps them in business.

However, the interests of economic actors need not always lead to a preference for aggressive policies. Indeed, economic actors who depend on peaceful relations with other countries in order to do business could press their governments to pursue friendly relations or even formal alliances with profitable partners. For

---

24. For a recent study arguing that the pro-Israel lobby wields a great deal of influence on U.S. foreign policy, see John J. Mearsheimer and Stephen M. Walt, *The Israel Lobby and U.S. Foreign Policy* (New York: Farrar, Straus & Giroux, 2007). This book generated a great deal of controversy not only because of the content of the claims, but also because of concerns about the quality of the evidence. For a sample of the dispute, see Robert C. Lieberman, "The 'Israel Lobby' and American Politics," *Perspectives on Politics* 7 (2009): 235–57, as well as the response by Mearsheimer and Walt in the same issue.

example, American banks and companies that had important trade, financial, and investment interests in Western Europe played a significant role in lobbying for a strong U.S. commitment to defend Western Europe at the outset of the Cold War. Similarly, banks that depended heavily on loans to Asia lobbied for strong alliance commitments to Japan and South Korea.[25]

More recently, U.S. corporations interested in selling goods to China have been a political force lobbying for more cooperative relations with that country. In fact, an extensive literature suggests that trade between countries decreases the likelihood of war between them, in part because businesses that profit from the trade lobby against policies that could lead to conflict.[26] In sum, depending on where and how they do business, economic actors can have an interest in peaceful relations with some countries and/or hostile relations with others.

How Can Small Groups Have a Big Influence on Policy?

We have seen that militaries seeking budgets and prestige, businesses seeking profits, and ethnic groups looking out for their kin may all, at times, see particular benefits to war. What is remarkable about each of these actors is how small they are relative to those who pay the costs of war. The generals and admirals who run military organizations are greatly outnumbered by the enlisted personnel who bear the brunt of the fighting, as well as by the rest of the population. Multinational companies and ethnic lobbies tend to make up a small fraction of society. Given how extensively they are outnumbered, when and how can these narrow interests prevail? The answer lies in the nature of the interactions between these different actors and the institutions that regulate their relations.

The military's influence on foreign policy decision making derives from the fact that it controls a large number of guns and people trained to use them. While militaries are generally created in order to defend a state from foreign threats, their capabilities inevitably make them key players domestically as well. In many states, the military plays a direct role in ensuring the continuation of the government. This role can either be very explicit (as with military dictatorships, in which military officers take direct control of executive power) or more subtle but no less potent.

In many countries, the military is able and willing to intervene in politics to ensure that the government is to its liking; as a result, a civilian government may have to cater to the military's interests in order to avoid being ousted in a coup d'état. A number of countries in Latin America, Africa, the Middle East, and Asia have experienced frequent alternations between direct military rule and civilian governments that lived under the constant threat of a coup. Moreover, authoritarian regimes that actively suppress popular dissent may rely heavily on the military to put down challenges to their rule. In such systems, the regime's dependence on

---

25. Benjamin O. Fordham, *Building the Cold War Consensus* (Ann Arbor: University of Michigan Press, 1998).

26. Stephen G. Brooks, "Economic Actors' Lobbying Influence on the Prospects for War and Peace," *International Organization* 67 (Fall 2013): 863–88.

In November 2017, the military in Zimbabwe unseated President Robert Mugabe in a coup d'état, prompting celebrations across Harare by Zimbabweans who welcomed the change in leadership. The ability to topple a government gives military organizations significant influence over foreign and domestic policies.

the armed forces for its continued survival gives military leaders a prominent role in decision making.

Even when the government does not depend so heavily on the military to stay in power, the military can have strong influence over foreign policy decision making. All political leaders rely on the information and expertise of bureaucratic actors within the state. No political leader is an expert in every policy area; even if that were possible, there would not be enough time for the leader to focus on every task of government. Instead, the job of making policy proposals and analyzing the implications of different decisions rests with the specialists who staff the bureaucratic agencies.

When making decisions about war, a leader has to rely on experts within the military and other agencies (such as those dealing with intelligence and diplomacy) to provide key pieces of information—what the country's capabilities are, what the capabilities of potential adversaries are, what plans there are to wage war with a given country—and deal with any contingencies that might arise. The political leader's dependence on the military for this kind of information gives military leaders the ability to shape decisions to their liking. A military bent on war could, for example, give the leader skewed advice about how easily the war could be won and how low the costs would be. Conversely, military officials opposed to war could give conservative estimates of the likelihood of success and magnify the potential costs. In this way, the military would shape the outcome by manipulating the information that the leader uses to calculate the expected value of war and its alternatives.

Organized interest groups also rely on their superior resources and access to information in order to exert influence over policy. Consider an intervention like the one in Guatemala mentioned at the outset of this chapter. In that case, intervention cost U.S. taxpayers about $3 million, and it protected property for which

United Fruit Company demanded $16 million. Given that the taxpayers who footed the bill vastly outnumbered the stockholders of the company that benefited, it is useful to think about why the latter would get their way at the expense of the former. How could economic interest groups "hijack" a state's foreign policy for their own narrow interests?

As suggested earlier, much of the answer lies in how the costs and benefits of international conflict are distributed in such situations. Precisely because taxpayers are more numerous, the costs of intervention to any individual are quite low. As a result, no individual citizen has much incentive to become informed about the situation, to call a member of Congress to weigh in on the policy, to go to Washington to bang on the doors of the State Department, and so on. Indeed, in the case of Guatemala and United Fruit Company, most U.S. citizens were likely unaware of what the CIA was up to (in arming and training Guatemalan rebels) and how much taxpayer money was being spent. By contrast, the company that stands to benefit from intervention has a very large stake in the outcome. Company representatives have every incentive to become informed, to lobby representatives, and to exploit contacts within the government. Hence, in the interaction between the many who pay the costs and the few who stand to benefit, the latter have a significant advantage.

Organized interest groups can prevail because they can provide political leaders with things they need and want in exchange for favored policies. Sometimes what interest groups provide is money, which leaders can use to line their pockets or, if that is prohibited, to finance political campaigns. Concerns about the military-industrial complex center around the flow of money: industries give money to elected officials, who then allocate taxpayer money to the military, which then spends the money in ways that benefit the industries, such as by purchasing their arms or intervening to protect their foreign assets.[27]

In democracies, interest groups also gain influence by promising the support of motivated voters. For example, the Cuban American lobby does not give large sums of money relative to big economic interest groups like companies, labor unions, and professional organizations. When representatives of this lobby go to Washington, they primarily remind politicians that 1 million Cuban Americans care enough about U.S. policy toward Cuba that they vote on the basis of that issue. Moreover, these voters are concentrated in Florida, a crucial state in U.S. presidential elections, where a margin of only 500 votes swung the 2000 election to George W. Bush. By contrast, most other voters pay little attention to this issue and do not base their votes on it. Hence, when representatives of the Cuban American or pro-Israel lobby say, "This is an issue our voters care about," politicians tend to listen.

In principle, then, interest groups can wield considerable influence over government policies, even if those policies come at the expense of broader national

---

27. This is an example of a larger phenomenon known in the American politics literature as an "iron triangle": the mutual dependence that arises among members of Congress, interest groups, and government agencies.

interests. So, to what extent does this mechanism explain foreign policy choices? Can the puzzle of war be resolved by finding some group within the state that actually benefits from the conflict? Though it can be tempting to see causal connections between policies and the groups those policies benefit, there are at least three reasons why we need to be cautious in jumping too hastily to interest-group explanations for wars.

The first reason has to do with evidence: How can we know that a particular policy was caused by interest-group lobbying? To put it another way, how can we be sure that government would have behaved differently if the interest group did not exist? The challenge here is significant. Just because Halliburton benefited from the invasion of Iraq, we cannot automatically infer that the company actively lobbied for the invasion or that President Bush chose to invade in order to benefit the company.

For most foreign policy decisions that bestow benefits on narrow groups, there are alternative justifications based on national interests. Hobson's theory of nineteenth-century imperialism has been disputed by scholars who argue that imperialism was a product of military-strategic competition among the principal powers.[28] U.S. interventions in Latin America during the Cold War were part of a larger pattern in which the United States sought to prevent the spread of communism, sometimes in countries in which U.S. investors had no significant assets. Thus, even though United Fruit benefited from the ouster of Arbenz, fears about his association with communism might have provoked U.S. intervention even without that company's lobbying efforts.[29] And even if oil helps explain the United States' intense interest in removing Iraq's regime in 2003, we have seen that exerting influence over oil-producing regions serves a variety of interests, not all of them unique to oil companies.

A second consideration to keep in mind is that in many issue areas there are multiple groups pushing in different directions. We already saw that economic considerations can just as readily create groups with an interest in peace as those with an interest in war or intervention. Arms manufacturers spend a great deal of political effort competing with each other for government contracts rather than banding together to promote general foreign policy objectives. In the case of U.S. policy toward the Middle East, pro-Israel sentiments sometimes compete with oil interests that favor closer relations with oil-rich Arab states. The United States has regularly sold advanced military technology to Saudi Arabia, even over the objections of the pro-Israel lobby. The existence of opposing groups and demands can make it much harder for any one group to "capture" the state's foreign policy.

The final important consideration is to recall, as before, that war is the product of a bargaining interaction between or among multiple states, not a choice made by a single leader or group. Thus, to evaluate the potential influence of groups that have hawkish interests, we need to revisit the bargaining model.

---

28. See, for example, Benjamin J. Cohen, *The Question of Imperialism* (London: Macmillan, 1974).

29. For an argument against the interest-group interpretation of these cases, see Stephen D. Krasner, *Defending the National Interest* (Princeton, NJ: Princeton University Press, 1978), esp. chap. 8.

How Do Domestic Interests Affect International Bargaining?

How could hawkish actors within a state affect the likelihood of war? The general answer is that domestic interests affect the likelihood of international conflict primarily by determining the extent of the state's ambitions. By influencing the costs and benefits of conflict, such interests can widen or narrow the scope of goods over which the state's leaders might be willing to wage war; they affect when and how often the state's foreign policy interests will come into conflict with those of other states; they determine the size of the demands that the state will make and the risks that it is willing to run.

In short, variation in the nature of domestic interests that influence policy making will increase or decrease the opportunities for conflict. Except in rare circumstances, however, these interests will not be sufficient to cause war in any given interaction. Thus, the influence of hawkish interests gives states more things they might consider worth fighting over, but these interests are generally not sufficient to explain why bargaining over those goods fails in some cases but not in others.

To illustrate this point, we return in Figure 4.5 to the bargaining model and ask what would happen if the interests of State A changed in response to the influence of hawkish actors. For example, imagine that the object in dispute is a piece of territory with oil in it. In the interaction depicted in the top panel, the government in State A is led by a party whose core supporters are pacifists. As a result, the government considers the costs of war over this territory to be rather high, as shown by the fact that State A's value for war (the portion of the bar to the left of the red dotted line) is far smaller than the share of territory it expects from the outcome of the war.

Recall that the costs of war are measured relative to the value of the good in dispute, so they are large when the human and economic costs of war loom large and/or when the benefit associated with possessing the territory is low. Because the dovish interests that control the state see war as very unattractive, they are highly unlikely to start a crisis over this territory. Only if the status quo distribution of the territory was located at the far left of the line—very far from State A's ideal point—would the government in State A see any potential benefit from sparking a crisis.

What happens to the international interaction if the dovish leader in State A is replaced by a leader of a party that draws support from oil companies that would profit from State A's control of the territory? Because of the influence of these actors, the new leader places more weight on the value of the land and less on the costs of war. In terms of our model, the costs of war relative to the value of the good are smaller. The lower panel shows how the value of war changes in the eyes of this hawkish government. Since the costs of war have gone down, State A's value for war shifts to the right.

Notice two things about the lower panel in Figure 4.5. First, status quo distributions that would have been tolerated by the dovish leader are unacceptable to the hawk. As a result, State A becomes more likely to initiate a crisis, and it will make larger demands on its adversary. Second, even after this shift, a bargaining range, shown in light green, still exists. As before, the costs of war ensure the existence of a set of mutually acceptable bargains.

FIGURE 4.5 *Domestic Interests and International Bargaining*

In the top panel, State A is led by a dovish government and considers the costs of war to be high relative to the value of the good in dispute. In the lower panel, State A is led by a hawkish government and sees the costs of war as less significant, placing more value on the good in dispute. Under hawkish leaders, State A is more likely to challenge the status quo, but a bargaining range still exists.

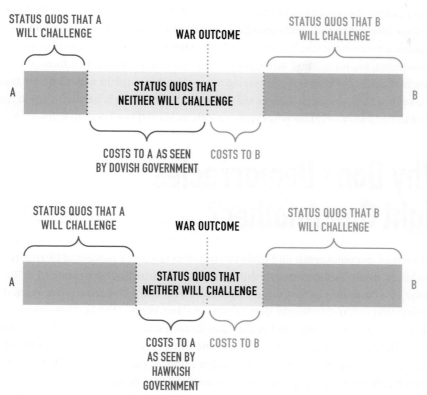

This means that absent the information, commitment, or divisibility problems discussed in Chapter 3, there is no reason why the shift from a dovish to a hawkish government should, on its own, lead to a war. However, the shift does create a danger of war that did not exist before. The new government in State A is more willing to threaten force to change the status quo. The change in governance increases the state's demands and creates a risk of conflict where none previously existed. Whether or not this potential conflict will lead to an actual war depends on features of the bargaining interaction, such as how information is distributed and whether the states can credibly commit to live by any deal they reach.

The one exception to this claim arises if there are actors who derive benefits from war that cannot be part of a negotiated settlement, as in the case of diversionary conflict. For example, assume that the leader of State A represents arms manufacturers. If there is a war, they get paid to build weapons and to replace those that are destroyed. Since they get these profits only if there is a war, then it is peace rather than war that these actors find costly. Would the influence of such interests change the logic we just outlined? As we saw when considering the diversionary incentive, the answer is yes—but only if the net benefits from war are high enough to offset *both* states' costs of war.

Hence, except in rare circumstances, the influence of groups within the state that place high value on the goods that can be acquired through force and/or see little cost to war does not itself ensure that war will happen. When such interests hold sway, they will make the state's foreign policy more belligerent, in the sense that the state will make larger demands and come into conflict with more states, but such interests alone are not sufficient to cause war in the absence of the strategic dilemmas discussed in Chapter 3. Thus, when we think about how oil interests influence U.S. policy in the Middle East, it is reasonable to say that they explain why there are issues in the region that American leaders are willing to fight over. It is harder to argue that these interests alone explain why crises over them sometimes become wars.

Why Don't Democracies Fight One Another?

For much of the nineteenth and early twentieth centuries, France and Germany were bitter rivals. France resisted the creation of a unified German state in 1870, and the two countries fought three major wars over the next century: the Franco-Prussian War (1870–71), World War I (1914–18), and World War II (1939–45). Millions died in these wars, and cemeteries in both countries are filled with those who fell in this rivalry. Today, however, France and Germany are close allies, and while they have differences of interest and opinion on important issues, it is almost inconceivable that there could be another war between them.

The turnaround in this relationship coincided with changes in the countries' political systems, which made them more democratic. France went into the Franco-Prussian War a monarchy, but it emerged with a more democratic system, which has become stronger over time. The change in Germany was even more dramatic. Ruled by a hereditary emperor in the nineteenth century, Germany devolved into a murderous dictatorship under Adolf Hitler in the 1930s. After World War II, however, Germany was divided and occupied by the victorious Allies, and what became West Germany was remade into a democratic country. When East and West Germany were reunified in the 1990s, the reborn German state inherited this democratic constitution.

There were, of course, a number of factors that helped solidify the relationship between these former adversaries after 1945, including the existence of a shared enemy in the Soviet Union; the reassuring presence of a common ally, the United States; and growing economic and financial ties that would make these two states central partners in a European Union. Nevertheless, the emergence of shared democracy helped pave the way for a dramatic shift in how these countries dealt with each other, to the point that war between the two is now unthinkable.

Far from being an isolated example, this case is part of a larger phenomenon that scholars and policy makers call the **democratic peace**. The term refers to a well-established observation that there are few, if any, clear cases of war between mature democratic states. Our choice of words reflects some caveats about this observation. We say "few, if any, clear cases of war" because the strength of the claim depends in part on how one defines democracy and what events one considers to be wars. Since there are some ambiguous cases, there is not a universal consensus on whether wars between democratic states are nonexistent or simply rare.[30] We say "mature democratic states" because some studies have suggested that countries in the process of becoming democracies do not fit this overall pattern.[31] Even taking these qualifications into account, this is still a remarkable observation: over the 200 or so years in which democracies have existed in their modern form, they seem not to have engaged in war with one another—or, at least, they have done so less frequently than we might expect, given the overall frequency of war.

Another noteworthy aspect of this observation is that democracies are not, overall, less war prone than other kinds of states. That is, while they rarely, if ever, fight wars against other democratic states, their overall rate of war participation is roughly the same as that of nondemocratic states.[32] This means that although democracies seldom find themselves at war with one another, they are more frequently at war with nondemocratic states. Hence, there is something special about the relationship among democracies that does not carry over to their relationships with other kinds of states.

This observation is so striking and important that it has entered into policy discussions in the United States and elsewhere. President George W. Bush argued that democracy promotion should be a central aspect of American policy in the Middle East because "democracies don't go to war with each other."[33] And during his 2009 speech accepting the Nobel Peace Prize, President Barack Obama emphasized the connection between peace and democracy in Europe and pointed out that "America has never fought a war against a democracy."[34] This interest in democratic peace has been particularly salient in recent decades, which have seen a remarkable growth in the number of democracies worldwide, as Figure 4.6 shows.

Is this absence of wars among democracies a coincidence, or is there something about democratic institutions that facilitates peaceful relations among states that have them? In what ways might shared democracy influence interstate bargaining?

democratic peace
The observation that there are few, if any, clear cases of war between mature democratic states.

---

30. For a discussion of the democratic peace finding, definitional issues, and some cases that raise questions, see Bruce Russett, *Grasping the Democratic Peace* (Princeton, NJ: Princeton University Press, 1993), chap. 1.

31. Edward D. Mansfield and Jack Snyder, *Electing to Fight: Why Emerging Democracies Go to War* (Cambridge, MA: MIT Press, 2005).

32. Although there has been some controversy over the issue, this statement reflects the general consensus in the literature. See, for example, Nils Petter Gleditsch and Havard Hegre, "Peace and Democracy: Three Levels of Analysis," *Journal of Conflict Resolution* 41 (1997): 283–310.

33. White House, Office of the Press Secretary, "President and Prime Minister Blair Discussed Iraq, Middle East," White House Press Conference, November 12, 2004, www.whitehouse.gov/news/releases/2004/11/20041112-5.html.

34. Barack H. Obama, "A Just and Lasting Peace" (Nobel lecture, December 10, 2009), www.nobelprize.org/nobel_prizes/peace/laureates/2009/obama-lecture_en.html.

FIGURE 4.6 **The Spread of Democracy, 1800–2016**

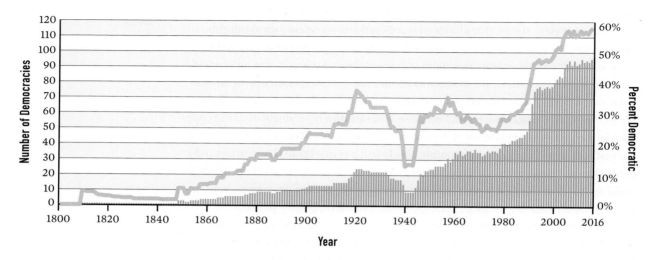

Figure source: Monty G. Marshall, Ted Robert Gurr, and Keith Jaggers, "Polity IV Project: Political Regime Characteristics and Transitions, 1800-2016," Center for Systemic Peace, http://www.systemicpeace .org/inscrdata.html (accessed 11/21/17).

democracy

A political system in which candidates compete for political office through frequent, fair elections in which a sizable portion of the adult population can vote.

autocracy

A political system in which an individual or small group exercises power with few constraints and no meaningful competition or participation by the general public.

What Is Democracy?

To answer these questions, we turn to the third leg of our framework: institutions. Domestic institutions determine the rules of political decision making within the state. They govern the relationship between the leadership and the people, and they help determine the extent to which citizens' interests matter when it comes to war and peace. Although there are many different kinds of political systems, the distinction that has attracted the most attention is that between democratic and nondemocratic systems.

A **democracy** is a political system in which candidates compete for political office through frequent, fair elections in which a sizable portion of the adult population can vote. This definition encompasses two major aspects of democracy: the ability of different individuals and groups to compete for political office and the ability of a large portion of the people to participate in the selection process through voting.

Nondemocratic countries, also known as **autocracies**, fall short of this definition in a variety of ways.[35] In some, leaders obtained office through hereditary succession, as in Saudi Arabia, or on the back of a military coup, as happened in Egypt in 2012. In others, such as China, only one political party is permitted to hold power, and competition from other parties is outlawed. Still others might hold elections among multiple parties but restrict competition so that the ruling party is all but certain to win. Such multiparty or electoral authoritarianism is the most common form of nondemocratic system in the world today; examples include Venezuela, Russia, Ethiopia, and Myanmar.[36] Map 4.1 on page 172 shows the type of regime in each country at the beginning of 2017.

---

35. Indeed, recent research in international relations has explored the effects of different kinds of nondemocratic governments; see, for example, Jessica L. P. Weeks, *Dictators at War and Peace* (Ithaca, NY: Cornell University Press, 2014).

36. There is an extensive literature on the nature and role of elections in authoritarian countries; see, for example, Jennifer Gandhi and Ellen Lust-Okar, "Elections under Authoritarianism," *Annual Review of Political Science* 12 (June 2009): 403–22.

Another term that often accompanies democracy is *liberal*, which we use here in its classic sense to refer to a philosophy that emphasizes the value of individual liberty. Most modern democracies are also liberal democracies, because in addition to allowing competition and voting, they have numerous protections for individuals' civil liberties and political rights, such as rights to free speech, religion, political association, and a free press. Hence, liberal democracies not only choose their leaders by democratic means, but they also impose restrictions on what those elected governments can do by giving citizens rights that cannot be transgressed. We should note that not all democratic countries are liberal, as some have restrictions on religious or press freedoms, or they give rights to ethnic or religious groups at the expense of individual rights. Indonesia, for example, has competitive and free elections, but it also has laws restricting the activities of civic and religious organizations, including a ban on the advocacy of certain ideas.[37]

With these definitions in place, we turn to the central question: How could democracies—especially mature, liberal democracies—be different when it comes to war and peace? Not surprisingly, the democratic peace observation has generated a great deal of scholarly interest in this question, and there is no single, settled answer. But the framework of this book suggests two broad ways in which domestic institutions can affect the likelihood of war: either by influencing the interests of states and their leaders or by influencing the bargaining interaction between and among countries.

Representation, Accountability, and Interests in War and Peace

A common argument for the distinctiveness of democracy is rooted in the idea that domestic institutions shape leaders' interests in war and peace. This argument starts with the observation that the costs of war are paid by society at large but generally not by the leader who makes the decision to wage war. It is the people who lose lives or loved ones on the battlefield, who suffer the economic hardship of wars, and who may have to pay higher taxes to support a war effort. The leader, by contrast, rarely has such direct exposure to the costs of war. This disjunction between the ruler and the ruled is humorously illustrated in the 2001 movie *Shrek*, when evil Lord Farquaad tells his knights that he is going to send them on a mission to rescue from a fire-breathing dragon a princess whom he wants to marry. Exhorting his men to combat, the prince declares, "Some of you may die, but it's a sacrifice I am willing to make."

Over 200 years before this scene was digitally animated, the German philosopher Immanuel Kant noted a similar dilemma. Kant wrote in the late eighteenth century, when most countries were ruled by monarchs. For such rulers, he noted, "The easiest thing in the world to do is to declare war." Kant reasoned:

> War does not affect [the ruler's] table, his hunt, his places of pleasure, his court festivals, and so on. Thus, he can decide to go to war for the most meaningless of reasons, as if it

---

37. For an assessment of political and civil rights in Indonesia, see Freedom House, Freedom in the World 2014, http://freedomhouse.org/report/freedom-world/2014/indonesia-0#.VCHKsRbTXpA (accessed 09/23/14).

MAP 4.1 *Regime Types*

This map shows the type of government in each country at the start of 2017. While democracy can be found on every continent, it is widespread in the Americas and Europe, present in parts of Asia, and scarce in Africa and the Middle East. Monarchies and military regimes are quite rare, while most autocratic regimes have limited multiparty competition.

GREENLAND (DENMARK)

ALASKA

CANADA

ICELAND

UNITED STATES

Pacific Ocean

Atlantic Ocean

CUBA

HAITI

MEXICO

DOMINICAN REPUBLIC

BELIZE

GUATEMALA

HONDURAS

EL SALVADOR

NICARAGUA

VENEZUELA

GUYANA

SURINAME

COSTA RICA

COLOMBIA

PANAMA

ECUADOR

PERU

BRAZIL

BOLIVIA

PARAGUAY

URUGUAY

CHILE

ARGENTINA

Regime Type:

■ DEMOCRACY

■ SINGLE-PARTY AUTOCRACY

■ MULTIPARTY AUTOCRACY

■ MILITARY

■ MONARCHY

Map source: Regime types in 2012 were sourced from Beatriz Magaloni, Jonathan Chu, and Eric Min. Autocracies of the World, 1950–2012, Version 1.0, Dataset, Stanford University, 2013. For more information on this dataset, see http://cddrl.fsi.stanford.edu/povgov/research/autocracies_of_the_world_dataset (accessed 01/20/15). Magaloni, Chu, and Min's coding rules were used to identify countries that had changed types by 2017.

Arctic Ocean

Pacific Ocean

Indian Ocean

RUSSIA

SWEDEN
FINLAND
NORWAY
UNITED
KINGDOM
IRELAND
GERMANY
BELARUS
UKRAINE
FRANCE
SWITZERLAND
ITALY
SPAIN
GREECE
BOSNIA
GEORGIA
KAZAKHSTAN
MONGOLIA
N. KOREA
S. KOREA
JAPAN
TURKEY
UZBEKISTAN
KYRGYZSTAN
TURKMENISTAN
TAJIKISTAN
SYRIA
IRAQ
IRAN
CHINA
MOROCCO
ISRAEL LEB.
JORDAN
KUWAIT
NEPAL
TAIWAN
ALGERIA
LIBYA
EGYPT
SAUDI
ARABIA
U.A.E.
OMAN
INDIA
MYANMAR (BURMA)
VIETNAM
MAURITANIA
ERITREA
YEMEN
PAKISTAN
THAILAND
PHILIPPINES
SENEGAL
MALI
NIGER
CHAD
SUDAN
AFGHANISTAN
BANGLADESH
LAOS
GUINEA
NIGERIA
CEN.
AFR.
REP.
S.SUDAN
ETHIOPIA
SRI LANKA
CAMBODIA
CAMEROON
UGANDA
KENYA
SOMALIA
MALAYSIA
GHANA
D.R.
CONGO
IVORY COAST
TANZANIA
INDONESIA
PAPUA NEW GUINEA
ANGOLA
MALAWI
ZAMBIA
MADAGASCAR
FIJI
NAMIBIA
MOZAMBIQUE
ZIMBABWE
AUSTRALIA
SOUTH
AFRICA
SWAZILAND
BOTSWANA
NEW
ZEALAND

173

were a kind of pleasure party, and he can blithely leave its justification (which decency requires) to his diplomatic corps, who are always prepared for such exercises.[38]

In other words, a basic problem in such political systems was that the interests of the ruler and the ruled were not aligned: the ruler enjoyed the benefit of war, while the people paid its costs. In Kant's view, the solution to this problem was to establish a representative government, one in which the ruler would be accountable to the people: if "the consent of the citizenry is required in order to determine whether or not there will be war, it is natural that they consider all its calamities before committing themselves to so risky a game."[39] In this view, political institutions that foster broad representation would serve to align the interests of the ruler and the ruled, making those with the power to decide on war sensitive to the costs that their decisions impose on others.

The primary mechanism through which political institutions influence decisions about war and peace is **accountability**, the ability to punish or reward leaders for their decisions. Even if political leaders do not directly bear the costs of war, they can be punished politically if they make decisions that harm the people or groups on whom they rely to stay in power. In a democratic system, elections and other practices provide a way for citizens to punish leaders for unpopular policies. Democratic leaders thus have to take into account the possibility that failed or costly wars can undermine their political support, jeopardizing their hold on office, as we saw in Figure 4.4. At the same time, by making it easier for voters to make their collective voice heard, electoral institutions weaken the potential influence of small groups that may see concentrated benefits but few costs from waging war. Thus, accountability to voters can raise the political risks of war to an elected leader and ensure representation of broader rather than particularistic interests.

Autocratic leaders may also be held accountable for their actions, but the key actors are different, so the interests that are represented in decision making are different. Though they do not face an electorate with real power to replace them, they may still be subject to removal by a "selectorate," the set of individuals and groups whose support is necessary for a leader to retain office. In nondemocratic systems, this selectorate can be quite small, often involving military, economic, or ethnic elites. Staying in power requires autocrats to prioritize policies that keep these actors satisfied, privileging particularistic interests over the public good. Autocrats are also protected by the fact that the actions needed to remove them, such as a revolution or coup, are risky to undertake. Thus, as long as members of the selectorate are sufficiently protected, paid off, or afraid, the leader can be politically insulated from the costs of war.[40] For example, after losing the first Persian Gulf War in 1991, Saddam Hussein was able to hold on to power, even in the face of popular revolts, because he was able to retain the loyalty of his elite military units and core supporters.

accountability
The ability to punish or reward leaders for the decisions they make, as when frequent, fair elections enable voters to hold elected officials responsible for their actions by granting or withholding access to political office.

---

38. Immanuel Kant, "To Perpetual Peace: A Philosophical Sketch," in *Perpetual Peace and Other Essays on Politics, History, and Morals*, trans. Ted Humphrey (Indianapolis, IN: Hackett, 1983), 113.

39. Kant, "To Perpetual Peace," 113.

40. See Bruce Bueno de Mesquita, Alastair Smith, Randolph M. Siverson, and James D. Morrow, *The Logic of Political Survival* (Cambridge, MA: MIT Press, 2003).

In this view, then, democracies are different because their leaders face systematically higher costs from war than do nondemocratic leaders. Given an equal probability of victory in war, a democratic leader values war less than the nondemocratic leader because the political implications of losing are worse. Given equal human and material costs of war, a democratic leader values war less, because that leader is more likely to be held accountable for those costs.

Although this logic is compelling, we must point out that losing office is not the worst or only consequence of losing a war. When democratic leaders lose an election, they can generally retire in good comfort, collect their pension, perhaps go on the lecture circuit, and even continue to participate in politics if they want. Nondemocratic leaders, by contrast, often find that life after losing office is not so pleasant. Because their removal often occurs through violent means, such as a coup or revolution, nondemocratic leaders often suffer additional punishment above and beyond simply losing office.

For the Russian tsar in 1917, the disastrous showing in World War I not only contributed to his removal from office, but he and his family were executed at the hands of the revolutionaries. The German emperor similarly faced popular uprisings in the wake of his country's defeat in that war, prompting him to abdicate his throne and flee into exile. And the leader of the military junta that led Argentina into the Falklands War was later tried for mishandling the war and spent five years in prison. Indeed, death, exile, and imprisonment are common punishments meted out to autocratic leaders who run afoul of their people. This suggests that the relationship between the political institutions and the costs of losing a war may not be as straightforward as the Kantian logic suggests.[41]

How would this argument about accountability explain the democratic peace? If, in fact, war is costlier for democratic leaders, the likelihood of war could be influenced in several ways. As we have seen, an increase in the costs of war diminishes a state's willingness to contest the status quo, reducing the opportunities for conflict. If there are fewer things that a state is willing to fight for, the scope for it to come into violent conflict with other states decreases. Moreover, the logic of political accountability suggests that democratic leaders should be more selective about starting wars; that is, they should be willing to wage war when their chances of victory are sufficiently high. Leaders in nondemocratic political systems may be more willing to gamble on wars in which they have a low chance of winning. This logic would lower the probability of war between two democratic states because in such interactions it is unlikely that both leaders would simultaneously judge their chances in war to be high enough.[42]

But how could this argument explain the fact that, overall, democratic states are just as war prone as other states, meaning that they are particularly likely to fight wars against nondemocracies? A possible answer lies in the

---

41. Goemans, *War and Punishment*.

42. See Bruce Bueno de Mesquita, James D. Morrow, Randolph M. Siverson, and Alastair Smith, "An Institutional Explanation for the Democratic Peace," *American Political Science Review* 93 (December 1999): 791–807.

In nondemocratic states, like Venezuela, a small group of leaders, sometimes including military officials, typically makes foreign policy behind closed doors, often limiting what can be reported to the media and the public. This lack of transparency can make it harder for foreign states to gauge the state's capabilities and resolve.

observation that constraints on the use of force can make democratic states appear to be tempting targets to their nondemocratic foes. Recall how Saddam Hussein dismissed U.S. deterrent threats prior to the Persian Gulf War: "Yours is a society which cannot accept 10,000 dead in one battle."[43] Although he did not say so explicitly, this statement seems to reflect a sense that American leaders would find war politically too costly to fight. This belief made Hussein more likely to resist U.S. efforts to coerce him out of Kuwait.

Similarly, Japanese leaders who decided to bomb Pearl Harbor in 1941 did so, in part, under the mistaken impression that the American public would respond by opposing a war and would therefore constrain President Franklin Roosevelt's ability to respond. In this view, the constraints that make democracies peaceful in their relations with one another can have the opposite effect when democracies square off against less constrained adversaries, who may seek to exploit democracies by making larger demands and discounting their threats, thereby increasing the risk of war.[44]

Democracy and the Bargaining Interaction

Another explanation for democratic peace focuses on how democracy influences bargaining interactions between states, increasing the chances that a peaceful settlement will be found. One version of this argument focuses on the ability of democratic states to overcome information problems. Recall from Chapter 3 that states may fail to find mutually beneficial bargains if they have incomplete information about the military and political factors that determine their value for war. Resolving this informational problem is challenging because states have an incentive to conceal or misrepresent their information in the hopes of getting a better deal.

There are several reasons to think that democratic institutions and processes make it easier to overcome informational problems. First, democratic political systems are much more transparent than nondemocratic systems because democratic processes are more open and observable. For example, major policy decisions are frequently subject to public and/or legislative debate. A relatively free press can disseminate information about what decision makers are thinking, the level of popular support for war, and even details about the state's military capabilities.

---

43. See Chapter 3, footnote 18.

44. Indeed, evidence suggests that conflicts between democracies and dictators are usually initiated by the latter; see Dan Reiter and Allan C. Stam, "Identifying the Culprit: Democracy, Dictatorship, and Dispute Initiation," *American Political Science Review* 97(May 2003): 333–37.

Opposition parties can freely voice approval of or dissent from the government's actions, thereby revealing the strength (or weakness) of the government's political support within the country. Such practices exist primarily to ensure that the public can scrutinize what its leaders are doing—an essential element of democratic accountability. A by-product of such openness is that foreign states can also glean relevant information about a democratic state's capabilities and resolve.

This is not to suggest that democratic states hide nothing—either from their own people or from outside eyes. Rather, the point is that democratic states are *relatively* more transparent than most nondemocratic systems, in which decision making occurs without broad participation, there are restrictions on what can be reported in the media, opposition groups are actively suppressed, and disagreements within the governing group are rarely aired in public. Thus, all other things being equal, there is less uncertainty about the capabilities and resolve of democratic states.[45]

In addition, democracies may be better able to send credible signals in crises. Recall from Chapter 3 that when states have private information, communicating their resolve in a credible manner often requires that they take costly actions—actions that a resolute state would be willing to take but an irresolute one would not. One way they can do so is by making statements or taking actions from which it would be difficult to back down. As we have seen, such threats are costly if leaders expect to lose domestic political support for failing to follow through on them.

Policy making in democratic states, like Canada, often involves public and legislative debate, resulting in a more open and observable process. Here, Prime Minister Justin Trudeau takes questions from legislators in the Canadian Parliament. This greater transparency makes it easier for other states to accurately assess the democratic state's capabilities and resolve.

A study of U.S. public opinion demonstrates this effect. One group of survey respondents was presented with a hypothetical scenario in which a president threatened to defend another country from invasion and then failed to do so. Another group was presented with a similar scenario, in which the president failed to defend another country but had never threatened to do so. When asked to assess the president's actions, respondents in the first group gave the president a lower approval rating than the rating given by those in the second group—a result that is consistent with the idea that it is politically costly to back down from a threat.[46]

If backing down creates public disapproval, then there is reason to think that democracy magnifies the political importance of this effect. Mechanisms of accountability mean that public disapproval is more likely to result in some kind of

45. Kenneth A. Schultz, *Democracy and Coercive Diplomacy* (Cambridge: Cambridge University Press, 2001). For a dissenting view on the effects of democratic transparency, see Bernard I. Finel and Kristin M. Lord, "The Surprising Logic of Transparency," *International Studies Quarterly* 43 (1999): 315–39.

46. Michael Tomz, "Domestic Audience Costs in International Relations: An Experimental Approach," *International Organization* 61, no. 4 (Fall 2007): 821–40.

punishment for the democratic leader, in the form of either diminished support for his agenda or a greater chance of losing office in the next election. Nondemocratic leaders, by contrast, are more politically insulated from whatever disapproval their actions might engender. If so, then public threats made by democratic leaders are more informative because they are costlier to make. This suggests that institutions of accountability make it easier for democratic leaders to credibly communicate their resolve with lower levels of escalation.[47]

While the previous argument suggests that democracies can make threats more effectively when they bargain, many scholars subscribe to a more ambitious argument that shared democracy changes the nature of the bargaining interaction altogether. In this view, democratic countries are unlikely to fight wars because they adhere to norms of mutual respect and nonviolence in their dealings with one another.[48] Relations among democratic states are fundamentally different from those among other kinds of countries because they regard each other as part of a community of states that share liberal values. This identity leads to greater levels of trust and more emphasis on resolving disputes through peaceful concessions rather than through threats of violence. By contrast, this courtesy is not extended to autocracies, which are seen as threatening and untrustworthy.

Several observations are consistent with this view. First, this logic helps explain why democratic states are peaceful with each other but are not more peaceful in general. While fellow democracies enjoy a presumption of friendship, autocrats are treated with suspicion and mistrust. In the extreme, autocrats may be seen as legitimate targets for regime change, as the United States argued in the case of Iraq under Saddam Hussein. Second, there is evidence that when democratic states get into disputes with one another, they are more likely to find a compromise solution and to bring in third parties to help manage the conflict peacefully.[49]

Finally, there is evidence that the publics in at least some democracies are less likely to support war against fellow democratic states. A survey of people in the United States and the United Kingdom showed that support for a hypothetical military strike against a state pursuing nuclear weapons was significantly lower if

---

47. James D. Fearon, "Domestic Political Audiences and the Escalation of International Disputes," *American Political Science Review* 88 (September 1994): 577–92. There is some controversy over whether democracies are really special in this respect or whether some kinds of autocrats may also be able to tie their hands by invoking audience costs. For example, Jessica Weiss argues that China manipulates nationalist protests as a way to signal its resolve in crises with Japan and the United States; see Jessica Weiss, *Powerful Patriots: Nationalist Protest in China's Foreign Relations* (Oxford: Oxford University Press, 2014). There is also a robust debate on whether domestic audience costs play an important role in the outcomes of international crises. For a critical view, see Jack Snyder and Erica D. Borghard, "The Cost of Empty Threats: A Penny, Not a Pound," *American Political Science Review* 105 (August 2011): 437–56. For evidence that democracies are not particularly effective at making credible threats, see Alexander B. Downes and Todd S. Sechser, "The Illusion of Democratic Credibility," *International Organization* 66 (2012): 457–89.

48. This discussion synthesizes several subtly different articulations of this idea. Main ones include Russett, *Grasping the Democratic Peace*, 30–38; Michael W. Doyle, "Liberalism and World Politics," *American Political Science Review* 80, no. 4 (December 1986): 1151–69; and Thomas Risse-Kappen, "Democratic Peace—Warlike Democracies? A Social Constructivist Interpretation of the Liberal Argument," *European Journal of Political Science* 1 (1995): 491–517.

49. See, for example, Michael Mousseau, "Democracy and Compromise in Militarized Interstate Disputes, 1816–1992," *Journal of Conflict Resolution* 42 (1998): 210–30; and William J. Dixon, "Democracy and Management of International Conflict," *Journal of Conflict Resolution* 37 (1993): 42–68.

respondents were told that the target was a democracy. People in these countries tended to view other democracies as less threatening and had greater moral reservations about attacking them.[50]

All of this evidence is consistent with the idea that bargaining among democratic states is guided by norms that favor compromise over the use of force, which could explain the marked absence of war between such states.

Does Democracy Cause Peace?

The preceding arguments all suggest that democratic institutions are the reason for the peace that has prevailed among states that possess them, either by altering leaders' incentives to wage war or facilitating the bargaining interaction.. There is a well-known adage, however, that "correlation does not imply causation," which in this context means that just because democracy and peace go together, we cannot automatically conclude that democracy *causes* peace. Why might that be? First, there could be some other factor that both causes states to become democratic and causes them not to fight. Second, it could be that the reverse is true—that is, that peace causes democracy. And third, there could be some other factor that causes peace among states that just so happened to be democracies. All three of these arguments have been made in the scholarly literature. We briefly introduce these arguments here both to show the richness of the debate and to stimulate thinking about what might actually be going on.

The relationship between democracy and peace could be a product of the fact that both democracy and peace share a common cause. What could this common cause be? One possibility is economic development. There is a strong tendency for democracy to emerge and survive in states that are relatively wealthy; in poorer countries, by contrast, democratic institutions are more likely to break down. While there is no general tendency for wealth alone to promote peace between countries, there is evidence consistent with a "capitalist peace" among countries with free-market economies.[51]

Another possibility is that peace causes democracy—that democracy is more likely to emerge in regions where countries already have peaceful relations with one another.[52] A menacing international environment and threats to the state's territory tend to empower the central government and the military, making it hard for democracy to take root. Thus, democracy is more likely to emerge after states have settled outstanding rivalries and territorial disputes with their neighbors. If so, then it is peaceful borders that make democracies, not vice versa.[53]

---

50. Michael R. Tomz and Jessica L. P. Weeks, "Public Opinion and the Democratic Peace," *American Political Science Review* 107 (November 2013): 849–65.

51. Erik Gartzke, "The Capitalist Peace," *American Journal of Political Science* 51 (2007): 166–91; Michael Mousseau, "The Democratic Peace Unraveled: It's the Economy," *International Studies Quarterly* 57 (March 2013): 187–97.

52. William R. Thompson, "Democracy and Peace: Putting the Cart before the Horse?" *International Organization* 50 (Winter 1996): 141–74.

53. Douglas M. Gibler, *The Territorial Peace: Borders, State Development, and International Conflict* (Cambridge: Cambridge University Press, 2012).

Finally, it has been argued that democratic peace is really a product of shared strategic interests among democratic states that have nothing to do with their domestic institutions.[54] From the late nineteenth century on, the main democratic countries were united against common threats, first against Germany and then against the Soviet Union. During the Cold War, most democracies had similar strategic interests because of a common perceived threat from the Soviet Union and the communist bloc (see Chapter 5).

Such common interests reduced the opportunities for conflict between democratic states and provided a strong incentive to resolve peacefully any conflicts that did arise. In addition to fighting with each other less often, democratic states in these periods also tended to form alliances with each other—an indication that they perceived common strategic interests. In this view, then, the bonds among democratic states arise not from their institutions or sense of shared identity, but from shared threats that produced common interests. Note that, to be compelling, this argument requires that the perception of threat is independent of the political institutions, rather than being shaped by them, as the survey evidence cited in the preceding discussion suggests.

In short, the democratic peace raises tantalizing questions for both scholars and policy makers, and we are likely to be debating this issue for some time. (See "Controversy" on p. 182.)

Conclusion: What if All the World Were Democratic?

When diplomats and state leaders come to the bargaining table with one another, they inevitably bring a great deal of baggage from their home countries. The interests that state representatives advance in international negotiations are themselves a function of interests, interactions, and institutions within the state. Political leaders may care about what is best for their country, but they also care about staying in office. As a result, they must think about how their foreign policy choices will impact the interests of important domestic constituents such as the military, organized interest groups, and in some cases, the general public.

When these actors have a stake in the outcome of international bargaining, and when they have the strategic and/or institutional resources to punish or reward the leader, then their interests will be represented at the bargaining table. In particular, when groups with hawkish interests have superior organization and resources, they can push the state toward greater international ambition and thus a greater risk of war. As we have seen, there are times when military organizations and economic or ethnic interest groups have both the interests and the ability to push foreign policy in such a direction.

---

54. Joanne Gowa, *Ballots and Bullets: The Elusive Democratic Peace* (Princeton, NJ: Princeton University Press, 1999).

In contrast, when interactions and institutions empower those who bear the costs of war, they can exert a pacifying effect at the international level. Economic actors that benefit from international commerce and investment may lobby for peaceful relations with profitable partners. Representative institutions give voice to the people who bear the costs of war, thereby weakening the influence of concentrated interests that might promote conflict for their own reasons. Free, fair, and frequent elections provide a relatively low-cost mechanism for people to punish leaders who engage in failed or costly wars. The relative openness and transparency of democratic political processes can reduce informational and commitment problems that can cause bargaining to fail. Although these features may make democracies tempting targets for autocratic foes, they also help account for the relative rarity of war among democratic states.

Does this mean that a world full of democratic states would be a world without war? Certainly, the evidence to date is encouraging, although not definitive. There are at least two reasons to be cautious. First, although the number of democracies in the world has generally increased over time, the spread of democracy has experienced reversals. There have been several periods during which democracy has broken down, particularly the 1930s (leading to the low point in 1940) and the 1970s. During these periods, economic and international upheaval caused some democratic systems to fail.

It is worth remembering that Adolf Hitler came to power in Germany through relatively democratic institutions—which he then subverted before embarking on his campaign of foreign expansion. Hence, democratic systems have given birth to forces that undermined democracy and engaged in aggressive foreign policies. Even if there are no cases of war between two democratic states, there have been wars between democracies and states that were once democratic.

A second reason for caution centers on the interests that will come to be represented by the spread of democracy. Recall that democratic institutions make leaders more sensitive to the interests of the citizenry. Kant, and those who follow in his tradition, assumed that citizens are generally cautious, since it is they who bear the costs of war. But what if the public is motivated by nationalist, ethnocentric, or even genocidal ideas? If fear and hatred of a rival are intense, accountability may induce belligerence rather than caution, and leaders may fear domestic political retribution for being overly "soft" toward the nation's ethnic or religious enemies.[55] The costs of war might, as a result, be offset by the political costs of compromise.

We already saw in the case of India and Pakistan that the fact that both were democracies in the spring of 1999 did not prevent a war from breaking out between them. (See "What Shaped Our World?" on p. 159.) A history of conflict and bloodshed, fueled by religious differences, has created a great deal of enmity between not just the governments but also the people in these states. Indeed, the Kargil War was popular on both sides; in Pakistan, people were disappointed only that their country did not prevail.

Hence, the international effects of democracy's spread may very well depend not only on the institutions that take root, but also on the interests of those they empower.

---

55. For evidence that leaders may be punished for making concessions to a rival, see Michael Colaresi, "When Doves Cry: International Rivalry, Unreciprocated Cooperation, and Leadership Turnover," *American Journal of Political Science* 48 (2004): 555–70.

Should We Prefer a Friendly Dictator or a Hostile Democracy?

On June 30, 2012, Mohamed Morsi (below right) was sworn in as the first democratically elected leader in Egypt's 5,000-year history. The emergence of a democratic government in Egypt followed a succession of demonstrations and protest movements throughout the Middle East starting in January 2011, which brought down or challenged long-serving authoritarian governments not only in Egypt, but also in Tunisia, Libya, Yemen, Syria, Jordan, and Bahrain. But hopes that this so-called Arab Spring would lead to more democratic and less repressive governments in the region were disappointed, as fundamental political reform in Egypt and other countries largely failed to materialize. After a year in power, Morsi faced a renewed wave of popular protest, and the Egyptian military took over in a coup d'état in July 2013. A year later, General Abdel Fattah al-Sisi, who had led the coup, was elected president in an election lacking real competition, and his government has clamped down on dissent, jailing political opponents and journalists.

Applying the Concepts

For the United States and other Western powers, the swing in Egypt from authoritarianism to democracy and back to authoritarianism created a foreign policy dilemma. On the one hand, American and other Western policy makers often stress the importance of promoting democratic **institutions** around the world because doing so leads to governments that are responsive to their citizens' needs and respectful of their human rights. Moreover, the democratic peace observation suggests that democratic states have more peaceful **interactions**. On the other hand, the majority of people in a country may have **interests** that are hostile to or incompatible with those of the United States and its allies. In such cases, it can be easier to deal with an autocratic leader who is free to ignore those views. In other words,

policy makers can be torn between liking democratic institutions but not the interests of those empowered by such institutions.

In the case of Egypt, this tension arises from the fact that many Egyptians do not like the United States and are hostile to Israel, a key U.S. ally. Under President Hosni Mubarak, Morsi's predecessor, Egypt had good relations with both countries on the basis of a 1979 peace treaty with Israel. In the ensuing years, Egypt became a strategic partner of the United States and a major recipient of U.S. aid. But the treaty was never popular among Egyptians, and American aid was seen as propping up a repressive government. Under the autocratic Mubarak, this popular opposition could be ignored or suppressed. The transition to democracy and the election of Morsi threatened this arrangement.

A poll taken in May 2013 showed that 63 percent of Egyptians wanted to annul the treaty with Israel and only 16 percent had a positive view of the United States.[a] Not only was there a danger that a more responsive government would be more hostile to Israel, but Morsi was also the leader of a party, the Muslim Brotherhood, that seeks

Mohamed Morsi speaks at a rally in Cairo.

to eliminate Western influences from the Arab world. During the Muslim Brotherhood's brief period of rule, Egyptian relations with Israel were strained. By contrast, the Sisi government has largely restored the strategic partnership.

How should countries that espouse democratic values manage this dilemma between institutions that are attractive but interests that are hostile? Should the United States continue to send military and economic aid to Egypt's military government, or should it push for the restoration of democracy?

One view is that a country's security interests outweigh any commitment to democracy. From the perspective of U.S. policy makers, democratic institutions are desirable in parts of the world where people have similar interests to America's, but they are dangerous where they empower people with very different interests and ideas. While this is not an ethically appealing argument, it is the position that has historically shaped U.S. policy. In the case of Egypt, the United States initially held back aid and military sales after the coup but later released them. President Obama even refused to label Morsi's ouster a coup, since doing so would have triggered a U.S. law barring aid to regimes that came to power that way.

The decision to prioritize security interests over democracy in this case was not new. During the Cold War, the United States feared that elections would empower communist parties that would then become allies of the Soviet Union; military dictatorships, though brutal to their own people, made more reliable partners. Thus, in several countries—Iran (1953), Guatemala (1954), Chile (1973)—the United States conspired in the overthrow of democratic governments by military dictators. Supporters of this position also argue that the elected leaders who were overthrown were likely to become dictators themselves. Morsi's opponents, for example, questioned whether the Muslim Brotherhood was committed to democracy or human rights. In fact, the military coup enjoyed a great deal of popular support because of dissatisfaction with the Morsi government and constitutional reforms that it had pushed.

The most common argument against placing security interests above democracy is based on moral considerations: people have a right to a government that is

A woman casts her ballot in the 2014 Egyptian presidential election that brought Abdel Fatah al-Sisi into office.

responsive to their interests and respects their civil liberties. By installing or supporting dictators, the United States is complicit in the human rights abuses committed by those regimes. In addition, one could argue that, in the long run, U.S. interests are best served by promoting democracy, even where it is inconvenient to do so in the short run.

By supporting authoritarian regimes like Egypt under Mubarak, the United States has stoked anti-American sentiment and contributed to the hostility of Egypt's people. In some cases, this hostility has fed the ranks of terrorist organizations like Al Qaeda that have targeted the United States and its interests. In this view, the United States would be safer in the long run if it did not prop up autocratic regimes in the region and gave more support to the self-determination of people there.

Thinking Analytically

1. Why might the United States care what kind of government Egypt has? Do democratic states have an *interest* in promoting democracy abroad, or does the preference for democracy only reflect a certain kind of *values*?

2. What are the risks of pressuring an allied government to make democratic reforms?

a. Pew Research Center, "Egyptians Increasingly Glum," May 16, 2013, www.pewglobal.org/2013/05/16/egyptians-increasingly-glum.

Study Tool Kit

Interests, Interactions, and Institutions in Context

- There may be actors within a state who perceive high benefits from war and expect to pay little or none of its costs. In particular, there are conditions under which political leaders, business and ethnic lobbies, and the military will see conflict as furthering their narrow interests.

- These actors have a variety of institutional and organizational advantages that make it possible for them to exert more influence than the general population can.

- Except in rare circumstances, these hawkish interests are not sufficient to cause war on their own. Rather, their main effect is to increase the aggressiveness of the state's foreign policy and the scope of its ambitions, thereby creating more opportunities for conflict.

- Democratic political institutions—in particular, free and fair elections, party competition, and free media—can diminish the influence of hawkish interests, increase the costs of war for political leaders, or change the bargaining interaction in a way that makes a peaceful settlement more likely.

Key Terms

bureaucracy, p. 146

interest groups, p. 146

rally effect, p. 150

diversionary incentive, p. 151

military-industrial complex, p. 156

democratic peace, p. 169

democracy, p. 170

autocracy, p. 170

accountability, p. 174

For Further Reading

Allison, Graham, and Philip Zelikow. *Essence of Decision: Explaining the Cuban Missile Crisis,* **2nd ed. New York: Longman, 1999.** Presents a classic study of the effects of bureaucratic politics on foreign policy making in one of the most dramatic crises of the Cold War.

Chiozza, Giacomo, and H. E. Goemans. *Leaders and International Conflict.* **Cambridge: Cambridge University Press, 2011.** Explores how democratic and autocratic leaders make decisions about international conflict with an eye toward staying in office and staying alive.

Doyle, Michael W. "Liberalism and World Politics." *American Political Science Review* **80, no. 4 (December 1986): 1151–69.** Offers an influential discussion of how liberal political systems might affect foreign policy choices; this analysis brought the study of the democratic peace to the forefront of political science.

Feaver, Peter D., and Christopher Gelpi. *Choosing Your Battles: American Civil-Military Relations and the Use of Force.* **Princeton, NJ: Princeton University Press, 2004.** Presents a systematic study of how civilians and military officers differ in their views about the use of force.

Fordham, Benjamin O. *Building the Cold War Consensus.* **Ann Arbor: University of Michigan Press, 1998.** Examines how different economic interests came together to underpin the United States' international commitments during the Cold War.

Russett, Bruce M., and John R. Oneal. *Triangulating Peace: Democracy, Interdependence, and International Organizations.* **New York: Norton, 2001.** Gives a comprehensive review and analysis of the effects of democracy, trade, and international institutions on violent conflict between states.

Saunders, Elizabeth N. *Leaders at War.* **Ithaca, NY: Cornell University Press, 2011.** Shows how the beliefs that U.S. presidents bring into office can shape the way they respond to foreign crises.

Snyder, Jack. *Myths of Empire: Domestic Politics and International Ambition.* **Ithaca, NY: Cornell University Press, 1991.** Explores how domestic interest groups and military organizations can push great powers to adopt expansionist foreign policies—often with disastrous consequences for the state as a whole.

Weeks, Jessica L. P. *Dictators at War and Peace.* **Ithaca, NY: Cornell University Press, 2014.** Explores the variation among autocratic governments and how different kinds of nondemocratic leaders weigh decisions about war and peace.

5

International Institutions and War

THE PUZZLE *In a well-governed country, the police prevent and punish acts of violence between individuals. Where are the police in international politics? Why is it so hard for the international community to prevent and punish acts of aggression?*

Above: Collective security organizations like the United Nations can influence interactions between adversaries in ways that promote peaceful outcomes. However, these institutions face significant challenges in achieving their goals.

When North Korea invaded South Korea in June 1950, the United Nations (UN) responded by authorizing member states to use military force to resist this act of aggression. Although North Korea had some influential supporters, including the Soviet Union and China, a coalition of 20 nations led by the United States successfully expelled the North Koreans from South Korea by October 1950. At that point, the UN expanded the forces' mandate and pushed into North Korea. This act provoked China to intervene in order to save its ally, and the Korean War dragged on for another three years.

Around the same time, Chinese forces also invaded Tibet, which neighbors China on the west. China had long claimed sovereignty over this vast, mountainous region, but Tibet had declared independence from China in 1911. Although China never recognized this declaration, Tibet was, in practice, an independent state for the next several decades as China, distracted by civil war and the Japanese invasion in the 1930s, was unable to resist. Not long after the Communists gained control of mainland China in 1949, they sought to reassert the country's historic claim over Tibet. Units of the People's Liberation Army swept into the region in October 1950, quickly defeating the Tibetan army

and forcing Tibet's leaders to accept Chinese rule. Tibet's political and religious leader, the Dalai Lama, appealed to the UN to meet the Chinese attack on Tibet with the same kind of response that it had mustered against North Korea. But in this case, the UN took no action, and the Chinese conquest of Tibet was allowed to stand.

In our everyday lives, we generally count on the police to protect us from acts of aggression by other people. If someone breaks into your house, you can call the police. Assuming you live in a place with an effective police force, the police may come in time to stop the person from harming you or your property. Even if the police cannot always stop a crime in progress, they can investigate and try to bring the perpetrator to justice. The existence of a police force has a deterrent effect on would-be criminals, who can be dissuaded from committing aggression by the expectation that they might be caught and punished. Although total security is rarely possible, people who live in societies with well-functioning police and judicial systems rarely experience acts of violence, and they rarely have to commit acts of violence to defend themselves. Unfortunately, the same cannot be said of actors in the international system.

Where are the police in world politics? The short answer is that the international system has no police force analogous to what exists in most countries. Each state possesses its own police and its own military, but there is no authoritative institution above states with an independent force that can police relations among them. As suggested by the Korean and Tibetan examples just described, this condition of anarchy means that there is variation in the ways the international community responds to acts of aggression. And this variation has real consequences for people living in the states where such aggression occurs. Thanks to the international efforts that kept it independent, South Korea is today a thriving and prosperous country, with a living standard that far exceeds that of the impoverished North. Tibet, on the other hand, remains a part of China in spite of the fact that many Tibetans want their independence and an active movement for independence continues to this day.

Understanding this variation in international responses requires that we explore the institutions that govern whether and how outside actors respond to acts of violence in the international system. The most obvious of these outside actors are bodies like the UN or its predecessor, the League of Nations (1919–46). Formally known as collective security organizations, these institutions are the closest approximation to a world government that we have. Collective security organizations try to govern relations among their members, providing them with tools for peaceful conflict resolution and a mechanism for organizing collective responses to acts of aggression. To answer the question "Where are the police in international politics?" collective security organizations are a natural first place to look.

For much longer than such organizations have existed, however, states have used an alternative institution to arrange for help from others: alliances. If collective security organizations are like governments, alliances more closely resemble neighborhood associations: relatively small groups of actors that work together to meet common threats or address common needs. Alliances are institutions that help states cooperate militarily, such as by coming to one another's defense in the event of war. In the absence of an effective world police, alliances represent attempts by small numbers of like-minded states to look out for one another.

This chapter continues our inquiry into the puzzle of war by examining how international institutions affect interactions between states as they try to cooperate to prevent or stop international and civil conflict.

Thinking Analytically about International Institutions and War

Alliances and collective security organizations both influence whether or not outsiders will intervene in the event that war breaks out. As a result, they play a role in the bargaining that precedes a war, the bargaining that seeks to end an ongoing war, and the bargaining that takes place in the aftermath of fighting. But, despite these common features, these two kinds of institutions also differ greatly in how they operate. They form in response to different kinds of interests that third parties have in international disputes. And while both kinds of institutions try to facilitate cooperation among states, they address different aspects of the strategic interactions that surround third-party involvement in international disputes. Hence, the factors that predict their success or failure are quite different.

Alliances form when states have compatible interests that motivate them to cooperate militarily. They often seek to influence bargaining interactions with some third party by influencing that adversary's beliefs about the allies' willingness to fight together in the event of war. A core function of these institutions is to strengthen the commitment that allies make to one another and to signal that commitment to others in a credible manner.

By contrast, collective security organizations like the UN form around a common interest, which all states are presumed to share, in reducing violence within and between countries. Their primary challenge is to facilitate collective action by the international community to deter, end, and prevent the recurrence of international and civil wars. The task is a daunting one, and international efforts can be stymied either by the opposition of leading states or by their unwillingness to pay the costs of intervention. As a result, collective efforts to keep the peace are uneven, but certainly better than if these organizations did not exist at all.

Alliances: Why Promise to Fight Someone Else's War?

World War II in Europe started as a territorial dispute between Germany and Poland but quickly grew into something much larger. After Germany invaded Poland on September 1, 1939, Britain and France responded two days later by declaring war on Germany. On September 17, the Soviet Union joined the fray, invading Poland from the east, and Poland was quickly swallowed up by its larger neighbors. Several months later, in June 1940, Italy joined the war on the German side and launched an invasion of southern France as German forces attacked France in the north.

In each case, states that joined the war were carrying out the terms of alliance treaties that they had signed earlier. France and Poland had long-standing promises, codified in treaties from 1921 and 1925, to help each other in the event of war with Germany. Britain made a similar commitment to Poland in March 1939. Italy and the Soviet Union, for their parts, had each signed treaties pledging support for German military activities. Italy and Germany forged the so-called Pact of Steel in May 1939. Germany and the Soviet Union unveiled the Molotov-Ribbentrop Pact (so named for the two countries' foreign ministers) only days before the invasion of Poland. In that treaty, the two countries pledged not to attack each other and agreed to divide Poland between them; in addition, Germany promised the Soviets control over Finland, Estonia, Latvia, and Lithuania.

Alliances are institutions that help their members cooperate militarily in the event of a war. Like all institutions, alliances specify standards of behavior, or expectations about how states are to behave under certain conditions. They may include provisions for monitoring and verifying each member's compliance and procedures for joint decision making. Alliances also codify bargains between their members that settle distributional issues, such as resolving conflicts that might get in the way of cooperation or specifying how much each member will contribute to the common cause.[1]

These provisions vary, depending on the interests of the allies. Some alliances are offensive, while others are defensive. An offensive alliance is an agreement between states to join one another in attacking a third state. The Molotov-Ribbentrop Pact is a classic example of such an agreement. It not only specified the nature of Soviet-German military cooperation, but it also spelled out how the spoils of conquest would be divided. More commonly, alliances are defensive: states pledge to come to one another's defense in the event that either is attacked. The British and French pledges to Poland had this character. Defensive alliances may be open-ended in the sense that allies pledge to defend

alliances

Institutions that help their members cooperate militarily in the event of a war.

---

1. The role of alliances in settling territorial conflicts among allies is noted by Douglas M. Gibler, "Control the Issues, Control the Conflict: The Effects of Alliances That Settle Territorial Issues on Interstate Rivalries," *International Interactions* 22 (1997): 341–68.

one another against any and all attackers, or they may be targeted only at specific countries. Alliances may also differ in what the member states are required to do in the event of attack. A typical defensive alliance requires states to come to one another's aid militarily—that is, to treat an attack on the ally as an attack on oneself. Other alliance agreements specify merely that the states will consult one another in the event of war.

The most comprehensive effort to collect and code information on alliances through history, the Alliance Treaty Obligation and Provision (ATOP) project, provides us with a sense of how common these different kinds of provisions are. ATOP researchers identified 538 alliance treaties between states in the period from 1815 to 2003.[2] Of these, just over half (277) involved promises of active military support in the event that one of the allies became involved in a conflict. The vast majority of these alliances (71 percent) were purely defensive in character, only 5 percent were purely offensive, and the rest (24 percent) had both offensive and defensive provisions. Of the agreements that did not provide for active military assistance, most (217) provided for consultation between the allies if either member became involved in military conflict. About a fifth of all alliances include a neutrality clause, which requires that each member promise not to join in any attack against an ally.

The United States currently has defensive alliances with a number of countries: South Korea, Japan, and—through the North Atlantic Treaty Organization (NATO)—Canada and many states in western and central Europe. If any of these states come under attack, they can invoke the U.S. alliance commitment and ask Americans to come to their aid. In turn, the United States can appeal to others if it is attacked. NATO invoked its mutual defense provision for the first time in the alliance's history after the terrorist attack on the United States in September 2001. European NATO members assisted in flying aircraft equipped with the Airborne Warning and Control System (AWACS) over U.S. skies from October 2001 to May 2002.

In addition to spelling out their offensive or defensive character, alliances may codify bargains over how much and what each state will contribute to the common defense. Some alliances are symmetrical, meaning that the members have similar responsibilities and contribute in roughly equal amounts. Other alliances are highly asymmetrical, typically because one of the members is much more powerful than the others. For example, while the United States has pledged to defend South Korea, there is little expectation that South Korea would be in a position to return the favor if the U.S. homeland was attacked. In exchange for protection, South Korea provides bases for American troops in East Asia, has contributed to U.S. military efforts in the region, and generally supports U.S. foreign policy diplomatically and economically.

---

2. The data collection is described in Brett Ashley Leeds, Jeffrey M. Ritter, Sara McLaughlin Mitchell, and Andrew G. Long, "Alliance Treaty Obligations and Provisions, 1815–1944," *International Interactions* 28 (2002): 237–60. The data and codebook are available at http://atop.rice.edu (accessed 07/26/11). The figures reported here do not include nonaggression pacts (that is, agreements to refrain from using force), since these do not meet the definition of an alliance.

The United States maintains numerous military bases in Japan, including this one in Fussa, west of Tokyo, as part of a defensive alliance between the two countries. Countries form alliances when they have compatible interests that motivate them to cooperate.

Interests and Alliances

Given that alliances can drag a country into other countries' wars, why do states sign them? Alliances form when states have compatible interests that provide the basis for cooperation. In some cases, states share a common interest in achieving the same outcome. In the lead-up to World War II, the leaders of Britain and France did not agree to defend Poland out of the goodness of their hearts; they did so because they feared that a German conquest of Poland would make Germany militarily stronger, economically more self-sufficient, and therefore a greater threat to their own security. Thus, Britain and France shared Poland's interest in its own survival. Similarly, the United States formed the NATO alliance after World War II because it believed that securing countries like Britain, France, and West Germany from Soviet domination was crucial to its own security.

In other cases, alliance partners might have complementary interests that serve as the basis for a deal. The alliance between the United States and South Korea rests on the fact that South Korea wants protection from North Korea and China, while the United States wants military bases and partners in projecting its power in East Asia. Thus, each partner can provide something that the other values.

Whatever the specific interests are that bring states together into alliances, allies generally have aligned interests in the context of bargaining with third-party states. Figure 5.1 shows how we can depict such an alignment in our bargaining framework. As before, the disputed good is shown as a horizontal bar, and any possible deal separates this good into shares enjoyed by States A and B. We now assume that there is some third state, State C, that also has a stake in the outcome of bargaining between States A and B. If, say, State C has aligned interests with State A, then State C's ideal point is, like State A's ideal point, at the far right end of the bar.

FIGURE 5.1 *Alignment of Interests*

If State C has common interests with State A, then both State A and State C prefer a deal as far to the right as possible. The more of the good State A gets, the happier State C is.

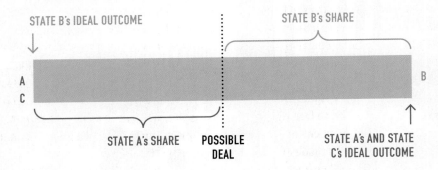

This means that the more of the good State A gets, the happier State C is. Thus, their interests are aligned, at least when it comes to this dispute with State B.

How these alignments arise is a complicated question without a single answer. A long tradition in the study of international relations holds that alliances form to create or preserve a **balance of power**—that is, a situation in which the military capabilities of two states or groups of states are roughly equal.[3] When a balance of power exists, no state or bloc has a clear military advantage over the other. A power imbalance, in contrast, is considered threatening to the weaker side's interests. According to this view, alliances form when two or more states need to combine their capabilities in order to match the capabilities of another state and thereby counter the threat to their security. Common interests thus arise from a common threat posed by the power of a stronger state or bloc.

In the late nineteenth century, both France and Russia feared the growing power and ambition of imperial Germany. Not only did each state want help in defending itself against a possible German attack, but each also feared that if Germany managed to conquer the other, then it would face an even more formidable foe in the future. As a result, each believed that its own survival depended in part on the survival of the other. The 1894 alliance between these states was formed on the basis of this common interest.

Although this dynamic can explain some aspects of alliance formation, the balance of power theory does not fully account for all alliance decisions. First, not all alliances form with the intent of balancing a stronger state. When the Soviet Union allied with Nazi Germany against Poland, it joined the stronger state, exacerbating rather than alleviating the imbalance of power in Central Europe. We refer to such

balance of power

A situation in which the military capabilities of two states or groups of states are roughly equal.

---

3. See, for example, Edward Gulick, *Europe's Classical Balance of Power* (New York: Norton, 1955). For an influential statement of the theory, see Kenneth N. Waltz, *Theory of International Politics* (Long Grove, IL: Waveland Press, 2010). For a historical analysis of balancing and its alternatives, see Paul Schroeder, "Alliances, 1815–1945: Weapons of Power and Tools of Management," in *Historical Dimensions of National Security Problems*, ed. Klaus Knorr, 247–86 (Lawrence: University Press of Kansas, 1976).

behavior as bandwagoning.[4] **Bandwagoning** occurs when states team up with the more powerful side in a dispute in order to share the spoils of conquest. Bandwagoning alliances are often offensive, as the shared interests that underlie them arise not from a common fear but from a desire to cooperate for a common gain.

A second limitation of the balance of power theory is that states can often choose many potential partners in order to balance the capabilities of a stronger state. The arithmetic of balancing capabilities does not explain why some partners are more desirable than others. For example, when Saudi Arabia sought allies against Egypt in 1957, why did it choose to ally with fellow Arab monarchies Jordan and Iraq, rather than with Israel, a state with much more impressive military capabilities and also reason to fear Egypt? The answer lies not in the balance of power, but rather in the ideological and religious incompatibility between Saudi Arabia and the Jewish state, which made an alliance between the two unthinkable.[5]

Conversely, shared cultural or religious identity can help explain why some pairs of states see each other as particularly attractive allies. Strategic cooperation between the United States and Israel, for example, is rooted in part in the perception that Israel is an outpost of Western cultural and democratic values in the Middle East and hence more "like" the United States than are other states in the region.[6]

A final problem for the balance of power theory is that not all strong powers provoke similar balancing responses. For example, ever since the collapse of the Soviet Union in 1991, the United States has been the most powerful country in the world, accounting in 2016 for 37 percent of all world military spending.[7] And yet, there has not been a significant tendency toward creating balancing alliances in response. Indeed, the U.S.-led NATO alliance, rather than falling apart after the collapse of the Soviet bloc, expanded both its membership and the scope of its missions (see "What Shaped Our World?" on p. 206).

A likely explanation is that while states sometimes complain about American arrogance and bullying, very few see the United States as an actual threat to their interests. Whatever differences the United States has had with France, for example, there is virtually no danger of war between them. Commercial, cultural, and ideological ties between the countries are strong, and there are no disputed goods in their relationship that are valuable enough to risk war over. In short, whether or not two states share a common interest vis-à-vis a third state depends on much more than whether the third state has an advantage in military capabilities. Other factors, such as geographic proximity, ideological and cultural similarity, and the existence (or not) of high-value disputes, play a large role in determining which states are considered threatening, and hence worth allying against, and which are not.[8]

bandwagoning
A strategy in which states join forces with the stronger side in a conflict.

---

4. Randall Schweller, "Bandwagoning for Profit: Bringing the Revisionist State Back In," *International Security* 19 (1994): 72–107.

5. Stephen M. Walt, *The Origins of Alliances* (Ithaca, NY: Cornell University Press, 1987), 204–6.

6. See, for example, Michael N. Barnett, "Identity and Alliances in the Middle East," in *The Culture of National Security*, ed. Peter J. Katzenstein, 400–47 (Ithaca, NY: Cornell University Press, 1996).

7. Stockholm International Peace Research Institute (SIPRI), "SIPRI Military Expenditure Database," https://sipri.org/databases/milex (accessed 07/10/17).

8. Walt, *Origins of Alliances.*

Alliances and Interstate Bargaining

The possibility of intervention by an ally influences international bargaining by changing the likely outcome and costs of war for each side. Returning to the three-state example introduced in Figure 5.1, imagine that if States A and B were to fight a war, the expected outcome would be as shown in the top panel of Figure 5.2. In this interaction, State B is assumed to be more powerful, so the war outcome is close to its ideal point. This means that State B can extract a favorable bargain from State A and is likely to challenge State A to try to realize that bargain (in other words, there is a large range of status quo outcomes in which State B will make a demand of State A). If State C is expected to join State A in this war, however, the outcome and costs will be quite different, as shown in the lower panel. With State C's power added to that of State A, the expected outcome shifts to the right, in State A's favor. Moreover, State B is likely to suffer higher costs in a war against two adversaries, whereas State A is likely to incur lower costs now that State C is carrying some of the burden.

FIGURE 5.2 *Alignments, Alliances, and Interstate Bargaining*

The bargaining interaction between State A and State B is determined by the expected outcome of a war between the two states.

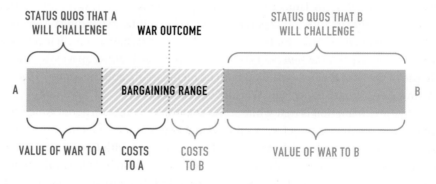

However, this interaction changes when State C is expected to join State A in the event of a war. As shown below, when State C's power is added to State A's, the expected war outcome shifts to the right, and State B's costs of war increase. As a result, the set of deals that are preferable to war shifts closer to the ideal point of States A and C, and the range of status quo distributions that State B will challenge shrinks.

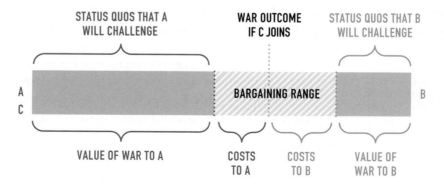

As before, the bargaining range is the set of deals that are preferred to war by both sides. Because of the change in the likely war outcome, the bargaining range has shifted to the right in the lower panel, benefiting States A and C. War is less attractive to State B, which can no longer extract a lopsided deal. State B's incentive to challenge State A also declines. By shrinking the range of status quos that State B can profitably challenge, the prospect of State C's participation deters State B from initiating crises in the first place. Hence, State C's willingness to intervene influences the bargaining interaction between States A and B by shifting each side's evaluation of war.

In addition, the possibility of intervention can affect whether the opposing sides reach a bargain. In the example just given, the shift in the bargaining range was based on the assumption that both States A and B believe that State C would intervene in the event of war. In other words, it assumed that the two sides form their expectations on the basis of the same information about State C's intentions. What would happen if this was not the case? For example, what if State A expected State C to join a war, but State B did not?

When the parties to a dispute have different information about what third parties will do, the uncertainty can heighten the probability that a bargaining failure will lead to war, for reasons discussed in Chapter 3. As we have seen, Iraq in August 1990 did not know whether the United States would defend Kuwait, and its doubts about U.S. threats to that effect helped bring about the Persian Gulf War. Similarly, we saw in the case of the Korean War that the United States was uncertain about whether China would come to the aid of North Korea if U.S. troops crossed the 38th parallel. In the lead-up to World War I, Germany was unsure until the last moment whether Britain would join its allies, France and Russia, in the event of war.

This observation suggests that alliances influence the bargaining interaction between states by influencing the states' beliefs about what third parties will do. While aligned interests are necessary for alliances to form, the main reason that states sign alliances is to signal those interests to others. After all, if it were completely obvious to everyone which states would come to the defense of others, there would be little need to negotiate and sign treaties to this effect.[9]

Because of their role as signals, alliances face the same challenge of credibility discussed in Chapter 3 with respect to threats. Indeed, an alliance entails an implied threat: "If you attack my ally, I will fight you." Just because a state has an interest in the outcome of its ally's bargaining interactions does not ensure that the state will actually fight alongside its ally in the event of war. As a result, an alliance commitment may be questionable for the same reasons that threats are questionable: they are costly to carry out, and there can be incentives to bluff. Alliances are not, after all, binding contracts. There is no external mechanism to compel states to fulfill their treaty obligations. Rather, the promise to come to another's defense in the event of war is precisely that: a promise, which may or may not be fulfilled. In fact, there are many instances in which allies have not lived up to their commitments.

---

9. James D. Morrow, "Alliances: Why Write Them Down?" *Annual Review of Political Science* 3 (2000): 63–83.

Allies may engage in joint military exercises in order to improve their ability to fight together and to publicize their commitment to do so. Here, American and South Korean soldiers engage in an April 2017 exercise near the border with North Korea.

Indeed, in June 1941, less than two years after signing the Molotov-Ribbentrop Pact, Germany broke its side of the agreement by invading the Soviet Union and grabbing all of Poland for itself.

This observation suggests that when we talk about alliances, we should be clear to treat them as institutions and not as actors in their own right. It sometimes serves as a useful shorthand to talk about alliances as cohesive actors; for example, we might say that "NATO intervened in Libya." However, we must remember that alliances are institutions formed by states in response to common interests. These institutions may shape states' interests in a way that helps them to act as a cohesive group, but at all times decision-making power rests with the states, not with the alliance itself.[10]

How Alliances Establish Credibility

Whether an alliance can successfully further the interests of allied states depends on the states' willingness to fight on one another's behalf and on their ability to signal this willingness in a credible manner. Therefore, alliances must accomplish two key tasks in order to enhance their chances of success. First, they must make it more likely that allies will fight on one another's behalf than they would in the absence of an alliance. This can be accomplished by decreasing the costs of fighting, increasing the benefits of fighting, and/or increasing the costs of not fighting—that is, of abandoning the ally. Second, alliances must do

10. This characteristic distinguishes alliances from empires and more hierarchical relationships between states in which the capabilities of two or more actors are combined but decision-making power rests in a dominant state. On security hierarchies, see David A. Lake, *Entangling Relations: American Foreign Policy in Its Century* (Princeton, NJ: Princeton University Press, 1999).

these things in a way that leads adversaries to believe that the allies will indeed fight together. Hence, the goal is both to heighten the allies' interests in aiding one another and to influence the interaction with the rival state by shaping its expectations.

Alliances typically have a number of features designed to further these goals. They increase the benefits and decrease the costs of war by improving the member countries' ability to fight effectively together. Allies may engage in joint military planning and joint military exercises, and they may station troops on one another's soil. For example, the United States has more than 20,000 troops stationed in South Korea and routinely engages in joint military exercises with the South Korean military. By doing so, it makes the expected value of the two states fighting together higher than it would be in the absence of an alliance. This coordination is publicly revealed (even if actual war-fighting strategies are not), which serves to put potential adversaries on notice. Some alliances also contain provisions for joint decision making that further enhance their collective war-fighting abilities. For instance, NATO appoints a Supreme Allied Commander, Europe, which is responsible for all troops under the organization's authority.

Alliances can also increase the costs of abandonment—that is, of failing to fight on an ally's behalf. Prior to the nineteenth century, it was common to cement alliances through a marriage between royal families—under the theory that a king would have special motivation to defend an ally if his daughter was married to that ally's monarch. More commonly, the fact that alliance treaties are generally made public—often accompanied by public signing ceremonies and, in some countries, open ratification processes—can bring states' reputations into play.[11] States may fear that the failure to come to an ally's defense, after making such a public commitment, would hurt their credibility in future conflicts. Such hand-tying strategies seek to bolster the credibility of alliances just as they do the credibility of other threats.

Despite the challenges of establishing credibility, states have historically honored their alliance commitments in war about 70 percent of the time.[12] Although it is hard to know with certainty how often states would have fought alongside their allies even without a formal alliance commitment, this is an impressive success rate, given the lack of any formal enforcement mechanism for treaties and the often substantial costs of war. Moreover, the states most likely to violate agreements are those that have experienced a significant change either in their power or in their domestic regimes. In the wake of such changes, the alignment of interests between the allies may no longer be as strong as it was when the alliance was first signed.[13]

---

11. This is generally true of defensive alliances. Offensive alliances, in contrast, may be kept secret if the intended target would otherwise take countermeasures to blunt the effectiveness of the alliance.

12. Brett Ashley Leeds and Sezi Anac, "Alliance Institutionalization and Alliance Performance," *International Interactions* 31 (2005): 192.

13. Brett Ashley Leeds, "Alliance Reliability in Times of War: Explaining State Decisions to Violate Treaties," *International Organization* 57 (Fall 2003): 801–27.

There is also evidence that states with defensive alliances are less likely to be targeted by militarized actions in the first place, suggesting that these agreements generally have the intended effect of deterring challenges.[14] These observations suggest that the institutional mechanisms just described are often effective at heightening states' interests in coming to their allies' aid and at signaling that commitment to potential adversaries.

Why Aren't Alliance Commitments Ironclad?

If states have compatible interests that lead them to form alliances and signal their commitments to one another, why is there often uncertainty about whether members will actually fulfill their obligations? Why do allies and other states that are the targets of alliances sometimes have different expectations about whether allies will actually come to one another's aid? To answer these questions, we need to think about the choices facing all sides of a strategic interaction.

While ironclad alliance guarantees can deter challenges to an ally, they also increase the risk that the ally will become more adventurous, making larger and riskier demands on other states. To see this, return to Figure 5.2 (p. 194). Alliances have two effects. As emphasized earlier, an alliance between States A and C deters a challenger, State B, by reducing the probability that it will win a war against the combined might of the two allies. This is why States A and C are interested in forging the alliance in the first place.

At the same time, the alliance strengthens State A in its bargaining with State B. As the expected war outcome moves to the right, the range of status quo outcomes in which State A has an incentive to challenge State B expands. As a result, State A is likely to demand a better bargain from State B and, following the risk-return trade-off explained in Chapter 3, run a risk of war to obtain its demands. In other words, while the alliance between States A and C weakens State B and deters it from challenging State A, the same alliance strengthens State A and gives it an incentive to demand more of State B.

Why might this situation pose a dilemma? A problem occurs if State C expects to pay greater costs of war than its ally, State A, perhaps because State A cares less about the good in dispute. In this case, there are some status quos that State C would prefer to war, but that State A has an incentive to challenge. If State A were to start a crisis under these conditions, then State C would be put in the undesirable position of having to either abandon its ally or risk being dragged into a war that it values less than the status quo. Thus, while State C wants to defend State A

---

14. Brett Ashley Leeds, "Do Alliances Deter Aggression? The Influence of Military Alliances on the Initiation of Interstate Disputes," *American Journal of Political Science* 47 (2003): 427–39. Because of the deterrent effect of alliances, the frequency with which states fight on behalf of their allies may understate the true reliability of alliances. We get to observe whether an alliance is honored only if it is challenged by an adversary; absent such a challenge, we do not know whether the allies would have fought together had they been challenged. But if third parties are most likely to challenge the alliances that are least credible, then the reliability of the alliances that are challenged is lower than the overall reliability of all alliances. See Alastair Smith, "To Intervene or Not to Intervene: A Biased Decision," *Journal of Conflict Resolution* 40 (1996): 16–40.

from challenges, it must also worry about becoming "entrapped" in a costly war by a reckless ally.[15]

In response to this dilemma, states attempt to avoid **entrapment** by limiting their commitments or leaving those commitments purposely ambiguous. In other words, in an effort to control opportunism by their allies, states rarely forge iron-clad agreements that they must fulfill. Rather, states attempt to reserve a measure of discretion for themselves on when, how, and to what extent they will meet their alliance obligations.

An important example of this challenge can be found in U.S. relations with China and Taiwan. Since 1949, the United States has sought to defend Taiwan from mainland China, which regards the island as a renegade province. China has repeatedly warned that if Taiwan officially declares independence, that act will be a cause for war. The dilemma for the United States has been this: how to deter China from attacking without, at the same time, making Taiwan feel that it could declare and win its independence with the help of the United States. On the one hand, China might attack if it believes the United States would abandon Taiwan. On the other hand, an ironclad promise to defend Taiwan might encourage pro-independence politicians there to take the fateful step that would risk a war. In order to navigate this dilemma, the United States has at times pursued a policy of "strategic ambiguity": making its intentions less than fully clear in the hopes that China will be deterred from attacking while Taiwan will act with restraint.

This dilemma shows that there can be a trade-off between the *credibility* of alliances (which requires ironclad promises) and efforts to *control* alliance partners (which can require ambiguity and flexibility). There is seldom any way to avoid this trade-off. The more credible the guarantee to an ally, the greater the incentive for that ally to behave opportunistically. But the greater the discretion that the state retains in an effort to limit the risk of entrapment, the less credible is the alliance and the less successful it will be in deterring challengers.

Analyzing the European Alliance System, 1879–1990

As we have seen, alliances are institutions that states create in order to facilitate cooperation in support of common interests. They form when states' interests are aligned to an extent that they may be willing to fight on one another's behalf. They work by making it more likely that the states will, in fact, fight together in the event of war and by signaling this willingness to the adversary. As a result, the success or failure of an alliance depends on (1) the strength of the interests that brought the allies together; (2) the ability of the alliance to alter its members' preferences so that in the event of war, fighting is preferable to abandonment; (3) the effectiveness of the alliance in convincing the adversary of this fact; and (4) the ability of the partners to limit the risk of entrapment.

entrapment
The risk of being dragged into an unwanted war because of the opportunistic actions of an ally.

---

15. On entrapment and other forms of opportunism by allies, see Glenn H. Snyder, "The Security Dilemma in Alliance Politics," *World Politics* 36 (1984): 461–95.

We can now use these concepts to analyze some of the major events of the last century through the lens of alliance politics. As noted in Chapter 1, the first and second halves of the twentieth century were markedly different in terms of warfare between the world's major powers. In both periods, international politics was shaped by conflicts among the large, industrialized countries in Europe. In both periods, states that felt threatened formed alliances in the hopes of protecting themselves from rivals. Yet the outcomes in these two periods were quite different. The first half of the century witnessed two world wars of unprecedented destructiveness; the second half was remarkable for the absence of war between the two superpowers, in spite of the intense hostility between them. Although a number of factors help explain this variation, part of the answer is that alliances played a stabilizing role in the second period, but not in the first. The logic developed here can help explain why.

Pre–World War I: Two Armed Camps

In the lead-up to the First World War, the major powers of Europe divided themselves into two competing alliance blocs. On one side was the Triple Alliance, composed of Germany, Austria-Hungary, and Italy; on the other side were Britain, France, and Russia, bound by an agreement that came be known as the Triple Entente. An entente, which comes from the French word for "understanding," is generally seen as a weak form of alliance, requiring consultation and coordination, not necessarily a strict commitment of military assistance. In Europe, the polarization into two blocs had been decades in the making and reflected the ambitions of a rising Germany, the fears of its neighbors to the east and west, and specific conflicts of interest of territory and colonies.

Although the apparent symmetry between the two alliances might have created a stable balance, the system was, in fact, fraught with danger. The alliance network created the possibility that any small conflict could drag all the European powers into war. Of course, since European decision makers understood that a small spark could lead to all-out war, this system did foster some caution and mutual deterrence by raising the expected costs of war to each side. And indeed, several crises in the first decade of the twentieth century were resolved peacefully, in spite of much saber rattling.

Nonetheless, the system had several features that made it unstable. First, as we saw in Chapter 3, the strategic situation created a number of preventive and preemptive incentives. Germany feared the rise of Russian power, causing some strategists to argue that war with Russia would be better now than later. In addition, Germany's need to plan for a two-front war—against France to the west and Russia to the east—gave rise to the Schlieffen Plan, the German war plan with precise timetables and preemptive logic (see the "What Shaped Our World?" box in Chapter 3, p. 126).

Second, the delicate balance made each of the major powers highly dependent on its allies for security; the prospect of losing an ally was seen as particularly dangerous. Hence, when Austrian archduke Franz Ferdinand was assassinated by a Serb extremist on June 28, 1914, the threat that Serb nationalism could rip the Austro-Hungarian Empire apart was also felt keenly in Germany. In the ensuing crisis, Germany gave its ally a blank check, promising to back Austria-Hungary in whatever the latter chose to do. This commitment, however, emboldened Austria-Hungary, leading it to issue a harsh ultimatum to Serbia.[16]

The set of interconnected alliances and Austria-Hungary's unwillingness to back down turned an otherwise local crisis into a war that consumed most of Europe. This process, whereby the actions of a small number of states drag all their allies to war, has been referred to as "chain-ganging," evoking the image of convicts chained together, forced to move in the same direction.[17] Finally, the sheer number of states involved magnified the possibility of miscalculations. Whether an ally would actually fight in the event of war was a crucial question in determining how hard a state could push or how much it should give. Uncertainty about who would join a prospective war created considerable scope for errors.

Probably the most important source of uncertainty in this event was how Great Britain would react in the event of war. Because it had the most powerful navy in the world—larger, in fact, than the next three largest navies combined— whether Britain would join a continental war was a crucially important question, and one over which there was a good deal of uncertainty until the very last minute. Although the Triple Entente committed Britain to consult with France and Russia in the event of war, the British public and many policy makers in government were not keen to shed British blood over what appeared to be a distant matter.

This uncertainty led German decision makers to believe for some time that Britain might stand aside while Germany took on France and Russia. Moreover, suggestions by British leaders that Britain would join its allies in war were discounted by German leaders as bluffs. It is unclear whether German leaders would have backed off from war, had they been certain that Britain would intervene; it is clear, however, that Germany was encouraged by British wavering to take an aggressive position in the crisis. When Britain belatedly made clear that it would join in the fight, the military actions and diplomatic commitments already made by Germany and Austria were hard to reverse. Once war started, the network of the alliances brought all of Europe into the conflict.[18]

The Coming of World War II, 1919–1939 Germany was defeated in World War I, but with Adolf Hitler's ascension to power in 1933, Germany once more posed a challenge to its neighbors. Although European powers again sought to contain the German threat through alliances, the effort was too little and too late to prevent another devastating war.

---

16. Some historians argue that Germany issued the blank check precisely to incite Austro-Hungarian stubbornness and thus provoke war. Among others, see Fritz Fischer, *Germany's Aims in the First World War* (New York: Norton, 1967).

17. Thomas Christensen and Jack Snyder, "Chain Gangs and Passed Bucks: Predicting Alliance Patterns in Multipolarity," *International Organization* 44 (Spring 1990): 137–68.

18. In a final example of how the alliance system failed, Italy refused to join its allies (Germany and Austria) when war broke out. After sitting on the sidelines for several months, Italy decided that the Triple Entente powers were more likely to win. Hence, Italy decided to side with the Triple Entente and, in May 1915, attacked its former ally, Austria-Hungary, with whom it had a long-standing territorial dispute.

In August 1939, Britain formed a defensive alliance with Poland. One month later, Germany invaded Poland, Britain stepped in to defend its ally, and World War II began.

Until the eve of war in 1939, the alliance system that formed to contain Germany rested on a few thin reeds, which easily snapped under Hitler's pressure. Under the terms of the Treaty of Locarno (1925), Britain pledged to defend Belgium and France in the event that either was attacked by Germany and to ensure that Germany respected the demilitarization of the Rhineland region, which bordered those countries. France also signed alliances with several of Germany's neighbors to the east: Poland, Czechoslovakia, Yugoslavia, and Romania. The first of these treaties was tested, and failed, in 1936 when Hitler remilitarized the Rhineland and Britain refused to support France in taking any action to stop the move.

The French guarantees to the eastern European countries lacked credibility because of the geographic separation between them. With most of the French forces positioned to defend a fortified line on the German frontier, France was in a weak position to defend its distant allies from the German threat. The weakness became all too clear in September 1938, when France and Britain acquiesced to German demands for a section of Czechoslovakia called the Sudetenland. Six months later, in March 1939, Germany invaded and conquered the rest of Czechoslovakia, and France did not lift a finger to save its ally. Not until Germany attacked Poland in September 1939 did France and Britain, which had pledged to defend Poland only days earlier, find the resolve to fulfill their commitments.

Hence, rather than being deterred by the states that sought to contain him, Hitler exploited weak alliances that were not backed up by sufficient resolve or capabilities, highlighting the lack of common interests and credible commitments among the allies. Bandwagoning alliances with Italy, the Soviet Union, and eventually Japan only strengthened his hand. The resulting imbalance between a bloc of revisionist powers and a fragmented group of buck-passing allies, combined with a leader ideologically bent on conquest, cast the world into war once more.

The Cold War: The "Long Peace" in Europe, 1945–1990

After the Second World War, European politics came to be dominated by the competition between two superpowers: the United States, which emerged from the war an unmatched industrial powerhouse, and the Soviet Union, whose large army sat astride much of Eastern and Central Europe. Once again, the countries of Europe sorted into alliances in response to the emerging rivalry. But this time, in the five decades that followed the end of World War II, there were no wars among the major European powers.[19] How did alliances contribute to stability in this period, when they had failed to keep the peace before?

Within 10 years after the end of World War II, most countries in Europe belonged to either the **North Atlantic Treaty Organization (NATO)** or the **Warsaw Pact** (see "What Shaped Our World?" on p. 206). NATO covered most of the states of Western Europe and bound them in a collective defense treaty with the United States. Its core provision was in Article 5 of the North Atlantic Treaty, which specified that each member would consider an attack against one or more members to be an attack against them all. The Warsaw Pact covered the states of Eastern Europe and the Soviet Union. Germany, which was split after the war into two countries, was also split between the blocs, with West Germany in NATO and East Germany in the Warsaw Pact.

Each bloc formed in response to a perceived threat from the other. NATO was established in 1949 in response to the Soviet military presence in Eastern Europe— a presence that the Soviets used to install puppet governments in those countries. The Warsaw Pact formed in 1955 after West Germany was admitted into NATO, raising the fear in Moscow that its enemy in the two world wars would again be rearmed and active on the European stage.

Although the experience of World War I would seem to suggest that two alliance blocs, roughly evenly divided, can be a cause of war, the Cold War alliance system had a number of features that made it different, and more stable, than what came before. First, the diplomatic landscape in 1914 was much more complicated, with several major powers in competition and highly dependent on their allies for security. During the Cold War, by contrast, the system was dominated by the two superpowers. This meant that there was less scope for miscalculation, since the outcome of any conflict was dependent on the choices of fewer key actors.

It also meant that neither superpower would be as threatened by the loss of an ally as the states of Europe were before 1914. Germany in the early twentieth century considered the possible loss of Austria-Hungary extremely threatening, worth risking war over. The United States and Soviet Union, by contrast, had less to fear from the possible defection of allies during the Cold War.[20] And indeed, France's departure from NATO's joint military command in 1966, Yugoslavia's defection from the Soviet orbit in 1948, and Romania's increasingly independent foreign policy starting in the 1960s did not upset the relatively stable equilibrium between the two sides.

A second major feature of the Cold War alliances was their highly institutionalized nature. Both NATO and the Warsaw Pact were more than just pieces of paper promising mutual aid in the event of war. Rather, they included a dense set of military, political, and economic relationships. The United States, in particular, needed to demonstrate that it would uphold its commitment to defend its allies an ocean away, since any uncertainty about the U.S. commitment was seen as inviting Soviet aggression against Western Europe.

North Atlantic Treaty Organization (NATO)

An alliance formed in 1949 among the United States, Canada, and most of the states of Western Europe in response to the threat posed by the Soviet Union. The alliance requires the members to consider an attack on any one of them as an attack on all.

Warsaw Pact

A military alliance formed in 1955 to bring together the Soviet Union and its Cold War allies in Eastern Europe and elsewhere; dissolved on March 31, 1991, as the Cold War ended.

---

19. John Lewis Gaddis, "The Long Peace: Elements of Stability in the Postwar International System," *International Security* 10 (Spring 1986): 99–142.

20. Waltz, *Theory of International Politics*, 169–70.

As a result, the NATO alliance provided for close integration of the American and European militaries, a joint command led by an American officer, and the basing of more than a quarter-million U.S. troops on European soil, primarily in West Germany. This forward deployment of U.S. forces served both military and political purposes. It ensured that the United States had capabilities in place to slow a Soviet offensive until much larger reinforcements could come across the sea. It also served to signal the American commitment to the region. In the event of a Soviet attack, U.S. troops would have been quickly involved in the fighting, ensuring that the United States could not remain indifferent.

This political aspect of the American presence in Europe was most clearly evident in the Berlin Brigade, a garrison of about 7,000 troops in West Berlin. Like the rest of Germany, the capital city of Berlin had been divided into western and eastern portions after the war. The city sat in the midst of Communist East Germany, however, so West Berlin was a small island of Western and American influence surrounded by a "red" sea. Given its geographic isolation, the American garrison would have been quickly overrun in the event of a war.

Nonetheless, its presence was seen as a crucial signal of the U.S. commitment to defend Western Europe. The theorist Thomas Schelling described its role vividly:

> The garrison in Berlin is as fine a collection of soldiers as has ever been assembled, but excruciatingly small. What can 7,000 American troops do . . . ? Bluntly, they can die. They can die heroically, dramatically, and in a manner that guarantees that the action cannot stop there. They represent the pride, the honor, and the reputation of the United States government and its armed forces; and they can apparently hold the entire Red Army at bay.[21]

Hence, the military presence was a kind of hand-tying strategy (see Chapter 3): an effort to ensure that if the American commitment to NATO was triggered by a Soviet attack, the United States would have little choice but to fulfill that commitment. The strength of this pledge, clearly signaled to the Soviet Union, had a deterrent effect that contributed to the relative stability of Europe during the Cold War. ("What Shaped Our World?" on p. 206 explores NATO's role since the Cold War.)

As this historical overview suggests, alliances were used frequently in twentieth-century Europe by states looking for partners in defense or conquest. Measured in terms of whether allies fought together when war came, most (but not all) of these alliances were successful. Measured in terms of whether they were able to prevent war in the first place, the track record is more uneven. By far the most successful alliances on this score were the Cold War alliance blocs. Anchored by two strong powers, held together by common security interests, and institutionalized through a variety of military, political, and economic ties, NATO and the Warsaw Pact contributed to a period of relative peace in Europe after World War II. By contrast, the alliances in the first half of the twentieth century either abetted aggression—in the case of the Japanese, Italian, and Russian alliances with

---

21. Thomas C. Schelling, *Arms and Influence* (New Haven, CT: Yale University Press, 1966), 47.

Hitler's Germany—or failed to contain it, contributing to the outbreak of two catastrophic wars. The inability of alliances to keep the peace would propel the search for a different kind of institution to serve this end: collective security organizations.

Collective Security: When Can the UN Keep the Peace?

As World War I was coming to a close, world leaders began to think about what the postwar world should look like. U.S. president Woodrow Wilson argued that the only way to prevent another such war was to change the nature of world politics. Wilson was convinced that the prewar pattern, in which major powers jockeyed for advantage against one another in shifting alliances, had to go. Alliances could not prevent wars; they could only cause wars to spread into larger, more destructive events. In their place, there should be a permanent institution that would enable countries to police the international system in the name of peace and security for all. From this vision, in 1919, the **League of Nations** was born; although it limped along until 1946, it effectively died in 1939 with the onset of World War II.

As World War II was coming to a close, world leaders once again turned their thoughts to the question of how to prevent another such war. Like his predecessor, U.S. president Franklin Roosevelt championed the idea of a permanent governing body that would enable the major powers to police the international system. The **United Nations (UN)** was created in 1945 as a successor to the League of Nations. The UN still functions to this day, but its track record in responding to acts of aggression is, at best, mixed. Why is this? Why have efforts to build an effective international organization capable of policing international politics failed to create a lasting peace?

The League of Nations and the UN are both examples of collective security organizations. Like alliances, **collective security organizations** are institutions that facilitate cooperation among their members. These two kinds of institutions, however, form in response to different kinds of interests. Alliances form when two or more states have a common interest in the outcome of bargaining interactions with an adversary or a set of adversaries and are based on alignments in interests that prompt states to cooperate against a common foe.

Collective security organizations, by contrast, form under the presumption that all states have a common interest in preventing war and aggression, regardless of who the perpetrator and victim are. Unlike alliances, their primary purpose is not to alter bargaining outcomes in favor of one state or another, but rather to ensure that changes to the status quo, if they occur, happen peacefully. They forbid the use of military force by one member state against another, and they generally provide mechanisms, such as mediators or arbitrators, to help member states resolve their disputes peacefully. An attack by one member against another is considered to be a threat to the whole community. As a result, the entire membership is responsible

League of Nations
A collective security organization founded in 1919 after World War I. The League ended in 1946 and was replaced by the United Nations.

United Nations (UN)
A collective security organization founded in 1945 after World War II. With over 190 members, the UN includes all recognized states.

collective security organizations
Broad-based institutions that promote peace and security among their members. Examples include the League of Nations and the United Nations.

The Future of NATO

When the Cold War ended in the late 1980s, many analysts thought that NATO's days were numbered. With the Soviet Union unable to maintain its control over Eastern Europe, the communist regimes in that region fell, and the Warsaw Pact dissolved. When the Soviet Union disintegrated in December 1991, it seemed plausible that the NATO alliance would crumble as well.

NATO's obituaries turned out to be premature. The United States did reduce its troop presence in Europe, but 62,000 U.S. military personnel remain stationed there today. Rather than withering away, NATO expanded eastward, adding 13 states that had been allies or republics of the former Soviet Union (see the map). The alliance also expanded its mission. In the 1990s, NATO intervened with air strikes in the wars that accompanied the breakup of Yugoslavia—not because a NATO member had been attacked, but to address the humanitarian crises those wars created (see pp. 222–225).

Its reach extended further after the September 11, 2001, terrorist attacks on the United States, when the alliance invoked Article 5 of the North Atlantic Treaty, declaring that the entire alliance had been attacked. NATO subsequently played an important role in efforts to stabilize Afghanistan after the U.S. invasion in 2001. In March 2011, NATO initiated a military campaign against Libya in response to that regime's violent crackdown against domestic opponents. How do we explain these developments?

Interests
Those who expected NATO to be thrown onto the ash heap of history believed that the common interests and fears that originally brought the alliance into being had vanished, and that without a clearly defined purpose, it would eventually disappear.[a] Subsequent events suggest that its members still share interests in common. These include a basic concern for security, but with an expanded conception of where the main threats lie: particularly, terrorism and the ability of terrorists to take root in chaotic, war-torn regions. Moreover, the operations in the former Yugoslavia and Libya showed that the alliance could act on a common commitment to stop massive violations of human rights. NATO members also had an interest in ensuring that former Soviet satellites in Eastern Europe developed stable, democratic, pro-Western regimes; many of those states, for their part, wanted the protection of NATO to guard against a resurgent Russia.

Institutions
NATO's persistence also reminds us that institutions often adapt to changing environments rather than die. Observers draw an analogy to the March of Dimes. This charity was originally formed to combat polio, but when that disease was largely eradicated following the discovery of a vaccine, the organization quickly expanded its agenda to include a host of other childhood illnesses. In taking on new missions and "out of area operations"—that is, operations not confined to territory of the member states—NATO has been transformed from a purely defensive alliance into something more akin to a collective security organization.

Interactions
Common interests and institutional adaptation do not preclude tough bargaining within the alliance. During the Cold War, NATO faced the collective action problem of providing the public good of common defense against the Soviet Union. Burden sharing was an essential principle of cooperation, but the United States—by far the largest member—was willing to bear a disproportionate share of the costs of collective defense. In return, Washington dominated alliance decision making.

In the last two decades, this bargain has come under strain. American leadership was questioned during the lead-up to the 2003 Iraq War, when key NATO allies, particularly France and Germany, refused to endorse the Bush administration's case for preventive war. Conflicting views and interests divided the alliance, preventing it from reaching a common policy toward Iraq.[b] In 2011, Germany refused to take part in the operation over Libya.

For its part, the United States has pressured European partners to increase their defense contributions.

---

a. For an example of this argument, see John J. Mearsheimer, "Back to the Future: Instability in Europe after the Cold War," *International Security* 15 (Summer 1990): 5–56.

b. See Philip H. Gordon and Jeremy Shapiro, *Allies at War: America, Europe, and the Crisis over Iraq* (New York: McGraw-Hill, 2004).

At U.S. urging, the alliance agreed that members should seek to spend at least 2 percent of their GDP on defense—a benchmark that, in 2017, only 5 of the 28 members reached. When he came into office, President Donald Trump suggested that the U.S. commitment to NATO might depend on its meeting this target. In response, many European governments have argued that military spending is a poor indicator of what they contribute to the common defense.

At the same time, the expansion of NATO up to Russia's borders has contributed to renewed conflict. Russian military advances into Georgia (2008) and Ukraine (2014)—both countries that at times courted NATO membership—created pressure on the alliance to cooperate in containing and sanctioning Russia. Whether the institution and the common but fraying interests of its members will remain sufficiently robust to overcome the more intense bargaining, both within the alliance and with Russia, remains an open question.

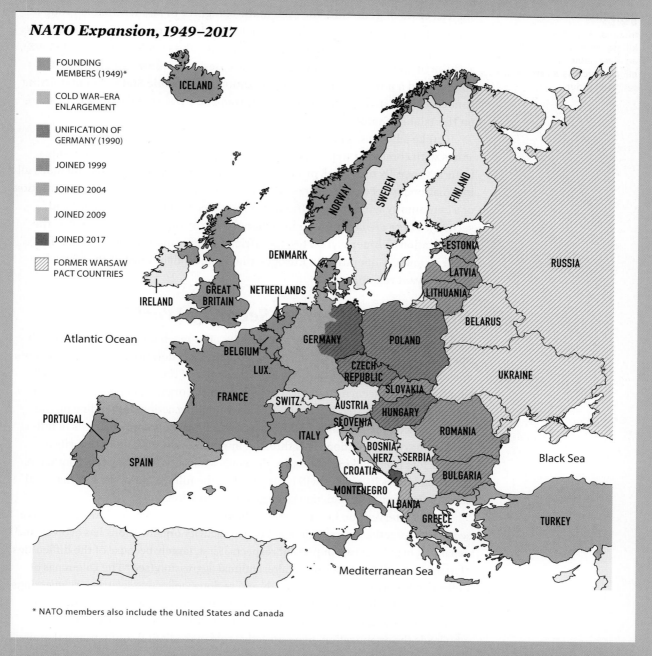

NATO Expansion, 1949–2017

FOUNDING MEMBERS (1949)*

COLD WAR–ERA ENLARGEMENT

UNIFICATION OF GERMANY (1990)

JOINED 1999

JOINED 2004

JOINED 2009

JOINED 2017

FORMER WARSAW PACT COUNTRIES

* NATO members also include the United States and Canada

for coming to the aid of the victims of aggression. This collective response is intended to deter would-be aggressors in the first place and, in the event that deterrence fails, ensure that those who wrong the community by engaging in war will not benefit from the transgression.

Although collective security organizations were born out of the desire to prevent interstate wars, they have also sought to prevent violence within states. Indeed, the UN has been quite active in dealing with civil wars and maintaining peace in their aftermath. In recent years, there also has been pressure to expand its scope to deal with gross violations of human rights, such as cases of **genocide**, the systematic slaughter of an identifiable group of people. In fact, genocidal conflicts have led to the sharpest criticism of the UN in recent years: for inaction in such places as Rwanda (1994), Bosnia (1992–95), and Darfur (2003–present; more on these cases will follow). In 2016, the UN condemned a nonstate terrorist organization, the Islamic State, for committing genocide against religious minorities in Iraq and Syria (see Chapter 6 for more on the Islamic State).

Unlike alliances, whose membership is restricted to a small number of states with common interests, the membership of collective security organizations is generally universal, or nearly universal. The UN, for example, includes all internationally recognized states. Universal membership reflects the presumption of a community with universally shared interests in international peace and security. There are also numerous regional security organizations—such as the Organization of American States, the African Union, and the Organization for Security and Co-operation in Europe—that include all or most of the states in each relevant region.

How Does Collective Security Work?

In theory, collective security works as follows. The mechanism is triggered when one state attacks or threatens to attack another. If it is determined that these events constitute an act of aggression—or, in the language of the UN, a "threat to international peace and security"—then all members of the organization are called on to act against the state that has committed the offending action. Depending on the circumstances, the prescribed action can range from economic sanctions to full-scale military intervention. This threat of intervention is intended primarily to deter actors from making aggressive demands against or attacking one another. A state that knows its actions will be opposed by the full weight of the international community should be reluctant to engage in aggression.

While intervention in interstate conflicts reflects the classic view of collective security, in practice the tool kit of collective security organizations has evolved and expanded in at least two important respects. First, largely because of the difficulties of mounting unified responses to international aggression (see "The Dilemmas of Collective Security" on p. 210), the UN and regional collective security organizations have developed alternative strategies that are intended to foster peaceful conflict resolution without requiring costly interventions. The UN secretary-general, who leads the organization, plays an active role in mediating conflicts and thereby

genocide

Intentional and systematic killing aimed at eliminating an identifiable group of people, such as an ethnic or religious group.

After civil conflict broke out in the Central African Republic in 2013, the African Union (AU), a regional security organization, deployed soldiers to help contain the violence and protect civilians. In September 2014, that mission was replaced by a larger UN peacekeeping operation. Here, Gabonese soldiers from the AU force, in green berets, confer with newly arriving UN troops, in blue.

helping states identify mutually beneficial bargains.[22] The United Nations also authorizes the deployment of peacekeeping forces—troops from neutral third parties—to help monitor and enforce peace agreements. We will say more about the theory and practice of peacekeeping in the discussion that follows.

Second, collective security organizations have in recent decades extended their mandate to include stopping or preventing civil conflicts and large-scale human rights abuses. Civil wars and genocides have at times been labeled as "threats to international peace and security," giving rise to **humanitarian interventions**, or collective interventions designed to relieve humanitarian crises. Ironically, while peacekeeping and humanitarian intervention do not fit the original view of collective security, they are, in practice, the bulk of what collective security organizations now do.

The various strategies employed by collective security organizations can influence the bargaining interaction between adversaries in at least three ways, all of them intended to foster peaceful outcomes. First, as with alliances, the prospect of outside involvement makes war less attractive by changing the likely outcome of the interaction between states or, in the case of civil wars, between groups. At the extreme, the combined weight of the entire international community means that the defeat of the challenger is virtually certain. (Consider what Figure 5.2 would look like if State C were replaced with the entire international community.) The status quo is stable if both sides know that they will surely lose if they attempt to change the status quo by force. Under such conditions, neither side can shift the bargain in its favor by threatening war.

humanitarian interventions

Interventions designed to relieve humanitarian crises stemming from civil conflicts or large-scale human rights abuses, including genocide.

---

22. Kjell Skjelsbaek and Gunnar Fermann, "The UN Secretary-General and the Mediation of International Disputes," in *Resolving International Conflicts*, ed. Jacob Bercovitch (Boulder, CO: Lynne Rienner, 1996), 75–104.

Second, outsiders can help resolve the commitment problems identified in Chapter 3 by promising to enforce what would otherwise be an unbelievable commitment by one state not to exploit its power against another. A shift in relative power between two states might be rendered less dangerous if the weakened state can count on others to defend it, thus diminishing any preventive incentive it might have. Likewise, a state may feel secure handing over a piece of strategic territory if it knows that others will come to its aid in the event that its adversary exploits this territory to attack or press further claims.

In other words, the state that is made more powerful by the deal can more credibly commit not to exploit its newfound power if it knows that any attempt to do so will be countered by the international community. For example, as noted in Chapter 3, Israel and Syria have a conflict over the strategically valuable Golan Heights, which Israel seized from Syria in 1967. Since control of this territory imparts a military advantage to its owner, Israel has been reluctant to return the land to Syria without guarantees that it (Israel) will remain safe from attack. In 1974, however, the two states agreed to withdraw their forces from the Golan Heights, and the UN inserted over 1,000 peacekeeping troops into observation posts in the hills between the two sides' positions.[23] For four decades, those troops helped ensure that neither side would deploy forces to the area, thereby easing a source of tension in the region. Starting in 2014, the peacekeepers came under attack by militant groups engaged in the Syrian civil war (see Chapter 6), but the mission has continued in spite of the risks.

Third, collective security organizations may play a positive role in promoting peace not through a threat of direct intervention for or against any particular side, but by serving as neutral observers and peacekeepers. Peacekeepers diminish first-strike advantages by interposing themselves between two adversarial factions, as in the Golan Heights. Such operations are particularly useful in cases in which previously warring parties have each pledged to disarm and demobilize, but each fears that if it disarms and the other does not, it will be at a dangerous disadvantage. As we will see in Chapter 6, the commitment problem associated with disarmament is a major obstacle to preventing and ending civil wars. The UN often deploys peacekeeping missions into precisely such situations in order to make sure that both sides uphold their promise to disarm and that neither side attempts to exploit the other in the process. For example, following the end of the civil war in Liberia, which claimed almost 150,000 lives from 1989 to 2003, the UN inserted 15,000 peacekeepers to facilitate disarmament and demobilization.

The Dilemmas of Collective Security

Regardless of where and how the organization chooses to intervene, it faces two major challenges: a collective action problem and a joint decision-making problem. The collective action problem arises from the fact that collective security

---

23. For more information on the UN peacekeeping mission in the Golan Heights, see www.un.org/en/peacekeeping/missions/undof (accessed 03/02/15).

organizations, unlike their members, do not have the power to tax anyone or to raise and field military forces. As a result, the organizations are wholly dependent on their members to provide troops, funds, and military equipment for any operation. The member states that contribute then face the costs and risks associated with sending troops into combat or forgoing trade because of economic sanctions.

Crucially, the international peace and stability that these actions are intended to provide is a public good. Recall from Chapter 2 that a public good can be enjoyed whether or not one actually contributed to its creation. If the community succeeds in preventing or reversing an act of aggression, all members of the community enjoy the benefit—whether or not they took costly action. After all, even if all states have an interest in seeing aggression halted, their first preference will often be to have the aggression halted by someone other than themselves.

Hence, collective security organizations necessarily face a free-rider problem: the temptation that member states face to let the burden of providing the public good fall on others. Because of this problem, even if everyone shares an interest in cooperating to stop or prevent a war, their collective effort may fall well short of what is required to do so. Indeed, UN peacekeeping missions are often underfunded and undermanned relative to their mandates; the temptation to free ride, to pass the costs to other states, leads to low levels of cooperation.

The challenges of joint decision making are also severe. Members of the organization need to be able to determine which acts constitute a threat to the community, which states are aggressors, and what actions to take in response. These determinations are not always straightforward, since collective security organizations permit states to use force in self-defense. Of course, states generally justify their military actions as being in self-defense, so determining which acts are acts of aggression and which are self-defense is necessary for the organization to function. Otherwise, the entire system can collapse as each side accuses the other of being at fault. A finding that a particular act constitutes a threat to international peace and security not only delegitimizes that act as a violation of community interests, but also grants legitimacy to those who use force to reverse it. As we will see, this grant of legitimacy can be an asset to states that operate under the organization's seal of approval.[24]

Determining whether a given act merits an international response is complicated by the mix of interests that member states have. Although they may share a general interest in halting aggression and promoting the peaceful settlement of disputes, they may also have specific interests that diverge in any particular conflict. Recall that collective security organizations, because of their universal membership, often include states with varying, even opposing, interests.

Whereas NATO during the Cold War included only states that perceived a common threat from the Soviet Union, the UN during this period included not only the United States and its NATO allies, but also the Soviet Union and

---

24. On the UN's legitimacy role, see Ian Hurd, *After Anarchy: Legitimacy and Power in the United Nations Security Council* (Princeton, NJ: Princeton University Press, 2007); and Alexander Thompson, *Channeling Power: The UN Security Council and American Statecraft in Iraq* (Ithaca, NY: Cornell University Press, 2009).

While the UN Security Council has the authority to identify and dictate the organization's response to international security threats, it is sometimes difficult for members with competing interests to agree on the best course of action. Here, Russia's ambassador to the UN vetoes a resolution that would have condemned the government of Syria, its traditional ally, for a fatal chemical weapons attack in April 2017.

its allies, as well as states that were neutral in the superpower rivalry. This mix of interests means that in many situations, the members of a collective security organization may not all be neutral outsiders to a particular military action. Some may have reasons to favor one side or the other in a dispute, meaning that some will be motivated to see aggression where others will not. Collective security works best when all states are satisfied with the current status quo—a condition that is rarely met.

Institutional Responses to the Challenges of Collective Security

The design of collective security organizations reflects the challenges posed by the dilemmas of collective action and joint decision making. Recall that institutions facilitate cooperation in situations that arise repeatedly. Rather than treating each new crisis in an ad hoc manner, requiring renegotiation of standards and rules each time, institutions embody a lasting set of standards and decision-making rules.

In the two most ambitious collective security organizations attempted in the last century—the League of Nations and the UN—the problems of collective action and joint decision making were addressed by vesting the main decision-making power in the hands of relatively small councils dominated by the strongest states in the system. These councils were given the authority to determine whether a particular action was a threat to international peace and security and to prescribe the organization's response. The League Council began with 4 permanent members— Great Britain, France, Italy, and Japan—and 4 nonpermanent members who were elected every three years. Germany later joined as a fifth permanent member,[25] and the council was expanded to 15.

When the UN replaced the League in 1946, its **Security Council (UNSC)** had a similar structure: 5 permanent members and 6 (later 10) nonpermanent members. The **permanent five (P5)** are the United States, Great Britain, France, Russia (formerly the Soviet Union), and China. In both cases, the privileged few shared a common trait: with the exception of Germany, which was admitted to the League only belatedly, they were the victors of the global wars that gave birth to these organizations.

The voting rules of both councils amplified the influence of these permanent members. In the case of the League Council, all decisions had to be unanimously approved by all 15 members. As a result, any member of the council could block the organization from acting by withholding its support. In other words, every member of the council had **veto power**, and permanent members had permanent veto power. This voting rule was modified in the Security Council. Enacting a substantive resolution in the Security Council requires a "yes" vote from at least 9 of the 15 council members *and* the support of every one of the P5. This change was intended to make decisive action easier—by eliminating the requirement that all members agree—but it also magnified the asymmetrical role of the P5, each of which can block a resolution it does not like.

These arrangements have several virtues. First, vesting decision-making power with a relatively small group of states means that it is not necessary to obtain consensus within the entire membership (which, in the case of the UN, now numbers 193). This both reduces the costs of coming to an agreement and, in theory at least, makes it possible for the organization to respond to crises quickly. Second, these rules ensure that when the organization acts, it does so with the consent of the strongest powers in the international system. This arrangement can help address the collective action problem by ensuring that any operation that is approved will enjoy cooperation and contributions from those members with the greatest resources and capabilities. Moreover, the veto ensures that at a minimum, the organization's actions will not be forcibly opposed by any of these powerful members.

As with all institutions, however, the effects of these rules are not neutral; rather, they bias policy outcomes in a direction that favors the states that were in a position to dictate the rules at the outset. The organization cannot act on its core mission without unanimity among the most powerful states in the system, any one of which can block action by exercising its veto. Such unanimity can be difficult to achieve. When the major powers disagree among themselves, the permanent-member veto introduces a bias toward inaction. The veto also ensures that the organization cannot act in ways that harm the interests of any of the permanent members.

As a result, the organization wields its policing powers unevenly: it may respond to the crimes of those who are weak, or who have no friends among the permanent members, while the crimes of the strong, or those with friends in high places, may go unpunished. In the case of Tibet, mentioned at the outset of this

Security Council (UNSC)

The main governing body of the UN, which has the authority to identify threats to international peace and security and to prescribe the organization's response, including military and/or economic sanctions.

permanent five (P5)

The five permanent members of the UN Security Council: the United States, Great Britain, France, Russia (formerly the Soviet Union), and China.

veto power

The ability to prevent the passage of a measure through a unilateral act, such as a single negative vote.

---

25. Originally, the United States was intended to be the fifth permanent member, but the United States never joined the League, because of congressional opposition.

Because of its institutional rules, the UN is unlikely to undertake missions that harm the interests of any of its most powerful members. For example, UN efforts to impose economic sanctions on the government of Sudan, in response to the genocide in the Darfur region, were blocked by China. As a big buyer of Sudanese oil, China has an interest in sparing Sudan from punishment.

chapter, any effective action by the UN against China could have been blocked by China's ally, the Soviet Union.[26] More recently, Russia has blocked efforts to sanction the government of Syria, a longtime Russian ally, for indiscriminate killing of civilians during the civil war that has raged in that country since 2011.

In sum, collective security organizations help states cooperate to further their collective interests in international peace by providing rules and standards to address challenges that complicate collective action and joint decision making. Nonetheless, these institutions operate under constraints that limit their ability to act effectively. Collective security organizations are most likely to succeed when two conditions are met. First, the powerful member states that are central to their decision-making processes must all agree on the desirability of collective action. At a minimum, none of these states can be sufficiently opposed that it will block such action.

Second, at least some members must value the collective good highly enough that they are willing to pay the costs in lives and money to ensure that the good is provided. This is most likely when the anticipated costs of intervention are low or when states have some private interest in contributing above and beyond the public interest in stopping aggression. In other words, collective security institutions are useful at promoting cooperation when their key members have strong common interests in protecting the peace; unfortunately, the existence of such common interests is not guaranteed.

The Experience of Collective Security: The United Nations

To see how these predictions have been borne out historically, we consider the experience of the most ambitious collective security organization ever created: the UN. This organization arose from the ashes of World War II with the aspiration, articulated in its founding charter, to "save succeeding generations from the scourge of war"—a goal that had become all the more pressing with the development of nuclear weapons, which have the capacity to kill millions in the blink of an eye.

26. Communist China was not, at that time, on the Security Council. Until 1971, China's seat on the council was held by Taiwan.

Although the world has not since seen a repetition of global warfare, or the nightmare of nuclear war, the role of the UN in preventing these outcomes is not clear. Indeed, the UN has had uneven success in fulfilling its creators' aspirations. In this section, we briefly review the experience of the UN. As we will see, the challenges facing collective security organizations described in the preceding discussion play a large role in accounting for this organization's limited success historically.

What Does the UN Do?

When countries join the UN, they sign on to the organization's charter.[27] Members pledge not to use force in disputes with one another and to seek assistance from the organization in resolving their conflicts peacefully. Chapter VII of the UN Charter authorizes the Security Council to identify acts of aggression and threats to peace and to determine what measures should be taken in response. The charter first provides for economic and diplomatic sanctions to be applied against aggressor states, but it also authorizes the Security Council to "take such action by air, sea, or land forces as may be necessary to maintain or restore international peace and security."

In practice, the Security Council can authorize two different kinds of military operations: peace-enforcement and peacekeeping. A **peace-enforcement operation** is intended to impose peace upon warring parties by intervening in an ongoing conflict, consistent with the traditional vision of collective security. The Security Council can authorize such an operation under Chapter VII of the charter, after finding that a particular situation is a threat to international peace and security. The invasion of one state by another is a classic example of the kind of act that was intended to trigger intervention under Chapter VII. In recent years, the Security Council has also authorized action under Chapter VII for purely civil conflicts when the state in question could not or did not request intervention.

peace-enforcement operation
A military operation in which force is used to make and/or enforce peace among warring parties that have not agreed to end their fighting.

Because peace-enforcement operations are generally targeted against one or more sides that are viewed as aggressors, they are not impartial, and the expectation is that troops involved in such operations will engage in combat. Hence, peace-enforcement operations tend to be heavily armed, and one or more P5 members may be centrally involved in providing the necessary resources. The UN efforts in the Korean War and the Persian Gulf War both fall within this category, as does the 2011 NATO-led intervention in Libya, which received UN approval under Chapter VII.

A **peacekeeping operation**, by contrast, typically follows the conclusion of an interstate or civil war. The combatants have agreed to end the fighting, but it is considered valuable to have an impartial force in place to make sure that the war does not resume. In such instances, the UN may assemble a multinational peacekeeping force with the mandate to verify that the terms of the peace agreement are kept: that the cease-fire holds; that any temporary cease-fire lines are respected; that troops are withdrawn or demobilized, if there are provisions to that effect; and so on. In the aftermath of civil conflict, peacekeeping forces have also helped to

peacekeeping operation
An operation in which troops and observers are deployed to monitor a cease-fire or peace agreement.

---

27. The entire UN Charter can be viewed at www.un.org/en/documents/charter (accessed 03/02/15).

administer elections and ensure their fairness. Their deployment typically requires that the parties to the conflict agree to invite them in—a requirement known as *host nation agreement*. Hence, except in rare cases, peacekeepers are not imposed on warring parties; rather, they deploy only with those parties' consent.

Although peacekeepers may be physically interposed between the adversaries or may patrol in areas where fighting could recur, they are typically lightly armed. Their purpose is not to fight a war, but to make sure that a war does not restart. For this reason, their main resource is not military power, but rather their perceived impartiality; that is, they are neutral brokers, favoring neither side in the dispute. As a result, peacekeepers are often drawn from distant countries with only weak interests in the conflict, and rarely from the P5. To illustrate, Table 5.1 provides a list of the top 10 contributors to peacekeeping missions in January 2018, none of which is a permanent member; the ranking of the permanent members is also shown. Interestingly, peacekeeping operations are not explicitly envisioned by the UN Charter. The difficulties of organizing peace-enforcement operations during the Cold War led the UN to innovate this less costly and less controversial strategy for conflict management.[28]

Cold War Paralysis   The UN was born with high hopes but soon found its most ambitious aspirations dashed by conflict among the powerful states in the system. The Cold War between the United States and the Soviet Union, which lasted from approximately 1946 to 1989, meant that the Security Council was largely incapable of dealing with issues that cut across this key divide. On many matters that came before the council, one side or the other had an interest in blocking effective action.

For example, when the United States put forward proposals in 1947 to help Greece in its civil war against communist rebels, the Soviet Union exercised its veto. The United States, for its part, wielded its veto quite frequently to stop resolutions that it saw as harmful to Israel, such as those censuring Israel for its treatment of Palestinians in the occupied territories. France, Great Britain, and China also exercised their vetoes, though on significantly fewer occasions. All in all, during the period between 1946 and 1989, there were 192 vetoes cast on substantive issues before the council. This compares to 646 resolutions passed in the same period. The UN was most active in cases that did not cut across the Cold War divide, in which case one or both superpowers had little direct interest.

The major exception to this generalization, the UN-sponsored intervention in the Korean War, is the one that proves the rule. Two days after North Korea invaded South Korea, the Security Council passed Resolution 83, authorizing member states to assist South Korea in repelling the attack. While the United States provided the bulk of the forces for this operation, it was joined by 19 other states. Given that North Korea was an ally of the Soviet Union, the latter should have been expected to veto the Security Council resolution. This act would not have prevented

---

28. When authorizing peacekeeping operations, the UN Security Council typically invokes Chapter VI of the charter, which provides for steps to peacefully resolve disputes that have the potential to threaten international peace and security.

TABLE 5.1 *Top Contributors to UN Peacekeeping Operations, January 2015*

RANK	COUNTRY	NUMBER OF PERSONNEL
1	Ethiopia	8,370
2	Bangladesh	7,053
3	India	6,695
4	Rwanda	6,476
5	Pakistan	6,216
6	Nepal	5,496
7	Egypt	3,256
8	Senegal	3,219
9	Indonesia	2,702
10	Ghana	2,675

Contributions of Peacekeepers from the P5

RANK	COUNTRY	NUMBER OF PERSONNEL
12	China	2,634
31	France	823
35	United Kingdom	729
67	Russia	83
72	United States	57

Source: UN, Department of Peacekeeping Operations, peacekeeping.un.org/sites/default/files/ranking_of_military_and_police_contributions.pdf (accessed 03/19/18).

American intervention, but it would have denied the operation UN blessing and perhaps some multilateral support.

The veto failed to materialize because the Soviet Union was boycotting meetings of the Security Council at the time, because of a dispute over China's representation on the body. When the UN was created, mainland China was ruled by a pro-American nationalist government. In 1949, however, Communist forces defeated the nationalists in a civil war, and the latter fled to the island of Taiwan. A year later, when the Korean War broke out, China's seat on the Security Council was held by a representative of the nationalist government on Taiwan. The Soviet Union argued that China's seat should be filled by a representative of the

TABLE 5.2 *The UN during and after the Cold War*

	COLD WAR (1946–89)	POST–COLD WAR (1990–2017)
Security Council resolutions approved	646	1,751
Vetoed resolutions*	162	39
Peacekeeping missions	18	53

*Vetoed resolutions include vetoes of draft resolutions, and not vetoes of amendments to or subsections of resolutions.

Sources: For information on UNSC resolutions passed, see www.un.org/en/sc/documents/resolutions; on vetoes, http://research.un.org/en/docs/sc/quick/veto; on peacekeeping operations, https://peacekeeping.un.org/en/past-peacekeeping-operations (all accessed 03/19/18).

Communist government on the mainland, and it refused to attend meetings of the Security Council until that demand was met. Hence, when Resolution 83 came to a vote on June 27, 1950, the Soviet representative was not present to cast a veto. The Soviet Union ended its boycott of the Security Council not long afterward.[29]

The Cold War divide thus crippled the UN for the first five decades of its existence. Although the organization did have a constructive role at times—brokering cease-fires on several occasions and deploying 18 peacekeeping missions—it sat on the sidelines of many of the most dangerous conflicts of this period.

The Gulf War and the "New World Order" The end of the Cold War created new possibilities for the UN. In 1989, the central source of the East-West rivalry, Soviet domination of Eastern Europe, receded. And in December 1991, the Soviet Union itself dissolved and was replaced by 15 new independent states, the largest of which, Russia, inherited the Soviet Union's seat in the UN, along with most of its military capabilities. The dramatic realignment of interests and reduction in conflict among the P5 meant that the UN could take on a more active role. And indeed, 1990 marks a major turning point in the activity of the organization. As Table 5.2 shows, the post–Cold War period saw a marked drop in the number of vetoes cast and a corresponding increase in the number of peacekeeping missions and resolutions passed by the Security Council. Map 5.1 on page 220 shows where UN peacekeeping missions were deployed in 2017.

Optimism about the UN's role in the post–Cold War period hit a high point very early on, in the wake of Iraq's invasion of Kuwait in August 1990. As we have seen, U.S. president George H. W. Bush committed almost immediately to ensuring that the conquest of Kuwait would not stand. Bush also made a concerted effort to line up UN support at every step of the way. Between Iraq's invasion of Kuwait and

---

29. China's seat on the Security Council remained in the hands of Taiwan until 1971, when warming relations between the United States and the People's Republic of China paved the way for the seat to be transferred to the mainland's control.

the U.S.-led military operation to reverse it, the Security Council passed 12 resolutions on the crisis. The most important of these, Resolution 678, authorized member states to use "all necessary means" to bring about the unconditional withdrawal of Iraqi forces from Kuwait if Iraq did not comply voluntarily by January 15, 1991.

The Security Council's approval of this resolution owed a great deal to the reduction of conflict in the international system with the end of the Cold War. The Soviet Union had long been an ally of Iraq, and in an earlier period it might have been expected to veto a resolution like 678. In the post–Cold War environment, however, when the Soviet Union desired better relations with the West, it was relatively easy to overcome that country's reluctance to approve the use of force against its former ally.

The blessing of the UN meant that the United States had substantial international assistance in the ensuing war. The coalition that fought Iraq included troops from 35 nations. As shown in Figure 5.3, the United States supplied the vast majority of the troops for the operation, but the multinational cast and UN blessing had political, if not much military, significance. The participation of a number of Arab and Muslim states was seen as important in blunting Iraq's argument that the United States was waging a war against Islam. The limited mandate of the operation—to liberate Kuwait and not to occupy Iraq—was intended to reassure states in the region that the United States did not have expansionist objectives. International support also reduced the financial costs of the war. Contributions from other countries covered about 90 percent of the $61 billion the United States spent fighting the war—making the Persian Gulf War the least expensive war in America's history on a per capita basis.

The successful operation of the UN machinery in this case led to great optimism about the role this organization could play in the new international environment.

FIGURE 5.3 *Allied Troop Contributions to the Persian Gulf War, 1990–91*

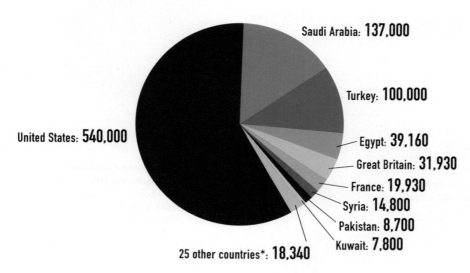

Saudi Arabia: **137,000**

Turkey: **100,000**

Egypt: **39,160**

Great Britain: **31,930**

France: **19,930**

Syria: **14,800**

Pakistan: **8,700**

Kuwait: **7,800**

United States: **540,000**

25 other countries*: **18,340**

Figure source: U.S. General Accounting Office, *Persian Gulf: Allied Burden Sharing Efforts*, GAO/NSIAD-92-71, Appendix II, 16-7, www.gao.gov/products/NSIAD-92-71 (accessed 10/20/08).

*Bangladesh, Morocco, Qatar, United Arab Emirates, Canada, Italy, Australia, Netherlands, Oman, Spain, Bahrain, Germany, Belgium, Senegal, Niger, Argentina, Philippines, Greece, Poland, South Korea, Czechoslovakia, Denmark, Norway, New Zealand, Hungary.

MAP 5.1 *UN Peacekeeping Operations Active in 2017*

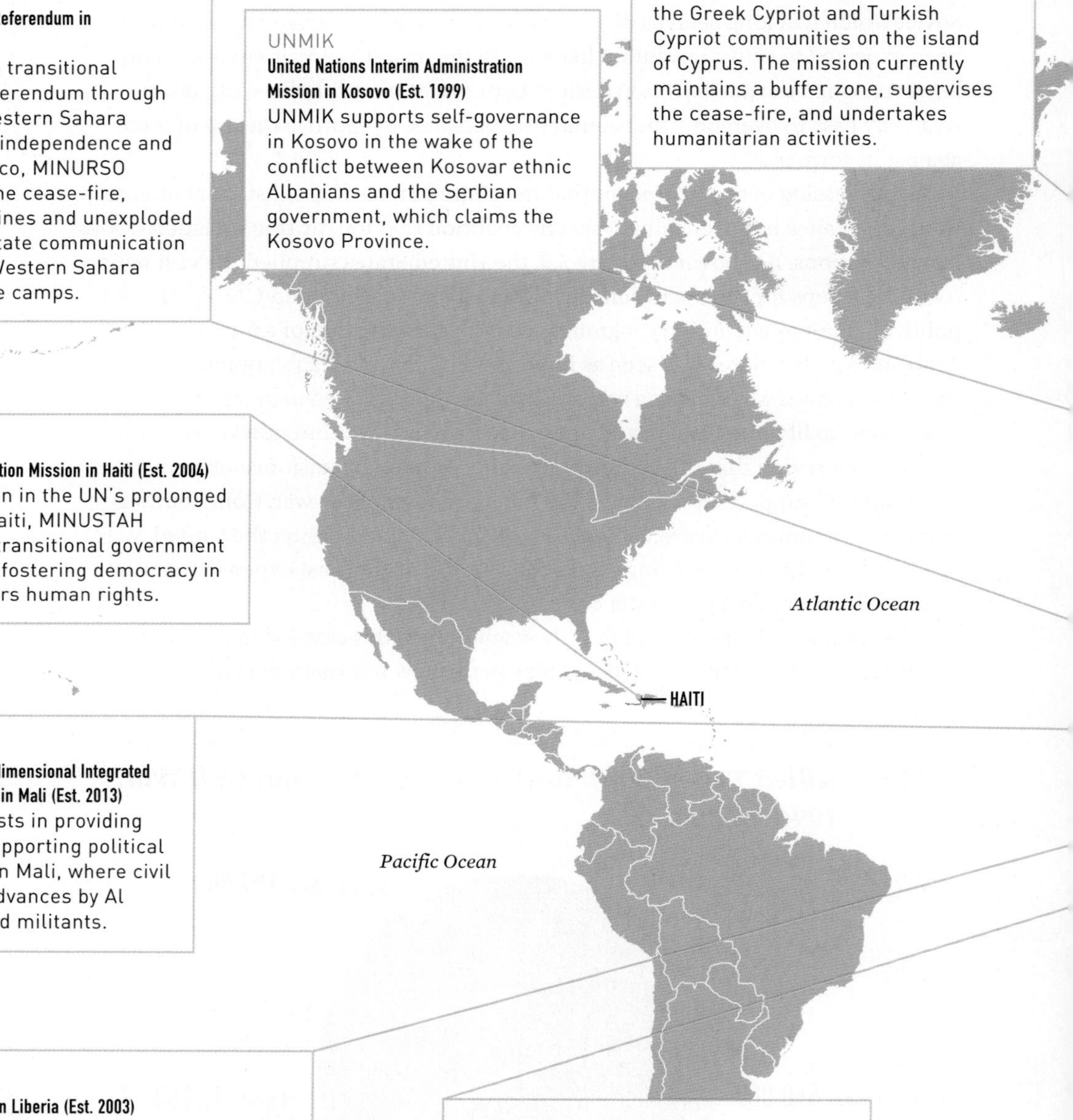

UNFICYP
United Nations Peacekeeping Force in Cyprus (Est. 1964)
UNFICYP was established to prevent the recurrence of violence between the Greek Cypriot and Turkish Cypriot communities on the island of Cyprus. The mission currently maintains a buffer zone, supervises the cease-fire, and undertakes humanitarian activities.

MINURSO
United Nations Mission for the Referendum in Western Sahara (Est. 1991)
Created to safeguard a transitional period to prepare a referendum through which the people of Western Sahara could choose between independence and integration with Morocco, MINURSO continues to monitor the cease-fire, reduce the threat of mines and unexploded ammunition, and facilitate communication between Saharans in Western Sahara and in Algerian refugee camps.

UNMIK
United Nations Interim Administration Mission in Kosovo (Est. 1999)
UNMIK supports self-governance in Kosovo in the wake of the conflict between Kosovar ethnic Albanians and the Serbian government, which claims the Kosovo Province.

MINUSTAH
United Nations Stabilization Mission in Haiti (Est. 2004)
The latest mission in the UN's prolonged involvement in Haiti, MINUSTAH supports Haiti's transitional government in governing and fostering democracy in Haiti, and monitors human rights.

MINUSMA
United Nations Multidimensional Integrated Stabilization Mission in Mali (Est. 2013)
MINUSMA assists in providing security and supporting political reconciliation in Mali, where civil unrest led to advances by Al Qaeda–affiliated militants.

UNMIL
United Nations Mission in Liberia (Est. 2003)
UNMIL supports the transition to democratic rule in Liberia following its civil war. It provides security, assists in reforming the military and police, and supports human rights activities.

MINUSCA
United Nations Multidimensional Integrated Stabilization Mission in the Central African Republic (Est. 2014)
MINUSCA protects civilians, facilitates humanitarian assistance, and promotes human rights in response to conflict in the Central African Republic.

Atlantic Ocean

Pacific Ocean

HAITI

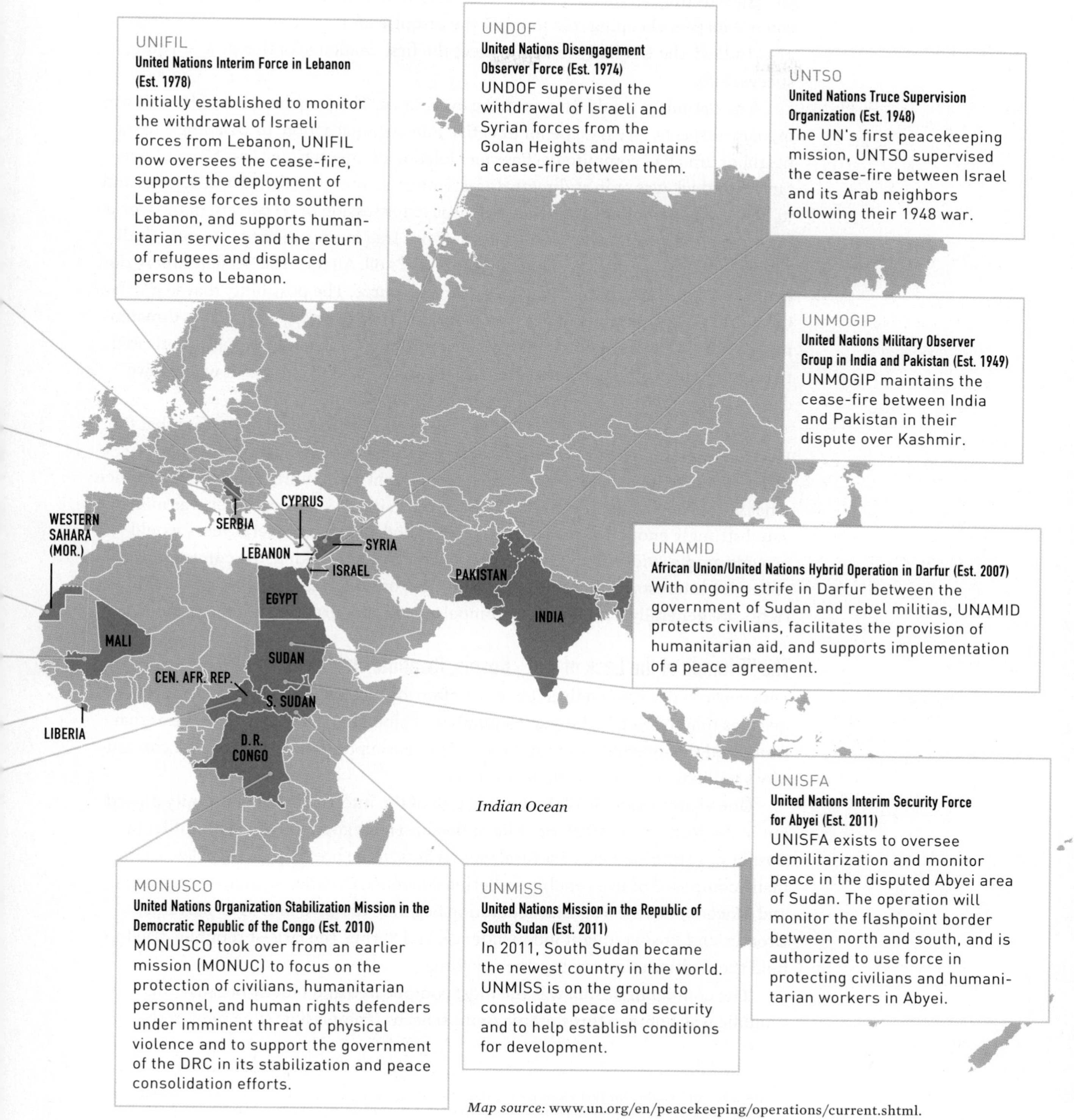

UNIFIL
United Nations Interim Force in Lebanon (Est. 1978)
Initially established to monitor the withdrawal of Israeli forces from Lebanon, UNIFIL now oversees the cease-fire, supports the deployment of Lebanese forces into southern Lebanon, and supports humanitarian services and the return of refugees and displaced persons to Lebanon.

UNDOF
United Nations Disengagement Observer Force (Est. 1974)
UNDOF supervised the withdrawal of Israeli and Syrian forces from the Golan Heights and maintains a cease-fire between them.

UNTSO
United Nations Truce Supervision Organization (Est. 1948)
The UN's first peacekeeping mission, UNTSO supervised the cease-fire between Israel and its Arab neighbors following their 1948 war.

UNMOGIP
United Nations Military Observer Group in India and Pakistan (Est. 1949)
UNMOGIP maintains the cease-fire between India and Pakistan in their dispute over Kashmir.

UNAMID
African Union/United Nations Hybrid Operation in Darfur (Est. 2007)
With ongoing strife in Darfur between the government of Sudan and rebel militias, UNAMID protects civilians, facilitates the provision of humanitarian aid, and supports implementation of a peace agreement.

UNISFA
United Nations Interim Security Force for Abyei (Est. 2011)
UNISFA exists to oversee demilitarization and monitor peace in the disputed Abyei area of Sudan. The operation will monitor the flashpoint border between north and south, and is authorized to use force in protecting civilians and humanitarian workers in Abyei.

MONUSCO
United Nations Organization Stabilization Mission in the Democratic Republic of the Congo (Est. 2010)
MONUSCO took over from an earlier mission (MONUC) to focus on the protection of civilians, humanitarian personnel, and human rights defenders under imminent threat of physical violence and to support the government of the DRC in its stabilization and peace consolidation efforts.

UNMISS
United Nations Mission in the Republic of South Sudan (Est. 2011)
In 2011, South Sudan became the newest country in the world. UNMISS is on the ground to consolidate peace and security and to help establish conditions for development.

Map labels: WESTERN SAHARA (MOR.), SERBIA, CYPRUS, SYRIA, LEBANON, ISRAEL, PAKISTAN, EGYPT, INDIA, MALI, SUDAN, CEN. AFR. REP., S. SUDAN, LIBERIA, D.R. CONGO, Indian Ocean

Map source: www.un.org/en/peacekeeping/operations/current.shtml.

Bush, in his State of the Union address just before the war, spoke of the opportunity to create "a new world order, a world where the rule of law, not the law of the jungle, governs the conduct of nations"—a world in which "a credible United Nations can use its peacekeeping role to fulfill the promise and vision of the UN's founders." Indeed, the UN had seemed to meet the first challenge of this new era quite successfully.

The optimism would turn out to be overblown. The Iraqi invasion of Kuwait was, in many respects, an easy case for effective international action. By invading a weak neighbor, Iraq had committed a flagrant violation of international law. More important, the attack was seen as directly threatening the interests of the United States and its allies. After gobbling up Kuwait, Iraq was in possession of 20 percent of the world's known oil reserves. Furthermore, the attack put Iraq in a position to threaten Saudi Arabia, home to another 25 percent of the world's oil. All told, the Persian Gulf region contained two-thirds of this valuable natural resource. The possibility that so much of the world's oil could come under the control of a hostile power was seen as threatening to vital American interests. As a result, the United States was strongly motivated to take forceful action to reverse the Iraqi invasion. In all likelihood, it would have done so even if it had been unable to secure UN approval.

Hence, the success of the UN in this case owed a great deal to the fact that the United States, the most powerful actor in the international system, perceived a direct threat to its own interests. The international community was, in this instance, what we called in Chapter 2 a privileged group, since a single member was motivated strongly enough to provide the public good. The next several years would provide ample evidence that when such incentives are lacking, the community's collective interests in stopping aggression and/or ending gross violations of human rights are generally not enough to compel effective international intervention.

The "Triumph of the Lack of Will": Bosnia, Rwanda, and Darfur The hard tests of the new world order came only a few years after the victory in the Persian Gulf. The decades that followed witnessed a number of bloody and heartrending crises that transfixed the international community but also exposed the limits of that community's willingness to do much about them.[30]

One visible example of the limited will of the international community played out in the former Yugoslav republic of Bosnia-Herzegovina. The civil conflict in Bosnia was the bloodiest of several violent acts in the breakup of Yugoslavia. Originally composed of five republics—Serbia, Slovenia, Croatia, Bosnia-Herzegovina, and Macedonia—the Yugoslav federation began to dissolve in 1991 as Slovenia, Croatia, and Bosnia sought independence, and Serbia, the largest republic, tried to hold the multiethnic state together by force.

The conflict in Bosnia was the most complicated and bloody because this republic was home to three ethnic groups: Serbs (comprising 31 percent of the

---

30. We take our heading for this section from the title phrase of an insightful analysis of this period; see James Gow, *Triumph of the Lack of Will: International Diplomacy and the Yugoslav War* (New York: Columbia University Press, 1997).

prewar population), Croats (25 percent), and Bosnian Muslims (44 percent), as shown in Map 5.2. Many Serbs did not want to live in an independent Bosnia; rather, they wanted to carve out portions of that republic and join with Serbia. The more radical Croats had similar thoughts of joining Croatia. When Bosnia declared its independence from Yugoslavia in March 1992, militant Serbs and Croats rebelled, triggering a three-way war.

The ensuing conflict, which lasted three years, was incredibly brutal, with 300,000 killed, mostly civilians, and at least 2 million refugees displaced from their homes. In addition, the combatants engaged in widespread atrocities against civilians: shelling cities, herding men and boys into detention camps where they were malnourished and mistreated, raping women and girls in order to terrorize the population. While crimes were committed by all sides, the greatest offenders were

Map source: University of Texas at Austin, www.lib.utexas.edu /maps/europe/balkans.jpg (accessed 06/02/15).

MAP 5.2 *Ethnic Divisions in the Former Yugoslavia, 1992*

Groups Comprising 50 Percent or More of the Population of a Given Area

ALBANIANS   CROATS   MACEDONIANS   MUSLIMS   SLOVENES   NO MAJORITY PRESENT

BULGARIANS   HUNGARIANS   MONTENEGRINS   SERBS

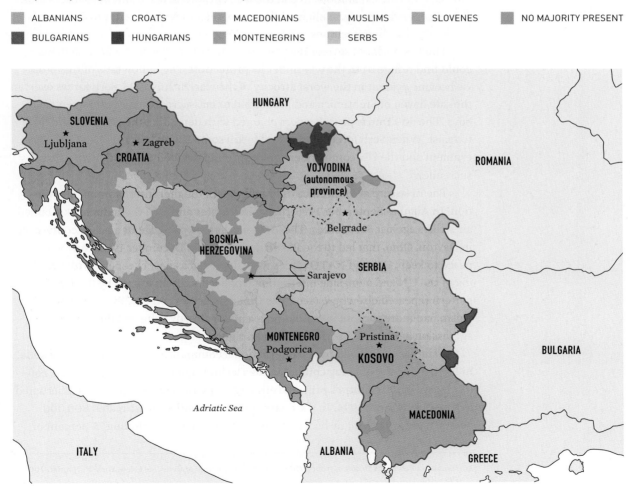

the Serbs, who engaged in a systematic campaign of what became known as "ethnic cleansing": clearing coveted territory of all non-Serbs by either killing them or scaring them into flight.

The international response to these events was feeble and at times counterproductive. Although there was unanimous condemnation of the violence, no one was willing to exert on behalf of Bosnia the kind of effort that had been marshaled to save Kuwait only one year earlier. Without compelling interests, such as securing an important natural resource (like oil), the UN, at the behest of the United States and European powers, responded in a half-hearted way. A peacekeeping force, comprising mostly European troops, was deployed to the area—despite the fact that there was no peace to keep.

Imposed into the war zone under Chapter VII, the UN Protection Force (UNPROFOR) nonetheless had many of the qualities of a traditional peacekeeping force: it was lightly armed, dispersed throughout the country, required to be neutral, and ordered to fire only in self-defense. Its main mission was to distribute food and medicine to civilians and to help keep them out of harm's way. Hence, UNPROFOR sought to treat the symptoms of the war, but it had neither a mandate nor the requisite capabilities to end the war. On several occasions Serb forces took peacekeepers hostage and chained them to artillery pieces in order to deter air strikes against their positions.

The UN declared several Bosnian cities to be "safe havens" where civilians could find refuge from the war under its protection. The hollowness of this promise became evident in the worst atrocity of the war. In July 1995, Serb forces overran the safe haven of Srebrenica and proceeded to massacre 8,000 Muslim men and boys. The 600 Dutch peacekeepers charged with defending the city could do little to resist. When Serb forces threatened to kill some Dutch hostages, the Dutch government and the UN commanders on the ground decided to negotiate their troops' surrender.[31]

The massacre at Srebrenica did finally spark tougher international intervention. In August–September 1995, the United States and NATO conducted sustained air strikes against Serb forces. These attacks helped bring about a peace conference in Dayton, Ohio, that led to the Bosnian war's end in December 1995. Now with a peace to keep, U.S. and NATO forces were deployed as peacekeepers, with the blessing of the UN and alongside international police forces organized by the UN. In a pattern repeated elsewhere (see "The Quiet Successes" on p. 225), the UN mechanism had more success in maintaining a peace already achieved than in ending aggression and gross violations of human rights.

A similar lack of will by the international community was apparent in Rwanda in 1994 and in the ongoing conflict in the Darfur region of Sudan. In Rwanda, conflict between the country's principal ethnic groups, the Hutus and the Tutsis, erupted in genocide in April 1994. In the course of three months, an estimated 800,000 people were killed—many hacked to death by machetes—including 75 percent of

---

31. Samantha Power, *"A Problem from Hell": America and the Age of Genocide* (New York: Perennial, 2002), 399–400.

In the case of Rwanda, the UN and the international community did little to stop ongoing fighting between the Hutus and the Tutsis, even when it became clear that civilians were being massacred. Here, Tutsi victims of a Hutu raid on a refugee camp in nearby Burundi are buried in a mass grave.

the Tutsi population. The international response to this tragedy was very weak. A small UN peacekeeping force already on the ground was overwhelmed. After 10 of its peacekeepers were killed on the first day of the conflict, Belgium withdrew its forces, and other nations followed suit. As the death toll rose, the international community stood by and watched. The killing stopped only after a Tutsi rebel force succeeded in defeating the Hutu forces responsible for much of the slaughter.

The case of Darfur is equally tragic. Since 2003, a bloody conflict has raged in western Sudan, where government-supported militias have carried out systematic killings of the people there. In another widely acknowledged genocide, it is estimated that 200,000–400,000 people have died, and up to 3 million have been displaced from their homes. In spite of widespread outrage, the response of the UN has been weak. Member states have been unwilling to support or contribute troops to a robust military operation to end the violence.

This discussion is not meant to imply that the UN mechanism never works. Rather, it suggests that absent compelling national interests, member states are reluctant to pay heavy costs or embrace high risks to further the community's interest in stopping aggression or ending humanitarian crises. In all these cases, the member states cared about the suffering, but they did not care enough to undertake the kind of military operation that would have been needed to end the conflicts that were the cause of the suffering. "Controversy" on page 226 discusses the NATO-led intervention in Libya (2011), and the challenges that international organizations face when it comes to such interventions.

The Quiet Successes In other cases, the costs of intervention are seen as relatively low, and the UN's track record has been more impressive. These cases generally

Should Outsiders Intervene Militarily to Stop Humanitarian Crises?

In 2011, Libyans revolted against the dictatorial rule of leader Mu'ammar Qaddafi. After initial successes by the rebels, Qaddafi's forces began to reclaim control as they moved east along the coast. The prospect of a bloodbath in Benghazi, Libya's second-largest city, spurred the international community to action. The UNSC passed a resolution authorizing member states to "take all necessary measures" to protect civilians in Libya, which allowed NATO to begin air operations and a naval blockade against Qaddafi's forces. With NATO support, the rebels beat back the loyalists at Benghazi. Qaddafi was captured and killed two months later.

The Libya operation is an example of armed humanitarian intervention, the use of military force by outsiders to stop mass killing or genocide within a country. Other notable examples include the UN-sponsored intervention to relieve a famine caused by civil war in Somalia in 1991–93 and, on a smaller scale, U.S. air strikes against Syria in 2017 to punish the regime's use of chemical weapons.

Applying the Concepts

The main argument for armed humanitarian intervention rests on the idea that everyone shares an **interest** in preventing suffering and death due to civil wars or murderous governments. But the practice remains controversial. Critics argue that (1) claims of humanitarianism disguise the self-interested reasons that actually motivate intervention, (2) military force is a poor instrument for influencing the strategic **interaction** between governments and civilians, and (3) existing **institutions** are not up to the task of deciding whether and when to intervene.

The case for armed humanitarian intervention rests on the moral imperative to protect unarmed civilians facing death at the hands of their government. When a state has failed in its basic obligation to protect its citizens from massacre, genocide, and other crimes against humanity, it has been argued that other states have a responsibility to intervene, by force if necessary (for more on the emergence of the "responsibility to protect" norm, see Chapter 11).

In the case of Libya, the looming attack on Benghazi reminded Western decision makers of their countries' failure to act under similar circumstances in June 1995, when Serb forces overran the city of Srebrenica in Bosnia and massacred 8,000 men and boys. If given the chance to prevent another such atrocity, why not act? A policy of intervention can not only save lives that are at immediate risk, but may also deter governments from committing atrocities in the first place.

While this argument seems compelling, the uncomfortable fact is that most humanitarian crises do not trigger this kind of response. Genocidal killings in Rwanda (1994), in the Darfur region of Sudan (starting in 2003), and against the Rohingya in Myanmar (starting in 2016) met international condemnation but not concerted military action. In Syria, where a civil war has claimed hundreds of thousands of lives, U.S. air strikes in 2017 were an exception to a policy that otherwise avoided direct confrontation with the Syrian regime as it bombed and starved civilian populations.

Because the international community cannot possibly protect everyone everywhere in the world, the application of this policy is bound to be inconsistent and influenced by interests other than humanitarianism. The fact that Qaddafi was a hostile and unpredictable leader with enormous oil wealth suggests that other interests contributed to the decision to support the rebellion. No comparable interests compelled intervention in Rwanda, Sudan, or Myanmar, and Russia's interest in preserving a friendly regime in Syria motivated it to block intervention efforts there.

Humanitarian intervention also threatens the interests that states have in exercising sovereign control over internal matters. While atrocities committed against civilians are unacceptable, states have a legitimate interest in maintaining order domestically and preserving their territorial integrity. Indeed, to some critics, the West's recent willingness to intervene looks a good deal like another, older practice: imperialism. Just as imperial powers claimed to bring "civilization" to the lands they conquered,

Benghazi, Libya

humanitarianism may be used to disguise self-interested efforts to undermine or take over unfriendly states.

Another concern about these operations is that military force is a blunt and costly instrument for influencing the interaction between governments and their citizens. Although the most direct way to protect civilians is to deploy troops to shield them from the government's security forces, outsiders are usually reluctant to put their own people in harm's way. For this reason, the Libya campaign was conducted entirely from the air, relying on bombs and cruise missiles. While this strategy was effective at preventing NATO casualties, it also limited NATO's ability to influence events on the ground. Even if an intervention succeeds in easing a crisis, an enduring solution requires a long-term commitment by outside actors that may not be credible. When the foreigners go home, conflict may erupt again. Indeed, Libya has fallen back into civil war as different factions vie to rule that country.

Finally, humanitarian intervention raises the institutional question of who should decide when the international community can get involved. The UN is the natural venue for such a determination. Even so, for the Security Council to authorize intervention in purely domestic conflicts requires an expansive interpretation of what constitutes a "threat to international peace and security." Two members of the Security Council—China and Russia—have been loath to endorse humanitarian intervention, in part because their own human rights records are spotty. Because of the threat of their veto, the Security Council

could not act against Sudan or Syria. In the case of Libya, the Security Council (with China and Russia abstaining) approved an operation to protect civilians but did not endorse the goal of ousting Qaddafi.

Supporters of humanitarian intervention have argued that NATO, as an alliance of democracies, is well qualified to act in support of human rights. But under international law, the alliance does not have the authority to undertake such an operation on its own, nor is it universally seen as an impartial force. Thus, while the international community has at times taken steps to protect people in harm's way, it still grapples with the question of how to perform this responsibility well.

Thinking Analytically

1. When do humanitarian interests override a state's interests in exercising sovereign control over its internal policies? Are there good criteria for deciding the answer to this question?

2. What are the advantages and disadvantages of vesting decisions about the legality of humanitarian intervention in the United Nations Security Council? If you could design an alternative institution to make this decision, what would its membership and voting rules be?

fall under the category of traditional peacekeeping: monitoring and assisting in the implementation of peace agreements. Because the existence of a peace agreement indicates that the opposing parties are ready to stop fighting and resolve their differences, the risks associated with getting involved are not that high. Keeping peace after a war is generally easier than making peace during a war.

For this reason, UN efforts have been most successful in the area of post-conflict reconstruction.[32] In the case of El Salvador, for example, a UN peacekeeping operation played an important role in that country's recovery from a 12-year civil war that had claimed 75,000 lives. The UN Observer Mission in El Salvador (ONUSAL) comprised about 700 military observers and civilian police from 17 countries, but it had an expansive mandate to help rebuild the country. ONUSAL not only helped to monitor the demobilization of the warring factions after a 1992 peace agreement, but it also assisted in implementing political reforms designed to address the root causes of the conflict, such as reforming the judiciary, forming and training a new civilian police force, and redistributing land to former combatants. ONUSAL also monitored an election in 1994 to ensure that it was free and fair and that all sides would respect the result. The mission's mandate ended in April 1995, leaving in its wake a country that is generally considered free and democratic.

Similar stories of success in post-conflict reconstruction can be found in Mozambique, Liberia, Sierra Leone, East Timor, Cambodia, and even Bosnia, where a NATO-led peacekeeping force with a UN blessing went in after the 1995 peace deal and was deemed to have fulfilled its mission and departed in December 2004.[33]

People following the news likely heard much more about the UN's failings in Bosnia, Rwanda, and Darfur than about the quieter victories in places like El Salvador and Bosnia after 1995. Bloodshed naturally draws more attention than do peace and reconciliation, so the failures of the UN get more publicity than do its successes. (See "How Do We Know?" on p. 229 for more evidence on the success of peacekeeping operations.)

From 9/11 to Iraq and After: Consensus Lost

During the 1990s, civil conflicts such as the ones in Bosnia and Rwanda were much more prominent on the UN agenda than were cases of international aggression like the Persian Gulf War. As we have seen, the main impediment to effective action in these cases was a lack of will— the absence of compelling national interests that could have justified committing resources and taking risks. The September 11, 2001, terrorist attacks against the United States changed this focus, exposing a threat that many UN member states, including all of the P5, had reason to fear. The unanimous condemnation of the terrorist attacks and international support for the United States' war in Afghanistan suggested that once again the UN mechanism could work effectively in the new international environment.

---

32. See Michael W. Doyle and Nicholas Sambanis, *Making War and Building Peace: United Nations Peace Operations* (Princeton, NJ: Princeton University Press, 2006).

33. The United Nations force was replaced by a European Union force (EUFOR Althea, named after the Greek goddess of healing).

Does Peacekeeping Keep the Peace?

Since its creation in 1946, the UN has undertaken 71 peacekeeping missions. About 3,600 peacekeepers have died in the course of these operations, whose total cost has been about $100 billion. At the time of this writing, over 112,000 uniformed personnel from 128 countries were deployed in 16 ongoing operations around the globe.[a] Given this expenditure of time, blood, and treasure, it is reasonable to ask: Do peacekeeping operations actually work?

A number of studies have sought to answer this question. Virginia Page Fortna collected information on cease-fires in interstate and civil wars since 1946. There is a good deal of variation in how long cease-fires last. Some break down almost immediately, others last for years, and still others form the basis for a permanent peace between the adversaries. To determine whether peacekeepers can affect how long a cease-fire will last, Fortna recorded, for each case, whether a peacekeeping force was sent in to monitor and/or enforce the agreement.

Even when other factors that influence the durability of a peace are taken into account, the presence of a peacekeeping operation has a substantial effect on the likelihood that a cease-fire will endure. Looking at the 48 cease-fires in interstate wars that ended between 1946 and 1998, Fortna found that the presence of peacekeepers reduced by 85 percent the probability that a cease-fire would break down in any given year.[b] Similarly, in an analysis of 94 cease-fires in 60 civil wars in the period 1989–99, Fortna found that the presence of peacekeepers reduced the risk of renewed fighting in any given year by about 60 percent.[c]

Another set of studies, by Lisa Hultman, Jacob Kathman, and Megan Shannon, looked more deeply into whether the size and composition of peacekeeping missions matters in civil wars. Combining information on the number of military, police, and unarmed observers in each mission, they showed that a larger presence of military forces reduces violence and lowers civilian deaths. By their estimate, increasing the peacekeeping presence from zero to 8,000 reduces the predicted number of civilian deaths in a country from about 100 per month to 2 per month.[d] Considering the enormous human and economic costs associated with warfare, peacekeeping operations appear to be well worth their price.

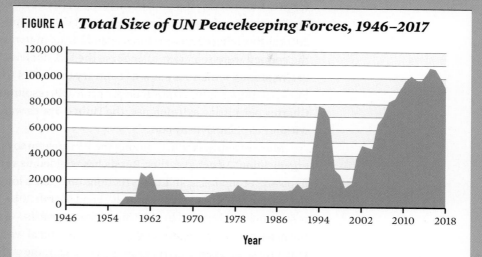

FIGURE A *Total Size of UN Peacekeeping Forces, 1946–2017*

Note: Highest month for each year. Figures include troops, military observers, and police.

Sources: Global Policy Forum, "Size of UN Peacekeeping Forces, 1947–2009," www.globalpolicy.org/component/content/article/102-tables-and-charts/40734-size-of-un-peacekeeping-forces-1947-2009.html (accessed 03/19/18). Updated through January 2018, using data from https://peacekeeping.un.org/sites/default/files/0_front_page_0.pdf (accessed 03/19/18).

a. Data are from www.un.org/en/peacekeeping/resources/statistics/factsheet.shtml (accessed 07/14/17).

b. Virginia Page Fortna, "Interstate Peacekeeping: Causal Mechanisms and Empirical Effects," *World Politics* 56 (July 2004): 481–519. See also Virginia Page Fortna, *Peace Time: Cease-Fire Agreements and the Durability of Peace* (Princeton, NJ: Princeton University Press, 2004).

c. Virginia Page Fortna, *Does Peacekeeping Work? Shaping Belligerents' Choices after Civil War* (Princeton, NJ: Princeton University Press, 2008), 105.

d. Lisa Hultman, Jacob Kathman, and Megan Shannon, "United Nations Peacekeeping and Civilian Protection in Civil War," *American Journal of Political Science* 57 (October 2013): 875–91. See also Lisa Hultman, Jacob Kathman, and Megan Shannon, "Beyond Keeping Peace: United Nations Effectiveness in the Midst of Fighting," *American Political Science Review* 108 (November 2014): 737–53.

This optimism would prove short-lived, however. Slightly over a year after the 9/11 attacks, the U.S. effort to mount a war against Iraq divided the Security Council and left the organization alienated from its most powerful member. Although all members were on record demanding that Iraq fully account for its past weapons programs, they parted ways on the desirability of using military force to enforce this demand. A majority of the Security Council members, including France, Russia, and China, refused to back a proposed resolution in January 2003 authorizing the use of force against Iraq, in part because many members of the council were reluctant to endorse the U.S. doctrine of preventive war (defined in Chapter 3), which they saw as contrary to the UN Charter's rules on the use of force. Claiming authorization under prior UN resolutions and Article 51 of the UN Charter permitting self-defense, the United States went ahead with the invasion without explicit UN support.

More recently, conflicts among the P5 threaten to once again sideline the organization. As noted earlier, Russia has wielded its veto to prevent the UN from imposing economic or military sanctions on Syria, a longtime Russian ally. Between the start of the Syrian civil war in 2011 and March 2018, Russia had vetoed eleven resolutions put forward by the United States and its Western allies condemning the mass killing of civilians and the use of chemical weapons. In the spring of 2014, when Russian tanks and troops moved into Ukraine and annexed Crimea, the Security Council debated the matter, but there was no chance that the institution would act against one of its permanent members. The two draft resolutions on Ukraine that came to a vote both fell victim to the Russian veto.[34]

In addition, there is little prospect of the Security Council getting involved in conflicts between China and its neighbors over disputed islands in the South China Sea—disputes that have the potential to become flashpoints for conflict between the United States and China (see Chapter 14). As a result of these rising tensions among the P5, the UN will once again find itself unable to act on key matters of international security.

As this overview suggests, the UN faces two essential requirements if it is to work as intended. First, none of the veto-wielding members can see a potential operation as threatening to its interests. If this requirement is not met—as was true through much of the Cold War and in the case of Iraq—then action can be blocked thanks to the voting rule. Second, member states, particularly the powerful member states, must care enough to devote the necessary resources and take the necessary risks. If those risks are low, as in the case of post-conflict peacekeeping, this requirement may not be hard to satisfy. In the more costly cases of reversing aggression or stopping genocides, a strong interest, such as existed in the Gulf War case, is necessary to ensure that sufficient resources are brought to bear. Thus, effective action can be thwarted in two ways: by self-interest, as in the case of Ukraine, or by apathy, as in the case of Rwanda.

---

34. An excellent resource on vetoed resolutions can be found at http://research.un.org/en/docs/sc/quick (accessed 07/14/17).

A cynical conclusion that one might draw from this observation is that the UN mechanism is most likely to be effective precisely when it is needed least—that is, when the powerful states agree enough and care enough to take action. In a case like the Gulf War, one could argue, the UN served simply to give a stamp of approval to actions that the United States would have taken anyway. Moreover, it is also clear from the experience of the Iraq War that the failure to get UN approval will not always stop a great power from taking actions that it wants to take.

In light of this conclusion, one might question whether the UN matters at all when it comes to war and peace. The answer is that although the UN matters less than one might hope, the organization does indeed make a difference. First, as already noted, it has played a constructive role in organizing peacekeeping missions to help countries reconstruct in the wake of conflict. In these cases, the UN's perceived impartiality bestows a legitimacy on peacekeepers' efforts that is needed for them to play the role of an honest broker.

Second, the American experience in its two wars against Iraq, in 1991 and 2003, shows that the UN's blessing can be a valuable resource. In the Gulf War, UN support helped build both domestic and international support for the war effort, which contributed to the United States' ability to prevail at low cost to itself. In the case of the Iraq War, the absence of UN support had important implications for the United States' ability to stabilize the country after toppling Hussein's regime. One study of post-conflict reconstruction showed that in order to have a nation-building effort in Iraq that was the same size per capita as the one that was deployed in Bosnia in 1995, the United States would have needed 480,000 combat troops and 12,600 international police.[35] The absence of UN backing, however, meant that some countries that often contribute peacekeeping or police forces to these kinds of missions, such as Pakistan and India, refused to do so in this case. As a result, the U.S.-led coalition had, in March 2004, 154,000 total combat troops, 85 percent of whom were American. And those troops had to serve double duty as an international police force, because there was no separate deployment of police. Hence, there are costs of going to war without the backing of the UN—even if these costs are not always sufficient to prevent a great power from doing so.

Finally, although cooperation is uneven, the UN facilitates joint decision making. Its rules of procedure in the Security Council and established mechanisms for fielding peacekeeping and peace-enforcement operations keep countries from having to "reinvent the wheel" each time a crisis arises. Vetoes may interfere with decision making, but without clearly established rules, decisions would be harder to reach even in those instances where cooperation has been successful. Indeed, if the UN did not exist, states would need to create an organization very similar to the one we already have.

---

35. James Dobbins, John G. McGinn, Keith Crane, Seth G. Jones, et al., *America's Role in Nation-Building: From Germany to Iraq* (Santa Monica, CA: RAND, 2003).

Conclusion: Are Poor Police Better than None?

At the outset of this chapter, we asked whether and when international institutions can prevent or stop wars between and within states. The track record of both alliances and collective security organizations has been uneven, at best, in this regard. Both are imperfect substitutes for an effective police force of the kind that we take for granted in a well-governed country.

Alliances form in response to common interests—generally, the perception of a common threat. For this reason, allies are often better able to work together in concert than are the more fractious members of, say, the UN. However, the existence of alliances does not ensure that allies will fight together, nor does it ensure that other states will be deterred from making threats. Not all alliances are created equally, as the capabilities and resolve underlying the commitment to defend an ally can vary quite considerably. When these are in doubt, as in the case of the French alliance to Czechoslovakia in the interwar period, the alliance can fail in both deterring threats and defending against them. When states are strongly resolved and take the necessary steps to lock in and demonstrate that commitment, as in the case of NATO, then the alliance institutions can be a source of peace through credible deterrence.

For collective security organizations, like the UN, the primary challenge involves providing a public good in an environment in which there can be competing private interests and the costs of providing the good may be more than anyone is willing to pay. Moreover, the joint decision-making rules set down by the organizations' founding members gave those states important privileges to block actions that they do not like. Hence, these organizations have been most effective only when there has been relatively strong agreement among the powerful states, and they have been crippled when those states are in conflict. They have had their greatest successes when at least one powerful state had a sufficient interest that it was willing to pay costs and take risks to provide the public good for everyone. They have also had more quiet successes when those costs and risks were relatively low, such as in cases of post-conflict reconstruction.

Former UN secretary-general Dag Hammarskjöld reportedly said, "The UN was not created to take humanity to heaven but to save it from hell."[36] This statement reflects a pragmatic understanding of the limits of governance in the international system. States have conflicts of interests that they are willing to fight over, as do people within states. In the absence of an impartial police force, the ability

---

36. The original source of this well-known quotation is unclear, and slight variations in wording can be found in the secondary literature, possibly because Hammarskjöld said something to this effect more than once. For a speech in which he made this point, see Andrew W. Cordier and Wilder Foote, eds., *Public Papers of the Secretaries-General of the United Nations*, vol. 2, *Dag Hammarskjöld* (New York: Columbia University Press, 1972), 301.

of third parties to enforce peace depends on whether those parties are willing and able to step in.

Do outsiders have an interest in intervening? Do the available institutions promote intervention by lowering the costs of getting involved or by increasing the costs of staying out? Does the intervention influence the interaction between combatants in a way that resolves the information and commitment problems that can lead to violence? All these questions have to be answered in the affirmative for outside intervention to have a chance at preventing or reversing acts of violence. In cases like the wars in Korea and the Persian Gulf, these conditions were met, and South Korea and Kuwait owe their continued existence to this fact. Similarly, in places like El Salvador and Liberia, effective outside assistance has helped these countries rebuild after decades of civil conflict. But in many other cases these conditions are not met, and the results can be disastrous, as in Bosnia, Rwanda, and Darfur.

And yet, as we survey this uneven record, Hammarskjöld's statement reminds us that even an imperfect police force may be better than none. Although the international system has no central authority analogous to that of a well-governed domestic system, the institutions that have developed in its place have a beneficial—albeit imperfect and uneven—impact on world politics. Alliances and collective security organizations are poor substitutes for an effective and neutral police, but it is likely that the world would be an even more violent place in their absence.

Study Tool Kit

Interests, Interactions, and Institutions in Context

- Alliances form when states have compatible interests that lead them to cooperate militarily. They are institutions created between or among states to facilitate cooperation for the purpose of influencing the outcomes of disputes with outsiders.

- Alliances are successful at deterring or fighting off challenges when allies have a strong interest in coming to one another's aid in the event of war, and when they are able to signal this interest to the opponent in a credible manner.

- Collective security organizations form around a common interest, which all states are presumed to share, in promoting peace. As broad-based institutions, their primary role is to facilitate collective action within the international community so that states can respond effectively to prevent or stop the outbreak of violence whenever and wherever it may occur.

- Collective security organizations are successful when leading states perceive a common and compelling interest in stopping an act of aggression. They fail when leading states have conflicting interests in the outcome of a particular dispute, or when they have too little interest in the matter to justify the costs of intervention.

Key Terms

alliances, p. 189

balance of power, p. 192

bandwagoning, p. 193

entrapment, p. 199

North Atlantic Treaty Organization (NATO), p. 203

Warsaw Pact, p. 203

League of Nations, p. 205

United Nations (UN), p. 205

collective security organizations, p. 205

genocide, p. 208

humanitarian interventions, p. 209

Security Council (UNSC), p. 213

permanent five (P5), p. 213

veto power, p. 213

peace-enforcement operation, p. 215

peacekeeping operation, p. 215

For Further Reading

Doyle, Michael W., and Nicholas Sambanis. *Making War and Building Peace: United Nations Peace Operations.* **Princeton, NJ: Princeton University Press, 2006.** Examines the track record of UN peacekeeping and peace-enforcement operations in civil wars; finds that while the UN is not well equipped to end wars, it has been helpful in peacekeeping and post-conflict reconstruction.

Lake, David A. *Entangling Relations: American Foreign Policy in Its Century.* **Princeton, NJ: Princeton University Press, 1999.** Considers the different ways that states can institutionalize their relationship with other countries, from empire to informal alignments.

Leeds, Brett Ashley, and Burcu Savun. "Terminating Alliances: Why Do States Abrogate Agreements?" *Journal of Politics* **69 (2007): 1118–32.** Offers empirical evidence about the conditions under which states decide to break or honor military alliances.

Power, Samantha. *"A Problem from Hell": America and the Age of Genocide,* **rev. ed. New York: Basic Books, 2013.** Graphically details the failings of the United States and the UN in the face of genocide, including the cases of Bosnia and Rwanda.

Snyder, Glenn H. *Alliance Politics.* **Ithaca, NY: Cornell University Press, 1997.** Offers a comprehensive presentation of theory and historical evidence on the origins and maintenance of alliances.

Voeten, Erik. "The Political Origins of the UN Security Council's Ability to Legitimize the Use of Force." *International Organization* **59 (Summer 2005): 527–57.** Seeks to explain why people care whether or not the UN authorizes a military operation.

Walt, Stephen M. *The Origins of Alliances.* **Ithaca, NY: Cornell University Press, 1987.** Tests balance of power theory and offers a reformulation that hinges on perceptions of threat, not just power.

Waltz, Kenneth N. *Theory of International Politics.* **Long Grove, IL: Waveland Press, Inc. esp. chaps. 6 and 8.** Presents a modern formulation of balance of power theory and argues that it explains the relative stability of the pre-1945 and Cold War international systems.

Weiss, Thomas G. *What's Wrong with the United Nations (and How to Fix It).* **Cambridge: Polity Press, 2009.** A very accessible and balanced survey of the strengths and weaknesses of the UN, with suggestions for how the institution could be improved.

6

Violence by Nonstate Actors: Civil War and Terrorism

THE PUZZLE *A great deal of politically motivated violence in the contemporary world is committed by or directed against nonstate actors, particularly rebel groups engaged in civil wars or terrorist networks. Why do some individuals and groups resort to violence against their governments or unarmed civilians?*

Above: Transnational terrorist networks, like the Islamic State (IS), use violence to advance their political goals. In July 2016, IS claimed responsibility for an attack in Nice, France, in which an assailant drove a cargo truck through a Bastille Day crowd, killing over 84 people and wounding hundreds of others.

On September 11, 2001, the United States experienced the worst attack on its homeland since the Japanese bombing of Pearl Harbor. On that day, the threat came not from the naval and air forces of a rival state but from 19 individuals armed with box cutters, who hijacked four airplanes and crashed them into the World Trade Center in New York and the Pentagon in Washington, D.C. Thanks to the heroic efforts of its passengers, a plane likely headed for the White House went down in a western Pennsylvania field. Nearly 3,000 people died in the attacks, which were perpetrated by a terrorist network known as Al Qaeda. In response, the United States launched a "global war on terror," a series of military operations around the world, including most prominently the invasion of Afghanistan, whose government had hosted Al Qaeda. The Bush administration then made the case for war against Iraq based partly on the argument (now largely discredited) that the regime there could transfer chemical, biological, or nuclear weapons to terrorists.

The wars in Afghanistan and Iraq both had two major phases. In the first, the United States and its allies quickly defeated the armed forces of the opposing states.

The Taliban regime in Afghanistan collapsed after two months; the Iraqi regime fell after six weeks. In both cases, however, victory in the interstate phase of the conflict was followed by much longer conflicts against a different kind of enemy. Both countries descended into civil war as rebellious factions, including elements of the previous regimes, took up arms against one another and the U.S.-installed governments. The United States' role thus shifted from trying to defeat the military of another state to trying to quell a domestic rebellion.

The civil phase of these conflicts lasted much longer and claimed more lives—American, Afghani, and Iraqi—than did the initial invasions. U.S. troops left Iraq in 2011, but the lingering conflict there gave birth to a new militant group—the Islamic State (IS)—whose activities drew the U.S. military back to the region only three years later. Since then, IS and related groups have organized or inspired terrorist attacks throughout the world, including Africa, Asia, Europe, and the United States. In short, the United States has spent much of the twenty-first century engaged in deadly conflict not with other states, but with nonstate actors—transnational terrorist networks and rebel groups within Afghanistan and Iraq.

The U.S. experience is representative of broader developments in world politics. Violence by and against nonstate actors has long been a prominent feature of international politics, but its importance has increased in recent years. A great deal of armed conflict in the contemporary world takes place not between states but *within* them (see Figure 6.1). Terrorism has also been a growing international concern, particularly since September 2001, which ushered in a period of increased terrorist violence (see Figure 6.3). How do we explain political violence by nonstate actors?

As a first cut, the tools used to understand interstate war are quite useful in understanding civil war and terrorism. Both phenomena arise when nonstate actors, such as rebel groups or terrorist organizations, have *interests* that bring them into conflict with states. These disputes can lead to conflict when these actors lack access to political *institutions* that could address their demands through peaceful means, leading to a bargaining *interaction* that can bring about violence owing to information problems, commitment problems, and/or issue indivisibility. While some of the specifics may change, we can learn a great deal simply by taking the models from earlier chapters and relabeling State A as "government" and State B as "rebel group" or "terrorist organization."

That said, there is a crucial difference between nonstate actors and states. To understand the problem that nonstate actors face, think of a cause that you care about, such as immigration or the quality of the food in your school's dining halls. Imagine that you wanted to form a group that would lobby the government or university administrators to enact policies that further your cause. To do so, you would have to convince people to volunteer their time and raise money to support your activities. It may be hard to find people who are committed to the same cause, and some may sympathize with your goals but not have spare time or money to donate. This challenge can be daunting, and many would-be activists give up.

Now imagine that pursuing your cause will require your supporters to take up arms against the police or military, plant bombs in shopping malls, or blow themselves up on a crowded bus. Finding people to contribute is likely to become quite a bit harder. You will also have to figure out how to buy guns, explosives, and other tools of rebellion. Along the way, there is the danger that people you approach will alert the police to your activities. What circumstances would lead you to take these risks? And how could you get others to follow you? This dilemma is the central challenge faced by rebel groups and terrorist organizations.

Thinking Analytically about Civil War and Terrorism

Rebel groups and terrorist organizations bring together individuals whose interests put them in conflict with either their own or some foreign government. If dissatisfied groups lack access to political institutions that might address their interests peacefully—or if their goals are too extreme to be accommodated by existing institutions—then they may resort to violence against the government and its citizens. But common interests alone are not enough to ensure that individuals will be able to act collectively to produce violence.

Actors who want to fight together face a collective action problem (see Chapter 2). For groups seeking to rebel against a government, or for terrorist organizations seeking to enlist people for dangerous, possibly suicidal, missions, getting support from like-minded individuals is an enduring challenge. Whatever substantive interests they seek to further, all such groups have an organizational interest in finding sympathizers and motivating them to participate in the fight. And governments in conflict with such groups have to implement strategies that diminish the pool of potential supporters and/or encourage free riding. These imperatives profoundly affect the likelihood, conduct, and outcome of violence involving nonstate actors.

Thus, we can understand both civil war and terrorism through a two-step process. In the first step, we consider what factors bring together groups of individuals who are able and willing to use violence to further their interests. In the second step, we ask why the interactions between these groups and their target states sometimes lead to costly, protracted conflicts. Understanding these processes can then help identify how different strategies and institutions can help prevent or defuse this kind of violence.

The Relationship between Civil War and Terrorism

A **civil war** is an armed conflict that occurs between organized actors within a state and that meets some minimum threshold for severity. In most cases, civil wars pit the government of the state against one or more rebel groups, who may also fight among themselves. In some cases, such as Somalia for much of the 1990s, there is no functioning central government to speak of, in which case the conflict involves several groups, each trying to assume that role. Scholars conventionally require a conflict to cause at least 1,000 battle-related deaths in order to qualify as a civil war, though lower thresholds are sometimes used.[1] Map 6.1 shows countries that experienced a civil war in the period 2010–16 (dark blue), as well as those that experienced a lower level civil conflict that caused at least 25 battle-related deaths (light blue).

Terrorism is the use of violence against noncombatant targets by individuals or nonstate groups for political ends. Terrorism generally consists of attacks by individuals or small groups against civilian targets such as airplanes, trains, schools, or restaurants. The purpose is not simply to kill the targets, but to create widespread fear in the hopes of achieving the group's goal. (We will expand on the definition of terrorism later in the chapter.) The orange dots on Map 6.1 show the location of each terrorist attack in the period 2010–16 that claimed at least one life.

As these definitions make clear, civil war is a kind of armed conflict that is distinguished by the nature of its participants, while terrorism is a strategy for using violence that is distinguished primarily by the nature of its targets. Thus, *civil war* and *terrorism* should not be equated or treated as synonymous. Nevertheless, we study civil war and terrorism in a single chapter for three main reasons.

First, they share a common underlying quality: the use of violence for political goals by nonstate actors. This pairing gives us the opportunity to think about the similarities and differences between these kinds of violence and violence that takes place between states—that is, interstate war. Many of the same tools and concepts used to explain interstate war in Chapter 3 will reappear here, though with some key differences.

More important, as nonstate actors, both rebel groups and terrorist organizations face the same fundamental problem: how to organize individuals and mobilize resources in order to engage in violence. States, almost by definition, have solved this problem. States generally have some capacity to raise money and to enlist or conscript people to fight their wars. Thus, when we consider the bargaining between states, we typically take it for granted that the participants have some ability to mobilize resources in order to wield power internationally. We cannot

civil war
A war in which the main participants are within the same state, such as the government and a rebel group.

terrorism
The use or threatened use of violence against noncombatant targets by individuals or nonstate groups for political ends.

---

1. In addition, to be a civil war, casualties need to be incurred by all sides, so one-sided killings—such as when a government massacres civilians—are not considered in this category.

MAP 6.1 *Civil War and Terrorist Attacks, 2010–16*

This map depicts the countries that experienced a civil conflict (causing at least 25 battle-related deaths) or a civil war (causing at least 1000 battle-related deaths) in the period from 2010 to 2016. Each dot represents the location of a terrorist attack that killed at least one person in that same period.

Aims of Rebel Groups:

- ▇ EXPERIENCED A CIVIL WAR
- ▇ EXPERIENCED CIVIL CONFLICT
- ● FATAL TERRORIST ATTACK

Map source: Data on civil wars are from UCDP/PRIO Armed Conflict Dataset version 17.1. Marie Allansoon, Erik Melander, and Lotta Themnér, "Organized Violence, 1989–2016," *Journal of Peace Research* 54, no. 4 (2017): 574–87. Data on terrorist attacks are from National Consortium for the Study of Terrorism and Responses to Terrorism (START), Global Terrorism Database [Data file], 2017, https://www.start.umd.edu/gtd.

Arctic Ocean

RUSSIA

UNITED
KINGDOM
NORWAY
SWEDEN
FINLAND
IRELAND
GERMANY
FRANCE
BELARUS
UKRAINE
KAZAKHSTAN
MONGOLIA
N. KOREA
S. KOREA
SPAIN
ITALY
BOSNIA
UZBEKISTAN
JAPAN
GREECE
TURKEY
KYRGYZSTAN
TAJIKISTAN
MOROCCO
ISRAEL
LEB.
SYRIA
IRAQ
TURKMENISTAN
CHINA
ALGERIA
LIBYA
EGYPT
IRAN
NEPAL
TAIWAN
SAUDI
ARABIA
MYANMAR (BURMA)
Pacific Ocean
MAURITANIA
MALI
NIGER
CHAD
SUDAN
YEMEN
PAKISTAN
INDIA
THAILAND
VIETNAM
PHILIPPINES
SENEGAL
AFGHANISTAN
BANGLADESH
LAOS
GUINEA
NIGERIA
CEN.
AFR.
REP.
ETHIOPIA
SOMALIA
CAMBODIA
GHANA
CAMEROON
S. SUDAN
UGANDA
KENYA
MALAYSIA
IVORY COAST
D. R.
CONGO
RWANDA
BURUNDI
PAPUA
NEW GUINEA
TANZANIA
INDONESIA
ANGOLA
ZAMBIA
MALAWI
Indian Ocean
MADAGASCAR
NAMIBIA
MOZAMBIQUE
ZIMBABWE
AUSTRALIA
SOUTH
AFRICA
BOTSWANA
NEW
ZEALAND

make the same assumption when dealing with nonstate actors. This challenge influences why some dissatisfied groups lead to rebellions or terrorist campaigns while others do not.

The second reason for studying these topics together is that the strategies that rebel groups and terrorists employ for using violence share some similarities. Both types of groups are, more often than not, weaker than the states they confront, and their strategies have to adjust to this fact. As we will see, rebel groups often use a tactic known as insurgency or "guerrilla warfare," which involves hit-and-run attacks against military, government, and civilian targets. Though not identical, both insurgency and terrorism are forms of **asymmetrical warfare**, or conflict between actors with highly unequal capabilities, that seek to circumvent the superior military strength of the target. These strategies share similarities in terms of how they are intended to work and the challenges they pose to states confronted by them.

Third, there is a very close empirical relationship between civil wars and the incidence of terrorism. As Map 6.1 shows, the overlap between the two kinds of events is striking. Every country that is coded as having a civil war or conflict also had at least one terrorist attack; only 38 percent of countries with no civil conflict experienced terrorism. Of the 29,864 recorded terrorist attacks in those years, 80 percent occurred in a country that had a civil war; another 17 percent occurred in a country that had a civil conflict. Only 3 percent occurred in a country that had no civil conflict. Thus, while neither is a necessary ingredient for the other, civil violence and terrorism go hand in hand.

Indeed, many violent nonstate actors are both rebel groups in a civil war and terrorist organizations. Virtually all rebel groups attack civilians to some degree, primarily to dissuade them from collaborating with the government or to coerce them into aiding the rebellion. Beyond that, a significant number of rebel groups systematically use violence against civilians as a strategy for coercing domestic or foreign governments to give in to their demands.[2]

The Islamic State, for example, is one of many rebel groups involved in the Syrian civil war that broke out in 2011, and it has used conventional means of warfare to seize and hold territory in both Syria and Iraq (for more on the origins of the Islamic State, see "What Shaped Our World?" on p. 256). At the same time, IS has planned and executed terrorist attacks not only in those countries, but also in other parts of the world, such as France, Belgium, and Britain. In addition, it has inspired terrorist attacks by individuals with no formal connection to the group, including mass shootings in San Bernardino, California (December 2015), and Orlando, Florida (June 2016). Similarly, Boko Haram is a rebel group that has sought to control large swaths of northern Nigeria. It also engages extensively in terrorist attacks throughout the country.

asymmetrical warfare

Armed conflict between actors with highly unequal military capabilities, such as when rebel groups or terrorists fight strong states.

---

2. Two studies, with somewhat different criteria, estimate that 25–30 percent of rebel groups use terrorism systematically. See Jessica A. Stanton, "Terrorism in the Context of Civil War," *Journal of Politics* 75 (2013): 1009–22; and Virginia Page Fortna, "Do Terrorists Win? Rebels' Use of Terrorism and Civil War Outcomes," *International Organization* 69 (2015): 519–56.

Given these observations, recent scholarship has moved away from an earlier tendency to study civil war and terrorism separately, and more frequently focuses on the relationship between these kinds of violence.[3] This chapter is guided by that view.

Why Does War Occur within States?

Figure 6.1 shows the number of states involved in interstate and civil wars in each year from 1816 to 2016. Except during periods of large, multilateral wars, in any given year generally more states are involved in civil war than in interstate war. The gap is even more pronounced in the most recent four decades, when civil wars have been much more numerous and have killed millions more people than interstate wars in the same period.[4]

Given that civil wars occur between a government and one or more rebel groups within the same country, why is this topic appropriate to study in a class on international relations, which typically deals with phenomena that cross state borders? There are two main reasons. First, as we will see in this chapter, the theoretical tools that we have developed to explain interstate wars are also very useful in explaining their intrastate counterparts. By examining them side by side, we start to see these two kinds of conflict as instances of a single, broader phenomenon: the use of violence by organized actors to pursue political interests. Seeing them in this way permits useful comparisons that deepen our understanding of both.

Moreover, civil war is an appropriate topic within international relations because, while the primary dynamic occurs within a single country, the determinants and effects of a civil war are rarely so contained. External actors often play a significant role in the onset, duration, and outcome of civil conflict. Foreign states with an interest in the victory of either the government or the rebels often give money, arms, training, and/or sanctuary to their preferred side. This aid can be critical in determining whether a rebel group forms in the first place, how long it can sustain its operations against the government, and which side wins. Indeed, most civil wars experience some outside assistance to the rebels, the government, or both.[5]

In addition, civil wars can have spillover effects beyond their borders. As Map 6.1 shows, civil wars often cluster together geographically. By one estimate, a state is twice as likely to experience a civil conflict if one or more of its neighbors is experiencing one.[6] To some extent, this clustering is due to the fact that some of the risk factors of civil war, such as low economic development, also cluster together: poor

---

3. See, for example, Stanton, "Terrorism in the Context of Civil War"; Fortna, "Do Terrorists Win?"; Michael G. Findley and Joseph K. Young, "Terrorism and Civil War: A Spatial and Temporal Approach to a Conceptual Problem," *Perspectives on Politics* 10 (June 2012): 285–305; and Jakana Thomas, "Rewarding Bad Behavior: How Governments Respond to Terrorism in Civil War," *American Journal of Political Science* 58 (October 2014): 804–18.

4. See, for example, James D. Fearon and David Laitin, "Ethnicity, Insurgency, and Civil War," *American Political Science Review* 97 (2003): 75.

5. See, for example, Patrick M. Regan, *Civil Wars and Foreign Powers: Outside Intervention in Intrastate Conflict* (Ann Arbor: University of Michigan Press, 2000).

6. Halvard Buhaug and Kristian Skrede Gleditsch, "Contagion or Confusion? Why Conflicts Cluster in Space," *International Studies Quarterly* 52 (2008): 215–33.

FIGURE 6.1   *Interstate and Civil Wars, 1816–2016*

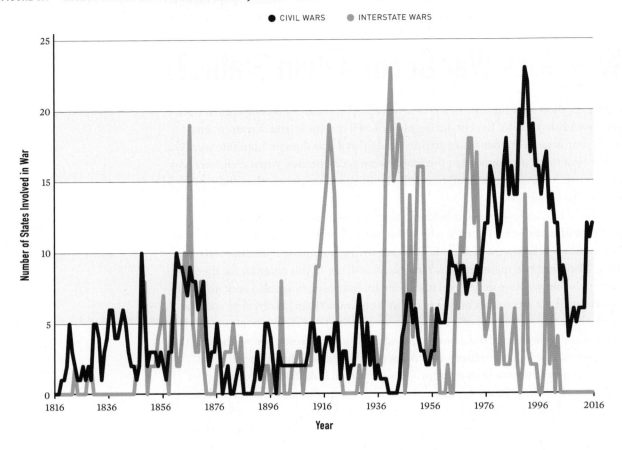

● CIVIL WARS   ● INTERSTATE WARS

Figure source: For 1816–2007, data are from the Correlates of War (COW) War Data, version 4.0; Meredith Reid Sarkees and Frank Wayman, *Resort to War: 1816–2007* (Washington, DC: CQ Press, 2010). Data for 2008–16 are from UCDP/PRIO Armed Conflict Dataset version 17.1. Marie Allansoon, Erik Melander, and Lotta Themnér, "Organized Violence, 1989–2016," *Journal of Peace Research* 54, no. 4 (2017): 574–87. Note that while these two datasets use somewhat different criteria for identifying conflicts, they agree reasonably well in their overall patterns.

states tend to have poor neighbors. But there is also reason to believe that civil wars, like diseases, can be contagious, particularly when the groups participating in a conflict straddle an international border. Civil wars also create refugee flows that can burden neighboring states, and they may involve widespread crimes against humanity that shock the consciences of those far away from the actual fighting.

These harms have led to greater international efforts at intervening to stop civil wars, with the United Nations (UN) increasingly citing purely domestic conflicts as "threats to international peace and security." Indeed, of the 71 peacekeeping operations undertaken by the UN from 1948 to 2017, 41 were deployed to conflicts that were within a single state, and another 12 dealt with conflicts having both international and civil dimensions.[7]

The long-running war in the Democratic Republic of the Congo (DRC) is an extreme but illustrative example of the interdependence between interstate and intrastate violence. The conflict that started in 1996 had its roots in the civil war and genocide that took place in neighboring Rwanda two years earlier (see Chapter 5).

---

7. Descriptions of UN peacekeeping operations can be found at www.un.org/en/peacekeeping/operations (accessed 12/08/14).

The genocide ended when the Tutsi-dominated Rwandan Patriotic Front ousted the Hutu-led government that had perpetrated the killings. Large numbers of Hutu militants then fled across the border into the DRC (then called Zaire) and started carrying out raids against their former homeland. In an example of cross-border contagion, the Rwandan government responded by arming Tutsis living in eastern Zaire, who then joined with other groups to form a broader resistance movement against the Zairian regime. Sensing a chance to rid themselves of a hostile neighbor, Rwanda, Uganda, and Angola openly intervened on the side of the rebels, who unseated Zaire's government in May 1997, at which point the country was renamed the DRC.

The civil war in the Democratic Republic of the Congo that began in 1996 was fueled by the intervention of neighboring states. The war claimed millions of lives, led to atrocities such as widespread rape and torture, and involved the forcible recruitment of thousands of child soldiers.

Conflict restarted the following year when the new government turned on its former allies and asked them to leave. The ensuing war, which officially ended in 2003 but has continued to smolder to this day, involved 25 different rebel groups supported directly or indirectly by eight different countries. In addition to claiming millions of lives, the war has led to massive atrocities, including horrific levels of rape. The resulting humanitarian crisis spurred the deployment of 20,000 UN peacekeepers in 1999, but these forces have been unable to stop the violence entirely. Given the scale and number of countries involved, this conflict has sometimes been called "Africa's World War,"[8] and it stands as a stark example of how civil conflicts can have their origins in international events and have effects that resonate beyond the borders of a single state.

Why Rebel?

At the root of all civil wars is some conflict of interests between the government and a subset of the population. The literature on civil wars generally classifies these interest conflicts as arising from two different sources: grievances and greed.[9] Grievances can arise when the policies of the government discriminate against members of a particular group, such as by repressing their language or culture, blocking their access to jobs or political office, or denying them government services, such as education, health care, and public infrastructure. These kinds of policies can lead to vast inequalities in wealth and quality of life among groups. Greed is a group's desire to control more of the country's economic resources, such as by having a greater share of the profits from natural resource extraction (such as oil or minerals) or privileged access to jobs and government largesse.

In either case, conflicts are rooted in individuals' and groups' basic interests in their economic and social well-being, autonomy, and power. When these interests

---

8. Gerard Prunier, *Africa's World War: Congo, the Rwandan Genocide, and the Making of a Continental Catastrophe* (New York: Oxford University Press, 2008).

9. Paul Collier and Anke Hoeffler, "Greed and Grievance in Civil War," *Oxford Economic Papers* 56 (2004): 563–95.

bring them into conflict with their government, dissatisfied groups have three options: they can try to leave the state, they can try to alter its policies, or they can try to take over the state altogether. Thus, intrastate conflicts give rise to demands over the same kinds of issues that we saw in interstate conflicts: territory, policy, and regime.

Territorial conflict in this context takes the form of separatism or irredentism. Both arise when a rebel group seeks to carve out a piece of the state's territory. A group is **separatist** if it wants to create its own independent state in the territory. Separatism generally arises when a group that is concentrated in a particular region of the country has grievances with the central government and expects to fare better under its own governance.

The newest state in the international system, South Sudan, achieved its independence from Sudan in 2011 after decades of separatist conflict that claimed more than 2 million lives (see "Controversy" on p. 248). Separatist conflicts also gave rise to East Timor, which separated from Indonesia in 2002; Kosovo, which declared its independence from Serbia in 2008; and Eritrea, which won its independence from Ethiopia in 1993. Most separatist conflicts are not as successful. Rebels in Chechnya have been fighting for that region's independence from Russia for over two decades, to no avail. The Liberation Tigers of Tamil Eelam (or Tamil Tigers) fought for a separate state in northern Sri Lanka from 1983 until their defeat in 2009. The United States also experienced a failed separatist movement when the Confederate states seceded in 1861 and were defeated in the ensuing civil war.

A rebel group is **irredentist** if members seek to attach their territory to that of a country next door. Irredentism usually arises when people of one state share ethnic or religious ties with the people in the neighboring state and therefore expect that their interests will be better served under its governance. For example, for much of the twentieth century, Great Britain faced a conflict with Catholics in Northern Ireland who wanted to join that region with the rest of Ireland, which is majority Catholic. The ongoing civil war in Ukraine is fueled by Russian speakers in the eastern portion of the country who would like to join Russia.

If leaving is impractical, a group motivated by grievances or greed may threaten civil war in order to change the policies pursued by the central government. Some minority groups in India, for example, have resorted to violence in order to get official recognition of their language—an act that confers a variety of political and social benefits. The civil war in Iraq pitted a variety of groups against each other and against the U.S.-led occupation in order to influence policies of the new state. Members of the Sunni Arab minority fought to preserve the privileges that they had enjoyed under Saddam Hussein (himself Sunni), including securing their share of Iraq's oil revenue and protecting their political, civil, and religious rights. Kurds, concentrated in the northern regions, sought to make sure that the new state would be highly decentralized, giving them autonomy in their region as well as influence over its oil.

Finally, dissatisfied groups might seek to seize control of the central government and establish a new regime. The civil war in Syria broke out in 2011 because of dissatisfaction with the repressive rule of President Bashar al-Assad. The Assad family, which has run Syria since 1970, comes from the Alawite sect of Islam, which makes up about 11 percent of the Syrian population but receives a vastly

---

separatist

An actor that seeks to create an independent state on territory carved from an existing state.

irredentist

An actor that seeks to detach a region from one country and attach it to another, usually because of shared ethnic or religious ties.

disproportionate share of influence and benefits. The numerous rebel factions that are seeking to oust Assad come from other, more populous groups that have been excluded from power. During the 1970s and 1980s, white minority governments in Rhodesia (now Zimbabwe) and South Africa fought civil wars against groups pushing for a democratic system that would lead to black majority rule. Political exclusion of a significant group is a common reason why rebels seek to overturn the existing polity.[10] Clashes over control of the central government are also common in newly independent states, when the retreat of the colonial power creates a space for groups to fight over control of the new state.

Members of the Kashmiri separatist group Hizbul Mujahideen have used terrorism to impose costs on India to compel an end to Indian rule in Kashmir so that the region can join Pakistan. Here, supporters of the separatist movement mourn the death of Burhan Wani, a commander of Hizbul Mujahideen who was killed in a confrontation with Indian forces.

It should be apparent from this discussion that rebel groups often form on the basis of ethnic and/or religious divisions: Catholic versus Protestant, Hutu versus Tutsi, Sunni versus Shiite, and so on. Indeed, the majority of civil wars have an ethnic or religious component to them. As a result, it might be tempting to assume that civil wars are caused by ethnic or religious differences and that countries divided in this way have a higher risk of conflict. In fact, this is not the case, and there are many diverse countries that do not experience internal violence.[11] Ethnic or religious differences alone do not cause the interest conflicts that underlie civil wars. It is when these differences give rise to discriminatory economic and social policies, inequality, political exclusion, and/or intolerance that demands for territory, policy change, or regime change can arise.[12]

When Does Dissatisfaction Lead to Armed Opposition?

Of course, most countries contain dissatisfied people who would like greater control over their territory, more influence over policy, privileged status for their language and culture, a bigger share of the country's wealth, a larger role in government, or a different kind of government altogether. And yet, civil wars are relatively rare. Grievances and greed are necessary to fuel the emergence of armed opposition groups, but they are clearly not sufficient. Why do some dissatisfied groups

10. Lars-Erik Cederman, Andreas Wimmer, and Brian Min, "Why Do Ethnic Groups Rebel? New Data and Analysis," *World Politics* 62 (2010): 87–119.

11. Fearon and Laitin, "Ethnicity, Insurgency, and Civil War."

12. See Donald L. Horowitz, *Ethnic Groups in Conflict*, 2nd ed. (Berkeley: University of California Press, 2000); and Lars-Erik Cederman, Nils B. Weidmann, and Kristian Skrede Gleditsch, "Horizontal Inequalities and Ethnonationalist Civil War: A Global Comparison," *American Political Science Review* 105 (2011): 478–95. The danger associated with excluding ethnic groups from power raises the intriguing question of why some leaders do it anyway. For an interesting analysis of this question, see Philip Roessler, *Ethnic Politics and State Power in Africa: The Logic of the Coup-Civil War Trap* (Cambridge: Cambridge University Press, 2016).

Should Every Group Have a State of Its Own?

On July 9, 2011, tens of thousands of people gathered in Freedom Square in Juba, South Sudan, to witness the birth of the international community's newest state. As the joyous crowd looked on, the flag of the Republic of Sudan came down, and the flag of the Republic of South Sudan was raised to the sound of the new national anthem. The country's first president signed its constitution and took the oath of office. Though the mood was jubilant, it was tinged with sadness, since the road to South Sudan's independence had been long and bloody.

South Sudan was the twenty-fifth state to join the international system since 1990, and in still many other places around the world, people are struggling for a state of their own, to no avail. The Israeli-held West Bank and Gaza Strip, South Ossetia and Abkhazia in Georgia, Russian majority areas in eastern Ukraine, Tibet in China, Aceh in Indonesia, Chechnya in Russia, Catalonia in Spain—all are regions whose people are seeking independence and that, in some cases, exercise de facto statehood that is not internationally recognized.

Applying the Concepts

Should all these regions get states of their own? The main argument in favor of statehood rests on the principle of self-determination: the idea that communities have the right to choose how they are governed and to which authority they are subject. Proponents argue that members of minority groups are more likely to have their **interests** met by a state whose boundaries conform to those of their group, rather than by one whose boundaries were imposed by outsiders. The argument against statehood is that it is rarely possible to carve out new states in a way that protects everyone's interests; that allowing secession can set off a chain reaction of conflictual **interactions**; and that groups' interests can instead be better met through **institutions** that protect minority rights.

The principle of self-determination stands in opposition to the practice of imperialism, whereby foreign powers exercise control over conquered lands, and self-determination movements were instrumental in bringing about the end of formal imperialism after World War II. Although few colonies remain in the world, the aftereffects of the imperial era are still ubiquitous in the existence of states whose boundaries were drawn by foreigners without much regard to the interests of the people living there. Such was the case with South Sudan. Originally colonized and jointly ruled by the British and the Egyptians, the region was joined with northern Sudan prior to gaining independence as the Republic of Sudan in 1956.

The union of the two Sudans was fraught with tension from the outset. Most northerners are Arabic-speaking Muslims, while most southerners either are Christian or practice indigenous religions. Home to the bulk of Sudan's population and urban centers, the northern region dominated the country's political and economic life and enjoyed the lion's share of its oil revenues. The south wanted greater autonomy, but the north wanted to hold on to the southern region, which contains about 80 percent of the country's oil reserves.

As a result of these conflicting interests, rebellion broke out in the south in 1955, shortly before the Sudan became independent, and the country experienced civil war for all but 10 of the next 50 years. A deal struck in 2005 provided for a popular vote on South Sudan's future, and in a referendum held in January 2011, 98.8 percent of the region's inhabitants voted for independence. Thus, the people of South Sudan had a very compelling case

A woman in Juba encourages people to vote in the January 2011 separation referendum.

for independence. Indeed, granting their demand earlier would have prevented a great deal of suffering and death. For this reason, some have advocated partition into separate states as a practical solution to ethnic civil wars.[a]

But what should be done if not all those living in the secessionist region would have their interests served by a new state? In the case of South Sudan, opposition to independence was minimal, but in Kosovo, which declared independence from Serbia in 2008, a significant minority of ethnic Serbs do not want separation and worry about their fate. In such cases, secession may give rise to further conflict, as newly created minorities struggle within the new state. Even if possible, a "clean" partition—that is, one in which no minorities are left on either side—may require large population transfers, which can themselves be quite brutal. South Sudan's border with Sudan is also contested in places, leading to militarized threats and violence.

Another concern is that allowing groups to secede can set off a cascade of further demands for secession. The principle of self-determination is silent with respect to what criteria a group should meet in order to merit its own state. Does everyone need to have the same religion, speak the same language, or have the same skin color? Can any collection of people, no matter how small, proclaim themselves a nation and seek recognition? In the absence of clear principles for drawing lines, the potential for violent conflict is high.

South Sudan is a case in point, since the new country is as much an artificial creation as the state it left. The people come from more than a dozen different ethnic groups, speak many different languages, and follow different religious faiths. Indeed, less than two years after independence was achieved, a political struggle between leaders representing the two largest ethnic groups cast the country into a civil war that had, by the end of 2017, killed over 50,000 and displaced 4 million people. Given these differences, there could be an argument for breaking South Sudan into ever-smaller units. But where does the process end? The international community's hesitation in recognizing new states rests in large part on similar concerns about a slippery slope that leads to the splintering of the entire system. Thus, partition may set off a chain of conflictual interactions, both within newly created states and between them.[b]

In the end, those sympathetic to the plight of "trapped" minorities might argue instead for institutions that protect those groups' interests without redrawing borders. Countries with heterogeneous populations have fostered civil peace through democracy, rules protecting minority rights, and institutions that give autonomy to regions where such groups are the majority. While partition may be necessary and desirable in some cases, it can be more practical instead to promote institutions that make it possible for diverse people to live together rather than granting every request to live apart.

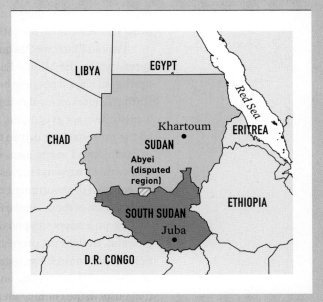

Thinking Analytically

1. What criteria should the international community use to decide when it should support the creation of a new state like South Sudan?

2. What are some alternatives to partition that might have addressed the interests of the people of South Sudan?

---

a. Chaim Kaufman, "Possible and Impossible Solutions to Ethnic Civil Wars," *International Security* 20 (1996): 136–75.

b. Nicholas Sambanis, "Partition as a Solution to Ethnic War: An Empirical Critique of the Theoretical Literature," *World Politics* 52 (2000): 437–83.

organize to further their interests through the threat or use of violence while others, indeed most, do not?

We can illustrate this question more concretely by considering the uprisings that spread across the Middle East and North Africa in winter/spring of 2011. The Arab Spring (so named not only because of the season in which it occurred, but also because spring denotes an awakening) involved mass protests in various countries, including Tunisia, Libya, Egypt, Syria, Yemen, and Bahrain. Though local circumstances varied, all the protests were driven to some degree by the same set of factors: a large number of unemployed young men, an increase in food prices, and long-standing dissatisfaction with corrupt and repressive governments. In all cases, the protesters demanded the removal of government officials and/or liberalization of the regimes.

In spite of these similarities, the outcomes varied quite significantly. In Tunisia and Egypt, leaders stepped down in response to mass protests that were largely peaceful. In Bahrain, protests were swiftly put down by the government. The opposition movement in Libya organized into an armed rebel group, which waged open war against the Libyan regime and ultimately succeeded in ousting it; in the power vacuum that ensued, the country then fell back into civil war. In Syria, a violent crackdown led to the emergence of a full-scale civil war that has claimed hundreds of thousands of lives, caused violence to spread into neighboring states, and, at the time of this writing, showed little sign of ending anytime soon. What might explain this variation?

In general, three sets of factors help explain the emergence of organized, armed opposition groups: features of the group and its interests, features of the country in which the group resides, and features of the international system that influence the possibilities for external support.

Group-Level Explanations   In some cases, the ability of groups to organize is aided by the nature of the interests for which they are fighting. Individuals may

Not all conflicts between dissatisfied groups and the government result in civil war. Mass protests in Tunisia led to the resignation of President Zine al-Abidine Ben Ali in January 2011 and the establishment of a new government without large-scale violence.

be motivated by very strong religious or ideological beliefs that lead them to see contributing to the cause as beneficial in its own right. In a study of why individuals participated in El Salvador's civil war, Elisabeth Wood found that many peasants were motivated by a sense of justice and a desire to do something meaningful with their lives.[13] When this is the case, there is no incentive to free ride and the collective action problem does not arise.

Similarly, individuals from the same ethnic or religious group may have higher levels of trust or collective solidarity and feel a stronger social disincentive to free ride when dealing with one another. Indeed, the majority of civil wars involve mobilization along ethnic lines, meaning that the rebels and the government tend to draw support from different ethnic groups.[14] As we already saw, this pattern may reflect interethnic tensions over the division of wealth and political power or the status of a particular religion, language, or culture. But even if ethnicity does not give rise to a grievance, it can be a resource for mobilizing people for or against the government. Because people of the same ethnic group tend to trust one another, it is easier to recruit fighters and raise funds from people of the same ethnicity than from outsiders. Indeed, when people trust their ethnic or religious kin more than they trust others, elites can strategically highlight and manipulate group differences in order to build a base of support.

Particularly when accompanied by violence, this strategy can cause a society to polarize along ethnic or religious lines, as individuals seek protection from their "own kind." This process of polarization played out rapidly and with tragic consequences in Iraq's capital city, Baghdad, following the American invasion. Before that, Baghdad was home to both Shiites and Sunnis, many living in mixed neighborhoods. In the aftermath of the invasion, radicals on each side started targeting those from the other group. Even if you were, say, a moderate Shiite who preferred to live in peace with your Sunni neighbors, the insecurity of knowing that you and your family might be attacked simply because of your religious identity would lead you to seek protection from other Shiites. This dynamic caused people to fill the ranks of Sunni or Shiite militias, thereby increasing the power base of the militia leaders who had sparked the violence in the first place. People also fled areas controlled by the other sect, causing mixed neighborhoods to all but vanish from the map.[15]

In addition, some traditional societies may be organized into tribes, which are substate groups with familial or ethnic ties. Tribes generally have their own systems of formal or informal governance, which facilitate collective action. If a tribal leader chooses to join a rebellion, he can bring along other members of the tribe.

---

13. Elisabeth Jean Wood, *Insurgent Collective Action and Civil War in El Salvador* (Cambridge: Cambridge University Press, 2003).

14. Fearon and Laitin, in "Ethnicity, Insurgency, and Civil War," report that 51 percent of civil wars in the 1945–99 period were fought along ethnic lines, and another 18 percent were mixed or ambiguous. Using different data and criteria, Nicholas Sambanis reports that 77 out of 109 civil wars from 1960 to 1999 were ethnic in nature; see Nicholas Sambanis, "Do Ethnic and Nonethnic Civil Wars Have the Same Causes? A Theoretical and Empirical Inquiry (Part 1)," *Journal of Conflict Resolution* 45 (2001): 259–82.

15. For some detailed maps showing the changes in the ethnic distribution in Baghdad from 2003 to 2009, see http://gulf2000.columbia.edu/maps.shtml (accessed 12/08/14).

The civil war in Libya stemmed in large part from the decision of several key tribes to withdraw their support from the government.

In the absence of strong ethnic ties or ideological motivations, groups that seek to mobilize against the government have to find other ways to encourage participation. One way is to compensate supporters materially. Rebel groups operating in areas of Africa with easy access to diamonds or other precious minerals can sell these goods on international markets, sometimes illegally, and funnel the proceeds to their fighters. The sale of so-called blood diamonds enriched rebels fighting in Sierra Leone (1996–99), while the long-running civil conflict in Colombia was fueled by the cocaine trade. Indeed, some rebel groups are essentially criminal gangs deeply engaged in smuggling, human trafficking, and extortion.[16]

Another way rebel groups may amass fighters is through forcible recruitment, or kidnapping. Men, women, and children may be taken from their homes at gunpoint and used as fighters, porters, messengers, spies, or sexual slaves. This practice was shockingly illustrated in April 2014, when nearly 300 Nigerian schoolgirls were kidnapped and forced to marry members of the rebel group Boko Haram. The UN estimates that tens of thousands of children under the age of 18 are participating in civil conflicts around the world.[17]

Country-Level Factors Certain features of a country can also contribute to the risk that armed opposition will emerge. Three in particular are important to note. The first deals with the country's political institutions or regime type. The incentive to threaten or use violence depends in part on whether the normal political process allows peaceful methods for redressing grievances. After all, fighting is very costly, so it makes sense to seek policy change or influence through existing political channels, if possible. If groups can pursue their goals by running candidates in elections or securing their rights through courts, then they have an alternative to taking up arms. This suggests that democratic countries should have a lower risk of experiencing civil wars, a hypothesis for which there is some evidence.[18]

Nevertheless, the relationship between a country's political institutions and civil war is complicated by another consideration: the ability of a rebel group to form depends in part on the government's repressive capacity—that is, how easily it can prevent, deter, or eliminate armed opposition. In this respect, authoritarian governments can have an advantage, owing to extensive police and surveillance activities, a greater willingness to use violence against their own citizens, and the absence of civil liberties. As a result of these competing considerations, there is reason to believe that the risk of civil war is highest in countries that are neither fully

---

16. See, for example, John Mueller, "The Banality of 'Ethnic War,'" *International Security* 25 (2000): 42–70.

17. For the UN program on children and armed conflict, see https://childrenandarmedconflict.un.org (accessed 08/28/17).

18. Håvard Hegre, Tanja Ellingsen, Scott Gates, and Nils Petter Gleditsch, "Toward a Democratic Civil Peace? Democracy, Political Change, and Civil War, 1816–1992," *American Political Science Review* 95 (2001): 33–48.

democratic nor strongly autocratic, because they lack both effective channels of peaceful participation and an effective apparatus of repression.[19]

A second factor that is known to influence a country's civil war risk is its wealth. That poor countries are much more likely to experience civil wars than rich countries is the strongest and most consistent finding in the scholarly literature. There is some disagreement, however, as to the mechanism underlying this relationship. One natural interpretation is that people in poor countries have greater reason to be unhappy with their lot. Poverty breeds desperation, and a lack of economic opportunities can also lead to a large pool of unemployed young men who can be recruited as fighters. By contrast, people in rich countries may find that their lives are too comfortable to undertake the risks associated with violent strategies.[20]

An alternative interpretation hinges on the government's capacity to prevent and defeat rebellions. Richer states tend to have better and stronger police and military forces, as well as a better ability to project their authority throughout the country. By contrast, poorer countries often have police and militaries that are not much better trained or equipped than their domestic opponents. With more limited resources, they may also have a hard time exerting their authority outside of one or two main cities. The inability to project forces throughout the country makes it possible for rebel groups to organize in places that are beyond the government's effective reach.[21]

This last insight has led scholars to think about a third set of country-level factors that can affect civil wars: those that make it easier or harder for governments to find and defeat rebels. Civil wars are more likely in populous countries, since rebels can more easily recruit from and hide in large populations. They are also more likely in countries that cover large areas, which are hard to police. Some scholarship has also suggested that civil war risk is higher in countries with rugged terrain, such as jungles and mountains. The difficulty of rooting rebels out of mountainous terrain explains why the English spent considerable effort during the thirteenth and fourteenth centuries incorporating the rebellious Welsh into their kingdom and why the United States in the twenty-first century has had such a hard time eliminating the Taliban from the mountains that straddle the Afghanistan-Pakistan border. Nevertheless, there is some debate among scholars about whether these kinds of examples generalize to a broader pattern.[22]

---

19. There is some controversy on this point. Hegre et al., "Toward a Democratic Civil Peace?" and Fearon and Laitin, "Ethnicity, Insurgency, and Civil War" both showed a high risk of civil war in "anocracies"—that is, states that are neither fully democratic nor fully autocratic. This view was called into question by James Raymond Vreeland in "The Effect of Political Regime on Civil War: Unpacking Anocracy," *Journal of Conflict Resolution* 52 (2008): 401–25. It may be that this relationship holds for some kinds of civil wars and not others. For example, Halvard Buhaug argues that "semi-democracies" have the highest risk of civil wars over government or policy, while democracies have a higher risk of territorial conflict; see Halvard Buhaug, "Relative Capability and Rebel Objective in Civil War," *Journal of Peace Research* 43 (2006): 691–708. For a recent review of this literature, see Håvard Hegre, "Democracy and Armed Conflict," *Journal of Peace Research* 51 (2014): 159–72.

20. Collier and Hoeffler, "Greed and Grievance in Civil War."

21. Fearon and Laitin, "Ethnicity, Insurgency, and Civil War."

22. Fearon and Laitin, in "Ethnicity, Insurgency, and Civil War," show that more mountainous countries experience higher civil war risk. But studies that look at variation within countries have found that mountainous regions are not necessarily more likely to be the site of civil conflict than nonmountainous regions; see, for example, Halvard Buhaug and Jan Ketil Rød, "Local Determinants of African Civil Wars, 1970–2001," *Political Geography* 25 (March 2006): 315–35.

U.S. soldiers search for Taliban rebels in the mountains on the Afghanistan-Pakistan border. Rough terrain makes it more difficult for government forces to find and defeat rebels.

International Factors Finally, rebel groups may be able to obtain resources if there are foreign countries that have an interest in their cause. Though civil wars pit rebels against a government within a state, most civil wars witness some meddling by other countries. Foreign states may intervene directly by sending their forces across the border to assist one side or the other; more commonly, sympathetic states may give arms, money, or training to rebel groups. Rebels may also operate from bases in neighboring countries, allowing them to organize and train in sanctuaries that are hard for the government to reach.[23]

There are several reasons why foreign governments might have an interest in supporting or hosting rebels. One possibility is that they share the interests of the rebel group. Just as two states with aligned interests may seek to cooperate militarily to improve the bargaining outcome (see Chapter 5), a state whose interests are aligned with those of a rebel group may look for ways to increase the group's fighting capabilities. Irredentist groups—that is, rebel groups seeking to join their land to that of a neighboring state—are likely to receive such support from the state they hope to join. During the civil war in the former Yugoslavia (see Chapter 5), Serbia gave aid to ethnic Serbs living in Bosnia and Croatia who wanted to carve out a "Greater Serbia" from these lands. Russia has given military support to ethnic Russians in eastern Ukraine who started a separatist war in 2014 with the goal of either joining Russia or creating a new Russian majority state.

More broadly, states or individuals may support rebellions that involve ethnic kin in other states.[24] For example, Irish rebels fighting British rule in Northern

23. Idean Salehyan, *Rebels without Borders: Transnational Insurgencies in World Politics* (Ithaca, NY: Cornell University Press, 2009).

24. Stephen M. Saideman, *The Ties That Divide: Ethnic Politics, Foreign Policy, and International Conflict* (New York: Columbia University Press, 2001). See also Lars-Erik Cederman, Luc Girardin, and Kristian Skrede Gleditsch, "Ethnonationalist Triads: Assessing the Influence of Kin Groups on Civil Wars," *World Politics* 61 (2009): 403–37.

Ireland received money from Irish Americans who sympathized with their cause. Rebel groups may also attract foreign support because of their ideology. During the Cold War, movements espousing communist ideals often received support from the Soviet Union or China. Similarly, Iran has, since its Islamic revolution in 1979, been active in supporting militant Islamist groups such as Hamas, a Palestinian group, and Hezbollah, which operates in Lebanon.

By giving support to groups with aligned interests, a foreign state can force the government to make greater concessions, or it can improve the chances that the rebels will replace the government altogether and implement policies closer to the foreign state's ideal point. This may be a particularly attractive strategy when the foreign state is weak relative to the target. In the 1970s, Somalia built up a separatist movement in Ethiopia after several attempts to seize Somali-inhabited territory through more conventional means failed. Thus, supporting rebels was seen as a way around Somalia's military weakness (though this strategy ultimately failed as well).

A second possibility is that outsiders may support rebels not because they care about the rebels' goals per se, but because they have other interest conflicts with the government. In these cases, support for rebels can be a relatively low-cost way for one state to impose costs on another in the hopes of either gaining concessions, to tie down some of the opponent's resources at home, or to hasten the ouster of a hostile government. For example, after Eritrea won its independence from Ethiopia, the Eritrean government gave support to other rebel movements in Ethiopia in order to strengthen its hand in a border dispute that arose after the separation. More generally, states that have long-standing disputes with their neighbors have a high likelihood of supporting and/or hosting rebel groups against their rivals.[25]

In some cases, the interests of outside parties can cause civil wars to become **proxy wars**, or conflicts in which two opposing states support opposite sides in a civil war within some third state. Such proxy wars were common during the Cold War, when the dangers of a direct confrontation between the superpowers were so great that conflict was often channeled through other actors. Thus, the Soviet Union and China supported communist rebels in South Vietnam, Laos, and Cambodia, while the United States gave support to the governments of those states. For its part, the United States supported rebels in countries with pro-Soviet governments like Nicaragua, Afghanistan, and Angola. The civil war that started in Yemen in 2015 has similarly become a battleground in a proxy war between Saudi Arabia and Iran. Unfortunately for the inhabitants of these countries, there is a significant cost to being a pawn in other states' conflicts: civil wars in which both the rebels and the government receive external support tend to last longer, thanks to additional fuel that outsiders bring to the fire.[26]

proxy wars
Conflicts in which two opposing states "fight" by supporting opposite sides in a war, such as the government and rebels in a third state.

25. Idean Salehyan, Kristian Skrede Gleditsch, and David E. Cunningham, "Explaining External Support for Insurgent Groups," *International Organization* 65 (October 2011): 709–44.

26. See, for example, Dylan Balch-Lindsay, Andrew J. Enterline, and Kyle A. Joyce, "Third-Party Intervention and the Civil War Process," *Journal of Peace Research* 45 (2008): 345–63.

The Rise of the Islamic State

The Islamic State (IS) burst onto the world stage in the summer of 2014, when it launched a dramatic invasion into Iraq from its strongholds in Syria. The crisis prompted the United States to initiate air strikes against IS positions and to coordinate a counterattack with Iraqi forces. How did this group arise?[a]

Interests The Islamic State is the latest version of a group that first formed during the civil war that erupted in Iraq following the 2003 U.S. invasion. The U.S. occupation met resistance from a variety of actors. Most important were members of the Sunni sect, who enjoyed a privileged position under the ousted regime of Saddam Hussein. Sunnis felt a political interest in spoiling the consolidation of a new regime that would be dominated by the majority Shia sect.

In addition, groups like Al Qaeda, which orchestrated the 9/11 attacks, aspired to create an Islamic "caliphate"—a territory under the rule of a Muslim religious leader—and they saw the removal of Western influence as a precondition to that end. The U.S. occupation of Iraq created an opportunity for individuals who shared that goal to fight Americans close to home. In 2004, a violent insurgent group of Sunnis and foreign fighters pledged allegiance to Osama bin Laden and became known as Al Qaeda in Iraq (AQI). In 2006, AQI joined with other militant groups to form the Islamic State of Iraq (ISI).

Interactions AQI and ISI employed violence for two main purposes. First, attacks on U.S. forces were intended to increase the costs of occupation and coerce an American withdrawal. Second, attacks on the Shia population were intended to provoke conflict between Shiites and Sunnis and thereby make any political reconciliation impossible. While the second part of the strategy succeeded in feeding a bloody sectarian war, the United States responded to the violence by increasing its forces in 2007. Combined with resistance from Sunni tribes who were repelled by AQI's harsh tactics, this troop surge decimated the group by 2008. ISI got a new lease on life, however, thanks to the United States' withdrawal of its forces in 2011 and the outbreak of civil war in neighboring Syria.

Institutions Syria's descent into civil war led to a dramatic contraction of the regime's reach and authority. Furthermore, in a move to justify harsh tactics, the Syrian government gave Islamist groups a relatively free hand in central and eastern Syria. ISI took advantage of this political vacuum and sent forces to Syria.

While the group's initial activity in Syria involved terrorist attacks against the regime and rival groups, growing strength allowed it to turn to a more ambitious goal: carving out a state in the Sunni regions straddling Syria and Iraq. In 2013, the group rebranded itself as the Islamic State of Iraq and Syria (ISIS) and focused its violence against other Sunni groups, including Al Qaeda affiliates.

ISIS also started to perform the tasks of a state within the areas it controlled: taxing and conscripting its inhabitants, providing services, issuing currency, and regulating people's behavior. In addition, it developed conventional military capabilities designed to conquer territory. This process of state building culminated in the 2014 offensive into Iraq. With large swaths of territory and several major cities under its control, the group declared itself the head of a new caliphate, the Islamic State.

Over the next several years, the United States and its allies fought to expel IS from lands it occupied. In 2017, U.S.-backed forces ousted IS from its self-declared capital in Raqqa, Syria. With its state apparently defeated, IS seemed likely to return to its roots as an insurgent group, sponsoring and inspiring terrorist attacks in the region and beyond.

---

a. Much of this history is based on William McCants, *The ISIS Apocalypse* (New York: St. Martin's, 2015).

All these factors contribute in some measure to explaining why Libya, of all the countries that experienced protests during the 2011 Arab Spring, had the most successful armed rebellion. The Libyan rebels benefited from the country's large size, combined with the regime's relatively weak grip on its eastern regions, where the rebellion took hold before the government could stamp it out. The strong tribal structure in Libya also facilitated collective action, since tribal leaders who went into opposition brought with them the resources and manpower of their tribes. Rebels also profited, literally, from their ability to seize oil production and exporting facilities. Sales of oil from rebel-controlled ports helped to finance arms purchases. Finally, and most notably, the Libyan rebels benefited from Western intervention on their behalf, which came in the form of air strikes against pro-government forces, arms, and training. Though intervention was justified primarily as a humanitarian act, the United States had long seen Libyan leader Mu'ammar Qaddafi as a hostile and unpredictable influence in the region and seized the opportunity to oust him. By contrast, rebels were less likely to oust governments backed by powerful foreign governments. The United States looked the other way when Bahrain, a key strategic ally, cracked down on its protesters, and Russia's support for the Syrian regime constrained the prospects of intervention in support of the rebellion there.

Civil War as a Bargaining Failure

We have seen that the potential for civil violence arises when (1) there are groups of people within the country motivated by greed or grievances that put their interests in conflict with those of the government; (2) those people cannot pursue their grievances through regular political institutions; and (3) those people can, owing to their own resources, foreign support, and/or the state's weakness, overcome the collective action problem to recruit enough fighters and purchase enough weaponry to pose a threat. Once these conditions are met, the interaction between the rebels and the government can start to look like the bargaining interaction introduced in the interstate context in Chapter 3: two actors with opposed interests bargaining in the shadow of threats to use force.

As with interstate conflicts, civil conflicts can, in theory, be resolved through compromises that would allow the actors to avoid the horrendous costs associated with these wars. A territorial dispute could lead to a negotiated secession or, more likely, a grant of autonomy that would give the rebel group many of the benefits of self-rule in its region.[27] Regime and policy disputes can be defused through policy concessions or power-sharing arrangements that give rebels greater representation in the government. Thus, once a capable opposition group has emerged, the puzzle of civil war is the same as the puzzle of international war: Why do the actors sometimes fail to reach bargains that would permit them to avoid the costs of war?

The three mechanisms discussed in Chapter 3—information problems, commitment problems, and indivisibilities—are all relevant in answering this question,

---

27. For evidence that granting autonomy can prevent the outbreak of violence, see Lars-Erik Cederman, Simon Hug, Andreas Schädel, and Julian Wucherpfennig, "Territorial Autonomy in the Shadow of Conflict: Too Little, Too Late?" *American Political Science Review* 109 (2015): 354–70.

though, as we will see, commitment problems loom particularly large in this context.[28]

Civil War from Incomplete Information
As in international bargaining, incomplete information can arise if the capabilities and resolve of each side are hard to observe. In the context of civil conflicts, it can be particularly difficult to gauge the size and effectiveness of rebel groups, which often organize covertly and take steps to hide their strength (or weakness) in order to avoid government crackdowns. Moreover, there may be less scope for prewar communication and diplomacy, since representatives of rebel groups do not enjoy the same protection from arrest or execution that international diplomats enjoy.

Still, most scholars find informational arguments to be less convincing as explanations for most civil wars because these conflicts tend to last so long. While the median duration of interstate wars since 1945 was three months, the corresponding figure for civil wars was six years.[29] Recalling the argument from Chapter 3 that wars can remove uncertainty about relative strength and resolve (see the "How Do We Know?" box on p. 124), it seems unlikely that these conflicts would last years, even decades, if the underlying problem was simply a lack of information.

Civil War from Commitment Problems
A more likely explanation for long civil wars is that they are rooted in commitment problems that are particularly difficult to resolve.[30] Several kinds of commitment problems are prevalent in civil conflicts. First, as we have seen, anticipated changes to the relative power of two sides can generate incentives for preventive war. When power is changing, the rising actor cannot credibly commit to not exploiting its power in the future to revise any deal made today; as a result, the actor that expects to grow weaker may prefer war now to a less desirable deal in the future.

In the context of civil conflicts, changes in the relative power of rebels and the government can arise regularly, because of the ups and downs of the state's economy. When the economy falters, the government's tax revenue falls, depriving it of resources that could be used to combat a rebellion; at the same time, popular discontent associated with a poor economy makes it easier for rebels to attract new recruits. As a result, a downturn in the economy creates a window in which rebels are relatively strong and have incentives to press demands. And the government, facing a strong rebellion, has incentives to make concessions.

However, economic downturns are generally temporary, often driven by short-term shocks, such as a change in the price of oil or, in countries that depend heavily on agriculture, too little or too much rainfall in a given year. If everyone expects the economy to recover in the near future, then the rebels' newfound strength is known to be temporary. The rebels may expect that any concessions the government

---

28. For a review of how bargaining theory applies to civil wars, see Barbara F. Walter, "Bargaining Failures and Civil War," *Annual Review of Political Science* 12 (June 2009): 243–61.

29. Fearon and Laitin, "Ethnicity, Insurgency, and Civil War," 75.

30. James D. Fearon, "Why Do Some Civil Wars Last So Much Longer than Others?" *Journal of Peace Research* 41(May 2004): 275–301.

makes under these conditions will be withdrawn once the economy improves. As with a rising state, the government may not be able to commit credibly to abiding by the deal once conditions improve. Hence, the anticipated economic recovery creates incentives for rebels to fight now in the hopes of obtaining an irreversible victory while they are relatively strong. This logic suggests that economic downturns should be associated with a higher risk of civil wars, and that is exactly what researchers have found.[31]

A second commitment problem results from the fact that the combatants in a civil war generally have to live together, in the same country, once their conflict is settled. When two states seek to settle a dispute or end a war, their armies can remain or retreat behind their respective borders. As a result, both sides retain the coercive power needed to sustain a deal. In the case of civil conflicts, however, this is usually not an option. A rebel group mobilizes and arms its members in order to make demands on the government. The government, hoping to avoid war, decides to make concessions but also requires, as part of the deal, that the rebels demobilize and disarm. This is a sensible demand to ensure civil peace and order; unless a new state is created through secession, rebel forces will have to be integrated into the existing state.

This demand, however, gives rise to a severe commitment problem: once the rebels have disarmed, how can they be sure that the government will continue to abide by the deal? The government might simply exploit the rebels' disarmament to crack down and eliminate them as a threat altogether. Hence, any deal that requires disarmament by the rebel group directly affects the future bargaining power of the actors. As we saw in the case of interstate conflict, this dynamic can create an insurmountable obstacle to reaching a negotiated settlement, either before or during conflict.[32]

Partly for this reason, civil wars rarely end with negotiated settlements. Indeed, the majority of civil wars end only when one side achieves an outright military victory or when the rebel group simply peters out from a loss of support. Indeed, one study found that only a quarter of civil conflicts since 1945 have ended with a peace agreement or cease-fire, compared to 50 percent of interstate conflicts that ended in one of those ways.[33]

Reaching an agreement either before or during fighting requires some mechanism to ensure that the government will live by the deal once the rebels lay down their arms. In some cases, it might be possible to craft power-sharing agreements that give all sides some control over the military after the conflict so that none can unilaterally exploit the others.[34] A more likely mechanism for these purposes, however, is the presence of some third party, such as peacekeepers from the UN, that can monitor and enforce the terms of the deal. We will revisit this issue shortly.

31. See, for example, Edward Miguel, Shanker Satyanath, and Ernest Sergenti, "Economic Shocks and Civil Conflict: An Instrumental Variables Approach," *Journal of Political Economy* 122 (2004): 725–53.

32. Barbara F. Walter, *Committing to Peace: The Successful Settlement of Civil Wars* (Princeton, NJ: Princeton University Press, 2002).

33. Joakim Kreutz, "How and When Armed Conflicts End: Introducing the UCDP Conflict Termination Dataset," *Journal of Peace Research* 47 (2010): 243–50.

34. See, for example, Caroline Hartzell and Matthew Hoddie, "Institutionalizing Peace: Power Sharing and Post–Civil War Conflict Management," *American Journal of Political Science* 47 (April 2003): 318–32.

Just as the government may have a hard time committing to abide by a deal, there can be commitment problems on the rebel side as well. Rebel organizations, unlike states, can often have a hard time controlling all their members. Even if the leaders are willing to accept some deal, they may not be able to guarantee that every member of the group will lay down their arms. Within any group, there may be some members with extreme, even fanatical, views, who are unwilling to accept a compromise and will continue fighting. Unless the rebels can credibly commit to rein in their extreme factions, the government may be unwilling to cut a deal, or bargains may be struck but will not hold. As long as each faction can, on its own, decide to reject a deal and continue the war, fighting will continue until there is a deal that is acceptable to the most extreme faction—or until one side or the other is decisively defeated. For this reason, rebellions that have more factions tend to generate longer wars.[35]

An example of this problem comes from the civil war that has raged since 2003 in the Darfur region of Sudan, a conflict that gained a great deal of international attention because of the genocide carried out by pro-government Arab militias against the non-Arab people of that region (see Chapter 5). Fighting on behalf of the latter are two main rebel groups, the Sudan Liberation Movement (SLM) and the Justice and Equality Movement (JEM), along with a number of smaller groups. Though both SLM and JEM purport to speak for the same people, they have disagreed over the terms of any peace deal, and there are factions with different preferences within each group as well.

The government of Sudan signed an agreement in 2006 with the SLM, but the JEM rejected the deal and continued fighting. The SLM withdrew from the deal in 2010, and since then there have been ongoing, but so far unsuccessful, negotiations between the government and numerous rebel factions, which at times work together and at other times compete. Though the failures of peace in this case are partly the result of the government's unwillingness to compromise, efforts to end the war have been complicated by the multitude of factions within the rebel movement.

Civil War from Indivisibilities

Finally, conflict might be unavoidable if the issue in dispute is valued in such a way that it is difficult to divide. As we saw in Chapter 3, governments and separatist groups might find it hard to compromise over pieces of territory that are imbued with religious or ethnic significance. The more common problem, though, is that the state may have incentives to treat its *entire territory* as indivisible, particularly if there are many possible groups with separatist interests. Consider the case of Russia, which has fought two bloody civil wars in the breakaway region of Chechnya since that republic's predominantly Muslim inhabitants declared independence in 1993. Given the costs of this war, which claimed tens of thousands of lives and sparked terrorist attacks by Islamic militants, Russia might have been better off letting the Chechens take their land and go.

---

35. David E. Cunningham, "Veto Players and Civil War Duration," *American Journal of Political Science* 50, no. 4 (2006): 875–92.

Rebellions that involve more factions tend to generate longer wars, as it is more difficult to get all groups to agree to a deal. In Sudan, the government signed a peace deal with the rebel group SLM in 2006, but another group, the JEM, kept fighting, and peace has eluded the region ever since.

If Russia faced a single possible separatist group, the dangers of such a concession might not be too large. But in a large, multiethnic country, concession to one group might encourage others to mobilize for similar reasons. Russia is home to more than 100 different ethnic groups, many of whom seek separation or greater autonomy from the central government in Moscow. If the government appears willing to let one group go, then all other potential claimants have incentives to make their own demands. Although any one set of concessions might not be too painful, the collective costs of making concessions to multiple groups could be quite large.

This dynamic means that a state might reasonably see its entire territory as an indivisible good, since the loss of a little can bring about the loss of enormous value. In such cases, a state has an incentive to resist making concessions to any challenger in order to convince all potential challengers that they will face similar resistance. This suggests that the more potential separatist groups a government faces, the less likely it is to make concessions to any one—a prediction that has been confirmed in recent research.[36]

Insurgency and Counterinsurgency: The Strategies of Civil War

If a civil war breaks out, how is it fought? To what extent does the strategy of using violence differ when it is employed by nonstate actors? For most Americans, the term *civil war* evokes memorable battles between Union and Confederate soldiers,

---

36. Monica Toft, *The Geography of Ethnic Violence* (Princeton, NJ: Princeton University Press, 2005), esp. chap. 5 on Russia and Chechnya; and Barbara F. Walter, *Reputation and Civil War: Why Separatist Conflicts Are So Violent* (Cambridge: Cambridge University Press, 2009). Technically, the dynamic described here is, at root, an information problem arising from uncertainty about the government's resolve to fight separatists. Treating the state's territory as indivisible is a strategy that the government employs to build a reputation for toughness, and not something intrinsic to the nature of the good. As we saw in Chapter 3, apparent indivisibilities are often rooted in strategic considerations.

blue uniforms against gray, marching against each other in formation—in other words, a conventional war that happened to be fought by people who previously considered themselves citizens of the same country. The majority of civil wars worldwide bear no resemblance to this image. Most rebel armies do not engage in direct combat with the government forces. Instead, most rebellions take the form of insurgencies.[37]

insurgency
A military strategy in which small, often lightly armed units engage in hit-and-run attacks against military, government, and civilian targets.

Insurgency is a military strategy in which small, often lightly armed units engage in hit-and-run attacks against military, government, and civilian targets. Unlike conventional military strategies, insurgency does not rely on capturing and holding territory. Instead, insurgents usually attack military bases, government buildings, or population centers and then melt back into rural areas, jungles, mountains, civilian populations, or across the border to take sanctuary in neighboring states. In order to blend into their surroundings, insurgents rarely wear distinctive uniforms. Indeed, the Chinese Communist leader Mao Tse-tung argued that insurgents should "swim" among the people just as fish swim in the sea—that is, hidden among the multitude.

The resort to insurgency is a direct response to the collective action problem facing rebel organizations. First and foremost, insurgency is well suited for groups that are small and weak relative to the adversary they face. Insurgency is a form of asymmetrical warfare, or conflict between actors with highly unequal military capabilities. Generally lacking the ability to raise a large fighting force or acquire sophisticated weaponry, rebels resort to tactics that avoid direct confrontations with usually larger and better-armed government forces. The purpose of insurgency is not to defeat the military, but rather to impose costs on the government in order to induce concessions. The hit-and-run strategy means that rebels rarely score decisive victories; at the same time, they are hard to defeat because they are hard to find. This elusiveness helps explain why civil wars often endure for years or decades, even when the rebel forces number only in the hundreds or low thousands.

The strategy of insurgency can also help address the collective action problem by increasing the pool of individuals who may be willing to side with the rebels. By attacking civilians or police stations, courts, and other official sites, insurgents seek to undermine confidence in the government and encourage people to join them for protection. The Taliban insurgency in Afghanistan, for example, has sought to undermine faith in the U.S.-backed government by making people feel insecure and then offering to provide protection in exchange for support.

Insurgents also, by hiding among the noncombatant population, seek to provoke government forces into attacking civilians, with the hope that these attacks will radicalize people into joining their cause. For example, Taliban fighters often

---

37. A recent study classified 147 civil wars in the period 1944–2004 into three types, depending on whether the government, rebels, or both used heavy weapons such as tanks and artillery. Conventional wars, in which both sides used heavy weapons, accounted for 34 percent of the cases. Insurgencies, in which the government used heavy weapons but the rebels did not, accounted for 54 percent. The remaining 12 percent were cases in which both sides lacked heavy weapons. See Stathis N. Kalyvas and Laia Balcells, "International System and Technologies of Rebellion: How the End of the Cold War Shaped Internal Conflict," *American Political Science Review* 104 (Autumn 2010): 423.

Many of the small armed groups involved in the Syrian Civil War, including the Al-Rahman Corps, have used insurgent strategies in their fight against the Syrian government.

fire on U.S. and Afghan government forces from populated areas, in the hopes that the retaliation will mistakenly kill civilians. The large number of Afghan civilians killed by U.S. air strikes has helped fuel opposition to the Western presence and has increased recruitment of new rebels. Far more Afghan civilians have been killed by the Taliban than by the United States and its allies, but the Taliban have been better able to exploit deaths caused by outsiders. This strategy of provocation is also used by terrorists and will be discussed further later in the chapter.

The nature of insurgency means that these kinds of rebellions can be hard to defeat through the conventional military strategies that characterize interstate combat. Highly mechanized modern forces with tanks, jet planes, and heavy artillery are effective for confronting an opposing force that operates out in the open but not for dealing with a stealthy adversary that hides in the shadows and among civilian populations.[38] One response to this challenge is to engage in indiscriminate attacks against the civilian populations that might be sympathetic to the rebels' cause. Recalling Mao's fish analogy, the purpose of such a policy is to "drain the sea" within which the rebels hide. Not surprisingly, when pro-government forces engage in this kind of strategy, civilian casualties are very high.[39]

Whether this strategy can be effective at defeating an insurgency has been the subject of mixed findings in the literature. On the one hand, indiscriminate attacks have been shown in some cases to decisively defeat militants or at least hinder their ability to operate; for example, the Sri Lankan government eliminated the

---

38. Jason Lyall and Isaiah Wilson III, "Rage against the Machines: Explaining Outcomes in Counterinsurgency Wars," *International Organization* 63 (2009): 67–106.

39. Benjamin Valentino, Paul Huth, and Dylan Balch-Lindsay, "'Draining the Sea': Mass Killing and Guerrilla Warfare," *International Organization* 58 (2004): 375–407.

Why Does War Occur within States?   **263**

Liberation Tigers of Tamil Eelam (LTTE) in 2009 in the course of an unrestrained offensive that killed as many as 40,000 civilians trapped in the war zone.[40] On the other hand, there is also evidence that attacks on civilians can be counterproductive, spurring people to join the rebellion out of revenge or decreasing the willingness of civilians to cooperate with government forces.[41]

An alternative response to insurgency is one that focuses on winning the support of noncombatant populations in order to undercut the insurgency politically. The basic idea of this strategy is to provide security and support to civilians so that they will not be tempted or coerced into joining the rebellion. To the extent that people see their interests as aligned with the government's, rebels have a harder time recruiting fighters. In addition, greater confidence in the pro-government forces creates incentives for civilians to help identify militants who are hiding among them, thereby neutralizing one of the insurgents' key advantages. Civilians often fear that if they were to "rat out" militants, the government would not be able to protect them from reprisals. Counterinsurgency (COIN) operations are intended to ease this fear by making the government's commitment to defend civilians credible.

Though not new, this idea was at the root of a major rethinking of U.S. military strategy in response to the challenges in Iraq and Afghanistan. Facing persistent insurgencies in both countries, the military articulated a COIN doctrine in 2006 that focuses on using military forces to protect the civilian populations and to create a secure space for economic reconstruction. Rather than emphasizing search-and-destroy missions against insurgent forces, the COIN doctrine prioritizes deploying troops within towns and cities, patrolling along with the national army and police forces, to provide security and create confidence in the governments on behalf of which the United States is fighting. The strategy also calls for steps to reduce the danger of accidentally killing civilians, for example, by relying more on ground forces and less on bombs and missiles launched from airplanes, which are responsible for a large share of civilian deaths. In addition, COIN operations involve not just military power but also an injection of economic resources to help jump-start development and undercut rebels' efforts to "buy" new fighters and supporters.

In short, the COIN doctrine is an attempt to defeat an insurgency by giving the population an interest in the survival of the government, thereby exacerbating the rebels' collective action problem and eliminating their informational advantages. This model had success in Iraq in 2007, when the deployment of more U.S. troops and the shift to the new COIN strategy helped bring about a dramatic reduction in

40. Jason Lyall, "Does Indiscriminate Violence Incite Insurgent Attacks? Evidence from Chechnya," *Journal of Conflict Resolution* 53 (June 2009): 331–62; Jacqueline L. Hazelton, "The 'Hearts and Minds' Fallacy: Violence, Coercion, and Success in Counterinsurgency Warfare," *International Security* 42 (2017): 80–113; and Lionel Beehner, "What Sri Lanka Can Teach Us about COIN," *Small Wars Journal* 6 (August 2010): 1–8.

41. Luke N. Condra and Jacob N. Shapiro, "Who Takes the Blame? The Strategic Effects of Collateral Damage," *American Journal of Political Science* 56 (January 2012): 167–87; Matthew Adam Kocher, Thomas B. Pepinsky, and Stathis N. Kalyvas, "Aerial Bombing and Counterinsurgency in the Vietnam War," *American Journal of Political Science* 55 (April 2011): 201–18.

FIGURE 6.2   *Estimated Civilian Deaths Due to Violence in Iraq, 2003–2017*

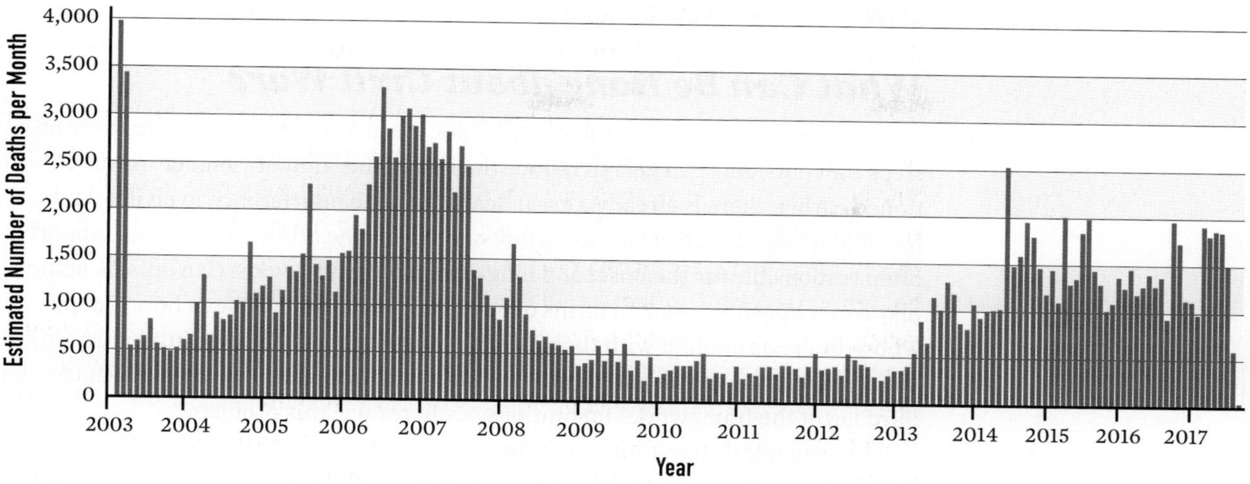

Figure source: The Iraq Body Count project, www .iraqbodycount.org/database (accessed 09/07/17).

Notes: Data for 2017 are preliminary. Year labels indicate January of each year.

insurgent activity and civilian deaths. This "surge" coincided with a split among the rebellious Sunnis, as some local leaders decided to assist the government in combating extremists who were responsible for much of the violence.

Though the United States was not primarily responsible for this turn, the surge made credible the American commitment not to abandon the government and enabled closer cooperation with local groups. The resulting reduction in violence paved the way for a significant withdrawal of American forces in Iraq, as well as their transition out of a combat role.[42] Figure 6.2 shows the trend in Iraqi civilian deaths due to the conflict, including the dramatic reduction after 2007. Taking advantage of this relative calm, U.S. forces left the country at the end of 2011. In the fall of 2009, President Barack Obama decided to try the same model against the Taliban insurgency in Afghanistan, increasing the U.S. troop presence there to 100,000 (together with roughly 40,000 troops from other countries) and implementing the COIN strategy.

Neither of these efforts brought about lasting solutions to those conflicts. As Figure 6.2 shows, only two years after U.S. forces left Iraq, the civil war there reignited, fed by the emergence of the militant group IS in neighboring Syria (see "What Shaped Our World?" on p. 256). In Afghanistan, the increased troop presence and new strategy had some successes, but there was no marked reduction in violence, nor much prospect that the Taliban could be defeated militarily. Despite limited progress, most U.S. and allied forces withdrew by the end of 2014, and those that remained transitioned away from combat roles. In 2017, President Donald Trump announced that he was sending as many as 5,000 additional troops

---

42. For an analysis of the various factors that brought down violence in Iraq, see Stephen Biddle, Jeffrey A. Friedman, and Jacob N. Shapiro, "Testing the Surge: Why Did Violence Decline in Iraq in 2007?" *International Security* 37 (Summer 2012): 7–40.

to Afghanistan to reverse worsening conditions there. The frustrations experienced in these countries by the world's most powerful state are a testament to the effectiveness of the strategy of insurgency.

What Can Be Done about Civil War?

Given the enormous human toll of civil wars, it is natural to ask whether there are steps that outsiders can take to reduce the risk of this kind of violence. As mentioned earlier, there is already a great deal of outside interference in civil wars, but much of it takes the form of supporting one side or the other; indeed, this support is often responsible for the onset and long duration of these wars. Can outside actors play a more positive role? In terms of our framework, we have seen how groups whose interests conflict with those of the government may engage in a bargaining interaction that sometimes leads to the outbreak of violence. To what extent can the third leg of the framework—institutions—help resolve this problem?

In principle, international institutions can help in several respects. First, international efforts could influence the bargaining between the government and domestic opponents in a way that increases the chances for a peaceful outcome. One such intervention would be to impose costs on actors that resort to force, much as collective security is intended to raise the costs of international aggression. As we saw in the previous chapter, collective security organizations like the UN have become increasingly active in intrastate conflicts. The track record has been, at best, uneven. Efforts to end ongoing conflicts in the former Yugoslavia, Rwanda, and elsewhere were ultimately hampered by the fact that few states had strong enough interests to motivate costly action, leading to halfhearted, ineffectual measures. In other cases, such as Syria, powerful states had conflicting interests that prevented collective action.

External efforts have played a much more positive role in keeping the peace once the combatants decide to stop fighting. As we have seen, agreements that require rebels to disarm create a severe commitment problem because of the government's incentives to renege on the deal once the rebels have complied. Peacekeepers may help alleviate this problem if they can credibly guarantee the safety of disarmed and demobilized rebels and help them reintegrate into society. International peace-building efforts may also help with the economic and political reconstruction of the country, which is important to long-term stability. For example, many peacekeeping missions after civil wars help organize and monitor elections, train the civilian police force, and bolster the judicial system. If successful, these efforts can lead to new political institutions through which future disputes can be handled without recourse to coercive bargaining. Evidence suggests that strong international efforts at peace building can not only prevent the resumption of violence, but also encourage the emergence of more democratic countries.[43]

---

43. Walter, *Committing to Peace*; Virginia Page Fortna, *Does Peacekeeping Work? Shaping Belligerents' Choices after Civil War* (Princeton, NJ: Princeton University Press, 2008); and Michael W. Doyle and Nicholas Sambanis, "International Peacebuilding: A Theoretical and Quantitative Analysis," *American Political Science Review* 94 (2000): 779–801.

There have also been some international efforts to reduce the ability of rebel groups to finance themselves through sales of drugs or minerals. For example, the Kimberley Process, initiated in 2003 (and named after the town in South Africa where the idea was hatched), is an international process that certifies rough diamonds that did not come from conflict zones. The hope is that if consumers purchase only diamonds that have the certification, the ability of rebels to finance themselves with so-called blood diamonds will be choked off.

Of course, most of these efforts are designed to end civil wars and prevent them from restarting after a peace deal; the ideal would be to reduce the likelihood that bloody and destructive civil wars will break out in the first place. There are several challenges to this aspiration. As already noted, most countries have dissatisfied groups and individuals that could provide the basis for armed opposition to the government. Although we know some of the factors that increase the risks of civil war, these conflicts are very hard to forecast with much certainty. As a result, it can be hard to correctly anticipate where the next civil war will break out and to target conflict management efforts appropriately. Moreover, there are truly repressive regimes that deserve the opposition of their people. In these cases, reducing the risk of armed rebellion can have the unintended effect of diminishing the government's incentives to liberalize.

In the long run, the best chance for a reduction in civil conflict hinges on changing interests and institutions within a country, particularly through economic development and democratization. Relatively wealthy countries have the lowest risk of civil war because their people have less to gain and more to lose by taking up arms and because wealthy governments are better able to buy off dissatisfied groups and/or deter the emergence of armed opposition. Well-functioning democracies provide institutions that enable groups and individuals to pursue their interests through peaceful political processes. Even so, these are long-run developments over which outsiders have only limited influence. Though states and international organizations constantly seek ways to promote development and democratization, these efforts, at best, support internal processes.

Moreover, the route to development and democracy can be rocky and dangerous. Though economic growth is good, it can have uneven effects as some groups within a country grow wealthy, while others remain mired in poverty. This kind of inequality can become a grievance that feeds civil conflict. Transitions to democracy can also be risky. During the period of transition, the regime may be too weak to deter violence while at the same time democratic institutions are not strong enough to channel political demands in peaceful ways. There is some evidence to suggest that periods of democratization are associated with an increased risk of civil war.[44]

The promotion of democracy by third parties also has to be done carefully. Some evidence suggests that foreign aid given for purposes of democracy building

---

44. See, for example, Lars-Erik Cederman, Simon Hug, and Lutz F. Krebs, "Democratization and Civil War: Empirical Evidence," *Journal of Peace Research* 47 (2010): 377–94.

can reduce the risk of civil war in countries that are already democratizing.[45] Bringing democracy to countries that are currently autocratic, on the other hand, requires some effort to destabilize the existing regime or, as in the case of the U.S. invasion of Iraq, remove it forcibly. As the U.S. experience vividly shows, however, the weakening or destruction of an autocratic regime can itself precipitate civil war.[46] The civil conflict in Iraq that followed the invasion is estimated to have claimed tens of thousands, if not hundreds of thousands, of lives. And, as we have seen, while U.S. forces helped bring about a reduction in violence after 2007, Iraq's civil war reignited only a few years after those troops left, dimming the prospects that Iraq will emerge prosperous and democratic.

Terrorism: Why Kill Civilians?

Though definitions abound, terrorism is conventionally defined as the premeditated threat or use of violence against noncombatant targets by individuals or subnational groups to obtain a political or social objective through intimidation of a larger audience.[47] Unlike conventional warfare, terrorism is an attempt to win concessions not by defeating the armed forces of another actor but by attacking civilians or civilian police forces or military units not engaged in combat. These attacks sow fear among some target population in the hope that this target will concede to the terrorists' political or social demands. The existence of such demands is crucial, as otherwise terrorism is no different from simple criminality.

Terrorism is transnational, and thus the subject of international relations, when it crosses an international border by involving a perpetrator and victim from different countries or when it aims to alter the behavior of a foreign government. Figure 6.3 shows the number of transnational terrorist attacks per year from 1970 to 2014, along with their estimated fatalities. Though terrorism rose to high levels in the 1970s and 1980s, it has increased considerably in the decade and a half since September 11, 2001, which marked the single bloodiest terrorist attack. Most terrorism, however, is purely domestic and does not cross national borders. Indeed, by one estimate, 89 percent of terrorist attacks since 1970 were domestic.[48]

---

45. Burcu Savun and Daniel C. Tirone, "Foreign Aid, Democratization, and Civil Conflict: How Does Democracy Aid Affect Civil Conflict?" *American Journal of Political Science* 55 (2011): 233–46.

46. For a general finding to this effect, see Goran Peic and Dan Reiter, "Foreign-Imposed Regime Change, State Power, and Civil War Onset, 1920–2004," *British Journal of Political Science* 41 (2010): 453–75.

47. This definition, used by scholars, is similar to that in the *United States Code*, title 22, chap. 38, sec. 2656f(d). Any definition of terrorism is itself a political statement. *Terrorist* is a term of opprobrium intended to delegitimize the action and, in turn, the cause for which violence is used. Thus, who is and is not a terrorist is often contested. State terrorism, which we do not consider here, involves the targeting of noncombatants by the government with the intent of influencing an audience. State-*sponsored* terrorism involves government funding or support of terrorists.

48. Kirssa Cline Ryckman and Mike Ryckman, "All Politics Is Local: The Domestic Agenda of Terror Groups and the Study of Transnational Attacks," *Journal of Global Security Studies* 2 (2017): 55–73. This estimate counts only attacks by known groups that conducted more than one attack.

FIGURE 6.3 **Transnational Terrorist Attacks and Fatalities, 1970–2014***

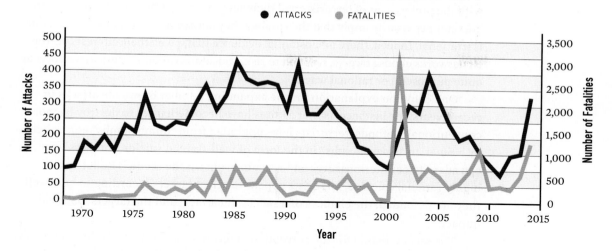

How can we understand people who hijack airliners and fly them into sky-scrapers or blow themselves up on crowded trains and buses? A common explanation for terrorism is that terrorists are hate-filled, irrational extremists who win glory by taking the lives of others. This is too simplistic. Rather, terrorism is a product of a strategic interaction between the terrorists and the governments they hope to influence. As such, violence can be understood as a bargaining failure prompted by incomplete information, commitment problems, and indivisibilities. At the same time, terrorists, like the rebel groups considered in the previous section, face a challenge in finding resources and recruits willing to undertake dangerous, possibly even suicidal, missions and in organizing collective action without being detected or ratted out. These organizational imperatives affect the nature of terrorist groups and the strategies they select.

Are Terrorists Rational?

Our framework usually starts by asking what interests motivate the relevant actors. In the context of terrorism, this immediately raises the question of whether terrorists can be thought of as actors who rationally pursue some interest. In popular discussions, it is often implied that terrorists are irrational, crazed "fanatics." If so, this characterization would significantly challenge our ability to analyze their behavior within the analytical framework developed in this textbook. At least three reasons for this perception must be examined before we turn to an explanation of terrorism.

First, groups that resort to terrorism often possess interests that are not widely shared, especially by the target audience. Describing terrorists as irrational may simply mean that terrorists rank alternative outcomes in ways that seem "unreasonable," at least from the broader population's perspective. However, as we saw in Chapter 2, *rationality* refers to purposive behavior or the strategies by which

Figure source: Attack data are from the National Consortium for the Study of Terrorism and Responses to Terrorism (START), Global Terrorism Database [Data file], 2017, https://www.start.umd.edu/gtd. Transnational attacks were identified using Kirssa Ryckman, "GTD Add-On: Terror Groups' Home," doi:10.7910/DVN/F6MTML, Harvard Dataverse, V1 (2016), UNF:6:1wXz57cxaKoR1/tmURSgdA== (accessed 09/06/17).

*The figure reports attacks directed against civilian targets (that is, not police or military) conducted by known groups that carried out more than one attack. Figures for 1993 are interpolated.

individuals or groups pursue their interests; the term *rational* is not a statement about the substance of an individual's or group's preferences. We may not agree with the preferences of terrorists and their supporters, but the fact that we disagree does not necessarily imply that the strategy they choose in pursuit of their interests is irrational. Indeed, there is substantial evidence that, given their interests, terrorist networks choose targets, respond to risk, and adjust to counterterrorist efforts in quite purposeful or rational ways.[49]

One common explanation for the expanding number of suicide attacks in recent years, for instance, is that as sites have become harder to destroy by more conventional methods, terrorists have upgraded from "dumb bombs" controlled by a timer, to "smart bombs" in the form of well-trained suicide bombers who can adapt to countermeasures and react to events at the scene.[50] Reflecting a highly rational calculus, terrorists appear to select targets according to how well they are defended, the chances of a successful attack, and the targets' political impact.

The second reason for the perception of terrorists as irrational is that a person's choice to become a terrorist—especially to become a suicide bomber—may entail costs larger than the gains to that individual and thus appears not to be an effective strategy for obtaining one's goals. Currently, we have no good explanations for why any particular individual chooses to become a terrorist or a suicide bomber. After all, the sacrifice of one's own life seems a high price to pay for any cause. However, we also lack complete explanations for why an individual would voluntarily choose to join a national military and go into battle to risk death for his or her country. For any individual, such choices may be irrational in that the personal costs (the risk of death) exceed the personal gains. Moreover, individuals may be motivated by goals that have nothing to do with the organization's political agenda, such as a desire for adventure or a feeling of belonging.[51] Acknowledging this point, however, does not imply that a terrorist organization lacks purpose and careful strategizing in how it deploys its forces.

The third reason for the perception of irrationality is that terrorist attacks sometimes appear to be random. In some cases, of course, it is clear why terrorists chose a certain target, as the selection of the World Trade Center and Pentagon as targets on 9/11 demonstrates. These sites were chosen because they represent the core of America's international power—business and the military. More generally, the most frequent targets of terrorists are businesses and diplomatic missions, which also serve as emblems of the target state's power. But certainly, some terrorist attacks are random, as when a suicide bomber selects one crowded pizzeria rather than another.

---

49. See, for example, Charlinda Santifort, Todd Sandler, and Patrick T. Brandt, "Terrorist Attack and Target Diversity: Changepoints and Their Drivers," *Journal of Peace Research* 50 (2012): 75–90.

50. Eli Berman and David Laitin, "Hard Targets: Theory and Evidence on Suicide Attacks," NBER Working Paper W11740, National Bureau of Economic Research, Cambridge, MA, November 2005.

51. See, for example, Max Abrahms, "What Terrorists Really Want: Terrorist Motives and Counterterrorism Strategy," *International Security* 32 (2008): 78–105.

Random selection of targets and times, however, is often part of a terrorist's strategy. After all, one objective of terrorism is to strike fear into the target population. If terrorist attacks are systematic and predictable, the population will adjust accordingly and avoid likely targets when an attack is anticipated. By selecting random times and places, terrorists can make people feel unsafe everywhere and greatly magnify the threat they pose and the fear they instill. In other words, randomness can be quite rational.

Why Terrorism?

A key point in understanding terrorism is that terrorist organizations are weak in two important senses: they are weak relative to the states they seek to coerce, and they are weak relative to the extensive demands they make.[52] This weakness arises from the nature of the interests that motivate them.

People and groups that use terrorism may be motivated by any number of interests. They may seek to overthrow a government, expel a foreign power from their homeland, or carve out a new utopian society based on some economic or religious ideology. Al Qaeda sought to eradicate Western influence from the Middle East in order to bring about Islamist governments in the region. Palestinian terrorist groups like Hamas have sought the destruction of the state of Israel. The Shining Path is a Marxist terrorist group that has operated in Peru since the 1980s and sought to destabilize the government and bring about a communist revolution.

Whatever interests they seek to promote, terrorists are typically **extremists** in the sense that their interests are not widely shared by others, or, at least, their willingness to pay costs to achieve those interests is not widely shared. In any population there is a range of individual interests in issues such as the most appropriate political system, the distribution of resources, proper religious beliefs, and so on. For most issues the range of interests is distributed in a bell-shaped curve, with most people being "moderate" and clustered in the middle of the distribution (Figure 6.4).

When we call someone extreme, we typically mean that his or her interests are significantly different from those of the majority. In the curve illustrated in Figure 6.4, extremists exist in the "tails" of the distribution to either the left or the right of the moderate majority. In fact, what it means to be an extremist is relative: someone who is an extremist in one society might not be in another. For example, moderates in Britain may have very different interests from moderates in Pakistan. But extremism implies that relatively few other individuals share the extremists' political preferences. And even if others share a group of terrorists' ultimate objectives—for example, many peaceful individuals in the Middle East

extremists
Actors whose interests are not widely shared by others; individuals or groups that are politically weak relative to the demands they make.

---

52. That terrorism is a "weapon of the weak" is conventional wisdom in academic and policy discussions, but we have to be precise about what this phrase means. Terrorism is an attractive strategy when relatively small groups confront powerful states with sophisticated militaries; see, for example, Cullen S. Hendrix and Joseph K. Young, "State Capacity and Terrorism: A Two-Dimensional Approach," *Security Studies* 23 (2014): 329–63. Among groups that are fighting a state, however, weaker groups are not necessarily more likely to resort to terrorism than stronger groups are; see Fortna, "Do Terrorists Win?"

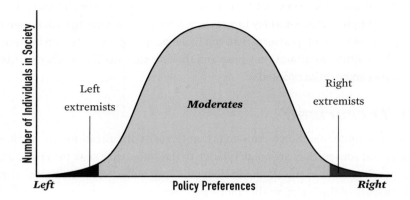

FIGURE 6.4 *Extremist Interests*

resent Western influence there and would like to see it end—they may not care so intensely that they are willing to kill or die for that goal.

Almost by definition, therefore, extremists are small groups of individuals who face a much larger majority that either does not share their goals or is unwilling to use violent means to achieve them. The result is that extremists tend to be weak politically relative to the demands they make. This condition means that the problem of recruitment is particularly acute, since the pool of motivated individuals is relatively small and extremists have difficulty convincing others to share their interests and join their causes. Moreover, their fringe status means that they will seldom be able to further their interests by participating in the normal political process, making use of existing institutions, even in a democracy. Instead, their hope lies in using violence to coerce concessions or somehow alter the status quo in their favor.

The resort to violence is further complicated by the fact that terrorists are weak not only relative to their demands, but also relative to their targets. States are nearly always stronger politically and militarily than the terrorist networks they face.[53] Whereas states have populations and economies they can tax for resources and standing militaries they can deploy, terrorist organizations are often starved for resources, quite small in numbers, and poorly armed, especially in their formative stages, when they are most vulnerable to government countermeasures. Like rebel groups, they often must resort to such criminal activities as drug running or bank robbery to acquire their initial funding, although some grow out of legitimate religious and service activities (such as Hamas) or depend on the personal wealth of their founders (such as Osama bin Laden in the case of Al Qaeda).

---

53. This is particularly true with transnational terrorism. Terrorism in the context of civil wars is often directed at weak states or takes place in the context of state failure.

Terrorists sometimes carry out seemingly random attacks on public places as a purposeful strategy to strike fear into the target population, as in the 2015 attacks on a suburban mosque and bakery in Beirut, Lebanon, which killed over 40 people.

This weakness is central to understanding why terrorism involves attacks on civilians, businesses, government embassies, and other official buildings. The object of terrorism is to bypass the other side's military and inflict pain and suffering on the target population so as to induce political change. In this sense, because it avoids a direct confrontation that would result in certain defeat, terrorism is like insurgency. As we will see, terrorism can also be used, like insurgency, to provoke government repression that increases the group's support base. The main difference between terrorism and insurgency is that the latter more commonly involves hit-and-run attacks on military units, whereas terrorism targets civilians or nonmilitary aspects of the government.

The relative weakness of terrorists also influences the way they choose to organize. Terrorists adopt organizational forms that make it difficult for traditional military forces to defeat them. First, they typically form networks of small, self-contained cells that are loosely connected to one another and, in some cases, to a central directorate.[54] Unlike states, which have internal hierarchies, terrorists are organized in networks of individuals and groups that cooperate to achieve common aims. Terrorists do not routinely share information within the network; each cell is largely responsible for its own activities and acquires resources and information from other cells or the central directorate only as necessary. This loose network insulates the individual cells and allows the organization to survive when penetrated or attacked. If the potential target state successfully infiltrates or destroys a cell, there is minimal impact on the rest of the network.[55]

In addition, transnational terrorist groups may try to spread their message through publications and social media in order to inspire followers into committing "lone wolf" attacks—that is, attacks by individuals who are not actually members of the group but who share its goals. The April 2013 attack on the Boston Marathon, which killed 3 people and injured over 250, was committed by two brothers who were allegedly radicalized by extremist propaganda and learned bomb-making skills from an online Al Qaeda publication. Similarly, IS has encouraged supporters in the West to drive vehicles into crowds of people—a tactic that has led to mass casualty attacks in a number of European countries. Such lone

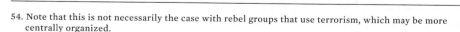

54. Note that this is not necessarily the case with rebel groups that use terrorism, which may be more centrally organized.

55. For an interesting analysis of how terrorists manage their organizations that draws on captured internal communications, see Jacob N. Shapiro, *The Terrorist's Dilemma: Managing Violent Covert Organizations* (Princeton, NJ: Princeton University Press, 2013).

IS has released numerous propaganda and training videos online designed to inspire lone wolf attacks by those who are sympathetic to, but not members of, the organization.

wolf attacks are rarely as lethal as those planned by an organization, but they are very hard to prevent, because the perpetrators have no observable connection to a terrorist group.

A second way that terrorists organize themselves to make it hard for traditional military forces to defeat them is by hiding within sympathetic populations, just as rebels take refuge in jungles, mountains, and cities. In cases where the group is not too extreme and thus has affiliated individuals who share its interests, or in which the local population has been radicalized and now shares the extremists' beliefs, terrorists can live within a larger population that protects and supports them. Palestinian extremists, for example, can blend into the wider Palestinian community, which supports many of their goals, if not always their methods. In other cases, terrorist groups can buy support from a corrupt, failed, or sympathetic state to gain refuge, as Al Qaeda did in Afghanistan prior to 9/11. Hidden within larger populations, terrorists are difficult to identify. Attempts to eliminate them, in turn, are likely to cause collateral damage to the larger population and thus raise the costs of any retaliatory or preemptive attack by the target state. Indeed, networks of loosely connected cells hidden in sympathetic populations make terrorist groups hard to eradicate.

Terrorism as a Bargaining Failure

Like states, terrorist organizations use violence or threats of violence to raise costs to the other side in hopes of eliciting concessions. In this way, terrorism and threats of terrorism are a form of bargaining. But if the target state knows the costs that terrorists can inflict on it, and the terrorists know that they are unlikely to defeat the state but can extract some concessions by threatening violence, why can't the two sides reach a compromise that reflects their relative bargaining positions? If such a bargain were possible, then the terrorists would be spared the costs of carrying out the attack and the target would not incur the damage and subsequent widespread fear. Given that the costs of violence theoretically make a mutually beneficial deal available, can we understand terrorism, like international and civil war, as the result of a bargaining failure?

One natural reaction against this view is that terrorists' goals may be so extreme that compromise is simply not possible. If terrorists want everyone in the target population to convert to a different religion, or they seek the elimination of the target state, then it may be difficult to imagine some compromise settlement that would be acceptable to both sides. In the extreme case where the adversary seeks your death or the obliteration of your identity, the costs of concessions and the costs of conflict may be indistinguishable, and there is little choice but to fight. But while we do not rule out the possibility of this extreme case—for example, Hamas and other Palestinian terrorist groups have called for the destruction of Israel—what separates terrorists from mass murderers is that they kill in order to advance a political objective, not as an end in its own right. Therefore, a mutually beneficial bargain generally exists in theory, even if there are significant barriers to identifying and achieving such a bargain in practice. As in the case of international and civil war, we can group these barriers as relating to information problems, commitment problems, and indivisibility.

Terrorism and Incomplete Information   Like states in conflict, terrorists have private information and incentives to misrepresent that information to targets. Precisely because terrorist networks are small, weak, and often shadowy organizations that hide within sympathetic populations or in fragile states, targets usually possess incomplete information about the size, capabilities, and resolve of those networks. Often, the first time anyone learns of a new terrorist group is after it claims credit for an attack. Even when targets have intelligence sources within the terrorist group, they may acquire relatively little information because the cell that is infiltrated or monitored may know little about other cells. Terrorist networks, in turn, have incentives to misrepresent their capabilities and resolve. By exaggerating claims of strength and commitment, these organizations seek to negotiate better deals from their targets.

As we now know, there were numerous hints about the impending attacks before 9/11, and bin Laden made no secret of the fact that he saw himself at war with the United States.[56] These warning signals were ignored, in part, because the separate agencies of the U.S. government were not able to put together the disparate pieces of the puzzle they had before them and because officials saw other threats as more important. But the warning signs were also downplayed because they could be interpreted as the normal blustering of terrorists whose aspirations seemed to far exceed their reach.

As we saw in Chapter 3, overcoming information problems requires finding ways for actors to communicate their capabilities and resolve in a credible manner. But the nature of terrorist organizations makes credible communication particularly difficult. Since their ability to carry out attacks against militarily more

---

56. See *The 9/11 Commission Report: Final Report of the National Commission on Terrorist Attacks upon the United States* (New York: Norton, 2004), 254–77.

powerful targets typically hinges on the element of surprise, terrorists cannot reveal their true capabilities or strategies in advance without undermining their effectiveness. If Al Qaeda had announced before 9/11 that unless the U.S. government conceded to its demands, it would fly hijacked airliners into the World Trade Center and the Pentagon, the United States would have quickly responded by grounding all airplanes (which it did immediately after the attacks) and surrounding New York and Washington, D.C., with constant air patrols. By tipping its hand in advance, Al Qaeda would have lost the ability to implement those very attacks on the United States.

The use of attacks to signal capability and resolve distinguishes terrorist organizations from states engaged in coercive diplomacy. States often communicate by using strategies short of force, such as public statements and mobilizations. Terrorist organizations cannot engage in the same kind of public displays without exposing themselves to the authorities and risking a crackdown. Instead, they tend to mobilize their efforts in secret, and the attack becomes the public signal.[57] Thus, unlike in interstate relations, there may be no bargaining between terrorists and states before the violence starts.

Terrorism and Commitment Problems

Problems of credible commitment also loom large in this context.[58] As part of any agreement reached before or after an attack, the target will insist that the organization promise not to employ violence in the future. After all, the whole point of making concessions is to reduce the threat and fear of future attacks. If the commitment to refrain from further attacks is not credible, however, this can prevent the conclusion of agreements that both sides prefer. Achieving credibility can be particularly hard in this context, since the target must judge not only the trustworthiness of the terrorist leadership, but also its ability to exert control over potential defectors within the group's ranks. Given their organization as decentralized networks of loosely connected individuals and cells, centralized control is often difficult for terrorists to achieve. Even if the group's leadership is willing to make a deal, it may not be able to rein in all the "loose cannons" that might want to continue the fight.

Terrorists can most credibly demonstrate their commitment to peace by publicly renouncing terror, disarming, and giving the target or some neutral third party full access to the network so as to alleviate any lingering information problems. This approach has been key to the still-fragile peace between Catholics and Protestants in Northern Ireland, where the Irish Republican Army (IRA) has disavowed terrorism, disarmed, and joined the political process.

As in the case of civil wars, however, the need for disarmament creates another commitment problem: If the terrorists disarm, how can they be certain that the target will honor its side of the agreement? After all, it was the fear of continuing

---

57. Harvey E. Lapan and Todd Sandler, "Terrorism and Signaling," *European Journal of Political Economy* 9 (1993): 383–97.

58. Ethan Bueno de Mesquita, "Conciliation, Counterterrorism, and Patterns of Terrorist Violence," *International Organization* 59, no. 1 (2005): 145–76; and Navin Bapat, "State Bargaining with Transnational Terrorist Groups," *International Studies Quarterly* 50, no. 1 (2006): 213–29.

attacks that gave terrorists power over the target in the first place. Once that ability is given up, the target no longer has any incentive to compromise with the terrorists. Credibly agreeing not to fight may be more difficult than credibly making threats in the first place. Indeed, the difficulties of committing to peace have been a source of continued fighting in many terrorist conflicts—including that between the Basque separatist group Euskadi Ta Azkatasuna (ETA) and Spain, where both sides appear to want peace but still have difficulty in credibly committing to a plan for disarmament.

States may also see fighting terrorists, rather than compromising with them, as a solution to a different commitment problem. A common argument for not negotiating with terrorists is that even if it makes sense to compromise with any one group, doing so will simply encourage others to emerge with new demands. After all, if any individual or group that threatens to detonate a bomb can wrest concessions from the target government, then a government faces a potentially endless list of demands from an ever-increasing set of adversaries. This is similar to the problem, mentioned earlier, of governments that face many potential separatist groups: though making concessions to any one might make sense, buying off every group is too costly. When faced with a large number of potential adversaries, the government would like to commit itself not to negotiate with any of them. Resisting any single group's demands, even at the risk of experiencing new attacks, is a way to signal this commitment and thereby deter the emergence of new challengers.

Terrorism and Indivisibilities Finally, bargaining may fail if the goods in dispute are such that they cannot readily be divided or subject to compromise. The view that it is not possible to negotiate with terrorists is often driven by the perception that the

Religiously motivated suicide bombers, like the perpetrators of the March 2016 Brussels airport attack, exemplify terrorists whose aims may not be subject to compromise.

goals of terrorist organizations are nonnegotiable. The connection between religion and terrorism furthers this perception, since goods that are connected to religious identities may be particularly hard to split.

Hamas and other Palestinian terrorist groups do not want a Jewish state on the land between the Jordan Valley and the Mediterranean Sea; if given the choice, they would institute an Islamic regime in what is now Israel. Most Israelis want their state to be a Jewish state, though one that permits other religions to be practiced openly. In principle, there are middle positions between a Jewish state and an Islamic state on this land. One could imagine a state with no officially sanctioned religion in which all faiths could be freely practiced or a state in which both religions were officially sanctioned. But while such compromises exist both in principle and in practice, there are those on both sides who see the state's religious identity as an all-or-nothing issue.

The connection between religion and terrorism is real but also should not be overstated. It is not the case that most terrorism is religiously motivated. Figure 6.5 breaks down international terrorist groups by the type of goal they were pursuing and shows the number of attacks and casualties (killed and wounded) caused by each type of group in the period 1968–2005. According to these figures, only 13 percent of terrorist attacks in this period were committed by religious terrorists. However, attacks by religious groups were particularly lethal, accounting for 42 percent

FIGURE 6.5 *The Number of Attacks and Fatalities by Group Goal, 1968–2005*

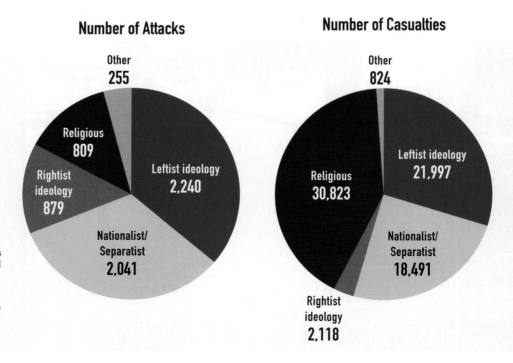

Figure source: James A. Piazza, "Is Islamist Terrorism More Dangerous? An Empirical Study of Group Ideology, Organization, and Goal Structure," *Terrorism and Political Violence* 21 (2009): 63. Leftist ideology includes groups whose goals were characterized as anarchist, antiglobalization, communist, socialist, and environmental. Rightist ideology includes groups whose goals were characterized as racist, right-wing conservative, and reactionary.

of all casualties. Religion also plays a pronounced role in suicide terrorism, as the belief that a reward is waiting in the afterlife seems important in motivating this kind of behavior. Though not all groups that use suicide terrorism draw on explicitly religious ideologies, most do, and the vast majority of suicide attacks involve perpetrators and targets from different religions.[59] If the individuals engaged in terrorism believe that they are pursuing ideals that cannot be compromised, then there may be little scope for bargaining.

How Can Terrorists Hope to Win? Strategies of Violence

We have already seen that terrorist organizations are generally weak relative to their adversaries, particularly those engaged in transnational terrorism against militarily powerful states. Given that they cannot defeat the target in any conventional sense, how can they hope to succeed? What purpose does killing people serve? (For more on whether terrorism is an effective strategy, see "How Do We Know?" on p. 282.)

When a group turns to terrorism, there are four principal strategies by which it may use violence to further its interests: coercion, provocation, spoiling, and outbidding.[60] These strategies are not mutually exclusive; any particular attack can involve elements of more than one. The key to understanding them is to recognize that terrorists act in front of at least two audiences: (1) the government and population of the target state and (2) the "home" population—that is, the people on whose behalf they claim to act. The different strategies of terrorism seek to impress these audiences in order to advance the organization's twin interests in wresting concession from the target and winning supporters among the home population. In particular, coercion and spoiling are intended to influence the beliefs of the target, while provocation and outbidding are intended to influence the beliefs of the home population.

Coercion Terrorists can attack or threaten to attack in order to coerce a target into making concessions. **Coercion** induces policy change by imposing costs—usually civilian deaths and injuries—on the target. More specifically, coercion works through the threat of future costs. The purpose of a terrorist attack is not simply to kill people or destroy buildings; rather, it is to create fear among the target population that there will be future attacks unless the terrorists' demands are met. By threatening to inflict harm on the target, terrorists aim to intimidate potential victims, thereby motivating individuals to press their own government to change its policy.

coercion

A strategy of imposing or threatening to impose costs on other actors in order to induce a change in their behavior.

---

59. Eli Berman and David D. Laitin, "Religion, Terrorism, and Public Goods: Testing the Club Model," *Journal of Public Economics* 92 (2008): 1942–67. See also Robert A. Pape, *Dying to Win: The Strategic Logic of Suicide Terrorism* (New York: Random House, 2005).

60. Andrew H. Kydd and Barbara F. Walter, "The Strategies of Terrorism," *International Security* 31, no. 1 (Summer 2006): 49–80. We combine their strategies of attrition and intimidation into a single strategy of coercion.

Since it is the fear of future attacks that may induce policy change, it follows that actual attacks occur primarily to make the threat of future violence credible. This is necessary, in turn, because the target is uncertain about the terrorists' capabilities or resolve and, as we saw above, it is difficult for terrorist organizations to signal their intentions peacefully. Thus, attacks are a form of costly signaling intended to make credible the terrorists' threats of future violence unless their demands are met. This type of signaling can entail small demonstration attacks such as bomb scares, which are designed not to kill people or destroy property, but rather to call attention to the network and signal that it has the ability to kill and destroy in the future, if its demands are not met.

In a form of pure signaling, the Basque separatist group ETA often gave warnings of its attacks so that people would not be killed. More spectacularly, Al Qaeda's attacks on 9/11 were an attempt to coerce the United States into withdrawing its troops from the Arabian Peninsula and ending its support for the Saudi regime. The simultaneous hijacking of four airliners and the destruction of the twin towers and severe damage to the Pentagon were intended to demonstrate an ability to carry out great violence at the core of America's centers of power.

Provocation Terrorists may attack in order to provoke the target government into a disproportionate response that alienates moderates in the terrorists' home society or in other sympathetic audiences. Particularly dramatic and heinous attacks often leave the target government with little political choice but to respond with a vigorous counterstrike. After 9/11, there was significant domestic support—even pressure—for the administration of President George W. Bush to strike back forcefully against Al Qaeda. The Israeli government has long maintained a policy of at least "an eye for an eye," responding aggressively to all terrorist attacks on its soil or citizens.

When terrorists are hiding within their home population, any counterstrike is likely to inflict collateral damage—that is, deaths and injuries to innocent bystanders. If the target government is already feared by the terrorists' home population, such a vigorous counterstrike can further radicalize that population and increase its support for the terrorists. Other audiences outside the terrorists' home society may also be alienated and possibly threatened by what are regarded as overly aggressive responses by the target. Thus, this strategy helps address the organization's collective action problem by creating a larger pool of extremists or sympathetic moderates.

Key to any strategy of **provocation** is the uncertainty of the terrorists' home population about the target's interests.[61] For example, many people in the Middle East fear that the United States is an imperialist state aligned with Israel to impose its will on their countries, with little regard for Muslim lives. This is precisely the message that groups like Al Qaeda and the Islamic State use to mobilize people to

provocation
A strategy of terrorist attacks intended to provoke the target government into making a disproportionate response that alienates moderates in the terrorists' home society or in other sympathetic audiences.

---

61. On provocation strategies, see Ethan Bueno de Mesquita and Eric S. Dickson, "The Propaganda of the Deed: Terrorism, Counterterrorism, and Mobilization," *American Journal of Political Science* 51 (2007): 364–81.

their cause. The group hopes that a disproportionate U.S. response that kills inno-cent civilians will essentially confirm this narrative.

After 9/11, the invasion of Afghanistan and the overthrow of the Taliban regime by the United States received generally broad support because the war could be understood as a response to the attacks; however, the subsequent invasion of Iraq, which had no role in the 9/11 attacks, was widely seen internationally as unjustified. In the words of a U.S. national intelligence estimate released in 2006, Iraq became a "'cause célèbre' for jihadists, breeding a deep resentment of U.S. involvement in the Muslim world and cultivating supporters for the global jihadist movement."[62] (To see how this contributed to the emergence of the Islamic State, see "What Shaped Our World?" on p. 256.) The war also led to increased anti-American sen-timent around the world, complicating the United States' relationships with other countries.

Disproportionate responses may lead the terrorists' home population to believe that it has more to fear from the target than from the extremists. Through multiple applications of this strategy, terrorist organizations hope to expand their base of support within their home populations and increase their political power over time.

Spoiling Terrorists may also attack to spoil, or sabotage, a prospective peace between the target and the moderate leadership from their home society.[63] Target states are often uncertain whether an opponent, even if led by moderates, wants to settle the conflict and can control its extremists. Targets want to negotiate with trustworthy and capable moderates who want to and can make peace; they do not want to negotiate with untrustworthy or incapable moderates who cannot or will not prevent further terrorist attacks. Unable to judge the sincerity or capabil-ity of the opponent's leadership, target governments watch for terrorist attacks to occur and break off negotiations when they do. By attacking, the terrorists can thus scuttle an agreement they oppose and hold out for terms they hope will be more favorable.

The purpose of the violence in **spoiling** is not to apply pressure on the target per se, but to play on doubts in the target state about whether the opponent can be trusted to implement a peace agreement and abide by it in the future. In this case the target is uncertain about the home population's interests and capabili-ties and whether it will be able to honor and enforce an agreement. When terror-ists attack the target, the latter learns that the terrorists' home government either does not want to or cannot control its extremists, and thus it is more likely to reject agreements as not credible. Attacks motivated by this logic are most likely to occur during or shortly after peace negotiations.

spoiling
A strategy of terrorist attacks intended to sabotage a prospective peace between the target and moderate leadership from the terrorists' home society.

---

62. Office of the Director of National Intelligence, "Trends in Global Terrorism: Implications for the United States," National Intelligence Estimate, April 2006, www.dni.gov/files/documents/Special%20 Report_Global%20Terrorism%20NIE%20Key%20Judgments.pdf.

63. Andrew H. Kydd and Barbara F. Walter, "Sabotaging the Peace: The Politics of Extremist Violence," *International Organization* 56 (2002): 263–96.

Does Terrorism Work?

Terrorism is effective at killing and maiming people and at creating fear within targeted populations. However, the purpose of terrorism is not simply to kill and terrorize, but to achieve some political or social objective. Is terrorism an effective strategy for advancing a group's interests?

A number of scholars have explored this question, and the results have been contradictory[a]. Among the many challenges in answering this question is properly specifying the alternative—that is, is terrorism effective compared to what? Even if terrorist groups rarely get their way, terrorism may be more effective for achieving some goals than is doing nothing or mobilizing peacefully or pursuing other strategies. There is also a concern that groups use terrorism because they are too small and weak to take on the target with more conventional means. If so, then it is the group's weakness, not the nature of its strategy, that would explain its failure.

In a recent study, Virginia Page Fortna sought to tackle these problems by taking advantage of the fact that some rebel groups engaged in civil wars use terrorism and others do not.[b] Civil wars provide a sample of groups that had a severe conflict of interest with the government and engaged in violent rebellion, but did so using different strategies. This observation permits a relatively clean comparison of the success rates of groups that relied on terrorism and those that did not. Fortna collected data on 104 rebel groups in the period 1989–2004. Of these, she estimated that 24 (about a quarter) routinely engaged in the deliberate and indiscriminate killing of civilians. Moreover, she found that there was no evidence within this population that relatively weaker groups used terrorism while relatively stronger ones did not.

Each conflict had one of five possible outcomes: (1) the rebels were defeated, (2) the rebellion fizzled out because of low activity, (3) the war was still ongoing at the time of the study, (4) the war ended with a peace agreement, (5) the rebels defeated the government. Figure A shows the distribution of outcomes for rebel groups that did and did not use terrorism. The evidence suggests that rebel groups that used terrorism were significantly *less* successful than those that did not. In particular, terrorist groups were more likely to be defeated by the government, had less chance of getting a peace agreement, and never won an outright victory.

Terrorism does seem to help with surviving: civil wars that involve terrorism are more likely to continue or fester, and they last significantly longer than those that do not. This suggests that terrorism, by avoiding the state's military capacity, can be an effective method for prolonging a struggle. In doing so, terrorism may also be good for preventing outcomes that a group dislikes, rather than compelling outcomes that it wants.

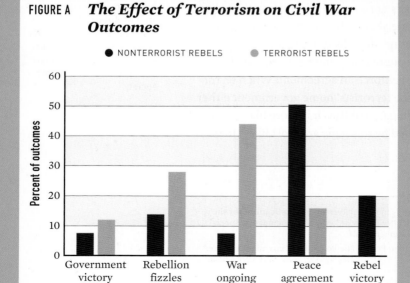

FIGURE A *The Effect of Terrorism on Civil War Outcomes*

● NONTERRORIST REBELS ● TERRORIST REBELS

Percent of outcomes

- Government victory
- Rebellion fizzles
- War ongoing
- Peace agreement
- Rebel victory

a. See, for example, Robert A. Pape, *Dying to Win* (New York: Random House, 2005); Andrew H. Kydd and Barbara F. Walter, "The Strategies of Terrorism," *International Security* 31, no. 1 (Summer 2006): 49–80; Jakana Thomas, "Rewarding Bad Behavior: How Governments Respond to Terrorism in Civil War," *American Journal of Political Science* 58 (October 2014): 804–18; Max Abrahms, "Why Terrorism Does Not Work," *International Security* 31, no. 2 (Fall 2006): 42–78; and Seth G. Jones and Martin C. Libicki, *How Terrorist Groups End* (Santa Monica, CA: Rand, 2008).

b. Virginia Page Fortna, "Do Terrorists Win? Rebels' Use of Terrorism and Civil War Outcomes," *International Organization* 69 (2015): 519–56.

Outbidding Finally, terrorist organizations may use violence to outbid potential rivals for support among their home population. In poker, a player may raise the bet to convince others that she is holding a stronger hand. Likewise, when two or more terrorist networks or factions compete for support within their home populations, they may attack a target in an effort to outbid the other and demonstrate their capability for leadership and commitment to the cause for which they are fighting. **Outbidding** arises when the home population is uncertain about which of several organizations is best able to represent and further its interests. In these cases, an organization may mount dramatic attacks not simply to coerce the target, but also to impress the audience at home.

Rivalries among different factions of the Palestinian movement have led to this kind of dynamic. Since the early 1990s, a number of groups—most prominently Fatah and Hamas—have competed for the support of the Palestinian people. Though originally a terrorist group, Fatah renounced violence and is no longer considered a terrorist organization; it has argued instead for a process of negotiation leading to the creation of a Palestinian state. Hamas has continued to engage in terrorist attacks, as have Islamic Jihad and other militant factions, some of which spun off from Fatah. For these groups, attacks against Israel are intended to demonstrate their credentials for leadership among Palestinians who are uncertain about which group best serves their interests.

These rivalries have led to cycles of escalation wherein attacks by one group require attacks by others so as not to be outdone; in some cases, multiple groups would claim credit for the same attack.[64] Similarly, when Peru returned to democratic rule in 1980, the Shining Path group turned to violence to distinguish itself from rival groups that chose instead to participate in the electoral process.

The actors we call *target*, *terrorist*, and *home population* are convenient abstractions but obvious simplifications. Within any particular instance, these actors may need to be disaggregated further to reveal internal divisions. Likewise, the four strategies of terror are not exclusive. Terrorist networks can attack simultaneously to coerce a target into making concessions, provoke the target into a disproportionate response that radicalizes their home population, undermine prospective peace agreements, and build support for their factions over others within their home populations. In any long-term struggle (such as that between Israel and the Palestinians or between the Tamil Tigers and the government of Sri Lanka), all four strategies are likely to be employed at some point. We isolate the strategies here merely to highlight their different logics. Understanding the multiple strategies of terrorism is also important in designing effective counterterrorist responses.

Can Terrorism Be Prevented?

Like the war on drugs, the war on poverty, or the war on crime, the "global war on terror" is likely to be a struggle without any clear end. As long as actors have different interests, and as long as individuals retain the ingenuity and ruthlessness that

outbidding

A strategy of terrorist attacks designed to demonstrate superior capability and commitment relative to other groups devoted to the same cause.

---

64. Mia M. Bloom, "Palestinian Suicide Bombing: Public Support, Market Share, and Outbidding," *Political Science Quarterly* 199 (2004): 61–88.

enabled 19 terrorists to use simple box cutters to transform airplanes into maneuverable kerosene-filled bombs, terrorism will remain a possibility. Extremism, combined with problems of incomplete information and credible commitment, will continue to lead terrorist organizations to launch attacks simply to demonstrate that they can.

As with civil wars, economic development and political liberalization might, in the long run, diffuse some of the grievances that fuel or enable terrorist violence, but there is actually little evidence that poverty, on its own, breeds extremism or drives people to join terrorist organizations.[65] Since ideological, religious, and nationalist extremists can arise in a variety of political and economic contexts, promoting development, while no doubt desirable, is also unlikely to be a magic bullet. Nonetheless, states can adopt certain counterterrorist strategies to make future attacks less likely and, perhaps, less destructive when they do occur. The same strategies also allow states to make smaller concessions to terrorists even when bargaining works and violence is avoided.

Can Terrorists Be Deterred? As discussed in Chapter 3, deterrence is a strategy to preserve the status quo by threatening challengers with unacceptable costs. Terrorism can, in principle, be deterred by potential targets threatening massive retaliation against terrorist organizations, should attacks occur. Although deterrence worked to avoid nuclear war between the superpowers during the Cold War, and although it may operate on a daily basis between states that might otherwise challenge each other if they thought the other would not fight back, many analysts are skeptical that, in practice, deterrence can work against terrorist networks.

Unlike states, terrorists do not possess a clearly identifiable location against which targets can respond. If a terrorist organization believes it can escape retaliation by hiding in unknown locations, it is less likely to be deterred from attacking. This consideration is real. However, investigative work can often find the trail leading back to a terrorist organization. In the event that terrorists turn to weapons of mass destruction, such as nuclear, chemical, biological, or radiological weapons, the materials may be traceable, and large nuclear processing facilities are hard to hide. Given today's advanced technological devices, it is quite likely that targets could, with time, identify who manufactured the weapons and where they originated. Thus, it is not the absence of a location against which to retaliate that undermines deterrence as much as two, more subtle, problems.

First, when terrorists use a strategy of provocation, retaliation by the target may simply play into their hands. Retaliating against a terrorist stronghold will likely kill a significant number of members of the home society, confirming for previously undecided moderates that the target really is a threat to their own security. Unless the retaliating target succeeds in eradicating the terrorist network, a cycle

---

65. See, for example, Alan B. Krueger and Jitka Male–cková, "Education, Poverty and Terrorism: Is There a Causal Connection?" *Journal of Economic Perspectives* 17 (Fall 2003): 119–44; and James A. Piazza, "Do Democracy and Free Markets Protect Us from Terrorism?" *International Politics* 45 (2008): 72–91.

of attacks and counterattacks may, over time, serve only to increase political support for the terrorists.

Second, and closely related, the threat of retaliation by the potential target may not be credible. Since terrorists hide in larger populations and massive retaliation would likely kill many individuals who are unrelated to the terrorist network, a target state may be unwilling to attack. If a terrorist set off a nuclear explosion in New York, would the United States be willing to annihilate hundreds of thousands of likely innocent people to destroy a terrorist cell operating in, say, Somalia? Or in a country allied with the United States in the global war on terror, such as Pakistan? Or perhaps even in another advanced democratic country, like Germany (where much of the planning for the 9/11 attacks took place)?

Nuclear deterrence in the Cold War, and especially extended deterrence in which the United States promised to launch a retaliatory attack against the civilian population if the Soviet Union invaded West Berlin or Paris, always rested on the possibility that the threat would be carried out. Although the United States might not have started another world war in response to a limited Soviet incursion in Europe, the risk that it might do so was sufficient to deter Russia. The risk that the United States or any other target would retaliate massively against terrorist attacks is not as likely or as clear. Knowing this, terrorists are less likely to be deterred than states.

Countries can attempt to stop terrorists before they strike—a strategy known as preemption. The United States has used remotely piloted drones to kill suspected terrorists in Pakistan, among other countries. This practice has bred resentment because of collateral damage from missile strikes.

Preemption If the threat of retaliation after an attack cannot deter terrorists, an alternative strategy is for states to take the initiative and attempt to disrupt or destroy terrorists and their networks before they attack. This strategy of preemption was the most distinctive response of the Bush administration to the attacks of 9/11. In his *National Security Strategy for the United States of America* outlined in September 2002, President Bush placed emphasis, for the first time, on preempting attacks from terrorists and states that may possess weapons of mass destruction.

The invasion of Afghanistan was not just in retaliation for the attacks, but was also intended to prevent future attacks. The goals of the war included capturing or killing the organization's leadership and foot soldiers and dismantling the infrastructure that had been used to plot and train for attacks. Although Afghanistan was the main theater of "Operation Enduring Freedom," this operation spanned the globe, leading to the killing and detention of suspected terrorists. The United States has also made extensive use of drones—remote-controlled aircraft armed with missiles—to kill suspected terrorists in a variety of countries, including Pakistan, Yemen, and Somalia. And, of course, the war in Iraq was justified by President Bush, in part, as a preemptive war on terror.

Preemption can also take nonmilitary forms. Surveillance—monitoring phone calls, e-mail, and other communications and tracking international financial transactions—can be used to identify terrorist networks and future attacks. Intelligence agencies may also detain and interrogate terrorism suspects in order to unravel plots or to identify other members of an organization. A report released by the U.S. Senate in 2014 detailed an extensive program of detention that was enacted after 9/11, as well as the use of interrogation techniques that are commonly understood to constitute torture.[66] In resorting to such methods, the United States is not alone. The use of torture, as well as other violations of civil rights, such as imprisonment without due process and extrajudicial killings, is not uncommon among states that are targeted by terrorism.[67]

Preemption is costly in many ways. The wars in Afghanistan and Iraq came at very high prices. By the end of 2016, the United States had spent over $3 trillion for costs related to those wars, which claimed the lives of over 7,000 Americans, more than 1,500 from allied countries, and hundreds of thousands in both Afghanistan and Iraq.[68]

Even less forceful measures entail costs. Surveillance is expensive relative to the number of attacks prevented. Like all police patrols, surveillance must be continuous—not just when attacks are under way—and comprehensive; otherwise, intelligence efforts are likely to be deployed elsewhere when actual attacks are being planned. Monitoring possible terrorist activities is akin to looking for the proverbial needle in the haystack, but in this case a potential terrorist attack is a well-hidden needle that we are not even sure exists. Moreover, surveillance is likely to infringe on the civil liberties of innocent civilians.

Preemption can also impose political costs by playing into the provocation strategy used by terrorists. Preemptive actions may be perceived by foreign populations as disproportionate responses that pose them a threat. U.S. drone attacks in Pakistan, Yemen, Somalia, and Libya have killed hundreds of noncombatants, breeding resentment that can feed terrorist recruitment.[69] There is also evidence that the systematic use of torture, extrajudicial killings, and imprisonment without due process can increase, rather than decrease, the number of attacks a country experiences.[70] Thus, in considering preemptive

---

66. Senate Select Committee on Intelligence, *The Senate Intelligence Committee Report on Torture* (New York: Melville House, 2014).

67. James A. Piazza and James Igoe Walsh, "Transnational Terror and Human Rights," *International Studies Quarterly* 53 (2009): 125–48. The authors find that terrorist attacks are associated with increased use of "disappearances" and extrajudicial killings, but not necessarily torture. They note, however, that the challenge of detecting and confirming torture complicates any analysis of this relationship.

68. Neta C. Crawford, "U.S. Budgetary Costs of Wars through 2016," Watson Institute for International and Public Affairs, Boston University, September 2016, http://watson.brown.edu/costsofwar/files/cow/imce/papers/2016/Costs%20of%20War%20through%202016%20FINAL%20final%20v2.pdf.

69. The actual number of civilian deaths from drone attacks is subject to controversy, and government-issued statistics have been challenged by nongovernment and media organizations; see, for example, Jack Serle, "Obama Drone Casualty Numbers a Fraction of Those Recorded by the Bureau," *Bureau of Investigative Journalism*, July 1, 2016, www.thebureauinvestigates.com/stories/2016-07-01/obama-drone-casualty-numbers-a-fraction-of-those-recorded-by-the-bureau.

70. James A. Piazza and James Igoe Walsh, "Physical Integrity Rights and Terrorism," *PS: Political Science and Politics* 43 (July 2010): 411–14.

Defensive measures against terrorists in Europe include enhanced security measures at many airports, including Istanbul's Ataturk airport, the site of a terrorist attack in June 2016. While these measures are designed to prevent future attacks, they are expensive and inconvenient for everyone, not just the terrorists.

action, targets must balance the probability that they will make themselves safer in the short term against the risk that they will increase terrorist recruitment in the long run.

Defensive Measures As an alternative to offensive or retaliatory military operations, states can and do employ defensive measures to guard against attacks. After a rash of airplane hijackings in the 1970s, airports around the world first installed metal detectors, leading to a dramatic drop in this kind of attack.[71] Even more elaborate security procedures were put in place after 9/11. In addition to enhanced screening at airports, American embassies abroad have been fortified; national monuments are protected by barrier defenses and, sometimes, armed guards; border security forces and inspection regimes have been expanded. Numerous sites remain vulnerable, including the nation's shipping ports, but across the country, homeland security efforts have been significantly increased. Similarly, after a campaign of suicide bombings, Israel constructed a wall separating it from Palestinian-controlled areas of the West Bank, with dramatic results in reducing the number of attacks.

Defensive measures work to reduce terrorism by raising the costs to groups of carrying out attacks. As it becomes more expensive to strike a target, whether in terms of resources deployed or time and effort consumed to evade security procedures, terrorism becomes less likely overall. Defensive measures can also have the advantage that they do not inflict collateral damage on the terrorists' home

---

71. See, for example, Walter Enders and Todd Sandler, "The Effectiveness of Antiterrorism Policies: A Vector-Autoregression-Intervention Analysis," *American Political Science Review* 87 (1993): 829–44.

population, though the Israeli security barrier in the West Bank has caused a great deal of hardship and resentment among Palestinians.

Defensive measures are not cheap. The United States has spent over half a trillion dollars on homeland security since 2001.[72] Indirectly, such measures may impose even greater costs on society. Passengers must now arrive at airports earlier to clear security before boarding their planes, making air travel less efficient and more unpleasant than before. Trucks are subject to longer delays at the nation's borders. Measured by hours of productivity lost, these indirect costs may well dwarf the direct costs. That said, when measured relative to the costs of the Iraq and Afghanistan wars, these costs may seem like a bargain.

Still, defensive measures will never be totally effective.[73] Target selection by terrorists is based on the difficulty of penetrating defenses and the likely success of carrying out their attacks. When the United States stepped up its internal security measures after 9/11, Al Qaeda shifted its attacks to embassies abroad and American troops in Iraq. The Islamic State encourages supporters to drive cars and trucks into crowds precisely because it is impossible to secure every market or busy street from such an attack. Given the many possible sites, it is prohibitively expensive to protect them all equally. And protecting some may only divert attacks to the next, less well defended target.

Criminalization States can criminalize terrorism and pursue specific individuals and groups for the attacks they have planned or carried out. Along with airport security measures, this was the primary response to the airplane hijackings that occurred in the late 1960s and early 1970s. By 1973, a series of international conventions on skyjackings had been put into place through which states agreed not to harbor hijackers and to turn them over to appropriate authorities. Individual terrorists and groups were pursued and brought to justice in criminal proceedings. Combined with the use of metal detectors at airports, this strategy led to a sharp decline in the number of airplane hijackings.

Criminalization is mostly reactive, seeking to arrest terrorists for attacks after they have been committed. By bringing individuals and groups to justice, states hope not only to disrupt terrorist groups, but to deter others from carrying out attacks as well. For transnational terrorism, this strategy hinges on effective international cooperation. Nearly all countries would agree that airplane hijackings are odious and against their interests. Even the United States and Cuba, which cooperate in few other areas, have been able to work together effectively in capturing and prosecuting hijackers; the two nations signed a bilateral pact in 1973 in which they agreed to return immediately any planes, passengers, crew members, and hijackers to the country of origin. The growth of transnational networks may require the development of new international institutions to combat terrorism in the future.

---

72. Crawford, "U.S. Budgetary Costs of Wars through 2016."

73. On the limits of defensive measures, see Robert Powell, "Defending against Terrorist Attacks with Limited Resources," *American Political Science Review* 101, no. 3 (2007): 527–41.

Yet countries do not always share such clearly compatible interests. States that sympathize with the goals pursued by terrorists and grant them safe haven, as Afghanistan did for the Taliban, or states that are too weak internally to prevent terrorist groups from operating from within their territory, like Somalia, can effectively undermine the ability of other countries to capture indicted terrorists. Even Pakistan, a country that is nominally allied with the United States in the war on terror, has chafed at U.S. efforts to track down Al Qaeda leaders there. The killing of bin Laden on Pakistani soil in 2011 added to tensions in the U.S.-Pakistan relationship.

The same forces of globalization that allow terrorists to attack anywhere around the world also permit terrorists to hide anywhere. To limit terrorism, states need to share intelligence and coordinate their counterattacks. While there has been progress in expanding efforts to track and prosecute terrorists, there are still few effective international institutions to secure compliance with antiterrorist efforts.

Negotiation and Compromise

Finally, states can attempt to negotiate and compromise on their differences with terrorist groups.[74] As explained earlier, bargaining failures are likely to be inevitable, and thus negotiations will not eliminate the problem of terrorism. Most states today maintain a policy of not negotiating with terrorists, for fear of recognizing the legitimacy of their demands and tactics—and for fear of being charged with appeasement by domestic critics. Another reason countries are reluctant to negotiate with terrorists is that they do not want to spur other groups into making greater demands. Thus, few explicit negotiations occur between states and terrorists.

Nonetheless, states have at times made concessions sought by terrorist groups. In the wake of terrorist campaigns, American and French military forces withdrew from Lebanon in 1983, and Israel withdrew from occupied portions of southern Lebanon in 2000 and from the Palestinian-controlled Gaza Strip in 2005.

In other cases, terrorist violence has been stemmed through a peace agreement. In the so-called Good Friday Agreement, signed in 1998, Britain made concessions favored by the IRA, granting Northern Ireland a great deal more autonomy and ensuring an influential role for republicans (that is, those seeking a united Ireland) in the region's governance. While some splinter groups continue to threaten violence to spoil the accords, the number of terrorist attacks by Irish nationalist groups dropped dramatically after the accords.

More recently, a 2016 peace deal between the Colombian government and the Revolutionary Armed Forces of Colombia (FARC) ended more than five decades of conflict. A rebel group that had made systematic use of terrorist attacks, FARC disarmed in 2017 under UN supervision and re-formed as a nonviolent political party. Although it can be painful reconciling with people who have committed atrocities against innocent civilians (the first version of the Colombian peace deal was

---

74. On bargaining, see Harvey E. Lapan and Todd Sandler, "To Bargain or Not to Bargain: That Is the Question," *American Economic Review* 78, no. 2 (1988): 16–21.

rejected by voters who thought it too lenient on FARC), allowing militant groups to enter the political process and compete for power through existing institutions can be an effective route to ending the violence.[75]

Conclusion: A Challenge to States?

Violence pursued by rebel groups and terrorist organizations represents a challenge to states in several respects. For the states that are targeted by these actors, insurgency and terrorism represent a threat to their people and to their ability to govern. Civil wars, in particular, exact a very high toll on the countries that suffer them—in terms of lives lost, resources spent and destroyed, and even death and disease, which linger long after the fighting stops.[76] Terrorism kills many fewer people but, by design, can lead whole nations to live in fear. Though in some cases we might share or sympathize with the interests that lead these groups to violence, the enormous costs involved are always tragic.

Rebellion and terrorism also pose a challenge to states in a more fundamental sense. Many models of international relations start with the assumption that states are the main actors in world politics. This assumption is sometimes made only to simplify the analysis, as we did in Chapter 3 when we used states as actors—a simplification that allowed us to focus on bargaining dynamics. In other theoretical approaches, however, particularly those derived from the realist school, the state-centric view represents a substantive claim about which actors really matter and, by implication, which do not. The pride of place given to states usually rests on two assertions: (1) interactions in international politics are dominated by the threat and use of force, and (2) states, particularly large states, are the main actors capable of mobilizing and wielding military power. In this view, then, the world stage is dominated by the clash of great powers.

The importance of rebellion and terrorism call this view into question. As we have seen, nonstate actors, while lacking the size and organizational advantages of states, have developed strategies of violence that can be quite effective. Insurgency and terrorism, the main weapons of asymmetrical warfare, seek to neutralize a state's power in several ways: by evading the target state's conventional military power; by exploiting vulnerabilities, such as civilians and other "soft" targets; and, at times, by using the state's power against it, by provoking counterattacks that may swell the ranks of the group's supporters. We have also seen that states often wield nonstate actors as a weapon against one another. When direct confrontation with another state is likely to be too costly (as during the Cold War) or ineffective (as when a weak state confronts a stronger one), sponsoring a rebel group or terrorist

---

75. See, for example, Aila M. Matanock, *Electing Peace: From Civil Conflict to Political Participation* (Cambridge: Cambridge University Press, 2017).

76. On this last point, see Hazem Adam Ghobarah, Paul Huth, and Bruce Russett, "Civil Wars Kill and Maim People—Long after the Shooting Stops," *American Political Science Review* 97 (2003): 189–202.

organization may be an effective alternative. Thus, even the bargaining interaction between states can be fundamentally influenced by the presence of nonstate actors willing to use violence.

In short, rebel groups and terrorist organizations violate the view that states monopolize the means of coercion in international politics. What strong states have is an institutional structure capable of overcoming the collective action problem inherent in wielding coercive power. This is no small matter, since many dissatisfied groups and extremist individuals will never mobilize the people, arms, and money necessary to make an impact. But those that have found a way to do so have managed to kill large numbers of people, consume vast resources, overthrow governments, and, at times, dominate the foreign policy agenda of even the most powerful states.

Study Tool Kit

Interests, Interactions, and Institutions in Context

- Civil conflict can arise when individuals have interests that conflict with those of the central government, leading to demands over territory, policy, or government composition. Whether a rebel group can overcome the collective action problem depends on its own resources, the capacity of the government, and the willingness of foreign states to lend support.

- Bargaining between a government and a rebel group can lead to war as a result of information problems, commitment problems, and issue indivisibilities. Particularly severe commitment problems often make civil wars hard to resolve without the outright victory of one side or the other.

- Domestic institutions that provide peaceful mechanisms for addressing groups' interests and international institutions that facilitate collective efforts to stabilize conflict-ridden countries both hold some promise for preventing civil conflicts from starting or reigniting.

- International terrorist organizations are composed of relatively small numbers of individuals with extreme preferences. Their weakness relative to their targets and relative to their goals drives their strategy of attacking civilians and their organization into loose networks that are hard to root out.

- Rebel groups and terrorists employ strategies of violence that are intended both to coerce their targets and to address their collective action problem by attracting supporters. For this reason, efforts to defeat these groups often require strategies that take account of their effects on noncombatants.

Key Terms

civil war, p. 239

terrorism, p. 239

asymmetrical warfare, p. 242

separatist, p. 246

irredentist, p. 246

proxy wars, p. 255

insurgency, p. 262

extremists, p. 271

coercion, p. 279

provocation, p. 280

spoiling, p. 281

outbidding, p. 283

For Further Reading

Bloom, Mia. *Dying to Kill: The Allure of Suicide Terror*. New York: Columbia University Press, 2005. A study of the origins of and motives behind suicide terrorism.

Enders, Walter, and Todd Sandler. *The Political Economy of Terrorism*. New York: Cambridge University Press, 2006. An excellent introduction to current research on terrorism.

Kilcullen, David. *The Accidental Guerrilla: Fighting Small Wars in the Midst of a Big One*. New York: Oxford University Press, 2009. An examination of counterterrorism and counterinsurgency doctrine as applied to the "war on terror."

Kydd, Andrew H., and Barbara F. Walter. "The Strategies of Terrorism." *International Security* 31, no. 1 (Summer 2006): 49–80. Develops the four strategies of terrorism explained in this text.

Mason, T. David, and Sara McLaughlin Mitchell, eds. *What Do We Know about Civil Wars?* Lanham, MD: Rowman & Littlefield, 2016. A collection of essays by leading scholars summarizing current scholarly understanding of the causes and outcome of civil wars.

Regan, Patrick M. *Sixteen Million One: Understanding Civil War*. Boulder, CO: Paradigm, 2009. An accessible blending of academic research on civil wars with a vivid account of the lives and motives of those who fight in them.

Salehyan, Idean. *Rebels without Borders: Transnational Insurgencies in World Politics*. Ithaca, NY: Cornell University Press, 2009. Examines how civil wars often spill over into neighboring countries owing to weak states, international rivalries, and refugee flows.

Shapiro, Jacob N. *The Terrorist's Dilemma: Managing Violent Covert Organizations*. Princeton, NJ: Princeton University Press, 2013. Examines how terrorist organizations try to control their members while balancing the needs for secrecy and control.

7

International Trade

THE PUZZLE *Virtually all economic analysis concludes that trade is economically beneficial. Why, then, does every country restrict trade in some way? Why have policies toward trade varied so much from country to country and over time?*

Above: Economies as a whole benefit from freer trade, but trade policies often create winners and losers. The Trans-Pacific Partnership (TPP), a sweeping trade agreement among 11 nations that border the Pacific Ocean, was met with protests in many of the original signatories, including Malaysia. Some critics of the TPP claim that its policies would enrich multinational corporations at the expense of workers.

The American steel industry employs about 80,000 people. Yet this relatively small industry has received massive assistance from the U.S. government, primarily in the form of protection from foreign competition. This trade protection raises the cost of steel in the United States and thus raises the cost that American consumers pay for goods made with steel. By one estimate, since 1970, protection and other aid to the U.S. steel industry have cost American consumers and taxpayers between $145 billion and $230 billion—a staggering amount for an industry with just 80,000 employees.[1]

The steel industry is hardly alone in being protected from imports, to the benefit of producers and the detriment of consumers. Footwear, dairy products, motorcycles, clothing, cotton, automobiles, and sugar are among the many other goods whose import has been restricted by the U.S. government. One group of scholars estimated that if all barriers to international trade were removed, the U.S. economy would gain some $540 billion by 2025, amounting to over $4,000 for each U.S. household per year.[2] And the United States is hardly alone in

erecting obstacles to international commerce; to varying degrees, every country has such trade barriers.

People have traded across borders for as long as borders have existed. In the modern world, international trade has been one of the two most important economic relationships among countries (the other is international investment, which we will examine in Chapter 8). Dramatic reductions in trade barriers and dramatic increases in international trade itself have been a major component of the evolution of the contemporary world economy since World War II. Yet governments have always attempted to control trade across their borders. In fact, trade policy—the restriction of imports and the promotion of exports—has long been one of the most important economic policies, foreign or domestic, that governments undertake. Those who sell or buy from abroad have a great deal at stake in international trade; so too do those who face competition from foreigners, which can threaten their jobs or businesses. Today's very high levels of international trade, the continued attempts of governments to control trade, and ongoing debates over the costs and benefits of international trade serve as the basis for this chapter's discussion.

We first ask why international trade takes the form it does. Most poor countries export almost exclusively farm products and raw materials, and they import manufactured goods. Most rich countries, in contrast, import much of their food and raw materials and export mainly manufactured goods. Those poor countries that do export industrial products typically sell such simple goods as clothing, footwear, and furniture; rich countries' manufactured exports include primarily sophisticated goods, such as commercial aircraft and elaborate machinery. How can we explain these patterns of international trade?

Our exploration of this question raises the additional question of why international trade is so commonly restricted. Although many of us take for granted that protecting national products is good, why should a government purposely raise the prices that domestic consumers pay?

Another question arises from the fact that barriers to international trade vary a great deal. Some countries restrict trade very little, while others come close to prohibiting it. Sometimes governments cooperate closely to maintain and expand their trade relations; at other times, bargaining among governments over trade policy is conflictual and even hostile. In addition, trade barriers have changed dramatically over time: both globally and in individual countries, trade has gone from generally unhindered to tightly regulated over relatively short periods. International trade has been quite free (that is, unrestricted) since the 1990s, but trade has become increasingly controversial over the past decade. Finally, government trade policies themselves often differ among industries, with some goods being strongly protected and others not at all.

1. William H. Barringer and Kenneth J. Pierce, *Paying the Price for Big Steel* (Washington, DC: American Institute for International Steel, 2000); and William H. Barringer, Kenneth J. Pierce, and Matthew P. McCullough, *Still Paying the Price* (Washington, DC: American Institute for International Steel, 2007).

2. Gary Clyde Hufbauer and Zhiyao (Lucy) Lu, *The Payoff to America from Globalization: A Fresh Look with a Focus on Costs to Workers*, Pieterson Institute for International Economics, Policy Brief 17-16, May 2017, https://piie.com/system/files/documents/pb17-16.pdf (accessed 07/20/17). It should be noted that these numbers have been questioned by other scholars, who think they are either too high or too low.

Thinking Analytically about International Trade

Because trade policy stands at the intersection of international and domestic politics, it involves powerful interests, important interactions, and influential institutions at both the domestic and international levels. Foreign trade has powerful effects on domestic producers, consumers, and others. The conflicts of interest between those in a country who want access to world markets and those who want protection from foreign competition help determine a nation's trade policy.

Domestically, trade interests interact in a battle over national policy, with supporters and opponents of freer trade squaring off according to their own economic interests. Interactions among contending domestic interests are mediated through the national political institutions of trade policy making: parties, legislatures, executives, and bureaucracies.

In addition, a given nation's trade policies affect other nations' trade, such that all national policies are made in interaction with those of other governments. Indeed, international trade interactions have often spilled into broader interstate relations—sometimes in a positive way, sometimes negatively.

A network of global and regional institutions has evolved to facilitate bargaining over trade policies. These institutions include treaties among countries, as well as regional and global trade agreements. The most prominent trade institutions have been the two international organizations that have governed world trade for 60 years: first the General Agreement on Tariffs and Trade (GATT); and since 1995, the World Trade Organization (WTO). At the regional level, trade-based institutions include the European Union (EU), which addresses many other issues in addition to those relating to trade, the North American Free Trade Agreement (NAFTA), and the Southern Common Market (Mercosur). All these factors help determine how open a country will be to trade and which domestic industries it will likely protect. When we consider global networks, these factors affect how open or closed international trade as a whole will be.

What's So Good about Trade?

Actors engage in foreign trade for the same reason that they trade with each other within countries: to realize the benefits of specialization. Only a household that produces everything it wants to consume, at a lower cost than available elsewhere, would have no reason to trade. But such a household is unlikely to exist. For example, a farm family could make its own tractor, but it is better off expending its energy in farming and using the proceeds to buy or rent a tractor. Modern societies are based on specialization—some people farm or manufacture, others transport or build—and on trade among people with different specialties. The division of labor permits diverse segments of society to focus on different economic activities in ways that benefit society as a whole. After all, if all households or all villages had to be self-sufficient, they would produce only a fraction of what they could if they specialized.

Specialization—the division of labor—was central to the argument made by Adam Smith in his 1776 founding text of classical economics, *The Wealth of Nations*. Smith and his fellow economic liberals argued, against the then dominant mercantilists, that self-sufficiency was foolish because a greater division of labor made societies wealthier. In a famous example, Smith pointed out that an individual pin maker working alone could make at best 20 pins a day. In the workshops of Smith's time, however, pin making was divided into about 18 steps, with each worker specializing in 1 or 2 steps. In this way, a pin factory with 10 workers produced 48,000 pins a day—making each individual some 240 times as productive as he would be if working alone.[3] Specialization increased productivity, and productivity fueled economic growth.[4]

The classical economists emphasized that specialization requires access to large markets; after all, a single village could hardly use 48,000 pins a day. They argued that restricting market size slows economic growth. A village cut off from the rest of the world and forced into self-sufficiency would have to produce everything it needed, but if that village was part of a larger national or global market, it could specialize in what it did best. Producers need ample markets in order to specialize; the division of labor depends on the size of the market.

The division of labor allows gains from international trade. In farming, temperate countries, such as the United States and Argentina, specialize in temperate crops, such as wheat, while tropical countries, such as Brazil and the Philippines, specialize in tropical crops, such as sugarcane. The nations around the Persian Gulf, with their rich oil deposits, base their economies on oil, while countries with plentiful iron ore gain economic advantages by mining it. Similarly, countries with many unskilled laborers, such as Bangladesh and Egypt, produce goods that require lots of

---

3. Adam Smith, *An Inquiry into the Nature and Causes of the Wealth of Nations* (New York: Modern Library, 1937), 4–5. Originally published 1776.

4. *Productivity* in this context refers to the amount produced by one unit of labor with the other factors of production—especially land and capital—at its disposal. In farming, for example, the same amount of labor is more productive on good soil than on poor, more productive with machinery and fertilizer and irrigation than without.

The Scottish thinker Adam Smith's ideas about division of labor help explain the benefits of trade.

comparative advantage

The ability of a country or firm to produce a particular good or service more efficiently than the other goods or services that it can produce, such that its resources are most efficiently employed in this activity. The comparison is to the efficiency of other economic activities that the actor might undertake, given all the products it can produce—not to the efficiency of other countries or firms.

absolute advantage

The ability of a country or firm to produce more of a particular good or service than other countries or firms do with the same amount of effort and resources.

unskilled labor, including clothing, footwear, and furniture. Countries with many skilled technicians, such as the European nations, produce goods that require sophisticated technical skills, such as complex machinery and aircraft. Such specialization among countries leads to economic gains based on trade.

Comparative advantage is the core concept of the economics of trade. (See the "Special Topic" appendix to this chapter, on p. 340.) It applies the principle of specialization to countries: like people, they should do what they do best. Thus, comparative advantage implies that a nation gains most by specializing in producing and exporting what it produces most efficiently. By doing so, it can earn as much as possible in order to pay for imports of the best products of other countries. The principle of comparative advantage leads to the conclusion that each country will be best off if it produces what it is best at producing and exchanges its products with other countries in return for imports of things it is not so good at producing.

The word *comparative* in the term *comparative advantage* refers to a comparison among the things a country can do—not between one country and another. Just as personal specialization implies that each individual should do what he does best—not what he does better than all others—the specialization involved in comparative advantage implies that countries should produce what they produce most cost-effectively. In other words, it is not necessary for a country to have an **absolute advantage** (the ability to do something better than others) in producing something for it to be profitable to produce and export that thing; all that is necessary is a comparative advantage.

The principle of comparative advantage has clear implications for free trade. Since a country gains from following its comparative advantage and engaging in exchange with other nations for goods in which it does not have a comparative advantage, and since barriers to trade impede its ability to do so, trade protection is harmful to the economy as a whole. Government policies that keep out imports force the country to produce goods that are not to its comparative advantage to produce. Indeed, trade protection raises the price of imports and reduces the efficiency of domestic production. Were national governments to follow the principle of comparative advantage, they would unilaterally remove trade barriers and implement free trade. In this state of affairs, trade policy would be fundamentally cooperative in that all countries would gain from the elimination of obstacles to international trade.

Many people find the economic argument for free trade counterintuitive. Policy makers often argue, like the mercantilists did 300 years ago, that exports are good because they create jobs, that imports are bad because they take away jobs, and that governments should stimulate the national economy by restricting imports and encouraging exports. Economic logic insists the opposite: that imports are the gains from trade, while exports are its costs. A country imports goods that it cannot make very well itself, allowing the nation to focus its productive energies on making (and exporting) the goods that it produces best.

Free trade induces a country to follow its comparative advantage, and economic logic implies that free trade is the ideal policy. This is true, according to economic thinking, even if free trade is pursued unilaterally. Protection serves only to raise costs to consumers. The fact that other countries impose trade barriers that raise prices to their own consumers is no reason for us to harm our own consumers in response. Countries should undertake open trade policies regardless of what other countries do.

There is a clear parallel, from this perspective, between the comparative-advantage argument and the choices available to a household. A farm family, for example, "exports" (sells its crops) in order to "import" (buy the goods and services it wants). Because the farm family wants to maximize the imports it buys, it needs to earn more; the best way to do so is to produce more of what it produces best. The principle of comparative advantage illustrates how farmers, workers, and firms gain by specializing and trading, just as countries do.

Why Do Countries Trade What They Trade?

The principle of comparative advantage suggests that countries should produce and export what they do best. But how can we know what a country does best, other than by observing what it exports? And if the only way to predict a country's exports is to observe them, the theory is not of much value—especially given that trade flows are affected by many noneconomic factors, such as trade barriers. In the 1920s, Swedish economists Eli Heckscher and Bertil Ohlin addressed this puzzle and extended the classical view.

The Heckscher-Ohlin approach tries to explain national comparative advantage and therefore national trading patterns. The two economists recognized that comparative advantage is not simply a result of effort; for example, the productivity of farmers depends primarily on characteristics of their land, not on how hard they work. In countries where land is in short supply and expensive, farming is costly; where it is plentiful and cheap, farming is low in cost.

Heckscher-Ohlin trade theory describes the basic economic characteristics of a country in terms of the material and human resources it possesses. Typically, these economic features are summarized according to basic factors of production, resources essential for economic activity. Such factors of production include:

- Land, an essential input into agricultural production

- Labor, usually meaning unskilled labor

- Capital for investment, which refers both to the machinery and equipment with which goods are produced and to the financial assets necessary to employ this machinery and equipment

- Human capital, which refers to skilled labor, so called because the labor has been enhanced by investment in training and education

Countries differ greatly in how they are endowed with these factors of production. Some are rich in land, others have abundant unskilled labor, others have abundant skilled labor (human capital), and still others are wealthy in investment capital. Heckscher-Ohlin trade theory relies on these "factor endowments" to explain what determines national comparative advantage and, in turn, what

Heckscher-Ohlin trade theory

The theory that a country will export goods that make intensive use of the factors of production in which it is well endowed. For example, a labor-rich country will export goods that make intensive use of labor.

countries produce and export. A country with a large population and poor farmland is likely to have a comparative disadvantage in farming; a country with few people but vast supplies of farmland is likely to have a comparative advantage in agriculture. Different products too require different mixes of resources: typically, farm goods require a lot of land, simple manufactured goods require a lot of unskilled labor, and complex machinery requires a lot of investment capital.

Heckscher-Ohlin trade theory argues that a country will export goods that make intensive use of the resources the country has in abundance, and it will import goods that make intensive use of the country's scarce resources. Countries with lots of land, where land is cheap, specialize in producing farm goods; for example, the United States in the nineteenth century was relatively sparsely populated but was rich in very fertile land and exported massive quantities of cotton, tobacco, and wheat. In contrast, countries with very little farmable land import many farm goods—such as Great Britain in the nineteenth century, which relied heavily on imports for its food. Countries rich in investment capital focus on making goods whose production requires a great deal of capital; for example, most North American and western European nations' industries today specialize in sophisticated manufactured goods, such as complex machinery, construction equipment, and commercial aircraft. Regions with abundant labor produce labor-intensive goods: China and other rapidly developing labor-rich nations concentrate on making products that require a great deal of labor, such as clothing, toys, furniture, and other relatively simple manufactures.

According to the Heckscher-Ohlin trade theory, developing countries that are rich in unskilled labor should export labor-intensive manufactured goods. Indonesia's primary exports are textiles and clothing.

This pattern of specialization leads to analogous trade patterns. Poor countries with little capital import the capital-intensive products they need. Today, for example, poor agricultural nations tend to import their farm machinery from capital-rich industrialized nations, just as the United States did in the early nineteenth century. China and India export their labor-intensive manufactures to North America and western Europe and import capital-intensive industrial goods—including the complex machinery needed to operate their domestic factories.[5] Within North America, the capital-rich United States exports capital-intensive machinery (and capital) to Mexico, while labor-rich Mexico sends labor-intensive manufactured products (and labor) to the United States.

Each of the *factors* of production can be associated with different socioeconomic *actors*. A country abundant in land will also, typically, have many farmers. Unskilled or skilled laborers have unskilled and skilled labor, respectively, to sell on the labor market. Investors hold much of the investment capital of a country. When we say a country that is abundant in land will export products that make great use of land, we are saying that farmers and farmworkers will be heavily engaged in producing goods for export. The relative abundance or scarcity of factors of production has a powerful impact on the economic activities of actors within a society.

The Heckscher-Ohlin theory helps explain the broad outlines of international trade. The industrial countries are rich in capital and skilled labor (human capital), and they export manufactured goods that make intensive use of these resources. Most developing countries are rich in land, raw materials, or unskilled labor (or some combination of the three), and they export agricultural products, minerals, or labor-intensive manufactures.

The theory also helps explain changes over time in a country's trade relations. A poor country with abundant land and labor but little capital will export farm goods and simple labor-intensive manufactures. As the country develops, it accumulates capital and its workers become more skilled, such that its endowments change and, with them, its export patterns. This explains, for example, why the United States in the nineteenth century exported almost exclusively raw materials and farm goods, yet today it exports almost exclusively goods and services that require large amounts of capital and skilled labor to produce. In addition to explaining aspects of world trade patterns, Heckscher-Ohlin trade theory has important implications for the domestic politics of trade policy, as we discuss later in this chapter.

There are other potential economic sources of the patterns we observe in international trade. A great deal of modern international trade is related to the activities of multinational corporations, such as sales among the far-flung subsidiaries of North American, Japanese, European, and other international corporations. In fact, it has been estimated that about one-third of all American trade actually takes place *within* a company, from one of its branches to another—say, from a Ford engine factory in Mexico to a Ford assembly plant in the United States.[6]

---

5. This argument applies to movements of capital and people, as well as to trade. Countries rich in capital should export capital, and countries rich in labor should export labor. (Land, of course, cannot be traded across borders without changing the borders!)

6. Kim Ruhl, "How Well Is US Intrafirm Trade Measured?" *American Economic Review*, 105, no. 5 (May 2015): 524–29.

Much international trade is in goods with internationally known and desirable brand names. South Korea, for instance, imports European-made cars, even though it has a vibrant automotive industry of its own.

This sort of "intrafirm" trade may not be due primarily to the forces that Heckscher-Ohlin trade theory suggests, but rather to production and distribution networks within companies. These kinds of production and distribution networks also exist among different companies. Indeed, much of world trade is now carried out in "global supply chains" in which parts and components are made in many locations around the world, to be assembled and sold in markets everywhere. One estimate is that more than two-thirds of all the trade of advanced industrial countries is actually this sort of "intra-industry" trade.[7] In this way, much of the manufacturing production that was once carried out in a single location, or a single country, has been "outsourced" to suppliers all over the world.

In addition, a great deal of international trade is in goods whose attraction to consumers has to do as much with brand name, reputation, or other related considerations as it does with price. North America, for example, both imports automobiles from Europe and exports automobiles to Europe. This sort of trade is not the result of fundamentally different factor endowments (and prices) between Europe and North America—both regions are rich in capital and skilled labor and poor in unskilled labor—but rather of European consumer interest in American car brands and American consumer interest in European car brands.

Other economic links among countries encourage trade. Countries that share a currency, such as those in the European Union that use the euro, trade with one another much more than those that do not. Countries that invest heavily in one another's economies also tend to trade heavily with one another.

7. Organisation for Economic Co-operation and Development, "Measuring Globalisation: OECD Economic Globalisation Indicators 2010" (Paris: OECD, 2010), www.oecd-ilibrary.org/docserver/download/9210031e .pdf?expires=1498499397&id=id&accname=guest&checksum=65E0F936C80321179F50E4510325B068.

Noneconomic factors also affect both what and with whom countries trade. Countries that are geographically close together trade more, since transport costs are lower. Diplomatic and military relations between nations also influence their trade patterns. Countries whose governments are hostile to one another are likely to trade little, whereas those on friendly terms are likely to trade more. There are two reasons for this. First, trade between hostile nations is riskier than trade between friendly nations: businesses avoid engaging in trade that may very well be disrupted by the outbreak of hostilities. Second, governments often pursue close economic ties with their allies in order to cement the alliance and help friendly nations. By the same token, if trade is good for a national economy, a government might shy away from encouraging trade with an unfriendly nation in order to keep from strengthening a potential enemy. During the Cold War, as we mentioned in Chapter 5 in our discussion of the North Atlantic Treaty Organization (NATO), the United States and its allies purposely limited their economic ties with the Soviet Union, just as they encouraged ties among themselves.

Some analysts believe that trade encourages friendly relations as much as friendly relations encourage trade. For example, Cordell Hull, U.S. secretary of state before and during World War II, wrote: "It is a fact that war did not break out between the United States and any country with which we had been able to negotiate a trade agreement. It is also a fact that, with very few exceptions, the countries with which we signed trade agreements joined together in resisting the Axis. The political line-up followed the economic line-up."[8]

After World War II, the two superpowers used their trade relations to reinforce their alliances: the United States and the Soviet Union each encouraged its allies to build a common trading order that excluded members of the other alliance. After the Cold War ended, many policy makers in Europe wanted to encourage trade with the former communist countries of Eastern and Central Europe as a way to encourage cooperative diplomatic relations with them. Regardless of the pattern of cause and effect, international diplomatic realities and international trade are closely related.

But the most important noneconomic source of international trade patterns is national trade policies undertaken to address the interests of domestic constituencies. Discussions of international trade often overlook the fact that while such trade takes place among countries, it really involves individuals and firms with well-defined interests. We say that "Mexico" exports a million tons of steel to "the United States," but in fact, companies in Mexico sell the steel to companies in the United States. Companies in one country profit from the sale, and companies in the other profit from the purchase. For trade is the stuff of domestic politics, as governments attempt to respond to the interests of corporations and consumers, farmers and workers, all of whom have something at stake in their countries' policies toward foreign trade.

We now consider how domestic political and economic factors affect trade policy and trade itself. In this context we examine the interests, institutions, and interactions that lead to national trade policies.

---

8. Quoted in Richard Gardner, *Sterling-Dollar Diplomacy in Current Perspective: The Origins and Prospects of Our International Economic Order*, expanded ed. (New York: Columbia University Press, 1980), 9.

protectionism

The imposition of barriers to restrict imports.

trade barriers

Government limitations on the international exchange of goods. Examples include tariffs, quantitative restrictions (quotas), import licenses, requirements that governments buy only domestically produced goods, and health and safety standards that discriminate against foreign goods.

tariff

A tax imposed on imports. Tariffs raise the domestic price of the imported good and may be applied for the purpose of protecting domestic producers from foreign competition.

quantitative restriction (quota)

A limit placed on the amount of a particular good that is allowed to be imported.

nontariff barriers to trade

Obstacles to imports other than tariffs (trade taxes). Examples include restrictions on the number of products that can be imported (quantitative restrictions, or quotas); regulations that favor domestic over imported products; and other measures that discriminate against foreign goods or services. "Buy American" laws that govern what state and local governments can buy, for example, are an implicit—but nontariff—obstacle to the purchase of imports.

Trade Restrictions Are the Rule, Not the Exception

Despite the powerful economic arguments for free trade, every country currently has at least some restrictions on trade with the rest of the world. Some countries have very high barriers to trade; others have much lower ones. Yet government policies to control and contain trade are the norm, today as in the past. **Protectionism**, the use of specific measures to shield domestic producers from imports, has long been one of the most common government policies worldwide. Most of today's rich countries were strongly protectionist at some point in their history.

Virtually all governments restrict at least some imports. For hundreds of years, governments have imposed a wide variety of **trade barriers**, impediments to the importation of foreign goods. Historically, the most common barrier is a **tariff**, a tax on imports levied at the border and paid by the importer. A tariff raises the price of the import directly, so a consumer of the imported good has to pay more for it. Another common form of trade barrier is a **quantitative restriction**, or **quota**, which limits the quantity of a foreign good that can be sold domestically. Because the reduced quantity typically causes an increase in its domestic price, a quantitative restriction has an effect like that of a tariff: it makes the imported good more expensive to domestic consumers. There are many other **nontariff barriers to trade**, such as regulations targeted at foreign goods or requirements that governments purchase from national producers. In all instances, the effect of these policies is to shelter domestic producers from foreign competition. Before we analyze the effects of these policies, it is important to emphasize how common they have been and continue to be.

The degree to which the world's major nations have been open to trade has varied greatly over time and among countries. As we saw in Chapter 1, for more than 300 years after 1492 the major European nations followed the trade policies of mercantilism, a system by which great powers used their military might to control trade with and extract wealth from their colonial possessions. The colonial powers' mercantilist regulations kept foreign goods out of their markets and reserved their colonies' markets for themselves.

Around the middle of the nineteenth century, however, Great Britain and other leading industrial countries moved in the direction of trade liberalization: they pursued policies that involved fewer restrictions on trade. Great Britain adopted free trade, permitting foreigners to sell anything to Britain without tax or restriction. More generally, from the 1860s until 1914, international trade among the principal industrialized nations was quite free. There were tariffs and other barriers, to be sure, and some countries were very protectionist—especially such industrializing nations as the United States, which had some of the world's highest trade barriers at the time. Nonetheless, most of the world's major economies were open, and world trade grew at a very rapid rate.

With the outbreak of World War I in 1914, however, international trade relations entered 30 years of crisis and closure. Efforts to rebuild the trading system after the war were not very successful, especially once the Great Depression hit in

1929. The major powers divided up the world into more or less hostile trading blocs: the British, French, Italian, Japanese, and other empires, along with the less formal German and American spheres of influence.

After 1945, the Western world under American leadership moved gradually to reduce trade barriers among the developed nations. The communist countries and most developing countries protected themselves from world markets, but the industrialized world significantly liberalized its trade. Although the reduction of trade barriers remained controversial, by the 1980s the rich countries had become very open to world trade, as part of the broader march toward economic globalization. Eventually, most developing and formerly communist countries joined the liberalizing and globalizing trend. Since the early 1990s, international trade has once more—as before 1914—been quite open. Thus, in terms of global trade relations over time, we see a pattern in which mercantilist closure gave way to freer trade, then to interwar closure, then to liberalization after 1945 and further liberalization leading to globalization after 1980.

Many nations have, at some point, gone from very closed to very open to trade, or in the opposite direction. Great Britain jettisoned mercantilism in the 1840s. The United States, one of the most protectionist nations in the world through most of the nineteenth and early twentieth centuries, started moving toward freer trade in the 1930s, and by the 1950s and 1960s was leading the charge for trade liberalization. As Figure 7.1 shows, trade became an increasingly large part of the U.S. economy after the 1960s. Developing nations such as Brazil and India were among the world's most closed economies until the 1980s, after which they reduced their barriers dramatically. Trade among European countries was quite free from the 1860s until 1914; in the 1920s and 1930s, the region's nations erected very strict barriers to trade among themselves; today, trade among the 27 EU members is completely unrestricted.

Figure source: World Bank, World Development Indicators, http://data.worldbank.org/indicator/NE.TRD.GNFS.ZS/countries/US?display=default (accessed 09/07/17).

FIGURE 7.1 *Importance of Trade to the U.S. Economy, 1960–2015*

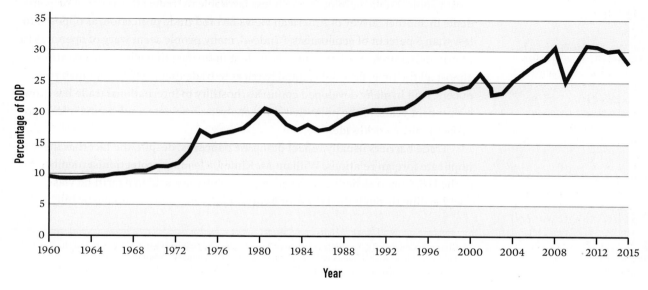

Even within a single country, there can be significant differences among policies toward trade in different goods—some protected and some not. Almost all developed nations protect agricultural producers much more heavily than manufacturers. Developing nations, meanwhile, tend to protect manufactured products more than farm products. The United States, as well as many other industrial nations, generally protects the steel industry more than most other industries. And despite the industrial countries' rhetoric in favor of freer trade, they have imposed restrictions on many goods that might be imported from developing nations. Why are some producers—farmers, or certain kinds of farmers; industries, or certain kinds of industries—more favored by trade policy than others? Why do different countries' trade policies vary so much? Why has the world's general openness to trade changed so dramatically over time? And, perhaps most central, why have governments almost always, and almost everywhere, ignored economic analysis and advice and imposed restrictions on foreign trade?

Why Do Governments Restrict Trade? The Domestic Political Economy of Protection

For over 200 years, economic analysis has been unambiguous about the benefits of trade for national income, output, and efficiency. This perspective is reflected in the opinions of professional economists, more than 90 percent of whom believe that barriers to trade reduce national well-being (according to one survey of American economists).[9] Yet economists' confidence in the benefits of trade is not shared by most people. Public opinion is much less favorable to trade: 60 percent of respondents in another survey of American views favored trade protection, as opposed to less than 5 percent of economists.[10] Indeed, many people seem wary of openness to international trade. Such wariness is evident in the fact that almost all countries, almost all the time, have substantial barriers to trade that protect their own producers. And in many developed countries, hostility to international trade has grown over recent years, to the point that some analysts anticipate a substantial return to protectionism worldwide.

Trade barriers usually reflect domestic concerns, despite the fact that they implicate foreign relations. William McKinley, a leading protectionist member of the U.S. Congress before he became president, once said of a tariff he was shepherding through the House of Representatives: "This is a domestic bill; it

---

9. Cletus C. Coughlin, "The Controversy over Free Trade: The Gap between Economists and the General Public," *Federal Reserve Bank of St. Louis Review* 84, no. 1 (January–February 2002): 1.

10. Coughlin, "Controversy over Free Trade," 1.

is not a foreign bill."[11] This statement remains a common view of protection for domestic interests.

Trade policy typically reaches the public consciousness, and the media, when some national producers complain that there is too much or too little trade in the goods they produce. Often, producers are concerned because imported goods cut into their profits or cost them their jobs. Other producers may complain that foreign barriers to their goods keep them out of markets abroad and similarly cut into profits and cost jobs at home. To understand the domestic politics of trade, we need to know the interests in question, the institutions through which these interests are expressed, and how competing interests interact with one another.

There are both benefits and costs to trade barriers. Virtually all tools of trade protection—tariffs, quotas, and other restrictions—make imports more expensive, which allows domestic producers to sell more of their products, to raise their prices, or both. When tariffs are imposed on foreign steel imported into the United States, American steelmakers can expand sales at higher prices. As a result, they may be able to increase profits, raise wages, and hire more workers. Quotas, which restrict the quantity of foreign goods sold in the national market, ultimately have a similar impact in that the reduction in imports reduces supply, thus raising prices. So, trade barriers assist national producers. What could be wrong with that?

The most direct cost of protection is to consumers of the protected good. Tariffs and quotas raise the domestic price of imported goods and may lead to price increases for similar domestically produced goods: for example, a barrier to steel imports makes imported steel more expensive and allows domestic steelmakers to raise prices too. Producers gain and consumers lose from protection; the *redistributive effect* is such that income is redistributed from domestic consumers to the protected domestic industry. But there is another cost as well—in this case to efficiency or the welfare of the society as a whole, the ability of society to use its resources most effectively. A trade barrier introduces economic inefficiencies. It leads domestic producers to make more goods that they are not particularly good at making (otherwise, they would not need protection), and it leads consumers to consume less of those goods that protection has made artificially expensive.

Trade protection also leads to an allocation of domestic resources—labor, capital, land, skills—that is not to the country's comparative advantage. Protection of European wheat leads European farmers to use their land for wheat farming when it might make more sense, from the standpoint of the region's overall economy, to use that land for

NAFTA imposes controls on trade that stipulate that a certain percentage of parts in any car must be made in the United States, Canada, or Mexico. Some car-part manufacturers, like Nemak, locate their factories in Mexico to take advantage of its lower labor costs.

---

11. Cited in David A. Lake, *Power, Protection, and Free Trade: International Sources of U.S. Commercial Strategy, 1887–1939* (Ithaca, NY: Cornell University Press, 1988), 111.

dairy or vegetable farming or to build houses. (For more on the economic effects of trade restrictions, see the "Special Topic" appendix to this chapter, on p. 340.)

Winners and Losers in International Trade

The domestic politics of trade is infused with battles between winners and losers from protection and with debates over the importance of any inefficiencies that protection may promote. The potential winners and losers constitute the principal actors in national debates over trade policy.

Domestic industries protected by trade barriers receive clear and concentrated benefits. Protection creates returns above the normal rate of profit by artificially restricting competition and supply. However, at least three groups of actors stand to lose from trade protection. First are consumers of the imported good. This group includes consuming industries, which—unlike average consumers—may be powerful and well organized. When the U.S. government imposed tariffs on imported steel in 2002, the American users of this steel—especially in the automobile industry—mobilized strongly against it (as did foreign governments), and the policy was eventually reversed.

A second group that tends to oppose protection is exporters. They worry that their country's protective barriers might provoke retaliation in foreign markets. American farmers, for example, have opposed American barriers to Chinese goods—largely to avoid Chinese retaliation against the many billions of dollars of American farm goods that China imports.

Third, citizens in general may be willing and able to punish politicians for the costs that protection imposes on them, especially if the connection is clear and the issue is prominent. In the 1980s, many people in Soviet-bloc (communist) countries blamed the stagnation of their economies on their governments' pervasive trade controls, and this perception may have created popular sympathy for the subsequent opening of these nations to international trade. In addition, there is evidence that consumers in developing countries favor freer trade because they understand that it will lead to reduced prices for themselves.[12]

Because of the diverse array of industries that compete with imports, use imports, and sell exports, as well as the range of producers and consumers, trade is politically controversial. Which actors do we expect to have an interest in supporting and opposing trade protection within national political systems?

Economic Interests and Trade Policy

The economic characteristics of a country, and of particular groups within it, help explain who might be in favor of and against trade. There are two leading theories of trade-policy interests; each predicts different sets of actors that will support or oppose trade protection.

---

12. See, for example, Andy Baker, "Who Wants to Globalize? Consumer Tastes and Labor Markets in a Theory of Trade Policy Beliefs," *American Journal of Political Science* 49, no. 4 (October 2005): 924–38.

The first theory, the Stolper-Samuelson approach, emphasizes the interests of broad factors of production—land, labor, capital. Remember that the Heckscher-Ohlin approach expects that a country's exports will make intensive use of resources that the country has a lot of. A labor-rich country will export labor-intensive goods; a capital-rich country will export capital-intensive goods. This pattern, in turn, affects which groups trade will help or hurt. If the country exports labor-intensive goods, for example, the demand for labor goes up, and so do wages. This first theory argues that trade affects primarily broad factors of production: labor, capital, land, skilled labor.

The second theory, the Ricardo-Viner approach, emphasizes specific sectors of the economy, such as the steel industry or cotton farmers. Both help us think analytically about support for and opposition to trade.

The Stolper-Samuelson Approach

The **Stolper-Samuelson theorem** is one explanation of who will support and who will oppose protection. It predicts that trade protection benefits the scarce factor of production. This is simply the counterpart of the argument that more trade helps the abundant factor: as discussed already, in a labor-rich country, labor benefits most from trade. The logical implication is that reducing trade in a labor-rich country will harm labor.

Consider Bangladesh, a poor country with lots of unskilled labor and very little capital. Bangladesh exports mainly clothing and leather goods, which make intensive use of its abundant unskilled labor; it imports such capital-intensive products as machinery, equipment, and chemicals. Trade barriers artificially make imported capital-intensive goods more expensive or harder to buy, which means that at least some of them will have to be produced in Bangladesh. Some Bangladeshi capital will have to be diverted from labor-intensive production in order to produce these capital-intensive goods (from garment factories to chemical plants, for example), which raises the domestic demand for capital and reduces the local demand for labor. This, in turn, raises the return on Bangladeshi capital (profits) and reduces Bangladeshi wages. Protection in a capital-scarce country helps owners of capital and hurts workers; we expect investors to support protection and workers to oppose it.

We can apply the Stolper-Samuelson theorem to a labor-scarce country, such as the United States. The opposite of Bangladesh, the United States has abundant capital but scarce unskilled labor. The United States imports labor-intensive goods, such as clothing and furniture, and exports capital-intensive goods, such as airplanes. Protection restricts the American supply of labor-intensive products and raises their price. This, in turn, increases American production of these labor-intensive products, raises the American demand for unskilled labor, and boosts the wages of American unskilled workers. By the same token, protection in land-scarce countries (such as those of western Europe, as well as Japan) helps farmers and hurts workers and owners of capital.

So, which actors would we expect to support and oppose trade barriers? We expect owners of the scarce factors of production in a country to be protectionist and owners of the abundant factors to favor free trade. In rich societies, which

Stolper-Samuelson theorem

The theorem that protection benefits the scarce factor of production. This view flows from the Heckscher-Ohlin theory: if a country imports goods that make intensive use of its scarce factor, then limiting imports will help that factor. So in a labor-scarce country, labor benefits from protection and loses from trade liberalization.

typically have abundant capital and skilled labor but are scarce in unskilled labor, capitalists and skilled workers should be free traders, while unskilled workers should be protectionists. In countries with abundant land, farmers should support trade; in countries where land is scarce, farmers should support protection. In poor societies, which typically have abundant unskilled labor and scarce capital, workers should support trade while capitalists should be protectionists. An important feature of the model is that actors' attitudes toward trade are not fixed, but vary with the country's resources of land, labor, capital, and human capital (skills). Thus, the model expects farmers to be protectionists in land-poor Japan but free traders in land-rich Argentina.

There is a great deal of evidence to support this model. Labor movements in the United States and other rich countries do seem to be relatively protectionist, while people with a lot of capital appear to find free trade more favorable. Japan and Europe have relatively little land, and their farmers are strongly protectionist; Australia and Canada are rich in land, and their farmers usually favor free trade. Notice that the Stolper-Samuelson predictions are about very broad groups or actors—owners of production factors (roughly the same as social classes) such as laborers, investors, and farmers.

But observers of economic policy making in the United States and elsewhere note that many demands for protection come from specific *industries*—the steel industry, sugar growers, shoe manufacturers. Often, everyone in an industrial sector—skilled and unskilled workers, managers, and owners of firms—works together to ask for trade barriers or support for their exports. For example, we tend to think of the American steel industry as relatively protectionist because we group together everyone associated with the industry. This assessment flies in the face of the Stolper-Samuelson focus on labor as a class or investors (capital) as a class. Many detailed studies of trade policy, and of attitudes toward trade, confirm the idea that the industry in which people work has a powerful impact on their trade-policy opinions.[13]

Ricardo-Viner (specific-factors) model

A model of trade relations that emphasizes the sector in which factors of production are employed rather than the nature of the factor itself. This differentiates it from the Heckscher-Ohlin theory, for which the nature of the factor—labor, land, capital—is the principal consideration.

The Ricardo-Viner (Specific-Factors) Approach A second way of predicting trade-policy preferences focuses on why whole industries often act together. The **Ricardo-Viner**, or **specific-factors**, **model** has one key feature that differentiates it from Stolper-Samuelson: some factors of production are tied to their industry; that is, they are *industry-specific*. The relevant actors thus are not classes, but industrial sectors. The approach is based on the principle that the factors of production are not very mobile, that it is difficult for labor or capital to move from use to use.

For example, capital in the steel industry largely takes the form of steel factories and machinery; it cannot simply be turned into capital in the food-processing industry. Since they are "stuck" in the steel industry, steel manufacturers care not about the profits of capital in *general* and in the country as a whole, but rather about the profits available only in steel. The same may be true of workers or farmers,

---

13. See, especially, Anna Maria Mayda and Dani Rodrik, "Why Are Some People (and Countries) More Protectionist Than Others?" *European Economic Review* 49 (2005): 1393–1430.

The U.S. steel industry, whose capital equipment is specific to the production of steel, often urges the U.S. government to provide protection from what it views as unfair "dumping"—that is, selling steel in the United States below the true cost of production. Cheap steel benefits consumers, but hurts the steel industry.

whose job skills or land can be inherently "specific to" (some might say "trapped in") a particular industry or crop. This gives the owners, workers, or farmers a strong incentive to safeguard their current use—for example, by obtaining government protection from foreign competition.

In this model, the interests of individuals flow from the sectors of the economy in which they are employed. Given the limited mobility of labor and capital, actors associate their interests with the sector in which they are employed. A worker or manager in an industry that faces stiff import competition will be protectionist; a worker or manager in an exporting industry will want free trade. Unlike in the Stolper-Samuelson approach, people's interests are tightly bound up with the interests of others in their sector of the economy, and the pertinent actors in domestic trade-policy debates are economic sectors, not factors.

A Firm-Based Trade Theory

A third approach to trade has gained theoretical and empirical support in recent years, motivated by the observation that international trade is dominated by a very few companies. Of the more than 5 million firms in the United States, for example, only 4 percent are exporters. Even in exporting industries, most of the exporting is done by a small number of companies: the top 1 percent of all exporting firms account for more than 80 percent of all American exports.[14]

This observation leads to an approach to trade, and to trade policy, that focuses on firms. The most productive firms in an exporting industry—typically also

---

14. Andrew B. Bernard, J. Bradford Jensen, and Peter K. Schott, "Importers, Exporters and Multinationals: A Portrait of Firms in the US That Trade Goods," in *Producer Dynamics: New Evidence from Micro Data*, ed. Timothy Dunne, J. Bradford Jensen, and Mark J. Roberts, 513–52 (Chicago: University of Chicago Press, 2009); and Andrew B. Bernard, J. Bradford Jensen, Stephen J. Redding, and Peter K. Schott, "Firms in International Trade," *Journal of Economic Perspectives* 21, no. 3 (2007): 105–30.

the largest—may be most likely to benefit from trade liberalization and to be politically active in the trade arena. Certainly, we are used to seeing very large firms—General Motors, Walmart, General Electric, Google—play a major role on all sides of trade-policy debates.

There is evidence for all three of these approaches in the politics of trade protection. Broad classes—farmers, workers—sometimes mobilize for or against protection. But at the same time, much lobbying for protection is industry-based, consistent with the view that the benefits of protection accrue to industries, not to broad classes or factors. And within industries, it is typically the largest firms that dominate debate. The accuracy of each view may vary among industries and countries, and over time. One study found, for example, that in the late nineteenth century, American labor was quite interchangeable, which contributed to the working class having a clear, distinctive interest in trade policy; in contrast, today's American working class is much more differentiated, so industry-based sectoral interests predominate.[15]

Groups may also support trade policies because they believe those policies help make possible other outcomes that they favor. The economist John Maynard Keynes wrote that protectionism "rests on the principle of making things relatively scarce. To those who are concerned with making these things, this is no doubt advantageous. But it causes an amount of distress more than equivalent elsewhere. The community as a whole cannot hope to gain by making artificially scarce what the country wants."[16]

This is a powerful argument; but later, in the midst of the Great Depression of the 1930s, Keynes came to believe that there could be equally powerful political arguments against free trade. In 1933, in fact, Keynes spoke in favor of "the policy of an increased national self-sufficiency . . . not as an ideal in itself, but as directed to the creation of an environment in which other ideals can be safely and conveniently pursued." Keynes had come to believe that trade barriers might usefully give national governments breathing space as they attempted to combat mass unemployment and economic collapse. Keynes felt that protectionism might permit governments to implement policy measures to alleviate the social and economic distress of the Great Depression.[17]

Understanding the economic interests that are in contention over trade is only a start to understanding national trade politics and policies. At best, this can tell us which actors want more or less protection and what the interests of different groups in trade policy might be. But what determines who wins and who loses in the battles among supporters and opponents of trade liberalization?

---

15. Michael Hiscox, "Commerce, Coalitions, and Factor Mobility: Evidence from Congressional Votes on Trade Legislation," *American Political Science Review* 96, no. 3 (September 2002): 593–608.

16. Cited in Robert Skidelsky, *John Maynard Keynes*, vol. 1, *Hopes Betrayed 1883–1920* (New York: Penguin, 1983), 227.

17. John Maynard Keynes, "National Self-Sufficiency," *Yale Review* 22, no. 4 (June 1933): 755–69.

Domestic Institutions and Trade Policy

Since there are always supporters and opponents of protection in any country, how are trade-policy decisions made? Why are some countries more open to trade than others? Why do governments protect some industries and not others? There are many steps between raw economic interests and the actual results in economic policy. Most of them have to do with the institutions of national politics, including the organization and representation of interests, and the ways in which policy decisions are made.

National political institutions can be of stunning variety and complexity, but a general rule of thumb can help orient our understanding of their implications for trade policy. A common view starts with the observation that trade protection tends to help relatively narrow and concentrated groups—the steel industry, skilled workers—but tends to harm the economy and consumers as a whole. It follows that those political institutional forms that are particularly responsive to the interests of more concentrated groups—a particular class, a particular industry—will be more favorable to protection, while those that respond especially to broad national pressures will be less favorable. So, an important question about domestic institutions has to do with whether they favor particularistic interests (in which case they would incline toward protectionism) or broad economic and consumer interests (in which case they would incline toward less protectionist policies).

The Organization of Interests Trade protection affects large groups both positively and negatively. This raises the possibility of free riding, a concept we introduced in Chapter 2. If a trade barrier is imposed, it helps all the beneficiaries of trade protection—whether a factor of production or an industry—regardless of whether they worked to get protection or not. This means that some members of the winning group—some companies, some individuals—have reasons to sit back and wait for others to fight for them. But if all the actors in a class or industry attempt to free ride, nothing will get done. In other words, both supporters and opponents of trade protection face problems of collective action.

As we've discussed in previous chapters, the logic of collective action implies that smaller groups will be better able to organize than larger groups can. We saw in Chapter 4 how smaller, highly motivated groups were better able to influence foreign policy in matters of war and peace. The same principle applies in matters of trade policy. There are typically relatively few producers and a great many consumers, which leads to the expectation that producers will win over consumers in many circumstances. This helps explain, for example, how a relatively small number of steelworkers are able to obtain a policy that benefits them at the expense of the vast mass of American consumers of goods that are made with steel.

Economic interests organize themselves very differently in different societies. In some western European countries, for example, most workers are members of a centralized labor federation that devises policies for virtually the entire labor movement. Even where workers in different industries might disagree, the existence of a class-wide labor federation helps create a common working-class political position and overcome collective action problems. In the United States, by contrast, labor unions tend to be organized by industry; even if there were common trade-policy interests among American workers, it might be difficult for them to express those interests in a common way.

The implication is that an organization reflecting the concerns of broad groups—such as all workers—is more likely to ignore the demands of specific groups or industries. In contrast, interests that are organized into narrower groups are more likely to pursue the particular goals of such special interests.

The Representation of Interests through Political Institutions

Just as narrowly based social groups are more likely to favor protection than broader ones are, so political institutions that are more closely tied to narrow interests are more likely to favor trade protection than are institutions that reflect broader interests. This is an example of the sort of bias that political institutions can create or intensify. Generally, to the extent that democracies reflect broad interests while dictatorships are restrictive, we would expect democracies to be less protectionist than dictatorships. Indeed, scholars have found that democratic developing countries are much more likely to liberalize their trade than dictatorships are.[18]

Apart from such broad institutional features as democracy, societies differ in the ways that their partisan, electoral, and legislative institutions represent the interests of their citizens, and these differences are likely to affect the way trade policy is made. For example, many European countries have strong class-based parties: the working class traditionally votes for the socialist parties, and other parties associate themselves more or less explicitly with farmers or business. Although the American labor movement has ties to the Democrats, working-class voters in the United States are somewhat less strongly connected to the Democratic Party as compared with working-class voters and left-leaning parties in Europe. This affects the parties' expression of interests and their bias toward special or general interests, and thus toward protection or freer trade.

National electoral systems vary greatly, and they may cause differences among national party structures. Most industrial countries are parliamentary and have a legislature elected on a proportional basis in which voters choose the party they prefer rather than an individual local candidate. American voters elect the president on a national basis but elect individual local candidates (for the House of Representatives and the Senate) whose ties to the national party may be weak. And there are systems in between, such as the Westminster system (in Great Britain) and hybrid presidential-parliamentary systems (in much of Latin America).

How might these institutions affect trade policy? Politicians with local political constituencies tend to be more responsive to local interest groups, while nationally elected politicians have less reason to cater to particular local concerns. Consider two otherwise identical countries: one with strong national parties and a powerful national executive and the other with weak national parties and a weak national

---

18. Helen V. Milner and Keiko Kubota, "Why the Move to Free Trade? Democracy and Trade Policy in the Developing Countries," *International Organization* 59, no. 1 (Winter 2005): 107–43.

executive. Politicians in the former are more likely to focus on national effects of policy and favor free trade, while politicians in the latter are more likely to emphasize local concerns and thus favor trade protection that benefits local special interests.

The same holds within a country, where one branch of government may be more sensitive to local pressures than another. The American president, elected nationally, has a strong incentive to consider the impact of trade policies on the country as a whole. Members of Congress, however, have little reason to think about anything other than the effects of the policy on their district. Traditionally, then, Congress is more protectionist than the president—although this relationship has changed in important ways more recently.

Partisan features of government can also affect trade policy, especially if parties are associated with well-defined social groups that have preferences for particular trade policies. For example, in the Stolper-Samuelson framework, labor has well-defined interests in trade: if labor is scarce, laborers will be protectionist; if labor is abundant, laborers will support free trade. In most of the world, labor typically supports left-wing parties. Given this observation, governments of the Left in labor-rich countries (mainly poor nations) should be more open to trade than are governments of the Left in labor-scarce countries (mainly rich nations). Similarly, because business typically is associated with right-wing parties, governments of the Right in capital-rich countries (usually rich nations) should be more open, while in capital-poor countries (usually poor nations) they should be more protectionist.

Thus, leftist governments should support free trade in poor countries and protection in rich countries; rightist governments should support free trade in rich countries and protection in poor countries. One study of a large number of countries indeed found strong support for this joint impact of partisan politics and Stolper-Samuelson interests. For example, Bangladesh and Senegal are similarly labor-rich and capital-poor, but in the 1980s, Bangladesh's right-wing (presumably anti-labor) government had tariffs twice as high as Senegal's left-wing (presumably pro-labor) government.[19]

Although theory and history tend to support these explanations of trade politics, a new mass politics of trade has emerged in many advanced industrial countries in the past decade. This trend is part of a broader backlash against globalization, which has entered mass and electoral politics in very striking ways. In the 2016 presidential campaign in the United States, for example, both political parties had candidates who were strongly and explicitly hostile to international trade. Democrat Bernie Sanders and Republican Donald Trump both criticized American trade policies, arguing that they had cost the country valuable manufacturing jobs and served primarily to enrich a corporate elite.

Donald Trump was elected president after a campaign that was more hostile to existing trade policy than any U.S. presidential campaign had been since the 1930s. The Trump administration has indeed pursued much more protectionist policies

---

19. Pushan Dutt and Devashish Mitra, "Endogenous Trade Policy through Majority Voting: An Empirical Investigation," *Journal of International Economics* 58 (2002): 107–33.

Proposed trade deals between the European Union and Canada (CETA) and between the European Union and the United States (TTIP) provoked demonstrations in Poland among citizens who were concerned about the deals' potential impact on domestic agriculture and consumer rights.

than any of its modern predecessors. The new American politics of trade has had its reflection in the rise of similarly "populist" movements, of both the Right and the Left, in other countries. In Europe, antiglobalization sentiment tends to take the form of opposition to the European Union or the euro, and it has been a powerful electoral force in countries from France to Poland. Similar attitudes clearly contributed to the British vote in June 2016 to leave the European Union.

It is probably too early to know whether the emergence of powerful mass and electoral pressures for trade protection in the past few years presage a fundamental change in the politics of trade. Concentrated special interests remain very powerful and continue to play a central role in trade policy. But it may be, at least in some rich countries, that large segments of the electorate now have strong enough views in favor of trade protection to have a significant impact on trade policy.

Costs, Benefits, and Compensation in National Trade Policies

Even if trade liberalization makes a country's economy as a whole better off, it can seriously harm groups within the country. Concentrated groups of potential losers with a lot at stake could conceivably block policy changes that would improve conditions for the nation overall. Indeed, the electoral success of antiglobalization candidates hostile to trade suggests that there is a widespread sentiment in some nations that many citizens have been harmed by freer trade. For those who believe that trade benefits the national economy as a whole, one implication is that the country could be better off if it "bought off" the actors whose interests would be harmed, to give them a reason to cooperate with trade policies that benefit the society as a whole. Such an approach would represent a movement toward the Pareto frontier in the model presented in Chapter 2.

Movement toward the Pareto frontier, called a Pareto improvement, makes everyone better off (or at least unharmed) and nobody worse off. While trade liberalization might hurt some people, the overall gains to the national economy are large enough that the losers can be fully compensated for their losses and the benefits will still remain for the rest of society. Indeed, it is not uncommon for a government to arrange compensation for people who lose from trade liberalization, in order to diminish opposition to a removal of trade barriers that the government wants to pursue. The United States, for example, provides Trade Adjustment Assistance to workers harmed by the country's foreign trade; the assistance ranges from tax credits, to money for retraining, to outright grants.

More generally, the very structure of the post-1945 political economy of most Western societies has, to some extent, been based on the logic of compensation. As the industrialized world substantially reduced trade barriers after World War II, its governments implemented sweeping social policies that provided a safety net to workers, farmers, and others who might be negatively affected by the reopening of world trade. This strategy reflects a kind of compromise between supporters of economic integration on the one hand, and defenders of the welfare state on the other.[20] The Bretton Woods System (introduced in Chapter 1) permitted, even encouraged, this compromise, and it was quite successful at achieving its goal of an integrated world economy and extensive social welfare policies in the industrialized nations.

The issue of compensation has attracted recent attention because many observers believe that trade has led to reduced wages for many workers in the industrial countries. Trade puts unskilled and semi-skilled American workers in direct competition with unskilled and semi-skilled workers in poor countries with much lower wages, which may depress the wages of the former. This is a clear implication of the Heckscher-Ohlin approach: trade will tend to make wages, profits, and other earnings more similar across countries. In this process, the prices of factors of production (the wages of labor, the profits of capital, the returns to land) tend to become more equal across countries. Trade leads countries to export goods that use factors of production in which they are well endowed: labor-rich countries export labor-intensive goods. This increases the demand for labor and raises wages. At the same time, labor-poor countries import labor-intensive goods rather than producing them at home, thus reducing the demand for labor and lowering wages. The implication is that wages in poor countries will rise toward the levels of those in rich countries, while wages in rich countries will fall toward the levels of poor countries.

20. John Ruggie called this compromise "embedded liberalism." See John Gerard Ruggie, "International Regimes, Transactions, and Change: Embedded Liberalism in the Postwar Economic Order," *International Organization* 36, no. 2 (1982): 379–415.

For example, the wages of unskilled workers in the United States have, in fact, been stagnant or declining since the early 1970s, and trade with developing countries may have contributed to this process. The issue is controversial; some analysts think that the decline in unskilled wages in the United States is due largely to technological changes that have made computer-based skills more valuable in the workplace. Nonetheless, there is little doubt that globalization has created winners and losers in rich countries and that working people are more likely to be on the losing side. This observation has led some analysts to suggest that rich countries will continue to face social and political conflict over economic openness that will be mitigated only if they develop more extensive social safety nets to reduce the negative impact of the world economy on some groups in society.

Clearly, the interests, interactions, and institutions that characterize different national political economies have a powerful impact on national trade policies. Nonetheless, a focus on the *domestic* sources of trade policies misses an important part of the story, because each country's trade relations are part of a broader international environment. While trends in French or Indian trade depend on French and Indian domestic politics, they also depend on the global economic and political situation.

It would be difficult to understand the French turn toward protectionism in the 1930s without the context of the Great Depression, that country's reduction in protection after 1950 without situating it within the Cold War, or its current trade policies without knowing France's place in the single market of the European Union. Similarly, it would be difficult to explain India's protectionism upon independence in 1947, or its turn toward freer trade in the 1990s, without knowing that in both instances it was following policies shared by most other developing countries. The *international* environment—especially the global strategic and institutional setting—has a powerful impact on national trade policies and patterns.

How Do Countries Get What They Want? The International Political Economy of Trade

What a national government wants from trade is only a starting point, for every country's commercial relations depend on the international environment. Certainly, a country can pursue a unilateral trade policy; it can open its borders or close them, regardless of what other countries do. But what a country achieves depends on the actions of others. How can governments get what their constituents want out of the world economy? How do factors abroad, including the policies of other countries, affect the ability of a national government to deliver goods to its people? What is the international political economy of trade?

International economic conditions, for example, have a powerful impact on both the policies a country might like to pursue and their likely effects. The collapse of the world economy in the 1930s drove many countries inward; foreign markets were small and shrinking, and the benefits of openness shrank with them. In contrast, the rapid expansion of world trade since 1945 has given many countries strong incentives to link their economies to dynamic world markets. In addition to global market conditions, the policies of other governments can have an enormous impact: for example, the opening of China and India to world trade has profoundly affected other developed and developing nations. How, then, can we understand the national politics of trade within the broader international context? How does the strategic and institutional environment affect whether countries get what they want from world trade?

Strategic Interaction in International Trade Relations

When governments make national trade policies, they take into account what other governments are likely to do in response. A government that raises tariffs dramatically, for example, might find other countries retaliating with even higher barriers to its exports—so that the benefits to domestic producers sheltered from imports might be canceled out by costs to exporters frozen out of foreign markets. In 1930, for example, the U.S. Congress attempted to provide relief to farmers by raising the tariff on eggs from 8¢ to 10¢ a dozen. This action reduced the already small number of Canadian eggs bought in the United States by 40 percent, from 160,000 to fewer than 100,000. The British imperial trade area (which included Canada) countered by increasing the tariff on eggs to the same 10¢ a dozen, from the previously low 3¢. This move drove down America's very considerable egg exports to Canada by 98 percent, from 11 million to fewer than 200,000. The British-Canadian response meant that American protectionism had backfired.[21]

By the same token, attempts to create regional trading areas such as the European Union or NAFTA, or to affect the international commercial order such as the United States did after World War II, rely on the joint behavior of different nation-states. One government cannot achieve many of its trade-policy goals without considering the actions of other governments. (See "What Shaped Our World?" on p. 320 for a discussion on the evolution of the European Union.)

Two or more governments involved in trade-policy negotiations are engaged in strategic interaction and must take into account the behavior of other governments in trying to do their best. For example, suppose that American farmers decide they would be better off if they had access to Europe's market for farm goods and are willing to reduce American agricultural trade barriers in return. American trade negotiators offer the Europeans a joint reduction of farm trade protection, and the Europeans agree.

---

21. Cordell Hull, *The Memoirs of Cordell Hull* (New York: Macmillan, 1948), 355–56.

The Single European Market: From Creation to Crisis and Beyond

In 1945, Europe emerged from the most devastating war in history, a conflict that tore the continent apart. Today, the countries of the European Union (EU) constitute a single market for goods, services, capital, and people, yet opposition to European integration has increased in recent years. How did the single European market emerge from such a troubled past? Why has it become controversial?

Interests European integration was based on the common interests among the states of Western Europe and the United States in the wake of World War II, as all countries looked for a way to rebuild from the war's devastation. At the same time, the Soviet Union had taken advantage of its control of Eastern Europe to install communist regimes. The threats of unrest from within and attack from without created shared interests among the Western European states in security and economic growth. Although these immediate threats dissipated with time, cooperation continued to rest on common interests, particularly the joint gains available through the free flow of goods, money, and people.

Interactions Although common interests are necessary for cooperation, they by no means ensure that cooperation will happen. In the aftermath of war, distrust among the states of Western Europe, particularly toward West Germany, complicated the interaction. The United States played a major role by providing security through the presence of U.S. troops and injecting money through the famous Marshall Plan. The Europeans had to cooperate among themselves to distribute U.S. aid, and this spirit of cooperation continued into the next decade. Given the emerging Cold War competition with the Soviet Union, an early priority of these cooperative efforts was the production of coal and steel, which were vital to both the economic development and the military might of the West.

Institutions From these modest beginnings institutional growth took off. Six original countries moved toward greater integration with the creation of the European Economic Community (EEC) in 1957, a customs union whose members allowed free trade among themselves and imposed a common external tariff on imported goods. However, trade in services remained outside the scope of

the EEC, as did many informal barriers to trade in goods, such as product standards and regulatory differences. The next institutional steps created a single European market for goods and services, along with capital and people. Today, the European Union is effectively free of barriers to trade, investment, and migration among its members. And 19 members of the EU share a common currency, the euro, with a common central bank, the European Central Bank (ECB).

Over the past decade, however, European integration has become more controversial. Many countries have political parties that are skeptical about or even opposed to their country's membership in the EU. The most striking demonstration of this was the June 2016 referendum in the United Kingdom in which British voters chose to leave the EU.

Some Europeans feel that their interests are not taken into consideration by EU officials, who are not directly accountable to national political movements. This feeling combines with a loss of confidence in EU institutions, which was intensified by the economic crisis that began in 2008. The eurozone debt crisis, along with an upsurge of immigration from the Middle East and North Africa, fed concerns that the European institutions were inadequate to the task of managing the complex conflicts of interests among and within member states.

The European Union remains a singular achievement—the first time in modern history that a large number of sovereign states have created a truly integrated single market for the movement of goods, capital, and people. Nonetheless, the EU confronts many difficult conflicts of interests that will tax its institutions over the coming decades.

The European single market allows produce from Spain to be sold alongside local produce in France without restrictions.

But the Americans are wary: the Europeans might find hidden ways to maintain their barriers, such as by imposing regulations that apply only to American crops. In fact, some American farmers argue that European bans on the import of genetically modified food, or of meat from animals whose feed contains hormones, are trade barriers in disguise. In other words, the Europeans might find ways to "cheat" on the agreement and gain greater access to the American market without providing anything substantial in return. The Europeans, for their part, have similar concerns: the United States, they fear, will promise them open markets but find devious ways to keep European goods out.

Given this threat, both the United States and the European Union decide not to take the chance, farm trade is not liberalized, and both sides are left worse off than they would have been with an agreement. This scenario is an example of how international trade bargaining problems can resemble a Prisoner's Dilemma (see the "Special Topic" appendix to Chapter 2, on p. 83): both sides would be better off cooperating to reduce trade barriers, but concern that the other side will cheat leads both sides to act noncooperatively, to their common detriment.

This sort of cooperation problem is common in trade relations among countries. To be sure, the logic of comparative advantage discussed earlier implies that countries would maximize their overall economic welfare by unilaterally liberalizing trade. However, governments respond to pressures other than that of the economy as a whole. For this reason, a government's first choice of trade policy is almost never to remove its trade barriers unilaterally; typically, it wants to get concessions from other countries in return for its own.

However, as the example of the Prisoner's Dilemma shows (see Chapter 2), it can be difficult for political actors to arrive at a mutually beneficial accord when there is no way to guarantee that all parties to the agreement will cooperate. Just as in the security relations among countries discussed in Chapters 3–5, in the international trade realm governments that want to collaborate may be hampered by the fear that they will be taken advantage of in an interaction that can have very high stakes. No government can take lightly the possibility that its farmers, companies, or workers might lose money or jobs because the government mismanaged an international trade negotiation. Countries face inherent difficulties in making credible commitments to abide by the terms of trade agreements; as in military matters, this can lead to a breakdown of trust and, eventually, an inability to cooperate.

Strategic problems can also arise when countries try to work out a common approach to a problem, such as which legal rules to use to govern trade. One of the most common difficulties arises when one country accuses another of unfairly subsidizing its exports with grants, loans, and other programs to raise profits artificially. Disputes in world trade often involve accusations that one country's exporters are *dumping* their goods—that is, selling them below the true cost of production in order to drive out competitors. Dumping is widely accepted to be an unfair trading practice, but it is extremely hard to define, let alone measure. Similarly, government subsidies to exporters encounter widespread disapproval. But such subsidies can take many indirect forms (such as regulation of shipping costs, complicated accounting or tax rules, or manipulation of the exchange rate), and there is often no easy way to determine whether, in fact, an actual subsidy is being used. In these cases, even where countries would like to work out their conflicts amicably, there may be serious disagreements about the standards to be used to govern fair trading relations.

For example, one of the longest-standing disputes in world trade has been between the United States and Canada, two countries with generally very friendly relations. Starting in the early 1980s, the U.S. government argued that the Canadian federal and provincial governments, which own most of the country's timber-bearing land, were charging lumber producers artificially low prices to harvest the wood. This would constitute an unfair subsidy to the country's exports of softwood lumber; the Canadians reject the charge. Both countries wanted to maintain their cooperative trade relations, but this cooperation was threatened by conflicting interpretations of trade rules. In these cases of coordination problems, the parties typically want to find a common position or standard but have trouble deciding which one is best.

Overcoming Problems of Strategic Interaction
The international politics of trade is full of examples of cooperation and coordination problems; it is also full of attempts to make it easier for governments to overcome these problems. In Chapter 2, we saw that several factors can facilitate cooperation and coordination: small numbers, information, repeated interaction, and linkage politics. These all affect international trade relations.

Small numbers make it easier for governments to monitor each others' behavior; there is likely to be less free riding among small groups of countries than in the world at large. An extreme version of this observation is the theory of *hegemonic stability*, which argues that the existence of a single very powerful nation facilitates the solution of problems of collective action and free riding; the hegemonic power is large and strong enough to be both willing and able to solve these problems for the world as a whole. In economic affairs, this approach argues that when there has been such a hegemonic power over the past two centuries (Great Britain after 1860 and the United States after 1945), trade liberalization was facilitated by the leadership of an overwhelmingly influential world economic power.

Less extreme versions of the approach suggest, more modestly, that smaller numbers of countries—privileged groups (see Chapter 2)—will find it easier to monitor and enforce trade agreements than will very large groups of nations or the world as a whole. Because of the greater ease of monitoring and enforcement, small numbers of countries are more likely to succeed at liberalizing trade.[22] This might help explain why so many trade agreements take the form of regional accords among a few neighboring nations, such as the European Union, NAFTA, and Mercosur.

Small numbers might also help explain why the United States and Canada have often been able to negotiate successfully even in the bitter dispute over softwood lumber, which involved billions of dollars and one of Canada's more important

---

22. For a reasoned summary, see David A. Lake, "Leadership, Hegemony, and the International Economy: Naked Emperor or Tattered Monarch with Potential?" *International Studies Quarterly* 37, no. 4 (December 1993): 459–89.

Mercosur began as a regional trade agreement among Argentina, Brazil, Paraguay, and Uruguay in 1991. However, it has not achieved the same level of success in the freer movement of goods, capital, or people as the European Union.

industries. In 1986 and again in 1996, despite long-standing conflict over whether Canada was, in fact, subsidizing its lumber industry, the two countries reached compromise agreements. In the first instance, the United States agreed to reduce its tariff on Canadian imports; in the second instance, Canada agreed to limit its exports to the United States.

Information can also be an important consideration in trade negotiations. Many failures of cooperation are due to fears of hidden actions—such as the fear that one government might use its superior knowledge of its own domestic conditions to take advantage of other governments. In the case of dumping and subsidies, decisions are often made by national bureaucratic agencies about which foreigners may know little.

For example, in 2001 the United States and Canada were unable to negotiate a renewal of the 1996 Softwood Lumber Agreement. Immediately after the agreement expired, the U.S. International Trade Commission and the Department of Commerce found that Canadian lumber was being subsidized, so the United States unilaterally imposed a 27 percent tariff on Canadian imports, triggering a new round of acrimonious conflict. If the Canadians had known about this finding, perhaps they might have reached an agreement with the Americans, but the Canadians did not have access to advance information about the American government's decision. This example suggests that transparency may lead to trade cooperation. It also suggests that establishing some manner by which partners can provide information to one another may facilitate cooperative relations.

Repeated interaction (iteration) between governments on a continuing basis provides a reason to avoid cheating, or even the appearance of cheating. The possibility that the collapse of a current deal might sour future deals can impose a powerful discipline on government behavior and can encourage greater efforts to cooperate. This is especially the case in a trading relationship, which is likely to go on indefinitely. By the same token, governments with a long history of dealing with one another are likely to have more information about each other—and, in good circumstances, more reason to trust one another.

Linking concessions granted in one arena to concessions received in another may also facilitate cooperation on trade. A government that would otherwise be uninterested in negotiating lower barriers in, say, steel might be willing to exchange concessions in steel if its partner gives it concessions in some other industry. Governments can, in other words, trade among trade policies—"giving" in an area they care less about, in return for "getting" in an area they care more about. These exchanges can benefit governments and their citizens. Countries might link agreements in trade (steel for apparel, for example), or they might link agreements in trade with agreements on something else, such as foreign aid or military cooperation.

All these considerations help explain why countries are more likely to have friendly, collaborative trade relations in some circumstances than in others. This is true of pairs or groups of countries: bilateral or regional trade agreements (RTAs) are more likely with smaller numbers, where information about the partners is readily available, where the partners have a long history of interaction, and where trade relations are linked to other economic or noneconomic relations. It may also be true for the world as a whole: when these conditions are met, at least for the leading countries in the international trading system, trade cooperation is more likely. But when there is great uncertainty about the true intentions of some of the major powers (such as Germany and Japan in the 1920s and 1930s), coupled with a real concern for the short term and the absence of a dense network of other relationships among the major powers, international trade cooperation is difficult or impossible.

Because it can be inherently difficult for governments to ensure cooperative trade relations among themselves, they have created international institutions that help overcome the variety of collective action and other strategic problems that have beset international trade relations. International institutions may indeed be the most powerful factor in affecting whether trade relations among countries are collaborative or conflictual. They run the gamut from global organizations, such as the WTO, to regional agreements, such as NAFTA, to bilateral treaties between countries. Most such institutional arrangements have the goal of facilitating trade cooperation among their member states.

International Institutions in International Trade

International organizations represent the principal systematic attempts to bring order to contemporary international trade policy. As we saw in Chapter 2, institutions can play an important part by providing a setting within which cooperation is facilitated. They can help mitigate all the problems that stand in the way of interstate cooperation on trade. Institutions can set standards of behavior that governments are expected to follow. They can gather information to assist member states in monitoring and enforcing compliance with their agreements. By providing an expectation of repeated interaction, they can restrain defection. International institutions can reduce the costs to governments of making joint decisions—a real problem in the very complex trade realm—and can help governments resolve disputes.

For all these reasons, over the years countries have developed institutional arrangements to facilitate their trade negotiations. One is the concept of **reciprocity**, by which a concession granted by one government is met by another—a sort of linkage politics that helps bind agreements. A more general provision of this nature has developed over the course of more than 100 years to serve a similar purpose: **most-favored nation (MFN) status**. Countries that grant one another MFN status agree to extend to each other the same concessions that they provide to all other nations with that status; for example, a tariff reduction given to one country is automatically given to all countries with MFN status. This system, called normal trade relations in the United States, serves to link negotiations between two countries to all their multilateral trade relations.

The World Trade Organization

The most important international institution in commercial relations has a global reach: the **World Trade Organization (WTO)**, which succeeded the **General Agreement on Tariffs and Trade (GATT)**. The GATT was created in 1947 as one of the original Bretton Woods institutions, and it oversaw a dramatic liberalization of trade relations, in particular among developed countries, for more than 40 years.[23] By the early 1990s, GATT members had come to believe that the GATT's somewhat loose structure was insufficient in an environment in which almost all countries—developed, developing, and formerly centrally planned—were joining the international trading system. The WTO, which opened its doors in 1995, is more structured, more formal, and more encompassing than the GATT, although its goal is very similar: to encourage the expansion of an open international trading system.

Both the GATT and the WTO have been enormously successful in their stated purpose of reducing barriers to trade among member nations, with world trade growing faster than world output for virtually all the postwar period. The principal achievement of both organizations has been to arrange a series of "rounds" during which member states negotiate multilateral reductions in trade barriers. The negotiations take place under a loose rule of reciprocity that balances the dollar value of concessions, which are then automatically extended to all other member states under the MFN rule. There are also rules about when and how countries can use safeguards to temporarily protect domestic industries.

Although all members of the WTO have a formally equal vote, in practice the negotiations are dominated by the largest trading states—in particular, the United States, the European Union (which negotiates as a single actor in the WTO), and

reciprocity

In international trade relations, a mutual agreement to lower tariffs and other barriers to trade. Reciprocity involves an implicit or explicit arrangement for one government to exchange trade-policy concessions with another.

most-favored nation (MFN) status

A status established by most modern trade agreements guaranteeing that the signatories will extend to each other any favorable trading terms offered in agreements with third parties.

World Trade Organization (WTO)

An institution created in 1995 to succeed the GATT and to govern international trade relations. The WTO encourages and polices the multilateral reduction of barriers to trade, and it oversees the resolution of trade disputes.

General Agreement on Tariffs and Trade (GATT)

An international institution created in 1947 in which member countries committed to reduce barriers to trade and to provide similar trading conditions to all other members. In 1995, the GATT was replaced by the WTO.

---

23. To be entirely accurate, the original Bretton Woods institution for trade was to be an "International Trade Organization," but it foundered and was never created; the GATT was an interim replacement that lasted far longer than its initiators expected.

Japan. The power of the largest members comes in part from their ability to set the agenda for negotiations. Their power also flows from the fact that they have more attractive outside options: they can more easily contemplate "going it alone" without the WTO. For all these reasons, developing countries have found it difficult to get their concerns onto the international trade agenda.

Conflicts between developed and developing nations have pervaded the most recent series of WTO negotiations, the Doha Round, which began with a meeting in Doha, Qatar, in 2001. Developing nations have accused the rich world of ignoring their concerns. Their principal demand has been for the liberalization of agricultural trade, as many developing countries would benefit from greater access to rich-country markets for food. Such liberalization has been blocked, however, by politically powerful farmers in the developed countries. For their part, developed countries would like greater liberalization of trade in services—most developed countries are major exporters of such services as finance and telecommunications—and stricter rules to protect intellectual property. The Doha Round has been stalled for many years, and there are widespread fears that it may never be completed.

The Doha Round has been a disappointment, and unequal power among countries has been a source of conflict; nonetheless, most WTO member states accept that the WTO, like the GATT before it, facilitates international cooperation: it helps to set standards of behavior, to verify compliance, to ease joint decision making, and to resolve disputes. The WTO makes available a great deal of information about trade and trade policies, including monitoring national compliance with international agreements.

The WTO monitors a country's compliance in two primary ways. First, members must report actions taken to restrict trade, as well as any RTAs they may enter into

Although the WTO has lowered barriers to international trade, it has often provoked opposition from actors whose interests may be harmed by trade liberalization. The 2009 demonstrations against the WTO in Geneva turned violent as angry protesters torched cars.

(such as NAFTA). Second, countries that believe that foreign exporters or importers are not complying with the rules can file a complaint with the WTO. Complaints are referred to the Dispute Settlement Body, composed of all member states, which then appoints a panel of experts in consultation with all parties to the dispute. The panel investigates the alleged rule violation and issues a report that becomes a ruling within 60 days. Each side can appeal (but not block) the ruling to the WTO's standing seven-member Appellate Body. If not overturned, the ruling becomes binding. A country held to be in violation of WTO rules must bring its policy into conformity with the rules; if it does not, it is subject to sanctions authorized by the organization itself.

However, Donald Trump was highly critical of the WTO and other trade agreements and institutions in his presidential campaign, and the Trump administration has expressed a desire to renegotiate American involvement in these organizations. This position is unpopular with most of the country's trading partners and has led to fears that the international trading regime might begin to unravel, since the United States has typically been a supporter of the WTO.

As the world's largest trader, the United States is the most frequent defendant at the WTO. The United States has usually abided by WTO rules and rulings, even when the complainant is a small country like Costa Rica that the United States could easily ignore. The reason probably is that previous American administrations believed that the United States was more likely to be a complainant than a target and wanted rulings in its favor to be obeyed, which was less likely to occur if the United States itself did not respect WTO rulings. The Trump administration has indicated that it believes the system has not, in fact, worked in America's best interests, and that it would like to see both the WTO and America's regional trade agreements reworked.

The Trump administration's stance has given rise to concerns in other countries. States usually obey the rules of the WTO because they value the WTO's promotion of an open trading system. Some believe that defiance of WTO rules and decisions, and attempts to restructure America's role in the WTO, would threaten the whole system of trade rules and the gains from trade.

Regional Trade Agreements   In addition to the WTO—and perhaps in reaction to some of the concerns about its organization and progress—many similar institutions have arisen at the regional level. In fact, the number and range of **regional trade agreements (RTAs)** has grown very rapidly in the past 20 years, and by 2011 the WTO counted 489 RTAs in force (Map 7.1). The three most prominent are the European Union, which started in 1958 as a customs union of 6 countries and now encompasses 28 nations in a single market; NAFTA, made up of the United States, Canada, and Mexico; and Mercosur, originally comprising Argentina, Brazil, Paraguay, and Uruguay. There are many other such RTAs, of varying size and involving varying degrees of commitment to openness among their members. Many are bilateral, involving only two countries; others involve dozens of countries.[24]

regional trade agreements (RTAs)

Agreements among three or more countries in a region to reduce barriers to trade among themselves.

---

24. For more information on RTAs, see the WTO's RTA website at www.wto.org/english/tratop_e/region_e/region_e.htm (accessed 01/02/12).

MAP 7.1 *Selected RTAs*

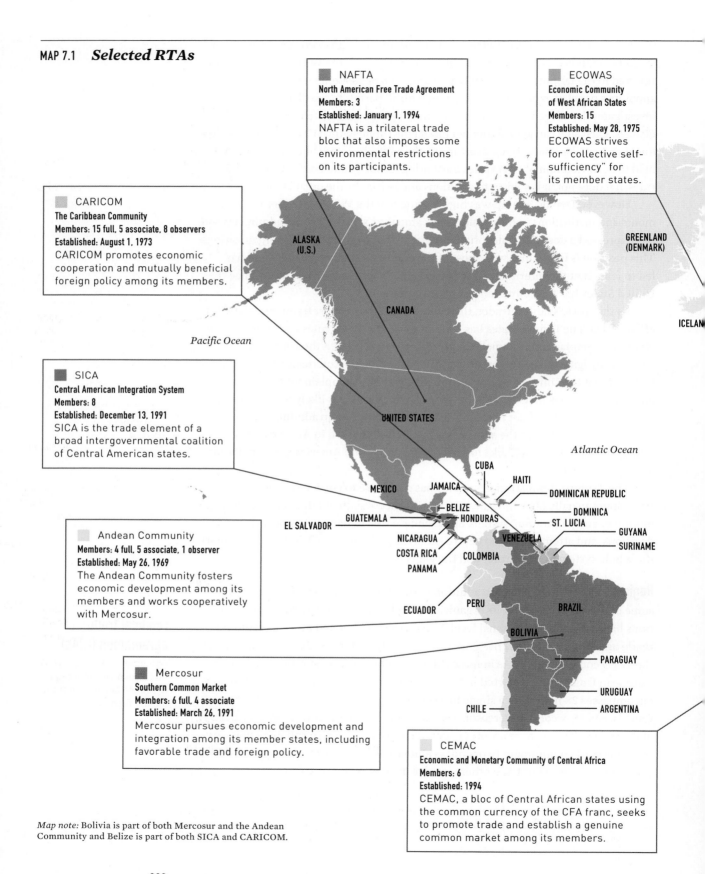

NAFTA
North American Free Trade Agreement
Members: 3
Established: January 1, 1994
NAFTA is a trilateral trade bloc that also imposes some environmental restrictions on its participants.

ECOWAS
Economic Community of West African States
Members: 15
Established: May 28, 1975
ECOWAS strives for "collective self-sufficiency" for its member states.

CARICOM
The Caribbean Community
Members: 15 full, 5 associate, 8 observers
Established: August 1, 1973
CARICOM promotes economic cooperation and mutually beneficial foreign policy among its members.

SICA
Central American Integration System
Members: 8
Established: December 13, 1991
SICA is the trade element of a broad intergovernmental coalition of Central American states.

Andean Community
Members: 4 full, 5 associate, 1 observer
Established: May 26, 1969
The Andean Community fosters economic development among its members and works cooperatively with Mercosur.

Mercosur
Southern Common Market
Members: 6 full, 4 associate
Established: March 26, 1991
Mercosur pursues economic development and integration among its member states, including favorable trade and foreign policy.

CEMAC
Economic and Monetary Community of Central Africa
Members: 6
Established: 1994
CEMAC, a bloc of Central African states using the common currency of the CFA franc, seeks to promote trade and establish a genuine common market among its members.

Pacific Ocean

Atlantic Ocean

ALASKA (U.S.)

CANADA

UNITED STATES

GREENLAND (DENMARK)

ICELAN

MEXICO

CUBA

JAMAICA

HAITI

DOMINICAN REPUBLIC

BELIZE

DOMINICA

GUATEMALA

HONDURAS

ST. LUCIA

EL SALVADOR

NICARAGUA

COSTA RICA

VENEZUELA

GUYANA

SURINAME

PANAMA

COLOMBIA

ECUADOR

PERU

BRAZIL

BOLIVIA

PARAGUAY

URUGUAY

CHILE

ARGENTINA

Map note: Bolivia is part of both Mercosur and the Andean Community and Belize is part of both SICA and CARICOM.

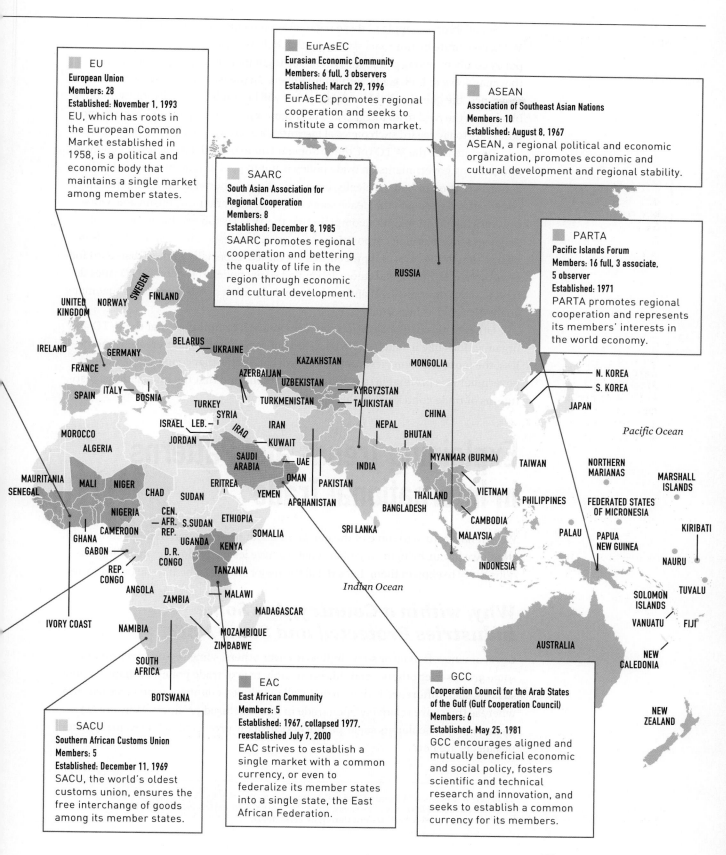

EU
European Union
Members: 28
Established: November 1, 1993
EU, which has roots in the European Common Market established in 1958, is a political and economic body that maintains a single market among member states.

EurAsEC
Eurasian Economic Community
Members: 6 full, 3 observers
Established: March 29, 1996
EurAsEC promotes regional cooperation and seeks to institute a common market.

ASEAN
Association of Southeast Asian Nations
Members: 10
Established: August 8, 1967
ASEAN, a regional political and economic organization, promotes economic and cultural development and regional stability.

SAARC
South Asian Association for Regional Cooperation
Members: 8
Established: December 8, 1985
SAARC promotes regional cooperation and bettering the quality of life in the region through economic and cultural development.

PARTA
Pacific Islands Forum
Members: 16 full, 3 associate, 5 observer
Established: 1971
PARTA promotes regional cooperation and represents its members' interests in the world economy.

SACU
Southern African Customs Union
Members: 5
Established: December 11, 1969
SACU, the world's oldest customs union, ensures the free interchange of goods among its member states.

EAC
East African Community
Members: 5
Established: 1967, collapsed 1977, reestablished July 7, 2000
EAC strives to establish a single market with a common currency, or even to federalize its member states into a single state, the East African Federation.

GCC
Cooperation Council for the Arab States of the Gulf (Gulf Cooperation Council)
Members: 6
Established: May 25, 1981
GCC encourages aligned and mutually beneficial economic and social policy, fosters scientific and technical research and innovation, and seeks to establish a common currency for its members.

Map labels:
SWEDEN, FINLAND, NORWAY, UNITED KINGDOM, IRELAND, GERMANY, FRANCE, SPAIN, ITALY, BOSNIA, BELARUS, UKRAINE, KAZAKHSTAN, AZERBAIJAN, UZBEKISTAN, TURKMENISTAN, KYRGYZSTAN, TAJIKISTAN, MONGOLIA, RUSSIA, CHINA, N. KOREA, S. KOREA, JAPAN, TURKEY, SYRIA, LEB., ISRAEL, JORDAN, IRAQ, IRAN, KUWAIT, SAUDI ARABIA, UAE, OMAN, YEMEN, AFGHANISTAN, PAKISTAN, NEPAL, BHUTAN, INDIA, BANGLADESH, MYANMAR (BURMA), THAILAND, VIETNAM, CAMBODIA, SRI LANKA, MALAYSIA, PHILIPPINES, TAIWAN, PALAU, INDONESIA, AUSTRALIA, NEW ZEALAND, NEW CALEDONIA, PAPUA NEW GUINEA, NORTHERN MARIANAS, FEDERATED STATES OF MICRONESIA, MARSHALL ISLANDS, KIRIBATI, NAURU, TUVALU, SOLOMON ISLANDS, VANUATU, FIJI, MOROCCO, ALGERIA, MAURITANIA, SENEGAL, MALI, NIGER, CHAD, SUDAN, ERITREA, NIGERIA, CEN. AFR. REP., S. SUDAN, ETHIOPIA, SOMALIA, CAMEROON, GHANA, GABON, REP. CONGO, D.R. CONGO, UGANDA, KENYA, TANZANIA, ANGOLA, ZAMBIA, MALAWI, MADAGASCAR, MOZAMBIQUE, ZIMBABWE, NAMIBIA, BOTSWANA, SOUTH AFRICA, IVORY COAST

Ocean labels: Pacific Ocean, Indian Ocean

Some observers applaud these regional agreements, arguing that they, like the WTO, constitute institutional structures that help mediate or avoid divisive trade-policy conflicts among countries. Others see them more negatively, believing that they may serve to limit trade with nonmembers. In the words of economist Robert Lawrence, the question is whether the RTAs will be "building blocks" or "stumbling blocks" on the road to an integrated world economy.[25] While questions remain, most observers today regard such regional institutions as complementary to the WTO.

To state that the WTO (or the European Union or NAFTA) facilitates cooperation among governments on trade policy is not to pass judgment on whether its actions are good or bad—ethically, economically, or otherwise. Governments may cooperate for purposes that leave some consumers, workers, or businesses worse off. Antiglobalization critics complain that the WTO is too pro-business, that it privileges international corporations over other interests. Those on the left often charge that WTO rules and procedures are biased, especially in their disregard for environmental, health and safety, labor, and social policies. Indeed, WTO rules do tend to focus on trade itself and exclude consideration of other concerns that many analysts regard as important.

Other critics of globalization, such as Donald Trump, argue that the WTO and organizations like it—such as NAFTA—do not serve American interests. Nonetheless, the most common view around the world remains that cooperation among governments is preferable to conflict among them, and that the international institutions of trade contribute to this cooperation.

Explaining Trends and Patterns in International Trade

We can now return to some of the questions about international trade relations with which we began, bringing together what we have learned from the preceding sections to try to explain them. Let's recall the major ways in which trade policies vary.

Why, within a Country, Are Some Industries Protected and Some Not?

Governments often favor some industries over others, some regions over others, some groups over others—and this is certainly true of trade policy. Perhaps the most striking such difference is that virtually all developed countries protect agriculture, whereas they have relatively open trade in manufactured products. Why are U.S. farmers (in particular, its sugar producers) strongly protected, while so many other producers are not?

---

25. Robert Z. Lawrence, "Emerging Regional Arrangements: Building Blocks or Stumbling Blocks?" in *Finance and the International Economy*, vol. 5, *The AMEX Bank Review Prize Essays*, ed. Richard O'Brien, 25–35 (New York: Oxford University Press, 1991).

We can look at the actors involved and their interests to determine which groups or industries are most likely to benefit from protection. Land is scarce in most developed countries, certainly relative to capital and skilled labor; this explains why their farmers are protectionist. We can then explore how well the actors are able to overcome their collective action problems; the more cohesive and powerful interests are likely to get more government support. Farmers are well organized, whereas consumers of food are rarely organized at all. Perhaps the country's political institutions are biased for or against some regions, classes, or industries. Many nations' electoral institutions favor farm regions over cities, as does the U.S. Senate, which allots a sparsely populated farm state the same number of senators (two) as a densely populated, mostly urban state. Farmers and their parties are often pivotal in parliamentary systems, as they occupy the crucial center of the political spectrum.

All these considerations help explain why some sectors receive more trade protection than others and, in particular, why farmers in rich countries are so commonly favored. In the case of American sugar producers, they have very high stakes in protection—the country's sugar farms might shut down without it—and their numbers are small enough to be extremely well organized and well represented in Congress. Figure 7.2 shows selected examples reflecting the protection of farmers in various countries.

Why Have National Trade Policies Varied over Time?

There have been many striking instances of countries shifting from openness to closure or from protectionism to trade liberalization. The United States in the 1920s was one of the most protectionist industrial nations on earth; starting after 1945, however, it led the Western world toward substantial trade liberalization. More recently, the Trump administration has shown itself to be sympathetic to higher levels of trade protection (see "Controversy" on p. 332). How can we explain such shifts?

Figure source: OECD, Producer and Consumer Support Estimates, www.oecd.org/unitedstates/producerandconsumersupportestimatesdatabase.htm#tables (accessed 09/07/17).

FIGURE 7.2 *Agricultural Subsidies in Selected Countries, 2016*

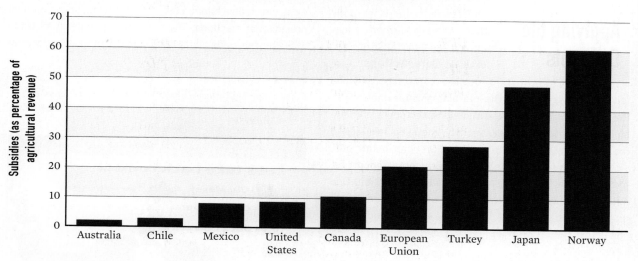

What Should Be Done When International Trade Harms Workers?

The 2016 American presidential election may have been the most anti-trade election campaign in the United States since the 1930s. Democratic candidate Bernie Sanders claimed that "trade is . . . a significant reason why Americans are working longer hours for low wages and why we are seeing our jobs go to China and other low-wage countries."[a] Republican Donald Trump expressed similar views, calling NAFTA "the worst trade deal in history" and arguing that "China's entrance into the World Trade Organization . . . enabled the greatest job theft in the history of our country."[b]

Such views are hardly unique to the United States. In the United Kingdom, many Britons voted to leave the European Union in June 2016, in part because of the EU's perceived impact on British workers. Elsewhere in the European Union, many trade union leaders oppose new international trade deals, such as one negotiated with Canada in 2017, because they believed it could threaten labor rights. What should be done when workers are hurt by international trade?

Applying the Concepts

Trade policy often divides actors in society: while some powerful groups have a strong **interest** in international trade and its benefits, there are many others who are harmed by foreign competition. These groups' domestic **interactions** have recently become especially bitter. The precise nature of the interactions often depends on the **institutions** that determine whether policy is made by the legislature, the bureaucracy, the executive, or—in the case of the European Union—by European institutions.

In Europe, the United States, and other countries, many workers have been hurt by trade competition. One influential study found that regions of the United States more exposed to imports from China experienced higher unemployment, lower wages, and more political polarization than other regions.[c] But we also know that many people, including many American workers, have an interest in maintaining or expanding trade. A government study found that exports created nearly 12 million American jobs in 2015.[d] So, this topic pits those with an interest in trade against those who are hurt by it.

How should a society weigh the positive effects of trade on some workers against the negative effects on others? These issues have informed political battles between supporters and opponents of trade in many different political arenas. Usually these interactions are limited to legislative or bureaucratic battles among special interests, largely out of the public eye. However, the economic crisis that began in 2008 heightened concerns about job losses in manufacturing due to import competition. Politicians responded to these concerns: those in areas more affected by imports became more protectionist—or they lost elections.[e]

Amid a broader backlash against globalization in advanced industrial countries, opposition to trade became a prominent issue in the 2016 American presidential race. Many of the communities most harmed by trade are in the American "rust belt"—industrial states of the Midwest, which also happen to be crucial swing states in most presidential elections. The general unpopularity of trade in these states contributed to Donald Trump's presidential

British member of Parliament Boris Johnson encouraged voters to support Brexit as a means for the United Kingdom to take back control of its trade policy.

In the 2016 U.S. presidential election, Donald Trump mobilized supporters in rust-belt states with a "Buy American, Hire American" platform.

victory and seemed to presage a more protectionist foreign economic policy in the United States.

However, in the United States the institutional separation of powers means that trade policy is determined not only by the president, but also by Congress and by such other trade-policy institutions as the International Trade Commission. Although President Trump promised higher trade barriers, individual members of Congress have powerful, perhaps competing incentives to represent their constituents. Rust-belt swing states may be especially important in a presidential election season, but in the making of trade policy, representatives from other states attempt to protect their own constituents—whether that means endorsing trade protection or opposing it.

Institutions have a significant influence on trade policy in other countries as well. One of the sources of British discontent with the European Union was that trade policy was being made by European, not British, institutions—within which the United Kingdom was only one among many actors.

Some analysts suggest an alternative to making the difficult choice between winners and losers from trade. If trade makes a country as a whole better off—as most economists believe—then the government should tax the winnings of the beneficiaries and use the revenue to compensate the victims. In this way, the country gains from trade, while those individuals and regions that are hurt are helped to overcome its negative effects.

This *Pareto improvement* makes theoretical sense, but in practice it is very difficult to overcome conflicts of interest mobilized by trade. In the United States, these conflicts have typically led to political polarization. But other countries, in particular some in northern Europe, have developed strong social and public institutions that address these concerns. These governments provide support for workers hurt by trade, such as retraining programs and assistance finding new jobs, which seems to limit political conflict. American politicians and voters have not typically supported these more active government responses to the social effects of trade. Perhaps, however, they will be a more prominent part of the political agenda as conflicts over the country's trade relations continue.

a. "Bernie Sanders on Free Trade," OnTheIssues, www.ontheissues.org/2016/Bernie_Sanders_Free_Trade.htm (accessed 07/24/17).

b. "Full Transcript: Donald Trump's Jobs Plan Speech," *Politico*, June 28, 2016, www.politico.com/story/2016/06/full-transcript-trump-job-plan-speech-224891.

c. David Autor, David Dorn, and Gordon Hanson, "The China Syndrome: Local Labor Effects of Import Competition in the United States," *American Economic Review* 103, no. 6 (October 2013): 2121–68; and David Autor, David Dorn, Gordon Hanson, and Kaveh Majlesi, "Importing Political Polarization? The Electoral Consequences of Rising Trade Exposure," December 2016, https://economics.mit.edu/files/11499.

d. Chris Rasmussen and Susan Xu, "Jobs Supported by Export Destination 2015," Department of Commerce, Office of Trade and Economic Analysis, November 8, 2016, http://trade.gov/mas/ian/build/groups/public/@tg_ian/documents/webcontent/tg_ian_005508.pdf.

e. James J. Feigenbaum and Andrew B. Hall, "How Legislators Respond to Localized Economic Shocks," *Journal of Politics* 77, no. 4 (October 2015): 1012–30.

Thinking Analytically

1. Why does international trade benefit some groups within a country more than others? Which groups tend to have an interest in protectionism? And which tend to have an interest in freer trade?

2. In what way do programs that mitigate the negative impacts of trade create a Pareto improvement? Why do you think there is relatively little support for such programs in the United States?

Interests may change; for example, a nation's ability to compete in world markets might improve, giving rise to more actors favorable to trade and reducing the concerns of actors opposed to trade. Institutions may change too: perhaps democratization gives more pro-trade groups, such as consumers, access to political influence and reduces a bias toward protectionist producers. Some such national changes may be driven by changes at the international level that affect the nation in question, such as a dramatic change in the price of its principal export product. The winners and losers from trade policy may change in such a way that affects national policy, as when one factor becomes more abundant or one industrial sector develops powerful export interests. And national political institutions can affect policy by strengthening the hands of groups that want to push policy in a certain direction.

The American experience is an example of how a country's policies can shift from very high levels of trade protection to support for liberalization—and how they might be shifting back. The turn away from protection after World War II was undoubtedly assisted by the wartime destruction of foreign economies: the United States faced very little serious industrial competition, which made it relatively easy for the country to opt for trade liberalization.

As the Cold War began, the geopolitical concerns associated with a desire to bind together a pro-American Western alliance reinforced support for an open Western trading system. At the same time, the rise of powerful American manufacturing industries interested in exporting and in investing overseas increased the range of actors in support of economic integration. This too was encouraged by institutional changes in the making of American trade policy in the 1930s, which gave the generally more trade-friendly president greater influence than the usually relatively protectionist Congress. All these factors and more may have affected American policy.

Why might trade protection have become more popular in the United States since 2000? Interests may have changed or become more intense: the rise of China as a trading power has certainly put major new pressures on many American industries and workers. Institutions play a role as well, since many of those most harmed by trade competition are in swing states in the American Midwest that play a major role in presidential elections. It remains to be seen whether these trends will lead to a thoroughgoing and lasting reorientation of American trade policy, and of the United States' place in the world trading order.

Scholars continue to present arguments and evidence for and against these hypotheses. They may not, in fact, be mutually exclusive. National policy changes may be better explained in some cases by the global context, in others by the domestic interests engaged, and in still others by domestic institutions.

Why Do Some Countries Have Higher Trade Barriers Than Others?

Even within a common international trading system, national policies can differ. In the late 1930s, as the United States and some Western European nations began moving away from trade protection and toward liberalization, most other industrial

Research has shown that democratization in developing countries is often associated with trade liberalization. Bolivia, which transitioned to democracy in the 1980s, has seen a significant increase in its exports of zinc and other mined minerals.

countries—especially Germany, Italy, and Japan—erected extremely high barriers to trade. In the 1980s, China became a global exporting powerhouse while many other developing nations remained very closed to trade.

Again, actors and their interests matter: these differences among nations may be driven by different factor endowments or sectoral features. In line with the Stolper-Samuelson approach, for example, the interests of landowners in two countries might be diametrically opposed: in favor of trade in a land-rich country, opposed to it in a land-poor country. If identical pro-farmer parties were in power in the two nations, one would reduce trade barriers while the other would raise them. A country whose economy is dominated by well-organized exporters will tend to be less protectionist than one that has very few exporters. In today's world, in which major portions of world trade are managed by huge international corporations, the role of individual firms can also have an impact on national trade policies.

The source of these differences, however, might be in national institutions, such as a party system or legislative structures biased in favor of the protectionist class (scarce factor) or protectionist sectors and regions, or—on the other hand—in favor of powerful exporting companies. A democracy might give labor or consumers more influence than a dictatorship would. (See "How Do We Know?" on p. 336 for the connection between democracy and free trade in developing countries.) Anything that affects the domestic interests, institutions, or interactions of a country may well affect its trade policies.

Why the Move to Free Trade in Developing Countries?

Beginning in the 1980s, many developing countries around the world reduced their barriers to trade and encouraged their producers to sell into global markets. One by one, countries as diverse as the Philippines, Bangladesh, Mexico, and Ghana reduced tariffs on imported manufactured goods and agricultural products and shifted to an export-oriented development strategy. This change puzzled many observers who believed that entrenched special interests would prevent governments in these countries from opening their economies to foreign competition and directing their industries toward foreign markets.

Helen Milner and Keiko Kubota tackled this important puzzle by demonstrating a connection between trade liberalization and democratization.[a] In authoritarian countries in which the majority of citizens cannot vote, many people who would benefit from free trade—such as unskilled workers in a labor-abundant country—are not able to directly influence the government's trade policies. Elites, however, such as owners of scarce capital and land, might have special channels in which to press the government for continued trade protection. Developing countries sustained high average tariff levels through the 1980s, creating a protectionist equilibrium. Milner and Kubota argue that the process of democratization—defined as a movement toward majority rule with universal voting in competitive elections—disturbed this historical equilibrium.

After a country transforms from autocratic rule to democracy, elected leaders must adjust their policies to respond to the preferences of the expanded electorate. Previously disenfranchised groups, including women, unskilled workers, and individuals who do not own land, are suddenly able to assert their preferences and influence trade policy. As the authors note: "Democratic political competition meant that leaders were likely to liberalize trade to appeal to these new groups to ensure their political survival."[b]

Testing this argument was no easy task. First, Milner and Kubota needed to find data on trade policy for a large number of developing countries. Trade-policy data for each country and each year over a long period are difficult to find because there are so many different ways to restrict trade, including tariffs, quotas, regulations, and other tools. The authors settled on two different measures: the average statutory tariff rate (used in Figure A), and a simpler binary indicator that takes the value of 1 (liberalized trade) if a variety of trade restrictions fall below certain thresholds, and 0 otherwise.

Second, the authors had to find a reliable measure of democracy. Here, they used a well-regarded index of democratization, from the Polity Project, that measures whether or not countries have regular competitive elections, universal suffrage, and a number of other indicators. Using these measures and a series of statistical models, the authors found that as countries transition to democratic rule, they are more likely to reduce their trade barriers.

a. Helen V. Milner and Keiko Kubota, "Why the Move to Free Trade? Democracy and Trade Policy in Developing Countries," *International Organization* 49, no. 1 (Winter 2005): 107–43.

b. Milner and Kubota, "Why the Move to Free Trade?" 113.

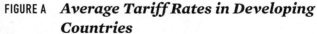

FIGURE A *Average Tariff Rates in Developing Countries*

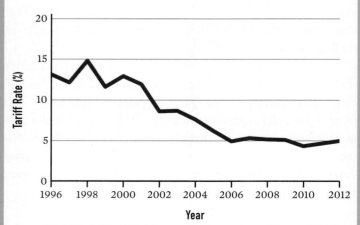

Source: World Bank, World Development Indicators, https://data.worldbank.org/indicator/TM.TAX.MRCH.WM.AR.ZS?locations=XO (accessed 1/3/18).

Why Has the World Trading Order Been More or Less Open at Different Times?

Global trends are usually best explained by international factors, and trade is no exception. Three causes of the ebb and flow of open trade relations are most prominent: international economic conditions, the role of one or a few very large countries, and the creation of international institutions. Forbidding world economic conditions in the 1930s were a major source of the protectionist turn of many countries' trade policies, just as global economic growth in the 1990s encouraged trade liberalization among developing and formerly communist countries, while the crisis that began in 2008 led to an upsurge in protectionist sentiment in many nations. The ability of one or a few large countries to organize a leadership role in international trade relations—Britain and France in the late nineteenth century, the United States and its principal allies after World War II— also appears to have been important in affecting global trade, which means that the change in American policies may remake the trading system. The presence of such institutions as the WTO has helped countries overcome some of the problems of cooperation that bedevil international trade relations, encouraging and facilitating collaborative trade ties among governments; current challenges to these institutions may lead to an erosion of these collaborative ties.

Conclusion: Trade and Politics

International trade is the centerpiece of international economic relations, and government policies toward trade have long been among the most hotly contested. They are controversial *within a country*, as supporters and opponents of freer trade clash. Trade policies can also be controversial *among countries*, as governments contend over their respective policies. This contention often breeds further discord; as the American statesman Cordell Hull said of the 1930s: "The political line-up followed the economic line-up."[26]

National policies toward foreign trade have been important to the development of the world economy and to international politics more generally. How open a nation is to trade affects its pattern of economic and social development, as well as its relations with other nations. In turn, a country's trade policies are determined by the nature of its prevailing economic interests and political institutions, and by its interactions with other nations. Today, international trade has become one of the more contentious issues in many nations—including, prominently, the United States—and the future of the international trading system is very much an open question.

---

26. Quoted in Gardner, *Sterling-Dollar Diplomacy*, 9.

Study Tool Kit

Interests, Interactions, and Institutions in Context

- Economists are virtually unanimous in concluding that international trade brings important benefits and that reducing trade barriers—trade liberalization—is good for a nation's economy.

- While trade may be beneficial for a country as a whole, it can harm the interests of groups and individuals in the society. Trade can create both winners and losers.

- The nature of a country's economy determines which groups have an interest in expanding or restricting trade with the rest of the world. National political institutions shape the outcomes when these interests come into conflict.

- The politics of international trade also involves strategic interaction among national governments. Governments can face difficult problems of bargaining and cooperation, which sometimes lead to trade conflicts among nations.

- The institutions of the international trading system can facilitate cooperation among governments as they confront the demands of both their own constituents and their foreign counterparts.

Key Terms

For Further Reading

Chase, Kerry. *Trading Blocs: States, Firms, and Regions in the World Economy.* **Ann Arbor: University of Michigan Press, 2005.** Describes and analyzes why countries decide to form RTAs such as NAFTA and the European Union.

Davis, Christina L. *Why Adjudicate? Enforcing Trade Rules in the WTO.* **Princeton, NJ: Princeton University Press, 2012.** Analyzes why countries tend to obey the WTO's dispute settlements, and more generally how international institutions contribute to more cooperative trade relations.

Destler, I. M. *American Trade Politics.* **4th ed. Washington, DC: Peterson Institute for International Economics, 2005.** Surveys and analyzes the political economy of trade policy in the United States.

Guisinger, Alexandra. *American Opinion on Trade: Preferences without Politics.* **Oxford: Oxford University Press, 2017.** An innovative look at how to understand the contradictory nature of American public opinion on trade relations, particularly relevant in light of current debates.

Hiscox, Michael. *International Trade and Political Conflict: Commerce, Coalitions, and Mobility.* **Princeton, NJ: Princeton University Press, 2002.** Evaluates the relative importance of factoral (class) and sectoral (industry) demands for protection and of variation among these considerations over time.

Hoekman, Bernard, and Michel M. Kostecki. *The Political Economy of the World Trading System.* **3rd ed. New York: Oxford University Press, 2009.** Comprehensive overview of the structure and functioning of the WTO and international institutions in the international trade arena.

Irwin, Douglas A. *Free Trade Under Fire.* **4th ed. Princeton, NJ: Princeton University Press, 2015.** Makes a strong argument for trade liberalization, addressing many common sources of opposition.

Mansfield, Edward D., and Helen V. Milner. *Votes, Vetoes, and the Political Economy of International Trade Agreements.* **Princeton, NJ: Princeton University Press, 2012.** Analyzes the domestic political forces that lead countries to undertake RTAs.

Rodrik, Dani. *Straight Talk on Trade: Ideas for a Sane World Economy.* **Princeton, NJ: Princeton University Press, 2017.** A leading economist assesses current debates over world trade, and the best ways policies might address them.

Rogowski, Ronald. *Commerce and Coalitions: How Trade Affects Domestic Political Alignments.* **Princeton, NJ: Princeton University Press, 1989.** Develops an analysis, based on the Stolper-Samuelson theorem, of how trade affects politics within nations.

Comparative Advantage and the Political Economy of Trade

Economists generally agree that international trade is good for the aggregate welfare of societies. Where does this consensus come from? In this appendix we introduce the concept of comparative advantage, which for centuries has been the backbone of economic thinking on international trade. We also illustrate the redistributive and welfare effects of opening the domestic economy to international trade and the countervailing effects of imposing a tariff.

Comparative Advantage

At the heart of economic analyses of international trade is *comparative advantage*. In short, the idea of comparative advantage implies that all countries benefit from trade if each country specializes in the production of certain goods. Which goods should countries produce? Economist David Ricardo[a] provided the straightforward answer in the early 1800s: countries should focus their production only on goods that they can produce most efficiently relative to other goods. If a country is good at mining copper or growing coffee beans or producing steel, then it should focus its productive capacities on producing these goods and rely on international trade to obtain all the other goods that it needs.

What if a country is not very good at producing anything? To answer this question, it is important to distinguish between *absolute advantage* and comparative advantage. A country has an absolute advantage if it can produce a good more efficiently than any other country. Comparative advantage, on the other hand, is determined within a country: of all the possible goods that a country might produce, it can produce some more efficiently than others. This means that *all* countries have a comparative advantage in something. A country might not be the most efficient in the world at producing coffee, but it still has a comparative advantage in coffee if it can produce coffee more efficiently than steel, airplanes, or any other good.

Consider the following example used by Ricardo himself to explain the concept of comparative advantage. Assume that there are two countries in the world, Portugal and England, and that these two countries can produce only cloth and wine. Further assume that the only input in the production process is labor, such that one unit of each good (a bolt of cloth or a barrel of wine) has a cost in man-hours. For example, in England it takes 15 man-hours to produce a bolt of cloth and 30 man-hours to produce a barrel of wine. In Portugal, it takes 10 man-hours to

---

a. The idea of comparative advantage—not the term itself—was introduced by David Ricardo in Chapter 7 of his *On the Principles of Political Economy and Taxation*, www.econlib.org/library/Ricardo/ricPCover.html (accessed 01/10/12).

COUNTRY	CLOTH	WINE
	Cost in Man–Hours per Bolt	Cost in Man–Hours per Barrel
England	15	30
Portugal	10	15

produce a bolt of cloth and 15 man-hours to produce a barrel of wine. Note that it takes fewer man-hours to produce both cloth and wine in Portugal than in England; indeed, in this example, Portugal has an absolute advantage in the production of both goods, cloth and wine (Table A.1).

To understand the impact of each country's choice of which goods to produce, it is helpful to examine the *opportunity cost of production*. This is the value that a country forgoes in order to make one product rather than another. The resources (in this example, labor) that each nation uses to make cloth are unavailable to make wine, so the country must forgo a certain amount of wine in order to make cloth. How many bolts of cloth must a country give up to produce a barrel of wine, and vice versa?

England must give up two bolts of cloth to produce an additional barrel of wine (30 ÷ 15); alternatively, it can give up a half barrel of wine to produce a bolt of cloth (15 ÷ 30). In contrast, Portugal must give up one and a half bolts of cloth to produce an additional barrel of wine; alternatively, it can give up two-thirds of a barrel of wine to produce an additional bolt of cloth. Table A.2 presents these results.

Note that the opportunity cost of producing cloth is lower in England than in Portugal, whereas the opportunity cost of producing wine is lower in Portugal than in England. From these figures we can conclude that England has a comparative advantage in the production of cloth, and Portugal has a comparative advantage in the production of wine.

What happens if these two countries engage in international trade? If England focuses all its man-hours on producing cloth, and Portugal does the same for wine, then the total world production of cloth and wine will be considerably higher than

TABLE A.2

COUNTRY	OPPORTUNITY COST OF PRODUCING . . .	
	One Bolt of Cloth	One Barrel of Wine
England	$1/2$ barrel of wine	2 bolts of cloth
Portugal	$2/3$ barrel of wine	$1^1/_2$ bolts of cloth

if the two countries did not specialize or engage in trade. Ricardo's simple model tells us that international trade based on comparative advantage increases aggregate welfare, measured by the total amount of goods produced in this two-country world. The increase in aggregate welfare occurs even though England does not have an absolute advantage in the production of either good.

Distributional and Welfare Effects of Trade

Economists largely agree that international trade makes society as a whole better off, whereas tariffs and other forms of trade protection are inefficient and costly for societies. A few simple graphs can illustrate the logic behind these claims. Consider first a country in a state of autarky, in which there is no international trade. The domestic price of any good is therefore determined by the intersection of the two lines of domestic supply and domestic demand. All else being equal, producers will supply more of a good as its price increases, and consumers will demand more of a good as its price falls. Therefore, the supply line slopes upward and the demand line slopes downward. The intersection indicates the good's domestic price (P) and quantity demanded (Q), as shown in Figure A.1.

The effects of the production of the good in autarky are measured by the concepts of *consumer surplus* and *producer surplus*. Consider first the fate of consumers. The downward-sloping demand line means that the lower the price, the more people demand the good. The shaded region represents the aggregate welfare benefit for consumers; it is called a surplus because it represents the gains to consumers who would be willing to pay more than P for the good. Similarly, there are some producers in the country who would happily supply the good at a lower price than P. The region beneath P and bounded by the two lines represents the producer surplus. This region captures the gains to

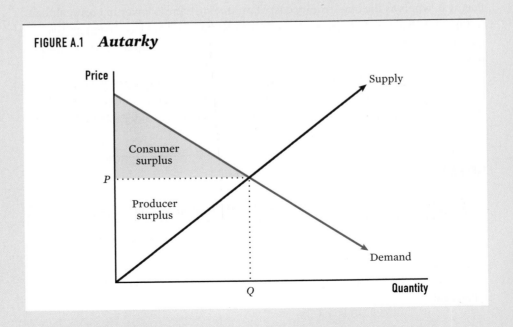

FIGURE A.1 *Autarky*

producers who benefit from a higher price than they would otherwise tolerate for selling the good.

Now consider how the price and quantity of the good change as the country begins to trade freely with other countries. Note that the world price of the good will be lower than the domestic price in autarky. The world price is determined by the intersection of global, not domestic, supply and demand. For simplicity, we assume that the country in this example is small relative to the world economy. In other words, it is a "price taker": its own domestic supply and demand of the good will not appreciably affect global supply or demand.

Figure A.2 indicates that the new domestic price declines to the (lower) world price (P_w) after the country moves from autarky to international trade openness. At this lower price, domestic consumer demand increases to Q_d because more people can enjoy the good at the new lower price. Domestic supply of the good decreases to Q_s because fewer producers are willing to produce the good at the lower price. The larger consumer demand is satisfied by imports from the rest of the world (equal to the distance between Q_s and Q_d).

Note that under free trade, the consumer surplus increases considerably because consumers are better off with the lower price. The regions labeled A and B represent the additions to consumer surplus that result from free trade. The producer surplus declines as a result of the lower world price. However, note that the combination of consumer and producer surplus—an overall measure of aggregate welfare—is larger under free trade than in autarky. There are two important implications: opening to trade redistributes income from producers to consumers, and opening to trade makes society as a whole better off.

As a final exercise, consider the implications to redistribution and to aggregate welfare of a tariff on the good. The tariff—which is a tax by the government on the imported good—increases the domestic price of the good to P_t, as shown in

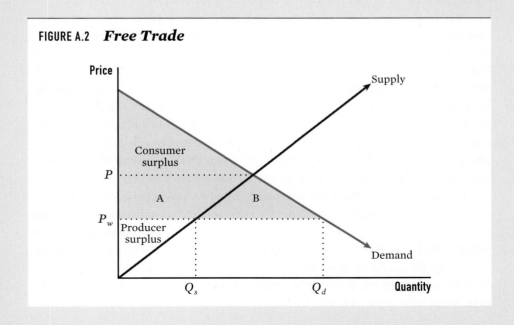

FIGURE A.2 *Free Trade*

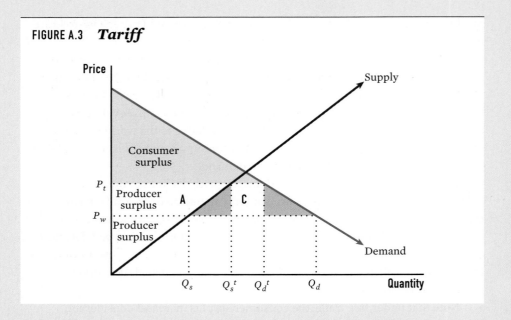

FIGURE A.3 *Tariff*

Figure A.3. The quantity demanded by consumers falls to Q_d^t because of the higher price, whereas the quantity supplied by domestic suppliers increases to Q_s^t. As expected, the consumer surplus declines, because many consumers who wish to purchase the good cannot afford the higher price. The producer surplus increases by the amount represented by Region A, as more producers benefit from a higher price than what they would normally receive. What of the remaining regions? The amount represented by Region C accrues to the government as a result of the tariff revenue. But the two dark triangular regions on either side of Region C do not benefit anyone! Known as the *deadweight loss* of the tariff, they represent the efficiency losses that trade protection imposes on society.

Where does the deadweight loss come from? The best way to understand this loss is to reflect on the concept of comparative advantage. The tariff causes an artificially higher price, which leads domestic producers to shift their production away from whatever they were previously producing and toward the higher-priced good. Suppose the country in question is England, which has a comparative advantage in the production of cloth. If England imposes a tariff on imported wine, then more English producers will shift their production away from cloth and toward wine to take advantage of the higher price, even though they are relatively inefficient in producing wine. In other words, a tariff interferes with the efficient allocation of production and works against the concept of comparative advantage.

By the same token, the artificially high price of the protected good leads consumers to reallocate their consumption away from it and toward a good they would not otherwise purchase, which is another loss to society. The losses to efficiency are represented by the dark triangles in Figure A.3. When we combine these efficiency losses with the decline in domestic consumption caused by the higher price, we can see why economists are generally in agreement that tariffs cause society as a whole to be worse off compared to free trade.

This simple set of graphs captures the essence of the political economy of trade policy. First, international trade improves aggregate welfare. However, certain producers who previously produced exclusively for the domestic market can be harmed when the country moves toward free trade. Trade tariffs lead to a decline in aggregate welfare and cause deadweight losses to society. They also result in an increase in the producer surplus and a reduction in the consumer surplus. If producer groups can successfully lobby the government for protection, they can reap great benefits. These benefits come at the expense of consumers, in the form of a reduced consumer surplus (owing to higher prices), and at the expense of the country as a whole, in the form of an efficiency loss.

8

International Financial Relations

THE PUZZLE *Every year, approximately $5 trillion is invested abroad. Why is so much money invested in foreign countries? And why do relations between foreign investors and the countries in which they invest often become hostile and politically controversial?*

Above: Argentina, like many developing countries, has had trouble servicing its loans to private investors. "Vulture funds" brought suit in American courts to try to force Argentina to pay, despite the costs to the Argentine economy. Here, a woman in Argentina is shown walking past graffiti that reads "country or vultures," while the Argentine government was engaged in conflict with such funds in 2014.

The global financial crisis that began in 2008 hit Europe almost immediately with a major debt crisis. Borrowers in a number of eurozone countries had built up large debts and appeared to be unable to service them. The crisis eventually came to be known as the European sovereign debt crisis (sovereign debt is debt owed by governments) and was the most serious sovereign debt crisis since the 1930s, endangering the international financial system and the world economy.

The four principal eurozone debtors were Greece, Ireland, Portugal, and Spain. In Spain and Ireland, households had borrowed heavily to finance a major housing and construction boom. When housing prices collapsed, the two national governments started borrowing heavily from abroad to finance national bank bailouts and to stimulate their economies. Greece, however, had been running budget deficits ever since the creation of the eurozone, with the government relying heavily on foreign borrowing to cover the shortfalls. Portugal was somewhere in between: both households and the government had been borrowing heavily.

The difficulties of the eurozone debtors were not just a problem for them, since major northern European financial institutions and investors were the ones that had made most of these loans. If the debtors defaulted, trillions of dollars in loans on the books of northern European banks, investors, and pension funds would go bad. The weight of so many bad loans and investments endangered the very integrity of the financial systems of even the richest European countries, especially Germany and France. The sovereign debt crisis threatened both the sovereign debtors and their creditors—and, in fact, the entire European economy.

Faced with this looming catastrophe, leaders of the eurozone member states put together a trillion-euro package to shore up the finances of the major debtors and the region's financial system. In return, they insisted that the debtor countries impose severe austerity measures, including raising taxes, cutting government spending, and selling off public enterprises. Mass protests rocked the debtor nations, and there were even talks of leaving the euro.

It took almost ten years for eurozone economic output to return to what it had been before the crisis. In the meantime the region's unemployment soared; in Greece and Spain, unemployment peaked at over 25 percent. The result was widespread dissatisfaction with both national governments and, more generally, the European Union

(EU). Political movements and parties hostile to or skeptical of European integration gained strength, culminating in Britain's June 2016 vote to leave the European Union. All over Europe, it seemed, 50 years of consensus in favor of European integration and a centrist vision of society had collapsed.

The eurozone crisis is an example of how international finance can become a highly political issue. Today, capital flows around the world in unimaginably large quantities. Nearly half of all the world's investment goes across borders—every year about $5 *trillion* in foreign loans and investments. Total international investments in 2014 were about $140 trillion, and *every day* many trillions of dollars in foreign currencies are traded. Even the United States has financed large trade and budget deficits with money from abroad, borrowing more than $5 trillion between 2005 and 2014—increasing its debt to foreigners in those years by more than $40,000 for every American household.[1]

International finance has long been the leading edge of global economic integration. Massive investment flows drove the integrated world economy of the nineteenth and early twentieth centuries; then they dried up during the years between World Wars I and II, when the world's nations turned inward. Since 1960, international finance has revived and is once again the most globalized component of the world economy, dwarfing international trade and migration.

Some analysts regard the emergence of a worldwide market for capital as one of globalization's main attractions. Companies, investors, and borrowers around the world now can tap into an enormous pool of capital. Home buyers in Arkansas can have their mortgages underwritten by investors in Germany; start-ups in India can be financed by Canadian pension funds; shopkeepers in South Africa can borrow money that comes from small savers in Japan.

Yet international finance is also extremely controversial, and critics of global economic integration have long targeted international bankers. Many policy makers in the developing world see international finance as a source of economic and political problems and as a potential threat to their nations' sovereignty.

A series of financial crises, culminating in the global economic crisis, has focused attention on how financial developments in one country can affect others. Problems that started in the market for housing finance in the United States in 2007 ended up causing the most serious international financial panic since the 1930s. Meanwhile, loans gone similarly bad in Europe threatened to tear the European Union apart. Even the world's largest and richest economies seemed highly susceptible to the volatility of international financial markets.

Thinking Analytically about International Finance

Governments, firms, and individuals sometimes pursue international finance avidly and sometimes attack it mercilessly. This disparity raises questions about why international investment is so controversial. As we will see, within borrowing nations, there are many actors who value access to foreign funds. However, there are others who resent the constraints and burdens that foreign investments sometimes impose on debtors. Similar conflicting interests exist within lending nations.

At the international level, lenders and borrowers have a shared interest in sustaining capital flows, but they may disagree about how the benefits from loans are divided. For example, most Europeans favor allowing capital to flow among EU member countries, but they may disagree profoundly about who should be asked to make the sacrifices necessary to resolve the region's debt crisis. Similarly, international investors and the recipients of investment may enter into conflict. These interactions frequently involve bargaining over the investments, as each side tries to get the best deal.

International institutions, such as the International Monetary Fund (IMF), structure interactions in the international financial realm. Like international finance generally, however, the role of the IMF is very controversial: some analysts think it contributes to the cooperative resolution of financial problems, while others think it takes unfair advantage of struggling debtor nations. In this chapter we take a closer look at these questions.

---

1. Except where otherwise noted, all data in this section are from M. Ayhan Kose, Eswar Prasad, Kenneth Rogoff, and Shang-Jin Wei, "Financial Globalization: A Reappraisal," *IMF Staff Papers* 56, no. 1 (2009); and the Updated and Extended External Wealth of Nations Dataset, 1970–2011, from Philip Lane and Gian Maria Milesi-Ferretti, "The External Wealth of Nations Mark II: Revised and Extended Estimates of Foreign Assets and Liabilities, 1970–2004," *Journal of International Economics* 73, no. 2 (2007), supplemented and updated from the IMF's International Financial Statistics and the U.S. Department of Treasury.

How and Why Do People Invest Overseas?

There are many ways in which those with capital can invest in foreign lands. There are two broad categories of foreign investment: portfolio and direct. A **portfolio investment** gives the investor a claim on some income but no role in managing the investment. Loans are portfolio investments. So are shares of a company's stock (equities), for each share of stock represents a minuscule portion of ownership in the corporation.[2]

If, for example, an investor buys the bonds of an Indian corporation or the Indian government, or if a bank lends money to an Indian corporation or the Indian government, the Indian debtor commits itself to make interest and principal payments but has no obligation to involve the creditor in figuring out how or when to use the borrowed money. Even if the Indian corporation or Indian government has a bad year, it is obligated to pay off its creditors at the preestablished interest rate.[3] Portfolio investors take little or no part in running their investment; their interest is simply in the rate of return.

A substantial portion of the portfolio investment that goes to developing countries is **sovereign lending**—that is, loans from private financial institutions to sovereign governments. Loans by European or American financial institutions to the governments of Indonesia or Brazil—or to government-owned or -controlled companies or agencies in those countries—are sovereign loans. So too are purchases by foreigners of French or American government bonds, for example. If the government provides a guarantee for loans made to private firms in foreign countries, these too can be considered to be sovereign loans.

Foreign direct investment (FDI) is made by a company that owns facilities in another country—facilities over which the company maintains control. For example, a Toyota truck factory in Thailand or a Disney theme park in France is an instance of an FDI. FDI differs from foreign portfolio investment most importantly because the investor maintains managerial control—and also bears the risk of the investment. If a Toyota truck factory in Thailand is not profitable, Toyota loses money. Direct investors have full authority to run their investments, but they take most of the associated risks as well.

portfolio investment
Investment in a foreign country via the purchase of stocks (equities), bonds, or other financial instruments. Portfolio investors do not exercise managerial control of the foreign operation.

sovereign lending
Loans from private financial institutions in one country to sovereign governments in other countries.

foreign direct investment (FDI)
Investment in a foreign country via the acquisition of a local facility or the establishment of a new facility. Direct investors maintain managerial control of the foreign operation.

---

2. Equities (stocks) can be ambiguous; an investor who owns enough of the company's shares might, in fact, take control of the company, making the investment direct. But almost all international equity investment is of the portfolio variety, meaning that it does not involve actual managerial control of the firm.

3. This distinction is blurred in instances in which foreigners buy large quantities of corporate equities—so at some point they could, in fact, exercise control over the corporation. Traditional portfolio investors, as discussed here, are not interested in control; they buy equities solely as financial instruments.

Why Invest Abroad? Why Borrow Abroad?

Banks, corporations, and individuals make investments overseas with a clear goal: to make money. Those with capital want to move their money from where profits are lower to where profits are higher. Thus, many international investors want to move money from capital-rich developed countries to capital-poor developing ones. Banks, corporations, and individuals in rich countries invest more than $800 billion every year in developing- and emerging-market nations, about two-thirds of it in direct investment from multinational corporations (MNCs), the other third in loans and investments in equities (stocks).[4] Figure 8.1 illustrates the rapid growth of foreign investment in emerging markets over recent decades.

The Heckscher-Ohlin theory presented in Chapter 7 explains why. A country's average profit rate depends on how plentiful capital is. Where land or labor is scarce, it is expensive; where it is plentiful, it is cheap. The same is true of capital, recognizing that the interest rate is the "price" of capital: more expensive capital means a higher rate of return. In a poor country, capital is scarce and therefore expensive: borrowers pay higher interest rates for something in short supply. In a rich country, capital is abundant, so interest rates and profit rates are much lower. For example, in 2014 the prevailing rate of interest on short-term loans in most developed countries was below 2 percent, while in Latin America it was typically 10 percent and often higher.

The greater scarcity of capital, as well as higher interest rates, in developing versus developed countries encourages capital to flow from richer to poorer countries. For example, Mexico is poor in capital, while the United States is rich in

Figure source: World Bank, World Development Indicators, http://data.worldbank.org/ indicator (accessed 09/07/17).

Note: Measures are "net inflows" in current U.S. dollars for low- and middle-income countries as defined by the World Bank. See http://data .worldbank.org/income-level/ LMY for countries included.

FIGURE 8.1 *Foreign Investment in Emerging Markets, 1970–2015*

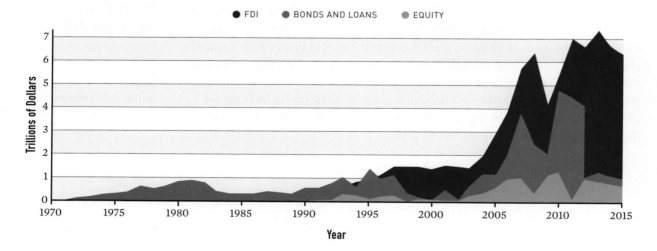

---

4. This is an annual average for 2007–2015 based on the data in Figure 8.1.

capital. Thus, profits and interest rates are higher in Mexico, which helps explain why American investors have, over time, accumulated investments worth over $300 billion there.

If the only considerations in international investment were differential rates of return, as in this simple Heckscher-Ohlin discussion, then all foreign investment would flow from capital-rich countries to capital-poor countries. But it decidedly does not. In fact, most international investment is among rich countries, and only a relatively small but growing fraction of international investment in the past couple of decades has gone to the developing world. The reason is the lower risk of cross-border investment in rich countries. International banks, corporations, and other investors care not just about the promised interest or profit rate on foreign investments, but also about the likelihood that they will actually get the money. See Figure 8.2 for a breakdown of FDI by region in recent years.

Although all investment is risky, international investment involves a very specific risk: that a foreign government over which the investor has no influence may do things that reduce the value of the investment. This is especially true about loans to a foreign government, which involve a government's promise to pay debt service (interest and principal). Unlike in domestic lending, this promise cannot be enforced by the threat of foreclosure or bankruptcy. For international corporate investment, the concern is that the local government will undertake policies that devalue the investment—up to and including taking over the investment itself.

Investment among rich countries is much less risky than investment in poor countries. After all, the industrialized nations are more economically and politically stable, and they have a longer and more reliable history of treating foreign

Figure source: United Nations Conference on Trade and Development, World Investment Report 2016, http://unctad .org/en/PublicationsLibrary/ wir2016_en.pdf (accessed 1/4/18).

Note: Measures are "FDI inward stock" in current U.S. dollars.

FIGURE 8.2 *Foreign Direct Investment by Region, 2000–2015*

The United Kingdom presents a low-risk environment for foreign investors because it is stable and rich. Many British brands and landmarks are owned by corporations based overseas, such as the London Taxi Company, owned by Chinese automotive manufacturer Geely.

investors well. For investors to be willing to take a chance on the greater risk in the developing world, they need either higher interest rates and profits or some reason to think that they can effectively manage the investment risks. This need can lead to negotiations, between lenders or investors on the one hand and developing countries on the other hand, to try to ensure a more reliable investment environment. This effort, in turn, draws international investment into international politics.

What's the Problem with Foreign Investment?

International investment is controversial because not only can it provide great benefits to both investors and the countries they invest in, but it can also impose real costs on both sides of the relationship. This is yet another example, discussed in Chapter 2, of how many issues in international politics contain elements of both cooperation and bargaining. Both sets of actors stand to gain by an amicable resolution of their differences, so they have an interest in cooperating, but each side wants to get as much as possible out of the relationship, which leads their interaction down the path to bargaining.

In international investment, there are many common interests among borrowers and lenders, among investors and the countries they invest in. Both sides of the interaction gain from successful international investments and loans. The receiving country gets capital it would not otherwise have. Companies that borrow from abroad can expand their businesses. Governments that borrow from abroad can finance projects that spur development, such as roads and power plants. An inflow of foreign funds can increase the availability of credit to small business owners and homeowners. Meanwhile, the foreign investor who has sent the money overseas gets higher profits than are available at home. Borrowing and lending nations alike gain from the ability of capital to flow across borders.

But there may also be major conflicts of interest between the two sides of the relationship. Each party wants to get as much as possible from the other and to give as little as possible. Lenders want their debts repaid in full, and corporations want to bring home high profits from their foreign investments. Debtor nations, however, would rather pay less of what they owe, and host countries would rather that foreign corporations have less to take away. This situation creates both a commonality of interests in maintaining a flow of capital and a conflict of interests in distributing the benefits of the flow.

Within countries, domestic politics may also contribute to conflict between capital-sending and capital-receiving nations. In most countries, there is little disagreement when money is flowing in. Foreign capital allows the country to consume more than it produces and allows the government to spend more than it takes in through taxes; the foreign capital increases domestic consumption, investment, and economic activity, and this outcome tends to be popular. Eventually, however, lenders must be repaid and profits taken out—an outcome that is less universally popular.

Making debt service payments can require raising taxes, reducing government services, restraining wages and consumption, importing less while exporting more, and generally imposing austerity on the national economy. Debt crises throughout history—including recent ones in both developing and developed countries—have been associated with slow growth, unemployment, cuts in social spending, and general economic hardship. And there is no guarantee that the people and groups who are asked to bear the greatest burden of austerity will be those who benefited most from the capital inflow. Even if foreign borrowing and foreign investment are unambiguously good for a nation, the benefits and costs do not accrue equally to all people in the country. This fact has made international finance a contentious issue within developing—and many developed—countries.

Overseas loans and investments can be controversial within lending and investing nations too. While those making the foreign investments stand to gain, there are also workers and firms that resent money going abroad that could be lent or invested at home. And when debt crises erupt, it is common for creditor-country governments to expend time, energy, and money to try to resolve the crisis. This is partly because a crisis abroad can have grave repercussions at home.

In the midst of the debt crisis of the 1980s, for instance, many Americans were shocked to learn that U.S. banks had lent more money to Latin American governments than the value of the capital base of the entire American banking system. This meant that the Latin American debt crisis could conceivably have bankrupted many of America's largest banks and caused a more general financial and economic crisis in the United States itself. Similarly, northern Europeans were startled to find out after 2008 that their banks, and often pension funds, had invested trillions of dollars in American, Spanish, and Irish mortgages and in the government bonds of Greece and Portugal—and that because these investments had gone bad, their financial systems were under serious threat.

But even if it is in the general interest of creditor nations as a whole to "bail out" their troubled banks and their borrowers, it may not be in the interests of everyone in these nations. So, international investment gives rise to plenty of potential sources of conflict, and these conflicts of interest give rise to complex interactions among the sources and targets of global capital movements.

Concessional Finance

There is another, smaller and somewhat less controversial, part of international finance: money lent to developing countries by government agencies and intergovernmental organizations. Rich countries give to poor countries, or lend to them at below-market interest rates, something on the order of $150 billion a year. Such concessional finance differs from that discussed in the preceding section because it is typically lent at interest rates well below those available in the marketplace; World Bank loans to the poorest nations, in fact, bear no interest.

Many of the countries that borrow these concessional funds would not be able to borrow from private creditors, who are wary of particularly poor and unstable nations. Most countries in sub-Saharan Africa and South Asia have little access to private loans; to the extent that they can borrow, it is from North American, European, and Japanese governments or from such institutions as the World Bank and the Asian Development Bank.

Concessional loans from foreign governments are more a form of aid than of finance. They reflect, as does aid generally, both economic and political motivations of the donors and lenders. The international development banks and related agencies—the World Bank, Inter-American Development Bank, Asian Development Bank, and so on—are somewhat less directly political, as they are controlled by a number of rich countries. Their lending programs emphasize basic development projects, such as economic infrastructure (power plants, dams, highways) and social infrastructure (schools, housing).

As we saw in Chapter 1, the two major international economic institutions established at Bretton Woods after World War II were the World Bank and the IMF. The **World Bank** (officially, the International Bank for Reconstruction and Development) was charged with making loans to promote economic development. The IMF was originally focused primarily on exchange rates and monetary relations, but, as we will see later in this chapter, its focus has shifted to international finance in recent decades.

Like the IMF, the World Bank is headquartered in Washington, D.C.; in fact, the two international financial institutions are across the street from each other. The World Bank gets most of its money by borrowing on major financial markets—typically at very low rates, as its bonds are guaranteed by the governments of the markets in which it borrows. Funds raised in this way are lent out to developing countries to help them build major infrastructural and other development projects. Because the World Bank can borrow at much lower interest rates than developing countries can, it can relend to them at very attractive rates. The World Bank also receives some money from developed member states that is lent out at extremely low or no interest to the poorest nations. The World Bank is oriented primarily toward financing long-term investments in such things as roads, dams, and power plants, all of which are considered essential for broader economic growth and development.

There has been less political controversy about concessional finance, as loans from individual governments are negotiated directly and, like loans from the World Bank and its related institutions, are relatively cheap. Nonetheless, countries with severe economic problems often complain about the cost of these loans, and for extremely poor nations concessional debt can be a heavy burden—despite the loans' lower interest rates.

World Bank

An important international institution that provides loans at below-market interest rates to developing countries, typically to enable them to carry out development projects.

This situation has led to calls for debt forgiveness, a measure that would alleviate some problems in very poor nations but that would come at the expense of rich nations' taxpayers. These issues, ethically important as they may be, do not have much impact on private international finance. The amounts at stake are relatively small, and private investors are typically not involved. In any case, much government-to-government concessional debt has been canceled, and the World Bank and IMF are in the process of writing off the debt of the most heavily indebted poor countries.[5] Moreover, the major economic and political issues related to international investment have to do with other, nonconcessional, finance.

Liberian Electricity Corporation workers string electric lines through Monrovia. To help moderate the high cost of electricity generation in West Africa, the World Bank approved a loan to facilitate the construction of an energy transmission network throughout the region.

Why Is International Finance Controversial?

Historically the most important—and most politically conflictual—component of international investment has been private lending to foreign governments. Shakespeare may have been right about the pitfalls of borrowing and lending when he wrote:

> Neither a borrower nor a lender be;
> For loan oft loses both itself and friend,
> And borrowing dulls the edge of husbandry.
> —Polonius, in Shakespeare's *Hamlet*

Indeed, the parties might end up enemies, and the borrowers could have little incentive to use the money wisely. However, there is nothing economically suspect about borrowing or lending, in principle. In the case of a private corporation, it makes sense to borrow if the borrowed funds are used in ways that increase the firm's earnings by more than the money costs. If General Motors borrows at an interest rate of 10 percent but uses the money to make investments that pay out only 5 percent, it will suffer a loss; but if the investments pay out 15 percent, both the borrower and the lender can benefit. The logic is similar for a government.

---

5. For further information on the reduction of debts owed by the heavily indebted poor countries (HIPC), see International Monetary Fund, "Debt Relief under the Heavily Indebted Poor Countries (HIPC) Initiative," September 20, 2014, www.imf.org/external/np/exr/facts/hipc.htm.

Who Wants to Borrow? Who Wants to Lend?

From the standpoint of the economy as a whole, it generally makes sense for a country to borrow if the borrowed funds are used productively, in ways that increase the country's output by more than it will take to repay the debt. Loans might be used to raise national output directly, such as to make productive use of a government-owned natural resource (oil or copper, for example). The money could also be used to increase national output indirectly, such as by building new roads that allow the opening or improvement of agricultural lands or by building a hydroelectric power plant that makes national industry more efficient. As national output rises, the government gets more tax revenue and can service its debts more easily. If borrowed funds are used to increase the productivity of the national economy, they can pay for themselves.

Because developing countries are by definition short of capital, most of their governments are eager to borrow abroad. The prospect of using borrowed money to speed growth and increase national output gives developing economies today a powerful interest in attracting loans from international investors, and it makes borrowing relatively uncontroversial within debtor countries—as long as times are good.

But sovereign debts can quickly become a burden to debtor nations, which makes them much less popular. Governments attempting to service their debts often impose unpopular measures. They cut spending and raise taxes in order to earn the money they need to pay off loans. They raise interest rates to restrain wages, profits, and consumption, which in turn reduces imports and increases exports, so that the country can earn more foreign currency to pay its creditors. These austerity measures typically weaken the domestic economy in order to allow the government to continue paying debt service to foreign creditors.

Such measures can cause a **recession** and or even **depression**, incurring the wrath of labor, business, and other groups. For example, in the wake of a 1997 debt crisis, the Thai government pushed interest rates to 25 percent, cut government spending by 20 percent, and raised taxes. The economy collapsed, shrinking by 12 percent in two years as unemployment more than doubled.[6] In Thailand, as in many such cases, people regarded debt-driven austerity as doubly unfair: they were being asked to sacrifice to repay borrowed money that did not help them, and their sacrifice was going to enrich huge international financial institutions.

One potential source of debt difficulties is international conditions, which can change in ways that make it harder for governments to pay their debts. Between 1980 and 1982, for example, American interest rates rose by 10 percent as the Federal Reserve attempted to reduce American inflation. Most of the debts owed by developing countries to international banks were at floating interest rates, adjusted every six months in line with American interest rates; as American rates went up, so did the cost of outstanding loans. This was, in fact, one of the causes of the debt crisis of the 1980s.

recession

A sharp slowdown in the rate of economic growth and economic activity.

depression

A severe downturn in the business cycle, typically associated with a major decline in economic activity, production, and investment; a severe contraction of credit; and sustained high unemployment.

---

6. Joseph Kahn, "I.M.F. Concedes Its Conditions for Thailand Were Too Austere," *New York Times*, February 11, 1998.

Similarly, an international recession that reduces demand for debtors' exports can make it hard to service loans: when the Great Depression of the 1930s drove down prices and demand for debtors' products, it caused almost every debtor nation to **default**. When circumstances, especially conditions beyond their control, make it harder for debtor governments to keep up their payments, some people in debtor nations prefer that their government simply default in order to force a reduction in the debt burden. There are, then, contending interests within debtor countries over whether to service foreign debt. Those who expect to benefit from maintaining access to international loans will disagree with those who have more to lose from the economic sacrifices required to maintain good relations with foreign creditors.

Within lending countries, when foreign debts are performing well there is usually little conflict over them. Some local companies and individuals may resent the fact that money that could be lent to them is being sent abroad, but this concern is counterbalanced by the profits being brought home. Overall, creditor countries and their governments tend to support their lenders.

Domestic conflict within creditor nations over foreign debts arises most commonly when the loans run into trouble. In these conditions, creditors and their governments often step in with billions of dollars of new loans and aid to alleviate a debtor country's financial crisis. They do so in the belief that if such a crisis were allowed to broaden and deepen, it could spread to other nations and eventually hurt the creditor nation itself. But many people in North America, Europe, and Japan resent their governments' spending of billions of dollars to "bail out" debtors and creditors whose plight may be the self-inflicted result of greed, venality, and bad judgment.

For example, in 1994, in the aftermath of another Mexican crisis, the U.S. government provided many billions of dollars to the beleaguered Mexican government to try to keep the crisis from spreading and affecting American domestic finances as well. In reaction, conservative Republican political activist Patrick Buchanan charged: "What's going down is not just a bailout of Mexico, but a bailout of Wall Street. [President] Clinton and Congress are rushing to recoup for Wall Street bankers and brokers their enormous losses from the plunderings of [Mexican] ex-President Carlos Salinas and friends."[7] From the Left, the liberal magazine the *Progressive* observed: "It's amazing how our government can find money for . . . bailing out some banks or shoring up some brutal regimes, but not for solving the pressing social needs of our own country, like health care, housing, and jobs at a living wage."[8]

Many people in creditor nations regard the trillions of dollars spent in financial rescue packages over the past 30 years as money doled out to undeserving banks and investors who benefited from their ability to put pressure on policy makers. In the aftermath of the Mexican and East Asian financial rescues, the U.S. Congress enacted a number of measures that limited the authority of the executive

default
To fail to make payments on a debt.

---

7. From Patrick J. Buchanan, "Congress Saves Wall Street's Bacon," Buchanan.org (blog), April 20, 1995, http://buchanan.org/blog/congress-saves-wall-streets-bacon-172.

8. "Bailout for Whom?" *Progressive* 62, no. 2 (February 1998): 9–10.

branch to use taxpayer money for such bailouts. Supporters of the bills presented the response to these crises as a clear case of Wall Street versus Main Street: bailing out banks while many small farms and businesses were allowed to go under.[9] Many American and European taxpayers were similarly angry with the financial rescues mounted by the governments of the United States and the European Union in the context of the global financial crisis that began in 2008.

Attitudes toward the IMF and other international financial institutions are often related to broader attitudes toward global economic integration. Both supporters and opponents of globalization tend to think of the IMF and its allies as important pillars of the contemporary international economy. Those wary of globalization distrust global finance and the IMF; those who favor globalization support them.

Whatever domestic disagreements there may be, in general the interests of debtor and creditor countries are clear. Both sides of the relationship stand to benefit from continued lending: borrowers get access to foreign money, and lenders get profits. But each side would prefer to gain more from the relationship. Thus, there are incentives to cooperate to keep the lending going and incentives to bargain for the best possible deal. This sets the stage for complex interactions between debtors and creditors.

Debtor-Creditor Interactions

In the modern era, there have been many cycles of lending and debt crises. All through the nineteenth and early twentieth centuries, rapidly growing countries borrowed heavily from the major European financial centers—primarily London, but also Paris, Amsterdam, and Berlin. Foreign borrowing was, in fact, important to the economic growth of the principal developing regions of the day: the United States, Canada, Australia, Argentina, Brazil, and others.

In most instances, debts appear to have contributed to economic development, but that did not diminish the attendant crises and political disputes. The United States, the world's largest borrower throughout the nineteenth century, was not immune: many of its state governments defaulted in the 1840s, and the state of Mississippi, whose banks borrowed heavily from London financiers in the 1830s and defaulted in 1841, has ever since continued to refuse to make payments on its London debt.

Concern about getting embroiled in debt disputes helps explain why today's private international financial flows to the developing world are restricted to the more advanced and successful developing countries. Countries facing severe developmental difficulties, or about which there is little reliable information, are simply unattractive to private creditors. For example, the government of Brazil is able to attract substantial loans from foreign investors (it had over $300 billion in outstanding debt to private creditors in 2015), whereas the governments of Burkina Faso, Nepal, and Yemen must rely overwhelmingly on concessional lend-ing from the World Bank and other aid agencies.[10] Even in the case of well-known

---

9. J. Lawrence Broz, "Congressional Politics of International Financial Rescues," *American Journal of Political Science* 49, no. 3 (July 2005): 496–512.

10. World Bank, World Development Indicators, http://data.worldbank.org/data-catalog/world-development-indicators (accessed 08/14/17).

This graffiti in Lisbon, Portugal, depicts German chancellor Angela Merkel manipulating the strings of Portuguese leaders. Many Portuguese blamed Merkel for the austerity measures that the government enacted in order to receive an emergency loan from eurozone partners during the crisis.

debtor countries, however, debtor-creditor interactions are inherently complicated by the strategic interactions that are in the relationship.

When debtors and creditors enter into conflict, each side in the interaction has clear interests at stake. For debtor nations in crisis, making prompt and full debt service payments can mean restraining consumption, increasing taxes, reducing government spending, and cutting wages—in a word, **austerity**. So, debtor governments want to reduce the amounts they have to pay so as to reduce the demands on their citizens. On the other hand, creditors' profits depend on the debt service payments they receive. So, creditors want to be paid in full for the loans they have extended. The two sets of interests are, of course, in conflict.

As we have seen, when two actors have conflicting interests, they engage in a bargaining interaction to determine whether a mutually acceptable deal is possible. Each side has tools in its arsenal that can be used to extract favorable terms. The principal bargaining weapon available to the debtor government is the threat of default, or suspension of payment on the debt.[11] In August 1998, the Russian government responded to national economic difficulties with a default that affected as much as $80 billion in foreign debt; in December 2001, the Argentine government defaulted on $93 billion in foreign debt, and controversy over its repayment continued for the next fifteen years.[12]

austerity
The application of policies to reduce consumption, typically by cutting government spending, raising taxes, and restricting wages.

11. Legally, a *default* is invoked by the creditor when the debtor misses payments, but the term is used more generally to describe a suspension of debt service.

12. The amounts involved are unclear, especially for Russia. See International Monetary Fund, *World Economic Outlook* (Washington, DC: International Monetary Fund, 1998), chap. 2. On Argentina's most recent default controversy, see Matt O'Brien, "Everything You Need to Know about Argentina's Weird Default," *Washington Post*, August 3, 2014, www.washingtonpost.com/blogs/wonkblog/wp/2014/08/03/everything-you-need-to-know-about-argentinas-weird-default.

Any sensible creditor would prefer to get some money rather than to get no money at all and therefore has an incentive to reduce the burden of debt. But creditors also have financial weapons available: they can cut off debtor governments from future lending, and they may be able to retaliate in related areas, such as freezing debtor governments' bank accounts or taking other government-owned properties. Creditors can also try to get their home governments to use broader foreign policy considerations to induce compliance, such as threatening a cut-off of aid or even military action. In short, each side can threaten to impose costs on the other in order to extract a better deal at the bargaining table. The ability of each side to get concessions from the other depends on how powerful and credible these threats are.

The bargaining between creditors and debtors over existing debt is analogous to the bargaining between countries that we described in Chapter 3, which can sometimes lead to war. Because of the costs associated with default and retaliation, there is usually a bargaining solution to their interaction that makes both sides better off than financial warfare. Both sides would prefer to restructure the debt so that payments can continue to be made; this is what negotiators, arbitrators, and bankruptcy courts do in the case of domestic debt problems.

However, as in the case of security relations, international debtor-creditor interactions are characterized by incomplete information. The debtor may claim not to be able to make payments, but the creditor does not know if the claim is true. Thus, creditors cannot know whether the threat to default will, in fact, be carried out in the face of potentially dire consequences for the debtor, which may simply be bluffing in order to get a better deal. The creditor, for its part, may threaten to retaliate, but the debtor does not know whether the threat will be carried out.

In these circumstances, cooperative relations between debtors and creditors can collapse into bitter conflict. Many debt conflicts drag on for years or even decades and can have a powerful impact on other dimensions of interstate interaction. Debt-related conflicts have even been blamed for invasions, wars, and colonialism. In some instances, the issue is resolved amicably with a negotiated settlement; in other instances, the parties remain far apart.

Of course, cooperation between debtors and creditors is not necessarily a good thing for everyone involved. This is especially the case when debtor or creditor governments pursue policies that impose major costs on domestic groups. Whether an amicable resolution of debtor-creditor interactions is a good thing or a bad thing, it is important to try to understand the conflict and how it develops. One prominent aspect of international debt interactions is that they have come to involve international institutions that can play an important part in debtor-creditor relations.

Institutions of International Finance

During the twentieth century, there were frequent attempts to regulate debtor-creditor relations by creating institutions to mediate their interactions and perhaps facilitate mutually acceptable outcomes. These institutions have, to a certain extent, helped alleviate the problems that can make lending difficult or impossible and that cause conflict when debtors run into trouble. In the interwar period, the League of Nations' Economic and Financial Committee attempted to work with debtors and creditors to manage the financial difficulties of troubled nations in central and eastern Europe, with mixed results.

The **Bank for International Settlements** was established in 1930 explicitly to help oversee relations between one of the world's most problematic debtor nations, Germany, and its international creditors. It too met with mixed results. Nonetheless, by the 1940s there was a common view that some form of international financial institution might be beneficial to the resolution of sovereign debt problems.

The International Monetary Fund
Today, many aspects of international financial affairs are overseen by one of the world's most powerful international organizations, the **International Monetary Fund (IMF)**. The establishment of the IMF was agreed on at Bretton Woods (see Chapter 1) in order to manage the international monetary system. After the Bretton Woods monetary regime collapsed in the early 1970s (as we will see in Chapter 9), the IMF gradually took on a more directly financial role. Today, its principal concern is financial crises in developing nations, although it has also played a role during crisis periods in developed countries.

The IMF's membership includes both borrowing and lending countries. All member states have a vote on its activities, but these votes are proportional to the member's financial contribution to the IMF resources, its "quota." These financial contributions are, in turn, a function of the size of the country's economy and its importance to world trade and payments. As a result, the United States provides nearly 18 percent of the IMF's total resources; the member states of the European Union provide another 32 percent. Because IMF decisions require an 85 percent supermajority, the United States and the European Union (acting as a group) can veto fund actions. This arrangement has led to complaints that the IMF is largely a tool of its richer and most powerful members—to which those members sometimes respond that this is appropriate inasmuch as they are the ones footing most of the bills.

The IMF, indeed, needs substantial funds to carry out its activities. The total of quotas from its members is currently about $650 billion, and the fund can call upon pledges from its members of another $1 trillion. This gives the IMF, in theory, access to over $1.5 trillion dollars, although it has never come close to using all these resources. Nonetheless, one of the things that leads many to regard the IMF as the most important and most powerful international economic institution is that it can mobilize an extraordinary amount of money in a relatively short time. And because debt crises often erupt suddenly, and often involve vast amounts of money, the IMF is uniquely suited to intervene in such crises.

Typically, a country facing debt difficulties turns to the IMF to negotiate a program of economic policies intended to address the sources of the difficulties. The conditions demanded by the IMF are often economically and politically difficult for the debtor government to enact, but in return for implementing a program that meets the IMF's standards, the debtor government receives relatively

Bank for International Settlements
One of the oldest international financial organizations, created in 1930. Its members include the world's principal central banks, and under its auspices they attempt to cooperate in the financial realm.

International Monetary Fund (IMF)
A major international economic institution that was established in 1944 to manage international monetary relations and that has gradually reoriented itself to focus on the international financial system, especially debt and currency crises.

When the Indonesian government sought the IMF's help during the 1997–98 Asian financial crisis, it was forced to cut spending on popular programs, and poor Indonesians suffered. These protesters in Jakarta hold a sign asking: "The country's debt—why should the people pay?"

inexpensive loans from the fund. Probably more important, the debtor country is "certified" as being in compliance with IMF norms, which makes it more attractive to creditors. This certification is meant to encourage private lenders to renegotiate with the debtor government and perhaps to extend it new loans to help it overcome temporary difficulties.

For example, during the debt crisis of the 1980s, the IMF signed dozens of agreements with troubled debtors, typically requiring policies of economic austerity and adjustment in return for assistance with working out their debt problems. The IMF's agreement with Indonesia in the midst of the 1997–98 Asian financial crisis obliged the Indonesian government to cut subsidies to—and therefore raise the prices of—sugar, wheat flour, corn, and soybeans, as well as fuel and electricity. All these factors imposed hardships on Indonesia's poor and working people. The IMF also required the government to shut down 16 banks controlled by relatives or cronies of the country's dictatorial president, Suharto. This move may have been less objectionable to ordinary people, but it was, of course, unpopular with the Indonesian government.[13]

While the IMF dealt mainly with developing debtor nations from the 1970s until the 2000s, the financial crisis that began in 2008 drove many industrialized countries to the fund. Over the course of the crisis, the IMF negotiated very large loans and austerity programs with Greece, Ireland, and Portugal, as well as with Ukraine, which experienced a severe crisis in 2014–15. The IMF's operations in these instances were similar to those in other debt crises, although in the European cases it worked in concert with EU authorities.

---

13. Stephan Haggard, *The Political Economy of the Asian Financial Crisis* (Washington, DC: Institute for International Economics, 2000).

The IMF, like other international institutions, can facilitate cooperative interactions among actors in a variety of ways. It provides a set of financial and macroeconomic standards, and a wealth of other information, that can be used to assess the behavior of debtor nations. By increasing the likelihood that debtor-creditor relations will be iterated (repeated), the fund can make cooperation more attractive. The IMF can also help verify a debtor government's compliance with commitments to pursue economic policies that creditors want to see. And the IMF can act on behalf of the collectivity of creditor nations, which might otherwise have difficulties working out common decisions about how to deal with financial crises.

In one sense, though, the IMF is unusual. While many international institutions act primarily to facilitate bargaining among nation-states, the IMF negotiates agreements directly with an individual country's government. And, perhaps even more unusual, the IMF's involvement is typically closely tied to relations between the debtor government and private international creditors. While the IMF does not represent foreign creditors, there is normally an understanding that an agreement with the IMF will facilitate agreement with private lenders, and sometimes the IMF, member governments, and private creditors make this connection explicit. In this sense, the IMF plays a major part, directly or indirectly, in negotiations between sovereign governments and private financiers. This unusual relationship has also led to charges that the IMF is biased in favor of creditors and against debtors (see "Controversy" on p. 364).

Supporters of the IMF believe that it plays an important role in managing the international financial system, allowing for an orderly resolution of debtor-creditor problems. They focus on the informational difficulties endemic in sovereign debt, as well as the need for reliable monitoring of compliance with agreements. Supporters emphasize how the IMF can help debtors and creditors arrive at cooperative arrangements. They believe that the IMF's power comes from its central role in resolving financial problems in ways that are beneficial to both debtors and creditors.

However, opponents see the IMF as a tool of international financiers. They regard the IMF as a biased agency whose actions reinforce the subordinate position of debtor nations and do little to assist them in achieving economic growth and development. Similar conflicts arise over the involvement of the home governments of creditors, primarily from North America, Europe, and Japan. Debtor nations often resent political pressure from these powerful governments, which they regard as unduly concerned with insisting that "their" bankers get repaid. Creditors can be politically influential at home, and defaults can threaten to bankrupt major financial institutions in industrial nations, which would, in turn, destabilize their own financial markets. This situation leads creditor governments and the IMF, in the eyes of many opponents, to serve as debt collectors for international banks.

Borrowing and Debt Crises

Lending to developing nations has been an important part of the international economy since the mid-1960s. At the same time, there have been many debt crises since international financial markets reopened to developing countries. The first

Is the IMF Biased against Developing Countries?

In February 1989, facing a protracted fiscal crisis, Venezuela's president, Carlos Andrés Pérez, negotiated a loan with the IMF. Going back on preelection promises he had made only weeks earlier, Pérez adopted market-based reforms recommended by the IMF as part of the loan deal: liberalizing trade, privatizing state companies, restricting state spending, relaxing price controls, and deregulating exchange and interest rates. Almost immediately, Caracas erupted in violent protests that eventually led to two failed coups, the impeachment of Pérez, and the rise of coup leader Hugo Chávez to the presidency. Chávez and the supporters of his "Bolivarian Revolution" became some of the strongest critics of the IMF, and in 2007 Venezuela pulled out of the IMF and the World Bank.

The IMF's supporters argue that its actions are in the interests of developing countries like Venezuela: the IMF assists nations in financial difficulty, and helps them maintain access to foreign capital that is vital to their development. But this claim is controversial. Why?

Applying the Concepts

The IMF typically is called upon when a country runs into debt trouble. These situations inevitably involve a conflict of **interests** between debtors (who want debt relief) and creditors (who want to be paid back). As an international **institution**, the IMF is charged with the task of safeguarding global financial stability, which it often interprets as demanding substantial economic reforms from debtor nations. Many people in the debtor nations see the IMF's demands for economic reforms as a threat to the important institution of national sovereignty. The **interactions** among the IMF, debtor countries, and creditors vary greatly in their nature: in some cases, they are cooperative and therefore not controversial; in other cases, they collapse into acrimonious conflicts. The IMF may facilitate international financial cooperation, but critics claim that it distributes the benefits and burdens of that cooperation unevenly across member nations.

The chief criticisms that Chávez leveled at the IMF reflect both conflicts of interest and institutional concerns.

Chávez's first main criticism derived from the "conditionalities" routinely attached to IMF loans. For decades, the IMF has required that countries requesting financial assistance commit to "structural adjustment programs" and economic austerity measures designed to address debtor nations' fiscal and financial problems. Critics argue that these conditions are not in the interests of debtor nations and often impose hardship on their poorest citizens, who face higher taxes, wage cuts, unemployment, and reduced social services.

The second charge is that the IMF as an international organization violates the institutional integrity of sovereign nations. This charge derives from the fact that IMF programs may include conditions associated not only with economic reforms, but also with changes to specific national political institutions. Pérez, for instance, was asked to institute direct elections of state governors in Venezuela in place of presidential appointments.

The IMF's critics also point out that the interaction between the IMF and debtor nations is highly unequal. Acceptance of IMF conditions is supposedly voluntary, but the high price of refusal—ineligibility for an IMF program—creates an impression of coercion. Indeed, debtor countries that turn to the IMF are typically in very weak bargaining positions; they are desperate for the IMF's financial assistance and the access to private loans it can help ensure.

Defenders of the IMF respond to these criticisms by stressing that both debtors and creditors have an interest in mutual gains from cooperation. The IMF's policy recommendations help debtor nations ensure economic recovery and restore access to foreign credit, and the benefits over the long term outweigh the temporary costs to the nation's citizens and the diminishment of a nation's sovereignty. Once these longer-term effects are taken into account, it becomes clear that it is in the interest of debtor nations to participate in the IMF.

Riots overtook Caracas in 1989 after the Venezuelan government imposed austerity measures recommended by the IMF. Here, people stand in line to buy food, looking on toward a victim of the violence.

Supporters further argue that the IMF provides essential institutional support to the international financial system, whose smooth functioning is equally in the interests of both debtor nations and creditors. If the IMF were not there to help guarantee creditors of good debtor behavior, creditors would not lend. Member states *voluntarily* go to the IMF because they want its seal of approval in order to gain access to global financial markets. Typically, governments have gotten into trouble because they pursued unsustainable policies, and the IMF can help them get back on track and regain access to international finance. Without the IMF, there would be little or no international lending, and poor nations would be far worse off.

Critics counter that the IMF worries primarily about the interests of creditors, even at the expense of social progress, economic growth, and equity. There is little moral justification for subjecting the people of a country to terrible austerity measures solely to pay billions to foreign banks and investors. Many IMF programs fail even on their own terms, providing little economic relief. The allegedly "voluntary" nature of IMF programs is a fiction; a developing country that does not "voluntarily" subject itself to IMF dictates will be punished. As a result, critics argue that the IMF is a tool of the creditor nations and

their investors, and its policies benefit only the rich and powerful.

The plausibility of these arguments depends on how well the IMF, in fact, delivers on its promises. If standard IMF measures actually rectify debtor nations' economic problems and contribute to economic growth, and this growth benefits the poor, then its operations may be regarded as fair and the bargains worth the cost. At this point, the evidence is mixed: while IMF programs may improve a nation's balance of payments, their record on economic growth and poverty reduction is unclear.

Thinking Analytically

1. How and why do the IMF's activities in the developing world lead to conflicts of interest?

2. As an international institution, what is the goal of the IMF? How does it try to achieve this goal?

3. Why might interactions between the IMF and debtor nations sometimes go smoothly, while ending up in acrimonious disputes at other times?

such crisis started in 1982, with the Mexican default. Like most financial crises, this one had a self-reinforcing nature. As in a bank panic, because lenders worried that developing-country governments might not repay them, they stopped lending. This left developing-country governments without a financial cushion, and in desperation they stopped making payments to their creditors—thereby scaring international bankers even further. The more the developing countries ran out of money, the less bankers lent; the less bankers lent, the more the developing countries ran out of money. In the space of weeks, some of the most rapidly growing economies in the world were suddenly cut off from the bank lending they had relied on for 15 years.

One after another, the major debtor governments struggled to generate the foreign currency and government revenue needed to pay their creditors, until eventually their economies collapsed. By 1983, as many as 34 developing and socialist countries were formally renegotiating their debts, and a dozen more were in serious trouble. Latin America was spending nearly half of its export earnings to pay interest and principal on its foreign debt, leaving little to buy the imports it needed. Most debtor economies remained depressed for years, and the crises were not fully resolved until 1990. Austerity programs and economic reforms in debtor nations, coupled with concessions from lenders to reduce the debt burden, gradually allowed the problems to be worked out. (See "What Shaped Our World?" on p. 367 for details about this debt crisis.)

Eventually, lending resumed, but debt crises continued to occur. In 1994, Mexican finances once again collapsed. In 1997–98, combined debt and currency crises hit a series of East Asian countries from Indonesia and Thailand to the Philippines and South Korea. This was a particularly startling shock, as these nations had long been regarded as models of developmental success. Their apparently endless potential had drawn in considerable amounts of foreign money: Thailand's foreign debt tripled, from $30 billion to $90 billion, in the three years leading up to 1996, while Indonesia's doubled from $25 billion to $50 billion. During the early 1990s, about $50 billion a year flowed into East Asia from global financial markets, with tens of billions more in direct investment from multinational corporations.

Once the crisis hit in the summer of 1997, however, money ran out of the East Asian debtor countries as fast as it had run in. The $50 billion annual inflow of the early 1990s turned into an outflow of over $230 billion between 1997 and 1999. After years of extraordinary growth—10 percent a year was common—the economies of Indonesia, Thailand, and Malaysia contracted by 15, 12, and 8 percent, respectively, in a matter of months. It would be years before they would recover their pre-crisis levels.

The East Asian crisis was followed by crises in Russia and Brazil in 1998–99, Argentina in 2000–2001, and others since then. In all these cases, intervention by the IMF alone was not sufficient; the debt problems were so large that creditor governments also stepped in, to the tune of over $50 billion for Mexico, almost $120 billion for the three principal Asian crisis nations (Indonesia, South Korea, and Thailand), and another $70 billion for Russia and Brazil. Critics charged that taxpayers were being forced to bail out foolish investors and dissolute governments, but financial leaders insisted on the need for a quick response to avoid financial contagion.

The Latin American Debt Crisis

In the 1960s, the governments of Latin America discovered a valuable resource: foreign loans. International investors had not lent money to developing countries since 1929, having been burned during the Great Depression when most countries stopped paying their debts. But by 1965 memories had faded, and international banks resumed lending to governments in the developing world.

Interests Latin American governments needed the money to build factories and roads, power plants and steel mills, schools and houses. For 15 years loans poured in, public and private projects lined up for money, and economies expanded. In the 10 years from 1973 to 1982, the region's total debt grew from $40 billion to $330 billion. The borrowing boom came to a crashing halt late in the summer of 1982. In August, the Mexican government announced that it could not pay the interest and principal on its $100 billion debt to foreign banks. International banks panicked. If Mexico, a major oil producer, couldn't or wouldn't pay its debts, perhaps other nations couldn't or wouldn't either. Investors stopped lending within weeks, and heavily indebted developing nations around the world were thrown into crisis. Within four months, about 40 countries had fallen behind on their debt payments.

Institutions The debt crisis that began in 1982 led to an economic collapse that was, for many countries, the most catastrophic in modern history. The crisis had dire effects on domestic political institutions. Latin America spiraled downward into recession and depression, unemployment, and hyperinflation (price increases of more than 50 percent a month). Governments collapsed all over the region.

At the international level, the governments of creditor and debtor nations, as well as the world's principal international financial institution, the IMF, all were important. The IMF orchestrated a multibillion-dollar bailout package even as it played an intermediary role between the creditor banks and the debtor nations. Debtor countries typically found themselves forced to enter an IMF program if they wanted to work out a better deal with their bank creditors.

Interactions The interplay among creditor governments, creditor banks, debtor governments, and the IMF made the politics of the debt crisis particularly complex. Lengthy and often bitter negotiations ensued over who would make the major sacrifices needed to address the accumulated debt burden. Most of the costs were borne by debtor nations. After decades of rapid growth, income per person in Latin America declined over the 1980s by 10 percent, real wages fell by at least 30 percent, and investment fell even further; inflation in many nations rose above 1,000 percent.[a] The 1980s became known in the region as the lost decade. Eventually, in 1989, creditor governments and banks offered some debt relief, governments began adopting new policies, and the region began growing again.

Domestically, throughout the developing world, protests erupted over the debt crisis and the unemployment, inflation, and government cutbacks it had brought. The economic and political crisis eventually drove most of Latin America's military dictatorships from power. But this advance was overshadowed by the fact that the debtor nations had fallen even further behind economically as they struggled to shoulder their debt. What had originally seemed a golden opportunity—readily available foreign loans—now seemed a terrible burden.

Banco de México, Mexico's central bank.

a. Eliana Cardoso and Ann Helwege, *Latin America's Economy: Diversity, Trends, and Conflicts* (Cambridge, MA: MIT Press, 1995).

The international politics of developing-country debt is a striking example of how actors with different interests interact strategically in a highly institutionalized context. The parties have not only clear conflicting interests, but also clear interests in common. Even though creditors want to be repaid and debtors want to pay as little as possible, both sides have an interest in continuing their relationship: the creditors to earn profits, the debtors to maintain access to foreign finance. This mix of cooperative and conflictual motives leads to complicated strategic interactions. And the role of the IMF highlights the role of international institutions—seen by some as effective at helping resolve conflicts, by others as tools of the powerful.

These debt crises in developing and transitional economies were dwarfed by a financial collapse that hit the advanced industrial economies in 2008. Some of the aspects of this crisis were familiar from previous debt crises—although it had been decades since an industrialized country had been so affected—while other features were very novel. Together, they plunged the world into the most serious economic downturn since the Great Depression of the 1930s.

A New Crisis Hits the United States—and the World

The 2008 financial crisis originated in the United States, the world's largest economy and most developed financial system. The country had embarked on a major foreign borrowing spree. In 2001, substantial tax cuts drove the U.S. federal government into a large deficit. Much of the deficit was financed by borrowing from abroad. Government borrowing spurred the economy, reinforced by a monetary policy of very low interest rates; in turn, these low interest rates encouraged American households to borrow heavily. Much of the borrowing went for housing, as many Americans refinanced their homes or bought new homes. Foreigners eager to buy American investments that they regarded as safe and profitable provided large portions of the lending directly or indirectly.

From 2001 to 2007, the United States experienced a traditional borrowing boom. Every year, the country borrowed between a half-trillion and a trillion dollars from the rest of the world. A significant portion of the debt went to finance the government budget deficit; much of the rest went into the flourishing housing market. As financial markets grew at a dizzying pace, banks developed ever-more-complex ways of investing, borrowing, and lending.

Some observers warned that not enough of the new debt was going into productive investments that would increase the efficiency of the U.S. economy, such as new factories or new technologies. Other observers were concerned that American regulators were inadequately supervising the freewheeling, increasingly complex financial system. However, the U.S. government resisted stricter financial oversight, especially given its general commitment to deregulation. Meanwhile, most Americans were happy to enjoy a dramatic expansion in consumption, reduced taxes, increased government spending, and a striking increase in housing prices—all made possible by foreign borrowing.

Between 2001 and 2007, Americans enjoyed increased consumption, reduced taxes, and more government spending, all made possible by foreign borrowing. When the debt-fueled expansion became unsustainable, the economy went into recession.

America's debt-fed expansion eventually became an unsustainable bubble, especially in the housing market. In some parts of the country, housing prices doubled in the space of four or five years. Much of the lending was predicated on the unrealistic expectation that housing prices would continue to rise at this pace. For example, financial institutions extended mortgages to borrowers who would otherwise not have qualified, because they expected that the homes being bought would rise in value. Both borrowers and lenders were thus gambling that housing prices would continue to go up.

Eventually, housing prices stopped soaring and began to fall. Overextended mortgage holders could not pay their debts; overextended lenders faced massive losses. During 2007 and 2008, financial difficulties spread, as hundreds of billions of dollars' worth of mortgages and related financial assets went bad. Fear spread from bank to bank, culminating in September 2008, when Lehman Brothers, one of the world's leading investment banks, collapsed. This was the largest bankruptcy in American history, and it caused near panic in financial markets.

Within a few months, the crisis was transmitted around the world, eventually coming to be known as the *global financial crisis*. Soon, virtually every economy was in decline. Some countries faced circumstances much like those of the United States: the United Kingdom, Spain, Portugal, and Greece. Also hard-hit were some developing and transition economies that had been borrowers over the course of the decade. When the U.S. spiraled downward into crisis, so did the other debtor nations. But the damage was even more widespread, because the collapse of the debtor economies affected the creditors who had extended trillions of dollars in loans to them. As the crisis spread from debtor to debtor, and from debtor to creditor, it became the first truly international financial crisis since the 1930s, resulting in the deepest global economic downturn since that decade.

Individual governments attempted to stem the decline. The U.S. government stepped in with trillions of dollars to bail out affected financial institutions and to try to get financial markets working again, taking over some of the country's largest financial corporations in order to avoid their collapse. And the U.S. government enacted a massive deficit-funded spending package to attempt to stimulate an economy in its steepest recession since the 1930s.

Within the United States, political battles broke out over the response to the financial crisis. The principal question confronting the nation was who would pay for the country's financial follies. Many Americans were furious that the government was spending taxpayer dollars to bail out imprudent banks and corporations. Others argued that attempts to stimulate the economy were simply throwing taxpayer money at the problem without any guarantee it would work. As in other debt crises, many felt that the interests of working-class and middle-class Americans were being sacrificed to address problems created by wealthy financiers. As the recovery stalled, political battles heated up, and the country became increasingly polarized over how best to confront the aftermath of the debt crisis and how best to distribute the burden of economic adjustment among Americans.

A similar dynamic played out in Europe, with the added complication that the problem divided the eurozone, the group of EU member countries that had created a common currency in 1999. As with the world at large, eurozone countries were divided into those that borrowed heavily during the decade before 2008, and those that lent heavily. The big borrowers were largely in southern Europe—Greece, Spain, Portugal, and Cyprus—but also included Ireland. They borrowed for different purposes: Greece to fund an overgrown public sector and huge budget deficits; the rest, like the United States, largely to fuel a consumption and housing boom. The big lenders were the northern Europeans, especially Germany.

Internationally too, the global financial crisis caused tension among contending interests. Governments everywhere scrambled to protect their economies, even at the expense of other countries. For example, the U.S. Congress insisted that government spending to stimulate the failing economy be used preferentially to buy American goods; trading partners insisted that this strategy was protectionist and violated the rules of the World Trade Organization (WTO). Developing countries complained that the heavy borrowing by industrialized-country governments to deal with the crisis was making it impossible for poor nations to get the funds they needed to confront their dire problems. The European Union was torn by conflicts among member states with widely different views as to the appropriate response to the crisis.

As the crisis unfolded, many observers wondered whether the deep recession that began in 2008 might spiral downward into a global depression similar to that of the early 1930s. It did not, in part because eventually, the world's major economic powers engaged in enough macroeconomic policy cooperation to limit the damage.

Nonetheless, the debt crisis in the eurozone dragged on for 10 years without a definitive resolution. And the crisis eventually fed into widespread dissatisfaction with domestic and international economic trends—dissatisfaction that had a profound impact on both domestic and international politics around the world. The global financial crisis once more demonstrated the potential for political controversy inherent in international financial affairs.

Foreign Direct Investment: What Role Do Multinational Corporations Play?

FDI is another important form of international capital movement. It differs from foreign lending because it is carried out explicitly by corporations that maintain control over the facilities they establish overseas; the corporations involved have come to be known as **multinational corporations (MNCs)**.[14] FDI occurs when Volkswagen sets up an auto factory in Brazil, or Telefónica de España buys the Czech telephone company, or ExxonMobil drills for oil in Angola. In all these instances, what is involved is far more than a simple transfer of capital. Volkswagen could export cars to Brazil but chooses to build them there instead; individual foreign investors could buy shares in the Czech telephone company, but instead a global telecommunications corporation adds the Czech system to its network; the Angolan government could borrow money to drill for oil but instead gives a concession to an American company.

multinational corporation (MNC)
An enterprise that operates in a number of countries, with production or service facilities outside its country of origin.

Why Do Corporations Go Multinational?

It is not easy for a corporation to set up facilities in a foreign country. As noted, Volkswagen could simply build cars in Europe and export them to Brazil rather than building them in Brazil, and one might imagine that a local company could run the Czech telephone system better than a Spanish company could. There must be a reason for firms to invest abroad rather than exporting, and for a foreign firm to have some advantage over a domestic one, despite the inherent difficulties of doing business abroad. What makes it attractive for a corporation to establish or purchase subsidiaries across borders, and what gives the host country an interest in permitting this foreign investment?

Corporations may want to establish overseas affiliates to gain access to the local market or to take advantage of local resources—in both instances presumably because doing so through trade is less attractive or impossible. Some FDI is driven

---

14. Some observers prefer the term *transnational corporation* to indicate that many of these firms transcend national boundaries. Most such corporations, however, maintain a clear national identity despite their global operations. In any event, both terms are commonly used and are largely interchangeable.

by resource location: American and European oil companies, with ample experience in exploring for oil, may be more effective at getting Angola's oil out of the ground than local entrepreneurs could be. The case of Volkswagen in Brazil illustrates that there are often advantages to producing in the local market: cheaper transport costs, or the ability to avoid trade barriers, or better access to market information. In the decades right after World War II, most FDI was by American manufacturers and was motivated by trade protection in Europe and developing countries. Ford, GE, and other big U.S. corporations faced tariffs and other restrictions imposed on their exports to Europe and the developing world. To get around these barriers, they established local affiliates.

As trade barriers were reduced in Europe and, eventually, in many developing countries, other motivations surfaced. MNCs today often place different components of their production network in different countries: the labor-intensive work is done in countries with cheap labor, such as Vietnam, while the work that requires more skilled labor and technicians is done in countries with ample skilled labor, such as Ireland. Other types of FDI, such as that by Telefónica de España, are in service sectors in which companies may have substantial experience or a famous brand name—banking or entertainment, for example. What ties all FDI together is that the corporations involved believe that overseas direct investment is profitable.[15]

Within the home countries of MNCs (that is, the countries in which they are headquartered), there is often support for their foreign activities. After all, American corporations are constituents of American politicians, and it is part of the job of the government to support their constituents, corporate or otherwise. So the U.S. government, like all governments, usually acts to promote and protect the interests of American corporations abroad.

However, FDI can be controversial in the countries from which it originates. Groups and people in North America and western Europe often fault MNCs for not investing at home. Labor unions in North America and western Europe often criticize MNCs, especially for "outsourcing" jobs to countries with lower wages. For his part, President Donald Trump has threatened American corporations that outsource with a 35 percent tax on the goods they try to sell in the American market: "If you go to another country," he told American corporate executives, "we are going to be imposing a very major border tax."[16]

The American labor federation, the AFL-CIO, has also complained: "In the global economy, multinational corporations move capital and jobs half-way around the world with the click of a mouse. These companies—many of them American—seek out the lowest possible labor costs and weakest worker protections. Even if the jobs are not moved, corporate executives use the threat of moving to coerce concessions from their U.S. workers."[17] Labor unions and others have demanded stricter controls

15. For more on the economics of FDI, see Richard Caves, *Multinational Enterprises and Economic Analysis*, 3rd ed. (Cambridge: Cambridge University Press, 2007).

16. C. E. Lee and D. Paletta, "Donald Trump Focuses on Trade and Jobs; President Withdraws from TPP Agreement, Promises Tax on Firms That Move Operations Overseas," *Wall Street Journal*, January 24, 2017.

17. From www.aflcio.org/issues/jobseconomy/globaleconomy/workersrights (accessed 10/07/11).

on "sweatshop labor" in the developing countries, reflecting both working-class solidarity and a more prosaic desire to reduce competitive pressure.

Some human rights activists and environmentalists also eye MNCs with apprehension. Just as corporations can seek lower wages, they can look for pollution-friendly regimes, dictatorships that allow violations of human rights, and other ethically lax governments. In the words of a European campaign to "clean up" the world garment industry: "Incentives for foreign investors include not only low wages, but also the suspension of certain workplace and environmental regulations. If a government does attempt to strictly enforce these regulations, you can bet that many investors will quickly pack their bags for another country that is even less strict and is more accommodating."[18] And there is a cultural component to some complaints about MNCs, arguing that MNCs reduce diversity and encourage the homogenization of world culture. Nonetheless, in general, home-country governments see their interests as closely tied to those of their corporations.

A factory worker in Shenzhen, China, inspects a motherboard in a manufacturing plant that supplies parts to Apple. Abundant cheap labor in countries like China makes it profitable for companies like Apple to invest in factories there.

Why Do Countries Let Foreign Multinationals In?

Most countries that host FDI have some interest in allowing MNCs to operate within their borders—otherwise, of course, they would keep the corporations out. Certainly, in the nineteenth century it was common for such rapidly growing nations as the United States, Canada, Argentina, Russia, and Australia to rely on foreign companies to build up such important industries as railroads.

Today, most governments welcome foreign corporations. This is because MNCs bring in managerial, technological, and marketing skills that might not otherwise be available, as well as investment capital. Some less developed countries (LDCs) lack the trained personnel and capital necessary to access and develop their own natural resources; without foreigners, they might not be able to profit from their resources. However, if they allow foreign companies to pump oil or to mine copper, the government can then tax some of the profits. Other poor nations with weak or small private sectors may welcome foreign corporations to provide jobs for their citizens and to gain access to world markets for their products.

Most nations are eager to attract the technological or other expertise that MNCs can mobilize. This may especially be the case in high-technology industries, where such multinationals as IBM or Siemens can be the sole source of crucial modern technologies. When Intel opened production facilities in Costa Rica in 1997,

---

18. From www.cleanclothes.org/intro.htm#7 (accessed 08/21/04).

it transformed that country's economy. The firm soon accounted for one-third of total exports, with Intel's sales alone surpassing the country's traditional banana and coffee exports. Overall, Intel invested about a billion dollars in a country of 3.5 million people, and it employed about 5,000 people directly or indirectly; it had a network of almost 500 local supplier companies; and its presence spurred the creation of a high-technology cluster with over 50 other companies. There were years when Intel's activities alone accounted for more than half of the growth of the Costa Rican economy.[19]

Yet host countries—the countries in which MNCs invest—do not always have such positive views of FDI. There is always scope for disagreement over the division of the benefits. Conflict can arise over how much in taxes an oil company should pay to the local government or over the wages an automobile factory should pay to local workers. Local competitors may complain about foreign firms' presence in the domestic market. Some people may be concerned that foreign managers will be insensitive to national social, cultural, and political norms. Developing-country governments have had particularly fraught interactions with MNCs. Many developing countries have gross domestic products (GDPs) smaller than the sales of the MNCs they host, which can make it difficult for them to adequately monitor the activities of these enormous corporations.

Even where there is agreement when the investment is made, views may change over time. One common pattern is that when countries are very poor, they are eager to attract FDI to bring natural resources and other national products to market. Over time, however, as the local economy becomes more sophisticated, local investors become better able to undertake the activities dominated by the MNCs. As the LDC develops, its government may want its own citizens to get more of the benefits of the investment. National businesses may come to resent the foreign competition, and local managers and technicians may feel they no longer need the MNC.

Even the case of Intel in Costa Rica is hardly clear-cut. Just as Intel's expansion spurred the country's economy, its difficulties have held it back: in 2000, when the firm's growth slowed, Intel's problems depressed Costa Rican growth to half of what it would have been otherwise. And in order to attract Intel, the Costa Rican government had exempted the company from all taxes for eight years and from half of its taxes for another four, and had freed it from many regulations that apply to other domestic and foreign firms. In 2014, Intel announced that it would close its main assembly facility in Costa Rica and move these operations to Malaysia, Vietnam, and China.[20] Costa Rica certainly gained from having Intel invest there; but the presence of this huge firm—whose total worldwide sales are larger than Costa Rica's GDP—also imposed real constraints on the small Central American nation, and the closure of its assembly plant caused job losses and economic contraction. In this context, there is plenty of scope for conflict between MNCs and host governments.

19. World Bank, Multilateral Investment Guarantee Agency, *The Impact of Intel in Costa Rica* (Washington, DC: World Bank, 2006).

20. See "Intel Outside," *Economist*, April 19, 2014, www.economist.com/news/americas/21600985-chipmaker-shuts-factory-slicing-away-one-fifth-countrys-exports-intel-outside. The company maintains a smaller research and development facility in Costa Rica, but the country lost some 1,500 jobs.

Host-Country Interactions with MNCs

Like debtors and creditors, foreign corporations and host-country governments have some common interests and some conflicting interests. This mix defines the scope of interactions between national governments and MNCs. As with foreign debt, each side has reasons to work to ensure that the investment can take place. But, again as with foreign debt, each side has strong incentives to bargain for a greater share of the benefits from FDI.

This bargaining can involve negotiations over tax rates, or the company's training of local citizens for more skilled jobs, or the MNC giving some of its business to local suppliers. The host country's weapons include its ability to regulate and tax companies within its borders, up to and including nationalizing them—essentially, forcing them to sell out to local investors or to the government itself. The MNC's weapons include withholding its capital, its technology, or its expertise and ultimately pulling out of the local economy.

Interactions between host countries and MNCs have gone through many phases. Among the most conflictual have been relations over FDI in the raw-materials sector. Before World War I, most FDI was in mining, agriculture, or utilities. These investments, which may have been popular at the outset, eventually became controversial. The case of the United Fruit Company in Central America (see Chapter 4) is a good example: many people in developing nations came to see plantation and raw-materials investments as exploitative. Indeed, after the 1920s, more and more LDCs tended to buy out, take over, or limit foreign investment in these sectors, favoring their own investors instead. One study of forcible takings of MNCs in developing countries between 1960 and 1976, for example, found that while FDI in extractive industries (agriculture and raw materials) and utilities was just one-fifth of the total, these sectors accounted for more than half of the takings.[21]

Political considerations about the role of FDI have added to purely economic concerns. Especially during the 1960s, LDC governments began to believe that large foreign corporations could have a powerful and unwelcome impact on local politics. The activities of the U.S.-based International Telephone & Telegraph (ITT) Corporation in Chile demonstrated the threat. ITT first tried to keep Socialist Party candidate Salvador Allende from being elected president in 1970, for fear that his government would nationalize its investments. When this attempt was unsuccessful, ITT participated in a series of plots to try to overthrow President Allende. The story ended with a coup that destroyed one of Latin America's sturdiest democracies and brought the murderous dictatorship of Augusto Pinochet to power. The notion that American companies could be complicit in such matters, long derided by Westerners as feverish imagining, was soon proved to be accurate by a congressional investigation, and this finding fueled sentiment against MNCs.[22]

---

21. Stephen J. Kobrin, "Foreign Enterprise and Forced Divestment in LDCs," *International Organization* 34, no. 1 (Winter 1980): 65–88.

22. Paul Sigmund, *Multinationals in Latin America* (Madison: University of Wisconsin Press, 1980).

For both economic and political reasons, many countries began restricting MNCs in the 1960s. This was even true of some developed nations: Canada monitored and controlled new investments, while both France and Japan limited foreign companies. But the most sweeping efforts were in the developing world, where foreign corporations were excluded from many industries, and foreign ownership was strictly limited, often to a minority share. Many developing countries nationalized foreign corporations, transferring ownership to local private companies or to the government. Others allowed FDI only if the foreign company did not compete with local firms, shared ownership with local investors, or agreed to reinvest most of its profits in the host country. The turn away from MNCs in the 1960s and 1970s went hand in hand with the turn toward foreign borrowing: by borrowing, developing countries could get foreign capital without allowing foreign ownership of the projects.

But the debt crisis of the 1980s, along with the increased acceptance of global economic integration in the 1990s, eroded resistance to multinationals. Developing countries were desperate for foreign capital, especially after loans dried up. And it appeared that attracting foreign corporations was important to ensuring a nation's integration into global markets. Previous restrictions on FDI were loosened or removed, and many LDCs actively sought to encourage foreign corporations to locate production facilities within their borders. The amounts involved were enormous: while MNCs invested about $2 billion a year in the developing world in the early 1970s, they have averaged over $450 billion a year since 2000. Even accounting for inflation, this is more than a 30-fold increase. As most developing countries have opened their economies to world markets, FDI has become less politically sensitive and more broadly desired.

This does not mean that MNCs are not controversial. Indeed, many people in the developing world continue to regard foreign corporations as economically, politically, or culturally undesirable. Restrictions persist on their activities in developing nations. In industrialized countries too, there are continuing concerns about the exporting of jobs, and in some quarters, about the possibility that foreign investors might compromise national sovereignty. Contemporary controversies over globalization are emblematic of the politically controversial nature of foreign direct investment.

Why Aren't There International Institutions Related to FDI?

There are no effective international institutions associated with FDI. This is in striking contrast to international lending, where there are both regional and global multilateral institutions: the IMF, the World Bank, the Inter-American Development Bank, and so on. One possible reason is that there are fewer (if any) widely accepted truly global concerns associated with FDI than with international finance. In the latter area, it has been generally agreed for over a century that there is a risk of financial crises in one country affecting other countries. This risk creates incentives for countries to find ways, including institutionalized ways, to cooperate to avoid such financial contagion, and international institutions facilitate cooperation in pursuit of these types of common goals. Such incentives are not as strong in the case of FDI.

Nor is there a particularly strong demand for cooperation among countries in bargaining with MNCs. Individual countries that wish to limit or regulate MNCs can do so on their own, and it is not clear that IMF-style international institutions would help with this effort. The role of international institutions in providing information or establishing standards seems less relevant in the case of FDI, where each investment has different characteristics and where host governments are often well equipped to supervise foreign companies.

There have been occasional suggestions that some international agreement or organization might help to create a common set of standards for FDI. Codes of conduct have been proposed, and there has been an increase in private voluntary compliance with such codes of conduct, but this falls far short of an organized intergovernmental institution. Initiatives to institutionalize and regularize relations between MNCs and host nations have made little progress. Thousands of **bilateral investment treaties** have been signed between two countries, providing protection for each other's investors, but nothing even remotely similar to an IMF has emerged.

Despite the absence of any multilateral institution, since the 1980s interactions between foreign corporations and nation-states have generally been less conflictual than they were before then. FDI today leads to much less debate than sovereign lending does. To be sure, in rich countries there remain concerns about the role of MNCs in exporting jobs, while many people in developing countries worry about the economic and political impact of large foreign corporations. Nonetheless, today FDI is widely accepted as an important component of an integrated world economy and as a generally positive factor in economic development.

bilateral investment treaty

An agreement between two countries about the conditions for private investment across borders. Most of these treaties include provisions to protect an investment from government discrimination or expropriation without compensation, as well as mechanisms to resolve disputes.

International Migration: What Happens When People— Rather than Capital— Move across Borders?

Like capital, labor is a factor of production that moves across borders. In fact, international movements of labor and capital can be thought of as responding to similar economic factors and having similar economic effects. Capital can leave one country so that workers can be hired in another; this is what happens when a corporation sets up production abroad. Alternatively, labor can leave one country in order to work for capital in another; this is what happens when workers migrate to a new country to be employed by a corporation there. Whether GM moves a factory to Mexico to hire Mexican workers, or Mexican workers move to Detroit to work for GM, the effect is similar. It therefore makes sense to think about the politics of immigration as part of the broader integration of the world economy.

Of course, the movement of people raises complex social, cultural, and political issues that are typically not present with most other cross-border economic relationships. In addition, there is a substantial difference between migration for economic reasons and the movement of refugees and asylum seekers. We address the noneconomic factors that drive the international movement of people in Chapter 14. For now, we focus entirely on the economic implications of immigration, analyzing it as simply another example of the movement of factors of production from country to country.

International migration has long been a feature of a globalized world economy. In the nineteenth and early twentieth centuries, international labor migration occurred at much higher levels than it does today. During the decades before World War I, some 100 million people left their homelands in Europe and Asia for other parts of the world. The cities of such rapidly growing countries as Canada, Australia, Argentina, and the United States were full of foreign-born workers. For the most part, before 1914 Europeans could move and work wherever they pleased, without complicated legal proceedings or documents (Asian immigration was much more heavily restricted). While international labor movements in recent years have been very large, they are proportionally smaller than those of the nineteenth and early twentieth centuries. However, labor migration has been significant—and also politically controversial.

Today, about one American resident in seven was born in a foreign country, approximately half of them in Latin America. The immigrant share of the population of other developed countries is generally similar to that of the United States (15 percent). It is a bit lower in some countries (10 percent in Italy, 12 percent in France) and substantially higher in some others (20 percent or more in Canada, New Zealand, and Switzerland).[23] Table 8.1 shows the countries with the largest number of immigrants. In almost every developed country, immigration is a politically contentious issue, with some residents favoring more open borders to immigrants and others wishing to limit immigration.[24] What explains these controversies over immigration?

The movement of labor from one country to another is similar to the movement of capital in many ways, and it can be similarly analyzed. Labor, like capital, responds to differential rates of return: higher wages in rich countries attract workers from poor countries. This is true of both unskilled labor and skilled labor, which is typically called human capital because its "owners" have invested in advanced skills. Unskilled workers from El Salvador or Morocco migrate to the United States or Germany in search of higher-paying jobs, just as unskilled workers from Italy and Sweden migrated to the United States and Australia a hundred years ago. Skilled

23. United Nations Population Division, "Trends in International Migrant Stock. The 2017 Revision," http://www.un.org/en/development/desa/population/migration/data/estimates2/estimates17.shtml (accessed 1/3/2018).

24. A useful resource on this highly controversial topic is the Migration Policy Institute, www .migrationpolicy.org (accessed 01/25/11).

TABLE 8.1 ***Countries with the Largest Number of International Migrants, 2017***

	TOTAL MIGRANTS	AS % TOTAL POPULATION
United States	49,776,970	15.3
Saudi Arabia	12,185,284	37.0
Germany	12,165,083	14.8
Russia	11,651,509	8.1
United Kingdom	8,841,717	13.4
United Arab Emirates	8,312,524	88.4
France	7,902,783	12.2
Canada	7,861,226	21.5
Australia	7,035,560	28.8
Spain	5,947,106	12.8

Source: United Nations Population Division, "Trends in International Migrant Stock. The 2017 Revision," http://www.un.org/en/development/desa/population/migration/data/estimates2/estimates17.shtml (accessed 1/3/2018).

workers from India or Argentina too move to Europe or North America in search of higher incomes.

In this sense, immigration can be explained in terms of the Heckscher-Ohlin theory discussed in Chapter 7. Countries with abundant unskilled labor will export unskilled labor; countries scarce in unskilled labor will import it. Differences across countries in labor endowments (and, consequently, wages) mean that there are economic incentives for a labor-rich country such as Mexico or China to export both labor-intensive goods and labor.

The economic impact of labor migration can also be understood in terms of the Heckscher-Ohlin theory. An inflow of unskilled labor from abroad will tend to reduce the wages of local unskilled workers, while an inflow of skilled labor will tend to reduce the wages of local skilled workers. Thus, for example, unskilled workers in developed countries are likely to be harmed by the immigration of unskilled workers from countries with lower wages. Concerns about this labor-market competition are one source of unease about immigration in developed countries (see "How Do We Know?" on p. 380).

This is not a new phenomenon. In the century before 1914, immigration probably also exerted downward pressure on wages in migrant-receiving countries: two scholars have estimated that in such countries as the United States, Australia, and

Explaining Public Opinion on Immigration

Immigration is one of the most politically controversial issues in developed countries. Both the Brexit movement in the United Kingdom and the Trump administration in the United States, along with many populist parties in Europe, have emphasized concern about immigration in their campaigns, and surveys suggest that immigration policy is an important issue for many voters. How do voters decide whether they favor or oppose immigration?

To answer this question, some scholars begin with the same frameworks used to analyze international trade. The Heckscher-Ohlin model, introduced in Chapter 7, demonstrates that the relative abundance or scarcity of factors of production (land, labor, and capital) are critical for understanding trade patterns. For example, countries that have abundant labor are likely to export labor-intensive products. The related Stolper-Samuelson theorem assumes that trade protection benefits the scarce factor of production.

The same logic can explain patterns of immigration and its distributional consequences. Labor-abundant countries, such as India, the Philippines, and Mexico, are likely to experience the largest out-migration of residents, and relatively labor-scarce rich economies, such as Britain, the United States, and Saudi Arabia, are likely to experience the largest inflows of people (see Table 8.1). By the same logic, restricting immigration benefits labor in the receiving country when it is scarce.

Political scientist Kenneth Scheve and economist Matthew Slaughter used the logic of the Heckscher-Ohlin model to explain American voters' responses to surveys about immigration policy.[a] They measured these preferences by responses to a question that appeared in successive American National Election Studies nationwide surveys in 1992, 1994, and 1996: "Do you think the number of immigrants from foreign countries who are permitted to come to the United States to live should be increased a little, increased a lot, decreased a little, decreased a lot, or left the same as it is now?" The authors assumed that respondents believed that U.S. immigrant inflows increase the relative supply of low-skilled workers, which

is a reasonable assumption given that nearly one-third of U.S. immigrants lack a high school diploma or equivalent.[b] The survey also asked respondents about their wages and years of education, which serve as useful proxies for respondents' skill levels.

Scheve and Slaughter analyzed the survey data using a statistical model and found that public opinion toward immigration reflects the logic of the Heckscher-Ohlin framework: respondents with lower skills prefer a more restrictive immigration policy, whereas high-skilled respondents prefer a more open policy. In their interpretation, domestic labor competition is key: unskilled workers—who constitute a relatively scarce factor in the United States—fear that low-skilled immigrants will cause a drop in their wages.

Scheve and Slaughter's findings caused considerable controversy among political scientists, some of whom were skeptical that voters could correctly calculate the income effects predicted by the Heckscher-Ohlin model. Other scholars were skeptical that wages and education actually measure skill level rather than noneconomic attributes like open-mindedness and experience with foreign cultures.[c] Public opinion toward immigration remains a very active research area, with political scientists devising new experiments to determine which economic or noneconomic factors drive individual preferences toward this highly politicized issue.

---

a. Kenneth F. Scheve and Matthew J. Slaughter, "Labor Market Competition and Individual Preferences over Immigration Policy," *Review of Economics and Statistics* 83, no. 1 (February 2001): 133–45.

b. See Pia M. Orrenius and Madeline Zavodny, "Immigrants in the U.S. Labor Market," Working Paper 1306, Federal Reserve Bank of Dallas, September 2013, www.dallasfed.org/assets/documents/research/papers/2013/wp1306.pdf.

c. See Jens Hainmueller and Michael J. Hiscox, "Attitudes toward Highly Skilled and Low-Skilled Immigration: Evidence from a Survey Experiment," *American Political Science Review* 104, no. 1 (February 2010): 61–84.

Argentina, unskilled wages were between one-eighth and one-third lower with immigration than they would have been without it.[25] While this outcome may have been bad for unskilled workers, it was probably good for the countries' economies as a whole, supplying them with much-needed labor.

Immigration benefits people in receiving countries in several ways. Employers gain from the lower wages they can pay. This is especially true for those who hire a lot of unskilled labor; in parts of the United States, sectors such as agriculture, restaurants, and construction have come to rely on cheaper immigrant labor. The economy as a whole profits from having a larger labor force and from the lower cost of production that lower wages can provide. As usual, the benefits for some are counterbalanced by costs to others: if immigration lowers the wages that employers have to pay, it also lowers the wages paid to native workers who compete with immigrants.

The domestic distributional effects of immigration, coupled with national political institutions, help explain changes in policies over time. In the nineteenth century, there was substantial anti-immigrant sentiment among workers in such countries as the United States, Canada, and Australia. But in the 1800s, employers were far more politically powerful than labor; after all, unions were barely organized. So, while there were some restrictions on immigration, especially from Asia, most countries remained open. As the political influence of labor grew, restrictions on immigration expanded and, until the 1960s, were very stringent. During the 1960s, labor shortages began to develop in industrialized nations, and pressure to permit more immigration grew. The result was a loosening of restrictions; this may also have been due to the rising influence of skilled workers in rich countries, who were less concerned about competition from unskilled immigrants.

The 1990s saw the rise of political movements that were less enthusiastic about, or downright hostile to, immigration. Concern about the economic impact of immigration rose with the financial crisis that began in 2008. In the United States and Europe, many people worried that immigrants from less developed countries were taking jobs away from native workers and driving wages down. A dramatic refugee crisis that grew out of civil war in Syria and unrest elsewhere in the Middle East and North Africa compounded these anxieties. The European Union, which had received about 200,000 requests for asylum in 2008, received 1.3 million in both 2015 and 2016, and many Europeans were concerned that their countries were being, or would be, flooded with refugees.[26] Concern about immigration was central to the rise of right-wing populism in Europe, to the Brexit campaign in the United Kingdom, and to the presidential campaign of Donald Trump in the United States (for more on these developments, see Chapter 14).

---

25. Kevin O'Rourke and Jeffrey Williamson, *Globalization and History: The Evolution of a Nineteenth-Century Atlantic Economy* (Cambridge, MA: MIT Press, 1999), Tables 8.1 and 8.3.

26. Eurostat, "Asylum and First Time Asylum Applicants—Annual Aggregated Data (Rounded)," http://ec.europa.eu/eurostat/tgm/table.do?tab=table&init=1&language=en&pcode=tps00191&plugin=1 (accessed 08/14/17).

The political economy of immigration involves additional economic considerations. One such concern is the potential cost of social programs that immigrants may use disproportionately, inasmuch as they tend to be poorer than natives. However, immigrants typically pay taxes, so the overall (net) effect may be hard to distinguish.[27] In some contemporary American and European debates, opponents of immigration express particular concern about the fiscal effects of large-scale immigration. Supporters and opponents of immigration often raise noneconomic issues as well, which we will discuss in more detail in Chapter 14.

Certainly, immigration is one of the more prominent and visible features of contemporary globalization. Today, there are many countervailing economic interests at play that drive opposing viewpoints: workers who would compete with immigrants and workers who would not, taxpayers concerned about the cost of immigrants and those who see them as beneficial, employers who depend on immigrant labor and those who do not. The topic promises to continue to be controversial.

Conclusion: The Politics of International Investment

International finance is the most globalized portion of the international economy. People and governments worldwide try mightily to attract foreign corporations and to qualify for loans from foreign lenders. There are substantial advantages to having access to the world's enormous pool of capital. This benefit gives governments powerful reasons to try to collaborate with foreign investors to smooth the path of capital as it moves from country to country.

However, international finance is not an unmitigated blessing. Foreign loans can be a boon to a developing nation, but they can become an oppressive burden that forces the population to make huge sacrifices in order for their government to keep up interest payments. Foreign investment by MNCs can bring a country valuable technology and expertise, but it can also impose severe constraints on how much room the host nation has to maneuver. Governments have many interests in common with international financiers, but they also have many conflicting interests.

International finance is inherently political because powerful private actors, governments, and international institutions all come together to bargain over the terms of international financial relations. Such negotiations—over foreign loans, debt bailouts, IMF packages, the role of MNCs, and other financial issues—can be

---

27. Like many other aspects of immigration, the fiscal costs and benefits of immigrants are hotly debated, even among scholars. For two contending views, both from conservative think tanks, see Robert E. Rector, Christine Kim, and Shanea Watkins, "The Fiscal Cost of Low-Skill Households to the U.S. Taxpayer," *Heritage Foundation Special Report* 12 (April 4, 2007); and Daniel Griswold, "The Fiscal Impact of Immigration Reform: The Real Story," *Free Trade Bulletin* 30 (May 21, 2007).

contentious. The policies associated with them are also often very controversial within nations, adding to the problems' politicization.

Many countries, past and present, have used foreign capital to finance rapid economic growth and development. And many individuals, groups, and companies have benefited from their access to international finance. However, when things go wrong in the international financial system, they can go spectacularly wrong in ways that can profoundly impact international politics—and the lives of billions of people.

Study Tool Kit

Interests, Interactions, and Institutions in Context

- Within borrowing nations, there are many actors who value access to foreign funds. However, there are others who resent the constraints and burdens that foreign investments sometimes impose on debtors. Similar conflicting interests exist within lending nations.

- At the international level, both lenders and borrowers, like investors and recipients of investment, have a common interest in sustaining capital flows, which benefit both sides. Nonetheless, they may enter into conflict—especially over how the benefits from the loans or investments will be divided.

- Lenders and borrowers, and investors and recipients, bargain over the investments that tie them together. There is frequent disagreement over debt payments to foreign creditors and profit payments to foreign corporations.

- An array of important and influential international institutions structure interactions in the international financial realm. The most prominent is the IMF, which has often played a major role in managing the problems of heavily indebted countries. Like international finance generally, the role of the IMF is very controversial: some analysts think it contributes to the cooperative resolution of financial problems, while others think it takes unfair advantage of struggling debtor nations.

Key Terms

portfolio investment, p. 349

sovereign lending, p. 349

foreign direct investment (FDI), p. 349

World Bank, p. 354

recession, p. 356

depression, p. 356

default, p. 357

austerity, p. 359

Bank for International Settlements, p. 361

International Monetary Fund (IMF), p. 361

multinational corporation (MNC), p. 371

bilateral investment treaty, p. 377

For Further Reading

Chinn, Menzie D., and Jeffry A. Frieden. *Lost Decades: The Making of America's Debt Crisis and the Long Recovery.* **New York: Norton, 2011.** Analyzes the politics and economics of the biggest financial crisis since the Great Depression.

Copelovitch, Mark. *The International Monetary Fund in the Global Economy: Banks, Bonds and Bailouts.* **Cambridge: Cambridge University Press, 2010.** Analyzes the politics and economics of the role of the IMF in resolving international debt conflicts.

McDowell, Daniel. *Brother, Can You Spare a Billion? The United States, the IMF, and the International Lender of Last Resort.* **Oxford: Oxford University Press, 2017.** Analyzes the role of the United States and the IMF in addressing debt and financial crises.

Mosley, Layna. *Labor Rights and Multinational Production.* **Cambridge: Cambridge University Press, 2011.** Assesses the impact of FDI on the rights and opportunities available to workers in developing countries.

Obstfeld, Maurice, and Alan Taylor. *Global Capital Markets: Integration, Crisis, and Growth.* **Cambridge: Cambridge University Press, 2004.** Provides a detailed description and analysis of the history and contemporary nature of international financial markets.

Pandya, Sonal. *Trading Spaces: Foreign Direct Investment Regulation, 1970–2000.* **Cambridge: Cambridge University Press, 2014.** Analyzes the politics and economics of national responses to foreign corporations.

Singer, David A. *Regulating Capital: Setting Standards for the International Financial System.* **Ithaca, NY: Cornell University Press, 2007.** Analyzes the economics and politics of international financial regulation in a world of global financial markets.

Tomz, Michael. *Reputation and International Cooperation: Sovereign Debt across Three Centuries.* **Princeton, NJ: Princeton University Press, 2007.** Explores the politics and economics of private lending to governments historically and in the present.

Walter, Stefanie. *Financial Crises and the Politics of Macroeconomic Adjustments.* **Cambridge: Cambridge University Press, 2013.** Explains the causes and consequences of financial crises, and government responses to them, with both historical and contemporary applications.

9

International Monetary Relations

THE PUZZLE *In the absence of global government, how are international currencies supplied and international monetary relations regulated?*

Above: International monetary relations are often controversial. Today, the European Central Bank in Frankfurt, Germany, implements monetary policies for the entire eurozone, which comprises 19 member countries that gave up their national currencies for the euro.

On December 18, 2001, rioters swept through the cities of Argentina. They were furious about three straight years of economic stagnation and government economic policies that seemed to make matters worse. Most recently, the government had frozen bank deposits so that Argentines could take only small amounts of cash out of their bank accounts—and nothing out of the very popular accounts that many people had in U.S. dollars.

In response to the rioting, President Fernando de la Rúa declared a state of siege, but the following day the disorder spread as hundreds of thousands of middle-class Argentines joined the protests in the streets. That evening, the economy minister stepped down. A day later, violent clashes with police led to more than two dozen deaths around the country, and huge crowds surrounded the presidential palace in Buenos Aires. At the end of the day, de la Rúa resigned and was evacuated by helicopter from the presidential palace to avoid the hostile crowds.

The president of the Senate, a member of the opposition Peronist Party that controlled both houses of Congress, assumed the interim presidency. Two days later, the Peronists installed provincial governor Adolfo Rodríguez Saá as president until national elections could be held.

Rodríguez Saá declared the largest default the world had seen—on $93 billion in sovereign debt. But he too faced protests, and resigned a week after taking office.

This time the president of the Chamber of Deputies, also a Peronist, stepped in as interim president. After further turmoil, the legislature appointed to the presidency Eduardo Duhalde, the Peronist candidate who had lost the 1999 presidential election to the now disgraced de la Rúa. Meanwhile, the country had entered full-fledged economic collapse. Argentine gross domestic product (GDP), which had declined by 8 percent over the three previous years of recession, dropped by 11 percent in 2002, and unemployment soared above 20 percent.

The ultimate reason for these extraordinary events—nationwide riots, five presidents in less than two weeks, the biggest default in history, economic disintegration—was the Argentine government's policies toward its currency. Ten years earlier, the government had made the Argentine peso equal to one U.S. dollar and fixed it at this exchange rate. The currency policy had led to rapid growth and many other economic achievements in Argentina. But by 2001, the commitment was dragging the economy downward. It was widely blamed for general economic stagnation and for the specific banking policies that provoked popular outrage. Argentina's fortunes rose dramatically, and fell even more dramatically, with its currency policies.

Many people who find currencies confusing or boring may be surprised that exchange rates could be responsible for such striking developments. But the Argentine events are not alone in illustrating the importance of currencies and currency policies to economics and politics—and to people's everyday lives. A couple of weeks after Argentine society exploded into violence over the exchange rate, and halfway around the world, came another, unrelated but equally remarkable, currency development. Twelve European countries abandoned their national monies, some of which had existed for centuries. In place of the Deutschmark, franc, lira, and other currencies, they adopted the euro (€), a common European currency. The creation of the euro dominated European politics and economics for most of the 1990s, and the early 2000s were spent consolidating, managing, and expanding the new currency.

Then, in 2008, the global financial crisis hit the eurozone. The international economic slowdown brought a European borrowing boom to an end and plunged the continent into recession. In the ten years that followed, the eurozone crisis dragged the entire European economy down into stagnation, threatened the existence of the euro itself, contributed to Britain's decision to exit the European Union (EU), and overall, constituted the gravest threat to European integration since the EU's formation. European currency politics—the euro's rise, creation, evolution, and crisis—have been central to the continent's political economy for 40 years. Argentina and Europe are not alone: in many countries, currency policy is one of the most hotly contested economic and political issues.

National governments have pursued very different policies toward their national currencies. Today, most governments choose among three monetary paths. One option is to give up the national currency in favor of another money—as has occurred in a number of Caribbean and Latin American countries, which have adopted the U.S. dollar, and in most European countries, which have adopted the euro. Other governments have tied the national currency's value to that of another country, such as the dollar or the euro (as we will discuss in more detail). Finally, many governments continue to maintain a separate national currency whose value is allowed to change in response to markets and other forces.

How and why do governments choose any one of these three monetary paths? The international monetary order has also varied enormously over the years. As we saw in Chapter 1, from the 1870s until 1914 most of the world's major economies were on a classical gold standard that tied their currencies together. After World War II, a revised version of this approach, the Bretton Woods monetary system, reigned until 1973. Since then, international and regional currency arrangements have been in flux.

Thinking Analytically about International Monetary Relations

This chapter makes several points about the interests, interactions, and institutions associated with international monetary policy. First, within each country there are many actors who have an interest in the country's monetary affairs, which leads to conflict over the appropriate currency policy to pursue. We will see, briefly, how national currency policies are set and which groups have a stake in those policies.

In addition to individual national choices, there are important global monetary issues. Indeed, international monetary affairs—the interrelationships among national monies—are central to the international economy and thus to world politics. Stable relations among national currencies allow actors in one country to make payments to actors in other countries, making it easier for goods, people, and capital to move across borders—all important forms of international interaction. Just as it is hard to imagine national economies without national money, it is hard to see how the modern world economy could function without some arrangement for cooperation in the use of money among countries.

Yet, while national governments supply national monies, there is no international government to organize international monetary affairs. Virtually everyone has an interest in the existence of a functioning international monetary system, but different arrangements benefit some actors more than others. This disparity leads to disagreements about how such a system should be organized. How is such a quintessentially governmental function as the provision of currencies carried out at the global level in the absence of global government?

What Are Exchange Rates, and Why Do They Matter?

A national monetary system allows for the convenient exchange of goods, services, and capital. It is a classic public good (see Chapter 2): it benefits everyone, but because people cannot be excluded from its benefits and charged for them, there is little incentive for private firms to provide it. This is why national governments typically determine the currency, print bills, mint coins, and control the money supply. It is also why governments try to instill trust in the national currency. Almost everyone in a country can agree on the desirability of a recognizable, trustworthy national money and stable prices.

But in addition to a currency's domestic use, it exists in relation to other national currencies. For example, the U.S. dollar can be used not only to buy goods and services in the United States, but also to buy euros, Canadian dollars, and Mexican pesos, among other currencies. The price of a national currency relative to other national currencies is its **exchange rate**, and like other prices, the exchange rate can go up or down. When the dollar goes up in value against some other currency—such that, for example, a dollar can buy more pesos—it is said to strengthen, or **appreciate**. When the dollar's value goes down against that of some other currency—such that, for example, a dollar can buy fewer pesos—it is said to weaken, or **depreciate**, or to be **devalued**.

When a country's currency appreciates, it is more expensive for foreigners to buy the country's goods and services; when the currency depreciates, it is cheaper to do so. The most direct experience that many people have with currency movements is as tourists or, if they live near a national border, with prices around the border. American travelers to Europe find, for example, that when the dollar is strong, local prices in Europe seem relatively low. The hotels they stay in, the restaurants they go to, and the souvenirs they purchase are relatively inexpensive. When the dollar weakens, however, local prices get much higher.

For example, in March 2017 an American staying in an Italian hotel that charged €100 a night would have paid about $105 a night, because the euro was worth $1.05; a year later, with the euro worth $1.24, the same hotel room at the same euro price would have cost 124 a night. Over the course of that year, the dollar had depreciated by about 18 percent against the euro, so goods and services in euro countries, such as Italy, cost 18 percent more. (See Figure 9.1 for an indication of how the value of the dollar has fluctuated against an average of other currencies.)

The same is true of goods bought and sold across borders. If a currency goes up or down, the prices that foreigners pay for goods priced in that currency rise or fall as well. So, a pair of Italian shoes that cost €100 in Italy in March 2017 could have been exported to the United States and sold for about $105 (plus shipping costs), while a year later, after the dollar had depreciated by about 18 percent, the same €100 Italian shoes would have sold for $124. When the U.S. dollar is weak against other currencies, foreign goods are expensive to Americans; however, when

---

exchange rate
The price at which one currency is exchanged for another.

appreciate
In terms of a currency, to increase in value relative to other currencies.

depreciate
In terms of a currency, to decrease in value relative to other currencies.

devalue
To reduce the value of one currency relative to other currencies.

FIGURE 9.1 **The Value of the U.S. Dollar, 1975–2016**

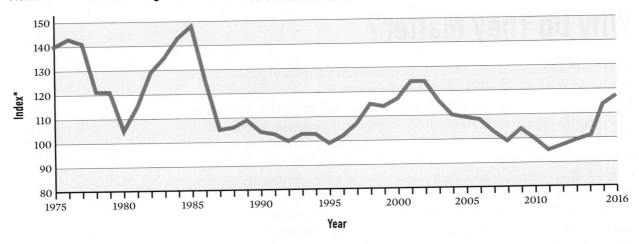

Figure source: World Bank, World Development Indicators, http://data.worldbank.org/ indicator (accessed 11/13/17).

*Real effective exchange-rate index. The real effective exchange-rate index is a measure of the value of the dollar against a weighted average of the currencies of the United States' major trading partners. The base year, 2010, is given the value of 100. Higher values indicate a stronger (more appreciated) dollar relative to the world's major currencies, and lower values indicate a weaker (depreciated) dollar.

the U.S. dollar is strong against other currencies, foreign goods are inexpensive to Americans.

Although the attractiveness of a given country to foreign tourists is not particularly important to most nations, the attractiveness of that country's goods, services, and investment opportunities is crucial. Thus, the exchange rate is a very important part of a country's international economic relations.

How Are Currency Values Determined?

Like other prices, an exchange rate goes up or down in response to changes in supply and demand. Many factors can affect supply and demand for a national money. Perhaps the most relevant is relative interest rates. As we saw in Chapter 8, foreigners considering investing in a country weigh relative interest rates; if U.S. interest rates are higher, investments in the United States are more attractive (everything else being equal).[1] But in order to invest in the United States, investors need dollars. Higher interest rates make it more profitable for people to put (or keep) their money in the country, so higher interest rates increase the demand for the currency and lead to its appreciation.

Of course, the relationship works in the opposite direction as well: if people want fewer dollars, the dollar's exchange rate will go down. Lower interest rates can lead to a depreciation of the currency, just as higher interest rates can lead to an appreciation. More generally, if foreigners want to invest in a country, they have to buy its currency; so if there is a lot of investment in an economy, demand for its currency will rise and the exchange rate will tend to appreciate. When foreigners invest heavily in the United States, all else equal, the dollar strengthens.

---

1. For convenience, we ignore trade-related sources of currency movements. It should be clear that anything that makes a country's goods and services more attractive to foreigners will increase demand for the country's currency and lead to an appreciation (and vice versa).

The relationship between interest rates and the value of the national currency is particularly important because governments routinely raise and lower interest rates as part of their **monetary policy**. Indeed, monetary policy is a powerful tool of national governments, which attempt to affect macroeconomic conditions—unemployment, inflation, overall economic growth—by manipulating monetary conditions.

In most developed countries, national monetary policy is implemented by a **central bank** (for example, the Federal Reserve in the United States). Central banks most commonly affect monetary conditions by raising or lowering interest rates. If the central bank wants to stimulate the economy, it lowers interest rates. Lower interest rates make it easier for people and companies to borrow, and allow the economy to expand. If the central bank wants to restrain the economy, typically because prices are rising and there is concern about inflation, it raises interest rates; this makes it harder to borrow and restrains demand.

Because interest rates also affect the exchange rate—higher interest rates make the currency more attractive and tend to raise its value—national monetary policy can also have a powerful impact on the value of the national currency. And this too can be a tool of national economic policy. For example, if a government wants to stimulate demand for its country's products in world markets, it can lower interest rates so that the currency depreciates. The weaker currency makes local goods cheaper to foreigners and spurs exports; it also makes foreign goods more expensive to local residents and reduces imports. In this way, a monetary policy that weakens the currency can help the nation's producers. Of course, a weaker currency means that citizens can buy less with their money, so the government has to choose which effects it finds most appealing.

Allowing the Exchange Rate to Change

There are other choices facing a national government with respect to its currency. Among these, the most important is whether and how to let the exchange rate change relative to others. The simplest choice is whether to "fix" the exchange rate or let it "float." A **fixed exchange rate** is one whose government promises to keep the national money at some established value in terms of another currency or in terms of a precious metal such as gold.

During the period of the classical **gold standard**, from the 1870s to 1914, a country's government "went on gold" by promising to exchange its currency for gold at an established rate (in the United States, it was one troy ounce of gold for $20.67). This move made the country's currency equivalent to gold and interchangeable at a fixed rate with the money of any other gold-standard country. Much of the world, as a result, essentially shared one currency. Gold-backed money invested by Germans in Japan, or by Belgians in Canada, would be paid back in equivalent amounts of gold-backed money. Contracted prices would not fluctuate, for exchange rates did not change.

A government that commits itself to a fixed exchange rate also commits itself to the policies necessary to maintain the set rate. For example, if the currency was posed to depreciate against other currencies, meaning the exchange rate would

monetary policy

An important tool of national governments to influence broad macroeconomic conditions such as unemployment, inflation, and economic growth. Typically, governments alter their monetary policies by changing national interest rates or exchange rates.

central bank

The institution that regulates monetary conditions in an economy, typically by affecting interest rates and the quantity of money in circulation.

fixed exchange rate

An exchange-rate policy under which a government commits itself to keep its currency at or around a specific value relative to another currency or a commodity, such as gold.

gold standard

The monetary system that prevailed between about 1870 and 1914, in which countries tied their currencies to gold at a legally fixed price.

The U.S. dollar was backed by gold from 1879 to 1933, meaning that the government needed to own enough gold to cover the dollars in circulation at a predetermined exchange rate.

fall, the government might raise interest rates to have money keep coming into the country—in other words, so that foreigners would buy the country's currency. This increase in demand for the currency would make the exchange rate go back up to the set level.

At the other extreme is a **floating exchange rate**, under which a currency's value is allowed to change more or less freely, driven by markets or other factors. This is the regime currently in place for most major currencies, including the U.S. dollar, the Japanese yen, and the euro. If a government chooses this exchange-rate regime, the price of the currency moves around in line with changes in supply and demand. Map 9.1 on p. 394 indicates which countries worldwide follow fixed versus floating exchange-rate regimes.

There are intermediate steps between a fully fixed currency and a freely floating one. A government can allow its currency to vary, but only within limits, or it can fix the exchange rate for short periods, changing the currency's value as desired. This approach avoids some of the costs of each system but also forgoes some of the benefits. At the global level, the **Bretton Woods monetary system**, which followed the classical gold standard and prevailed from 1945 to 1973, was something of a compromise. It was based on a fixed rate and a gold standard for the United States and on a "fixed but adjustable rate" for other currencies that were on a dollar standard. This system of fixed but adjustable rates (an **adjustable peg**) required that governments keep currency values fixed for relatively long periods but permitted them to alter ("adjust") currency rates if and when they found it desirable to do so.

In practice, the Bretton Woods monetary system meant that the U.S. dollar's value could not change (it was fixed at $35 per ounce of gold). Other governments also fixed their currency against the dollar, but the national government of a country other than the United States could devalue or readjust its currency's value if it felt a change was necessary. Typically, such changes were infrequent, occurring once every five to seven years. The Bretton Woods monetary system was seen as a middle ground between gold-standard rigidity and complete unpredictability. As under the gold standard, exchange rates were stable enough to encourage international trade and investment. As under a more flexible system, the exchange rates could be varied as necessary, albeit rarely.

As these examples indicate, a national government's decisions about the exchange rate often depend on international monetary conditions. While national policies are important, from the standpoint of international economics and politics more generally, it is the *global* nature of international monetary relations that is most relevant. We will return to these international issues later in the chapter. First, however, we evaluate the potential for *domestic* conflicts of interest over exchange-rate policy.

floating exchange rate

An exchange-rate policy under which a government permits its currency to be traded on the open market without direct government control or intervention.

Bretton Woods monetary system

The monetary order negotiated among the World War II Allies in 1944, which lasted until the 1970s and which was based on a U.S. dollar tied to gold. Other currencies were fixed to the dollar but were permitted to adjust their exchange rates.

adjustable peg

A monetary system of fixed but adjustable rates. Governments are expected to keep their currencies fixed for extended periods but are permitted to adjust the exchange rate from time to time as economic conditions change.

Who Cares about Exchange Rates, and Why?

A national government's decision about its exchange rate leads the country to take other policies to support its decision. Both the initial currency policy and the other economic measures needed to sustain it affect different domestic groups differently. This disparity can lead to disagreement over the appropriate currency policy to pursue.

Governments

A government deciding what to do with its currency must consider important trade-offs and domestic interests that are often in conflict. One dimension of conflict involves whether the currency should be fixed, floating, or in between. Each choice helps some domestic actors and hurts others.

Fixed exchange rates, such as the gold standard or a peg to the dollar, provide currency stability and predictability, which greatly facilitate international trade, investment, finance, migration, and travel. Under the gold standard, businessmen, investors, and immigrants did not have to worry about changes in exchange rates or about major impediments to moving money around the world. The stimulus to trade was substantial; being on gold in this period is estimated to have raised trade between two countries by 30–70 percent.[2] Generally speaking, a fixed currency provides stability that facilitates international economic exchange; it also provides a monetary anchor that keeps prices stable. A fixed currency is thus very much in the interest of those engaged in cross-border trade, investment, finance, and travel, as well as those who want to keep inflation low.

However, there are costs to fixing the exchange rate, so some people and governments are strongly opposed to it. By definition, a government on a fixed exchange rate is committed to maintaining its currency's value, even if economic conditions could be improved with a change. A fixed rate reduces or eliminates a government's ability to have its own independent monetary policy, which can be costly. For example, if an economy is in recession, a common economic policy response is to lower interest rates and thereby promote borrowing to expand consumption and investment. This move stimulates the economy, as mentioned earlier, and may help alleviate the recession.

But if a country is on a fixed exchange rate, its interest rates are dictated by the need to keep the currency's value constant. For example, the government will raise interest rates if the exchange rate threatens to depreciate, in order to encourage investors to buy the currency. This is the case even in difficult economic

---

2. See, for example, A. Estevadeordal, B. Frantz, and A. M. Taylor, "The Rise and Fall of World Trade, 1870–1939," *Quarterly Journal of Economics* 118 (May 2003): 359–407; and J. Ernesto Lopez-Cordova and Christopher M. Meissner, "Exchange-Rate Regimes and International Trade: Evidence from the Classical Gold Standard Era," *American Economic Review* 93, no. 1 (2003): 344–53.

MAP 9.1 *Exchange-Rate Regimes, 2015*

Today, several of the world's major economies, including the United States and Japan, allow the value of their currency to float independently. However, exchange-rate regimes around the world span a wide spectrum, from those that have given up their national currency, such as countries in the eurozone, to those that peg the value of their currency to the dollar, the euro, or other currencies. Countries with a "crawling peg" or "managed floating currency" can be considered to have a floating exchange rate, though with some limits on changes in the value of the currency.

FIXED RATE REGIMES

No national currency

- USES DOLLAR
- USES EURO
- USES CFA FRANC

Fixed peg arrangements

- PEGGED TO DOLLAR
- PEGGED TO EURO
- PEGGED TO "OTHER"

FLOATING RATE REGIMES

- CRAWLING PEG
- MANAGED FLOATING CURRENCY
- INDEPENDENTLY FLOATING CURRENCY

Map source: International Monetary Fund, *Annual Report on Exchange Arrangements and Exchange Restrictions 2016*, October 2016, www.imf .org/en/Publications/Annual-Report-on-Exchange-Arrangements-and-Exchange-Restrictions/Issues/2017/01/25/Annual-Report-on-Exchange-Arrangements-and-Exchange-Restrictions-2016-43741.

Arctic Ocean

RUSSIA

SWEDEN
FINLAND
UNITED
KINGDOM
NORWAY
NETH.
GERMANY
BELARUS
IRELAND
UKRAINE
FRANCE
KAZAKHSTAN
MONGOLIA
GEORGIA
N. KOREA
ITALY
SERBIA
UZBEKISTAN
S. KOREA
PORTUGAL
SPAIN
GREECE
TURKEY
TURKMENISTAN
KYRGYZSTAN
JAPAN
TAJIKISTAN
CHINA
MOROCCO
ISRAEL
LEB.
SYRIA
IRAQ
IRAN
NEPAL
BHUTAN
HONG KONG
Pacific Ocean
JORDAN
KUWAIT
ALGERIA
LIBYA
EGYPT
SAUDI
ARABIA
UAE
MYANMAR
(BURMA)
TAIWAN
OMAN
INDIA
MAURITANIA
MALI
NIGER
CHAD
ERITREA
PAKISTAN
VIETNAM
SENEGAL
YEMEN
THAILAND
PHILIPPINES
GUINEA
NIGERIA
SUDAN
AFGHANISTAN
BANGLADESH
LAOS
PALAU
CEN.
AFR.
REP.
S. SUDAN
ETHIOPIA
SRI LANKA
CAMBODIA
CAMEROON
MICRONESIA
GHANA
UGANDA
SOMALIA
MALAYSIA
IVORY COAST
D.R.
CONGO
KENYA
INDONESIA
PAPUA NEW GUINEA
TANZANIA
Indian Ocean
ANGOLA
MALAWI
ZAMBIA
MADAGASCAR
NAMIBIA
MOZAMBIQUE
ZIMBABWE
AUSTRALIA
SOUTH
AFRICA
BOTSWANA
NEW
ZEALAND

A currency exchange-rate board, like this one in Tehran, Iran, is a familiar site for the foreign traveler. Travelers to foreign countries find that their money goes further when their country's currency is strong relative to the local currency. The same is true when goods are traded across borders; buyers find that foreign goods are less expensive when their own currency is relatively stronger.

times, when there can be strong pressures for the government to allow the currency to depreciate so as to make the country's goods more attractive to foreign consumers. The government's commitment to a fixed exchange rate makes this impossible.

A fixed exchange rate, of course, makes the central bank—the institution charged with running domestic monetary policy—much less influential, and central bankers may have reservations about giving up their ability to control interest rates. More generally, producers of goods that compete on import or export markets might want the government to be able to change the currency's value so that it becomes easier for them to sell their products. But this is impossible with a fixed exchange rate.

Both of these fixed-currency constraints were at work in the run-up to the 2001 Argentine crisis, and in the eurozone crisis that began in 2008. In 2001, the Argentine peso had been tightly fixed to the U.S. dollar for 10 years, but the Argentine economy was in great distress. There were powerful pressures for the government to address broader economic conditions—in particular, to lower interest rates and to depreciate the currency so that Argentine goods would become more competitive on international markets. To carry out this strategy, the Argentine government needed to loosen the peso's link to the dollar. But at the same time, many Argentines did not want to see the peso's value change; among them were millions of homeowners whose mortgages were in dollars and who would have had to pay substantially more in pesos if the currency was devalued. With powerful interests on both sides, the Argentine government was paralyzed.

Members of the eurozone faced a similar instance of the constraints of a fixed exchange rate after 2008. As the global financial crisis deepened and the European debt crisis worsened, some countries that used the euro, such as Greece, Ireland, Spain, and Portugal, faced severe economic difficulties. If those countries had had their own national monies, they could have loosened monetary policy and depreciated their currencies. This action would have made their goods cheaper for other countries, increasing the amount of goods they exported, and thus bringing more money back into the country. By selling more, their economies would have grown faster, and perhaps they could have exported their way out of recession. But these nations were part of a multicountry currency union, whose monetary and exchange-rate policies were set in Frankfurt by the European Central Bank (ECB) on behalf of the entire eurozone. This meant that the governments of these nations simply did not have the tools of monetary and exchange-rate policy in their arsenals as they attempted to confront the crisis.

The problems that a fixed exchange rate caused for the Argentine and eurozone governments demonstrate one important advantage of a floating exchange rate: it gives a government more freedom to pursue its own monetary policies, as it is not hampered by the need to keep the exchange rate fixed. But this advantage is countered by the fact that floating exchange rates can move around a great deal, which can impose costs on those engaged in international trade and investment, and which more generally can impede international economic exchange. Volatility (that is, frequent significant shifts) in currency values almost certainly makes international trade and investment, travel, and finance more difficult.[3]

Consumers and Businesses

Different actors have different interests, and often conflicting views, about how the national currency should be managed, depending on their position in the economy. Those whose economic activities are entirely domestic are likely to favor a floating exchange rate because they are indifferent to currency fluctuations but want the government to be able to affect the national economy as necessary. Those with international economic concerns have an interest in a fixed currency because too much volatility in exchange rates can be harmful to their activities.

Just as people, firms, and groups may have conflicting interests over whether a currency should be fixed or floating, actors' interests may also differ over a currency's desirable value (that is, whether it should be stronger or weaker). Government policy can have a powerful impact on whether a currency's value rises or falls in the short and medium run, which in turn can affect important domestic interests.

A strong exchange rate allows consumers and others to buy more of the world's products, thereby increasing national purchasing power. But there is a trade-off: a strong exchange rate makes domestic goods more expensive to foreigners, which harms national producers who compete with foreigners on local or world markets. This is why manufacturers and farmers typically complain about a strong currency: it leads to a surge of cheaper imports, and it dampens exports.

For example, the U.S. dollar appreciated by more than 50 percent between 1981 and 1985. This rise in value was associated with a big increase in Americans' purchasing power and ability to buy goods from the rest of the world—all of which contributed to a sense of prosperity among American consumers. However, the strong dollar led to a flood of cheaper imports into the United States and made U.S. exports more expensive to foreigners. As a result, serious problems arose in American manufacturing industries, and 1.5 million manufacturing jobs were lost.

The strong dollar was particularly damaging to firms that either sold many of their products abroad or competed with imports; it led the president of one such firm, Caterpillar Tractor, to call the strong dollar "the single most important trade issue facing the U.S." Under this pressure, in 1985 the Senate passed a unanimous

---

3. The specific constraints on exchange-rate policy are known as the Mundell-Fleming conditions, after the two economists who pioneered the approach. They imply, simply put, that in a financially integrated country, the government must choose between a stable exchange rate and an independent monetary policy; it cannot have both. See, for example, Jeffry A. Frieden, "Invested Interests: The Politics of National Economic Policies in a World of Global Finance," *International Organization* 45, no. 4 (Autumn 1991): 407–31.

resolution calling on the administration to depreciate the dollar.[4] Eventually, the dollar did decline, and complaints subsided.

A weak currency gives a big boost to national producers. This is why countries that are trying to encourage exports—such as many developing countries—typically keep their currencies weak. It is also why manufacturers and farmers, who compete with foreign producers both at home and abroad, have an interest in a relatively weak exchange rate. But there is a trade-off here too: a weak currency reduces national purchasing power, making consumers worse off. As the dollar declines, Americans can buy fewer of the world's products—and tourists cannot afford foreign vacations so easily. Declines in a currency's value and increases in prices of foreign goods can also contribute to overall price rises and inflation.

Both strong and weak currencies have advantages and disadvantages, and there is no particular reason that one or the other is better for a country. A strong currency helps consumers (and tourists) but hurts producers who compete with foreigners; a weak currency helps producers but hurts consumers. These conflicts of interest make currency policy controversial within countries and can make governments sensitive to the domestic political and economic effects of their currency arrangements.

Such conflicts are evident when the possibility arises that a government might devalue its currency. Because the devaluation makes foreign goods more expensive and domestic goods relatively cheaper, it is in the interests of national producers. But the devaluation also reduces consumers' ability to buy goods and services. In this context, it is perhaps not surprising that governments in democratic systems typically avoid currency devaluations or depreciations in the run-up to elections, for fear that the negative impact on consumers will cost them votes.[5]

A government's interest in exchange-rate policy depends on the structure of its economy, its interest groups, and its political system. In a country with many firms and individuals engaged in economic activities across borders, the government is likely to face powerful pressure to stabilize or fix the currency's value. This is why the smaller economies of Europe that were extremely open to trade with other European countries (the Netherlands, Belgium, Luxembourg, Austria, Ireland) were among the strongest supporters of the creation of the euro. However, some larger European economies that traded and invested less across European borders (like France and Italy) were less enthusiastic.

This is also why, in the Western Hemisphere, small countries that are tightly tied to U.S. trade, investment, and tourism (such as Caribbean island nations, El Salvador, and Panama) have been the most likely to adopt the U.S. dollar or to fix their currencies to it. Larger, more self-sufficient economies (like Mexico and Brazil) have typically allowed their currencies to vary.

One currency policy that has been the source of much controversy in recent decades is the tendency of some governments to keep their currency very weak over

---

4. Jeffry A. Frieden, "Economic Integration and the Politics of Monetary Policy in the United States," in *Internationalization and Domestic Politics*, ed. Robert O. Keohane and Helen V. Milner, 127–30 (Cambridge: Cambridge University Press, 1996).

5. S. Brock Blomberg, Jeffry Frieden, and Ernesto Stein, "Sustaining Fixed Rates: The Political Economy of Currency Pegs in Latin America," *Journal of Applied Economics* 8, no. 2 (November 2005): 203–25.

long periods of time in order to stimulate their exports. The most prominent example is that of China, which after 1979 organized its development strategy around the promotion of manufactured goods for export. A major part of this strategy involved keeping the Chinese currency, the renminbi, artificially weak. The export promotion policy was very successful, and China has become one of the world's greatest exporters.

But if the government had let the dollars its exporters earned come back into the Chinese economy, they would have been used to buy renminbi for local purchases, and the renminbi would have appreciated against the dollar. This, in turn, would have made Chinese exports less attractive on world markets. So the Chinese government used a series of measures to keep its currency depreciated. It controlled capital flows and the domestic market for foreign currency, and it held very large reserves of dollars overseas (keeping them from coming back to China to be spent).

The Chinese government's currency policies were very successful at promoting the nation's exports. But they created problems both at home and abroad. Within China, the weak-currency policy effectively taxed consumers to benefit export producers. An artificially weak renminbi meant that Chinese residents had artificially low purchasing power. There were complaints from Chinese consumers and the country's growing middle class that the average Chinese person had not gotten the full benefit of the country's rapid economic growth and that disproportionate benefits had gone to the export producers.

Another set of problems was international: China's trading partners, in particular the United States, complained with increasing vehemence that the artificial weakness of the renminbi was an unfair trading practice. This dispute threatened to break into open trade conflict between the United States and China on many occasions since 1990. (For more on recent developments, see "Controversy" on p. 400.)

Countries with unstable economies may choose to fix their currency's value to that of a more stable currency, like the U.S. dollar or the euro. Other countries have no national currency at all. In Zimbabwe, for example, the U.S. dollar is the most widely used of the country's legally acceptable currencies.

Should Countries Be Allowed to Manipulate Their Currencies?

During his 2016 campaign for the presidency, Donald Trump promised that, as president, he would "label China a currency manipulator" within his first 100 days in office.[a] In April 2017, however, just before the hundredth day of his term, President Trump announced that he would not, in fact, follow through on this threat. Why had then candidate Trump been concerned about China manipulating its currency? What did his threat to label them manipulators imply? Why did he not carry out his promise? More generally, what is currency manipulation, and should it be discouraged, even punished, by other countries or by international institutions?

Applying the Concepts

A country may have an **interest** in "manipulating" its currency, or intervening in currency markets to alter the currency's value, in order to give its producers a competitive advantage in international markets. This policy often leads to bitter **interactions** between the country and its trading partners, who resent the policy's impact on their own producers. There are domestic and international **institutions** in place that are meant to address currency manipulation. Nonetheless, the issue remains controversial: some leaders and analysts believe that national governments should be permitted to set their currency's value as they wish.

Controversies over currency manipulation typically arise when a government sells its own currency (and buys other currencies) in order to weaken its exchange rate. A weaker (depreciated) currency reduces the price of domestic goods to foreigners and makes it more attractive for foreigners to buy the country's goods. Many developing countries purposely keep their currencies weak because they want to stimulate exports. East Asian countries, in particular, have often kept their exchange rates artificially depreciated as part of their attempts to encourage domestic manufacturers to produce for world markets. Japan, South Korea, and Taiwan have all pursued this strategy at different points in their histories.

Most governments oppose currency manipulation by their trading partners. Although their own consumers benefit, they usually face a backlash from domestic producers, who, when confronted with cheaper imports, demand that their government do something to relieve the competitive pressure on them. As a result, nations often strongly criticize countries that manipulate their currencies. In some cases, these conflicts lead to threats of retaliation and other countermeasures.

After China opened to the world economy in 1979, and especially after 1990, there were many accusations that it was manipulating its currency—the *renminbi*—in order to give Chinese manufacturers an advantage in world markets. Most analysts would agree that Chinese government policy did artificially weaken the renminbi. Chinese export manufacturers benefited from this policy because it enabled them to sell more of their goods abroad. Producers who competed with Chinese exports—including many European and American manufacturers—believed they were harmed by China's policy. Chinese consumers were also hurt by a weak currency, because it reduced their purchasing power, and European and American consumers benefited because they could buy Chinese goods more cheaply.

---

a. "Donald Trump's Contract with the Voter," https://assets.donaldjtrump.com/_landings/contract/O-TRU-102316-Contractv02.pdf (accessed 10/10/17).

In an effort to avoid conflicts over currency manipulation, the IMF and the World Trade Organization (WTO) have rules against it. Despite the importance of these international institutions, however, they have little enforcement power in this realm. These issues are usually dealt with in bilateral interactions between the country accused of manipulating its currency and that country's trading partners.

American interactions with countries that it considers to be currency manipulators have often been conflictual. Under then existing U.S. law, the Treasury Department found that Japan was a currency manipulator in 1988, Taiwan in 1988 and 1992, and China between 1992 and 1994. In these cases, the United States put pressure on the countries to stop the practice, and eventually the Treasury Department found that the manipulation had ceased. But complaints persisted, especially as China's exports to the United States continued to grow.

A 2015 law gave the U.S. government more tools to punish alleged manipulators, including the ability to cut off some government funds to the country in question and the option to reevaluate existing trade agreements. When Donald Trump promised to label China a currency manipulator, he was threatening to impose these, and potentially other, sanctions on a country that he regarded as harming American economic interests.

Why didn't Trump follow through? For one thing, by the time President Trump took office, most economic analyses indicated that China was not trying to weaken its currency. In fact, the Chinese government appeared to be trying hard to prevent weakening of the renminbi. For another thing, the Trump administration felt that labeling China a currency manipulator would interfere with its own efforts to secure China's cooperation in dealing with an increasingly troubling problem: North Korea's acquisition of nuclear weapons. For both economic and diplomatic reasons, then, President Trump did not label China a currency manipulator.

The broader question remains: Should international institutions, or individual governments, try to punish a government for manipulating its currency? After all, many analysts believe that poor countries should have weak currencies to stimulate exports and production more generally, and consumers in rich countries benefit when they can buy more inexpensive goods from weak-currency countries. Others, however, argue that a government that artificially weakens its currency is putting unfair competitive pressures on producers in other nations, thereby potentially provoking protectionist retaliation.

China has faced accusations that it was artificially weakening the value of its currency, the renminbi.

To some extent, currency manipulation is simply a clash of interests. It helps exporters in the country whose currency is weak, and it helps consumers in other nations. These benefits come at the expense of producers in other countries, and of consumers in the manipulating country. Normally, currency manipulation might simply be the source of conflictual interactions within and between countries. However, when the country accused of manipulating its currency plays a large role in international trade—such as China, or Japan in earlier years—conflicts over currency manipulation can spill over into trade conflicts. To the extent that these disagreements become a source of friction in international trade and other economic relations, they may be of broader international importance.

Thinking Analytically

1. Which groups within the United States are most likely to be harmed by Chinese currency manipulation to lower the value of the renminbi? Why? Are there U.S. groups that benefit when the renminbi is weaker relative to the dollar?

2. Why might China have decided at a certain point that changing course and propping up the value of its currency was in its economic interest?

3. When it comes to the role of international institutions, what are some arguments for their punishing currency manipulators? What are some arguments against their doing so?

National currency policy implicates contending interests and complex institutions within countries. As disputes over China's currency indicate, the matter is doubly complicated because one government's exchange-rate policy inevitably affects other countries' policies. This observation takes us to the international level, where national governments with interests in conflict, and in common, interact over the structure of the international monetary system.

International Politics and International Monetary Relations

A monetary system is crucial to any modern economy; this is also true of the international economy, which requires some institutional arrangement to permit trade, investment, and other payments across borders. A *national* monetary order provides predictability in the value of a trusted money and thus in the prices of goods; this is widely seen as one of the core functions of the institutions of national government. An *international* monetary order does the same for prices across borders—which means that it has to provide predictability in currency values.

If traders, investors, tourists, and others had no idea what exchange rates would be tomorrow or next week, they would be very reluctant to engage in exchange across borders. For the international economy to work well, there must be some predictability to currency values so that people can reasonably expect that the dollar or peso they are earning today will be worth something tomorrow.

A stable and predictable monetary arrangement that allows firms and people to compare prices and transact business from one nation to another benefits almost everyone. Governments and people tend to share a desire for a general commitment to a common international monetary order. In this sense, a common regime is a Pareto improvement over a world in which there is no agreement on global monetary relations; that is, it makes all countries better off—or at least as well off—and none worse off. Agreement on a monetary regime thus has many features of a public good: everyone benefits if there is a smoothly functioning way to carry out international economic transactions.

As with most public goods, however, the provision of this monetary order is not automatic or easy. Since there is no one global institution to provide a global monetary order, a functioning order requires conscious efforts by individual national governments to alter their policies, or to contribute funds to stabilize currencies, or to otherwise help sustain the system. In the absence of a world government and a world money, many institutional arrangements have emerged to provide this global public good. Under the classical gold standard of the nineteenth and early twentieth centuries, gold was the common denominator for international transactions. Under the Bretton Woods monetary system, which prevailed from 1945 to 1973, the dollar was the centerpiece of the monetary order.

But there can be disagreements over the nature of the international monetary system and every country's place in it; the different actors in the international political economy may have conflicting interests about the kinds of international monetary institutions they would like to see in place. Governments and people often differ on the standard they would prefer. During the days of the classical gold standard, for example, many people and governments—including some powerful political movements—preferred a silver standard to a gold standard.

Supporters of silver typically believed that if silver, which was plentiful, served as money, prices would be higher than they would be with gold, which was scarce. Adoption of a silver standard rather than a gold standard, they believed, would thus help raise the prices of goods they produced. By the same token, during the decades of the Bretton Woods monetary system, Americans were quite satisfied with a system that put the dollar at its center, but Europeans were less enthusiastic. International monetary relations are infused with this tension between sources of conflict and reasons for cooperation.

International Monetary Cooperation and Conflict

Just as there are conflicting interests within countries over national policy, there are trade-offs and conflicts of interests among countries over international monetary arrangements. It can be difficult to organize collaboration among governments to provide the public good of international monetary stability, because there are powerful incentives to free ride on the efforts of others. Governments of smaller countries might reason that their contributions are too trivial to matter and thus not participate; if enough governments follow this path, cooperation will break down. For example, a global fixed-rate system such as the gold standard can facilitate international trade and investment, but the government of a small country might decide that it can benefit from the global system without fixing its own currency and tying its hands. If enough countries take this route, the system will collapse.

A successful international monetary regime depends on interactions among the governments of the world's major economies. The behavior of these governments sets the standards for the regime as a whole, and they need to address problems as they arise. However, governments also face major temptations to "cheat" on their international monetary commitments. In a fixed-rate regime, for example, one government might decide to devalue in order to make its producers' goods more competitive on world markets. Other countries might respond by also devaluing to allow their producers to match.

The result is akin to the undesirable outcome of a Prisoner's Dilemma game (see the "Special Topic" appendix to Chapter 2, on p. 83). If every nation engages in competitive devaluations, all currencies end up being devalued, and nobody gains any advantage. Meanwhile, the currency turmoil can throw international monetary relations into disorder and uncertainty, thereby interfering with normal economic activities.

Interactions among national governments, facing incentives both to cooperate and to enter into conflict, have determined the character of international monetary relations, including the emergence of global and regional monetary institutions. In the following section, we take a closer look at the evolution of international monetary arrangements over the past couple of centuries.

International Monetary Regimes

international monetary regime

A formal or informal arrangement among governments to govern relations among their currencies; the agreement is shared by most countries in the world economy.

National government decisions to float or to fix their currencies interact to create an **international monetary regime**—that is, an arrangement, which may be formal and institutionalized or informal, that is widely accepted to govern relations among currencies, and that is shared by most countries in the world economy. There may also be regional monetary regimes that prevail in particular geographic regions, such as in Europe with the euro.

The existence of a generally accepted international monetary regime has clear benefits for the international community in general, since it facilitates international economic exchange. It may come, however, at the cost of national sacrifices, as we will see. First we will define the characteristics of international monetary regimes.

International monetary regimes have two principal features. The first makes clear whether currency values are expected to be fixed, floating, or a mix of both. As discussed already, the classical gold standard and the Bretton Woods monetary system were international fixed-rate regimes (although the Bretton Woods monetary system allowed for occasional adjustments). The contemporary regime is based on floating rates; there is no general agreement that national currency values should be fixed.

The second feature of an international monetary regime is agreement about whether there will be a mutually accepted benchmark against which values are measured—some common base or standard to which currencies can be compared. Three such standards have been used over time: a commodity standard, a commodity-backed paper standard, and a national paper currency standard.

A *commodity standard* uses a good with value of its own as the basic monetary unit. Typically, this good is a precious metal such as gold or silver. Under the classical gold standard that prevailed from the 1870s until 1914, for example, all major national currencies had a fixed value in terms of gold, and they could be exchanged freely on the basis of their gold equivalent. This was a fixed-rate regime based on gold as the commodity standard.

A *commodity-backed paper standard* is similar to the Bretton Woods monetary system that prevailed from 1945 to 1973. Under such a regime, national governments issue paper currency with a fixed value in terms of gold (or some other commodity). This is one step removed from a pure gold standard, as it requires that governments be able to commit credibly to stand ready to redeem the currency for gold. Nonetheless, under such a standard, national currency values are comparable because they are all expressed in terms of a common commodity: gold. Under the Bretton Woods monetary system, the U.S. dollar was fixed to gold, while all other currencies were fixed to the dollar.

Under a *national paper currency standard*, national currencies are backed by only the commitments of their issuing governments to support them. In this context, people want to know that the government will act to ensure that the national currency continues to be valuable. This may not mean committing to a fixed rate; it does mean committing to the currency not losing so much value as to become undesirable. Foreigners who hold dollars or euros, or who accept promises to pay in dollars or euros, do so with the expectation that even if exchange rates do change, dollars and euros will continue to be valuable national monies. Typically, only a few major currencies are used for international exchange—usually, the currencies of the world's most important trading and financial powers. This is the system that has prevailed since 1973. Today, most international exchange is measured and conducted in the dollar and the euro.

A Short History of International Monetary Systems

The modern international economy has experienced all three of these kinds of international monetary regimes.

The Gold Standard Under the classical gold standard, most of the world's major economies had gold or gold-backed currencies tied together at exchange rates that did not change for decades. The portion of the world that was on gold—which eventually came to include every major economy except China and Persia—effectively had a common money: gold.

The stability of the classical gold standard relied on close ties among the three leading financial powers of the day—Britain, France, and Germany—along with support from smaller European nations. For example, when the 1890 collapse of Barings, a major British bank, threatened to destabilize the London markets, the central banks of France and Russia lent large sums to the Bank of England. The mere knowledge that enough money was available to address the problem helped calm investors. In 1898, the British and French helped stabilize German financial markets; a few years later, the Austrians helped calm the Berlin market. And at least seven more times between 1900 and 1914, the French stepped in to assist the British in order to stabilize the gold standard.[6]

The gold standard provided currency stability and predictability, which greatly facilitated international trade, investment, finance, migration, and travel. Most of the world's governments and many countries' citizens agreed that this common monetary standard was generally beneficial. Such confluence of interests among the major financial centers allowed them to interact cooperatively to sustain the gold standard for many decades.

However, the costs to being on gold made some people and governments less enthusiastic. As we saw in our discussion of a fixed-rate system, a government on the gold standard gave up its ability to run its own independent monetary policy, which implied a serious loss of economic policy influence. In the United States, the gold standard was very controversial; in fact, the 1896 presidential campaign was largely fought around it. William McKinley and the Republicans ran in favor of maintaining the American commitment to gold, but many Americans were hostile to the gold standard. The anti-gold forces, led by the Populists, wanted the government to take the dollar off gold and put it on silver at a different rate.

The move to silver would have accomplished two things: it would have devalued the dollar, making American exports more competitive, and it would have

---

6. For a classic account of the gold-standard era and the interwar collapse of the gold standard, see Barry Eichengreen, *Golden Fetters: The Gold Standard and the Great Depression, 1919–1939* (New York: Oxford University Press, 1992).

raised American prices. Farmers in particular liked the idea of a devaluation, as many of them produced for export markets. They, and others, also liked the idea of raising prices, as many of them were heavily indebted, and an increase in prices could have reduced their debt burden (the debts would have remained the same, while prices for farm products would have risen). Therefore, the Democratic Party and the Populists united around William Jennings Bryan, who famously said to gold supporters, "You shall not crucify mankind upon a cross of gold!"

Bryan lost in 1896 and again in 1900 and 1908, although the anti-gold movement he represented remained strong. (See "What Shaped Our World?" on p. 407 for more on this episode of U.S. history.) Nonetheless, there was enough domestic political support for the international cooperation necessary to sustain the gold standard that it was solid and extensive for almost 50 years, from the 1870s until 1914.

In the 1920s and 1930s, attempts to restore the classical gold standard were largely unsuccessful. Most countries did go on gold again after World War I ended, but the sort of international monetary cooperation that had allowed the classical gold standard to succeed had become difficult to organize. Countries such as France and Germany were on very poor terms diplomatically, which created an atmosphere of distrust that impeded efforts to negotiate monetary collaboration. As interests diverged, interactions among the major financial players became more hostile.

This failure to cooperate in the 1920s was exacerbated by the Great Depression, which began in 1929. Faced with massive crises, governments were unwilling to forgo an economic policy that might allow them to alleviate the suffering of their citizens. After 1929, virtually all the governments that had gone on gold in the 1920s went back off it as they tried to resuscitate their failing national economies. The result was a floating-rate system based on paper national currencies. This system led to a great deal of currency volatility and instability, including many competitive devaluations, and probably contributed to the overall collapse of the international economy in the 1930s. In any case, monetary disorder was overwhelmed by the economic and military conflicts of the 1930s and 1940s.

The Bretton Woods Monetary System As World War II drew to a close, the United States and Great Britain led the victorious Allies in designing an international monetary order—called the Bretton Woods monetary system because the agreements were negotiated at the Bretton Woods resort in New Hampshire—that represented a fundamental reform of the gold standard.[7] The Bretton Woods monetary system was organized around the U.S. dollar, and the dollar was tied to gold at the fixed rate of $35 per ounce. While other currencies were tied to the dollar, and thus indirectly to gold, they were permitted to be adjusted as necessary.

This system was seen as a middle ground between gold-standard rigidity and interwar insecurity. Like under the gold standard, exchange rates were stable

---

7. The term *Bretton Woods System* is sometimes used to describe the post–World War II international economic order more generally; we use the term *Bretton Woods monetary system* more narrowly to describe the currency order.

The Wizard of Oz and the Gold Standard

The gold standard was a central institution of the late nineteenth and early twentieth centuries. This international monetary system, and political battles over it, was so prominent that one of the most famous children's stories of all time may well be a parable about the politics of exchange rates in the gold-standard era.

The book *The Wonderful Wizard of Oz* was first published in 1900; it was turned into the film in 1939. The story chronicles the adventures of Dorothy, a girl from Kansas whose house is swept up in a tornado and transported to a magical place populated by munchkins, witches, and other strange creatures. The Good Witch of the North counsels Dorothy to follow the yellow brick road to the Emerald City and seek the help of the Wizard of Oz to return home to Kansas. The Good Witch also gives Dorothy a pair of magic slippers. Dorothy skips along the yellow brick road and meets a brainless scarecrow, a tin man without a heart, and a cowardly lion. Together, this motley team battles the Wicked Witch of the West to gain access to the venerable wizard. At the end of the story, they realize that the wizard is a fraud, but fortunately the Good Witch reappears and informs Dorothy that she can return home simply by clicking together her magic slippers.

What does *The Wizard of Oz* have to do with exchange-rate politics? A little background on the gold standard will help to elucidate the symbolism in the story.

Institutions Starting in the 1870s, the U.S. government officially agreed to exchange dollars for gold at a fixed rate of one ounce of gold for $20.67. This institution was intended to facilitate international trade and financial flows. However, one problem with this policy was that the domestic money supply was fixed to the availability of gold. If businesses produced more goods and services but the stock of gold remained steady, then prices would fall. This was indeed the case throughout much of the 1880s and 1890s. Because the United States was on the gold standard, it was not able to lower interest rates or allow the currency to depreciate, both of which would have boosted prices and stimulated the economy.

Interests Falling prices harmed nearly everyone, but they were especially harmful to farmers who sold their grain on world markets and borrowed money from banks to finance their operations. With the price of grain declining, farmers had difficulty earning enough to repay their debts. Industrial workers also faced tough times as unemployment increased. The dire economic conditions of the 1890s helped to fuel the populist movement, led by Democratic presidential candidate William Jennings Bryan. He wanted to replace the gold standard with an alternative system that would help increase the money supply—in particular, a system that included silver, a much more plentiful commodity. Bryan ultimately lost the 1896 election to William McKinley, a Republican who supported the gold standard.

Interactions With this background in mind, it is easy to see the symbolism in *The Wizard of Oz*, which was written just a few years after the 1896 election. Dorothy, representing the naive American public, believes that her problems will be solved if she simply follows a winding road paved with gold bricks. She meets a scarecrow (a farmer), a tin man (an industrial worker), and a lion whose roar masks his cowardice (Bryan). When Dorothy finally meets the Wizard (McKinley), she realizes that he is a fraud. In response, she simply clicks her slippers together to transport herself back home. In the original book, the slippers were silver.

The symbolism in *The Wizard of Oz* (note that *oz* is an abbreviation for *ounce*) reflects the political and cultural importance of different monetary systems.

Representatives of 44 countries met at the Bretton Woods conference in 1944 and negotiated a new monetary system organized around the U.S. dollar. After the turbulence of the interwar years and World War II, the Bretton Woods monetary system succeeded in bringing stability to currency values.

enough to encourage international trade and investment. Unlike under the gold standard, governments other than the United States could change their currencies' values as needed, although frequent changes were frowned upon. The Bretton Woods monetary compromise kept currency values stable and currency markets open, contributing to the growth of international trade and investment while allowing national governments to pursue national policies in line with national conditions.

Like the gold standard, the Bretton Woods monetary system relied on collaboration among its leading members. It was sustained in large part because the Western allies after World War II saw it as an important component of their economic and military alliance structure, just as the West's willingness to undertake international trade liberalization was related to its geopolitical alliance. There was thus a confluence of both economic and noneconomic interests among Western nations that facilitated cooperation. This cooperation was reminiscent of that which prevailed during the classical gold standard: under Bretton Woods, as under the gold standard, for example, it was common for the world's major national central banks to lend money to each other in times of crisis.

Under the Bretton Woods monetary system, the International Monetary Fund (IMF) was established as the principal institution to monitor interstate interaction on exchange rates. During this period, the IMF was charged with overseeing currency relations and with providing support to countries in need of short-term assistance in keeping their exchange rates stable. The IMF made information available to members and provided standards of behavior that countries were expected to follow with respect to their currencies. The backing of the major Western financial powers, along with the institutional support of the IMF, was central to the stability of the Bretton Woods monetary system.

Eventually, however, international monetary cooperation failed because of fundamental disagreements among countries. By the early 1970s, the U.S. government was unwilling to make the sacrifices necessary to keep the dollar fixed to gold. President Richard Nixon felt that the Bretton Woods commitments constrained American economic policy more than was acceptable. The U.S. government felt itself too restricted by the rigid link between the dollar and gold, eventually breaking that link in order to give itself more monetary independence.

Today's International Monetary System

Since 1973, international monetary relations have been based on floating exchange rates among a small number of major currencies, typically those of the principal industrial and financial nations (especially the United States, Japan, Germany, and Great Britain). While today's international monetary system does not depend on explicit commitments to fixed exchange rates, its orderly functioning still requires the major national governments to work together, especially in times of crisis.

And although the IMF was originally designed to monitor and assist the functioning of a modified fixed-rate international monetary order, the fund has remained important even after the shift to floating rates. When the major governments believe that exchange rates are fluctuating too wildly, they can coordinate their monetary policies to try to reduce these wide swings; the IMF sometimes serves as the venue for discussions about this sort of coordination. At times, currency problems in developing countries have led the major financial powers to intervene to attempt to stabilize exchange rates and keep a crisis from spreading; again, the IMF frequently participates in such attempts at crisis management and sometimes leads them.

Different alignments of national interests, and different patterns of strategic interaction among states, help account for different international monetary outcomes. It is striking that both the gold standard and the Bretton Woods monetary system each relied in major ways on the leadership of one country—Great Britain and the United States, respectively. Nonetheless, the participation of other major financial and monetary powers was needed to keep the systems going, so a sense of common interests was also crucial. As the collapse of both systems indicates, such participation can be difficult to sustain. It can be impeded by fundamental disagreements over how to share the costs of stabilizing the system or by a lack of trust among governments that the commitments of others will be honored.

Today's world of floating exchange rates presents a related set of problems. While the major powers do interact, generally cooperatively, to try to avoid major monetary disturbances, exchange rates still fluctuate quite widely. Since 1980, for example, the U.S. dollar has risen and fallen by very large amounts against other major currencies. While few people in the United States seem overly worried about this volatility, in smaller countries that trade more with the rest of the world, these currency fluctuations can be widely unpopular.

The current system is not monolithic (as was the gold standard) or organized (as was Bretton Woods), but it does have some clear defining features. Countries can allow their currencies to float freely, and large countries typically do; but smaller countries appear less enthusiastic about this currency volatility, and they often link their currency to that of a larger nation or bloc. The absence of an established global monetary system has, in fact, led some countries to try to develop regional monetary systems that can at least stabilize exchange rates among groups of countries.

Regional Monetary Arrangements: The Euro

In the absence of a global agreement on stabilizing currencies, some countries have tried to work out regional arrangements. Where countries can resolve problems of cooperation, a more orderly system can be maintained regionally even as it disintegrates globally. This was the strategy pursued by most of the members of the European Union after the collapse of the Bretton Woods monetary system. Most EU countries trade and invest a great deal with one another—an arrangement that leads them to want to limit exchange-rate fluctuations. Starting in 1973, they committed themselves to stabilize exchange rates among EU member countries and eventually to work toward a common currency.

But the road to the euro was not an easy one, for both domestic and interstate political reasons. Within countries, some interests were often less than enthusiastic about a common monetary policy. In practice, fixing EU exchange rates meant pegging them to the German currency (the Deutschmark), for Germany was the largest economy in the European Union and had a long-standing commitment to keeping its currency, as well as its prices, stable.

In countries with higher inflation than Germany had, pegging the currency to the Deutschmark meant that governments would have to bring inflation down. The typical approach was to raise interest rates and implement austerity measures, such as restraining wages and cutting government spending. In France and Italy, labor unions and public employees, especially, felt that their interests would be sacrificed to the currency peg. It was not until 1985 that supporters of a fixed rate won out in these two countries. In Great Britain and Sweden, there were even fewer supporters of a fixed rate, and for most of the period these two nations kept their distance from the growing currency union.

At the regional level, interactions among the governments of the European Union were complex and often conflictual. Because other EU currencies were fixed to the Deutschmark, Germany's monetary policy had to be followed by other countries. This arrangement was satisfactory as long as they all agreed on the course of German policy. In 1991, however, in the aftermath of the reunification of the eastern and western parts of Germany, the German central bank was very concerned about inflation. To restrain prices, it raised interest rates very high. This measure, taken for entirely domestic reasons, forced the rest of the currency bloc to make a difficult choice. They could raise interest rates and drive their economies into recession; or they could keep interest rates low, in which case money would flow out of their countries, toward Germany's higher interest rates, and force them to leave the peg. The eventual result was a currency crisis (discussed in more detail shortly)—and the decision by many EU members to break the Deutschmark link.

Movement toward currency union continued, nonetheless, because there was a domestic consensus in most EU countries on the desirability of stabilizing currencies—even at the cost of giving up a national policy and even, in many cases, a powerful national symbol, the currency. The next move was to plan for a common currency, the euro, to be managed by a common ECB. This measure appealed to countries other than Germany, because it meant that European monetary policy would be made by a European, rather than a German, central bank and would presumably take European conditions as a whole into account.

Germany went along for several reasons. First, the ECB was to be based in Frankfurt, and its constitution was drafted so as to ensure that it would be very similar to the German central bank. These facts helped allay German fears that the new institution would stray too far from the low-inflation principles that Germans preferred. Second, Germany itself wanted a reduction in currency volatility in Europe, and it was clear that other EU members would not accept a continuation of the Deutschmark-based system. Third, the creation of the euro and the ECB was connected to a broad array of cooperative ventures among EU member governments on a wide range of issues. Just as economic cooperation between the United States and western Europe was facilitated by their military alliance, monetary union among western European countries was facilitated by the fact that they had come to cooperate in so many other dimensions, from trade policy and antitrust law to foreign policy.

The combination of gradually emerging domestic consensus within most EU member countries and increasingly cooperative interaction among EU governments led to the adoption of the euro and its successful introduction as Europe's circulating money in 2002. As of 2018, 19 of 27 EU members share the euro, which is used by nearly 350 million people. (See Map 9.2 for members of the eurozone in 2018.)

The United Kingdom, which has voted to leave the EU, was never a eurozone member. Denmark has not adopted the euro but has fixed its own currency against the euro very tightly. Sweden remains outside the eurozone, as do six other, newer members of the European Union in central and eastern Europe (Bulgaria, Croatia, the Czech Republic, Hungary, Poland, and Romania). Many in these countries are wary of how eurozone membership would restrict their ability to manage their own monetary policies. This wariness has been heightened by the fact that the eurozone itself was recently wracked by a crisis that threatened its very unity (discussed shortly).

The creation of this regional currency union reflected the interests of many countries to stabilize their exchange rates in a time of turbulence. There are several other such regional currency arrangements. For example, 14 central and western African countries share a common currency, which is pegged to the euro; and eight Caribbean island nations and territories share a common eastern Caribbean dollar, pegged to the U.S. dollar.

Many other countries deal with concern over currency volatility by pursuing unilateral measures, such as adopting another currency (for example, Panama, Ecuador, and El Salvador use the U.S. dollar as their currency) or linking their currency to that of another country. All these strategies are aimed at achieving the desired balance between currency stability and policy independence—either on one's own or in collaboration with other national governments. While they may succeed in reducing threats to individual countries or groups of countries, these strategies do not address problems at the global monetary level, which some analysts regard as a matter for concern. Nor do they address the continuing problem of spreading currency crises, to which we turn in the next section.

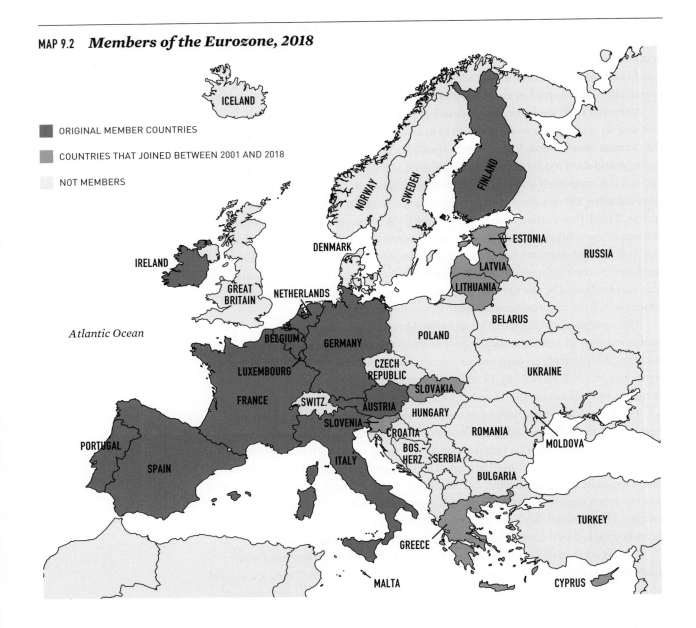

MAP 9.2 *Members of the Eurozone, 2018*

ORIGINAL MEMBER COUNTRIES

COUNTRIES THAT JOINED BETWEEN 2001 AND 2018

NOT MEMBERS

ICELAND

NORWAY

SWEDEN

FINLAND

ESTONIA

RUSSIA

LATVIA

LITHUANIA

DENMARK

BELARUS

IRELAND

GREAT BRITAIN

NETHERLANDS

POLAND

Atlantic Ocean

BELGIUM

GERMANY

CZECH REPUBLIC

UKRAINE

LUXEMBOURG

SLOVAKIA

FRANCE

SWITZ.

AUSTRIA

HUNGARY

SLOVENIA

MOLDOVA

CROATIA

ROMANIA

PORTUGAL

BOS.-HERZ.

SERBIA

SPAIN

ITALY

BULGARIA

TURKEY

GREECE

MALTA

CYPRUS

What Happens When Currencies Collapse?

Even those who pay little attention to international monetary affairs notice the occasional spectacular currency crises, such as those that affected Europe in 1992–93 and again in 2011, East Asia in 1997–98, or Argentina in 2001. Indeed, currency crises have been a frequent feature of the modern international political economy. They are one of the more dramatic effects of national currency policy. Currency crises have been closely related to the financial and debt crises discussed in Chapter 8 and have been associated with all-encompassing economic and political upheavals.

Currency crises usually result when government exchange-rate commitments are not fully credible. In this sense they are analytically comparable to crises in military affairs that result when the threats and promises of governments are not fully credible (see Chapter 3). In the case of currency affairs, when private economic actors do not believe the promises of a government with respect to its exchange rate, they can react in ways that cause a major crisis.

Effects on Government

Up to now, we have assumed that when a government fixes its exchange rate, it stays fixed until the government decides, on its own, to alter the arrangement. But we also know that it can be economically and politically difficult for a government to sustain a fixed currency, because a government with a fixed exchange rate may not be able to undertake monetary policies desirable to address national economic conditions.

This was the problem in Argentina in 2001, when the tight dollar-peso link made it virtually impossible for the Argentine government to reverse a three-year recession. It was also the problem in a number of countries in the eurozone in the aftermath of the crisis that began in 2008, for the fact that they had given up their national currencies made it very difficult for them to act to ease the impact of the Great Recession. In these circumstances, expectations that the government will not be able to sustain its commitment to a fixed rate or to membership in a currency union can create concern among economic actors about the future course of the currency. And this concern can feed on itself until it becomes a panic.

A typical currency crisis follows a fairly predictable trajectory. In order to reap the benefits of a fixed currency, the government commits itself to a particular fixed exchange rate—a peg to gold, the dollar, or the euro at a specific rate. This move presumably has all the advantages we have identified, but it also imposes costs. Over time, for some reason, the government faces economic and political difficulties in maintaining a fixed exchange rate. Perhaps the local economy is doing poorly, or exporters are clamoring for a devaluation that will make their goods more attractive abroad, or the country's main exports are losing markets to competitors.

As the government faces increasing pressures to devalue the currency, people begin to lose faith in the government's commitment to keep the exchange rate stable. This unease gives investors strong reasons to sell the nation's currency. After all, nobody wants to hold on to an asset, in this case a currency, that is going to lose value. So, investors at home and abroad start converting the local currency into more reliable foreign currency. The government usually continues to assure the public that the exchange rate will be maintained, in an effort to keep people from selling the currency. But as doubts about the government's credibility grow, more and more people may go to the banks to exchange their local currency for more reliable dollars or euros.

When the Argentine government devalued the peso in 2001, many homeowners whose mortgage was denominated in dollars saw the value of their debt triple compared to their salary (paid in pesos) in a span of just two months. This result fueled public anger.

The government itself is torn. On the one hand, there are powerful domestic interests in favor of keeping the currency's exchange rate where it is. Companies and others that have borrowed in a foreign currency, for example, are anxious to make sure the national currency is not devalued. For those with foreign-currency debts, a devaluation would increase the cost of their debt by requiring more of the national currency to buy the foreign currency they must use to repay the debt. In addition, a devaluation would reduce national purchasing power—an unpopular move with consumers, who would have to pay more for many goods as a result. On the other hand, there are good reasons to allow the currency's value to drop: it might alleviate economic distress and help national farmers and manufacturers compete with foreigners. ("How Do We Know?" on p. 415 looks at the decision to devalue the currency in several European countries.)

At the same time, sustaining the fixed rate can be very difficult. The government would have to take some action to convince people to hold on to the national currency rather than buying dollars or some other foreign currency. Most commonly, a government trying to convince investors and others to hold on to the national money has to raise interest rates in order to make the local currency more attractive—and raising interest rates is likely to exacerbate the country's economic difficulties.

Eventually, the government runs out of time, money, or patience, and the currency is devalued. A drop in a currency's value may have a positive effect by helping national producers compete with foreigners. But it also usually has some very powerful negative effects. Anyone in the country with substantial foreign-currency debts, including the government, faces serious trouble. As the local currency drops in value, the burden of foreign-currency debt rises.

In early 2002, the Argentine peso's value dropped from one to the dollar to three to the dollar in two months, so a $1 million debt went from being a 1-million-peso debt to a 3-million-peso debt. In such circumstances, large numbers of debtors go bankrupt, which in turn leads many banks to fail because their customers cannot pay their debts. A recession almost always ensues, which can even turn into a deep financial and debt crisis. Indeed, most currency crises eventually turn into broader banking crises. This scenario has been repeated hundreds of times, from the nineteenth century through the present in developed and developing countries.

International Repercussions

The international aspect of currency crises can be particularly troubling. Currency crises can be transmitted from one country to another as uncertainties about one country feed uncertainties about others. Investors looking at countries that are

Devaluation or Depression in the European Union

When the global financial crisis hit in 2008, governments in central and eastern Europe had to figure out how they would respond. These nations had recently entered the EU, and many of them were on track to adopt the euro. Most had currencies that were tightly tied to the euro.

As the world economy spiraled downward, each faced a serious exchange-rate policy choice. On the one hand, in order to move forward toward adoption of the euro, the government could hold fast to its peg to the euro. However, doing so would restrict it from adopting an independent policy, such as devaluing its currency. And this was a major restriction; one of the typical recommendations for small open economies in crisis is to devalue in order to make national goods more attractive on world markets and stimulate exports. On the other hand, if the government chose to devalue, it would forgo the opportunity to join the eurozone.

Political scientist Stefanie Walter analyzed the political economy of this choice.[a] She focused on the interests at play in different central and eastern European societies and, in particular, on their citizens' debts in foreign currency. In the Baltic states of Estonia, Latvia, and Lithuania, for example, between 60 and 90 percent of total loans were in foreign currency. A devaluation would have dramatically increased the cost of this debt. If a Latvian homeowner took out a €100,000 mortgage in 2005, this would have been equal to about 70,000 Latvian lats (at the then current exchange rate of 1.00 lat to €1.42). But if the lat had been devalued by 30 percent (so that the lat and the euro were approximately equivalent), the mortgage would have increased in local value to about 100,000 lats.

TABLE A   *Foreign-Currency Debt and Currency Depreciation*

	LOANS IN FOREIGN CURRENCY[a]	MAXIMUM DEPRECIATION OF NATIONAL CURRENCY[b]	REAL GDP GROWTH RATE, 2009[b]	CHANGE IN UNEMPLOYMENT RATE, 2007–10[b]
Latvia	88.4%	1.2%	−17.7%	13.3%
Estonia	85.3%	0%	−14.3%	12.2%
Lithuania	64.0%	0%	−14.8%	13.5%
Poland	32.6%	43%	1.6%	0%
Czech Republic	13.6%	21%	−4.7%	2%

a. Martin Myant and Jan Drahokupil, "International Integration, Varieties of Capitalism, and Resilience to Crisis in Transition Economies," *Europe-Asia Studies* 64, no. 1 (2012): 1–33.

b. Stefanie Walter, *Financial Crises and the Politics of Macroeconomic Adjustments* (Cambridge: Cambridge University Press, 2013), Table 7.1.

In some other countries, citizens had not borrowed very much in foreign currency. In Poland, foreign-currency debts were barely 30 percent of the total, and in the Czech Republic there were few foreign-currency debts. People in these countries were less vulnerable to devaluation.

Walter argues that the countries whose economic interests were most vulnerable to devaluation chose to keep their currency peg (Table A). Lithuania, Estonia, and Latvia, in fact, underwent massive recessions; unemployment approached 20 percent, and GDP dropped by over 15 percent in just one year. Nonetheless, they held on to their euro dreams, and all three countries are now in the eurozone.

Poland and the Czech Republic, whose economic interests were less vulnerable to devaluation, opted to devalue their currencies. Their exports boomed, and as a result, they experienced little or no increase in unemployment. The Czech Republic had only a shallow recession, and Poland had none. On the other hand, both countries largely foreclosed their option to join the eurozone—a step they did not particularly favor in any case.

a. Stefanie Walter, *Financial Crises and the Politics of Macroeconomic Adjustments* (Cambridge: Cambridge University Press, 2013), 181–217.

economically or politically similar may believe that the collapse of one country's currency portends the collapse of others like it.

Throughout the nineteenth century, currency crises (often originating in the United States, then a heavily indebted developing country) had repercussions all over the industrialized world. When, in 1931, Austria was hit by a currency and banking crisis, the resulting fears soon affected neighboring Hungary, leading to a follow-on crisis there. Then the crisis hit Germany, then the rest of Central Europe, then Great Britain; eventually, most of Europe was brought down by a "contagious" currency crisis that almost certainly deepened the Great Depression.

In the past 30 years, there have been many rounds of currency crises. The first was associated with the less developed countries' sovereign debt defaults of the early and middle 1980s. In this case, the currency crises followed, rather than led, the larger financial crisis. As country after country found itself unable to sustain its currency's value in the face of massive debt problems, currencies collapsed as well. Since the early 1990s, it has become more common for currency crises to be the source of broader financial and economic difficulties.

Case Study: Europe, 1992 One of the first major modern currency crises affected European countries that were moving toward currency union. In this process, most EU countries had pegged their currencies to that of Germany, the Deutschmark. In 1991, the German central bank raised interest rates quickly and steeply to keep prices from rising after the eastern and western parts of the country had been unified.

This action presented the other European countries whose currencies were tied to the Deutschmark with a difficult choice. On the one hand, they could keep interest rates low, which would cause investors to pull their money out of other countries in favor of the higher German interest rates. As investors pulled out and sold the non-German currencies, these countries would eventually have to devalue their currencies against the Deutschmark and break the peg. On the other hand, the other countries could raise interest rates along with Germany, which would shove them into a recession made in Germany. In sum, German policy confronted European governments with a stark choice between continued membership in the Deutschmark bloc on the one hand, and avoiding a recession on the other. The rest of Europe was already mired in slow growth and double-digit unemployment, and there was little enthusiasm for more austerity measures that would slow inflation but also reduce wages and public spending.

In the summer of 1992, investors and currency traders began anticipating that Great Britain and Italy would not maintain their currencies' pegs to the Deutschmark. Investors sold off their holdings of these currencies, thus intensifying speculation that the pound and the lira would be devalued. The British and Italian governments pushed interest rates up to try to convince investors to hold on to their pounds and liras, but in the end, the cost seemed extreme, and both devalued their currencies. Foreign-exchange traders started selling off other currencies in the months that followed. Governments tried to hold on to the link to the Deutschmark (at one point, the Swedish central bank pushed interest rates to 500 percent), but the cost was too high.

Eventually, six other European nations followed Britain and Italy in devaluing their currencies. The damage to monetary unification was repaired quickly and effectively enough to move forward with plans for the euro. But it was clear that even the world's richest nations were not immune to currency crises that could force governments to devalue and change policies. The perception began to grow that there might be a common interest in trying to limit the negative effects of currency crises, since they could be transmitted from nation to nation.

Case Study: Mexico Within a year of the European currency crisis, the idea that currency crises could cross national borders was brought home to Mexico. With the North American Free Trade Agreement (NAFTA) in effect, the Mexican government wanted to hold the peso steady against the U.S. dollar. And in the run-up to a hotly contested presidential election campaign, the government wanted to keep the peso strong and Mexican incomes high. But in January 1994, a rebellion broke out in southern Mexico, and in March, one of the ruling party's leading presidential candidates was assassinated. These events worried investors, who came to believe that the government's position was shaky. As the election year of 1994 wore on, the government struggled to maintain its commitment to the peso, both to uphold its reputation and, through the strong peso, to increase the purchasing power of Mexican consumers.

But currency traders did not believe that the government could hold to its promises. Investors became more and more skittish, and the narrowness of the victory won by the ruling Partido Revolucionario Institucional (PRI), or Institutional Revolutionary Party, in the August 1994 presidential election was not reassuring. The PRI's secretary-general was assassinated in September, further scaring investors, who worried that the new government would be too unstable to commit credibly to the currency peg.

As the new government took office in December, currency traders sensed they could take a "one-way bet" against the peso: if it was devalued, they would win; if it wasn't, they wouldn't lose. As the speculators sold off the currency, the government tried desperately to keep the currency stable, but a few days before Christmas 1994, it floated the peso—which promptly sank. Yet another government had been forced to devalue its currency.

Following the common pattern of currency crises leading to financial crises, Mexico was next hit by a crippling banking crisis as a result of the currency collapse. When the peso was strong, many banks and companies borrowed heavily in dollars. The devaluation of the peso triggered mass bankruptcies as the real cost of dollar debts soared. The peso's value dropped in the space of a month from about 30¢ to about 15¢, so the real burden on a Mexican company of a $1 million foreign debt doubled from about 3.3 million pesos to 6.6 million.

Many indebted firms collapsed, followed by their domestic bankers, and within weeks the country was in the throes of a financial panic. The country's output dropped by 6 percent, and inflation soared above 50 percent. The fallout of the Mexican crisis affected all of Latin America, which was plunged into recession.

Case Study: East Asia The next round of currency and financial crises was even more dramatic. In 1997, the East Asian economies were booming, as about $50 billion a year flowed into East Asia from global financial markets, with tens of billions more in direct investment from multinational corporations. The region seemed well on the way to rapid economic development. But there were a few warning signs of slowing growth and a bubble in housing and financial markets. By 1996 and early 1997, exports were lagging, inflation was rising, and banks were taking on more and more debt. Soon, investors began to anticipate devaluations and started selling off East Asian currencies.

In a now familiar spiral, the movement away from the region's currencies became a flood, then a stampede, then a panic. The sell-off spread from Thailand and the Philippines to Indonesia and Malaysia, then to Taiwan and Korea. The size and efficiency of international financial markets seemed to facilitate the attacks by making it remarkably easy for investors to speculate against government attempts to defend their currencies. Joseph Stiglitz, then chief economist at the World Bank, gave an example of the process:

> Assume a speculator goes to a Thai bank, borrows 24 billion baht, which, at the original exchange rate, can be converted into $1 billion. A week later the exchange rate falls; instead of there being 24 baht to the dollar, there are now 40 baht to the dollar. He takes $600 million, converting it back to baht, getting 24 billion baht to repay the loan. The remaining $400 million is his profit—a tidy return for one week's work, and the investment of little of his own money. . . . As perceptions that a devaluation is imminent grow, the chance to make money becomes irresistible and speculators from around the world pile in to take advantage of the situation.[8]

As more and more investors did as Stiglitz described, expectations of devaluations grew. Since no investor wanted to hold on to currencies that would lose value, billions of dollars flooded out of the East Asian economies, and eventually governments were, in fact, forced to devalue. Within weeks of the initial attack, the currencies of Korea, the Philippines, and Malaysia dropped by 40 percent, that of Thailand by 50 percent, and that of Indonesia by 80 percent. The political fallout was also intense: the government of Thailand fell, and after more than 30 years in power, the Suharto dictatorship in Indonesia collapsed.

Case Study: Europe, 2011–2015 The most recent major currency crisis in Europe was different from the early-1990s crisis: it involved the threat that a multicountry currency union might break up. The member states of the eurozone have very different economies and have grown at different rates, but as long as the zone as a whole was growing, these differences did not cause many problems. When the

---

8. Joseph Stiglitz, *Globalization and Its Discontents* (New York: Norton, 2002), 94–95.

global financial crisis began in 2008, however, it put major strains on the very structure of the euro.

A group of eurozone member states—especially Greece, Ireland, Portugal, and Spain—had borrowed very heavily after the euro was created. Their economies had boomed, but at the same time, these debt-financed booms raised prices and wages and made it harder for these countries to compete. Faced with the worldwide recession, the major debtor countries had trouble servicing their debts. Soon they were in full financial crisis and had to be bailed out by their EU partners, to the tune of over a trillion euros (see Chapter 8).

As the debt crisis dragged on, it appeared that it might threaten some countries' membership in the eurozone. The hardest-hit member state, Greece, certainly might have benefited from the ability to devalue its currency—except that it no longer had a currency

As a member of the eurozone, Spain didn't have a national currency to manipulate in the face of a growing financial crisis in 2011–15. Other EU countries required austerity measures in Spain as a condition of their support, leading many citizens of Spain to protest the euro.

to devalue. And it was not clear that the other members of the eurozone were enthusiastic about Greece staying in. Indeed, in 2015, Greece appeared to come very close to being forced out of the eurozone, because of its continuing difficulties in servicing debts to banks and governments in other eurozone member countries. Nonetheless, the threat of the breakup of the euro helped push the eurozone's leaders toward a resolution of the crisis, involving a combination of painful austerity measures in the debtor nations, bailouts from the rest of the eurozone, and a small amount of debt restructuring. Thus far, the euro's unity has been preserved, but at a very high cost.

The dramatic economic and political effects of the crises in Europe, Mexico, Argentina, and East Asia, and of others in Turkey, Russia, Brazil, Venezuela, and elsewhere, caught the world's attention. So too did the fact that currency and banking crises could spread quickly from country to country, as they did in East Asia in 1997–98. This realization led many of the world's economic leaders to see these currency crises as threats to the international monetary order and the world economy more generally. One nation's currency collapse could be transmitted to others, to an entire region, or to the whole world. Currency and financial instability had, after all, lengthened and deepened the Great Depression of the 1930s. The currency crises of the 1990s and the early 2000s led many to believe that in a globalized financial system, such attacks had the potential to destabilize the entire world economy.

Containing Currency Crises

Concern that currency crises can have broad international effects makes attempts to counter them something of an international public good. Thus, major governments have a common interest in containing such crises—although, as with all public goods, there is often conflict over how to distribute the cost of providing such containment. This challenge has given rise to complex interactions in which governments, private investors, and international institutions both cooperate and contend over attempts to limit the damage caused by currency crises.

Indeed, over the past 20 years, governments of the major financial centers and the leading international financial institutions have often cooperated to try to slow the spread of currency crises. The IMF, other international institutions, and creditor governments have often mobilized tens of billions of dollars to try to support governments facing a currency crisis. The reasons for major governments to cooperate in the face of currency crises are closely related to the reasons for cooperation to address sovereign debt crises, as discussed in Chapter 8. Cooperation among national governments can help avoid, or mitigate the international impact of, currency crises; indeed, developed-country governments and the IMF have spent hundreds of billions of dollars since 1980 in attempts to control these crises.

However, such cooperation has not always been easy to organize and sustain. As with all public goods, there are incentives for each government to free ride and hope that other governments will pay the price of stabilizing the monetary order. Even more, many people believe that it is not a good idea to spend billions to support a failed or failing currency; such an effort may prop up undeserving governments and banks. This issue highlights the fact that currency crises can be controversial in domestic politics; governments are often blamed for allowing the crisis to take place, for not dealing with it effectively, or for inappropriately setting the currency in the first place.

Supporters have regarded these currency crisis interventions as striking examples of international cooperation to sustain the global monetary order, and with it the global economy more generally, with a quick response to avoid the proliferation of contagious crises. But critics have charged that taxpayers were being forced to bail out foolish investors and overextended governments, encouraging a continuation of irresponsible government and private behavior. The clash has largely pitted contending interests against one another (see Chapter 8 for similar debates over financial bailouts), and it is sure to continue. The mix of common interests and contentious issues ensures that currency crises, and controversies over them, will continue to plague many currencies and globalized financial markets.

Conclusion: Currencies, Conflict, and Cooperation

Argentines and Greeks are not alone in learning from experience that currency policy can make a significant difference to economic and political life. Over the past 20 years, billions of people in dozens of countries have experienced both the positive and negative effects of national currency policies. The exchange rate is controversial within countries because its impact differs among groups, firms, regions, and individuals with competing interests. There are many who benefit if the currency is fixed, and others who are harmed. For every firm that gains as a currency depreciates, there is another that loses. This clash of interests, mediated through national political institutions, determines national attitudes toward the exchange rate.

International monetary relations too have a profound impact on international economic and political affairs. There is a reason that the classical gold standard and the Bretton Woods monetary system gave their names to entire economic eras: the ordering principles of these currency regimes were central to their respective international economies. Without functioning international monetary arrangements, global economic activity would be immensely difficult.

Governments have powerful reasons to collaborate in devising international monetary arrangements, but they also have significant interests that conflict. Inasmuch as an international monetary regime is a public good, governments have strong incentives to free ride and let others provide it; they also have strong reasons to try to make sure it is provided, and they have reasons to want the regime to be organized in ways favorable to themselves. Such a mix of incentives for cooperation and incentives to bargain hard characterizes the politics of international monetary relations today, as it has for centuries. This connection can be seen through the currency policy issues that are likely to preoccupy national governments, and the world community, over the coming years.

The first contentious issue has to do with the overall structure and functioning of the international monetary system, and also cooperation among the world's major financial and monetary powers. Many scholars believe that more organized collaboration among major governments is desirable to avoid future problems and crises. Certainly, there is a desire among many governments to collaborate in devising a new monetary order. Yet there are also powerful interests in conflict, since governments disagree about the desirable characteristics of such an order.

In the absence of global agreement on international monetary relations, many countries in specific geographic regions continue to devise regional currency arrangements. The eurozone remains intact, and some of the EU's newer members are still considering whether to join. Many countries in Africa and the Middle East have already linked their currencies to the euro or plan to do so. There have been similar proposals for informal or formal currency unions in Latin America, North America, and parts of Asia.

Because many governments find these regional proposals an appealing way to reduce currency instability, some observers have suggested that we may be heading toward a world of currency blocs: an expanded eurozone eventually including much of the Middle East and Africa, and parts of Asia; a dollar zone in the Western Hemisphere; and an East Asian currency area. The future of such arrangements depends both on the interests that governments have in developing them and on their interactions to pursue their monetary goals. Whether national governments come together on the global level to forge a new international monetary regime, or devise regional arrangements such as the euro, international monetary relations will profoundly shape the world economy.

Study Tool Kit

Interests, Interactions, and Institutions in Context

- There are many contending interests over monetary affairs within countries, which leads to domestic conflict over the appropriate currency policy to pursue.

- Although every country can set currency policy as it wants, the fact that exchange rates value currencies relative to one another means that outcomes are the product of interactions among countries' policies. As a result, countries may have reasons to cooperate with one another to create arrangements that are mutually beneficial.

- Virtually everyone has an interest in the existence of a functioning international monetary system. But different arrangements benefit some actors more than others, which leads to disagreement about how such a system should be organized and about how the burdens and benefits should be distributed among countries.

- International monetary institutions, such as the gold standard, the Bretton Woods monetary system, or the eurozone, can create rules that facilitate cooperation in international monetary policy.

Key Terms

exchange rate, p. 389

appreciate, p. 389

depreciate, p. 389

devalue, p. 389

monetary policy, p. 391

central bank, p. 391

fixed exchange rate, p. 391

gold standard, p. 391

floating exchange rate, p. 392

Bretton Woods monetary system, p. 392

adjustable peg, p. 392

international monetary regime, p. 404

For Further Reading

Eichengreen, Barry. *Exorbitant Privilege: The Rise and Fall of the Dollar and the Future of the International Monetary System.* **New York: Oxford University Press, 2011.** Surveys the rise of the U.S. dollar as an international currency and evaluates how the dollar's role—and international monetary relations—is likely to evolve in the future.

Eichengreen, Barry. *Globalizing Capital: A History of the International Monetary System.* **2nd ed. Princeton, NJ: Princeton University Press, 2008.** Presents a general historical survey of the economics and politics of the international monetary order.

Eichengreen, Barry. *Golden Fetters: The Gold Standard and the Great Depression, 1919–1939.* **New York: Oxford University Press, 1992.** Serves as a classic analysis of how the gold standard collapsed in the interwar period.

Frieden, Jeffry A. *Currency Politics: The Political Economy of Exchange Rate Policy.* **Princeton, NJ: Princeton University Press, 2015.** Explains the politics and economics of government exchange-rate policy choices, with applications to the gold standard, European monetary integration, and Latin American currency policies and currency crises.

Klein, Michael, and Jay Shambaugh. *Exchange Rate Regimes in the Modern Era.* **Cambridge, MA: MIT Press, 2010.** Analyzes the different exchange-rate policy choices available to governments, and explores how and why they chose their currency regimes.

Schelkle, Waltraud. *The Political Economy of Monetary Solidarity: Understanding the Euro Experiment.* **Oxford: Oxford University Press, 2017.** Analyzes the problems and prospects of the eurozone, and compares it to the creation of an American monetary union.

Varoufakis, Yanis. *Adults in the Room: My Battle with the European and American Deep Establishment.* **New York: Farrar, Strauss and Giroux, 2017.** A controversial inside look at the eurozone crisis, by the equally controversial former Greek finance minister.

10

Development: Causes of the Wealth and Poverty of Nations

THE PUZZLE *Why are some countries rich and others poor? How do international politics and economics affect development?*

Above: Despite the overall growth of the world economy in recent decades, billions of people still live in poverty. For example, citizens of Zambia are significantly worse off today than they were when Zambia achieved independence in 1964. The average Zambian lives on the equivalent of less than $1,200 per year.

In 1964, the African nation of Zambia and the East Asian country of South Korea were at roughly equivalent levels of development. Indeed, when Zambia achieved its independence in 1964, its prospects appeared far more promising than those of South Korea. Zambia was rich in copper, and its newly elected president, Kenneth Kaunda, was popular at home and respected abroad for his intelligence and seriousness of purpose. South Korea, in contrast, had no resources to speak of, was ruled by a despised and ridiculed military dictatorship, and depended heavily on American aid, which was being cut back.

More than five decades later, the two countries could not be more different. The economy of Zambia has failed miserably. In the thirty years after Kaunda's election, Zambian income per person fell until, by the mid-1990s, the average Zambian had barely half the income he'd had at independence. Faced with this development failure, Zambians voted Kaunda out of office amid substantial political unrest and widespread food riots. The government's failures were compounded by the AIDS epidemic that swept Africa in the 1990s.

While conditions have improved somewhat since then, Zambia still has one of the lowest standards of living in the world. Life expectancy is just 61 years; more than one-third of the adult population is illiterate; child labor rates are high, with over 40 percent of children ages 5–14 in the workforce; and two-thirds of the population lives below the international poverty line, on less than $1.90 a day.[1] Today, Zambia is a developmental disaster.

Meanwhile, South Korea has become a modern industrial nation. In 1996, the Organisation for Economic Co-operation and Development recognized Korea's progress and made the country a member of this club of rich countries. South Korea had "graduated" from the developing to the developed world. It now has a standard of living comparable to that of France. Life expectancy is 82 years, adult literacy is practically universal, and per capita income is close to $35,000 a year. Although the two nations had similar starting points 50 years ago, today South Korea is an industrialized, developed nation, while Zambia is desperately poor.

This comparison illustrates two realities of contemporary economic development. First, billions of people live

---

1. Data from the UN Human Development Reports 2016, http://hdr.undp.org/en/ (accessed 11/01/17).

in conditions of poverty. For example, average incomes in Africa today are comparable to what they were in western Europe 200 years ago; African life expectancy and literacy rates are similar to those of western Europe 100 years ago. In sub-Saharan Africa, nearly one-third of all children under age five are malnourished, just over one-third of children of secondary school age attend school, and one-third of the population lacks access to clean water.

Second, developmental experiences have varied widely. In 1960, countries such as South Korea and Taiwan were dismally poor—poorer than most of Africa. Today, these two nations are advanced industrial countries with per capita incomes comparable to those in western Europe. And the world's two most populous countries, China and India—home to over one-third of the world's people—have been growing very rapidly for over 30 years. China's living standards are today 15 times higher than they were in 1990; India's are 5 times higher. The differences among developing nations are enormous; for example, the gap between Latin America and sub-Saharan Africa is substantially bigger than the gap between Latin America and the industrialized nations.

In fact, the proportion of the world's population living in abject poverty has declined since the 1980s. Most international organizations use an international absolute poverty line equivalent to about $1.90 a day per person in today's dollars, taking into account differences in the cost of living across countries. By this measure, while 52 percent of the developing world's population lived in absolute poverty in 1981, by 2013 the proportion was 11 percent.[2] This improvement is largely the result of successful development in China and India.

Nonetheless, the stark fact remains that nearly 6 billion of the total world population of about 7 billion live in poor countries. While not everyone in poor countries is poor, these nations have an average income per person of just one-quarter that of the rich countries. Most of the world's people are poor.

The continued poverty of much of the world's population leads us to ask why so many countries are poor. Why have some countries developed successfully while others have stagnated? Why have the experiences of less developed countries differed so widely? Within these questions lie related issues about the relationship between developing countries and international politics: How has the international political economy affected the development of poor nations? Has it been a hindrance or a help to them?

Thinking Analytically about Development

This chapter makes several points about the politics and economics of development. We note that although everyone in poor countries prefers more development to less, individuals and groups within countries may have conflicting interests with respect to how development is achieved. Powerful domestic groups that pursue policies to enrich themselves might prevent the adoption of other measures that would improve economic conditions for everyone else. Domestic social and political institutions can have a major impact on how such conflicts of interest among different domestic groups affect a country's development. Some institutional arrangements empower special interest groups, while others overcome those who would stand in the way of development. In addition, a country's institutions can either facilitate or impede cooperation to promote policies that are conducive to economic growth.

At the international level, rich and poor nations generally have a common interest in accelerating the economic growth of the developing world. As poor nations grow, their demand for the products of rich nations grows, and they are better able to supply rich nations with goods and services they need. However, there have been many instances of rich countries supporting policies and institutions that disfavor less developed countries. For example, agricultural policies in Europe, North America, and Japan help farmers in rich countries at the expense of farmers in poor countries.

Given these conditions, successful economic growth requires that a country overcome both the domestic obstacles posed by interests and institutions that are detrimental to development, and the international obstacles created by conflicts of interest with wealthy nations.

---

2. The best source on the issue, from which most of these data are taken, is Branko Milanovic, *Global Inequality: A New Approach for the Age of Globalization* (Cambridge, MA: Harvard University Press, 2016). The numbers cited here are from the World Bank, www .worldbank.org/en/topic/poverty/overview (accessed 11/01/17).

If Everyone Wants Development, Why Is It So Hard to Achieve?

Less developed countries (LDCs) want to develop, and few people would deny them the opportunity to do so.[3] However, steps to improve a nation's developmental prospects sometimes threaten the interests of certain actors at home or abroad. Recognizing this fact, we can identify three prominent approaches that explain why such a universally accepted goal appears to be so difficult to attain. These approaches consider geography, domestic factors such as a nation's political economy, and domestic institutions.

less developed countries (LDCs)
Countries at a relatively low level of economic development.

Geographic Location

One view is that the geographic realities of some countries impede their growth. The fact that the world's tropical regions are generally poor, while its temperate regions are generally rich, suggests that geography and climate affect development, directly or indirectly. There is little doubt that such factors play some part in explaining patterns of development.

Landlocked countries, regions with diseases that are difficult to control or cure, and areas that are very far from major markets for their goods are all at a developmental disadvantage—and this disadvantage was probably greater in an earlier era, when medical knowledge was limited and transportation and communications costs were much higher. By virtue of weather and disease, tropical environments in particular may be less conducive to urbanization and industrialization than temperate zones. Some scholars ascribe a substantial portion of the developmental problems of tropical regions like sub-Saharan Africa, for example, to geography itself.[4]

But geographic factors cannot be the whole story, as there is a great deal of variation among countries within the same regions. Indeed, if we compare LDCs that have very similar geographic characteristics, we find that some have done extremely well, while others have done very poorly (see "What Shaped Our World?" on p. 428). While the climate and geography of a nation shape its development, they do so by way of their impact on the people, social structures, politics, and policies of the nation. Later in this chapter we return to analyses in which geography plays a part in the development process in conjunction with other socioeconomic and political factors.

---

3. Observers use a variety of terms for these countries. During the Cold War, it was common to refer to them as *third world*, to distinguish them from the capitalist *first world* and the communist *second world*. Today it is more common to use the label *less developed country* or, more optimistically, *developing country*; some observers refer to the more successful of these countries as *emerging markets*. Another convention is to refer to these countries collectively as *the South* because they tend to be located geographically to the south of the richer countries. We will use some of these terms interchangeably.

4. For prominent statements on geography and development, see Jared Diamond, *Guns, Germs, and Steel* (New York: Norton, 1997); David Bloom and Jeffrey Sachs, "Geography, Demography, and Economic Growth in Africa," *Brookings Papers on Economic Activity* 2 (1998): 207–95; and Jeffrey Sachs, Andrew Mellinger, and John Gallup, "The Geography of Poverty and Wealth," *Scientific American*, March 2001, 70–75.

Paths to Development

Why have some countries prospered, with their economies growing over time, while others have stagnated or even declined? One way to understand the interests, interactions, and institutions that lead some countries to prosper while others struggle is to compare countries that began their modern developmental experience under similar conditions, especially when they now diverge substantially.

Consider the cases of Zambia and Botswana. These two southern African countries gained their independence from Great Britain in 1964 and 1966, respectively. Both countries are landlocked and have substantial mineral wealth. At independence, Zambia was much richer than Botswana, perhaps twice as rich, but today Zambia remains very poor, while Botswana is thriving.[a] Why?

Interests The interests that dominated Zambian politics were largely urban: the business community and the urban middle and working classes, along with workers in the country's major copper mines. In contrast, the new Botswanan government presided over an economy with few initial natural resources: the main economic activity was cattle ranching, with most cattle in the hands of indigenous political leaders (the tribal chiefs). This difference meant that the Zambian government had incentives to channel its resources from the countryside and the copper belt to the cities, while the Botswanan government had incentives to develop the country's cattle-ranching economy.

Institutions Following independence, the new Zambian government created institutions that centralized power. The country's rulers institutionalized a single-party state, destroying most of the country's democratic institutions. The government also created institutions to take over the country's copper mines from private owners. This monopoly of power allowed the government to use its copper earnings to award benefits to its core supporters. It also permitted the government to discriminate against farmers to provide cheap food to urban interests that were its

The Botswanan parliament in Gaborone.

power base, and raise high barriers to imports to encourage local industries. Thus, Zambian political institutions served the interests of the business community and the urban middle and working classes, while leaving other domestic groups, notably farmers, in poverty.

The new Botswanan government pursued a different path. Rather than centralizing power in the hands of one political party, it maintained and strengthened democratic political institutions. It invested in public goods to promote farming, especially cattle ranching; spent heavily on education and infrastructure; provided a stable environment for private investment; and encouraged foreign investment in the country's natural resources. Eventually, rich diamond deposits were discovered, which helped speed up economic growth.

Interactions The structure of Zambia's dominant interests, and the institutions that allowed them to control political power, led the government to pursue policies that served primarily to reinforce the position of the minority of urban dwellers to the detriment of the society as a whole. In contrast, the principal interests in Botswana led the government to encourage agrarian development and maintain inclusive democratic institutions. Today, Botswana is a thriving, democratic nation with a 2016 per capita GDP of $6,788, while Zambia is an economically, politically, and socially troubled country, whose 2016 per capita GDP was $1,178—less than one-fifth that of its neighbor.

There are many reasons why one country develops while another does not. Whether it is divergent domestic interests, different national political institutions, or varied interactions among them, they all have a powerful impact on government policies and domestic politics.

---

a. Real GDP per capita here and elsewhere in this section comes from Alan Heston, Robert Summers, and Bettina Aten, Penn World Table Version 7.0, Center for International Comparisons of Production, Income, and Prices, University of Pennsylvania, Philadelphia, May 2011, http://pwt.econ.upenn.edu/php site/pwt_index.php (accessed 11/01/17); and World Bank, World Development Indicators, http://data.worldbank.org/country (accessed 11/02/17).

Two other approaches dominate attempts to explain patterns of development. One focuses on domestic factors, another on domestic institutions. International factors are relevant as well, and we return to them later in the chapter. However, the fact that there is so much variation among countries that are similarly situated and that face similar international conditions implies that domestic factors and institutions are crucially important.

Domestic Factors

Within developing nations, there are interests, interactions, and institutions that can speed or impede economic growth. While every country is different and every experience is unique, certain common features of national political economies can help explain why some nations have been more successful than others. At the outset, it is crucial to recognize that a government's policies have a powerful impact on economic growth, either encouraging or slowing it. In fact, almost all explanations of development and underdevelopment consider the results of the actions (or inactions) of governments.

A very important policy that governments can undertake to boost development is to provide public goods that contribute to economic growth and prosperity. One such public good is the economic **infrastructure**, including a physical infrastructure of roads, railroads, airports, utilities, ports, and the like, which are necessary to allow trade and exchange; and such economic institutions as financial and monetary systems, which permit people to make payments and investments easily. A social infrastructure too—public health and sanitation, education, urban planning— can encourage growth and development by allowing citizens to focus their efforts on economic activity in a productive way. In contrast, if the government does not build and maintain roads and schools, impedes normal banking operations, allows prices to spiral out of control, and fails to control disease and social problems, it is hard to imagine how the economy can develop.

Another crucial function for government is to ensure the security of property. After all, economic growth requires everyone from farmers to factory owners to invest in improving their ability to produce, and such improvements are unlikely to be made if property rights are not safe. Secure property rights—which people in developed countries take for granted—mean that a property owner can be confident that his or her material goods will not be seized arbitrarily.

A commitment to protect private property is not necessarily something that benefits only the rich; in most poor societies, the principal property owners are farmers. To take advantage of new economic opportunities, farmers must set aside time, energy, and money to improve the soil. They have to put their livelihood on the line in order to plant coffee trees, clear woodland, or irrigate. How can they undertake such risky investments if they cannot be sure that the benefits will come back to them? If marauders can steal their animals and torch their fields? If local government officials can extort any wealth they see being earned? If the national government taxes away all their earnings?

Long-term economic growth requires a stable and reliable environment within which people can make economic plans for the future. A government that invests

infrastructure
Basic structures necessary for social activity, such as transportation and telecommunications networks, and power and water supply.

Some countries, including Indonesia, have recently chosen to pursue a policy of infrastructure development to facilitate trade and exchange, attract foreign investment, grow their economies, and ultimately join the ranks of wealthy nations.

in education and public health, creates an efficient economic infrastructure, and ensures a stable monetary and financial system can do a great deal to facilitate economic growth. People need a credible commitment that the government will abide by its promises to provide such public goods. Governments that cannot or will not credibly promise to provide important public goods inhibit their citizens' ability to take advantage of economic opportunities.

Why might a government not be willing or able to commit to creating a favorable environment for economic growth? After all, even the most selfish rulers presumably stand to benefit from a prosperous economy. And all societies have workers, farmers, and businesspeople with an interest in active and effective government policies to expand the range of economic opportunities.

Some countries' governments might simply lack the technical expertise to manage modern economic growth, in which case foreign assistance, in the form of both money and skills, may be needed. More often, unfortunately, the answer is not so easy.

In many societies, certain actors have interests that go against broad-based economic development. This is not to say that such actors consciously desire to limit growth, but that a pursuit of their own interests can ultimately harm the economy. (This phenomenon is not specific to LDCs, of course; every country has actors with an interest in manipulating the economy to benefit themselves, even at the cost of slowing economic growth.)

In developing countries, such actors are often engaged in traditional economic sectors whose livelihood would be threatened by the growth of a more modern economy. For example, wealthy landowners may prefer that the property rights of poor farmers not be protected, so that the rich can encroach on the land being farmed by the poor. Owners of labor-intensive plantations or mines may have little reason to support urbanization, industrialization, or education, because these developments would draw workers away and raise labor costs. Powerful corporations that receive generous subsidies and protection want to maintain them, even if they are a burden on taxpayers and consumers. Bureaucrats who can extort bribes in return for favors have nothing to gain from a more open and efficient administration.

The dismal experience of sub-Saharan Africa since independence provides an example of how actors whose interests are at odds with the general social interest can impede economic growth. As Map 10.1 shows, many of the world's poorest countries are found in sub-Saharan Africa. Development policy in this region has served largely to benefit small groups and to harm the rest of society. For decades, governments systematically drained resources from the countryside in order to channel them into the cities, by taxing farmers directly, by keeping farm prices artificially low, or by other means.

These policies were often justified as a way of speeding urbanization and industrialization, and they may indeed have had that effect. But in societies that were 80 or 90 percent rural, this process amounted to impoverishing the masses to benefit a narrow urban elite. However, the urban elite was a politically important base of support for African governments. It included urban businessmen, government employees, and the military, on which many governments relied to stay in power. As a result, many African governments pursued economic policies that depleted the farm sector—which represented most of the population and most of the meaningful economic opportunities—in the interest of catering to inefficient urban enterprises and bureaucracies.[5]

Self-serving groups whose goals conflict with those of the rest of society can significantly impede development, but interests alone are insufficient to explain countries' different paths of development. After all, every country has powerful special interests, including groups that may be opposed to broader development, but every country also has masses of farmers, workers, businesspeople, and others who stand to benefit from policies that promote economic growth. What ultimately determines the character of government policies toward development is not just the interests in play, but also the nature of their interactions: how politicians, social groups, and the public bargain, fight, cooperate, and negotiate their way toward an outcome.

Conditions in some societies may make it easy for actors to come together in pursuit of shared goals, but other societies may have endemic divisions that make this collaboration very difficult. Hostility and conflict among ethnic or regional groups can impede both political stability and effective national government policies if rivalries between groups overcome a concern for the common good. Because many LDCs have boundaries that were determined by colonial powers without regard to preexisting ethnic, religious, and racial features of the population, they can be very diverse, and competition among groups can complicate the making of economic policy in these countries.[6]

Generally speaking, as we saw in Chapter 2, the larger the group, the more difficult collective action is. This means that, as we saw with respect to trade

---

5. Robert Bates, *Markets and States in Tropical Africa* (Berkeley: University of California Press, 1981), is the classic examination of this process.

6. For a survey, see Alberto Alesina and Eliana LaFerrara, "Ethnic Diversity and Economic Performance," *Journal of Economic Literature* 63 (September 2005): 762–800. This is not a problem only for poor countries, but it can be particularly troubling there.

MAP 10.1 *Economic Activity around the World*

This map shows that per capita Gross Domestic Product (GDP), the most widely used measure of economic activity, varies greatly around the world. People in many African and South Asian countries live on less than $4,000 per year on average, a small fraction of the per capita GDP of North American and European countries. However, per capita GDP tells only part of the story, as it is an average. Some countries with relatively high per capita GDP, such as Brazil or South Africa, nonetheless have serious problems with poverty owing to the highly unequal distribution of income and wealth within the country.

GREENLAND (DENMARK)

ALASKA

CANADA

ICELAND

Pacific Ocean

Atlantic Ocean

UNITED STATES

BAHAMAS
HAITI
MEXICO
CUBA
BELIZE
GUATEMALA — HONDURAS
EL SALVADOR
NICARAGUA
COSTA RICA
PANAMA
VENEZUELA
GUYANA
SURINAME
COLOMBIA
ECUADOR
PERU
BRAZIL
BOLIVIA
PARAGUAY
URUGUAY
ARGENTINA
CHILE

Per capita GDP, 2015

- $1,314 OR LESS
- $1,315–$3,828
- $3,829–$8,053
- $8,054–$19,220
- $19,221 OR MORE
- NO DATA

Map source: World Bank, World Development Indicators, http://data.worldbank.org/indicator (accessed 11/28/17).

Arctic Ocean

UNITED
KINGDOM
NORWAY
SWEDEN
FINLAND
IRELAND
GERMANY
BELARUS
UKRAINE
RUSSIA
FRANCE
GEORGIA
KAZAKHSTAN
MONGOLIA
N. KOREA
S. KOREA
PORTUGAL
SPAIN
ITALY
GREECE
TURKEY
UZBEKISTAN
KYRGYZSTAN
TURKMENISTAN
TAJIKISTAN
CHINA
JAPAN
MOROCCO
TUNISIA
ISRAEL
LEB.
SYRIA
IRAQ
IRAN
NEPAL
BHUTAN
MACAU
Pacific Ocean
ALGERIA
LIBYA
JORDAN
EGYPT
SAUDI
ARABIA
UAE
OMAN
MYANMAR
(BURMA)
HONG KONG
TAIWAN
MAURITANIA
MALI
NIGER
CHAD
SUDAN
ERITREA
YEMEN
AFGHANISTAN
PAKISTAN
INDIA
THAILAND
VIETNAM
SENEGAL
LAOS
PHILIPPINES
GUINEA
NIGERIA
CEN.
AFR.
REP.
S. SUDAN
ETHIOPIA
BANGLADESH
CAMBODIA
GHANA
CAMEROON
UGANDA
SOMALIA
SRI LANKA
MALAYSIA
IVORY COAST
D.R.
CONGO
KENYA
MALAWI
INDONESIA
PAPUA NEW GUINEA
TANZANIA
ANGOLA
ZAMBIA
MADAGASCAR
Indian Ocean
NAMIBIA
MOZAMBIQUE
ZIMBABWE
AUSTRALIA
SOUTH
AFRICA
BOTSWANA
NEW
ZEALAND

433

policies in Chapter 7, broad social interests are less likely to be organized than narrower special interests. Thus, special interest groups have an advantage in influencing policy. Nonetheless, sometimes the existence of a powerful common national goal (such as national unification or resistance to an external threat) can lead groups to set aside their differences and focus together on developmental requirements. It has been suggested that South Korea and Taiwan, for example, were strongly motivated to grow rapidly in part because of their competition with North Korea and China, respectively. The economist Mancur Olson was optimistic that development could be spurred, and self-interested special interests denied, when societies were dominated by encompassing coalitions—that is, alliances that include enough of society to be concerned for broad social welfare.[7]

Whether important social actors interact in a cooperative manner to spur development also depends on domestic political institutions. These institutions affect the influence of those pressing for the public interest and for the goals of specific groups. More representative political institutions, for example, are likely to give more weight to broad public concerns about overall economic growth. Countries with more democratic political institutions appear to provide more public goods than do authoritarian political systems—more basic education, more public health, more equitable and efficient distributions of land.[8] In fact, part of the problem in postcolonial Africa has been the very undemocratic nature of most of the region's political systems, which allowed a narrow urban elite to use the government to exploit the masses of farmers and other rural dwellers.

However, the relationship between democracy and development has been contested. While some believe that democratic regimes are more conducive to development than authoritarian ones are, others argue that authoritarian regimes may be better suited to force-march their countries toward development. Still others believe that there is no clear relationship between regime type and development.[9]

Domestic Institutions

How and why have certain societies developed institutions that are conducive to economic growth, while others have not? The interests that characterize a society, the interactions among them, and the institutions that develop within the society are all interrelated. Nonetheless, some scholars emphasize how the human and material resources that societies possess give rise to interests and institutions that may be more or less favorable to development.

7. Mancur Olson, *The Rise and Decline of Nations: Economic Growth, Stagflation, and Social Rigidities* (New Haven, CT: Yale University Press, 1982).

8. See, for example, David A. Lake and Matthew A. Baum, "The Political Economy of Growth: Democracy and Human Capital," *American Journal of Political Science* 47, no. 2 (April 2003): 333–47; Nancy D. Lapp, *Landing Votes: Representation and Land Reform in Latin America* (New York: Palgrave/Macmillan, 2004); David Stasavage, "Democracy and Education Spending in Africa," *American Journal of Political Science* 49, no. 2 (2005): 343–58; and David S. Brown and Wendy A. Hunter, "Democracy and Human Capital Formation: Education Spending in Latin America, 1980 to 1997," *Comparative Political Studies* 37, no. 7 (2004): 842–64.

9. An excellent summary of the debate and the evidence is James A. Robinson, "Economic Development and Democracy," *Annual Review of Political Science* 9, no. 1 (2006): 503–27.

This view incorporates the geographic features of different regions of the world into a broader interpretation of developmental paths. For example, societies that rely on the exploitation of rich natural resources with the use of plantation agriculture or mining are often dominated by powerful elites whose interests work against development. Elites in these societies can create political institutions that are strongly biased against popular participation and that serve to retard broad-based participation in economic growth (see "How Do We Know?" on p. 436).

This perspective helps explain the surprising fact that many regions that are extremely rich in natural resources are developmental disasters. The relationship between resource wealth and underdevelopment is strong enough to have prompted theories of a "resource curse," in which initial wealth gives rise to subsequent poverty. One such idea is that the government of a country with a natural resource that can be easily and lucratively exploited may have few reasons to encourage productive activities other than those associated with that resource. Another, related, view is that when a country experiences massive inflows of funds, whether through the private or the public sector, there are greater incentives for people to use those funds to engage in such corrupt practices as buying favors from government or extorting bribes from private companies.

In contrast, the government of a country with few natural resources, if it wants economic growth, has little choice but to undertake measures that will make the economy more productive. Recalling the comparison of Zambia and South Korea noted at the outset of this chapter, it may be that Zambia's copper wealth gave its rulers little incentive to increase the country's ability to produce anything other than raw materials by improving education, public health, and the economic

Many countries that are rich in natural resources remain poor. Nigeria is one of the world's largest oil exporters, but the average Nigerian has hardly benefited from this natural wealth. Poor Nigerians frequently risk death to pilfer oil from pipelines.

Explaining Developmental Differences: North and South America

What explains the major developmental differences among countries with relatively similar economic starting points? One instructive comparison is between North and South America. The two regions were colonized by Europeans at roughly the same time and got their independence within a few decades of each other; since then, however, they have diverged in important ways.

Two economic historians, Stanley Engerman and Kenneth Sokoloff, have argued that the kinds of economic activities the regions undertook early in their history had a lasting impact on their subsequent social, political, and economic evolution. The early patterns of economic organization created powerful interests that could craft institutions with an enduring effect on subsequent political, social, and economic development. Engerman and Sokoloff have brought many different kinds of evidence to bear in comparing North and South American developmental paths.[a]

Many Latin American colonies and countries were drawn into the world economy on the basis of plantation agriculture (such as sugar, cotton, or coffee, as in the plantation pictured here) or labor-intensive mining (silver, gold). These economic activities created highly unequal societies made up of wealthy landowners or miners on the one hand, and poorly paid workers or slaves on the other. Naturally, the wealthy landowners and miners were the dominant interests in these societies. These powerful interests played a major part in creating undemocratic

political institutions, which reflected and reinforced the great inequalities in society and helped the wealthy hold on to power.

The bias in colonial and postcolonial political institutions can be seen in their rules on who was eligible to vote. All 13 original colonies that made up the United States restricted voting to those with property, sometimes substantial property. But over the decades after independence, these property ownership requirements were gradually relaxed and eventually eliminated. By 1850, white male adult Americans could vote whether or not they owned property or were literate, while every Latin American country restricted voting to those who both owned property and were literate.

As a result, at a time when 13 percent of the American population voted in elections, the proportion in Latin America was at most 1 or 2 percent. To be sure, the United States at that time would not qualify as a democracy by our current standards: African Americans and women could not vote. Nonetheless, the difference in the extent to which politicians faced a broad electorate is striking. The image on the next page depicts a lively scene from the 1852 U.S. elections.

These differences in the right to vote persisted for decades, even centuries. Around 1900, 18 percent of Americans voted—although this advance was marred by the fact that the southern states, controlled by white supremacists,

a. A summary of their work is in Stanley Engerman and Kenneth Sokoloff, "History Lessons: Institutions, Factor Endowments, and Paths of Development in the New World," *Journal of Economic Perspectives* 14, no. 3 (2000): 217–32. Other components can be found in Stanley Engerman and Kenneth Sokoloff, "Factor Endowments, Institutions, and Differential Paths of Growth among New World Economies: A View from Economic Historians of the United States," in *How Latin America Fell Behind*, ed. Stephen Haber, 260–304 (Stanford, CA: Stanford University Press, 1997); Stanley Engerman and Kenneth Sokoloff, "The Evolution of Suffrage Institutions in the New World," *Journal of Economic History* 65, no. 4 (December 2005): 891–921; and Kenneth Sokoloff and Eric Zolt, "Inequality and the Evolution of Institutions of Taxation: Evidence from the Economic History of the Americas," in *The Decline of Latin American Economies: Growth, Institutions, and Crises*, ed. Sebastian Edwards, Gerardo Esquivel, and Graciela Márquez, 83–136 (Chicago: University of Chicago Press, 2007).

had imposed literacy requirements in order to restrict the voting rights of African Americans. In most Latin American countries, the proportion voting was still below 5 percent. Even in 1940, the share of Americans voting was still two to four times as great as the share of Latin Americans.

The institutions that restricted the access of Latin Americans to the political system had a powerful effect on what governments had incentives to do. Where only the wealthy could influence politics, policies reflected the interests of the wealthy. In Latin America, governments dominated by elite interests lacked policies to improve education, public health, or the economic opportunities of the poor. Biased institutions and the lack of developmentally oriented policies retarded economic growth.

In most of North America, however, early economic activities created fewer inequalities. Small-scale wheat farming in the United States and Canada, for example, produced a class of independent family farmers and a society that was quite equal. This equality was reflected in democratic political institutions, as well as in substantial government investments in infrastructure, education, and other economically important activities. Here, the developmentally oriented institutions and policies encouraged economic growth. As early as 1850, literacy for white adults in the United States was above 90 percent—a level that many Latin American countries have reached only recently, if at

all. Of course, because literacy was actively discouraged (even prohibited) among slaves, literacy among African American adults in the United States was under 20 percent.

In fact, the experience of the American South underscores the argument that economic activities affect interests, which in turn affect institutions, which in turn affect developmental paths. In the southern United States, unlike in the North and Midwest, there were substantial slave plantation regions growing cotton and tobacco. In this aspect, the South was more like Latin America than like the North. Engerman and Sokoloff show that in the former plantation areas in the eighteenth and nineteenth centuries, inequalities were much greater than elsewhere in the United States; the right to vote was much more restricted, and of course these restrictions persisted for a century after slavery was abolished; and there was much less spending on education and other public works. The highly unequal nature of southern American society, Engerman and Sokoloff argue, created an enduring legacy that was reflected in the South's institutions and that held back its economic growth for many decades.

The experiences of Latin America and of the American South demonstrate how domestic economic, political, and social interests and institutions created early in a region's economic history can have a long-lasting impact on its subsequent development.

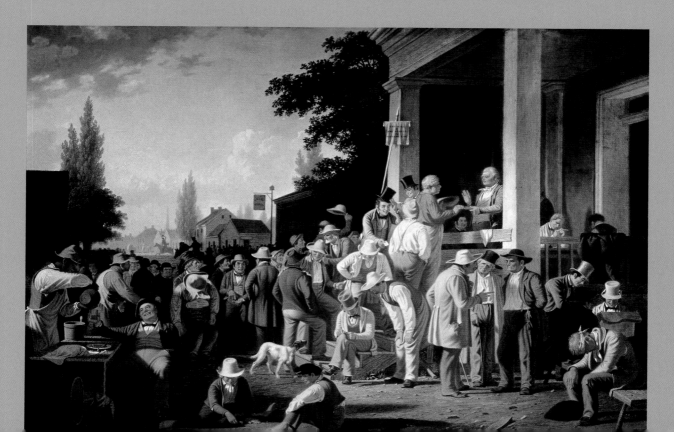

infrastructure. By contrast, South Korea's lack of any major exportable raw materials forced its government to focus on improving the productive capacities of its people.[10] The broader point is that geographic and other inherent features of a country are important for subsequent development inasmuch as they have a substantial impact on the kinds of interests and institutions that arise on their basis.

In sum, to understand why countries have developed in a certain way, we need to understand people's interests and their ability or inability to interact in ways that foster cooperation, as well as the political institutions that determine how people's interests are translated into policy. Domestic factors, and especially national government policies, are crucial to understanding national developmental success or failure.

In addition to domestic factors, the international environment shapes the constraints and opportunities faced by developing countries in various ways. Many people in LDCs argue that international conditions have not been helpful to their prospects and, indeed, that the current poverty of much of the world is due to the structure of the international system.

How Do Rich Countries Affect the Developing World?

There is evidence that interests, interactions, and institutions at the international level are responsible for at least some of the current problems of poor nations. While developed and developing countries have many interests in common, there are also many real and potential conflicts of interest among them.

Rich and poor nations have many shared interests. Economic growth in the developing world can create enormous opportunities for wealthy countries. As we saw in Chapters 7, 8, and 9, rich-country corporations can profit from investing in and selling to developing nations, while poor countries can benefit from the capital, technology, and expertise that such corporations bring. LDC exports provide cheap goods for industrial-country consumers while they make money for the exporters. Banks from the industrialized world are eager to make loans to developing countries, in part because poor countries that are short of capital are willing to pay higher interest rates than can be earned elsewhere. The growth of poor countries' economies expands investment opportunities and markets for rich-country businesses. All these factors suggest why the relationship among rich and poor nations could be cooperative and the scope for mutually beneficial exchange very large.

---

10. See, for example, Michael Shafer, *Winners and Losers: How Sectors Shape the Developmental Prospects of States* (Ithaca, NY: Cornell University Press, 1994); Halvor Mehlum, Karl Moene, and Ragnar Torvik, "Institutions and the Resource Curse," *Economic Journal* 116 (2006): 1–20; and Macartan Humphreys, Jeffrey D. Sachs, and Joseph E. Stiglitz, eds., *Escaping the Resource Curse* (New York: Columbia University Press, 2007). For a different view, see Yu-Ming Liou and Paul Musgrave, "Refining the Oil Curse," *Comparative Political Studies* 47, no. 11 (September 2014): 1584–1610.

By the same token, all countries have a common interest in the successful management of international economic affairs. Developed and developing countries alike benefit from well-functioning international trading, financial, and monetary systems. Few, if any, nations stand to gain from a breakdown of the international economy or from the transmission of financial crises from one country to another. International collaboration to smooth the operation of the world economy and to deal with problems that may arise is generally in the interest of all countries. Indeed, most international economic organizations—including the International Monetary Fund (IMF), the World Bank, and the World Trade Organization (WTO)—have both rich and poor nations as their members.

However, the interests of developed and developing countries may also clash. As we have seen in other areas of international politics, agreement over the desirability of cooperation coexists with disagreement over how to distribute the benefits of cooperation. A multinational mining company and an LDC government have a common interest in getting minerals out of the ground and to market, but they are likely to disagree about the division of the profits. Similarly, LDC companies and governments may appreciate being able to borrow from international banks, but there is likely to be political controversy about making the sacrifices necessary to pay back their debts—especially in hard times. The fact that rich-country corporations can profit from low wages in the LDCs means that they may have little interest in encouraging development that will raise wages.

Such a mix of interests in common and in conflict is central to the international political economy of development. It can be seen in the historical dynamics of colonialism and many contemporary examples.

This 1933 French illustration shows an idealized vision of colonialism—one in which the European settlers fostered development through education and industry. In reality, however, the interests of colonial rulers were often at odds with local development.

Did Colonialism Hamper Development?

One aspect of the international order that is often blamed for underdevelopment is the legacy of colonialism. As we discussed in Chapter 1, from the sixteenth through the twentieth centuries colonial rule was often justified as being in the interests of both the colonial powers and the colonized. Indeed, in many instances colonialism encouraged broad-based economic growth in poor countries, for sometimes the interests of rulers and ruled were similar. Some colonial regimes supplied roads, railroads, ports, and other infrastructure both to facilitate their rule and to gain access to the colonies' resources; this infrastructure facilitated the economic and political development of the colonial society overall. Some of today's most developed nations—the United States, Canada, Australia, New Zealand—were longtime colonies.

Nonetheless, the interests of the colonizers and the colonized were frequently in conflict, so the enduring impact of colonialism was often negative. Most imperial powers wanted to use their colonies for the mother country's benefit, even if this was not beneficial to the colonial society. They often reserved economic advantages to their own citizens and restricted the access of colonial subjects to economic opportunity. And when the colonial rulers' interests were inconsistent with local development, it was the rulers' interests that prevailed. This situation led to interactions that subordinated colonial societies and economies to the needs of the empire.

Colonialism, indeed, institutionalized a relationship in which the interests of the colonies were secondary to those of the mother country. For example, colonial policy commonly directed colonial trade toward the mother country, restricted manufacturing in the colonies, and otherwise gave trading privileges to the colonial power. (This was true of British policy toward the 13 colonies in North America; see Chapter 1.) Such preferential policies were intended in part to benefit residents of the great power, and in part to deny benefits to real or potential enemies in other empires. This approach can hardly have been beneficial for development, and it may have been highly detrimental.

There are many instances of colonial rule that was negligent at best, predatory at worst. One famous example is that of Leopold II, king of Belgium, in the Congo (the former Belgian Congo, now known as the Democratic Republic of the Congo). When the European powers colonized Africa in the late nineteenth century, they permitted Leopold to turn the Congo into his own personal possession. For decades, Leopold exploited the indigenous people mercilessly, forcing them to gather ivory, rubber, and other raw materials and turn them over to his own colonial government.[11]

In one study, three scholars analyzed how the form colonialism took had a systematic impact on subsequent development. Daron Acemoglu, Simon Johnson, and James Robinson suggest that the countries and regions of the colonial world can be divided into two types. The first includes countries where European settlers could live easily, without fear of high mortality owing to tropical diseases or other threats. In these regions, settlers from the colonial powers, the scholars write, "went and settled in the colonies and set up institutions that enforced the rule of

---

11. A classic analysis of the Congo's experience is Adam Hochschild, *King Leopold's Ghost* (Boston: Houghton Mifflin, 1998).

LA NOUVELLE YORCK.

...dans l'Amérique septentrionale dans l'Isle de Manahatan près l'embouchure du fleuve hudson, Les Hollandois commencèrent à la bâtir en l'année ...merent nouvelle Amsterdam, mais en 1666. ils en furent privés par les Anglois, qui la nommerent la nouvelle Yorck.

In regions with climates hospitable to European immigrants, such as the Atlantic coast of North America, settlers moved in and established political institutions that set the stage for successful economic development.

law and encouraged investment."[12] European settlers, in other words, went where they could survive, and they established social, political, and economic institutions that were conducive to economic growth. These institutions persisted, and in such countries as Canada and Australia the result was successful development.

In regions of the second type, where European settlers were much more likely to die of disease or other factors, the colonial powers engaged in predatory policies. There, the scholars say, the Europeans "set up extractive states with the intention of transferring resources rapidly to the metropole. These institutions were detrimental to investment and economic progress."[13] In other words, where large-scale European immigration and settlement were not feasible, the colonial powers simply exploited the region for their own benefit, establishing institutions that were not conducive to economic growth. These institutions too persisted and served to impede successful development.

To evaluate their argument, Acemoglu, Johnson, and Robinson looked at the death rates of early European settlers in colonial regions between the 1600s and the 1800s. There is little reason to think that these death rates would in themselves have a direct impact on modern economic growth, but in fact the settlers' mortality rates were strongly correlated with underdevelopment today. This is powerful evidence for the kind of effects the three scholars anticipated.

12. Daron Acemoglu, Simon Johnson, and James Robinson, "The Colonial Origins of Comparative Development," *American Economic Review* 91, no. 5 (December 2001): 1395.

13. Acemoglu, Johnson, and Robinson, "Colonial Origins of Comparative Development," 1395.

It seems clear that different types of colonial experiences, and the different institutions put in place by colonial powers, have had enduring effects on development. Where the common interests of colonial powers and people in the colonies predominated, the impact of colonialism was favorable (or at least neutral). But where the colonial powers' interests went against those of the local population—such as in extracting labor and resources from the colony by force—and the colonialists imposed their will, the impact of colonialism was detrimental.

Although the lasting effects of colonialism explain some of the disparity between rich and poor nations, they cannot explain all of it. After all, most Latin American nations have been independent for nearly 200 years—longer than many developed countries have been in existence—and even most former colonies in Africa, Asia, and the Caribbean have been independent for nearly 60 years. Some poor countries—such as China, Thailand, Iran, Liberia, and Ethiopia—have never been colonies[14] and yet have suffered from severe developmental problems. However, other international factors are often invoked as barriers to development as well.

How Does the International Economy Affect LDCs?

Some analysts believe that general features of the international economy impede the development of poor nations. One prominent argument was made in the 1950s by Raúl Prebisch, an Argentine economist and for many years the head of the UN Economic Commission for Latin America (ECLA).[15] Prebisch accepted that, in principle, trade was good for both rich and poor countries. However, he noted that LDCs produced mostly raw materials and agricultural products, while rich countries produced mostly manufactured goods. He contended that this very fact meant that trade worked against the interests of the LDCs and in favor of the interests of the developed countries.

The problem, Prebisch said, was that the prices of the LDCs' products tended to decline over time relative to the prices of the industrialized countries' products. This disparity arose because LDCs sold mainly **primary products**—that is, agricultural goods and raw materials. And because markets for the LDCs' primary products were very competitive (there were millions of cocoa or coffee farmers), prices moved up and down very easily. However, markets for manufactured goods (automobiles, machinery) were controlled by a few large, **oligopolistic** firms—that is, firms that could control their markets. These firms could ensure that prices rose whenever possible and did not fall even in adverse market conditions.[16]

The result was that the **terms of trade**—the relative movement of export and import prices—of countries that specialized in primary products deteriorated: they got less for what they sold, and they paid more for what they bought. Countries that specialized in producing raw materials and farm products for world markets, Prebisch and his supporters argued, were thus at a fundamental disadvantage.

primary products

Raw materials and agricultural products, typically unprocessed or only slightly processed. The primary sectors are distinguished from secondary sectors (industry) and tertiary sectors (services).

oligopoly

A situation in which a market or industry is dominated by a few firms.

terms of trade

The relationship between a country's export prices and its import prices.

---

14. However, parts of China were occupied by foreign powers, and Ethiopia was invaded and occupied by Italy for several years.

15. For a survey and analysis, see Joseph L. Love, "Raul Prebisch and the Origins of the Doctrine of Unequal Exchange," *Latin American Research Review* 15 (1980): 45–72.

16. Prebisch also observed that because manufacturing was usually unionized, wages were also less flexible, which contributed to the rigidity of industrial prices.

Prebisch and his followers in ECLA concluded that the very structure of the world economy was biased against the developing world. In this view, the industrialized countries had an interest in maintaining a structure of international trade that was detrimental to the LDCs. Although many scholars were skeptical of the argument, it was very popular in the developing world. Indeed, it justified policies that many LDCs were pursuing—of protecting the home market and artificially spurring industrialization.

Are International Institutions Biased against LDCs?

Even among those who accept that the world economy can benefit LDCs, many scholars believe that international political factors are responsible for exacerbating the problems of development. They emphasize the relative powerlessness of developing nations in their interactions with richer countries. In this view, the principal obstacle facing LDCs is not global markets, but the character of the international order and of international institutions whose rules are written by rich nations in order to serve their own interests.

While all countries can benefit from international economic exchange, the greater power of rich countries to influence patterns of international trade and finance can certainly work against the interests of LDCs. Indeed, rich countries often pursue their own interests in ways that harm prospects for development in poor countries. The problem is not that the industrialized nations purposefully or maliciously attempt to impoverish poor countries. Rather, it is that rich countries' policies to safeguard their own interests (or at least the interests powerful enough to matter to their governments) create problems for poor countries.

Farm trade policy is a good example. As we saw in Chapter 7, almost all industrialized countries extensively subsidize and protect their farmers. This policy has the effect of restricting the opportunities of LDC farmers, many of whom would otherwise be able to undersell farmers in North America, western Europe, and Japan. There is no intellectual or economic justification for these protectionist policies; they are simply the result of the interests of American, European, and Japanese farmers, which are in conflict with the interests of developing-country farmers.

American cotton policy illustrates the point. The U.S. government spends several billion dollars a year to subsidize American cotton farmers. This policy is lucrative for the recipients of the subsidies and politically attractive for U.S. politicians. The subsidy program pays farmers extra to produce cotton, which increases American output of cotton beyond what it would otherwise be; it therefore raises the world supply of cotton and lowers its price.

Farmers in the developing world have a comparative advantage in providing agricultural products (like cotton) to world markets, but Western governments subsidize their farms so heavily that developing nations' farmers are hampered in their ability to compete.

These effects, in turn, drive down the price received by cotton farmers in developing countries, who may be lower-cost producers than the American farmers but who do not have the luxury of expensive farm support programs.

The upshot is that the U.S. government has, since 1995, paid about $2 billion a year in subsidies to American cotton farmers—almost all of which has gone to about 25,000 farmers. Cotton farmers in Texas alone have received nearly $11 billion in subsidies since 1995.[17] Meanwhile, several million cotton farmers in Africa, Asia, and Latin America have had their incomes cut by the resultant reduction in the world price of cotton.

The power disparity between rich and poor countries clearly works against LDCs. The governments of the developing world have been almost entirely unsuccessful at getting their farmers greater access to the markets of the industrialized nations. Meanwhile, the governments of rich countries have been quite successful in getting LDCs to open their markets to manufacturers, multinational corporations, and international banks from the developed world. The weakness of LDCs relative to developed nations means that they often lose out in international interactions of this sort, to the ultimate detriment of their economic prospects.[18]

The same pattern prevails within the major international economic institutions. While LDCs participate in international economic institutions—most are members of the IMF, the World Bank, and the WTO—these institutions are dominated by rich countries, and it is no surprise that their policies largely reflect the interests of their dominant members—even when these policies may be in conflict with the interests of poor nations.

We saw in Chapter 9 that many critics in the developing world regard the IMF as a tool of rich nations. Indeed, in the IMF, voting is weighted by the financial and economic size of the member states, such that rich countries effectively control the institution (Figure 10.1). In fact, the United States has enough votes to veto any proposal, as do the member states of the European Union. This means that the rich countries can bend IMF policies and procedures in their favor—for example, to deal lightly with their allies or harshly with their enemies—even when such action is not generally consistent with the IMF's own rules.

International trade agreements similarly reflect the interests of the rich and powerful. Initiatives of developing countries are frequently ignored, even when they clearly would go in the direction of the WTO's purported goal, trade liberalization. Many developing-country exports face protectionist barriers in industrialized nations, provided at the behest of affected industries that do not want to face such stiff competition.

Perhaps most important is the attempt by developing nations (and a few industrial countries that export farm products) to push for the WTO to encourage greater openness to farm products, especially on the part of the highly protectionist rich countries. Agricultural trade liberalization would open up important new

---

17. Full data are available at http://farm.ewg.org/progdetail.php?fips=00000&progcode=cotton (accessed 01/05/15).

18. Joseph Stiglitz discusses many such examples in *Making Globalization Work* (New York: Norton, 2006); see pp. 85–86 for the cotton example.

FIGURE 10.1 *Voting Power in the International Monetary Fund, 2017*

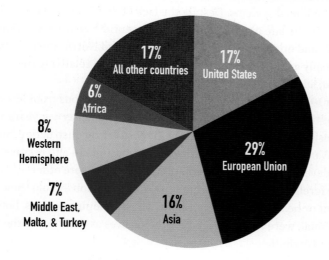

17%
All other countries

17%
United States

6%
Africa

8%
Western
Hemisphere

7%
Middle East,
Malta, & Turkey

29%
European Union

16%
Asia

Figure source: International Monetary Fund, www.imf.org/external/np/sec/memdir/members.aspx#E (accessed 11/08/17).

opportunities to farmers in developing countries, many of whom are low-cost agricultural producers. But because the principal losers would be farmers in developed countries, the rich nations have adamantly resisted including trade in farm products on the agenda for liberalization.

The interests of developed- and developing-country governments clash in many arenas. The power disparities between rich and poor countries typically mean that interactions among them are decided in favor of the rich. Moreover, the institutions that govern the international economy were created largely by rich and powerful countries, so their policies and decision rules reflect their own concerns. In all these ways, the alignment of interests, interactions, and institutions in the international order can limit the prospects for successful development of poor nations.

Development Policies and Development Politics

Over the past century, poor countries have experienced many changes in the domestic and international spheres that have affected their development. Conditions both at home and abroad have had an impact on the interests, institutions, and interactions that structure the development process. Before 1914, most developing regions—whether they were independent, as in Latin America, or colonial, as in most of the rest of the world—focused their efforts on primary products (agricultural goods and raw materials). Dominated as they were by those with interests in selling their goods abroad, they welcomed access to global markets and foreign capital as they strove to develop their mineral wealth and their farmland.

The importance of export-oriented interests was reinforced by their control over political institutions—a situation that occurred in both autocratic, independent countries and colonial systems. Despite the lack of democracy, many poor nations did quite well in the late nineteenth and early twentieth centuries, selling copper, coffee, cotton, and other primary goods to Europe and North America. In the process, they usually accepted general economic openness: relatively free trade, the gold standard, and inflows of foreign capital.

But after 1914, as the world economy experienced serious trouble, most developing regions turned inward. World War I, the troubled interwar years and the Great Depression of the 1930s, World War II, postwar reconstruction, and the start of the Cold War all kept the developed world preoccupied—and relatively uninterested in the developing regions. International investors were otherwise engaged at home; the foreign markets into which LDCs had previously sold their products were stagnant or heavily protected, or both. The developing regions, both independent and colonial, were forced to fend for themselves as their ties to the developed world began to dwindle.

Import-Substituting Industrialization

In the context of these international trends, beginning in the 1930s a different set of interests came to the fore in many developing countries. With the collapse of foreign markets, export interests could no longer claim primacy, and initiative often shifted to economic groups interested in domestically oriented growth. Many developing countries therefore adopted policies that encouraged industrial development so that domestic producers could supply goods that had previously been imported. Latin America led the way in practice as in theory, adopting measures to stimulate industry.

The initial turn inward may have been forced by international events, the dislocations of the two world wars, and the Great Depression, but eventually it became a more conscious strategy. As domestic industrial interests grew in size and strength, they were able to push for a complex of policies known as **import-substituting industrialization (ISI)**. These policies had the goal of substituting local products for imports. It was in this context that Raúl Prebisch and his followers argued that such enforced self-sufficiency was actually desirable and should be deepened.

There were powerful domestic interests in favor of ISI. Most generally, developing-country governments wanted their economies to move away from primary production (raw materials and agricultural products) and toward industry. This interest grew out of theoretical conceptions, like those of Prebisch, that accelerated industrialization would aid broader development; out of the belief that modern societies required a manufacturing base; out of a national security desire for indigenous industrial capacity; and out of other broad goals.

At the same time, there were more specific interests in favor of the new policies. The previously predominant emphasis on primary production for export was associated with the political dominance of producers of these goods—copper miners, oilmen, plantation owners, ranchers. As foreign markets collapsed, these

import-substituting industrialization (ISI)

A set of policies, pursued by most developing countries from the 1930s through the 1980s, to reduce imports and encourage domestic manufacturing, often through trade barriers, subsidies to manufacturing, and state ownership of basic industries.

internationally oriented groups lost influence. They were supplanted by such pro-industrial groups as the urban business and middle classes and the industrial working class, who strongly supported ISI. The institutional evolution of developing societies, particularly the emergence of more representative political systems—democracies, in some cases—reduced the influence of the old exporting elites and increased the power of the urban groups.

Both broad and narrower interests in ISI were also at play in the former colonies in Africa and Asia as they won their independence. Colonialism had been associated with selling primary products to the colonial power, but decolonization was associated with efforts to replace raw materials and agricultural production with urban manufacturing. And just as colonial societies were often dominated by colonial or local miners, oilmen, or farmers, postcolonial societies came to be dominated by such urban interest groups as businessmen, the middle classes, labor, and government employees.

For these reasons, after 1945 almost all the long-independent developing nations of Latin America and the newly independent ones of Africa, Asia, and the Caribbean reduced their economic ties with the rest of the world, protected and subsidized local manufacturing, and attempted to stimulate domestic industrial development. In important ways, these policies reflected the view that engagement with the world economy could be an impediment to national economic development.

For decades, most LDCs followed the broad outlines of import substitution, including:

- Trade barriers to protect domestic manufacturers from foreign competition and encourage national industrial development

- Government incentives to industry, including tax credits, cheap loans, and other subsidies to draw investors into the modern industrial sector

- Government provision of basic industrial services by public enterprises—electric power, telecommunications, transport, finance—to supplement or replace private provision that was seen as too expensive or too limited

All over the third world, government policies encouraged the development of large state sectors behind high protectionist barriers. The result was rapid industrialization in many areas. Between 1950 and 1970, for example, Brazil and Mexico developed large automobile industries where none had previously existed, and by the 1970s the two countries were producing a million cars a year. By the 1970s, indeed, most of the larger developing countries pursuing ISI—India, Brazil, Mexico, Argentina—were nearly self-sufficient in manufactured products.

However, ISI had weaknesses. The industries it encouraged were not efficient and had difficulty selling their goods abroad. After all, they had grown up in protected markets and were not originally expected to be competitive in international markets. Over time, as countries continued needing to earn money to pay for essential imports, the difficulties the new manufacturers encountered in exporting were worrisome.

As problems accumulated, the inward-looking self-sufficiency of ISI began to lose support. In part, the Prebisch-ECLA view declined for intellectual reasons: evidence accumulated that the argument might not be correct or that economic ties with developed countries might not have as negative an impact as had been suggested. There were also pragmatic and political reasons why the LDCs turned toward global integration. Many producers with previous interests in ISI came to believe that selling only to a small and poor home market restricted their potential. The insularity of protected markets left many manufacturers technically backward, making products of low quality—a fact that became increasingly worrisome with the rise of modern electronics and computing.

The bias against producing for export meant that developing countries sold little in world markets. Therefore, they could not buy much abroad, which left them vulnerable to crises when, for example, oil prices skyrocketed in the 1970s. And the ISI bias against agriculture impoverished many farmers, leading to mass internal migrations that flooded the cities with the formerly rural poor. By the early 1980s, ISI was in trouble.

Export-Oriented Industrialization

export-oriented industrialization (EOI)

A set of policies, originally pursued in the late 1960s by several East Asian countries, to spur manufacturing for export, often through subsidies and incentives for export production.

There was an alternative to ISI that a handful of countries in East Asia had tried. Beginning in the mid-1960s, South Korea, Taiwan, Singapore, and the British colony of Hong Kong had turned toward **export-oriented industrialization (EOI)**. These governments had encouraged their manufacturers to produce for foreign, especially American, consumers. They used many techniques to push exports, including low-cost loans and tax breaks to exporters, and a very weak currency to make their products artificially cheap.

Like those countries pursuing ISI, the export-promoting governments typically used substantial state intervention in the economy to achieve their goals. Yet, while the rest of the third world used government involvement in the economy to turn industry inward in the 1960s and 1970s, the governments of export-oriented countries pushed it outward. This approach meant relying on often volatile international markets, but it had the advantage of forcing national manufacturers to produce goods that met rigorous technological, quality, and price standards.

By the late 1970s, the four EOI economies of East Asia were flooding world markets with toys, clothing, furniture, and other simple manufactures. South Korean exports skyrocketed from $385 million in 1970 to $15 billion in 1979, 90 percent of them manufactured goods. On this basis, South Korea's government pursued heavy industrial development by sponsoring modern steel mills, chemical factories, and a new auto industry. By the early 1980s, the country had the world's largest private shipyard and largest machinery factory.[19]

---

19. Jeff Frieden, "Third World Indebted Industrialization: International Finance and State Capitalism in Mexico, Brazil, Algeria, and South Korea," *International Organization* 35, no. 3 (Summer 1981): 426.

A strategy of export-oriented industrialization led some developing countries to produce high-quality goods to be sold overseas. By the 1980s, this strategy had proved highly successful for countries like South Korea. Here, a worker in a South Korean factory inspects washing machines for export.

The Turn toward Globalization

Although the EOI model was pursued by a relatively small number of countries prior to the 1980s, only a decade later it became the dominant strategy throughout the developing world. The devastating debt crisis that hit the developing world in the early 1980s (see Chapter 8) dealt a fatal blow to ISI. For one thing, the ISI economies were particularly severely affected because they had so much trouble increasing exports and generating the money they needed to service their debts. But the East Asian EOI economies weathered the crisis with less trouble.

The East Asian businesses were used to selling abroad and could increase exports rapidly to service their debts. After a couple of difficult years, the so-called Asian Tigers—South Korea, Taiwan, Singapore, and Hong Kong—resumed rapid growth. Meanwhile, the deep crisis in the ISI economies eventually drove them to turn toward export promotion themselves. By the late 1980s, almost all developing countries had abandoned ISI and opted to integrate their economies into global markets. The positive experience of EOI, and the negative experiences of ISI, seemed to point the way toward a new, globalized economic future for the developing world.

The debt crisis also left the LDCs vulnerable to pressure from the industrialized countries—and from such international institutions as the IMF and the World Bank—to change their economic policies. In return for having their debts restructured, LDCs came under pressure to implement reforms favored by governments and institutions from the rich world. For both domestic and international reasons, then, over the course of the 1990s many LDCs adapted to the new interest in globalization. The economist John Williamson dubbed the complex of policies associated

Washington Consensus

An array of policy recommendations generally advocated by developed-country economists and policy makers starting in the 1980s, including trade liberalization, privatization, openness to foreign investment, and restrictive monetary and fiscal policies.

with this transformation the **Washington Consensus**, which came to connote the general acceptance of market-oriented policies.[20]

Among the policies that were, in varying degrees, adopted by the LDCs were the following:

- *Trade liberalization*, the removal of many barriers to imports and exports in an attempt to make national producers more competitive in world markets

- *Privatization*, the selling off of many government enterprises to private investors who would presumably run them more efficiently

- *Fiscal and monetary policies* to avoid large deficits and high inflation

- *Openness* to foreign investment and to international capital flows more generally

These policies were also generally embraced by the governments of countries in eastern and central Europe and the former Soviet Union, as they made their way from communist central planning toward market societies in the 1990s.

The shift away from economic nationalism toward economic openness had both international and domestic sources. As the rest of the world economy grew rapidly, and as globalization advanced elsewhere, it was hard for poor nations to continue denying themselves access to the opportunities the world economy might make available. Powerful domestic actors in the developing world increasingly saw their interests as being served by tapping into global markets, global capital, and global technologies. And economic integration seems to have worked relatively well.

Countries such as China and India have grown very rapidly since they turned toward world markets, and they have been followed by dozens of other LDCs. Meanwhile, demands from the developed countries and the international institutions they dominate have pushed even many reluctant LDCs in the direction of globalization. This move highlights the fact that many actors in the developing world resent the perceived bias of international economic institutions and that many LDC governments have attempted to counter the power imbalance with the power of numbers.

Attempts to Remedy the Bias of International Institutions

Developing countries confronted their problems at the international level, as well as through national policies. Beginning in the 1950s, many countries in Asia, Africa, and the Caribbean that gained their independence after World War II grouped themselves into an international organization focused on economic and political issues that are of concern to developing nations, the Non-Aligned Movement, and pledged to avoid alliances with either the American-led West or the Soviet-led East.

---

20. John Williamson, "What Washington Means by Policy Reform," in *Latin American Readjustment: How Much Has Happened*, ed. John Williamson (Washington, DC: Institute for International Economics, 1989).

The Non-Aligned Movement eventually gave rise to developing-country coalitions at the UN and in international institutions more generally. The UN variant was formed in 1964 with 77 members and has since been known as the **Group of 77** (although it currently has over 130 member countries). These developing-country-based institutions attempt to use the collective power of numbers in the world political arena to reform the economic order in favor of the developing world.

The most systematic efforts along these lines came in the 1970s, when developing countries fought in the UN and elsewhere for what they called the New International Economic Order (NIEO). The NIEO's purpose was to renegotiate the bargain that had constituted the international economic order so that it would be more in line with the economic needs of poor nations. The proposals included curtailing the rights of foreign investors in developing countries, revising trade agreements to favor the products of the developing world, and enhancing the influence of LDC governments in international economic organizations. These efforts resulted in some UN resolutions and other initiatives, but little of a concrete nature was accomplished.

The LDCs were more successful at using their control over natural resources to strengthen their bargaining position with rich nations. The most striking example came from members of the Organization of the Petroleum Exporting Countries (OPEC), a group of developing-country oil producers whose creation in 1960 had gone almost unnoticed. But in 1973, in the midst of a war between Israel and its Arab neighbors, OPEC's Arab members doubled the price of oil to more than $5 a barrel, then two months later doubled it again to nearly $12 a barrel. They did so by purposely restricting their supply of oil to world markets, a move that drove up world oil prices.

As the price increases persisted, it was clear that a small group of developing countries had dramatically changed the terms on which they sold their goods. Tens of billions of dollars flowed into the coffers of developing-country governments, and for the first time a group of developing nations appeared to have the upper hand in economic dealings with the West. In the wake of this electrifying development, other third-world commodity producers—of copper, coffee, iron ore, bauxite, and bananas—tried to emulate OPEC in creating international **commodity cartels**, organizations of producers who cooperate to restrict the supply and raise the price of their products.

Some of the other commodity cartels had an impact, but the oil sector was unique in the scale of its achievements. Oil producers were particularly successful for several reasons. There were few readily available substitutes for oil, so price increases did not reduce consumption very much. In addition, just a few OPEC members controlled a very large share of the world's oil: Saudi Arabia, Kuwait, Qatar, and the United Arab Emirates together had nearly half the world's oil reserves. They did not need to sell oil quickly and could hold it off the market to keep prices high. An additional source of power was the solidarity of OPEC's Muslim members in and around the Middle East, who shared cultural and political ties.

OPEC was able to obtain enormous amounts of money for its members. Some of this income was shared with other developing countries, although many poor

Group of 77

A coalition of developing countries in the UN, formed in 1964 with 77 members, that seeks changes to the international economic order to favor the developing world. It has grown to over 130 members but retains the original name.

commodity cartels

Associations of producers of commodities (raw materials and agricultural products) that restrict world supply and thereby cause the price of the goods to rise.

countries that did not have oil themselves were harmed by the oil shocks. In addition, oil states were able to leverage their resources into increased influence at the IMF and World Bank. For a while, it appeared that commodity cartels would have a more general effect on third-world power, strengthening demands for a new economic order. But, by the early 1980s LDC attempts to achieve far-reaching international reforms had largely failed. Some natural resource producers had gotten richer, but the underlying institutions of the international political economy had not fundamentally changed.

The very rapid growth of some large developing countries—in particular China, India, and Brazil—has led to their gradual inclusion in some of the international discussions that had previously been the sole domain of rich countries. In fact, in the aftermath of the global financial crisis that began in 2008, the Group of 20 Finance Ministers and Central Bank Governors played a major role in attempting to address the crisis. The Group of 20 includes representatives of nine developing nations: Argentina, Brazil, China, India, Indonesia, Mexico, Russia, Saudi Arabia, and Turkey.

Many observers believe that this expansion of the "leadership group" in international economic affairs reflects an opening up of at least some global discussions to the concerns of developing countries. Nonetheless, the countries represented tend to be the largest and richest nations in the developing world, and on balance, LDCs still find themselves subject to international economic trends and constrained by international institutions over which they have little or no control.

Is Foreign Aid an Answer?

Many people believe that problems of development could be substantially alleviated by increased foreign aid from the rich nations of the world (see "Controversy" on p. 454). And there are certainly examples of places and projects where foreign aid has made a difference to the quality of life of people in poor nations. However, foreign aid is unlikely to play a major role in overcoming problems of underdevelopment for at least two reasons.

First, the amounts of aid given are quite small and are unlikely to grow. In recent years, total foreign assistance has been about $100 billion a year. This may seem like a lot, but it averages out to less than $20 per person in the LDCs, and it is dwarfed by the amounts of private investments and loans that come into the developing world from abroad. Although rich countries have often expressed support for increasing aid, few countries have followed through in practice. In 1970, the rich nations set a target of 0.7 percent of their GDP as aid, but the actual number today is about one-third of that target. There is very little popular support for foreign aid in most developed nations, and there seems to be little prospect that the situation will change.

Second, and perhaps more important, there is good reason to believe that even increased levels of aid would not go very far toward solving the basic problems of developing countries. LDC governments that act in the narrow interests of themselves or their supporters are likely to use the aid they receive for similarly narrow purposes. There is substantial evidence that much foreign aid is misused by recipient governments. By the same token, there is evidence that much foreign aid is given by developed-country governments for geopolitical and military reasons and not to alleviate poverty.

To be sure, humanitarian assistance can make a difference in the lives of people in the developing world. However, sustained economic development provides the best hope for achieving the broader goal of lifting poor countries out of poverty. Governments that are willing and able to pursue policies aimed at stimulating growth may use aid effectively as a supplement to good policies. But aid alone, especially in the small amounts currently available, cannot go far toward satisfying the massive needs of impoverished people in developing countries.[21]

Globalization and Its Discontents

Over the past 25 years, developing countries have gradually committed themselves to more engagement with the global economy. In this context, they may share more interests in common with developed nations. The LDCs have also tended to participate more fully in international economic institutions, reflecting a widespread acceptance of the desirability of economic integration and a broader belief that there is scope for some of the common interests of developed and developing nations to create opportunities that will speed economic growth and development in Africa, Asia, and Latin America.

But the turn toward globalization in the developing world has not been without difficulties and critics. One source of stress has been the series of financial and currency crises that have affected a score of developing countries (see Chapters 8 and 9). While such developing countries as Mexico, Thailand, and Argentina benefited from massive inflows of capital, they also suffered debilitating crises when these flows stopped. As developed countries had themselves discovered, integration into world markets has costs as well as benefits, creates losers as well as winners. The depth of the currency and financial crises led many observers to question whether the benefits of openness to international investment truly outweighed its costs.

The threat of crisis was heightened by the concern that the new economic openness was not delivering the kind and rate of economic growth that many analysts had anticipated. Economic reform was, in the minds of many, justified by how rapidly such countries as South Korea had rushed to modernity and how relatively equitable their societies had become in the process. This justification was attractive to people in developing countries whose economies had been stagnant and in which the gap between rich and poor had been growing.

---

21. For two divergent views on aid, see William Easterly, *The White Man's Burden: Why the West's Efforts to Aid the Rest Have Done So Much Ill and So Little Good* (New York: Penguin, 2007); and Jeffrey Sachs, *The End of Poverty: Economic Possibilities for Our Time* (New York: Penguin, 2006).

What Helps the Global Poor Best: Aid or Trade?

In the year 2000, HIV, malaria, and tuberculosis killed millions of people in the developing world. These diseases reached epidemic proportions in some regions of Asia and Africa and were endemic (consistently present) in many others. That year, the rich countries of the world began the process of creating the Global Fund to Fight AIDS, Tuberculosis and Malaria. Since 2002, the Global Fund has spent over $60 billion to help poor countries in the fight against these deadly diseases. It is estimated that by the end of 2019, these efforts will have saved some 36 million lives and will have averted nearly 200 million new cases of AIDS, malaria, and tuberculosis.[a] The quality of life of hundreds of millions of people has been measurably improved by aid to promote global public health.

Such funds comprise only a fraction of the aid given to the developing world overall. Indeed, over the past 60 years the rich countries of the world have given over $3 trillion in aid to poor countries. While there have been some major successes in improving public health, foreign aid targeting other developmental goals has often failed to produce a lasting improvement in living conditions. More than a billion people in the developing world still live in abject poverty, barely at or below the income level necessary to guarantee subsistence. Is aid the most effective way to help the world's poor? Might there be a better way?

Activists, policy makers, and scholars have long argued about how best to help the world's poorest people. Some emphasize how foreign aid from rich nations can have a powerful, beneficial impact on the living standards of the poor. Others downplay the potential for aid to make a difference, and emphasize the need for economic reforms so that poor countries can take advantage of international trade. The debate is often characterized as one between aid and trade: whether it is more effective to give money to developing countries, or to encourage them to pursue better economic policies.

Applying the Concepts

This disagreement has to do with how aid, or trade, might affect the **interests** of people and policy makers in poor countries. And the effect on interests, in turn, depends on the social and political **institutions** of the poor countries—in particular, whether governments are set up in such a way that they are willing and able to put aid money to appropriate uses. Central to this issue is the nature of **interactions** between donors and the recipient governments, and whether the donors are themselves willing and able to ensure that their money is used productively to improve the lives of the poor.

Supporters of foreign aid argue that aid has important economic and political effects. Economically, they believe that the prospect of receiving aid can give policy makers in the developing world reasons to pursue policies to alleviate poverty and spur economic development. By loosening some of the tight financial constraints that governments of poor countries face, aid may also encourage these governments to pursue policies that benefit the poor. And while policy makers may not have an interest in alleviating poverty, especially if national political institutions are undemocratic or otherwise do not reflect the interests of the poor, donor countries and nongovernmental agencies can use financial incentives to encourage recipient governments to adopt better policies.[b]

Politically and socially, supporters of foreign aid also hope that aid will reduce some of the extreme pressures

Aid from the Global Fund has supported malaria prevention programs and provided mosquito nets to people in many developing countries, including the Ivory Coast.

---

a. www.theglobalfund.org/en/impact (accessed 12/01/17).

on these countries' populations, so that they can more fully participate in national life. The Global Fund, in alleviating the burden of disease on developing countries, shares this goal. Jeffrey Sachs, a prominent economist and strong supporter of more generous aid, argues that "development aid, when properly designed and delivered, works, saving the lives of the poor and helping to promote economic growth."[c]

Aid skeptics question whether governments in developing nations will do the right thing with the aid they receive. They argue that many of these governments do not rely on the poor for political support and so have little interest in pro-poor policies. Aid money may go to benefit only their supporters, such as powerful interest groups or corrupt politicians. As Nobel laureate Angus Deaton writes: "Aid undermines what poor people need most: an effective government that works with them for today and tomorrow."[d]

Those who are pessimistic about the positive impact of aid may quote the old saying: "Give a man a fish, and he can eat for a day; teach him to fish, and he can eat for the rest of his life." Their general view is that it is important for developing countries to adopt policies that lead to economic growth and development—especially policies tying them to the world economy so that they can take advantage of the opportunities offered by international markets.

There is evidence to support both positions. Scholars have typically found that aid does not spur development *unless* the assisted governments adopt appropriate policies.[e] On the other hand, even skeptics accept that foreign aid can make a difference to the lives of the poor; Deaton writes: "Foreign aid . . . has much to its credit, particularly in terms of health care, with many people alive today who would otherwise be dead."[f]

Some economists have suggested a third position: that aid should be focused not on broad national policies, but rather on targeted interventions that affect particular aspects

Some argue that developing countries are better served by policies that promote trade. Here, workers at a factory in Bangladesh manufacture clothing for export.

of the lives of the poor. These might include finding more effective ways to deliver medicine or education to poor villages, or developing measures to encourage poor farmers to adopt more efficient techniques.[g] While this approach seems to have achieved some success, it largely abandons attempts at thoroughgoing changes to the development process.

In light of these arguments, how can well-meaning people, and governments, in the rich countries of the world best help the global poor? Aid transfers money to the developing world but may not be effective in the long run. Trade—and economic reforms in general—may hold out long-term promise, but the problem of poverty is pressing and unlikely to be alleviated quickly by policy change. Wherever the answer lies, the quality of life of a billion and more people is at stake.

b. Jeffrey Sachs, *The End of Poverty: Economic Possibilities for Our Times* (New York: Penguin, 2006).

c. Jeffrey Sachs, "The Case for Aid," *Foreign Policy* 21 (2014).

d. Angus Deaton, "Weak States, Poor Countries," Project Syndicate, October 12, 2015, www.project-syndicate.org/commentary/economic-development-requires-effective-governments-by-angus-deaton.

e. Craig Burnside and David Dollar, "Aid, Policies and Growth," *American Economic Review* 90 (2000): 847–868.

f. Deaton, "Weak States, Poor Countries."

g. Abhijit Banerjee and Esther Duflo, *Poor Economics: A Radical Rethinking of the Way to Fight Global Poverty* (New York: Public Affairs, 2011) presents a prominent argument for this position.

Thinking Analytically

1. How might foreign aid affect the interests of recipient governments? Would these effects be good for the poor?

2. How might domestic political institutions affect the ways in which foreign aid would be put to use in recipient countries?

3. How do interactions between donors and recipient governments affect the ways in which foreign aid could help the poor?

Between 1987 (top) and 2013 (bottom), China increased its GDP per capita from just $250 to $6,810. These images show the effects of economic development on Shanghai's Pudong district. However, extreme economic inequality has accompanied the rapid development.

But even after opening more to the world economy, many developing countries grew only slowly or not at all—an outcome that disappointed those who had hoped to see tangible results of the economic reforms. Even more disturbing was the increasingly unequal distribution of income in many of the reformed developing countries. Then there were true developmental disasters, countries that seemed to be sinking ever further into destitution and, in some cases, social chaos.

Although there have been success stories, the overall picture is still troubling. Many of the developing world's people remain in poverty. While the impoverished are a smaller share of the LDC population than they were 25 years ago, because of population growth the ranks of the poor have increased by about 100 million people. In addition, many developing countries—including some of the fastest growers—have become more unequal as they have grown.

Disappointment with the results of 30 years of reform-oriented development policies and outcomes has contributed to something of a backlash against the economic reforms of the 1980s and 1990s—a backlash that in some ways is similar to what many developed nations experienced over the past decade. Some of this backlash has taken the form of electoral successes by politicians who have been critical of the current pattern of globalization. The governments of Venezuela, Bolivia, and Iran, for example, are highly critical of the trend toward economic openness and integration into international markets. Even governments that remain committed to engagement with the world economy have searched for ways to reduce the social costs of this integration and to address the political discontent that has become common in much of the developing world.

Conclusion: Toward Global Development

At the human level, the most pressing issue today is how to improve the living standards of the billions of people in the developing world who live in or near poverty. This is why so many nongovernmental organizations (which we discuss more in Chapter 11) focus on development issues. Generally, finding an effective path toward the goal of broad-based economic development requires a clear understanding of how and why countries have failed or succeeded in developing. While scholars and others continue to debate the matter heatedly, the preceding discussion points to several components of a reasonable diagnosis of the sources of underdevelopment and offers suggestions about what might be done to overcome them.

Addressing International Factors

While developed and developing countries have many interests in common, there are also important areas in which their interests conflict. And interactions between developed and developing countries almost always favor developed countries. Industrialized nations are richer and more powerful than LDCs and can usually get their way in bilateral and multilateral negotiations. Although scores of developing nations have been involved in international trade bargaining rounds, the outcomes of these interactions have been far more reflective of developed-country concerns than of developing-country preferences.

International institutions tend to reflect inherent power relations among nations, which means that they favor developed over developing nations. The principal international economic organizations—the IMF, the World Bank, the

WTO—all have an implicit or explicit bias toward the interests of rich nations. Sometimes the bias is formal, as when votes are weighted by economic size in the IMF; sometimes it is informal, based only on the greater wealth and power of the industrialized world. Either way, the policy bias of these international institutions can bend outcomes in ways that are not favorable to the developmental prospects of poor nations.

Developed countries are unlikely to cede influence over the outcome of international bargaining, or over international institutions, for purely humanitarian reasons. Yet there are common interests between rich and poor nations, and there may be scope for agreement on reforming international institutions to make them more responsive to LDCs. Indeed, the IMF and World Bank have undertaken reform efforts to address some LDC criticisms of their activities. But many observers believe that reform of international institutions has to go further in order to have a substantial impact on development prospects.[22]

To the extent that these international factors impede LDC progress, addressing them might speed it up. Because both the developed and the developing world can benefit from faster growth and more stability in LDCs, there is scope for LDC and developed-country interests to emphasize shared goals over individual ones. However, a diagnosis of failures of development that rests too strongly on international constraints faces the reality that the same international conditions seem to allow for strikingly different national economic outcomes—for example, Botswana and Zambia. While the external environment may not be as favorable as LDCs might like, it has permitted the emergence of some very striking success stories in addition to spectacular failures. This observation leads us back to the conclusion that domestic forces are probably the principal factors affecting economic growth and development.

Addressing Domestic Factors

As we have seen, interests within a poor country can stand in the way of its overall economic progress. Powerful groups may hamper the government's ability to improve education, social services, or the economic infrastructure. But even the most malevolent interests can impede economic progress only if they are successful in dominating society and politics. Where the impact of self-interested groups is countered by broad public pressure, the result is less likely to impede economic development. Where groups can cooperate to support the provision of public goods, rather than fighting over private benefits, all of society will be better off in the long run.

Likewise, the political institutions of developing nations have a powerful impact on whether their citizens are able to overcome obstacles to development. A well-functioning electoral democracy, for example, can reduce the impact of venal private interest groups and can serve as a brake on the activities of corrupt public employees.

---

22. Joseph Stiglitz's *Making Globalization Work* is a prominent statement of the position that lays much of the blame on the structure of the international order and that presents proposals for global reform.

The conclusion that domestic features of LDCs are key to understanding their problems is cautiously optimistic. It is optimistic because it suggests that the future of developing nations is largely in their own hands, rather than being hostage to geographic destiny or the nature of the international system. Indeed, a growing number of countries have succeeded in narrowing the development gap. But this optimism must be guarded. For where economic development has been held back for decades—even generations—by domestic interests, interactions, or institutions, it is likely to be difficult to change these conditions. Nonetheless, this would appear to be the most promising path forward in the continuing effort to reduce the enormous disparity between the world's rich minority and its poor majority.

Study Tool Kit

Interests, Interactions, and Institutions in Context

- Although everyone in poor countries prefers more development to less, individuals and groups within countries may have conflicting interests with respect to development policy. The pursuit of private interests by powerful groups can impede the adoption of measures that would spur economic growth.

- Domestic social and political institutions can have a major impact on how these conflicts of interest affect development. They can either empower or overcome special interest groups that stand in the way of development. They can either facilitate or impede the ability of actors to cooperate to promote government policies conducive to economic growth.

- At the international level, rich and poor nations generally have a common interest in accelerating the economic growth of the developing world. However, there have been many instances of rich countries supporting policies and institutions that disfavor less developed countries.

- Successful economic growth requires that a country overcome both the domestic obstacles posed by interests and institutions that are detrimental to development, and the international impediments created by conflicts of interest with wealthy nations, which can draw on superior reserves of economic and political power.

Key Terms

For Further Reading

Acemoglu, Daron, and James Robinson. *Why Nations Fail.* **New York: Crown Business, 2012.** Presents a strong theoretical argument for the importance of political institutions in affecting economic development, along with a range of empirical evidence to illustrate the theory.

Banerjee, Abhijit V., and Esther Duflo. *Poor Economics: A Radical Rethinking of the Way to Fight Global Poverty.* **New York: Public Affairs, 2011.** Presents both illuminating analyses of poverty in developing countries and concrete proposals for policies to alleviate poverty, based in large part on the authors' many years of work in the field.

Engerman, Stanley, and Kenneth Sokoloff. *Economic Development in the Americas since 1500: Endowments and Institutions.* **Cambridge: Cambridge University Press, 2012.** Demonstrates how differences in the underlying economic characteristics of different societies in the Americas had a profound and lasting effect on their socioeconomic and political organization, and on their subsequent economic development.

Milanovic, Branko. *Global Inequality: A New Approach for the Age of Globalization.* **Cambridge, MA: Harvard University Press, 2016.** Provides a data-intensive and historically informed summary of the level of and trends in international inequality.

Rodrik, Dani. *One Economics, Many Recipes: Globalization, Institutions, and Economic Growth.* **Princeton, NJ: Princeton University Press, 2007.** Presents a prominent economist's ideas about how globalization can be made more compatible with the needs of developing countries.

Stiglitz, Joseph. *Making Globalization Work.* **New York: Norton, 2006.** Provides a critical look by the Nobel laureate and former World Bank chief economist at how the contemporary international economic order impedes economic growth and development and what might be done about it.

11

International Law and Norms

THE PUZZLE *In a world of sovereign states, how can the international community constrain states' actions? When and why do states do what is "right"?*

Above: The international community's failure to stop the genocide that took place in Rwanda in 1994, which killed 800,000 and exiled millions, inspired a reexamination of the norms related to intervention. United Nations secretary-general Kofi Annan (far right) visited Rwanda in the years after the massacres as part of a "healing mission" and reevaluation of the UN's initial response to the genocide.

Shocked by the suffering of wounded soldiers after the Battle of Solferino, fought in 1859 as part of the Italian wars of unification, Swiss social activist Henry Dunant began a campaign to reform and limit the conduct of states during wartime. The result of Dunant's efforts, and the efforts of many others mobilized to the cause, was the first Geneva Convention, on the treatment of wounded soldiers, adopted in 1864. This agreement was followed by a second convention, on the treatment of members of armed forces at sea, in 1906; and a third convention, on the treatment of prisoners of war, in 1929. These three agreements were revised in 1949 and joined by a fourth convention, on the protection of civilians in wartime.

This set of treaties outlining the laws of war is typically referred to as the Geneva Conventions, and it forms one of the most clearly articulated and respected bodies of international law in today's world. War between states might seem an unlikely interaction to be governed by such an international institution. At the same time that states are sending their soldiers into battle to kill their enemies and possibly die for their country, they generally follow international laws regulating how that killing is done and how prisoners and civilians are to be treated.

The Geneva Conventions are monitored and supervised by the International Committee of the Red Cross, part of the International Red Cross and Red Crescent Movement. The conventions have now been ratified by all 193 members of the United Nations (UN), firmly establishing their provisions as nearly universally acknowledged and respected international law.

The conventions, however, have not ended all atrocities, especially within countries. In 1994, Hutu extremists in Rwanda began a mass murder of ethnic Tutsis. Although a minority, Tutsis had been favored under colonial rule and remained politically dominant within Rwanda. A civil war that began in 1990, which pitted Hutus against Tutsis, ended with the Arusha Accords in 1993, signed by then president Juvénal Habyarimana. Seeking to overturn the agreement, Hutu extremists allegedly killed the president and then carried out systematic killings of Tutsis and Hutus who they believed had collaborated with the regime. Roughly 800,000 people are believed to have been killed within 100 days, although estimates range from 500,000 to 1,000,000. A small UN force deployed in Rwanda to implement the Arusha Accords was overwhelmed and proved ineffective at controlling the violence. The killings ended only when the Rwandan Patriotic Front, a militia of mostly Tutsi rebels who had originally started the civil war, reentered the conflict and seized control of the country.

The international community watched and condemned this unmistakable act of genocide but did little to stop it. In 1999, then UN secretary-general Kofi Annan challenged the international community to define its obligations to protect endangered peoples when their governments either cannot or will not protect vulnerable populations themselves. Grasping the lead, Canada sponsored the International Commission on Intervention and State Sovereignty in September 2000. In December 2001, the commission issued its report with the provocative title *The Responsibility to Protect*.[1] The report argued that the international community not only must prosecute crimes against humanity, but also has a responsibility to protect at-risk populations through military means if necessary. This new obligation was quickly dubbed R2P, after the title of the report. In April 2006, the UN Security Council affirmed R2P, recognizing it as a new norm of international behavior.

The Geneva Conventions are international treaties in which states consent to treat armed personnel and civilians in humane ways. The conventions have had an important impact, but the agreements do not diminish the sovereignty of states, as the principle of sovereignty includes the right to freely enter into agreements that constrain one's actions. R2P stands in stark contrast to this principle. The UN, with the consent of its member states, has championed a new international norm that explicitly limits national sovereignty in cases of widespread human rights abuses and state-sponsored violence. This is important because it legitimizes the intervention of states in the internal affairs of other states whether or not the targets give their consent. The Geneva Conventions and R2P are both part of a growing collection of laws and norms, respectively, that are broadly referred to as *global governance*.

The puzzle, though, is this: Why would sovereign states agree to be bound by international rules? This is especially curious in the case of norms like R2P, to which individual states have not necessarily agreed to bind themselves but on which they may be held to account. As we saw in Chapter 2, sovereignty implies that states are the ultimate authorities over their own territories. Yet states today are increasingly governed by laws and norms promoted by the international community in general, and by nongovernmental organizations (NGOs) in particular. Why and how do states collectively constrain their own behavior? How are other, private actors, who are supposedly subject to states under the concept of sovereignty, able to alter state behavior?

Thinking Analytically about International Law and Norms

International law and norms are institutions that seek to shape how states understand their interests and that constrain the many ways in which states interact. States create and abide by international law because of the cooperation it facilitates. Indeed, where we observe strong international laws, the benefits of cooperation to states are generally large enough that international laws are often self-enforcing, or in the interests of states to follow willingly. International law clarifies the obligations of states, defines violations that are subject to retaliation, and sometimes provides for independent tribunals to resolve disputes. Through these mechanisms, international law helps states to understand, meet, and manage their obligations to one another.

International norms affect world politics by changing how individuals and, in turn, states conceive of their interests and appropriate actions in their interactions with other states. Norms are standards of behavior that reflect a community's beliefs about what is appropriate behavior for an actor in a specified condition. Norms affect interactions because they are understood by states to be rules of conduct that are right and morally correct.

As we will see, transnational advocacy networks (TANs) have an important effect on world politics by promoting normative values, which are then reflected in international law or norms. In addition to changing conceptions of interest, TANs facilitate cooperation between states by providing information about international agreements and monitoring compliance.

---

1. The full report is available at http://responsibilitytoprotect.org/ICISS%20Report.pdf (accessed 02/01/14).

What Is International Law?

International law is established by states through either custom or convention as a way to facilitate international cooperation. The Geneva Conventions are one example, but others abound. For instance, the World Trade Organization (WTO) sets rules on the exchange of goods and services and increasingly on investment and property rights; the UN Convention on the Law of the Sea (UNCLOS) governs the use of the oceans and seabed resources; and the Convention on the Prohibition of the Use, Stockpiling, Production, and Transfer of Anti-Personnel Mines and on Their Destruction, more simply known as the Ottawa Convention, outlaws the use and production of land mines and mandates the clearing of existing minefields.

International human rights law, which we will examine in more detail in Chapter 12, intrudes deeply into national political practices. Precisely because the specific rules of international law matter, states often bargain intensely over the rules and their interpretation. Law does not mean the end of conflict between states but is itself the product of political interaction and struggle. Nonetheless, international law is valued and typically followed for the cooperation that it helps bring about.

International law is "a body of rules which binds states and other agents in world politics in their relations with one another and is considered to have the status of law."[2] This definition might appear circular at first, with law being constituted by rules having the status of law, but two aspects of the definition help us understand international law more precisely.

First, international law is a *body of rules* linked together in a common logical structure. Law is not simply an ad hoc list of rules issued or even enforced by some authority. Rather, to stand as law, rules must be woven together by one or more unifying principles. In contemporary international law, the primary unifying concept is sovereignty, especially the notion that all states have equal rights to make international law and can be bound by law only by their own consent. Even though sovereignty is often violated in practice, it still forms the foundation on which rules governing state and nonstate behavior become international law.

Second, to have the *status of law*, a body of rules must include both primary and secondary rules.[3] Primary rules are the negative and positive rules regulating behavior. They may take the form of "Don't do *x*," where *x* is some more or less clearly specified action. The Ottawa Convention, for instance, explicitly prohibits the use of land mines. Or, primary rules may require that actors "must do *y*," where *y* is also some specified action. The Ottawa Convention also stipulated that states destroy their stockpiles of land mines within four years of the treaty's coming into

international law

A body of rules that binds states and other agents in world politics and is considered to have the status of law.

---

2. Hedley Bull, *The Anarchical Society: A Study of Order in World Politics* (New York: Columbia University Press, 1977), 127.

3. This conception of the status of law follows from H. L. A. Hart, *The Concept of Law* (Oxford: Clarendon, 1961).

States cooperate under the Ottawa Convention to clear existing minefields. Although the treaty was ratified in 1999, there is still much work to be done. Here, a member of the Danish Demining Group works to clear a field in Ukraine, which had the highest rate of anti-vehicle mine explosions in the world in 2016.

force, which finally happened on March 1, 1999, when Burkina Faso became the fortieth country to ratify the agreement.

To have the status of law, primary rules must be made in accordance with secondary rules. One can think of secondary rules as akin to a constitution; secondary rules structure the making of primary rules, just as a country's constitutional rules structure the making of other rules in that country. In other words, secondary rules are the rules about how rules are made. To be governed by the "rule of law" is thus to set and enforce primary rules in ways that are consistent with secondary rules. It is the existence of primary rules enacted in compliance with existing secondary rules that gives a rule the status of law. In international law, the principle of sovereignty implies a secondary rule about how other rules are made: under sovereignty, only states can bind themselves to international law. In the case of the Ottawa Convention, its primary rules become law because it was negotiated and ratified by sovereign states as an international treaty.

As a body of rules, duly enacted under secondary rules, international law is distinct from norms (taken up later in this chapter) and other international institutions. Norms are often singular rules, disconnected from any larger body of rules, and can contradict secondary rules, especially sovereignty. Thus, R2P is an emerging norm and not law, even though it was affirmed by the UN Security Council, because it explicitly violates the principle of sovereignty by calling for intervention into the internal affairs of states under some circumstances and has not been accepted as binding by the states most likely to be subject to those interventions.

How Is International Law Made?

States establish and abide by international law, like any other institution, because it facilitates cooperation. States may also bargain over international law, with some preferring one rule over another. For instance, UNCLOS, enacted in 1982, took 9 years of hard negotiations, largely over rules on the exploitation of mineral resources on the ocean floor. It did not come into force until 12 years later, after being ratified by the required 60 countries. Even though 165 countries have now joined the treaty, and it is widely acknowledged as international law governing the use of the seas, the United States was so opposed to some of the provisions that it has refused to sign the final document. Most of the time, however, it is the benefits of cooperation made possible by rules and adherence to those rules that lead states to create and abide by international laws.

In international relations, there are two principal mechanisms for making international law.[4] The first is custom, or accepted practice, which is carried out by states on the basis of a subjective belief that an action is a legal obligation. **Customary international law** usually develops slowly, over time, as states recognize some practices as appropriate and correct. The law of diplomatic immunity, whereby ambassadors and other embassy staff are exempt from a host nation's law, is a classic example. This practice became law by custom because it was in the interests of both home and host countries.

Diplomatic immunity permits embassy personnel to carry out their jobs of reporting on the host country, negotiating with host country representatives, and generally promoting the interests of their home country without fearing possibly politically motivated prosecutions for "trumped-up" crimes. It also prevents potential misunderstandings between countries over the activities of their diplomats from escalating into larger disputes. Countries have learned that rather than imprisoning and punishing diplomats, it is best just to send them home if they violate national laws. Despite occasional abuses, such as diplomats racking up a large number of parking tickets for traffic violations, the practice of diplomatic immunity was sufficiently beneficial to home and host countries that, over time, it came to be recognized as international law.

Although in effect for centuries, this law was codified in the Vienna Convention on Diplomatic Relations enacted in 1961. Freedom of the seas is another important rule that was accepted as customary international law long before it was codified in UNCLOS. Finally, the concept of crimes against humanity also developed largely as customary law and was finally codified in the Rome Statute of the International Criminal Court (ICC), which went into effect in 2002 (see "What Shaped Our World?" on p. 468).

Secondary rules for the establishment of customary international law remain vague, however. The number of countries that must recognize a practice as legitimate and the length of time before it is accepted as law are not specified by any other rule. Increasingly, as the examples of diplomatic immunity, freedom of the seas, and crimes against humanity suggest, customary international law is, for this reason, being codified in formal international agreements.

The second mechanism for creating international law, as just suggested, is international treaties, which are negotiated and then ratified by states. International treaties typically originate in a convention that brings together a large number of states, but not necessarily all countries, to negotiate a new agreement. Some agreements are easily reached, such as the first Geneva Convention (though the original negotiations involved just 12 states). As in the UNCLOS negotiations, however, hard bargaining may ensue precisely because substantial gains are at stake and states seek deals more favorable to their interests.

As explained in the next section, agreements differ in their obligations, precision, and delegation, sometimes in order to address differences in interests that

customary international law
International law that usually develops slowly, over time, as states recognize practices as appropriate and correct.

---

4. The sources of international law are formally defined by Article 38 of the Statute of the International Court of Justice. In addition to conventions and custom, discussed here, the statute allows for law to follow from "general principles of law recognized by civilized nations" and, as a subsidiary means, "the teachings of the most highly qualified publicists of the various nations." The statute is available at www.icj-cij.org/documents/index.php?p1=4&p2=2&p3=0 (accessed 08/13/11).

Crimes against Humanity

The concept of crimes against humanity is one of the most significant developments in international law of the last century.

Institutions The Rome Statute of the ICC, adopted in 1998 and entered into force in 2002, defines crimes against humanity as any of the following acts when committed as part of a planned and systematic attack directed against any civilian population: (1) murder; (2) extermination; (3) enslavement; (4) deportation or forced population transfer; (5) imprisonment or other severe deprivation of liberty in violation of fundamental rules of international law; (6) torture; (7) rape and other forms of sexual violence; (8) persecution against any identifiable group based on political affiliation, race, nationality, culture, religion, or gender; (9) enforced disappearance of persons; and (10) apartheid. In contrast, war crimes are single, isolated instances of abuse carried out during armed conflict. Crimes against humanity are intentional, systematic violent acts against civilians.

Interests The interests of states in prosecuting crimes against humanity have evolved and grown over time. The first known use of the phrase *crimes against humanity* was in the 1860 Republican Party platform, on which President Abraham Lincoln was elected; it described the reopening of the African slave trade as "a crime against humanity and a burning shame to our country and age." In May 1915, the Allied powers in World War I denounced the Armenian genocide carried out by the Ottoman government as a "crime against humanity." The term, however, was first developed systematically in the London Charter of the International Military Tribunal, under which the Nuremberg trials of Nazi leaders were conducted after World War II.

A traditional understanding of war crimes did not allow for the prosecution of government officials for crimes carried out against their own citizens. The Holocaust, in which 6 million Jews were systematically exterminated by the Nazi regime, was not then illegal under international law. Faced with an interest in punishing officials of the Nazi regime for the Holocaust and other atrocities, the drafters of the London Charter gave first real form to the doctrine of crimes against humanity.

The doctrine was carried over into the International Military Tribunal for the Far East and the so-called Tokyo trials, which prosecuted Japanese government officials for atrocities carried out during the war as well, especially the Nanking Massacre, in which hundreds of thousands of Chinese civilians and disarmed soldiers were murdered and tens of thousands of women were raped by the Japanese Imperial Army. As is clear from this history, the concept of crimes against humanity originated in the desires of the victors of World War II to punish the losing states for atrocities conducted in the course of the conflict and to prevent similar behaviors from recurring in the future.

Interactions Through the charters and military tribunals created after World War II, crimes against humanity became international law largely through custom, being formally codified only when the Rome Statute created the ICC. Government officials are now held responsible for widespread abuses of their own citizens, potentially subject to punishments for violations of basic rights and possibly even to armed intervention to halt abuses.

This relatively recent innovation in international law is important because, like human rights law more generally (see Chapter 12), it defines international law as resting on a common humanity that is superior to the policies of any state. This law clearly constrains the rights and, more important, actions of states within the international community. R2P is an extension of the doctrine of crimes against humanity. It not only allows for the prosecution of such crimes after they have happened, as at Nuremberg and Tokyo, but calls for active responses by the international community to stop the abuses.

As of March 2018, there are 11 official investigations underway, and 24 cases in eight countries have been brought before the ICC, most including indictments of individuals for crimes against humanity. Some of these investigations are aimed at high-level government officials, including Presidents Omar Hassan al-Bashir of Sudan and Uhuru Kenyatta of Kenya. The first conviction by the ICC was handed down in early 2012 against Thomas Lubanga Dyilo for war crimes in the Democratic Republic of the Congo. Having lost his appeal, Lubanga is now in prison serving a 14-year sentence. The indictment of heads of state for crimes against humanity confirms the status of international law in this area and puts leaders on notice that the international community will hold them responsible for abuses of their citizens.

would otherwise prevent agreement. Once finalized by international negotiations, the agreement must then be ratified by each member state in accordance with its domestic constitutional provisions. By ratifying treaties like the Geneva Conventions, states voluntarily take on the constraints of international law. This is not interpreted as a violation of the principle of sovereignty. With international conventions, the secondary rules of international law are quite clear. Countries that sign an international convention are bound to respect the terms of the agreement.

Is All International Law the Same?

Even when states have a shared interest in establishing international law to facilitate cooperation, they must still agree on what form the law will take. International law varies across several dimensions. First, international law varies in **obligation**, or the degree to which agents are legally bound by a rule. High-obligation rules "must be performed in good faith regardless of inconsistent provisions of domestic law" and changing state interests, subject to certain exceptions, such as self-defense or necessity.[5] High-obligation laws, like the Geneva Conventions or crimes against humanity, are unconditional and, if breached, require reparations to an injured party. Low-obligation laws are merely aspirational, urging states to live up to some standard of behavior. As we will explain in Chapter 12, much early human rights law took this form.

Even high-obligation laws are often contingent or contain escape clauses. The 1994 Framework Convention on Climate Change (FCCC), which we will discuss in Chapter 13, requires parties of the agreement to reduce greenhouse gas emissions, but only after considering "their specific national and regional development priorities." Likewise, the Limited Test Ban Treaty enacted in 1963, which outlaws certain forms of nuclear weapons testing, permits states to withdraw from the agreement if they decide "extraordinary events" jeopardize their "supreme interests."

A second dimension on which international law varies is its **precision**, or how specific the obligations that states incur are. More precise laws narrow the scope for reasonable interpretation. An important aspect of precision is that "for a set of rules, precision implies not just that each rule in the set is unambiguous, but that rules are related to one another in a noncontradictory way, creating a framework within which case-by-case interpretation can be coherently carried out."[6]

Before the concept of crimes against humanity was codified in the Rome Statute of the International Criminal Court, these crimes were first prosecuted by tribunals formed in the aftermath of World War II. The International Military Tribunal for the Far East tried the leaders of Japan for crimes committed during the war.

obligation

The degree to which states are legally bound by an international rule. High-obligation rules must be performed in good faith and, if breached, require reparations to the injured party.

precision

The degree to which international legal obligations are fully specified. More precise rules narrow the scope for reasonable interpretation.

---

5. We owe these dimensions, and the examples used here, to Kenneth W. Abbott, Robert O. Keohane, Andrew Moravcsik, Anne-Marie Slaughter, et al., "The Concept of Legalization," in *Legalization and World Politics*, ed. Judith L. Goldstein, Miles Kahler, Robert O. Keohane, and Anne-Marie Slaughter (Cambridge, MA: MIT Press, 2001), 25.

6. Abbott et al., "Concept of Legalization," 29.

Much of international law is quite precise, with international treaties running to hundreds and sometimes thousands of pages of definitions, terms, and rules. The UNCLOS treaty, for example, contains 17 parts, 320 articles, and 9 annexes, plus an additional agreement (with 9 more annexes) elaborating on Part XI of the treaty. States often seek to retain control over international law, and to limit future interpretations, by being as precise as possible in the treaty itself.

Other agreements, however, are remarkably imprecise. Commercial treaties, for instance, typically require states to create "favorable conditions" for investment and avoid "unreasonable regulations." Such imprecise terms are usually not the product of poor legal draftsmanship, but rather reflect continuing disagreement between states over the exact nature of the obligations being specified. Vague terms ensure that law will not bring bargaining to a close and that states will continue to negotiate, albeit now within a legalized framework.

Finally, international law also varies in its degree of **delegation** to third parties, wherein courts, arbitrators, mediators, or others are given the authority to implement, interpret, and apply the rules specified; to resolve disputes over the rules; and to make additional rules. In domestic law, courts often have tremendous delegated powers to interpret the law and, in so doing, to fill in legal gaps left in the original statutes. When delegation is high and statutes are imprecise, courts through their interpretations may actually make new law—a result sometimes decried by critics as judicial activism.

In international relations, states are generally reluctant to delegate significant legal authority to third parties. The power to interpret law and possibly make new law has the potential to bind states in ways they did not anticipate and would not have approved if considered in advance. In dispute settlement, delegation ranges from international courts with relatively broad jurisdiction, binding decision-making powers, and the ability to set legal precedents (as in the ICC in the enforcement of crimes against humanity) to limited dispute settlement bodies with more narrow mandates and national vetoes of decisions (as under the old General Agreement on Tariffs and Trade, or GATT). Having even less delegated authority are various arbitrators and mediators, who can recommend more or less binding solutions to disagreements.

In rule making and implementation, administrative bodies can have sweeping powers, usually found only in specialized agencies like the International Civil Aviation Organization (ICAO). In most cases, administrative bodies have more conditional powers subject to override by states, as in the International Monetary Fund (IMF) and World Bank.

By considering these three dimensions—obligation, precision, and delegation—we can distinguish between hard and soft law.[7] Hard law is obligatory, precisely defined, and delegates substantial authority to third parties, particularly international courts. Soft law is aspirational, ambiguous, and does not delegate significant powers to third parties. Countries often adopt soft law because it is easier to achieve, is more flexible and therefore better suited to dealing with uncertain

delegation

The degree to which third parties, such as courts, arbitrators, or mediators, are given authority to implement, interpret, and apply international legal rules; to resolve disputes over the rules; and to make additional rules.

---

7. Kenneth W. Abbott and Duncan Snidal, "Hard and Soft Law in International Governance," in Goldstein et al., *Legalization and World Politics*, 37–72.

futures, infringes less on state sovereignty, and facilitates compromise. Soft law is not a failure of lawmaking, but reflects intentional choices by states to write law appropriate to the issue area or to the extent of cooperation they are currently prepared to accept.

Although there is no guarantee that soft law will lead to hard law, agreements in new issue areas often begin as soft law that sets goals for states and creates frameworks for continuing negotiations, and may eventually become hard law as states gain experience, bargain over specific issues, and write more detailed treaties. A clear example is the FCCC, which was dismissed by critics as toothless when first signed, but later led to the effective Montreal Protocol, in force since 1999, and to the Kyoto Protocol (see Chapter 13). At the extreme, soft law blends into international norms, like R2P, which we will consider further later in the chapter.

Under some international laws, states agree to delegate extensive rule-making powers to specialized agencies, such as the ICAO. The ICAO establishes rules and standards that help states cooperate on the common goal of safe and orderly air transport.

Does International Law Matter?

Can international law "domesticate" international politics? That is, can international law become more like domestic law found within states? Can the use of force in international relations be tamed by international law? Perhaps no questions have vexed scholars of international relations and diplomats more.

Supporters of international law view it as an effective—perhaps essential—tool in facilitating cooperation and managing conflicts. According to international lawyer Louis Henkin, "almost all nations observe almost all principles of international law and almost all of their obligations almost all of the time."[8] Sometimes high levels of compliance result from more or less explicit enforcement mechanisms in international law. Yet, states may comply with international law even without enforcement provisions.

International lawyers Abram Chayes and Antonia Chayes argue that states typically do comply with international law, and when they fail to do so, it is either because the law itself is imprecise or because they lack the capacity to fulfill their obligations.[9] In their view, states want to observe, say, the Geneva Conventions on the rules of war, but they may not have effective control over their own soldiers, who may abuse prisoners, as in the infamous Abu Ghraib scandal that shocked the world in 2004 when pictures of American soldiers abusing Iraqi prisoners surfaced on the Internet. Proponents point to the high rates of compliance as evidence of

8. Louis Henkin, *How Nations Behave: Law and Foreign Policy* (New York: Columbia University Press, 1981), 47. Italics omitted.
9. Abram Chayes and Antonia Handler Chayes, "On Compliance," *International Organization* 47, no. 2 (1993): 175–205.

international law's potential. In this view, law can be a significant constraint on the interactions of states.

More skeptical observers see international law as unrealistic and utopian, or at least a reflection of state interest, rather than as a severe constraint on state action. Two main problems exist. First, law is seldom precise enough to deal with every possible interaction between actors. Indeed, in domestic politics, lawyers earn their livings from and courts are clogged with cases where the parties disagree on what the law says or requires in their specific circumstances. We should hardly expect international law to be more precise and less open to creative interpretation than domestic law is.

In one telling instance, when NATO was considering intervening in Kosovo in 1999, British foreign secretary Robin Cook told U.S. secretary of state Madeleine Albright that he had "problems with our lawyers" over using force without the approval of the UN Security Council. Albright responded that he should "get new lawyers."[10] Albright's sentiment still applies today. If international law is malleable and can be interpreted to justify whatever states might want to do, it is a weak constraint, at best, on their actions.

Second, as we have seen, international law is the product of states' interests and interactions. States decide the rules by which they will constrain themselves, including the degree to which these rules are obligatory, precise, and delegated. That states therefore comply with rules they have written is, at one level, hardly surprising. This is sometimes described as the "selection problem" in international relations.[11]

For skeptics, therefore, international law does not constrain states, despite seemingly high levels of compliance with the law. Rather, countries only sign agreements and make laws that serve their interests and obligate them to undertake actions they would want to do anyway. With states crafting the laws that constrain them and then interpreting the meaning of those laws for their own purposes, it is very difficult for scholars to demonstrate conclusively that international law has an effect on state behavior over and above state interest.

The truth likely lies somewhere between these extremes. The questions here are how, when, and why international law alters state behavior. International cooperation requires that states often subordinate their short-term interests for long-term benefits. Can international law constrain states to act in ways that are not in their short-term interests?

Enforcement provisions in international agreements vary widely. As shown in Figure 11.1, nearly 40 percent of economic and human rights agreements contain clauses empowering members to punish noncompliance, while less than 10 percent of environmental agreements include such provisions.[12] We should note, however, that just because agreements do not contain explicit enforcement provisions does not mean that states cannot use informal mechanisms to punish noncompliance.

---

10. Michael J. Glennon, *Limits of Law, Prerogatives of Power: Interventionism after Kosovo* (London: Palgrave Macmillan, 2003), 178.

11. George W. Downs, David M. Rocke, and Peter N. Barsoom, "Is the Good News about Compliance Good News about Cooperation?" *International Organization* 50, no. 3 (1996): 379–406.

12. Barbara Koremenos, *The Continent of International Law: Explaining Agreement Design* (New York: Cambridge University Press, 2016), 229.

FIGURE 11.1 **_Treaties Containing Punishment Provisions_**

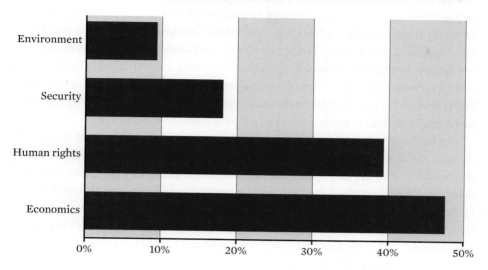

Figure source: Barbara
Koremenos, *The Continent of
International Law: Explaining
Agreement Design* (New York:
Cambridge University Press,
2016).

Even though enforcement provisions may be specified in an agreement, the enforcement of international law ultimately depends on the principle of national self-help. It is a truth of world politics that there is no central authority higher than the state that can enforce law between all states. As we discussed in Chapter 5, there are no police in international relations. At most, international law sets the terms and conditions under which victims can legally and legitimately retaliate against countries that violate rules of behavior.

Even in world trade, an area of international relations with strong and well-developed international laws, the WTO only permits victims of illegal trade barriers to retaliate by imposing punitive duties on goods purchased from the violator. The WTO cannot punish violators itself, nor can it mandate that other states punish violators. Each victimized country must, on its own, decide whether to seek and carry out retribution for clearly illegal acts. This dependence on self-help necessarily limits the effectiveness of international law.

At the same time, international law is generally followed because of the very real and important benefits of cooperation that it enables. Like all institutions, international law facilitates cooperation by setting more or less obligatory standards of behavior, helping to verify compliance by articulating more or less precise rules, lowering the costs of decision making by creating rules that do not need to be renegotiated for each interaction, and managing disputes.

In analyzing the problem of restraints on violence during war, as one example, the political scientist James Morrow argues that cooperation depends on reciprocity.[13] A state is more likely to treat enemy prisoners of war (POWs) well if it expects its opponent to treat its captive soldiers well, and violations by one state are likely

---

13. James D. Morrow, *Order within Anarchy: The Laws of War as an International Institution* (New York: Cambridge University Press, 2014).

to provoke retaliation by another. The Geneva Conventions, especially when ratified by both parties, make clear that the states understand, accept, and are likely to follow international laws regulating the treatment of POWs. This makes it easier for states to presume that others will treat POWs humanely, and for them to do the same for theirs, and it defines relatively clearly what constitutes a violation that would then be punished through retaliation. By setting rules that help clarify expectations on both sides, the Geneva Conventions reinforce the equilibrium (treating POWs well as long as the other state treats POWs well) that might otherwise prove more fragile or tend to erode under the stress of war.

In facilitating cooperation, obligation and precision may be the most important dimensions of international law, for, as just explained, they set expectations for the behavior of others and reduce the range within which states can argue that the law does not apply to their interactions in a particular instance. Simple words matter here because they define which behaviors are consistent with cooperation and which are not. It is the anticipated benefits of cooperation that lead states to create international law in the first place, and it is the actual benefits of cooperation that lead them to comply with the rules once they are in place.

Widespread transgressions of law undermine the gains from cooperation that states seek, and states fear that the set of rules will unravel and destroy cooperation. This fear of cooperation breaking down prevents states from violating laws in pursuit of their short-term interests. The greater the benefits of cooperation, and the more evenly these benefits are shared, the more international law will constrain the policies of all states. The more states have to lose, the more international law will shape their interactions and alter outcomes.

International law is also more effective when it is delegated to courts, arbitrators, and other tribunals. When states disagree on what the law says, or how it should be applied in specific situations, referring the dispute to an independent body for decision can help prevent conflicts from escalating. The international adjudication procedures of the WTO are one highly developed example of how delegations to a supranational institution can mitigate disagreements that might otherwise undermine international trade relations.[14]

Domestic courts, however, are also important to the enforcement of international law. In many countries, including the United States, international treaties are superior to domestic laws, meaning that once enacted, they override domestic laws that contradict their provisions and cannot be changed by subsequent legislation. The treaty thereby becomes part of "domestic" law and is enforced in the same way as all other laws in the ratifying country.

Domestic courts are also increasingly appealing to international law in interpreting strictly domestic statutes. In *Roper v. Simmons* (2005), which overturned laws on the death penalty for juvenile offenders in the United States, the U.S. Supreme Court cited as support the UN Convention on the Rights of the Child, previously signed by the president but never ratified by the Senate. Writing for

---

14. Christina L. Davis, *Why Adjudicate? Enforcing Trade Rules in the WTO* (Princeton, NJ: Princeton University Press, 2012).

the majority, Justice Anthony Kennedy argued it was "proper that we acknowledge the overwhelming weight of international opinion against the juvenile death penalty. . . . The opinion of the world community, while not controlling our outcome, does provide respected and significant confirmation of our own conclusions."[15] As international law is directly and indirectly incorporated into domestic law, the enforcement powers of states within their own jurisdictions are being harnessed to it.

In addition, some international law also creates *compliance constituencies* within states that then have interests in ensuring that their governments follow the rules.[16] Even when some domestic groups might benefit from breaking international laws, other constituencies have a strong interest in upholding the law. WTO law, for instance, opens foreign markets to trade and helps ensure nondiscriminatory treatment for goods from different countries. Although import-competing industries that favor protection might advocate policies that violate WTO rules, export industries that are dependent on foreign markets have an interest in ensuring that their governments uphold their obligations. Similarly, militaries are often staunch advocates of upholding the Geneva Conventions, especially with regard to the treatment of prisoners. TANs that propagate norms that are subsequently embedded in international law, as discussed in the next section, are also likely to be continuing advocates for compliance.

Thus, the benefits of cooperation, both to states as a whole and to particular groups within states, can make international law self-enforcing. Although still reliant on and limited by the principle of self-help, states have an interest in following international law so as to help ensure that other states also follow the rules. In this way, international law can significantly influence and constrain the interactions of states even without any external enforcement mechanism. Nonetheless, international law is unlikely to end the bargaining failures that lead states into war or resolve other sources of conflict.

Like other institutions, international law facilitates cooperation, but it does not ensure that cooperation will always prevail. It is a useful tool in altering the interactions of states in more constructive directions and in bringing about desirable outcomes in world politics, but it is not a panacea. The difficulty of demonstrating the independent effect of international law, however, ensures that the debate about how effective law is will continue. As we will see in Chapter 12, the selection problem is central in the debate about the effectiveness of international human rights law.

What Are International Norms?

International norms are also a type of institution that constrains states. **Norms** are standards of behavior for actors with a given identity defined in terms of rights and obligations. They rest on a community's beliefs about what is appropriate for an

norms
Standards of behavior for actors with a given identity; norms define what actions are "right" or appropriate under particular circumstances.

---

15. Quoted in Robert Delahunty and John Yoo, "Against Foreign Law," *Harvard Journal of Law and Public Policy* 29, no. 1 (2005): 291–330. The trend toward citing foreign law is strongly opposed by conservatives, who see it overturning democratic processes within the United States.

16. Miles Kahler, "Conclusion: The Causes and Consequences of Legalization," in Goldstein et al., *Legalization and World Politics*, 283–84.

actor under some specified condition. Norms may be codified into international law, but norms as institutions can exist and be respected by members of a community even when they are not written down in formal agreements. In our everyday life, many of our interactions are regulated by norms that have nothing to do with law. You are not required by law to hold an elevator for others, for instance. But to intentionally—or even unintentionally—allow the doors to close on someone rushing to the elevator is regarded as rude, and you may even apologize for letting the door close, even though the now excluded passenger cannot hear you.

Similarly, and with greater political importance, norms of fairness—which are not required in any way by law but reflect deep-seated social understandings—shape political appeals and policies in many countries, although exactly what is "fair" is not always clear and has varied considerably over time. In this same way, many now recognize a nuclear "taboo" in international relations—a normative prohibition against the use of nuclear weapons—even though the norm is nowhere found in international law.

Like law, international norms shape the behavior of states in important ways. Norms affect the interactions of states because they are understood by people within those states to be rules of conduct that are right and morally correct. In other words, norms define what it is we *should* do and thereby shape our understanding of our interests. In our everyday lives, of course, individuals and countries do many things they should not. Norms are often violated. They are standards of behavior, not prohibitions or straitjackets. But even if we choose to violate norms, we must then excuse our behavior, justify it, or risk being ostracized by the community.

We can group most norms into three broad categories. The first category, which we refer to as *constitutive norms*, defines who is a legitimate or appropriate actor under what circumstances. What it means to be a state, for instance, is defined largely by norms.[17] At the level of everyday diplomacy, all states have flags, national anthems, and—even in the poorest states—ministries of science and technology. No law requires this, but there is remarkable similarity in the form and practices of states in the world today. To show that they are indeed modern states, many countries also buy advanced military equipment for which they have little use and even less ability to maintain—most notably fighter jets, which appear to have enormous symbolic value. More broadly, norms shape what it means to be sovereign at any point in history. This includes evolving ideas about when states can legitimately intervene in one another's "sovereign" areas of control, as reflected today in the new norm of R2P.

The second category, *procedural norms*, defines how decisions involving multiple actors should be made. As such, procedural norms are analogous to secondary rules in international law. In domestic politics, procedural norms are often well structured. In legislatures, for instance, ramming through a major

---

17. Statehood and sovereignty are defined as law through the UN Charter and other international agreements. The "rights" that sovereignty entails, however, have varied dramatically over time, depending on how states choose to interpret the law.

bill late at night without due warning to the opposition, though permitted by the rules, is usually regarded as unfair and illegitimate and taints the resulting legislation.

In international relations, procedural norms are generally less robust. Sovereignty implies that all states are formally equal, and thus each state is entitled to an equal voice in world affairs—at least in principle. This is an important support for multilateralism, the practice of "diffuse reciprocity" in international relations in which states are expected to offer one another roughly equal benefits over time.[18] Yet, more powerful states are often acknowledged to have special rights and greater responsibilities in recognition that their support is necessary for multilateralism to be effective. The United States and other major donors are often consulted, for instance, by IMF staff before loan agreements are formally presented to the executive directors for approval.[19] Such procedural norms give more powerful states a larger voice in diplomatic circles than the formal equality of sovereignty otherwise allows.

The possession of advanced military equipment has come to be a powerful symbol of legitimate statehood, even for countries that have little need for it. Venezuela, for instance, owns dozens of fighter jets.

Finally, the third category, *regulative norms*, governs the behavior of actors in their interactions with other actors. R2P is one example, as is the norm of election monitoring. The nuclear taboo is also a regulative norm.[20] Although the United States did drop two atomic bombs on Japan in 1945, ending World War II, no country since has used nuclear weapons, despite the fact that at least nine countries are now believed to possess workable bombs. Although nuclear weapons are held in reserve as the ultimate defense—a lingering threat to all enemies—political leaders are reluctant to contemplate using them, even when they are technically feasible and possibly efficient. To destroy hardened underground bunkers—whether of the type that hid Saddam Hussein during the Iraq War or those that protect the Iranian or North Korean nuclear programs—the United States has devoted considerable resources to developing large conventional "bunker-busting" bombs, even when existing tactical nuclear weapons could likely accomplish the same task more effectively.

That countries do not use nuclear weapons for fear of retaliation is undoubtedly part of the explanation for this norm. But such weapons are not used—and not contemplated for use—even when the target does not have nuclear weapons or the

18. John Gerard Ruggie, ed., *Multilateralism Matters: The Theory and Praxis of an Institutional Form* (New York: Columbia University Press, 1993), 11.

19. Randall W. Stone, *Controlling Institutions: International Organizations and the Global Economy* (New York: Cambridge University Press, 2011).

20. Nina Tannenwald, "The Nuclear Taboo: The United States and the Normative Basis of Nuclear Non-use," *International Organization* 53, no. 3 (2003): 433–68.

The taboo against the use of nuclear weapons is an example of a regulative norm. Since the U.S. bombing of Hiroshima (above) and Nagasaki in 1945, no country has resorted to a nuclear attack, at least in part because of the international norm against the use of such weapons.

capacity to retaliate against the user directly. Deterrence alone cannot explain the taboo. Leaders appear reluctant to cross the nuclear threshold for fear of being branded as immoral, either personally or on behalf of their country.

Norms are often difficult to identify. When not written down, they exist only by collective assent. In turn, when norms are deeply internalized, actors typically do not even consciously contemplate violating them, meaning that behavior consistent with the norm appears entirely voluntary or as the exercise of free will. To take an extreme example, nearly all societies have strongly internalized norms against cannibalism, yet this norm almost never appears to affect our conscious choices. We do not wake up in the morning and consider eating our neighbor for breakfast. That we do not want to violate the norm is not evidence that the norm is unimportant, but rather that it is so deeply internalized that we are not even aware that it constrains our behavior.

In a far less extreme form, the nuclear taboo works in similar ways. That nuclear first strikes are not on the list of options that leaders in diplomatic disputes consider does not mean that the norm is not having an effect, but instead suggests that the norm is sufficiently internalized that we are not aware of how fundamentally it shapes our interests and interactions.

Norms are often most easily observed when they are violated. Their presence is revealed both by the censure of others and, usually, by the justifications or excuses given by the offending party. For example, since 1945 there has been a growing norm against changing international borders through the use of force, described as the "territorial integrity" norm.[21] When Saddam Hussein invaded and seized Kuwait in August 1990, the international community quickly condemned his actions. Although Hussein challenged the prior border as an anachronism of British colonial rule—in an attempt to reframe the issue as one of decolonization—and proclaimed Kuwait to be the long-lost nineteenth province of Iraq, his justifications for the land grab were broadly rejected by the rest of the international community. The United States and a coalition of other states fought a war to return Kuwait to sovereignty.

---

21. Mark W. Zacher, "The Territorial Integrity Norm: International Boundaries and the Use of Force," *International Organization* 55, no. 2 (2001): 215–50.

Similar objections were raised when Russia annexed the Crimea from Ukraine in 2014, claiming it as part of its historical territory. Although no state or coalition rose to reverse Russia's action in this case, it was nonetheless the reactions of norm-abiding others and the types of justifications or excuses offered by Russia that display most clearly the territorial integrity norm at work. No actor needs to justify its behavior to others unless it is at risk of transgressing a norm held by the community it belongs to.

Unlike law, norms need not be consistent with one another or with secondary rules. Indeed, the norm of national self-determination conflicts with sovereignty: if the state is the ultimate authority within a territory, how can a nation within that territory freely decide to secede? We have already discussed how R2P conflicts with sovereignty, and the same holds for many of the human rights norms examined in the next chapter.

The tension between norms creates opportunities for actors to interpret rules selectively for their own advantage. When faced with two morally just but conflicting rules, which one do you follow? Germans faced exactly this kind of choice in deciding whether to back NATO's intervention in Kosovo. On the one hand, many Germans were committed to a foreign policy that eschewed war and the use of force; on the other, they had pledged to never again stand idly by as a genocide unfolded. Despite contradictions such as these, however, norms—as with law—can serve as important constraints on states in their interactions.

How Are International Norms Created?

For a principle or idea to become institutionalized as a norm, the standard of behavior it specifies must be accepted as morally right and appropriate by a sufficiently large proportion of any given population, although that proportion is not always clear. Norms change. Where once it was acceptable to own slaves, we now find the practice morally repugnant—though many people around the world are still held in various forms of bondage, not least in the sex trade.

Something is not considered immoral until a sufficiently large number of us decide that it is wrong or objectionable. Child labor is one such principle that remains contested and thus has failed to attain the status of a norm (see "Controversy" on p. 480). Once we agree, in turn, practices that once might have been common become odious or at least inappropriate and even sometimes unimaginable. Over time, norms can develop a taken-for-granted quality, an unquestioned and perhaps unquestionable status. But all norms were originally just principles or ideas without widely accepted moral implications.

Some principles become norms simply by the force of their own inherent moral standing. The nuclear taboo may be one such example of a principle that so obviously improves human welfare that almost everyone accepts it. Other norms are propagated by powerful states or through international organizations. The Washington Consensus on economic liberalism (see Chapter 10, p. 450), which

Toys Made for Children, by Children

Tariq was 12 years old, stitching soccer balls for the equivalent of 60¢ apiece in Pakistan. It took him all day to make one ball, for an average of about 6¢ per hour. Featured in *Life* magazine in 1996, Tariq became the face of child labor in the developing world and sparked a major global civil society action to stop the commercial exploitation of children. Today, over 168 million children ages 5–17, about one in six worldwide, are still engaged in some form of child labor.[a] Children work in a host of occupations, including rug weaving, the production of surgical instruments, mining and construction, and—like Tariq—the making of toys for other children.

Applying the Concepts

As TANs have directed attention to child labor, consumers in developed countries have acquired new **interests** in ethical consumption; more consumers are making informed purchases to reward improved working conditions and practices. These market **interactions**, however, are more complex than they may seem. If the norm or **institution** prohibiting child labor takes hold, we must take into account the opportunities that poor workers, especially children, have in their societies.

Since Tariq appeared in *Life*, a norm against child labor has indeed emerged, at least in developed countries. Consumers in rich countries are increasingly avoiding goods that are known to be produced by child labor. For many people in developed countries, the concept of child labor is now abhorrent, nearly unthinkable, and assumed to be exploitative. Nonetheless, this principle has probably not yet hit the tipping point where enough individuals accept the principle that it acquires a broad moral status. Why?

The issue of child labor is more complicated than it first appears. Clearly, the economic exploitation of children is wrong. But the evil of child labor must be balanced against the alternatives to work for children in the poorest countries. These alternatives are often quite dismal. Most children and their families are not choosing between work and play or even education, but between work and starvation.

Although low, the wages earned by children are often essential to supplement the meager incomes of their parents. In families living on mere dollars a day, a child's earnings might be the difference between subsistence and starvation. In turn, for most villages where children work, schools are typically few and far away. Moreover, families dependent on child labor can rarely afford even the small fees required for schooling where it exists. In the end, banning child labor may only force child workers further into the informal economy—outside government oversight and regulation, where they are even more easily exploited—or into the sex trade.

Indeed, after the Child Labor Deterrence Act was introduced in the U.S. Senate in 1992, the mere threat of prohibitions on child-produced garments led business owners in Bangladesh to summarily dismiss many children from their jobs. According to a unique follow-up study that tracked those children, some were forced to take jobs "in more hazardous situations, in unsafe workshops where they were paid less, or in prostitution."[b] Thus, the core problem is the lack of other opportunities for child laborers.

A toy-making factory in Bangladesh.

---

a. International Labour Office, *Marking Progress against Child Labour: Global Estimates and Trends, 2000–2012* (Geneva, Switzerland: International Labour Office, 2013), 3–5. The number of child laborers is down from 246 million in 2000.

Under these circumstances, banning child workers can be seen as another form of Western cultural imperialism—a projection of values that are now dominant in the richest countries onto individuals and families struggling to sustain themselves in some of the world's poorest areas. After all, minimum age requirements for employment in the United States were not enacted until 1938. In 1910, 2 million children were employed outside the agricultural sector in the United States—a number that would be much larger if we included farm labor.

Although the states had moved individually to regulate child labor, only during the Great Depression—when unemployment rates rose to extraordinary levels—could Progressives finally enact national minimum age standards for workers. This standard, combined with free primary schooling, led the proportion of children working to drop rapidly to less than 1 percent. Child labor was common in the now developed countries before they became rich. Why should consumers or voters in these countries now seek to deny employment to children in the poorest countries?

Clearly, it is not enough to simply ban child labor. Advocates must couple ending child labor with expanded educational opportunities and financial support for poor families to replace lost income. This task will be expensive, at least in the short term. The International Labour Organization demonstrates clearly that the long-term benefits of shifting children from work to education are enormous. More education not only frees children from labor but increases their earning capacity over the course of their lifetimes. But paying to educate cohorts of children, monitoring compliance with anti–child labor laws, and subsidizing families to replace the income lost incurs substantial net costs for approximately the first 20 years of any program.[c]

Only after generations of children have completed their educations and entered the adult workforce do the economic gains begin to outweigh the costs. Politicians everywhere are notoriously shortsighted. To bear costs for 20 years before the gains arrive is a challenge, and one that even farsighted leaders may not easily manage.

To ask the poorest countries to incur such costs over two decades is, perhaps, to expect too much.

Though the norm against child labor that is taking hold in developed countries hardly seems objectionable, these consumers and politicians who advocate for this norm on moral grounds may not actually be helping children unless they also support expanded education and income transfers to those they leave with fewer—rather than more—opportunities in the world's poorest countries.

b. UNICEF, *The State of the World's Children* (New York: Oxford University Press, 1997), 23, www.unicef.org/sowc97/report.

c. International Labour Office, *Investing in Every Child: An Economic Study of the Costs and Benefits of Eliminating Child Labour* (Geneva, Switzerland: International Labour Office, 2003), 6.

Thinking Analytically

1. How does a growing interest in ethical consumption affect others, especially producers? Do the interests of consumers and producers always coincide?

2. Should rules and norms prevalent in rich countries be followed by poor countries? Should certain institutions be universal? If so, which ones and why?

held broad sway in the 1990s and early 2000s, was heavily promoted by the United States through its policies and the IMF and World Bank. Still other norms may be championed by virtuous leaders seeking to distinguish themselves from the perhaps less virtuous. These leaders' efforts to signal their commitment to democracy have been a factor in spreading the norm of inviting monitors to oversee elections in other new democracies (see Chapter 2, p. 72).

Norms typically begin with individuals or groups who seek to advance a principled standard of behavior for states and other actors. Transnational advocacy networks (TANs) are central to spreading norms throughout the international system. Comprising individuals and NGOs deeply committed to ethical beliefs, TANs aim to persuade other individuals and groups to share their commitment. We call these individuals and groups **norms entrepreneurs**.

norms entrepreneurs
Individuals or groups that seek to advance principled standards of behavior for states and other actors.

The International Campaign to Ban Landmines (ICBL), for instance, is a clear example of how a group of committed activists were able to call attention to an issue and convince many other people around the globe that existing practices were morally wrong. The ICBL is a network of hundreds of NGOs in some 100 countries, working to outlaw and remove land mines, which still kill and maim over 6,000 people worldwide each year. It was the primary force behind the negotiation and adoption of the Ottawa Convention.

The convention was negotiated and signed in 1997 and entered into force in March 1999. As of March 2018, 164 countries have joined the convention, and only 32 countries remain outside the treaty entirely, including China, Egypt, India, Israel, Pakistan, Russia, and the United States.[22] In 1997, the ICBL and its coordinator, Jody Williams, were awarded the Nobel Peace Prize for their work. In bestowing the award, the Norwegian Nobel Committee applauded the campaign for moving the ban from "a vision to a feasible reality" and acclaimed the organization as a model for international disarmament and peace.

Once norms are adopted, supporters of those norms then hold their governments accountable to acceptable standards of international behavior. Political leaders who hold deep normative commitments may decide to rule out certain policy options, deeming them immoral in the face of these international standards. Even if tempted to violate norms, leaders may fear punishment by their constituents for violating widely accepted standards of behavior. Political leaders may also be held to account by citizens of other states, who press their governments to enforce compliance to norms they hold dear, as in the anti-apartheid movement, which we will discuss in Chapter 12. In this way, even authoritarian governments that are not accountable to their own people can be pressed to uphold international norms.

transnational advocacy network (TAN)
A set of individuals and nongovernmental organizations acting in pursuit of a normative objective.

TANs: Changing Minds, Altering Interests Transnational advocacy networks (TANs) are, as the name implies, sets of activists allied in the pursuit of a common normative objective, including (in the contemporary era) human rights; the

---

22. See www.icbl.org/en-gb/the-treaty/treaty-status.aspx (accessed 08/03/17).

FIGURE 11.2　*Issue Focus of Transnational Advocacy Networks, 2000**

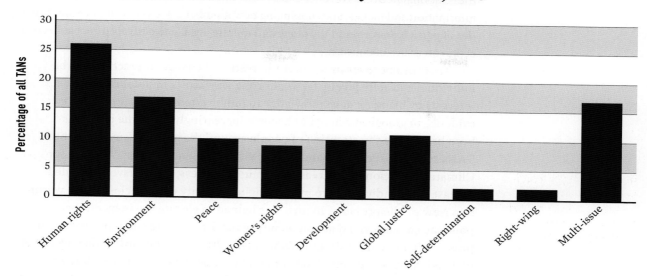

Figure source: Jackie Smith, "Exploring Connections between Global Integration and Political Mobilization," *Journal of World System Research* 10, no. 1 (2004): 266, Table 2.

*The most recent data available are from 2000 but are still useful in providing a sense of the issue areas that contemporary TANs focus on.

environment; economic and social justice; democracy; women's rights; and abortion rights or, conversely, the right to life (Figure 11.2). The actors that make up TANs may include (1) international and domestic NGOs involved in research and advocacy; (2) local social movements; (3) foundations and other philanthropic organizations; (4) the media; and (5) churches, trade unions, and consumer and other civil organizations.[23] The number of TANs has grown dramatically over the past 50 years: in 1953, there were about 100 identifiable TANs; today, they number well into the thousands—so many, in fact, that a proper count is nearly impossible.[24]

Nearly all the major issues that engage citizens within countries now have an international counterpart. For example, the Planned Parenthood Federation of America, often on the front lines of the movement to make or keep abortion legal, has 10 foreign affiliates and cooperates with hundreds of other organizations and countless individuals worldwide in the women's rights and legalized abortion movement. Heartbeat International, a network of pro-life pregnancy centers, has affiliates in more than 47 countries and works with many churches and other organizations to promote the right to life. First gaining momentum in the United States,

23. Margaret E. Keck and Kathryn Sikkink, *Activists beyond Borders: Advocacy Networks in International Politics* (Ithaca, NY: Cornell University Press, 1998), 9. We exclude international organizations and governments from this list, although individuals in these organizations may interact with transnational networks. On public transnational networks, see Anne-Marie Slaughter, *A New World Order* (Princeton, NJ: Princeton University Press, 2004).

24. For the latest available figures, see Kathryn Sikkink and Jackie Smith, "Infrastructures for Change: Transnational Organizations, 1953–1993," in *Restructuring World Politics: Transnational Social Movements, Networks, and Norms*, ed. Sanjeev Khagram, James V. Riker, and Kathryn Sikkink, 30, Table 2.1 (Minneapolis: University of Minnesota Press, 2002); and Jackie Smith, "Exploring Connections between Global Integration and Political Mobilization," *Journal of World System Research* 10, no. 1 (2004): 266, Table 2.

the struggle over abortion has now become an international political issue with transnational networks on both sides of the question coordinating action, sharing information and tactics, and mobilizing new members. TANs coordinate the activities of participants around the globe and initiate, lead, and actively direct collective action on issues of concern.

TANs promote norms to alter interests and change interactions at the individual and state levels. TANs alter the way actors first define their interests by bringing new knowledge to public attention. For example, as evidence of global warming has become increasingly clear, the issue has been brought to the attention of people around the globe by environmental TANs such as Greenpeace and former vice president Al Gore's Alliance for Climate Protection. By increasing public awareness, TANs have persuaded at least some individuals to place a higher priority on reducing global warming. New public pressure, in turn, has helped to elevate the issue on the political agenda, even if action on policy remains halting and tentative. Such pressure helped promote agreement on the 2016 Paris Accord, under the terms of which many countries pledged to reduce greenhouse gas emissions. This pressure, however, did not sway President Donald Trump, who indicated that he intended to withdraw from the agreement negotiated by his predecessor (see Chapter 13).[25]

Yet scientific or technical knowledge seldom translates directly into policy change. Expert consensus can call attention to new problems and point to possible solutions, but groups negatively affected by the proposed policy changes will also mobilize politically to influence government decisions. For example, the scientific community agreed for decades on the hazards of smoking before the tobacco industry lobby in the United States was finally defeated and the policy altered. In many countries, government policy still favors smokers, even in the face of nearly universal scientific agreement on the harmful effects of smoking.

Similarly, despite widespread scientific concern about carbon dioxide emissions into the atmosphere, policies to limit global climate change are often blocked by countries and industries that use carbon intensively. American oil and gas industries' support for President Trump, for instance, was likely a key factor in his withdrawal from the Paris Agreement. Knowledge is power—but it alone may not be enough to create a norm or set policy.

Perhaps more important, TANs also change how actors conceive of their interests by promoting new moral values. In essence, TANs urge actors to have preferences over certain practices—owning slaves, using land mines—rather than thinking only about the possible outcomes of those practices, such as greater wealth or victory on the battlefield. Of course, norms existed and spread throughout the world system prior to the recent proliferation of TANs. After all, not all norms are connected with TANs and their activities. But one important function

---

25. Communities of technical experts who create and promote new knowledge are often called epistemic communities but are, in practice, similar to TANs. See Peter M. Haas, ed., *Knowledge, Power, and International Policy Coordination* (Columbia: University of South Carolina Press, 1997).

of TANs is to encourage and support socially appropriate behavior and help spread norms across national borders. Martha Finnemore and Kathryn Sikkink, two leading scholars of norms in international relations, posit a three-stage **norms life cycle** that can help us understand how TANs shape norms and interests and, thus, political outcomes.[26]

In the first stage, norms entrepreneurs actively work to convince a critical mass of other individuals in other states to embrace their beliefs. The norm that medical personnel on the battlefield and wounded soldiers be treated as neutral noncombatants, now embodied in the Geneva Conventions, was rooted in the crusade by Henry Dumont, a Swiss banker, who helped found the International Committee of the Red Cross.

Similarly, the National Rifle Association (NRA) is working globally to promote the principle that owning a gun is a natural right. Although its charter prohibits the organization from funding groups in other countries, it is building a network of like-minded organizations around the world. Whether the NRA will succeed in establishing gun ownership as a right outside the United States is not clear, but its efforts helped defeat a national gun control law in Brazil in October 2005.[27] It is during this first stage of the norms life cycle that most TANs become vehicles for the dissemination of new norms.

Norms entrepreneurs frame "issues to make them comprehensible to target audiences . . . [and] attract attention and encourage action."[28] Perhaps most important, they find creative ways to connect the behavior they wish to encourage to other, preexisting norms; because these norms are already widely accepted, audiences are likely to see the value in the desired behaviors or ends. Activists "win" by framing principles they want to promote so that they connect to principles that are already accepted in a community.

One effective frame is to redefine undesirable behaviors as perpetrating violence against innocent persons, which is nearly universally abhorred. The women's rights movement, for instance, failed to make progress for many years in the 1980s and 1990s because it was caught among three competing frames: one of discrimination, emphasizing the principle of gender equality articulated in the 1979 Convention on the Elimination of All Forms of Discrimination against Women; one of economic development and the need to improve the quality of life for women; and one of general human rights, claiming that civil and political rights for everyone could not be secured without protecting the rights of women as well, adopted at the 1993 World Conference on Human Rights. Seeking to build an integrated transnational movement, activists finally framed the issue as one of violence against women and made this approach the centerpiece of the UN's World Conference on Women in Beijing in 1995, successfully bridging the competing orientations and rallying

norms life cycle
A three-stage model of how norms diffuse within a population and achieve a taken-for-granted status.

---

26. Martha Finnemore and Kathryn Sikkink, "International Norm Dynamics and Political Change," *International Organization* 52, no. 4 (1998): 887–917.

27. David Morton, "Gunning for the World," *Foreign Policy* (January–February 2006), 58–67.

28. Keck and Sikkink, *Activists beyond Borders*, 2–3.

the women's rights network behind a unified message of opposition to all forms of violence against women.[29]

In the case of female genital cutting, opponents framed the practice simply by changing the name from *female circumcision* (thereby breaking its association with the traditional practice of male circumcision, which does not produce the same long-term health problems) to *female genital mutilation*, which carries stronger connotations of violence against women. Traditionalists, in turn, attempted to frame the issue as one of local culture against Western values imposed by colonial governors and Christian missionaries.[30] By connecting the practice to the larger anticolonial struggle, they ensured some continuing support among local communities and, thus, continuing controversy.[31] Similarly, the NRA attempts to frame the issue of gun ownership by linking it to the concept of human rights, while advocates of gun control emphasize firearm safety and the threat to children.

During the second stage of the norms life cycle, once a new frame has taken hold, a *norms cascade* occurs as the number of adherents passes a tipping point beyond which the idea gains sufficient support that it becomes a nearly universal standard of behavior to which others can be held accountable. The tipping point is often hard to identify in advance; it is determined not only by the number of actors that adopt the new belief, but also by those actors' leadership or visibility within the international community. Conformity to the new norm can then be established through coercion (such as economic sanctions in the case of human rights norms) or through socialization (a process akin to peer pressure in which, say, states adopt new behaviors because that is what "good" states do).

The norm of national election monitoring appears to have recently crossed this threshold. Although this norm was essentially unknown before 1978, virtually all democratizing states now invite other governments or transnational NGOs to monitor their first elections (see the "How Do We Know?" box in Chapter 2, p. 72). It is not clear, given the prominent countries that have not yet committed to eliminate their use, whether the ban on land mines has reached this stage.

In the third stage of the cycle, norms are internalized or become so widely accepted that they acquire the taken-for-granted quality that makes conforming almost automatic. Indeed, even contemplating violation of the deeply internalized norms against, say, cannibalism or eating certain foods can make some people feel ill. Norms against slavery or violence against political prisoners, once the subjects of TAN activity, are now at least partially internalized within many countries, although violations still occur. Few norms governing

---

29. Keck and Sikkink, *Activists beyond Borders*, chap. 5.

30. See, for example, Makau Mutua, *Human Rights: A Political and Cultural Critique* (Philadelphia: University of Pennsylvania Press, 2002).

31. Keck and Sikkink, *Activists beyond Borders*, 67–71.

interactions between states have reached this final
stage, although the nuclear taboo may be close. Were
North Korea to use a nuclear weapon, for instance, it
would likely be strongly condemned by the international community for violating the norm, indicating the
robust presence of the taboo and its role as a constraint
in other cases.

Once internalized, norms affect the way actors conceive of their interests. Prior to this stage, norms are
enforced by the sanctions or moral disapproval of others.
These forms of punishment raise the costs of engaging
in behaviors that violate the norm, thereby affecting the
choices actors make in particular interactions. But once a
norm is internalized, certain actions are simply not considered, because they are normatively prohibited (taboo),
and others are favored as appropriate or correct. At this
deepest level, internalized norms lead actors to recon-
ceive their interests by reordering how they evaluate
alternative political outcomes and the appropriate means
of achieving them.

Do Norms Matter?

Norms constrain states and other actors in two principal
ways, first by redefining interests, and second, by changing their interactions. In both cases, isolating the effects
of norms on policy is difficult. To the extent that norms
define how individuals and states perceive their inter-

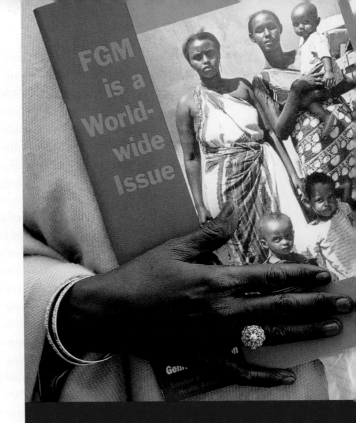

TANs and other groups try to frame issues in
a way that will win sympathy for their position.
In the case of female circumcision, opponents
have framed it as female genital *mutilation* to
emphasize the violence of the practice.

ests, the selection problem identified in the preceding discussion of international
law becomes even more acute. If norms shape interests, and states act on those
interests, distinguishing the independent effect of norms on action is nearly
impossible. Nonetheless, there is reason to believe that the effects of norms on
state action may be considerable.

Norms define interests by shaping what actors believe is right and appropriate behavior under specific circumstances. Countries as a whole may respect
norms out of concern for their reputations as honorable or norm-abiding states.
Such a reputation may have intrinsic value. It may also be valued because it
facilitates cooperation with other countries. As individuals, leaders may seek
for their own egotistic reasons to be seen as moral and "upstanding." Other
leaders may do the right thing simply because it is right. Even if leaders are
cross-pressured by circumstances or self-interested groups to act in ways that
contravene norms, however, they can be held to account by their own citizens,
and especially by voters.

TANs play an important role in enforcing norms, by calling attention to violations of widely held beliefs—a practice known as naming and shaming. States and

their leaders typically value their reputations as "good" countries or individuals that respect and comply with standards of appropriate behavior. By calling attention to violations of norms, TANs mobilize domestic citizens, as well as the "court of world opinion," to castigate and shame states into altering abhorrent behavior. They also challenge and potentially damage the reputations of offending states. If countries violate norms frequently and are called to account repeatedly by TANs, they risk becoming international pariahs that other states will be reluctant to trust. Although naming and shaming might seem like a weak tool to leverage good compliance from otherwise strong states, over the long run it can severely weaken a state's reputation and put potentially profitable cooperation at risk.

Norms also change the interactions of states and their outcomes by invoking the coercive power of other states. In the **boomerang model** proposed by Margaret Keck and Kathryn Sikkink, NGOs in one state are able to activate transnational linkages to bring pressure from other states to bear on their own governments (Figure 11.3).[32] This process is most likely to be effective when NGOs are blocked from influencing their own governments, as is common in many nondemocratic regimes. Unable to appeal to their own governments, NGOs activate their transnational network and bring their plight to the attention of NGOs and individuals in other countries, who, in turn, press their governments or, perhaps, international organizations into action. These other governments then demand that the first state alter its behavior or remove the block on its own NGOs. In this way, foreign states are mobilized to try to influence the offending state.

Reflecting the importance of domestic political institutions, the boomerang model is most likely to be activated by NGOs originating in nondemocratic regimes and directed at NGOs in more democratic states, where governments are more sensitive to social demands pressed by their voters. New forms of social media have likely accentuated the strength and speed of the boomerang effect as news and often graphic video of state repression can be transmitted broadly across the globe instantaneously (see "How Do We Know?" on p. 490).

The anti-apartheid movement in South Africa is a good example of the boomerang model in action (see Chapter 12). Excluded from power and influence in the White-dominated government, Black South Africans, their NGOs, and their allies in the society appealed to foreign TANs in their struggle. These advocacy networks mobilized opinion and voters in other countries—mostly in Western democracies—whose governments placed sanctions on South Africa and eventually helped topple the apartheid regime. As this example suggests, the essence of the boomerang process involves domestic NGOs bringing greater pressure to bear on their government than they would be able to exert on their own. The process does not require any actor to alter its perceived interests; instead, the activation of transnational ties changes the nature of the political interactions in which the domestic actors are engaged and makes socially inappropriate behavior more costly.

boomerang model
A process through which NGOs in one state are able to activate transnational linkages to bring pressure from other states on their own governments.

---

32. Keck and Sikkink, *Activists beyond Borders*, 12–13.

FIGURE 11.3 *The Boomerang Model*

This stylized depiction of the boomerang model shows how NGOs that are blocked from influence within their own state (State A) can appeal to other transnational NGOs, which can press their states (State B) or an international organization to press State A to change its policy.

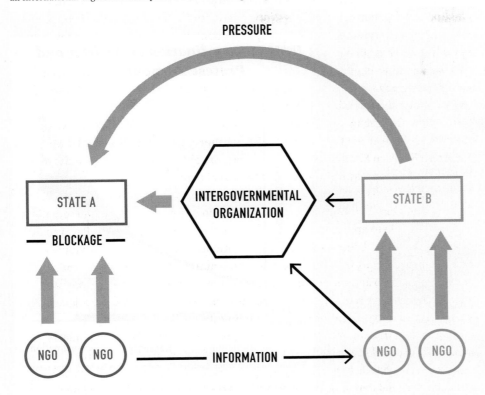

Figure source: Margaret E. Keck and Kathryn Sikkink, *Activists beyond Borders: Advocacy Networks in International Politics* (Ithaca, NY: Cornell University Press, 1998), 13.

Beyond Norms: TANs and International Cooperation

In addition to promoting norms, TANs can affect behavior and outcomes by providing information to states both as endorsers before a final agreement is reached and as monitors afterward. In both cases, the information provided by TANs facilitates interstate cooperation that would otherwise fail. In this way, TANs provide important support for international cooperation that goes beyond their role as norms entrepreneurs.

TANs as Endorsers International agreements can be quite complex. We assume that the negotiators themselves know and agree on the terms of any given treaty or executive agreement they sign, although many agreements contain imprecise language to paper over differences between parties, or do not consider all possible contingencies under which the agreement might hold. But members of the legislature that must ratify the agreement or implement its terms typically

Social Media and the Arab Spring

Starting in Tunisia in December 2010, political protests rolled across North Africa and the Middle East. In a matter of months, as protests spread, regimes were toppled in Tunisia, Libya, and Egypt. Meanwhile, the government in Bahrain cracked down on demonstrators, deterring further protests, and civil war broke out in Syria. Many of these events played out across social media platforms, including Facebook and Twitter, where protesters posted video, provided commentary, or simply communicated with friends and family. Indeed, social media were believed to be so central at the time that the Arab Spring was also called the "Twitter revolution." Yet, some have pushed back against the importance of social media as a political force, pointing out that "Twitter cannot stop a bullet."[a] What role did social media play in the Arab Spring?

Zachary C. Steinert-Threlkeld examined the effect of tweets on protest activity in 16 countries during the Arab Spring.[b] In any protest, there is safety in numbers—especially when the government is likely to target demonstrators. In considering whether to attend a protest, each person must anticipate whether others will attend as well, making protest a highly strategic interaction with other protesters and the state. Because the stakes are so high, individuals rely on many signals about the likely behavior of others. In the past, such signals included conversations with family and friends, declarations made in coffee shops, and encouragement from local religious or union leaders. Today, social media allow for broader communication in real time. Does wider communication make a difference?

Steinert-Threlkeld begins by distinguishing between "core" members of a community with numerous followers on Twitter, many of whom are likely political activists working with various transnational advocacy or nongovernmental organizations, and "peripheral" members, who have few followers. Core members, he argues, tweet a lot, are highly visible, and may be essential for planning protests. The 5 percent of Twitter users in Syria with the most followers,

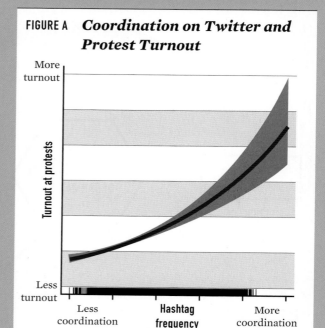

FIGURE A *Coordination on Twitter and Protest Turnout*

Source: Adapted from Zachary C. Steinert-Threlkeld, "Spontaneous Collective Action: Peripheral Mobilization during the Arab Spring," *American Political Science Review* 111, no. 2 (May 2017): 379–403.

for instance, sent out nearly 50 percent of all tweets in that country surrounding the 2011 protests. But protest turnout, he shows, is driven by peripheral individuals.

The more that peripheral members coordinate their activities, measured by the use of the same hashtags on Twitter, the more protests occur. Figure A shows that as individuals with fewer followers (the periphery) tweet using the same hashtags, representing more coordination, more protestors participate the next day. Conversely, frequent tweeters—core members—do not affect protest turnout; the corresponding graph (not shown) is essentially flat.

Frequent tweeters may be essential for planning protests, yet it's the tweets from everyday people that inspire protesters to show up. Rather than getting their information only from the local bar or market, protesters may coordinate their activities today more effectively through social media. Although we cannot know what would otherwise have happened in the Arab Spring, Twitter may have raised overall turnout—and helped to bring down several governments.

---

a. Jared Keller, "Evaluating Iran's Twitter Revolution," *Atlantic*, June 18, 2010, www.theatlantic.com/technology/archive/2010/06/evaluating-irans-twitter-revolution/58337.

b. Zachary C. Steinert-Threlkeld, "Spontaneous Collective Action: Peripheral Mobilization during the Arab Spring," *American Political Science Review* 111, no. 2 (May 2017): 379–403.

do not have a detailed understanding of its provisions. Furthermore, the voters who must reelect the executive who negotiated the deal, or the legislators who concurred, almost certainly do not know much about the agreement undertaken in their name.

Legislators and voters can learn whether to support or oppose an agreement from TANs that track the negotiations, study the final text, and endorse or reject its provisions. Legislators or voters need not know a great deal about the substance of the policy issue or the agreement, but they can make informed choices by taking cues from groups that (1) share their preferences or have some external incentive (such as penalties for lying) to truthfully reveal what they know and (2) possess real knowledge about the agreement.[33] Thus, in considering whether to support a proposed environmental treaty, a legislator need not study the text closely, but can observe whether representatives of a trustworthy TAN have endorsed the agreement and decide how to vote accordingly. Legislators who support tighter environmental regulations will vote for treaties endorsed by, say, the Sierra Club, Greenpeace, and similar organizations; those who prefer less stringent regulations will vote against treaties endorsed by those same groups.

The endorsements by TANs provide an informational shortcut that allows legislators and voters to make decisions (nearly) identical to those they would make if they were completely informed. TANs are often particularly effective endorsers precisely because they are perceived as principled actors with strongly held normative beliefs. When they speak for or against an issue on which they are perceived to possess expertise, their voices are typically quite loud and are heard clearly by legislators and voters.

By helping voters or legislators to make appropriate decisions on the basis of limited information, TANs enhance the prospects for cooperation between states. Whenever a domestic legislature must ratify an international agreement, the effect is to make cooperation between two countries either equally as likely or less likely than it is when only the executive is directly involved.[34] If the legislature is uncertain about the content and meaning of the agreement negotiated between the executive and the foreign state, it may mistakenly reject agreements that all three parties would prefer. Similar to the problem of bargaining in war (see Chapter 3), uncertainty makes bargaining inefficient and more likely to fail. TANs can reduce such uncertainty and improve the likelihood of cooperation by providing information to all the parties. In this way, TANs facilitate cooperation between states that would otherwise not occur.

---

33. This discussion draws on Arthur Lupia and Mathew D. McCubbins, *The Democratic Dilemma: Can Citizens Learn What They Need to Know?* (New York: Cambridge University Press, 1998).

34. See Helen V. Milner, *Interests, Institutions, and Information: Domestic Politics and International Relations* (Princeton, NJ: Princeton University Press, 1997). The existence of an effective legislature never makes cooperation more likely.

TANs as Monitors

TANs can also monitor whether and how states comply with international law and other agreements, as well as international norms. By revealing information about compliance, TANs allow states to have greater confidence that present and future agreements will be honored.

Having enacted a law, reached an agreement, or recognized a norm, states acquire information about compliance in one of three ways. First, they can rely on the self-reports of others. Many international agreements depend on this mechanism, requiring states to report on their efforts to reduce atmospheric emissions, for instance. This mechanism is, in fact, relatively weak, as states that have incentives to cheat on agreements are also likely to have incentives to lie about their cheating. Self-reports are useful only when they can be verified by one of the other mechanisms.

Second, states can monitor one another's behavior directly. For example, the arms control agreements negotiated between the United States and the Soviet Union during the Cold War depended on direct monitoring. Yet, direct monitoring is often quite expensive, as each state must expend resources in collecting information about often hard-to-observe behaviors by others. Direct monitoring is sometimes likened to police patrols actively circulating on their "beats" looking for violations of the law.[35] Such direct monitoring can be inefficient, since monitors must be in the field even when violations are not occurring. It can also be imperfect, since monitors may be occupied or distracted elsewhere when violations do occur. Nonetheless, this practice is a common means of monitoring compliance in international relations.

Third, states can monitor indirectly by listening to the testimony of trustworthy third parties. Here TANs can be useful in identifying and calling attention to violations of international agreements. Having championed the ban on land mines into international law, the ICBL now monitors state compliance very closely. Indirect monitoring is common in the human rights issue area, where organizations like Amnesty International and Human Rights Watch track practices globally and issue calls to their members and states when violations are observed.

Similar practices are emerging in the issue area of the environment. Nearly 10,000 NGOs were officially permitted to participate in the 1992 Earth Summit, the largest-ever gathering of national leaders to discuss protecting the environment. Not only did these organizations conduct a parallel summit and make policy proposals to the interstate meeting, but through their participation they were accredited and legitimized as the watchdogs of the agreements made at the conference. With its new acceptance and prominence, this transnational environmental network has played an important role in calling international attention to poor environmental policies and practices worldwide.

---

35. See Mathew D. McCubbins and Thomas Schwartz, "Congressional Oversight Overlooked: Police Patrols versus Fire Alarms," *American Journal of Political Science* 28, no. 1 (February 1984): 165–79.

TANs may protest complex international laws to draw broader public attention to policies that they find objectionable. Greenpeace frequently stages outsize demonstrations that it knows will attract an audience against laws that it sees as harmful to the environment.

Indirect monitoring is similar to fire alarms: when problems arise, concerned parties pull the alarm and alert others who respond, but only when necessary.[36] When trustworthy monitors are available, indirect monitoring is far less expensive to states and more efficient than the alternatives. By facilitating monitoring and reducing its costs, TANs help promote cooperation that states would otherwise be reluctant to pursue.

Conclusion: Can States Be Constrained?

Can state behavior be changed by international law and norms? This remains a lively debate in which scholars do not have settled answers. On one side, traditionalists argue that international law binds states only to the extent they want to be bound; in turn, transnational networks exist only because states that might otherwise regulate, control, and limit the interactions of those networks permit them to flourish. From this perspective, international law is at best a soft constraint, and TANs and the norms they promote reflect the interests and international prominence of liberal, democratic states that have active domestic civil societies and project these onto the global system. Were these states to weaken or choose otherwise,

---

36. McCubbins and Schwartz, "Congressional Oversight Overlooked." On the credibility of transnational NGOs, see Peter Gourevitch, David A. Lake, and Janice Gross Stein, eds., *The Credibility of Transnational NGOs: When Virtue Is Not Enough* (New York: Cambridge University Press, 2012).

both international law and international norms might be undercut by less supportive governments.[37]

On the other side, globalists argue that international law and transnational networks are emerging as effective forms of global governance. In this view, political authority previously exercised by states is migrating to new supranational authorities, which can regulate states through international law, and to TANs, which are gradually assuming some responsibilities formerly fulfilled by states.[38] Here, law is respected because of the large gains from the cooperation it facilitates, and TANs are promoting new norms of global civil society and pressing states to change their behavior. For the globalists, international law and norms are increasingly constraining states in their actions both at home and with one another.

As with all such debates, there are no easy answers. The growth of international law and norms does appear to be changing patterns of state interaction in some issue areas, including human rights and the environment, discussed in the following chapters. International law constrains some actions of some states at least some of the time, punishing or at least sullying the reputation of states that violate legitimate rules. TANs make cooperation between countries more likely by serving as endorsers and monitors of international agreements. They perform essential roles in supporting and observing compliance with both the international human rights and environmental regimes.

Although the traditionalists may be correct in their view that states, in principle, still have the authority to set international law and control transnational groups, it is not clear that they retain the ability or political will to do so. Precisely because international law and norms are often useful to states, it will become increasingly difficult for states to ignore their restraints.

Globalists, however, may exaggerate the extent to which international law and TANs can substitute for government at the global level. International law is still hampered by the need for self-enforcement. TANs that are active in promoting social causes are voluntary associations that cannot legally bind their own members, much less others. Lacking the political authority attributed to states, they must rely on voluntary compliance from their targets, which is often uneven.

Despite the hopes of some, international law and norms appear not to have displaced the central role of states on the world stage. States make international law. Even though TANs are influencing interests, the norms advocated

37. Among other traditionalist sources, see Robert Gilpin, *Global Political Economy* (Princeton, NJ: Princeton University Press, 2001), chap. 15; and Stephan D. Krasner, "Power Politics, Institutions, and Transnational Relations," in *Bringing Transnational Relations Back In: Non-state Actors, Domestic Structures and International Institutions*, ed. Thomas Risse-Kappen, 257–79 (New York: Cambridge University Press, 1995).

38. See David Held, Anthony G. McGrew, David Goldblatt, and Jonathan Perraton, *Global Transformations: Politics, Economics, and Culture* (Stanford, CA: Stanford University Press, 1999), esp. chap. 1; Walter Mattli, "Public and Private Governance in Setting International Standards," in *Governance in a Global Economy: Political Authority in Transition*, ed. Miles Kahler and David A. Lake, 199–225 (Princeton, NJ: Princeton University Press, 2012); and Virginia Haufler, "Globalization and Industry Self-Regulation," in Kahler and Lake, *Governance in a Global Economy*, 226–52.

by TANs are still very much norms about appropriate *state* behavior. It is the human rights, environmental, economic, and political practices of *states* that TANs typically seek to change. Similarly, although TANs activate transnational linkages, they do so to mobilize foreign groups to urge their *states* to press the offending state to change its policy. Finally, although TANs facilitate cooperation, it is cooperation between and among *states* that is altered, and the information the TANs provide is about states to other states. Even as law and TANs have proliferated and grown in prominence, world politics remains very much an arena of states.

Study Tool Kit

Interests, Interactions, and Institutions in Context

- International law and norms are institutions that seek to shape how states understand their interests and to constrain the ways in which they interact.

- States create and abide by international law because of the cooperation it enables. Although states are typically dependent on "self-help" for enforcement, the benefits of cooperation to states are often large enough that international laws are self-enforcing, or in the interests of states to follow apparently willingly.

- International norms affect world politics by changing how individuals and, in turn, states conceive of their interests and appropriate actions in their interactions with other states.

- TANs have an important effect on world politics by promoting normative values. TANs also alter interactions between states and facilitate cooperation by providing information about international agreements and monitoring compliance.

Key Terms

international law, p. 465

customary international law, p. 467

obligation, p. 469

precision, p. 469

delegation, p. 470

norms, p. 475

norms entrepreneurs, p. 482

transnational advocacy network (TAN), p. 482

norms life cycle, p. 485

boomerang model, p. 488

For Further Reading

Abbott, Kenneth W., Jessica F. Green, and Robert O. Keohane, "Organizational Ecology and Institutional Change in Global Governance," *International Organization* 70, no. 2 (April 2016): 247–77. Explains the role of private transnational regulatory organizations in global environmental politics.

Adler-Nissen, Rebecca. "Stigma Management in International Relations: Transgressive Identities, Norms, and Order in International Society." *International Organization* 68, no. 1 (2014): 143–76. Demonstrates that international order is formed in part by stigmatizing nonconforming and norm-violating states.

Goldstein, Judith L., Miles Kaher, Robert O. Keohane, and Anne-Marie Slaughter, eds. *Legalization and World Politics*. Cambridge, MA: MIT Press, 2001. Some of the best contemporary research on international law by political scientists.

Guzman, Andrew T. *How International Law Works: A Rational Choice Theory*. New York: Oxford University Press, 2008. Explains how international law can succeed through reciprocity, reputation, and retaliation even in the absence of third-party enforcement.

Hathaway, Oona A., and Scott J. Shapiro. *The Internationalists: How a Radical Plan to Outlaw War Remade the World*. New York: Simon and Schuster, 2017. A lively historical account of the 1928 plan to abolish war through international law, with relevance to today.

Keck, Margaret E., and Kathryn Sikkink. *Activists beyond Borders: Advocacy Networks in International Politics*. Ithaca, NY: Cornell University Press, 1998. A classic study of the growth and role of TANs.

Morrow, James D. *Order within Anarchy: The Laws of War as an International Institution*. New York: Cambridge University Press, 2014. Examines how law conditions expectations and state behavior in the context of the Geneva Conventions.

Stroup, Sarah S., and Wendy H. Wong. *The Authority Trap: Strategic Choices of International NGOs*. Ithaca, NY: Cornell University Press, 2017. Explores how leading NGOs command deference from various powerful audiences and influence the practices of states, corporations, and other organizations.

Towns, Ann E. *Women and States: Norms and Hierarchies in International Society*. New York: Cambridge University Press, 2010. Examines the changing international norms that govern the relationship between women and their states.

12

Human Rights

THE PUZZLE *Why do states undertake costly actions to protect the human rights of people outside their borders? In light of the widespread support for the principle of human rights, why has the movement to protect those rights not been even more successful?*

Above: Since the end of apartheid in the early 1990s, South Africa's Black majority has held control of the country's government and institutions. Here, supporters celebrate at a rally for the ruling African National Congress, the party of Nelson Mandela.

For over 40 years, the White-dominated government of South Africa pursued a strict policy of racial segregation and inequality called apartheid. Distinguishing among Whites, Indians, Coloureds, and Africans or Blacks, this policy assigned everyone to a "homeland" within the territory of the state, regulated movement into the cities and employment, and created a system of racial discrimination designed to perpetuate the political and economic dominance of the White minority. Human rights abuses under apartheid were widespread. In addition to denying the political, economic, social, and cultural rights of more than three-quarters of the country's population, the White government engaged in arbitrary arrests and detentions without trial, as well as torture and executions without judicial review. The full extent of the abuses perpetrated by the regime was revealed only by the post-apartheid Truth and Reconciliation Commission.[1]

Transnational advocacy networks (TANs; see Chapter 11) worked closely with South African opposition groups to bring international pressure against the apartheid regime. In November 1962, the United Nations (UN) General Assembly adopted Resolution 1761 condemning apartheid and calling for all countries to terminate economic and military relations with South Africa. The country was excluded from the Organization of African Unity at the institution's founding in 1963 and was expelled from Olympic Games membership in 1968. The UN Security Council adopted a mandatory embargo on weapons sales to the White regime in 1977.

As domestic unrest flared in 1984 following constitutional reforms that gave political rights to Indians and Coloureds but not to Africans, the government began a brutal crackdown. To signal their displeasure with the widespread human rights abuses, by 1986 all of South Africa's major trading partners—including the United States—had adopted economic sanctions. Often under pressure from student protests that forced universities to flex the power of their endowments, some foreign firms ended their investments in South Africa.[2]

1. David Black, "The Long and Winding Road: International Norms and Domestic Political Change in South Africa," in *The Power of Human Rights: International Norms and Domestic Change*, ed. Thomas Risse, Stephen C. Ropp, and Kathryn Sikkink (New York: Cambridge University Press, 1999), 80.

2. Audie Klotz, *Norms in International Relations: The Struggle against Apartheid* (Ithaca, NY: Cornell University Press, 1995).

Increasing internal dissent, both nonviolent and violent, combined with international censure to finally end apartheid in 1990 and start the peaceful transition to Black-majority rule in 1994. Primary credit for the repeal of apartheid goes to the brave South African men, women, and children of all backgrounds who stood up against the racist regime. Nonetheless, the anti-apartheid struggle stands out for two larger effects on the global human rights movement.

First, the national struggle played out on a global stage. Blocked at home from influencing the White regime, the Black majority appealed to allies abroad for support. By documenting and publicizing abuses and by mobilizing activists worldwide, TANs helped bring about the end of the long-standing practice of systematic racial discrimination. The struggle against apartheid set a visible precedent for TAN activity and success in the broad area of human rights.

Second, the anti-apartheid struggle demonstrated that states are, at times, willing to bear costs to express their disapproval of other governments and to support the victims of widespread human rights abuses. Not all states cooperated in the movement to repeal apartheid, and some were pushed into doing so only by vigorous pressure from activists. Nonetheless, opposing apartheid was an important turning point for states in using their influence to isolate and punish regimes that systematically abuse their own people.

Despite the success in ending apartheid, the effort to promote human rights in other countries is highly uneven. Concerns remain about human rights practices in many places, including China, Myanmar, Russia, Syria, and even the United States with regard to the death penalty and the treatment of detainees in the global war on terror. Although nearly everyone supports human rights in principle, and many rights are codified in international law, disagreement continues on what constitutes a human right and when human rights should be protected.

Human rights violations in one country rarely affect the material welfare of other peoples, the principal exception being when political conflict within a country generates significant refugee flows into other countries. Moreover, noninterference by others in a state's internal affairs is a defining and often highly treasured principle of national sovereignty—a principle that the apartheid regime appealed to repeatedly in an effort to insulate itself from foreign scrutiny. By condemning the human rights abuses of others, states not only violate this norm of noninterference, but risk opening themselves to foreign interference. Why do states undertake costly actions, such as sanctioning South Africa, with no immediate benefit to themselves or their own citizens?

As the example of South Africa makes clear, human rights practices around the globe are undoubtedly better than they would be without broad support for human rights, international laws governing how states treat their citizens, TANs "naming and shaming" abusers, and states occasionally punishing violators with sanctions. Yet few countries respect all human rights, and a significant number of countries violate many of these rights. Why isn't international human rights law more effective?

Thinking Analytically about Human Rights

In addressing this puzzle, our discussion considers the interests, interactions, and institutions involved in international human rights. First, we will see that international human rights law is an institution created by and largely reflecting the political norms and values of Western, liberal democracies. The norms embodied in these laws are not shared equally by all countries and have not yet been internalized by many societies and governments. Thus, even when formally codified, they remain controversial.

The interests and interactions involved in enforcing human rights help explain both why some actors work hard to promote human rights abroad and why states that violate human rights do so despite international norms. Individuals have an interest in international human rights, and this is why they sometimes encourage their leaders to take action to punish states that violate rights. But, as we will see, these interests are rarely strong enough to compel states to pay the high costs to protect vulnerable individuals and groups outside their own borders.

Thus, states that violate human rights anticipate that in their interactions with other states, they probably will not face serious consequences for their behavior and, therefore, can abuse individuals and groups without significant penalties. Unfortunately, these states are most likely correct. International human rights law does indeed promote improved practices. Its full promise, however, has not yet been realized.

What Are International Human Rights?

Human rights are rights that all individuals possess by virtue of being human, regardless of their status as citizens of particular states or members of a group or organization. These rights are, by definition, universal and apply to all humans equally.

The concept of human rights has a long philosophical tradition, dating from the Enlightenment in the eighteenth century. English philosopher John Locke (1632–1704) first developed the modern notion of natural rights, the idea that people are by nature free and equal and, therefore, possess certain basic rights that are not contingent on the laws, customs, or beliefs of any particular society or government. This idea then informed the American and French Revolutions, embodied in the famous second sentence of the Declaration of Independence, which states "that all men are created equal, that they are endowed by their Creator with certain unalienable rights, that among these are life, liberty and the pursuit of happiness."

The first concrete international steps toward regulating how governments treat their citizens were undertaken in the UN Charter, adopted in 1945. This movement was spurred by the atrocities of World War II, especially the Holocaust, in which at least 6 million Jews and other minorities were systematically "dehumanized" and killed. Article 55 of the charter states that "based on respect for the principle of equal rights and self-determination of peoples, the United Nations shall promote . . . universal respect for, and observance of, human rights and fundamental freedoms for all without distinction as to race, sex, language, or religion."

Soon after the United Nations was founded, work began on an effort to clarify which rights Article 55 embodied and which rights states would be expected to protect. The **Universal Declaration of Human Rights (UDHR)**,[3] adopted by the UN General Assembly in 1948, is the product of those deliberations. Defined as a "common standard of achievement for all peoples" and broadly accepted as the foundation of modern human rights law, its 30 articles identify a diverse set of rights. Although governed only by soft law (see Chapter 11), the UDHR is today considered to be the authoritative standard of human rights.

René Cassin, one of the main authors of the UDHR, described the document as having four pillars, supporting "dignity, liberty, equality, and brotherhood." Each of the pillars represents a different historical principle and philosophy of human rights. The first two articles of the UDHR stand for a timeless human dignity shared by all individuals regardless of race, religion, nationality, or sex. Articles 3–21 of the declaration define a first generation of civil liberties and other rights founded in a Western philosophical and legal tradition begun during the Enlightenment, such as freedom of speech and association, and equal protection and recognition before the law.

human rights

The rights possessed by all individuals by virtue of being human, regardless of their status as citizens of particular states or members of a group or organization.

Universal Declaration of Human Rights (UDHR)

A declaration, adopted by the UN General Assembly in 1948, that defines a "common standard of achievement for all peoples" and forms the foundation of modern human rights law.

---

3. See www.hrweb.org/legal/udhr.html (accessed 11/5/2017).

The UDHR establishes that everyone has a right to education and that elementary education shall be free. The United Nations estimates that 58 million children do not have a school to go to.

Articles 22–26 focus on political, social, and economic equality—a second generation of rights that emerged during the Industrial Revolution and that is often associated with socialist thought. This second generation includes the rights to employment, to an adequate standard of living, to forming trade unions, and to education.

Articles 27 and 28 address rights of communal and national solidarity, first developed in the late nineteenth century and championed by the states emerging from colonialism.[4] This last generation of rights, however, is far less developed in the UDHR than the first two generations are.

In tandem with the UDHR, the UN negotiated the Convention on the Prevention and Punishment of the Crime of Genocide, the first human rights treaty with clearly defined obligations and precise rules. The term *genocide* was coined by Raphael Lemkin, a Polish lawyer of Jewish descent who immigrated to the United States in 1941, to capture the essence of what happened during the Holocaust. It combines the Greek word *genos*, for "race" or "people," with the Latin word *cidere*, "to kill." The Genocide Convention, as the UN initiative is widely known, follows Lemkin closely in defining genocide as "acts committed with the intent to destroy, in whole or part, a national, ethnical, racial or religious group."

Pushed to the forefront of the human rights agenda because of the Holocaust, the Genocide Convention became the first piece of hard international human rights law. With 148 state parties to the agreement, this is one of the more widely recognized and supported treaties ever written.[5] The United States signed the treaty in

4. Micheline R. Ishay, *The History of Human Rights: From Ancient Times to the Globalization Era* (Berkeley: University of California Press, 2004), 3–4.

5. See https://treaties.un.org/Pages/ViewDetails.aspx?src=IND&mtdsg_no=IV-1&chapter=4&clang=_en (accessed 09/24/17).

1948 but did not ratify it until 40 years later. Senator William Proxmire (Democrat from Wisconsin), a major supporter, was well known for his daily speeches in favor of ratification (a total of 3,211), given on the floor every day the Senate was in session between 1967 and the Senate vote on the treaty in 1986.

After negotiating the UDHR and the Genocide Convention, the UN then began the much more difficult task of translating the UDHR into legally binding and internationally enforceable treaties. Unfolding over 18 years, the negotiations eventually produced two separate agreements: the **International Covenant on Civil and Political Rights (ICCPR)** and the **International Covenant on Economic, Social, and Cultural Rights (ICESCR)**.[6]

Although there was nearly universal agreement on the UDHR, the attempt to write hard international law protecting human rights got caught, like so many other attempts at cooperation, between the superpowers during the Cold War. The solution was to write two separate treaties: one focusing on the civil and political rights of liberty then favored by Western states, the other focusing on the economic, social, and cultural rights of equality and brotherhood supported by the then Communist states and others in the developing world. As formal treaties completed in 1966 and in force from 1976, the twin covenants are considered legally binding for all states that have signed them.

The ICCPR details the basic rights of individuals and nations, defining in sometimes more precise terms the political and civil rights first claimed in the UDHR. The ICCPR affirms the rights to life, liberty, and the freedom of movement; the presumption of innocence; equal standing before the law; legal recourse when rights have been violated; and privacy. In addition, all individuals are guaranteed freedom of thought, conscience, and religion; freedom of opinion and expression; and freedom of assembly and association. The covenant forbids torture and inhumane or degrading punishment, slavery and involuntary servitude, and arbitrary arrest and detention. It also prohibits propaganda advocating war or hatred based on race, religion, or national origin.

The ICCPR also provides for the right of all people to choose freely whom they will marry and to found a family, and it requires that the duties and obligations of marriage and family be shared equally between partners. It guarantees the rights of children and prohibits discrimination based on race, sex, color, national origin, or language. It restricts the death penalty to the most serious of crimes, guarantees condemned people the right to appeal for commutation to a lesser penalty, and forbids the death penalty entirely for people under 18 years of age.

As of March 2018, 170 of the UN's 193 member countries were parties to the ICCPR. The United States ratified the treaty in 1992, but only after declaring that its provisions were "not self-executing"—meaning that although the agreement is binding as a matter of international law, its provisions would not automatically become domestic law without further legislation by the U.S. Congress. Human rights practices under the covenant are monitored by the UN Human Rights

International Covenant on Civil and Political Rights (ICCPR)

The agreement, completed in 1966 and in force from 1976, that details the basic civil and political rights of individuals and nations. The ICCPR and ICESCR together are known as the "twin covenants."

International Covenant on Economic, Social, and Cultural Rights (ICESCR)

The agreement, completed in 1966 and in force from 1976, that specifies the basic economic, social, and cultural rights of individuals and nations. The ICCPR and ICESCR together are known as the "twin covenants."

---

6. For more information on the covenants and their texts, see www.ohchr.org/EN/ProfessionalInterest/Pages/InternationalLaw.aspx (accessed 09/24/17).

There are 84 parties to an optional protocol to the ICCPR aimed at abolishing the death penalty. The protesters here delivered a petition to the U.S. embassy in Hong Kong, calling for the United States to stop executions.

Committee, a group of 18 experts who meet three times a year to consider periodic reports submitted by member states on their compliance with the treaty and interstate complaints of violations.

The parallel ICESCR reiterates and affirms the basic economic, social, and cultural rights of individuals and nations, including the right to earn wages sufficient to support a minimum standard of living; equal pay for equal work; equal opportunity for advancement; the right to form trade unions and strike; paid or otherwise compensated maternity leave; free primary education and accessible schools at all levels; and copyright, patent, and trademark protection for intellectual property. The treaty forbids the exploitation of children and requires all countries to cooperate to end world hunger. Each nation that has ratified this covenant is required to submit reports on its progress in providing for these rights to the secretary-general of the UN. The ICESCR currently has 165 members. The United States signed the covenant in 1977 under President Jimmy Carter but has never ratified it, because of continuing opposition to provisions that would go substantially beyond existing domestic laws.

Together, the UDHR and the twin covenants are often referred to as the **International Bill of Rights**. Over time, additional rights have been added through supplementary conventions, as summarized in Table 12.1. The agreements listed in the table highlight the range of rights that are now more or less protected under international law, including, in certain cases, the right of individual petition through which victims of human rights abuses can seek redress directly from international courts. In short, as the list demonstrates, the international community now possesses an extensive body of international human rights law, albeit one that remains controversial and possesses varying degrees of national support for different provisions.

International Bill of Rights

The UDHR, ICCPR, and ICESCR collectively. Together, these three agreements form the core of the international human rights regime.

Why Are Human Rights Controversial?

Because of differing legal traditions, domestic political regimes and institutions, and philosophies, states often have different interests in human rights. Even though human rights are by definition universal, states do not necessarily have the same interests in promoting the same rights to the same extent. States have interests in supporting rights that they already respect domestically and in fighting against new rights that they see as costly to protect. They also have an interest in preserving their own sovereignty. States may also have a strategic interest in promoting rights that their adversaries will deny or find costly to implement.

Many of the rights defined in the UDHR—especially many of the economic and social rights—are drawn directly from President Franklin D. Roosevelt's New Deal,

TABLE 12.1 *UN Human Rights Agreements*

TREATY	DATE SIGNED/IN FORCE	BRIEF DESCRIPTION
Universal Declaration of Human Rights (UDHR)	1948	Outlines basic human rights.
Convention on the Prevention and Punishment of the Crime of Genocide	1948/1951	Bans acts committed with the intent to destroy, in whole or part, a national, ethnic, racial, or religious group.
International Convention on the Elimination of All Forms of Racial Discrimination (ICERD)	1965/1969	Bans all racial discrimination, with particular attention to policies and practices of apartheid.
International Covenant on Economic, Social, and Cultural Rights (ICESCR)	1966/1976	Details the basic economic, social, and cultural rights of individuals and nations.
International Covenant on Civil and Political Rights (ICCPR)	1966/1976	Details the basic civil and political rights of individuals and nations. Optional protocol (1966/1976) permits petitions from individuals. Second optional protocol (1989/1991) commits state parties to abolish the death penalty.
Convention on the Elimination of All Forms of Discrimination against Women (CEDAW)	1979/1981	Bans discrimination against women, focusing on education, employment, health, marriage, and the family. Optional protocol (1999/2000) permits petitions from individuals.
Convention against Torture and Other Cruel, Inhuman or Degrading Treatment or Punishment (CAT)	1984/1987	Bans torture under all circumstances. Optional protocol (2002/2006) establishes regular visits to monitor state practice.
Convention on the Rights of the Child (CRC)	1989/1990	Details the special rights of children. Optional protocol (2000/2002) bans children in the armed forces from participating in hostilities. Second optional protocol (2000/2002) prohibits the sale of children, child prostitution, and child pornography. Third optional protocol (2011/2014) allows the submission of complaints by individual children.
International Convention on the Protection of the Rights of All Migrant Workers and Members of Their Families (ICRMW)	1990/2003	Details the special rights of workers outside their country of origin.
Convention on the Rights of Persons with Disabilities (CRPD)	2007/2008	Mandates equal status and treatment for individuals with disabilities. Optional protocol (2007/2008) permits petitions from individuals.
International Convention for the Protection of All Persons from Enforced Disappearance	2007/2010	Prohibits arrest, detention, or abduction of individuals without acknowledgment by the state.

Note: For texts and updated membership information, consult www.ohchr.org/EN/ProfessionalInterest/Pages/InternationalLaw.aspx (accessed 07/24/17).

adopted during the Great Depression of the 1930s. Through the 1950s, many people in the United States and other Western countries remained supporters of economic and social rights. As the New Deal lost popularity, however, support for enshrining many of its progressive policies into international law diminished.

Human rights also became caught up in the Cold War competition of ideas. In public forums, Western states tended to emphasize first-generation civil and political rights already enshrined in their own systems, while the countries of the Soviet bloc and many countries in the developing world trumpeted their superior progress on second-generation economic, social, and cultural rights. This Cold War division and historical legacy continues to undermine support for the ICESCR in the United States today. Many U.S. conservatives, for instance, question whether economic, social, and cultural rights are actually rights at all, since they pertain to particular classes or groups of people (for example, workers) rather than to all human beings.[7]

Critics of the rights specified in the UDHR point to their origin in a Western, liberal philosophical tradition that emphasizes first-generation individual rights over second- and third-generation collective rights. This is correct—to a point. The modern idea of human rights is rooted in a moral vision that sees all humans as equal and autonomous individuals. Political scientist Jack Donnelly observes that "it is a relatively simple matter to derive the full list of rights in the Universal Declaration from the political principle of equal concern and respect."[8]

Although the rights founded in this tradition may now be accepted because of their status as international standards and law, the philosophical tradition itself is not universally shared. An alternative philosophy, for example, is the notion of "Asian values," which elevates the rights of families and communities and the goal of social and political stability over the rights of individuals (see "What Shaped Our World?" on p. 507). The debate over which rights individuals have continues, under-scoring the point that rights are an institution that evolves over time. International human rights are not fixed, but are a product of struggle, debate, and social inter-ests. Although nearly everyone may agree that some human rights exist in principle, debate continues on exactly which rights humans possess.

This continuing debate also demonstrates that human rights have not been internalized as norms in all societies and governments. Although more deeply held in Western, democratic countries, few human rights have obtained the taken-for-granted quality in which violations are considered taboo or inappropriate, except in the most dire circumstances. Freedom from torture is likely one of the most widely and deeply held human rights, but the ongoing debate in the United States on the treatment of terrorist suspects suggests that even for some Americans, torture or practices that border on torture remain acceptable instruments of government policy.

---

7. Jack Donnelly, *Universal Human Rights in Theory and Practice*, 3rd ed. (Ithaca, NY: Cornell University Press, 2013), 40.

8. Donnelly, *Universal Human Rights in Theory and Practice*, 63.

The Asian Values Debate

Although there is broad agreement that human rights are important, as reflected in the near-universal support for the UDHR and the twin covenants, exactly which rights should be priorities remains contested. Some of the most controversial questions about promoting human rights arose in the Asian values debate of the 1990s, a controversy that continues today in slightly altered form.

Interests For many human rights advocates, the *Universal Declaration of Human Rights* is aptly titled. However, an alternative, "Asian values" approach to human rights was propounded by Southeast Asian leaders in the 1990s, most visibly Mahathir Mohamad of Malaysia and Lee Kuan Yew of Singapore. As East Asian countries began to develop more rapidly, often under authoritarian governments and with a notable degree of state guidance of the economy, their leaders asserted a distinct and, in their view, superior "Asian" approach to human rights.

Interactions The key articulation of the Asian values approach was the Bangkok Declaration of 1993. This document affirmed the commitment of signatories to the UDHR, while also stressing the principles of sovereignty and noninterference. The Bangkok Declaration departed from the standard approach, however, in calling for greater attention to economic, social, and cultural rights and downplaying political rights and civil liberties. Proponents argued that Asian societies were founded on a philosophy that emphasizes the welfare of the community over individual freedoms. Rooted in Confucian thought, Asian values were said to prioritize respect for authority and social harmony.

Critics of this position charged that it was simply cover for the authoritarian rule of Mahathir, Lee, and other political leaders within the region. Lee had been in power since 1959, and though he was often described as a "benevolent dictator," he detained without trial hundreds of alleged extremists, and he ruthlessly crushed political opposition. Mahathir was criticized for imprisoning political activists, including his rival Anwar Ibrahim, and for undermining the independence of the judiciary.

As their countries succeeded economically, these leaders pushed back against their critics by appealing to different political principles and cultural affinities. Mahathir in 1997 called the UDHR an "oppressing" instrument by which the United States and other countries tried to impose Western values on Asians, adding that Asians needed stability and economic growth more than civil liberties.[a]

Institutions The Asian values debate was a significant attempt to alter the underlying norms of human rights that had developed largely under the influence of Europe and the United States in the postwar period. As an institution, the UDHR was broad enough that all could see their respective priorities within it, so the controversy was really over priorities.

As the debate unfolded, however, Lee of Singapore went further and criticized Western individualism for the perceived decadence of Western societies, including high rates of crime, drug abuse, and family breakdown. The debate was eventually cast not just as one of cultural differences over human rights priorities, but as one of cultural superiority. This change in focus hardened differences on both sides of the debate. Support for Asian values as a distinct approach to human rights waned after the Asian financial crisis of 1997, which called into question the economic success on which much of the movement rested.

Today, emphasis on a distinct Asian understanding of human rights is once again building under China's growing international leadership. As with the earlier Asian values campaign, appeals to Confucius—this time from China's Xi Jinping, among others—affirm party authority and subordinate political and civil rights to the need for political stability and growth. Even when nearly all countries sign on to a human rights institution like the UDHR, the specific rights that will be prioritized in practice remain contested.

---

a. Stephen Chapman, "Is Democracy Foreign to 'Asian Values'?" *Chicago Tribune*, July 31, 1997, http://articles.chicagotribune.com/1997-07-31/news/9707310080_1_asian-values-southeast-asian-nations-human-rights.

Some human rights activists have argued that the U.S. government has violated the rights of the 41 remaining detainees held at Guantánamo Bay, Cuba. They are concerned about harsh interrogation methods and the lack of due process of law.

The power of the anti-torture principle was evident in the attempt by President George W. Bush's administration to deny that it was engaging in torture by redefining some practices, such as waterboarding, as not inconsistent with international law—an interpretation not supported by most other states. President Donald Trump has taken an even more aggressive stance and publicly defended torture while on the campaign trail. "Only a stupid person would say it doesn't work," he stated. And even if it does not, he concluded, those being tortured "deserve it anyway, for what they're doing."[9]

Actual practice suggests that the norm against torture is, in fact, ambiguous and fails to significantly constrain government behavior. That human rights norms have not yet been internalized or, at best, are only weakly internalized implies that individuals and states still act on human rights and enforce laws only when it is in their self-interest to do so.

Are Some Rights More Important than Others?

Although the UDHR specifies a wide range of rights, it appears that (to paraphrase George Orwell's *Animal Farm*) although all rights are equal, some are more equal than others. Few, if any, human rights are internalized as norms, but some rights in the UDHR and ICCPR do have a special status in international law and, along with the Genocide Convention, appear to have broader support than others.

In the ICCPR, Article 4 permits the suspension of some rights in cases of social or public emergency, but it simultaneously identifies a small number of other rights that cannot be suspended for any reason. These **nonderogable rights** include freedom from torture or cruel and degrading punishment; recognition as a person before the law; and freedom of thought, conscience, and religion.[10] In contrast, none of the rights identified in the ICESCR are nonderogable, and all can be limited by states acting under the law. Despite their special status, however, nonderogable rights are not automatically enforced more than other rights, as the continuing practice of torture in countries around the world makes clear.

In turn, many of these nonderogable rights have gained special support within human rights TANs. Amnesty International, generally considered the world's leading human rights organization, identifies its core mission as protecting individuals from torture; cruel, inhuman, or degrading punishment; and arbitrary arrest, detention,

nonderogable rights
Rights that cannot be suspended for any reason, including at times of public emergency.

9. Adam Serwer, "Can Trump Bring Back Torture?" *Atlantic*, January 26, 2017, www.theatlantic.com/politics/archive/2017/01/trump-torture/514463.

10. Specifically, Article 4 prohibits the suspension of Articles 6 (inherent right to life, referring to the death penalty), 7 (torture), 8 (paragraphs 1 and 2, on slavery and servitude), 11 (imprisonment from contractual obligation), 15 (ex post facto criminal offenses), 16 (recognition before the law), and 18 (freedom of thought, conscience, and religion).

and exile, as well as defending the freedoms of thought, conscience, religion, opinion, and expression.[11] Individuals imprisoned solely for the peaceful expression of their beliefs are what Amnesty International calls **prisoners of conscience (POCs)**. One prominent POC was the recently deceased Nobel Peace Prize winner Liu Xiaobo, who was jailed in 2009 simply for coauthoring a proposal for political and legal reform in China.

The focus of Amnesty International, overlapping to a considerable extent with the nonderogable rights of the ICCPR, is shared by many human rights organizations. In focusing on these more limited rights and publicizing violations of only these rights, Amnesty has done much to influence notions of what human rights are today. To the extent that certain rights have become or moved toward becoming international norms, as explained in Chapter 11, Amnesty International and the other major human rights organizations that make up the TAN have had much to do with shaping this process. Building support for human rights and changing conceptions of interests for both individuals and states on human rights practices has been a major achievement of TANs.

Finally, by examining when states are willing to incur costs in order to punish human rights violations in other states, we can infer something about which rights are most important to them. Economic sanctions are a common tool that states use to punish violators of human rights (see "Controversy" on p. 510). For example, states may limit trade, loans, or travel to the target country in order to put pressure on the government to improve political and civil rights. Since sanctions also inflict costs on states that impose them, these states must weigh their interest in defending certain rights against their other priorities. Indeed, many violations of human rights go entirely unpunished, sometimes even unnoticed. Actual sanctions by states against violators are relatively rare. But when states have taken steps to impose sanctions against human rights abusers, these steps have almost always been for unfair political detentions and torture, and the suspension of peaceful political opposition.[12]

For instance, the United States imposed sanctions on South Korea and Chile in 1973 for the detention and treatment of political prisoners, and on Paraguay, Guatemala, Argentina, Nicaragua, El Salvador, and Brazil in 1977 for the same issues. Even in the case of South Africa, sanctions were not imposed against the country for its policy of apartheid in general, but only after the insurrection began and the South African government brutally repressed political opponents. States clearly act to enforce some rights more frequently than others. In practice, the rights that states appear ready to defend are narrower than the full range of rights articulated in the UDHR and may, in fact, be limited to the nonderogable rights identified in the ICCPR.

Overall, as an institution, international human rights remain a work in progress. Although codified in at least soft law, rights are themselves objects of

prisoners of conscience (POCs)

Individuals imprisoned solely because of the peaceful expression of their beliefs. The term was coined by the human rights organization Amnesty International.

---

11. Articles 5, 9, 18, and 19 of the UDHR.

12. See David A. Lake and Wendy Wong, "The Politics of Networks: Interests, Power, and Human Rights Norms," in *Networked Politics: Agency, Power, and Governance*, ed. Miles Kahler (Ithaca, NY: Cornell University Press, 2009), 148.

Should Economic Sanctions Be Imposed on Governments That Violate Human Rights?

In 2017, the United States imposed new or continuing economic sanctions on nearly 20 countries, often for human rights violations by the governments. However, sanctions also affect the ordinary people living in the target countries. Using economic leverage to try to promote better protection of political and civil rights poses a difficult moral question: If sanctions can reduce human rights abuses by governments, but only at the cost of increased suffering by average citizens, are they justified?

Applying the Concepts

Sanctions are most often imposed when countries have opposing **interests**, whether the differences are over human rights practices, the development of new weapons, or some other issue. Restricting trade, travel, or new loans is an **interaction** or, more specifically, a form of coercion, intended to raise the cost of certain actions to the target state, and thereby change its behavior. Since sanctions must be imposed by many, if not all, countries to be effective—as the target can otherwise obtain needed commodities or finance from nonparticipating countries—they are most likely to be effective when coordinated through a multilateral **institution**, like the United Nations. Because countries may not have similar interests, much as the United States and Russia differ on the war in Syria and the sanctions against the regime of Bashar al-Assad, getting agreement at the UN or elsewhere can be difficult.

One of the most troubling cases of sanctions were those imposed against Iraq after the Persian Gulf War of 1991. Four days after Iraq's invasion of Kuwait, the UN Security Council passed a resolution imposing economic sanctions on Iraq, including a trade embargo on all exports to the country other than basic food and medical supplies.[a] Although the war ended quickly, the sanctions continued for the next 12 years.

One justification for maintaining the policy was that restrictions on international trade and finance would sap Saddam Hussein's power and thereby end the human rights abuses that the autocrat had inflicted on the Iraqi people. Yet the World Health Organization reported in March 1996 that, among other detrimental effects, sanctions-related deprivations in Iraq had caused infant mortality to rise by a factor of six, equivalent to the deaths of hundreds of thousands of children under age five.[b] Denis Halliday, the UN humanitarian coordinator for Iraq, condemned the sanctions. Resigning in 1998 after a 34-year career with the United Nations, he described the program in Iraq as "satisfying the definition of genocide."[c]

In light of the suffering imposed on Iraqis by the sanctions, many countries now seek to use targeted, or so-called smart, sanctions limited to specific government leaders and their supporters. Indeed, most U.S. sanctions are now limited to specified elites. Targeted sanctions aim to freeze assets that certain individuals hold abroad, prohibit travel, or otherwise penalize leaders for their behavior. The aim is to impose pain only on the regime's

Iraqi women wait in line to receive food rations in 2003 amid sanctions imposed against the country.

supporters, so that they will want to change policy to alleviate their own suffering. Even with such smart sanctions, however, it appears difficult to impose sufficient pain on the elite that they will turn against the regime, since they are its primary beneficiaries. It is also hard to limit the effects of sanctions to the elite alone. Even smart sanctions, however carefully designed they may be, will nearly always impose some costs on society as a whole.

The issue is not just whether sanctions work to bring about improved human rights practices, although the more effective they are, the stronger the case is for their use. The record on success is mixed.[d] However, the more perplexing moral question is, how much pain is political change worth to members of the target society? And who has the right to determine the answer to this question? In the case of South Africa, the political opposition to White-minority rule actually called for and supported sanctions. As Bishop Desmond Tutu, a South African leader in the anti-apartheid movement, wrote in the *New York Times* in June 1986: "There is no guarantee that sanctions will topple apartheid, but it is the last nonviolent option left, and it is a risk with a chance."[e]

The Iraq case was different. The sanctions were imposed not at the request of opposition groups within Iraq (who at the time were still heavily repressed by the regime), but by the United States and its allies. In the midst of the sanctions against Iraq, then U.S. ambassador to the United Nations Madeleine Albright was asked in a *60 Minutes* interview about the possibility that up to half a million Iraqi children had died as a result of the trade and financial restrictions. Albright responded that "we think

The United States has imposed smart sanctions on select Russian elites, including government official Sergei Ivanov (left), in response to Russia's annexation of Crimea.

the price is worth it." Although she later said she had been asked a "loaded" question and regretted her answer, she did not disavow it.[f] But of course the "we" here was the United States, not necessarily the Iraqi people.

The issue arises with any sanctions attempt, including those currently directed at Syria because of the brutal civil war being waged by the Assad regime against a highly factionalized opposition. Even if some groups in Iraq might have supported sanctions against the regime, despite some suffering by the people, who gets to decide whether it is "worth it"?

Thinking Analytically

1. Which groups within a target country are most directly impacted by, say, a general trade embargo? In what ways could these impacts be expected to influence leaders' behavior?

2. Should sanctions ever be used to force governments to improve their human rights practices? If yes, when and under what conditions?

3. Does it make a difference if the conflict of interest is not over human rights but, rather, over an economic or security issue? On what issues and toward what kinds of countries might sanctions ever be an appropriate tool of diplomacy?

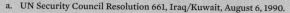

a. UN Security Council Resolution 661, Iraq/Kuwait, August 6, 1990.

b. World Health Organization, "The Health Conditions of the Population in Iraq since the Gulf Crisis," WHO/EHA/96.1, March 1996.

c. John Pilger, *Paying the Price: Killing the Children of Iraq* (documentary), directed by Alan Lowery (Carlton Television, 2000).

d. The classic study on the effectiveness of sanctions is Gary Clyde Hufbauer, Jeffrey J. Schott, and Kimberly Ann Elliott, *Economic Sanctions Reconsidered: History and Current Policy*, vol. 1, *History and Current Policy*, 2nd ed. (Washington, DC: Institute for International Economics, 1990).

e. Desmond Tutu, "Sanctions vs. Apartheid," *New York Times*, June 16, 1986.

f. Madeleine Albright, *Madam Secretary: A Memoir* (Norwalk, CT: Easton Press, 2003), 274–75.

political struggle, defining what is and is not acceptable government behavior toward its own citizens. Countries differ in their views on which rights they are bound to protect. They also differ on which rights they should seek to enforce when abused by others. Thus, we must examine not just human rights law, but also the interests and interactions of states to account for the politics of international human rights.

Why Do Individuals and States Care about the Human Rights of Others?

Proponents of improving human rights, including TANs such as Amnesty International, Human Rights Watch, and hundreds of other nongovernmental organizations (NGOs), clearly suggest that individuals and states possess and act on an interest in the human rights of others around the globe. But the puzzle still remains. Why would individuals and states care about the way other states treat their citizens? Why is it in their interests to promote and potentially enforce laws governing the human rights practices of other states? In turn, as sovereign entities, why would states want to constrain the way they deal with their own people and open themselves to the scrutiny of others? In answering these questions, we begin by addressing why states violate human rights in the first place.

Why Do States Violate Human Rights?

States violate human rights for many reasons. Some violations arise from a lack of state capacity. Many poor countries, for instance, may sincerely want but simply cannot afford to provide free primary schooling to everyone, as required under the ICESCR. Other governments may not be able to control their militaries or police sufficiently to stem human rights abuses. Even though it was not official policy, the United States was appropriately criticized when its troops, apparently acting under their own volition, abused prisoners at Abu Ghraib prison in Iraq during the 2003 war. Recognizing varying capacities to implement standards, many human rights are soft law, understood to be aspirations or goals toward which states should strive rather than strict rules to which they can and should be held accountable.[13]

In other cases, however, states violate human rights in defense of their national security. Violent or potentially violent opposition to the state is illegal everywhere, and thus it counts as criminal, not political, behavior. Amnesty International specifically excludes as POCs any individuals who use or advocate violence. Nelson Mandela, a leader of the anti-apartheid movement in South Africa, was originally designated a POC in 1962 after his arrest for organizing strikes to protest apartheid.

---

13. See Wade M. Cole, "Mind the Gap: State Capacity and the Implementation of Human Rights Treaties," *International Organization* 69, no. 2 (2015): 405–41.

But Mandela's status was revoked by Amnesty after he was convicted in 1964 of trying to overthrow the government violently. Yet the dividing line between criminal and political activities is often ambiguous, and some states prosecute individuals as criminals for political actions that would be considered legal elsewhere. Even when actions are clearly criminal, however, prosecution and punishment may be abusive when individuals are not given due process under the law.

When under attack or perceived attack, states are sometimes tempted to violate the rights of groups or individuals that they fear may be allied with a foreign power. Thus, the United States violated the civil and political rights of many of its own citizens in the infamous Red Scare of 1917–20, following the Bolshevik revolution in Russia. During the first Red Scare, between 3,000 and 10,000 individuals were arrested, denied due process, and sometimes beaten during questioning. The United States also violated the rights of approximately 110,000 Japanese Americans who were interned in concentration camps following the attack on Pearl Harbor and the start of World War II. And, in the second Red Scare (1947–57), the U.S. government blacklisted, jailed, and deported Americans suspected of following a communist or other left-wing ideology.

Today, following the terrorist attacks of September 11, 2001, the United States has been criticized for violating the human rights of citizens or residents accused of planning additional attacks or associating with terrorist organizations abroad.[14] Targeted drone attacks that President Obama authorized against U.S. citizens abroad accused of planning terrorism were especially controversial. Other countries have responded similarly to attacks on their own people or soil. Indeed, the existence of an interstate or civil war is strongly associated with increased human rights violations.[15] In justifying these violations, governments often claim that national security trumps the human rights of individuals.

Governments also violate the human rights of their citizens to preserve their own rule. This motivation differs from the national security rationale just described. In these cases, the country is not under attack, but political opponents are abused in an effort to suppress internal dissent. To weaken and deter opponents, governments in essence declare war on their own citizens. One of the most egregious cases of such abuse occurred in Argentina following a military coup in March 1976. The three-man junta, led by General Jorge Rafael Videla, immediately began a seven-year campaign known as the Dirty War against suspected political dissidents and opponents of the military regime. Although some were publicly detained, many more individuals were "disappeared."

While denying any official knowledge or involvement, the Argentine military eventually kidnapped, tortured, and killed nearly 10,000 perceived political

---

14. The United States is also accused of violating international humanitarian law, specified in the Geneva Conventions, when it treats foreign detainees as "enemy combatants" supposedly outside international law. On the Geneva Conventions and laws of war, see James D. Morrow, "The Institutional Features of the Prisoners of War Treaties," *International Organization* 55, no. 4 (2001): 971–91.

15. Steven C. Poe and C. Neal Tate, "Repression of Human Rights to Personal Integrity in the 1980s: A Global Analysis," *American Political Science Review* 88, no. 4 (1994): 853–72; and Matthew Krain, "State-Sponsored Mass Murder: The Onset and Severity of Genocides and Politicides," *Journal of Conflict Resolution* 41, no. 3 (1997): 331–60.

Argentina's Dirty War, which began in 1976, provoked a strong response from a vast transnational human rights network. Here, the Mothers of the Plaza de Mayo in Argentina gather to protest abuses by the junta and to demand information on their "disappeared" children.

opponents.[16] Many of the disappeared, we now know, were taken on death flights on which they were pushed from airplanes high above the Atlantic Ocean. As many as 500 newborns were taken from their imprisoned mothers and given to childless military families because, as General Ramón Camps (head of the Buenos Aires Provincial Police) later attempted to explain, "subversive parents will raise subversive children."[17] This was government-sponsored cruelty on a dramatic scale intended to crush and intimidate political opponents and keep the military regime in power. Like the case of apartheid in South Africa, the Dirty War in Argentina was critical in mobilizing the human rights TAN, and that network, in turn, was instrumental in bringing about political change in Argentina.

Fear of "others" within a society who may undermine the state, as well as fragile governments seeking to preserve their rule, often come together in genocides, the most extreme form of human rights abuse, in which entire identity groups are singled out for systematic persecution and murder. Genocide is one of the extreme crimes against humanity. The Armenian Genocide in Turkey during World War I and the Holocaust perpetrated by Germany during World War II led to the concept of genocide and modern human rights law.

---

16. The Argentine National Commission on the Disappeared provides an "official" figure of about 9,000 "disappeared" between 1976 and 1983. Internal documents from the Argentine security services suggest a figure of 22,000. Human rights organizations estimate that the total number of casualties of this Dirty War may be as high as 30,000.

17. Translated from Nancy Berger-Levraut, *Disparus: Rapport à la Commission indépendente sur les questions humanitaires internationales* (London: Zed Books, 1986), 29. For more on Camps, see "Ramon Camps, 67, Argentine General in the 'Dirty War,'" *New York Times*, August 23, 1994, www.nytimes.com/1994/08/23/obituaries/ramon-camps-67-argentine-general-in-the-dirty-war.html; and Francisco Goldman, "Children of the Dirty War," *New Yorker*, March 19, 2012, www.newyorker.com/magazine/2012/03/19/children-of-the-dirty-war. There have been 77 documented cases of kidnapped newborns.

More recently, genocides have occurred in Rwanda (see Chapters 5 and 11); in the former Yugoslavia, where perpetrators of the Srebrenica massacre were prosecuted for the crime; and in Sudan, where President Omar Hassan al-Bashir has been indicted by the International Criminal Court (ICC) on three counts of genocide.

More generally, autocracies and unstable democracies are significantly more likely to violate the human rights of their citizens than are established democracies, where political competition is respected and channeled through regular elections in which incumbent governments accept defeat and leave office.[18] Overt acts of torture (and possibly other human rights abuses as well) are most likely to occur in multiparty dictatorships. In single-party or personalist dictatorships, political opponents are sufficiently repressed that fewer acts of torture are necessary. These states might use torture if necessary, and broad civil liberties are typically denied, but opponents are deterred from challenging the government; thus, the regime does not often need to use violence against individuals to maintain its rule. In multiparty dictatorships, however, the political opposition usually remains visible and viable, and the government is tempted to use torture to suppress opponents so that it can stay in power.[19] In all cases, the weaker or less legitimate the government, the more likely it is to abuse human rights.

There is no single explanation for why countries violate human rights. In turn, there is no single explanation for why individuals, groups, and states seek to protect human rights at home and abroad. Repressing human rights is a political strategy that states and governments employ to protect themselves from real and perceived threats. It should be no surprise, then, that protecting human rights is also a political strategy that a variety of political actors use for a variety of aims.

Why Do States Sign Human Rights Agreements?

Some states have an interest in imposing human rights law on themselves as a means of demonstrating their commitment to democracy and political liberalization. While some governments have an interest in repressing human rights to retain political power, liberal or liberalizing governments often have an interest in promoting human rights as a means of committing themselves and their successors to political reforms.

Political scientist Andrew Moravcsik argues that democratizing states that sincerely seek to shed their autocratic and possibly abusive pasts sign human rights

---

18. Christian Davenport, "Multi-dimensional Threat Perception and State Repression: An Inquiry into Why States Apply Negative Sanctions," *American Journal of Political Science* 39, no. 3 (1995): 683–713; and Steven C. Poe, C. Neal Tate, and Linda Camp Keith, "Repression of the Human Right to Personal Integrity Revisited: A Global Cross-national Study Covering the Years 1976–1993," *International Studies Quarterly* 43 (1999): 291–313. Todd Landman, *Protecting Human Rights: A Comparative Study* (Washington, DC: Georgetown University Press, 2005), finds that states whose democratic status is more recent are more likely to engage in human rights abuses.

19. James Raymond Vreeland, "Political Institutions and Human Rights: Why Dictatorships Enter into the United Nations Convention against Torture," *International Organization* 62, no. 1 (2008): 65–101.

agreements in an attempt to lock in their new institutions and improved practices.[20] By committing to international agreements that may carry some cost if they are violated—even if that cost is only a loss of international reputation—new democratic leaders and coalitions attempt to make political backsliding more costly and, thus, less likely.

By obliging themselves to follow international human rights law, newly democratizing states aim to commit themselves credibly to political reform. This observation implies that the countries most eager to ratify human rights treaties should be newly democratic or democratizing states—a proposition for which Moravcsik and others find some support. In this conception, international human rights law is a tool that states use strategically to alter their own domestic political incentives.

This notion of using international human rights treaties to lock in domestic political reforms also explains the weaker tendency and sometimes outright reluctance of established democracies to ratify human rights agreements. To the extent that human rights are already secured at home through constitutional protections and the rule of law, stable democracies have less need to bind themselves through international agreements.[21] Thus, with its own Bill of Rights and stable democratic institutions, the United States, for instance, relies on its own, internal processes for protecting human rights and is reluctant to cede any authority to international treaties like the ICCPR or international bodies like the UN Commission on Human Rights or the ICC (see the next section) to oversee its practices.

Increasingly, however, democracies are recognizing the contradiction inherent in advocating human rights for others while failing to ratify international human rights treaties themselves. Established democracies are now signing agreements they had previously rejected and shrinking the difference in treaty ratification between new and established democracies. The United States remains a visible exception to this trend, however, in its continuing reluctance to accept international human rights accords.

Finally, some states may sign international human rights treaties because they are induced to do so by contingent rewards provided by others—a form of linkage (see Chapter 2). Established democracies often provide inducements for new democracies to join such regimes. Inducements may include financial assistance or the promise of future membership in international organizations, such as NATO, that provide benefits on other dimensions. The European Union, for instance, has required countries applying for membership to sign and comply with a host of human rights treaties before being accepted. Turkey's human rights practices—especially its repression of the Kurds—have been one of the major stumbling blocks in its attempt to join the European Union. By imposing human rights standards as a condition for assistance or membership in international organizations, other states

---

20. Andrew Moravcsik, "The Origins of Human Rights Regimes: Democratic Delegation in Postwar Europe," *International Organization* 54, no. 2 (Spring 2000): 217–52.

21. These states will, however, also have lower costs for signing agreements that already accord with domestic practice. See Jay Goodliffe and Darren G. Hawkins, "Explaining Commitment: States and the Convention against Torture," *Journal of Politics* 68, no. 2 (2006): 358–71.

Many supporters of human rights abroad are motivated by compassion for the suffering of others. The plight of the Rohingya refugees, driven from their homes in Myanmar by armed violence, inspired people around the world to demand action by their own governments and the UN.

hope to facilitate the lock-in of democracy in transitional governments—and to use the threat of expulsion to persuade states to keep their promises.

As the example of the established democracies suggests, states also ratify international human rights treaties not to bind themselves, but to constrain the human rights practices of others. They accept international oversight of their own affairs in order to secure their ability to scrutinize others. There are both altruistic and self-interested reasons why individuals and states seek to influence human rights in other countries.

Moral and Philosophical Motivations

Many individuals identify with a common humanity and feel personally affected by the welfare and treatment of others, including those in countries other than their own. As social animals, humans possess a degree of empathy that is weaker in some, stronger in others, but present in all.[22] The sense of empathy is evident most dramatically in the international responses to natural disasters when individuals across the globe donate to relief efforts. The hurricanes that battered the Caribbean in late summer and fall of 2017 generated outpourings of support and donations to victims, although for months later Puerto Rico remained without many essential services and little assistance from the mainland. When others suffer, we may hurt as well; this response can be a profound motivator of political action.

Empathy produces support not only for victims of natural disasters, but also for victims of human rights abuses. Indeed, human rights for all, and especially for the

---

22. For more on social preferences in humans, see Samuel Bowles and Herbert Gintis, *A Cooperative Species: Human Reciprocity and Its Evolution* (Princeton, NJ: Princeton University Press, 2011).

disadvantaged, is a cause that many individuals feel deeply about and are driven to try to protect by strong feelings of empathy. Gross violations of human rights, like genocide, strongly affect and motivate individuals and states to respond.

Closer to home, our own human rights depend on state respect for the individual. It is our status as humans that creates and sustains our rights. It follows in the views of some philosophers and human rights advocates that we cannot secure these rights domestically unless we also seek to promote respect for rights abroad. If it is acceptable for some governments to abuse the rights of some people, what principled defense can we give if our own government wants to abuse our rights? In this view, human rights are secure only if they are universal not merely in principle, but also in practice.

Finally, as much as, if not more than, on other issues, we have been socialized to identify with universal human rights. Human rights NGOs and the larger human rights advocacy network have played a critical role in educating the public about human rights and human rights practices, calling attention to human rights abuses, and eventually bringing pressure to bear on states.

As discussed in Chapter 11, the human rights TAN has successfully framed the issue of international human rights in terms that resonate with the political freedoms and civil rights that already exist in established democracies. Given the wide acceptance of these principles within states, it is easier to persuade people to actively defend these rights abroad. The international human rights TAN has vigorously promoted concern with human rights among broad publics and has emphasized to many groups and individuals the extent to which human rights practices abroad affect our daily lives. It is in framing issues and socializing individuals to see their interests in different ways that TANs may have their greatest impact on the international politics of human rights.

Self-Interest Motivations   Even if we do not have altruistic interests in protecting the human rights of others, we do have self-interests in promoting peace and prosperity, which, in a globalizing world, cannot flourish at home without flourishing abroad too. Recall that modern human rights originated in the depths of the Great Depression and World War II. Reflecting on the causes of these twin disasters, President Roosevelt and others drew the conclusion that protecting human rights against fascism and other forms of totalitarianism was essential to the maintenance of international peace.

By connecting human rights to the epic struggles against totalitarianism that defined much of the twentieth century, Roosevelt laid out the case that promoting human rights abroad was in the self-interest of both Americans and the citizens of other countries. This observation may be no less true today. As the democratic peace discussed in Chapter 4 shows clearly, there is an increasing recognition that democracy and the protection of political freedom can promote peace, economic interdependence, and growth that are of direct benefit to all countries.

More immediately, to the extent that suppressing human rights creates domestic political unrest and possible insurrection, such civil conflicts may spill into neighboring states either directly or indirectly. As a result, all states have an interest in preventing abuses in neighboring countries. The United States was forced to become involved in Haiti's internal political unrest in 1994 to stem the flow of people escaping by boat to southern Florida over treacherous waters. European countries sent troops into Bosnia to prevent political instability and ethnic violence in the former Yugoslavia from spilling over into the rest of the Balkans and possibly beyond. Much of the current concern about the ongoing civil war in Syria is driven by refugee flows into neighboring Turkey and, especially, into the European Union. In an interdependent world, political instability and repression in one country can have direct consequences for others.

In addition to general self-interest motivations, particular interests within countries have promoted human rights law abroad for their own instrumental purposes. This is most evident in the labor movements within the United States and Europe, which now demand that human rights (and environmental) clauses be inserted into nearly all regional trade agreements (RTAs).[23] The North American Free Trade Agreement (NAFTA), for instance, includes extensive labor provisions that guarantee freedom of association and the right to organize, the right to bargain collectively and strike, freedom from discrimination, access to labor tribunals, and effective employment standards and minimum wage laws; it even establishes a tri-national ministerial commission to monitor the labor provisions of the agreement.[24]

Labor unions promote such clauses to level the political and economic playing fields on which their own workers compete. To protect their ability to organize and strike for higher wages at home, unions want to ensure that workers in labor-abundant and low-wage countries have similar rights and, indeed, possess the broader political rights necessary to protect their ability to form effective trade unions. In this way, the economic self-interest of workers in developed states can dovetail with the interests of citizens in developing countries in more effective protections for human rights.

Labor demands for human rights clauses, however, may also disguise a form of trade protectionism. By inserting human rights clauses into RTAs, the unions may be making free-trade pacts less appealing to foreign trading partners and, therefore, less likely to be approved. For example, the Mexican government strongly opposed the human rights clauses of NAFTA. Moreover, human rights provisions open up the opportunity for subsequent claims that the trading partner is violating the terms of the agreement and that the trade concessions made by the home country should be withdrawn. For labor in the developed countries, human rights provisions in RTAs may be "poison pills" that are used to prevent further movements toward free trade.

Together, these various motivations for protecting human rights abroad suggest that interests are multiple and often quite complex. Each reason, however, prompts individuals or groups to press their governments to promote international human rights law. One person may be particularly motivated by a general concern for human well-being, another by a concern with protecting democracy at home, and

---

23. Emilie M. Hafner-Burton, "Trading Human Rights: How Preferential Trade Agreements Influence Government Repression," *International Organization* 59, no. 3 (2005): 593–629.

24. Collectively, the labor provisions of NAFTA are referred to as the North American Agreement on Labor Cooperation. See www.dol.gov/ilab/trade/agreements/naalcgd.htm (accessed 09/27/17).

a third by a hidden desire for trade protection, but all combine to bring pressure to bear on their governments to make international human rights a priority.

Such pressure on governments may be increasing. As human rights NGOs grow and succeed, as they have done in a more globalized world, they influence the views of more and more individuals. In turn, the same technology that facilitates the growth of TANs also brings the horror of human rights abuses to immediate public attention. The genocide in the Darfur region of Sudan was brought into our homes via television and the Internet. In the summer of 2014, protests of democratic activists in Hong Kong were watched in real time around the globe. The Syrian government's use of barrel bombs and sarin gas against its own people is documented on the nightly news.

It is now much harder to ignore human rights abuses or to deny that we knew about the violations while they were occurring. This realization heightens awareness and may prompt individuals to demand that their governments be more aggressive in promoting international human rights. This greater awareness was an important driver of the Arab Spring protests that diffused across North Africa and the Middle East in 2010–11 (see Chapter 11).[25]

Rarely would we expect governments to promote human rights abroad to the exclusion of all other interests that they might be seeking in their relations with other states. Nonetheless, founded in the tragedy of World War II, supported by a growing transnational human rights movement, and accelerated by new technologies that bring abuses to the public's immediate attention, individuals and groups now increasingly recognize international human rights as part of their nations' interests and demand that their governments act accordingly.

Do States Observe International Human Rights Law?

Given a now extensive body of international law, broad agreement on human rights norms, and growing interests in promoting rights, do states actually protect human rights abroad? Is interest reflected in practice? In the case of human rights practices, we can view the proverbial glass as half empty or half full. Although international human rights institutions are being developed, large-scale abuses continue to occur. Maps 12.1, 12.2, and 12.3 graphically illustrate the extent of the problem. While it can be difficult to measure such rights, and some of the information in the maps may seem surprising, the data reflected in the maps are the best available and, on the whole, indicate that human rights violations still occur across the globe. (See "How Do We Know?" on p. 526 about the difficulty of measuring human rights practices.)

At the same time, however, it appears that human rights practices have improved substantially since 1980. Even if, in the view of optimists, the glass of human rights practices is half full, it is still possible to ask: Why has there not been even greater

---

25. Zachery C. Steinert-Threlkeld, "Spontaneous Collective Action: Peripheral Mobilization during the Arab Spring," *American Political Science Review* 111, no. 2 (May 2017): 379–403.

MAP 12.1 **Respect for Freedom of Religion by Public Authorities, 2016**

- ■ NOT RESPECTED
- ■ WEAKLY RESPECTED
- ■ SOMEWHAT RESPECTED
- ■ MOSTLY RESPECTED
- □ FULLY RESPECTED
- □ NO DATA AVAILABLE

improvement, given the development of a body of robust international human rights law, an extensive transnational advocacy network, and growing norms of appropriate state behavior?

The most frequent and deadliest form of violence in the world today is by governments against their own citizens (including governments fighting civil wars). In violation of the ICCPR, governments continue to inflict violence against political dissidents. Defying the ICESCR, governments also violate the human rights of their citizens by misguided economic or social policies that lead to widespread suffering and deaths. For example, the Great Leap Forward in China (1958–62) created a nation-wide famine and left as many as 38 million people dead. R. J. Rummel, who coined the word *democide* to describe such government-sponsored killing, graphically writes:

> In total, during the first eighty-eight years of [the twentieth] century, almost 170,000,000 men, women, and children have been shot, beaten, tortured, knifed, burned, starved, frozen, crushed, or worked to death; or buried alive, drowned, hung, bombed, or killed in any other of the myriad ways governments have inflicted death on unarmed, helpless citizens or foreigners. . . . This is as though our species has been devastated by a modern Black Plague.[26]

Note: The data in this map measure the extent in 2016 to which individuals and groups had the right to choose a religion, change their religion, and practice that religion in private or in public, as well as to proselytize peacefully without being subject to restrictions by public authorities.

Map source: Michael Coppedge, John Gerring, Staffan I. Lindberg, Svend-Erik Skaaning, et al., "V-Dem Codebook v7.1," Varieties of Democracy (V-Dem) Project, www.v-dem .net/en/data/data-version-7-1 (accessed 09/25/17).

26. From www.hawaii.edu/powerkills/POWER.ART.HTM (accessed 07/24/17).

MAP 12.2 **Respect for Norms against Torture by Public Authorities, 2016**

■ NOT RESPECTED   ■ SOMEWHAT RESPECTED   FULLY RESPECTED

■ WEAKLY RESPECTED   ■ MOSTLY RESPECTED   NO DATA AVAILABLE

Note: The data in this map measure the extent in 2016 to which state officials or other agents of the state purposefully inflicted extreme pain, whether mental or physical, on individuals in a state of incarceration with an aim to extract information or intimidate victims.

Map source: Michael Coppedge, John Gerring, Staffan I. Lindberg, Svend-Erik Skaaning, et al., "V-Dem Codebook v7.1," Varieties of Democracy (V-Dem) Project, www.v-dem .net/en/data/data-version-7-1 (accessed 09/25/17).

According to political philosopher Thomas Hobbes (1588–1679), states were created to lift humans out of the state of nature in which life was "solitary, poor, nasty, brutish, and short." This statement may be true; we do not know how dangerous life would be without states to provide a measure of social order and protection against other individuals—although failed states like Somalia suggest that life in the state of nature may be close to that envisioned by Hobbes. But today, governments around the world may themselves be the biggest threats to our human rights and, indeed, to our very lives.

Rummel's data do show that the twentieth century appears to have been more violent and deadly than past centuries, but this may have more to do with the "improved" technology of state killing than with any change in state intent or practice. The best evidence indicates, however, that human rights practices on average have improved fairly significantly in recent decades, especially in South America, which enjoyed a wave of democratization in the 1980s, supported in part by popular outrage at the human rights abuses of the prior military regimes, and Central and Eastern Europe, which democratized in the 1990s after the fall of communism.

MAP 12.3 *Respect for Women's Freedom of Discussion by Public Authorities, 2016*

NOT RESPECTED   SOMEWHAT RESPECTED   FULLY RESPECTED

WEAKLY RESPECTED   MOSTLY RESPECTED   NO DATA AVAILABLE

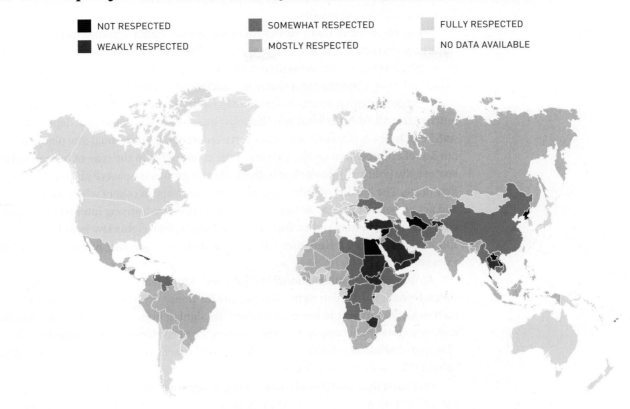

Does International Human Rights Law Make a Difference?

Given the pattern discussed in the previous section, does international human rights law make a difference? Even if abuses continue to occur, do countries that sign human rights treaties protect the rights of their citizens better than those that have not signed the agreements? Do these human rights institutions constrain state behavior in significant ways?

The accumulating evidence on the impact of international human rights agreements on state practice is mixed. This question is, as discussed in Chapter 11, a difficult problem for researchers because the countries most likely to sign human rights agreements are also those most likely to respect human rights. If we simply examined the relationship between signing agreements and protecting human rights, we would conclude, perhaps incorrectly, that the agreements were having a huge effect on practice when, in fact, these two factors simply occur together as a reflection of some underlying trait, such as democracy and a concern for political and civil rights, that leads states both to sign agreements

Note: The data in this map measure the extent in 2016 to which women were able to engage in private discussions, particularly on political issues, in private homes and public spaces without fear of harassment by other members of the polity or the public authorities; includes restrictions by the government and its agents, as well as cultural restrictions or customary laws that are enforced by other members of the polity, sometimes in informal ways.

Map source: Michael Coppedge, John Gerring, Staffan I. Lindberg, Svend-Erik Skaaning, et al., "V-Dem Codebook v7.1," Varieties of Democracy (V-Dem) Project, www.v-dem .net/en/data/data-version-7-1 (accessed 09/25/17).

and to protect those rights. As a result of these difficulties, as well as the measurement problems discussed in the previous section, different analysts have found different results.

Some researchers find that international human rights agreements make no difference on practice, or even have a negative effect once other factors (like income per capita and economic growth) that affect state practice are taken into account. This implies that signing agreements is associated with worse human rights practices,[27] suggesting that international human rights law just might not matter very much. After all, international law, like most international agreements, depends on self-help. In the absence of any third-party enforcers, international law places the burden of enforcement on the victims of the crime, who, in the case of human rights law, are the politically powerless individuals and groups who were abused in the first place. The burden of enforcement, therefore, rests on others who can speak and act on behalf of these victims. Yet not all states have a strong interest in penalizing violators of human rights; thus, international human rights law is, at best, sporadically enforced. Knowing this, states can choose to violate human rights with a degree of impunity.

As described by international law professor Oona Hathaway, countries may sign international human rights agreements for their "expressive value" rather than as a commitment to better behavior.[28] By signing human rights agreements, she suggests, states may hope to give the appearance of conforming to civilized norms of behavior while continuing to engage in actual practices that violate human rights behind the scenes or out of the public eye.

Our most developed explanation for the negative effect of international agreements on practice comes from political scientist James Vreeland. Focusing on the Convention against Torture and Other Cruel, Inhuman or Degrading Treatment or Punishment (CAT), Vreeland shows that the negative relationship is rooted primarily in multiparty dictatorships that both sign the CAT and use torture at higher-than-average rates. Multiparty dictatorships, he argues, are pressed by domestic political opponents, who have some influence, to ratify international conventions in hopes of changing the government's behavior over the long run. But since domestic opponents remain viable and their rule is unstable, dictators are also most likely to abuse human rights, including by using torture against insurgents.[29] In the case of the despotic rule of Paul Biya in Cameroon, for instance, levels of torture were rated as "isolated" and infrequent, but once multiple parties were permitted in 1992, the practice became "common."[30] Putting these two trends together appears to explain why multiparty dictatorships sign human rights agreements and are also more likely to abuse those rights.

---

27. Linda Camp Keith, "The United Nations International Covenant on Civil and Political Rights: Does It Make a Difference in Human Rights Behavior?" *Journal of Peace Research* 36, no. 1 (1999): 95–118; Oona A. Hathaway, "Do Human Rights Treaties Make a Difference?" *Yale Law Journal* 111, no. 8 (June 2002): 1935–2042; and Daniel W. Hill Jr., "Estimating the Effects of Human Rights Treaties on State Behavior," *Journal of Politics* 72, no. 4 (2010): 1161–74.

28. Hathaway, "Do Human Rights Treaties Make a Difference?"

29. Vreeland, "Political Institutions and Human Rights."

30. See Vreeland, "Political Institutions and Human Rights," 76, for this and other examples.

By contrast, other researchers find that signing international human rights agreements actually improves practice.[31] They reach this conclusion either by modeling the selection process directly or by adjusting for the changing standards of human rights over time (see "How Do We Know?" on p. 526).

Others find that the effects of international agreements are contingent on or exist only when combined with certain other factors. Agreements "work" in essence only when combined with specific domestic political institutions, strong domestic courts and the rule of law, large NGO contingents, the expected tenure of political leaders, and legal standards of proof for particular rights violations.[32] Taken together, this more recent research appears to be gaining the upper hand, indicating that international human rights law is having a positive effect, but in subtle ways and only under certain limited conditions.

As reflected in these inconsistent results, however, it is very difficult to isolate the effect of international human rights agreements on state behavior. Joining human rights conventions might indeed be leading to better protections of human rights than otherwise, but at the same time, the effect on practice is overwhelmed by a number of countries signing agreements to hide their practices and insulate themselves from international pressure. Isolating the impact of international institutions from the underlying interests of states to join agreements is difficult. Although additional research is still necessary, there may be some grounds for optimism by advocates of international human rights law.

Even if international human rights institutions have only a limited effect in the short term, they may exert a more beneficial effect on human rights norms and practices in the long run.[33] Rather than just binding states, international human rights law also empowers social actors to conceive of their interests in new ways, provides a shared vocabulary of judgment, and emboldens societies to advocate for their own rights, sometimes leading to massive political change.

For instance, the Helsinki Final Act of 1975, which established the applicability of human rights in all of Europe, served as the opening wedge that allowed

---

31. In *Protecting Human Rights*, p. 157, Todd Landman uses a broader set of agreements and longer time period than other studies do, as well as a nonrecursive model, and reports a positive effect of human rights agreements on practice. In a later survey of this debate, however, he concludes judiciously that no definitive evidence exists; see Todd Landman, *Studying Human Rights* (New York: Routledge, 2006), 103. Using his dynamic standard measure (see "How Do We Know?" on p. 526), Christopher J. Fariss, in "The Changing Standard of Accountability and the Positive Relationship between Human Rights Treaty Ratification and Compliance," *British Journal of Political Science* (forthcoming), finds consistent support for a positive relationship. See also Yonatan Lupu, "The Informative Power of Treaty Commitment: Using the Spatial Model to Address Selection Effects," *American Journal of Political Science* 57, no. 4 (2013): 912–25.

32. Eric Neumayer, "Do International Human Rights Treaties Improve Respect for Human Rights?" *Journal of Conflict Resolution* 49, no. 6 (2005): 925–53; Beth A. Simmons, *Mobilizing for Human Rights: International Law in Domestic Politics* (New York: Cambridge University Press, 2009); Amanda N. Murdie and David R. Davis, "Shaming and Blaming: Using Events Data to Assess the Impact of Human Rights INGOs," *International Studies Quarterly* 56, no. 1 (2012): 1–16; Courtenay R. Conrad and Emily Hencken Ritter, "Treaties, Tenure and Torture: The Conflicting Domestic Effects of International Law," *Journal of Politics* 75, no. 2 (2013): 397–409; and Yonatan Lupu, "Best Evidence: The Role of Information in Domestic Judicial Enforcement of International Human Rights Agreements," *International Organization* 67, no. 3 (2013): 469–503.

33. The statistical evidence on long-term effects is, at best, ambiguous as well. See Emilie M. Hafner-Burton and Kiyoteru Tsutsui, "Justice Lost! The Failure of International Human Rights Law to Matter Where Needed Most," *Journal of Peace Research* 44, no. 4 (2007): 407–25.

Measuring Human Rights Practices

Observing trends in human rights practices is quite tricky. Violations of human rights are typically not advertised by governments, and some, like torture, are usually carried out in secret with few witnesses or traces of physical evidence. Even when observers suspect that governments are violating human rights on a fairly widespread and persistent basis, lawyers often lack the kinds of evidence necessary to prosecute offenders in traditional courts of law.[a]

Amnesty International and the U.S. Department of State track violations as best they can, drawing on many forms of evidence, including local sources, and they issue annual reports on human rights practices for every country. Political scientists, in turn, have developed scales of human rights violations based on these reports, which then give us an approximate measure of the pattern over time and across countries.[b] In Figure A, the light-gray line represents rights practices around the globe based on the Amnesty and State Department reports. The "whiskers" around the estimates indicate the degree of uncertainty about them. This gray line is essentially flat, indicating that there has been virtually no improvement since 1946, despite the considerable efforts of the international community. Estimates such as this one have fueled controversy about the effectiveness of international human rights law.

Recently, however, Christopher Fariss has developed a new measure of human rights protection that uses the available information on actual, observed violations of human rights, and compares this to the traditional measure based on the Amnesty and State Department reports. He finds that the standards used by Amnesty and the State Department for assessing and including information about violations have changed in subtle ways over time, perhaps because of better information

and monitoring. It now takes fewer cases of documented torture by governments, for instance, to be rated as a "frequent violator" than it did in the past. It may also be the case that as practices actually have improved, the international community, as reflected in these annual reports, has become less tolerant of violators.

When rescaled to reflect these changing standards, depicted in the blue line in Figure A, we see that human rights practices have improved considerably, especially since the late 1980s. Overall, this is good news for international human rights. Even though it reminds us that human rights practices are difficult to measure accurately and consistently, this research suggests that those practices really have improved over the last generation.

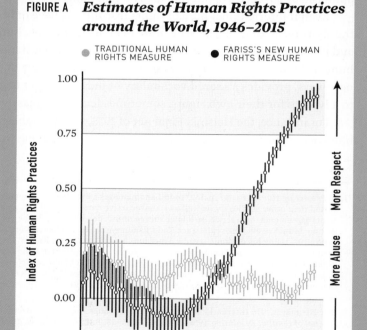

FIGURE A *Estimates of Human Rights Practices around the World, 1946–2015*

● TRADITIONAL HUMAN RIGHTS MEASURE   ● FARISS'S NEW HUMAN RIGHTS MEASURE

Source: Christopher J. Fariss, "Respect for Human Rights Has Improved over Time: Modeling the Changing Standard of Accountability," *American Political Science Review* 108, no. 2 (2014): 297–318. Updated to 2015 by Christopher Fariss.

a. Yonatan Lupu, "Best Evidence: The Role of Information in Domestic Judicial Enforcement of International Human Rights Agreements," *International Organization* 67, no. 3 (2013): 469–503.

b. See David L. Cingranelli and David L. Richards, The Cingranelli-Richards Human Rights Dataset, http://humanrightsdata.com (accessed 09/18/14).

S DROITS HUMAINS SONT MA FIERTE

AMNESTY INTERNATIONAL

Human rights TANs, including groups like Amnesty International, promote public awareness of human rights issues and monitor states' compliance with international laws. In these ways, they pressure other states to take action against governments that violate human rights.

human rights activists to mobilize within the communist bloc countries of Eastern Europe. Three years earlier, the 35-country Conference on Security and Co-operation in Europe had convened to resolve political and territorial issues left over from World War II, and to expand economic contacts between East and West. Much against the wishes of the communist regimes, the countries of Western Europe insisted on the inclusion of human rights on the agenda. Trading concessions on other issues, the Western states were eventually able to gain the assent of their Eastern counterparts to the principle of "respect for human rights and other fundamental freedoms, including freedom of thought, conscience, religion or belief."[34]

Although the communist countries first attempted to suppress publication and discussion of this principle, word spread and domestic groups began to agitate for their rights and make contact with their transnational counterparts in the West. In the bright lights of public awareness, the societal groups activated by the Helsinki Accords were eventually able to mount effective challenges to the autocratic regimes that had long suppressed all dissent. Although many factors contributed to the fall of the communist regimes in Eastern Europe in 1989, the political freedom first created by the Helsinki agreement is broadly seen as a contributing cause of that political earthquake.[35]

In addition, international human rights law permits TANs to bring pressure to bear on governments to enforce human rights standards. Human rights TANs, of course, have no legal standing to issue mandatory sanctions or other punishments,

---

34. Conference on Security and Cooperation in Europe, Final Act, Helsinki, 1975, sec. 1, (a) VII, www.osce .org/helsinki-final-act?download=true (accessed 09/20/14).

35. Daniel C. Thomas, "The Helsinki Accords and Political Change in Eastern Europe," in Risse, Ropp, and Sikkink, *Power of Human Rights*, 205–33.

but they do exert an important influence by naming and shaming violators of human rights.[36] Equally important, if not more so, by promoting public awareness and monitoring state human rights practices, TANs create political pressure that may eventually force states to act. TANs are not superseding the role of the state, but they do shape the political context in which states interact with their citizens and one another. Thus, even if international human rights law may not cause governments to change their behavior in the short run, it may lead to significant political change over time by legitimizing and encouraging the mobilization of domestic political forces.

What Can Lead to Better Protection of International Human Rights?

Few human rights violators are actually punished. States do sanction one another for human rights abuses, as discussed already, but such penalties remain rare. Although states may be named and shamed by transnational human rights organizations, and some may modify their behavior to avoid public condemnation, most escape any significant costs for violating the rights of their citizens.

The key problem in human rights is that the gains from cooperation that make international law self-enforcing, as explained in Chapter 11, are small or nonexistent, meaning that states have few incentives to bear high costs for enforcing the law. States that violate human rights have no interest in enforcing the law against themselves. This much is obvious. But although other states have interests in supporting human rights in principle, few gain directly from better human rights practices abroad, as discussed shortly. They have some interest in enforcing human rights standards, but only if the costs are not too high.

This combination of mostly empathetic interests in human rights practices abroad and few incentives to actually punish violators produces, for most states, an inconsistent human rights policy. Even the United States, a strong promoter of human rights, has often chosen not to act against abuses by states it supports—including the use of poison gas against Iraq's Kurdish minority in the late 1980s by Saddam Hussein, who was then being backed by the United States in his war against Iran, as well as widespread abuses by the military junta in Chile following an American-backed coup in 1973. At the same time, the United States did press human rights concerns against the White-majority regime in South Africa, contributing to the peaceful revolution that eventually led to Black-majority rule, and spoke out in support of the pro-democracy protesters in Egypt and Libya during the Arab Spring in 2011.

---

36. The effectiveness of naming and shaming is open to debate. See Emilie M. Hafner-Burton, "Sticks and Stones: Naming and Shaming the Human Rights Enforcement Problem," *International Organization* 62, no. 4 (2008): 689–716.

This inconsistent enforcement may explain why international human rights law is often ineffective. Facing opposition to their rule at home, states may be willing to take the small risk of international punishment to secure their tenure in office. That is, for some governments the temptation to ignore human rights law to secure their hold on power may be stronger than the fear of international penalties. With regime survival as a strong core interest and minor punishments carried out only a small percentage of the time by the international community, few leaders may feel tightly constrained by international human rights institutions or the laws that they themselves have accepted as binding.

It is costly for states to enforce international human rights laws. Naming and shaming may anger a violator whose cooperation is needed on some other diplomatic issue. Pressing the human rights provisions of the Helsinki agreement, for instance, meant that European states gave up bargaining leverage on other issues they also cared about. Economic sanctions impose costs on the target state, but they also impose costs on exporters within the home state, who lose a potential market for their goods. Businesses strongly resisted divesting from South Africa when it meant forgoing access to raw materials, cheap labor, and Africa's wealthiest consumers. If sanctions hurt the target state, they will also hurt the home state (see "Controversy" on p. 510). Promoting human rights always carries a price. States do sometimes act to punish human rights violations, but under what conditions?

When Do States Take Action on Human Rights?

States are most likely to pay the costs of enforcing human rights law under three conditions. First, states act when faced with domestic pressure to do something to stop human rights abuses. As noted already, few governments have intrinsic interests in promoting international human rights, and most do so only in response to domestic political pressure. Governments normally weigh demands to stop abuses, however, against costs to business interests or other diplomatic initiatives. Domestic pressure often produces merely toothless condemnations of the abuse or loose and ineffective economic sanctions.

Nonetheless, the more outrageous the abuse, the greater the domestic pressure on governments to act. In a particularly extreme case, when President Bashar al-Assad of Syria used chemical weapons against his own civilians in April 2017, U.S. president Donald J. Trump punished the regime by launching 59 cruise missiles against the Shayrat air base near Homs. Although President Trump had derided foreign military interventions during the campaign, this use of force against Syria received broad support at home.

The boomerang effect (described in Chapter 11) employed by TANs also plays an important role in protecting human rights. Victims or other advocates in one country who are blocked from influencing their own states can bring their plight to the attention of concerned others in foreign countries, who can then press their own governments into action against the offending regime. Domestic pressure also explains why democratic states are typically the most important promoters of international human rights. Not only are such rights more consistent with the states' own practice, but also they are more susceptible to the demands of the states' citizens to undertake costly efforts to advance human rights abroad.

In turn, domestic demands for action are more likely when citizens are better informed about abuses in other countries. It is here, as monitors of practices around the globe, that human rights TANs play perhaps their most important role. Almost by their very nature, human rights abuses are hidden. They are typically perpetrated against individuals and groups that, though perhaps a potential threat to the regime, are nonetheless excluded from political power. Governments that violate human rights, in turn, are also likely to control access to the international media and other routes by which the abused might publicize their plight. It is through the links between domestic activists, who are often the victims of abuses, and transnational activists, who largely operate out of established democracies, that human rights violations are most often brought to light.

Amnesty International's annual reports are an important vehicle for documenting state practice. Even though the U.S. Department of State issues its own annual reports, many of the abuses in those reports are first uncovered and brought to public attention by TANs. Without TANs, many more governments would be able to abuse their citizens, confident that their odious practices would escape international scrutiny. This is one issue area where the networks of individuals and groups promoting new international norms, and pressing their governments to make greater efforts in pursuit of those goals, have had a significant effect on state practice.

The second condition under which states are more likely to act against human rights violators is when doing so serves larger geopolitical interests. Raising human rights issues as part of the Helsinki Accords was applauded by many in the West as another way to bring pressure to bear on the Soviet Union and its allies for political and economic reform. Saddam Hussein's human rights record became an issue in the relations between Washington and Baghdad only after the Iraqi dictator invaded Kuwait in August 1990. His human rights violations later became one of several reasons given by President George W. Bush to remove Hussein from power in the Iraq War of 2003. Likewise, President Trump might have been more reluctant to punish Syria for using chemical weapons against its citizens if it were not aligned with Russia and Iran. Raising human rights concerns and demanding policy change in other states can be goals in themselves, but they may also be instruments in larger political and economic struggles.

The third condition making the action of states against human rights violators more likely is when the gap between the principle of sovereignty and international human rights law can be bridged. Central to the concept of sovereignty is the principle of nonintervention, which is often jealously protected by precisely those states most likely to be sanctioned by the international community for their violations of human rights law. States are, therefore, reluctant to criticize one another, except when the principle of nonintervention can be reconciled with other principles. The anti-apartheid movement was broadly supported, for instance, because it was framed not as foreign intervention, but as an anticolonial struggle; thus, it fell under the right to national self-determination guaranteed in the ICCPR and ICESCR.

Although attitudes are changing slightly as various regional organizations, like the African Union, move toward support for their own versions of the responsibility to protect (see Chapter 11), the postcolonial states remain among the states most committed to the principle of nonintervention. Under many circumstances, they would have been reluctant to intervene in the affairs of South Africa, for fear of legitimizing external intervention in their own domestic politics. A key move in the anti-apartheid struggle was defining it as an anticolonial struggle against one of the last White-minority regimes on the continent.[37] With the issue framed in this way, Black-majority-rule states not only could join the sanctions against South Africa, but also could actively press Western states to join in the liberation struggle.

Countries do promote international human rights and punish violators, even if only in a weaker or more episodic way than some advocates desire. When faced with strong domestic pressures and lower costs, states do act to further human rights abroad. Yet states are often inconsistent in their human rights policies. Human rights are seldom the only motivation behind a state's foreign policy. The inconsistency of enforcement may make international human rights law comparatively ineffective and, thus, may explain why international human rights treaties appear to have mostly a contingent effect on human rights practices.

Will Protection of Human Rights Improve in the Future?

As with all international cooperation, efforts to promote more effective collaboration between and among states involve building better international institutions. There are at least four ongoing innovations in international human rights institutions that may have important implications for the future.

Transitional Justice New forms of transitional justice are important innovations in international human rights practice. Following World War II, the focus of international human rights law was the criminal prosecution and punishment of individuals found to have engaged in human rights abuses. Starting in the 1980s and 1990s, however, emphasis has shifted to noncriminal and nonjudicial forms of reconciliation, which are believed to provide a better and more solid long-term foundation for rebuilding societies after major civil conflicts involving human rights abuses.

These new forms include truth and reconciliation commissions that aim to document and publicize past human rights abuses; reparations to repair the suffering of human rights victims; memorials that seek to preserve evidence and commemorate victims of abuse; and institutional reforms, especially strengthening civilian control of the police and military. Also common is *lustration*, the government policy of limiting members of the previous regime from serving in political, bureaucratic, or sometimes even civil positions.

---

37. On the construction of a norm of self-determination, see Neta C. Crawford, *Argument and Change in World Politics: Ethics, Decolonization, and Humanitarian Intervention* (New York: Cambridge University Press, 2002). On the norm of racial equality in mobilizing support for the anti-apartheid movement, see Klotz, *Norms in International Relations*.

The Truth and Dignity Commission of Tunisia collected approximately 62,000 submissions between 2014 and 2016 as part of its investigation into human rights violations perpetrated by the Tunisian dictatorship beginning in 1955.

Advocates of transitional justice argue that it is better for the society to acknowledge and publicize past human rights abuses than to focus on criminal prosecutions. Criminal proceedings are adversarial, pitting prosecutors who may not have strong evidence of abuses that the previous government intentionally hid from public view against defendants who have no incentive to admit past wrongdoing or provide information. Criminal prosecutions may also create incentives for human rights abusers to fight longer and harder to stay in power, lest they be accused in court and likely punished.[38] To ease the transition to democracy and the rule of law, advocates suggest, revealing past abuses can heal a society and allow it to move forward rather than remain mired in prior conflicts.

The most difficult issue in transitional justice deals with amnesty, especially for the most serious crimes against humanity. Amnesties pardon individuals who committed human rights abuses or other political crimes, typically as part of an effort to move on by putting past conflicts to rest. Amnesty was common in Latin American countries undergoing transitions to democracy in the 1980s. Conditional amnesties grant forgiveness to individuals in return for their full and truthful accountings of their role and knowledge of past abuses.

One of the most successful conditional amnesty-granting institutions was the South African Truth and Reconciliation Commission, which ran from 1995 to 2002, following the end of apartheid. Its goals were laid out in the 1993 Interim Constitution, which stated that "there is a need for understanding but not for vengeance, a need for reparation but not retaliation, a need for ubuntu [the essence of being human] but not for victimization."[39] Conditional amnesties are also frequently combined with lustrations. All amnesties, however, conflict with laws proscribing crimes against humanity, which can be prosecuted internationally, and with the new ICC, which defers to national courts only when a criminal investigation has been carried out in full, as we will see. The tension between international human rights law and the desire of countries to move beyond the past through transitional justice has not been resolved.

individual petition

A right that permits individuals to petition appropriate international legal bodies directly if they believe a state has violated their rights.

Individual Petition   One of the most important developments in international human rights law was the right of **individual petition** to a supranational court, found most prominently in the European Convention on Human Rights (ECHR),

---

38. For a contrary view, see Kathryn Sikkink, *The Justice Cascade: How Human Rights Prosecutions Are Changing World Politics* (New York: Norton, 2011).

39. Quoted in Simon Chesterman, *You, the People: The United Nations, Transitional Administration, and State-Building* (New York: Oxford University Press, 2004), 158.

adopted in 1950 by the Council of Europe and its now 47 member states.[40] Though it preceded the ICCPR by 26 years, the ECHR recognizes many of the same rights ultimately in the ICCPR. It does not incorporate economic, social, or cultural rights into the corpus of rights that it protects. The ECHR's most innovative features are the European Court of Human Rights and its right of individual petition.[41] The court currently consists of 47 judges from the member states of the Council of Europe. It hears cases, offers decisions that are binding on members, and awards damages. Although there is no formal mechanism for ensuring compliance, responsibility for enforcing the decisions of the court rests with the Committee of Ministers of the Council of Europe. Enforcement is informally overseen by the European Union.

Since 1998, individuals in all member states have possessed the right to petition the court for redress. Prior to this date, an optional protocol allowed individuals to petition the European Commission of Human Rights, which could then launch cases in the court on their behalf. By adopting the measure known as Protocol 11, all members are now required to allow individuals to petition the court directly if they believe a state has violated their rights as specified in the ECHR. This provision is nearly unique in international law, in which states—not individuals—are normally the subjects. In the court, individuals can now bring suit against their own governments for violations of internationally recognized human rights.

In the year before the new provisions took effect, 5,891 petitions were filed with the commission—already a large number. In 2001, the first full year under the new rules, 13,845 petitions were filed, representing an increase of approximately 138 percent. In 2016, the most recent year for which data are available, 53,500 applications were filed, of which 1,926 were ultimately decided by the court.[42] Today, nearly all petitions before the court are from private individuals, and the success rate is over 50 percent, indicating that petitioners quite often win their cases against their own states. The ECHR is clearly having a profound effect on human rights practices in Europe, and especially in the relatively new democracies of eastern Europe.

Without the right of individual petition, states act as gatekeepers, blocking international courts from hearing cases that they might lose. Some human rights activists advocate expanding the right of individual petition to other supranational courts as a check against human rights abuses. This move would open channels to international courts now blocked by states and would likely lead to greater attention to, if not better enforcement of, human rights violations.

---

40. Rights of individual standing are also found in several optional protocols (see Table 12.1). In all cases, however, states must actively declare their willingness to allow the appropriate UN review committee to accept petitions from individuals. On how the right of individual petition can "trap" countries that sign agreements but do not intend to honor them, see Heather Smith-Cannoy, *Insincere Commitments: Human Rights Treaties, Abusive States, and Citizen Action* (Washington, DC: Georgetown University Press, 2012).

41. On the court, see www.echr.coe.int/Pages/home.aspx?p=home (accessed 09/20/14).

42. On the court's caseload, see European Court of Human Rights, Analysis of Statistics 2016, www.echr .coe.int/Documents/Stats_analysis_2016_ENG.pdf (accessed 09/25/17). Although the courts themselves have different rules, procedures, and roles for comparison, the U.S. Supreme Court for the 2015 term (the most recent for which data are available) received 6,475 case filings, of which 70 were decided. See the annual report of the Supreme Court at www.supremecourt.gov/publicinfo/year-end/2016year-endreport.pdf (accessed 09/25/17).

The right of individual petition is now found in several optional protocols to international human rights treaties, such as the ICCPR (see Table 12.1 on p. 505). Ratified by fewer states than the main agreements, these optional protocols are a significant step forward.

International Criminal Court (ICC)

A court of last resort for human rights cases that possesses jurisdiction only if the accused is a national of a state party, the crime took place on the territory of a state party, or the UN Security Council has referred the case to the prosecutor.

The International Criminal Court The **International Criminal Court (ICC)** was established in 1998 and came into force in July 2002 after receiving the necessary 60 ratifications of its founding treaty. Today, more than 124 states have accepted the jurisdiction of the ICC and thus have become "state parties." The ICC possesses jurisdiction only if the accused is a national of a state party, the crime took place on the territory of a state party, or the UN Security Council has referred the case to the prosecutor. Moreover, the ICC is a court of last resort, meaning that it cannot act if a national judicial authority has genuinely investigated or prosecuted a case—regardless of the outcome of that investigation or prosecution. The ICC can act only when a state cannot or will not act itself. As of March 2018, 24 cases in eight countries have been brought before the ICC for investigation or trial.[43]

Although the number of prosecutions by the ICC has been relatively small, this does not necessarily mean the court is ineffective. The real question is whether the existence of the court, and the possibility of prosecution, deters human rights abuses. In principle, the most effective court is one that does not need to hear any cases, because no crimes are committed, but we know this is not the case for human rights abuses. Does the ICC make any difference at all? Emerging research suggests that the ICC can deter at least the most egregious human rights violations in some circumstances. Both ratification of the ICC and prosecutions by the court have been found to reduce state-sponsored violence, while prosecutions reduce rebel group abuses.[44] These findings indicate that the court is deterring some abuses, at least at the margin.

This effect, however, may not be entirely positive. Other research finds that involvement by the ICC in a conflict prolongs the strife and killings, especially when the risk of prosecution at home is relatively low. Similar to the gambling-for-resurrection logic explained in Chapter 4 (p. 151), the risk that the leader who loses the conflict will face arrest and prosecution by the ICC creates an incentive to fight on longer than would otherwise be the case.[45] We will get a clearer picture of the ICC's effects on human rights as the court develops and investigates more cases.

The ICC remains highly controversial. As it begins to investigate and prosecute possible crimes against humanity, critics point out that all the cases are

---

43. For the most recent updates, see www.icc-cpi.int/en_menus/icc/situations%20and%20cases/pages/situations%20and%20cases.aspx (accessed 07/24/17).

44. Hyeran Jo and Beth A. Simmons, "Can the International Criminal Court Deter Atrocity?" *International Organization* 70, no. 3 (2016): 443–75. Stephen Chaudoin, in "How Contestation Moderates the Effects of International Institutions: The International Criminal Court and Kenya," *Journal of Politics* 78, no. 2 (2016): 557–71, argues that the ICC only enhances compliance when pro- and anticompliance groups are roughly balanced within states.

45. Alyssa K. Prorok, "The (In)compatibility of Peace and Justice? The International Criminal Court and Civil Conflict Termination," *International Organization* 71, no. 2 (2017): 213–43.

from Africa, yet severe human rights violations are found elsewhere as well.[46] This pattern of prosecutorial conduct, they charge, reflects either blatant racism or, perhaps less insidiously, a willingness by the court to proceed only in regions where the major states do not have significant interests. Many African countries are quite critical of the ICC and are threatening to withdraw. Either way, the ICC risks becoming a political entity rather than a true court of last resort.

The United States remains highly critical of the court. The treaty establishing the ICC was signed by President Bill Clinton shortly before he left office, which permitted the United States to participate in further negotiations on the court's rules of procedure. Almost immediately on taking office, however, President George W. Bush "unsigned" the treaty—a largely symbolic act.

The U.S. government raises many objections to the ICC.[47] Foremost is the fear of frivolous and politically motivated prosecutions against political leaders or American military personnel for actions taken to protect the security of the United States or on peacekeeping or peacemaking missions abroad. Given what is often seen as the special role of the United States in maintaining international peace and security, and real anti-Americanism in many countries, some skeptics of the ICC fear a string of political prosecutions in which leaders are tried not for violations of law, but merely for "show" or because others disagree with their policies.

There is also concern that leaders would be constrained by fears of future politically motivated prosecutions. Although the United States could avoid prosecution by the ICC by undertaking a genuine investigation or prosecution under its national laws, in defining what constitutes an adequate national-level inquiry the statute is sufficiently ambiguous that politically motivated prosecutions might still be possible.

The U.S. government also claims that the ICC is insufficiently accountable and lacks oversight mechanisms for both the judges and the prosecutors. On the dimensions of international law discussed in Chapter 11, critics fear that the ICC has been delegated too much power to interpret still-imprecise laws. Without the ability to remove activist judges, opponents are concerned that personnel at the ICC may escape political control and develop too much independence. In addition, international human rights case law and precedent are thin. Without adequate guidance from state parties on the intent of international law, the court might not just interpret, but essentially make, international law itself. Finally, given its prosecutorial and judicial independence, critics claim that the ICC might clash with the more political and problem-solving approach of the UN Security Council. Whereas diplomacy must be flexible and aware of context,

---

46. David Bosco, "Why Is the International Criminal Court Picking Only on Africa?" *Washington Post*, March 29, 2013, www.washingtonpost.com/opinions/why-is-the-international-criminal-court-picking-only-on-africa/2013/03/29/cb9bf5da-96f7-11e2-97cd-3d8c1afe4f0f_story.html. There is an open investigation in the country of Georgia, suggesting that a case may be filed soon.

47. See the statement by John R. Bolton, then undersecretary for arms control and international security at the Department of State, and later U.S. ambassador to the United Nations, http://2001-2009.state.gov/r/pa/prs/ps/2002/9968.htm (accessed 09/20/14). For a review, see the Congressional Research Service's report, www.fas.org/sgp/crs/misc/RL31495.pdf (accessed 09/20/14).

In March 2012, Thomas Lubanga Dyilo (seated, back right) became the first person to be convicted by the ICC. He was sentenced to 14 years in prison for the crime of forcibly recruiting child soldiers in the Democratic Republic of the Congo. Though Lubanga has appealed his conviction, he began serving his sentence in December 2015.

judicial proceedings that stress precedent, statutory interpretation, and equity across similar cases may conflict with the UN Security Council's charge to maintain peace and security.

After the ICC entered into force in 2002, the administration of President George W. Bush worked aggressively to exempt American nationals from the court's jurisdiction. Most important were the Article 98 agreements that were urged—some might say forced—on other countries. Article 98 of the ICC exempts a country from handing over a foreign national to the court if it is prohibited from doing so by a bilateral agreement with the national's country of origin. Under President Bush, over 100 countries signed such bilateral agreements with the United States under threat of losing all foreign and military aid or having American peacekeeping forces withdrawn. Despite sometimes significant aid cutoffs, other countries, including Barbados, Brazil, Costa Rica, Peru, Venezuela, Ecuador, Saint Vincent and the Grenadines, and South Africa, refused to sign these agreements. Although the Obama administration softened the U.S. stance toward the ICC, it did not move toward becoming a state party and accepting the court's jurisdiction. There is much concern that President Trump will seek to further undermine the ICC, though he has not made any statements one way or the other about the court.

Harnessing Material Interests

A final source for optimism is the proliferation of RTAs with human rights provisions. As we saw in Chapter 7, nearly every country in the world now belongs to at least one RTA, and nearly all RTAs contain some provisions on human rights. Some agreements are soft, or merely declarative, and appear to have no effect on behavior. Increasingly, though, RTAs contain obligatory and precise human rights provisions that bind states to international standards of behavior and threaten to withdraw trade and financial benefits if periodic reviews find substantial abuses of human rights. These hard provisions link concrete, material benefits of market access to a state's human rights practices. Unlike human rights agreements in general, and even soft RTAs, these hard provisions do have a significant, if small, effect on the level and extent of human rights violations.[48]

Ironically, protectionist groups that are looking to insulate themselves from import competition by including human rights provisions in free-trade agreements may have devised effective weapons to protect human rights abroad—and their self-interest in seeing benefits revoked may make threats to use these weapons

---

48. Hafner-Burton, "Trading Human Rights."

credible. Human rights advocates would do well to find other ways by which to harness often instrumental, material interests to the cause of promoting better human rights practices.

Conclusion: Why Protect Human Rights?

The puzzle of why states seek to protect the human rights of people outside their own borders is explained primarily by the interests of states. Whether because of concern for the well-being of others, an understanding of common humanity and the need to preserve democracy, or purely instrumental goals, individuals, groups, and thus states do have interests in promoting human rights abroad. TANs have been critical to the spread of international human rights norms in recent decades and in activating citizens to press their governments to act more forcefully to protect human rights. The facts that human rights are an issue today in international relations and that states concern themselves with human rights abroad is testament to the activities of the human rights TANs.

International human rights law is itself an institution. The likely positive but still-limited effectiveness of this institution in constraining abuses, in turn, follows from strategic interaction—or perhaps more precisely from the lack of real and consistent enforcement. While states have interests and are willing to pay some cost to protect human rights within other countries, rarely are they willing to make human rights a priority. As a result, states may publicly condemn abuse but impose few penalties on those who violate human rights. Knowing this, states abuse their citizens with little fear that they will be sanctioned.

The fact that the human rights clauses of RTAs do improve practice, however, suggests that institutions that link behavior to real consequences can have important effects. Current issues in international human rights law focus largely on the breadth and depth of the law itself—individual petitions, the ICC, and inclusion of obligatory human rights provisions in trade and other treaties. Given the modest effect of international human rights law on practice, perhaps human rights advocates would do better by focusing on designing more effective enforcement institutions.

Interests, Interactions, and Institutions in Context

- International human rights law is an institution created by and largely reflecting the political norms of Western, liberal democracies. The norms embodied in these laws remain controversial, are not shared equally by all countries, and have not yet been internalized in many societies and governments. Nonetheless, there is new evidence that international human rights law is improving practice in some specific contexts.

- Individuals and states have an interest in international human rights, and thus they undertake costly acts to punish states that violate the rights of their citizens. These interests are rarely strong enough to compel states to pay high costs for the protection of vulnerable individuals and groups outside their own borders. Human rights practices, in turn, may be more affected by TANs that change how both individuals and states conceive of their interests.

- States that violate human rights reason that, in their interactions with other states, they will probably not face serious consequences for their behavior and, therefore, can freely abuse individuals and groups. Unfortunately, these states are most likely correct. Although international human rights law does appear to promote improved practices, it remains of only limited effectiveness in altering the actions of states. Despite increasing support for human rights, international law by itself is not a panacea.

Key Terms

human rights, p. 501

Universal Declaration of Human Rights (UDHR), p. 501

International Covenant on Civil and Political Rights (ICCPR), p. 503

International Covenant on Economic, Social, and Cultural Rights (ICESCR), p. 503

International Bill of Rights, p. 504

nonderogable rights, p. 508

prisoners of conscience (POCs), p. 509

individual petition, p. 532

International Criminal Court (ICC), p. 534

For Further Reading

Brysk, Alison. *Speaking Rights to Power: Constructing Political Will.* **New York: Oxford University Press, 2013.** Surveys the conditions for successful human rights campaigns by NGOs.

Donnelly, Jack. *Universal Human Rights in Theory and Practice.* **3rd ed. Ithaca, NY: Cornell University Press, 2013.** Presents a general overview of the philosophy and practice of international human rights law.

Forsythe, David. *Human Rights in International Relations.* **New York: Columbia University Press, 2000.** Offers an introduction to international human rights, with detailed analyses of international courts, regional human rights agreements, and other issues.

Hafner-Burton, Emilie. *Making Human Rights a Reality.* **Princeton, NJ: Princeton University Press, 2013.** Argues against the current universalistic and legalistic approach to human rights and for an alternative model based on human rights "stewards" who focus their efforts on issues and places where progress is possible.

Hopgood, Stephen. *The Endtimes of Human Rights.* **Ithaca, NY: Cornell University Press, 2013.** A critique of the assumption that human rights are universal and of current practices of human rights promotion.

Ishay, Micheline R. *The History of Human Rights: From Ancient Times to the Globalization Era.* **Berkeley: University of California Press, 2004.** Provides a comprehensive analysis of human rights philosophy and practice from ancient Greece to the present.

Sikkink, Kathryn. *The Justice Cascade: How Human Rights Prosecutions Are Changing World Politics.* **New York: Norton, 2011.** Examines the origins and consequences of international human rights prosecutions.

Simmons, Beth A. *Mobilizing for Human Rights: International Law in Domestic Politics.* **New York: Cambridge University Press, 2009.** Examines the critical role of domestic institutions in promoting effective human rights practices.

Wong, Wendy. *Internal Affairs: How the Structure of NGOs Transforms Human Rights.* **Ithaca, NY: Cornell University Press, 2012.** Demonstrates how the organizational structures and incentives of human rights NGOs shaped the transnational advocacy movement and its effectiveness.

13

The Global Environment

THE PUZZLE *Nearly everyone wants a cleaner and healthier environment. Why, then, is it so hard to cooperate internationally to protect the environment?*

Above: Though Bangladesh is responsible for only a small fraction of the carbon emissions driving global climate change, low-lying areas of the country are especially vulnerable to one of climate change's primary consequences: rising sea levels. The disproportionate effects of climate change on countries around the world, with some of the largest emitters facing fewer consequences, has hampered cooperation among members of the international community on environmental issues.

On June 1, 2017, President Donald J. Trump announced that he planned to withdraw the United States from the Paris Agreement. Under this agreement, which took effect only months earlier, nearly all nations committed to undertake plans to combat climate change. The agreement also provides enhanced support for developing countries in this effort. Many analysts see the accord as a major step forward in the fight against global warming, but Trump argued that its terms were not sufficiently favorable to the United States.

Despite Trump's stated intent to withdraw, not one of the 197 other countries that signed the Paris accord has announced a similar move. The rest of the world appears to be standing firmly behind the agreement. Within the United States, a growing number of states, municipalities, and businesses have affirmed that they still plan to abide by the terms of the agreement. The same day that President Trump announced his withdrawal plans, the governors of California, New York, and Washington State announced the formation of the United States Climate Alliance to bring together states, cities, and companies committed to meeting the nation's previous Paris commitment. The efforts of these groups, in combination with changes in the U.S. economy (especially the falling costs of alternative energy sources), make it likely that the United States will, in fact, meet the goals set under the Paris Agreement—regardless of the president's actions.[1]

Successfully addressing environmental challenges requires coordination and cooperation at many levels. As a global agreement that relies on commitments to concrete actions by each individual country, the Paris Agreement embodies this complex reality. It was decades in the making, having grown out of the United Nations Framework Convention on Climate Change (UNFCCC), which was signed in 1992. As its name implies, the UNFCCC created only a framework for further negotiations that would address specific issues, including the reduction of greenhouse gas emissions and financing for poor countries to adapt to climate change.

1. Harriet Agerholm, "US Will Meet Paris Accord Commitments Even If Donald Trump Withdraws, Says Report," *Independent*, July 17, 2017, www.independent.co.uk/environment/renewable-energy-cheapest-power-form-country-2020-paris-agreement-climate-change-us-donald-trump-a7844671.html.

The framework was followed in 1997 by the Kyoto Protocol, in force since 2005, which committed only the 24 most developed countries to reductions in greenhouse gases. Kyoto faltered after the United States withdrew in 2001. While many observers have been skeptical of the Paris Agreement because commitments are "bottom up," designed by each country rather than adhering to a global formula, it may be this very flexibility combined with its planned ability to adapt over time that will allow it to succeed.

In recent decades, the international community has also made substantial progress on other environmental issues. International treaties have restricted shipments of hazardous waste across borders, established protections for countless plant and animal species, banned some of the most harmful fishing practices, and protected the ozone layer. But addressing climate change remains a major challenge. The Intergovernmental Panel on Climate Change (IPCC) estimates that the earth has already warmed by an average of 0.85°C since 1880, that this increase is clearly attributable to human-caused emissions of greenhouse gases, and that the planet will continue to warm with accumulated greenhouse gas emissions. How much future warming we can expect is highly dependent on continued emissions.

The global community agreed in the Paris Agreement to "pursue" a limit of 1.5°C of total warming above preindustrial levels. But while people around the world are already feeling the effects of global warming, from more typhoons in the Pacific to wildfires in California, countries have found it difficult to balance the strong measures required to address climate change with fears that such restrictions will inhibit economic growth. Even if countries meet their Paris Agreement commitments, global temperatures are still expected to rise 3°C by 2100, with serious consequences.[2]

So, while the Paris Agreement, as the first universal climate accord, represents progress, it also demonstrates how difficult it is to coordinate global action.

Thinking Analytically about the Global Environment

This chapter aims to explain the sources of and impediments to international environmental cooperation. First, we will see that despite widely shared interests in the quality of the environment, the interactions among individuals and countries suffer from problems of collective action. Although each person and each country has an interest in a world without climate change, for instance, they also prefer to free ride on the efforts of others, saving themselves the cost of reducing emissions while benefiting from the cutbacks of others. In the absence of any international authority that can mandate improved performance, free riding produces less overall environmental cooperation than individuals and countries collectively desire.

Second, individuals, groups, and countries have conflicting interests over who bears the costs of mitigating harmful environmental practices, with rich countries typically demanding universal cuts and poorer countries claiming they should be largely exempt from costly restrictions until their incomes have risen. When President Trump announced his intent to withdraw the United States from the Paris Agreement, he argued both that he wanted to preserve and possibly expand jobs in coal and other carbon fuel–based industries and that other countries should bear more of the costs of addressing climate change. How environmental policies distribute costs affects how likely actors are to cooperate successfully on issues relating to the environment.

Finally, international institutions facilitate environmental cooperation, primarily by enhancing information and verifying compliance. Transnational advocacy networks (TANs) and other nongovernmental organizations (NGOs) now play an essential role in monitoring compliance with environmental agreements. The clearer and more easily verified the standard, the more likely states are to cooperate successfully.

2. United Nations Environment Programme, "The Emissions Gap Report 2016," November 2016, http://uneplive.unep.org/theme/index/13#egr.

Why Are Good Intentions Not Good Enough?

As we have noted, international cooperation on **global climate change** has made significant progress in the past several decades—from the foundational **United Nations Framework Convention on Climate Change (UNFCCC)** signed in 1992, to the **Paris Agreement** signed in 2016. Despite broad-based interests in environmental quality, however, cooperation is sometimes thwarted by interactions in which it is difficult to coordinate large numbers of individuals or, at the international level, moderately large numbers of states.

We might personally care about the environment and want to improve the quality of the world we inhabit—that is, we have an interest in environmental cooperation—but our individual actions have little effect on the local or global ecosystem. This problem is sometimes referred to as the **tragedy of the commons**, after a famous article by the ecologist Garrett Hardin.[3]

Imagine a meadow in old England where all the villagers graze their sheep. It is open to all—the village "commons" as it was called. This is the end of the Middle Ages, a long period where nothing much seemed to change. The human population was stable, and families raised the same number of sheep for generations. But now imagine that people start to have new sources of income, and some invest in sheep. There is new demand for wool and meat. Villagers choose to raise more and more lambs to adulthood and graze them on the land.

An individual farmer—let's call him Smith—is deciding whether to raise more sheep this year. He takes a look at the land. It is starting to become degraded; sheep pull grass up by the roots, so each year as there are more sheep, there is less grass in the meadow. To protect the land, Smith knows it would be better to graze fewer sheep. But even if he puts fewer sheep out to graze, he anticipates that other farmers will continue to increase the size of their flocks. In fact, he worries, if he waits until next year, there might not be enough grass for anyone. So, Smith reasons, better to raise more sheep this year and make a profit while he can. Every farmer is making the same calculation as Smith, and as a result, the once flourishing meadow gets further degraded, and over time the farmers can graze fewer and fewer sheep.

This dilemma, where individual action cannot prevent the environmental harm, has been known for centuries. In fact, the scenario just described is exactly what happened in countless villages all over England between the end of the Middle Ages and the beginning of the Industrial Revolution. It led to a change in practice and law known as the enclosure movement, the privatizing of formerly common land. We will explain in the next section how private property is one way to resolve the tragedy of the commons.

global climate change

Human-induced change in the environment, especially from the emissions of greenhouse gases, leading to higher temperatures around the globe.

United Nations Framework Convention on Climate Change (UNFCCC)

An international agreement enacted in 1992, and entered into force in 1994, that provides an overall framework for intergovernmental efforts on climate change.

Paris Agreement

An agreement negotiated under the UNFCCC in 2015, signed by 197 countries, and entered into force in 2016. It was the first agreement to require commitments for the control of greenhouse gas emissions from all signatories.

tragedy of the commons

A problem that occurs when a resource is open to all, without limit. No one has an incentive to conserve, because others would use the resource in the meantime, so the resource suffers degradation.

---

3. Garrett Hardin, "The Tragedy of the Commons," *Science* 162, no. 3859 (December 3, 1968): 1243–48.

An overgrazed meadow is the classic example of the tragedy of the commons, in which individual farmers graze sheep according to their own self-interest, consequently depleting the amount of grass in the meadow and disadvantaging all farmers.

The tragedy of the commons is not just an interesting tale from history. It describes many of our current environmental challenges. Some are local. A fishery in a lake or a forest shared by villagers is often degraded from overuse: no one has an incentive to leave the immature fish or saplings for later if others will take them today. The water in the lake itself can be subject to such a tragedy, either from overuse of the water (drawing too much for irrigation purposes) or from the dumping of pollutants into it. Each person's small amount of waste seems harmless enough, but added together, it can destroy the lake. The tragedy of the commons is a classic Prisoner's Dilemma (see Chapter 2).

We now face tragedies of the commons on a global scale. Take the earth's atmosphere and global climate change as one example. When only a small number of people drove automobiles, the carbon dioxide from burning gasoline did not build up significantly in the lower atmosphere or threaten the planet with global warming. But now, as more and more people own cars, the accumulation of pollution threatens the health of humans, as well as of plants and animals, and the buildup of carbon risks causing permanent climate change (see Figure 13.1).

No single individual's or small group's changes in behavior can solve these problems. We face similar problems with the loss of species or degradation of forests around the world. For one small town, cutting down a forest to make way for more agricultural land or a new factory might make economic sense. But globally, these individual choices have added up to a loss of forest area about the size of South Africa between 1990 and 2015.[4]

Because we can benefit from others' efforts to preserve the environment while having only a marginal effect ourselves, we often avoid changing our personal behaviors or incurring costs to reduce pollution. In short, even though we prefer a cleaner environment, we nonetheless seek to free ride on the efforts of others. Since everyone makes the same calculation, we individually defect from environmental efforts and collectively produce a suboptimal outcome for society as a whole (also known as a Pareto suboptimal or inferior outcome; see the "Special Topic" appendix to Chapter 2, on p. 82). Thus, even though we may all have a shared interest in protecting the environment, our incentives to free ride usually win out, and through our interactions we collectively degrade the ecosystem.

The same logic applies at the international level. Most countries' efforts to conserve resources or limit pollution have only a small effect on the global

---

4. Food and Agriculture Organization of the United Nations, *Global Forest Resources Assessment 2015: How Are the World's Forests Changing?* 2nd ed. (Rome: FAO, 2016), 3, www.fao.org/3/a-i4793e.pdf.

FIGURE 13.1 *The Greenhouse Effect*

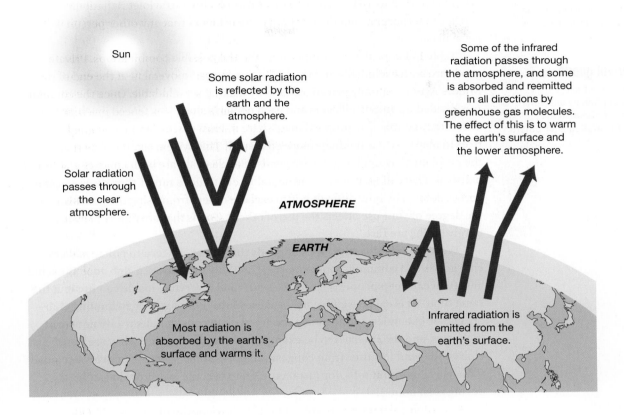

Sun

Some solar radiation is reflected by the earth and the atmosphere.

Some of the infrared radiation passes through the atmosphere, and some is absorbed and reemitted in all directions by greenhouse gas molecules. The effect of this is to warm the earth's surface and the lower atmosphere.

Solar radiation passes through the clear atmosphere.

ATMOSPHERE

EARTH

Most radiation is absorbed by the earth's surface and warms it.

Infrared radiation is emitted from the earth's surface.

Figure source: www.seai.ie/ images_upload/Schools/ Secondary_Schools/Subjects/ CSPE/Lesson_Plans_for_CSPE/ Climate_Change_facts/ greenhouse%20effect.jpg (accessed 09/20/14).

environment. Because the costs of their pollution fall on others as well as on themselves, they do not bear the full consequences of their decision to pollute. Similarly, if they sacrifice income by imposing tighter environmental controls on themselves, they create benefits for other countries that have not paid a similarly high price. Thus, countries seek to free ride on other countries, and the global environment suffers.

Collective Action and the Environment

Most of the environmental benefits we wish to gain or the harms we wish to avoid come in the form of **public goods** or **common-pool resources**. All goods, whether they are individually owned items, like your car, or goods that we can enjoy collectively, like clean air, can be defined along two axes. First, goods are defined by whether they are excludable, or by how easily you can be kept from using them. Second, goods are also classified by whether they are rival, or if your use of them precludes their use by others.

Your car is a private good. You can exclude others from using it—just hold on to your key—and if you lend it to your friend to drive, you cannot drive it

public goods

Products that are nonexcludable and nonrival in consumption, such as clean air or water.

common-pool resources

Goods that are available to everyone, but such that one user's consumption of the good reduces the amount available for others. Common-pool resources are rival but nonexcludable.

nonexcludable goods

Goods that, if available to be consumed by one actor, cannot be prevented from being consumed by other actors as well.

nonrival goods

Goods for which consumption by one actor does not diminish the quantity available for others.

somewhere else. Clean air and the ozone layer, by contrast, are public goods. They are **nonexcludable** and **nonrival** in consumption. If the ozone layer is strong and protective, we all benefit from its sun-screening effects. If it is diminished, we all are subject to an increased risk of cancer from higher ultraviolet radiation. Whether you get skin cancer or not does not affect the chances that any other person will get skin cancer.

Table 13.1 depicts these dimensions and the possible combinations. Private goods are both excludable and rival. The "enclosure" movement at the end of the Middle Ages essentially privatized land by making it excludable. Once the commons was divided up among villagers and each person's share was fenced in—with the aristocracy getting a disproportionate share in most cases—landowners had incentives to manage their holdings more efficiently. This system significantly reduced the problem of overgrazing. Public goods, like clean air, are both nonexcludable and nonrival. These dimensions are, in actuality, continuous rather than discrete categories, defined by how difficult it is to exclude others from using the goods and how the degree of your use affects the use of others. Goods that are purely private or purely public are rare.

We also find two other types of goods that are of concern to policy makers: club goods and common-pool resources. As Table 13.1 shows, a club good is excludable (you can keep people out), but it is not rival (everyone inside can use it at the same time). It is called a club good because clubs—like a golf or swimming club—are classic examples. In the policy sphere, we can consider electricity networks, highways, and the Internet to be examples of club goods. Since they are nonrival, club goods tend to suffer from congestion unless some users are actively excluded ("freeways" without tolls, for instance, tend to become overcrowded, at least during rush hours).

Common-pool resources are essentially the opposite of club goods. One person's use does impinge on another's, so they are rival. But it is very difficult to exclude people from using them. These are goods like the old-fashioned village commons, a forest, or a fishery. Global fisheries suffer greatly as common-pool resources. It is difficult to exclude anyone from fishing on the high seas, but a fish caught by one boat cannot simultaneously be caught by another. Like the village commons before enclosure, common-pool resources tend to be overexploited, often leading to environmental degradation.

Most of the environmental challenges we face today relate either to public goods or to common-pool resources. Public goods arise partly from nature. Because the earth has a single atmosphere, we all suffer from a thinner ozone layer and a warmer

---

TABLE 13.1 *Private versus Public Goods, and Their Variants*

	EXCLUDABLE	NONEXCLUDABLE
RIVAL	Private goods	Common-pool resources
NONRIVAL	Club goods	Public goods

climate. Public goods and common-pool resources are also produced by social practice and law. The village commons described earlier is one such social practice that was altered through enclosure, a different social practice, and a new set of laws.

Similarly, the **Kyoto Protocol** created a carbon trading system that, in essence, privatized what was previously a public good. Before Kyoto, the atmosphere was treated as a global commons, free for anyone to use, even when that use produced harmful greenhouse gas emissions. The Kyoto Protocol, however, limited the total amount of carbon pollution allowed and then divided that resource among the parties through rights to pollute. The fact that social practice and laws can change the incentives and, thus, the interests of actors is a foundation on which better environmental practices can be built.

Common-pool resources like fish in the ocean or water in a lake are frequently exploited to the point of devastation because everyone benefits from using the resource but no one actor bears specific responsibility for ensuring its survival.

Solving Collective Action Problems

Public goods are undersupplied by market forces. People want the public good, like clean air or clean water. Since they benefit from the public good, once supplied, there is a demand for it. The problem arises on the supply side. Because you cannot be excluded from enjoying the good if it is provided by others, nor does your use diminish the quantity of the good available to others, you have little incentive to voluntarily provide the good yourself or to contribute to its provision by the community. You can, in short, "free ride" on your neighbors, your fellow citizens, or the global community.

Resolving or at least mitigating the tragedy of the commons requires one or sometimes both of two possible strategies. Actors can create private property rights, as in the enclosure movement, or actors can regulate their behavior through laws, norms, or cooperative agreements. Before doing either, however, actors must first recognize the problem and agree that action is necessary.

Kyoto Protocol

An amendment to the UN Framework Convention on Climate Change, adopted in 1997 and entered into force in 2005, that established specific targets for reducing emissions of carbon and five other greenhouse gases through 2020.

Five Factors in Cooperation As explained in Chapter 2, international environmental cooperation is affected by at least five factors. First, the magnitude of collective action problems typically varies by group size.[5] The larger the group of actors, the more likely they are to free ride on one another, as the contribution of each will be a proportionally smaller percentage of the total. The smaller the group, the more likely actors are to contribute to solving the problem.

---

5. Mancur Olson, *The Logic of Collective Action: Public Goods and the Theory of Groups* (Cambridge, MA: Harvard University Press, 1965).

This helps explain why acid rain, a problem in the 1970s, was relatively easy to address. Acid rain is produced when sulfur dioxide and nitrogen oxide are emitted into the atmosphere and subsequently absorbed by water droplets, creating a mild solution of sulfuric and nitric acid that eventually falls to the earth as precipitation. The highly acidic rain affects the chemical balance of soil, lakes, and streams. Indeed, acid rain killed many forests and both plant and aquatic life in lakes before being brought under control. Acid rain is primarily a regional phenomenon, however, falling mostly downwind of large coal-burning industrial centers. Thus, emissions from the United States fell mostly on itself and Canada; British emissions, on Scandinavia; western European emissions, on eastern Europe; and so forth. Although restricted to countries downwind of large polluters, the same problem occurs in many different regions.

The limited number of countries in each acid rain region was a key factor in facilitating negotiations for the Convention on Long-Range Transboundary Air Pollution (CLRTAP) and its optional protocol, completed in 1979 and now possessing 51 members from across several acid rain regions. Together, the member states have reduced sulfur emissions by more than 60 percent below 1980 levels.[6] Small numbers do not guarantee success, however. East Asian countries were never able to copy the CLRTAP example. While Chinese air pollution has started to decline, it continues to cause smog problems in both Japan and Korea.

The second factor affecting international environmental cooperation is the complexity and magnitude of the problem. Some environmental problems are defined narrowly. In 1995, the Governing Council of the United Nations Environment Programme (UNEP) decided that 12 particular chemicals, the "dirty dozen," were particularly hazardous. Not only did these chemicals persist and move around in the atmosphere, but they accumulated in animals and humans. This narrowly defined problem moved to a rapid solution. Negotiations began in 1998 on the Stockholm Convention on Persistent Organic Pollutants. A treaty was completed in 2001 and entered into force in 2004. Most countries, 181 to date, have ratified the treaty—a figure similar to the ratification numbers for more difficult treaties like the Paris Agreement and the Montreal Protocol. Similar issue-specific treaties, like the Basel Convention on the Control of Transboundary Movements of Hazardous Wastes and Their Disposal, were also negotiated quickly.

Third, as we saw in Chapter 2, groups that interact repeatedly (iteration) or frequently on other issues (linkage) will be able to induce greater contributions from one another through strategies of reciprocal punishment in which contributors sanction noncontributors by withholding future cooperation. The resolution of the acid rain problem in North America and Europe was facilitated because the neighboring states interacted frequently on many dimensions (Canada and the United States are among each other's largest trading partners, for instance) and

---

6. Keith Bull, M. Johansson, and M. Krzyzanowski, "Impacts of the Convention on Long-Range Transboundary Air Pollution on Air Quality in Europe," *Journal of Toxicology and Environmental Health. Part A* 71, no. 1 (2008): 51–55.

expected to interact intensely into the foreseeable future. Downwind states whose lakes were slowly dying from acid rain thus expected to have plenty of opportunities to punish their upwind neighbors if the latter did not live up to the terms of the CLRTAP.

Fourth, when public goods come bundled with private goods for which actors are willing to pay, cooperation is also facilitated. These are called joint products.[7] Rain forests absorb significant amounts of carbon and thus help reduce the problem of global climate change, and they are home to many different species, thereby enhancing biodiversity. Saving acres in a rain forest to preserve a global carbon sink (absorber of greenhouse gases) and promote biodiversity also provides erosion control to local landowners and opportunities for ecotourism, and those landowners are free to pursue such measures for those private benefits.

In an analogous situation, the DuPont company saw an opportunity for increased profits as the pressure to ban CFCs began to increase in the 1980s. DuPont was a leading producer of CFCs, accounting for nearly 50 percent of all production in the United States and 25 percent of global production. But as the leading innovator of alternatives for CFCs as well, DuPont was also well positioned to gain from a CFC ban.[8] In this case, eliminating the production of CFCs also provided a private profit for DuPont. For all joint products, the public good is provided as a by-product of efforts to obtain the private good. The larger the private benefits are relative to the public good, the less free riding we will observe.

Fifth and finally, when actors vary in size (as states do) or in the intensity of their preferences for public goods, a privileged group may emerge (see Chapter 2). A privileged group comprises one or a small number of actors who receive sufficient benefits themselves from the public good that they are willing to bear the cost of providing that good for all. The benefits of reducing ozone depletion were sufficiently large to the United States, for example, that it was willing to bear the initial costs of banning CFCs unilaterally and of leading the international fight against their use. The United States produced 30 percent of the world's CFCs, and the savings to the country alone from reduced instances of skin cancer were sufficient to justify a major effort to limit CFC emissions. After some initial reluctance, the United States took a leadership position in the negotiations that produced the effective **Vienna Convention** and **Montreal Protocol** (see "What Shaped Our World?" on p. 550). The developed countries were then collectively motivated enough to pay for the transition to safer chemicals in developing countries.

Climate change is an especially difficult environmental problem because it (1) affects all countries on the globe, although not necessarily to the same extent, given differences in elevation, latitude, and other factors; (2) centers on the burning

Vienna Convention
A framework convention adopted in 1985 to regulate activities, especially emissions of CFCs, that damage the ozone layer.

Montreal Protocol
An international treaty, signed in 1987, that is designed to protect the ozone layer by phasing out the production of a number of CFCs and other chemical compounds.

---

7. They are also called selective incentives. See Todd Sandler, *Global Challenges: An Approach to Environmental, Political, and Economic Problems* (New York: Cambridge University Press, 1997), 45–46.

8. Karen Litfin, *Ozone Discourses: Science and Politics in Global Environmental Cooperation* (New York: Columbia University Press, 1994), 123–27.

The Montreal Protocol and the Protection of the Ozone Layer

The 1974 finding that human-made chemicals called CFCs (chlorofluorocarbons) were destroying the stratospheric ozone layer (Figure A) initiated the most rapid and successful international environmental effort in history.[a] Countries responded to this threat quickly with steps that included banning aerosol sprays in 1978. At the same time, the United States and other countries pushed for international action. As the predictions of scientists became more dire, their fears were dramatically confirmed with the unexpected discovery of the enormous Antarctic ozone hole in 1984. The Vienna Convention, signed in 1985, established a framework for limiting CFCs. Two years later, the Montreal Protocol established a strict global phaseout plan.

And the London Amendment to the Montreal Protocol, adopted in 1990, accelerated the timeline for phasing out CFCs. Since then, as the science has progressed, more chemicals have been added to the phaseout list.

The Montreal Protocol has worked. Emissions of ozone-depleting substances (ODS) have decreased dramatically. Although ODS remain in the atmosphere for decades and continue to cause damage to the ozone layer (see Figure B), scientists have identified "fingerprints of

FIGURE A *The Chemistry of Ozone Depletion*

Ultraviolet radiation strikes a CFC molecule...

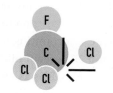
...and causes a chlorine atom to break away.

The chlorine atom collides with an ozone molecule...

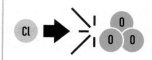

...and steals an oxygen atom to form chlorine monoxide and leave a molecule of ordinary oxygen.

When a free atom of oxygen collides with the chlorine monoxide...

...the two oxygen atoms form a molecule of oxygen. The chlorine atom is released and free to destroy more ozone.

Note: C: carbon; Cl: chlorine; F: fluorine; O: oxygen.

healing" of the ozone layer and predict it will recover to its pre-1980s levels by 2070.[b]

Interactions The ozone layer is a classic example of a public good. Everyone can share equally in its benefits of protection from the sun's harmful ultraviolet light. However, once humans became capable of polluting it, the ozone layer was subject to the tragedy of the commons. Unless everyone agreed to protect the ozone layer together, no single group of people or country could enjoy its benefits.

To figure out how much human activity needed to be curtailed required scientific input. But determining who would reduce, by how much, and who would pay required active bargaining among governments often concerned about companies within their borders. That the United States, the wealthiest and most powerful nation, was cutting its own emissions first made these interactions easier, forcing reluctant countries to stay at the table and enabling the global community to find solutions to these challenges.

a. Mario J. Molina and F. Sherwood Rowland, "Stratospheric Sink for Chlorofluoromethanes: Chlorine Atom-Catalysed Destruction of Ozone," *Nature* 249 no. 5460 (1974): 810–12.

b. Susan Solomon, Diane J. Ivy, Doug Kinnison, Michael J. Mills, et al., "Emergence of Healing in the Antarctic Ozone Layer," *Science* 353, no. 6296 (2016): 269–74; and Paul A. Newman, Eric R. Nash, S. Randolph Kawa, Stephen A. Montzka, et al., "When Will the Antarctic Ozone Hole Recover?" *Geophysical Research Letters* 33, no. 12 (2006).

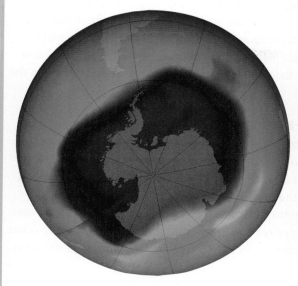

FIGURE B *Ozone Hole on September 24, 2006*

This image depicts the largest ozone hole ever observed: 11.4 million square miles. Purple and blue identify areas with the least amount of ozone; green and yellow areas have more ozone.

Figure source: www.nasa.gov/images/content/160657main_OZONE_large.jpg (accessed 07/02/07).

Interests

The global community had a clear interest in protecting the ozone layer and thus reducing the emissions of ODS. However, the problem we face in any tragedy of the commons is that it is always better for you if someone else goes first. Moreover, different publics and different businesses had very different priorities. The American public was concerned about ODS by the late 1970s, and U.S. companies had developed some alternative products. By contrast, the European public was not yet focused on the issue, and manufacturers in France, Italy, and the United Kingdom still wanted to produce CFCs and related chemicals. As a result, the initial negotiations were a tough fight between the United States and Europe.

By the time of the Montreal Protocol, interests had changed again, with British prime minister Margaret Thatcher (a former chemist) and U.S. industrial leaders schooling President Ronald Reagan on the importance of the agreement. The major challenge then was how to ensure that developing countries that were not yet major manufacturers would go along with the ban instead of jumping in to take advantage of a deserted market.[c]

Institutions

The Montreal Protocol is managed by the UN Environment Programme (UNEP). The cornerstone of the agreement is the phaseout of ODS, but developing countries were allowed to phase them out at a slower rate. When the parties to the treaty agreed to accelerate the phaseout in the London Amendment, they also agreed to what became known as the Multilateral Fund, a special fund designed to compensate developing countries for the cost of phaseout and provide technical and financial assistance with the transition to other chemicals. To date, the Multilateral Fund has spent over $3 billion.[d]

The Montreal Protocol is today the only global treaty with universal membership. All 193 UN members are parties to the treaty. The treaty has both carrots and sticks. In addition to offering developing countries financial assistance and access to technology, the treaty was designed to be costly to those who did not join. Countries outside the treaty were no longer able to purchase ODS from treaty members. In effect, since most developing countries were not manufacturers, they would face an immediate cutoff rather than a gradual and financially cushioned phaseout.

The phaseout has not been without criticism. In particular, the slow phaseout of another ODS, called methyl bromide, was an issue of contention for years, with the United States seeking and receiving special protection for a substance that made tomatoes and strawberries easier to transport over longer distances.[e] In the end, while experts had recommended a phaseout by 2001, the chemical was not fully phased out until 2015. Critics argued that the United States had used its considerable power, which earlier had pushed through the agreement, to protect its own industry.

Despite these challenges, the Montreal Protocol is widely viewed as successful because of its design. The agreement is flexible and dynamic and intended to be informed by the latest scientific research. It has also relied heavily on the willingness of developed countries to pay the cost of the entire global public good. While $3 billion may sound like a lot, that figure is spread out over 26 years. Thus, the amount, while unprecedented in an international environmental agreement, was relatively modest. By contrast, the transition to a non-carbon-based global economy is estimated to cost in the trillions.

c. Richard Elliot Benedick, *Ozone Diplomacy: New Directions in Safeguarding the Planet* (Cambridge, MA: Harvard University Press, 1998).

d. www.multilateralfund.org/default.aspx (accessed 07/20/17).

e. Brian J. Gareau, "A Critical Review of the Successful CFC Phaseout versus the Delayed Methyl Bromide Phase-out in the Montreal Protocol," *International Environmental Agreements: Politics, Law and Economics* 10, no. 3 (2010): 209–31.

of fossil fuels, the major source of energy today, and therefore touches on all aspects of nearly every country's economy and society, rendering any solution enormously complex; and (3) to date lacks leadership by the world's single largest producer of greenhouse gases, the United States. On the positive side, because fossil fuels are ubiquitous, there are many joint products and opportunities for iteration and linkage. These features of the climate change problem have resulted in only tentative progress, first in the UNFCCC, then in the Kyoto Protocol, and most recently in the Paris Agreement.

Creating Property Rights: Cap-and-Trade Systems

Most economists agree that the most efficient way to overcome the collective action problems inherent in addressing climate change is to tax carbon emissions, thereby forcing polluters to pay a price for emitting carbon into the atmosphere. If taxed, the price of carbon fuels would more fully reflect the costs imposed on society. Such carbon taxes, however, are politically unpopular with both industries that emit carbon and consumers, who would pay higher prices for these industries' products. As with other environmental problems, efforts have focused instead on creating property rights and regulations.

In implementing the Kyoto Protocol, Europe essentially created property rights in greenhouse gas emissions. Since 2005, Europe has used an Emissions Trading Scheme (ETS) to regulate emissions. In the current phase of the program, the system includes 11,000 facilities in the electric power and industrial sectors, as well as civil aviation, and covers some 45 percent of Europe's emissions. The ETS is what is known as a **cap-and-trade system**. Cap and trade works very well for large emitters, where emissions can be measured. For other sources, like individual automobiles, the European Union (EU), like the United States, uses an efficiency standard.

In previous phases of the EU's ETS, firms were issued free credits to emit a set amount of greenhouse gases based on their prior emissions, and the firms then could buy and sell the credits. The credits created ownership over an amount of greenhouse gases that could be released into the atmosphere in any given year—in essence creating a property right to a certain quantity of pollutants. The number of credits drops a bit each year to force a reduction in total emissions. In the current phase, the majority of credits will be sold at auction, although there continue to be some free credits.

Given a cap-and-trade system, economists believe that selling credits at auction is the most efficient way to allocate them. Those who find it most difficult to reduce their greenhouse gas emissions will bid for the credits. Others may find that there are less expensive alternatives, such as improving energy efficiency or investing in renewable energy. Once the credits are issued, companies can buy and sell them if they find they need more or fewer than they originally thought. Starting from a 2005 baseline, the goal of the European Union's ETS is to achieve a 21 percent reduction in emissions by 2020, and a 43 percent reduction by 2030. While not a party to the Kyoto Protocol, the state of California also uses a cap-and-trade system for its state-established carbon goals.

cap-and-trade system

A cap-and-trade system sets limits on emissions, which are then lowered over time to reduce pollutants released into the atmosphere. Firms can sell "credits" when they emit less than their allocation or must buy from others when they emit more than their allocation.

In addition to buying and selling credits within Europe, European countries can buy credits from developing countries. A similar system exists in Japan. Since developing countries do not have a carbon cap under the Kyoto Protocol, these emissions savings are documented through a program known as the Clean Development Mechanism (CDM). In order to sell credits through the CDM, a project in the developing country has to clearly document that it is reducing emissions from what would otherwise be business as usual.

Since the reduction in emissions in developing countries is offset by an increase in allowed emissions in Europe (or elsewhere within the Kyoto Protocol), the CDM does not reduce total global emissions. The real goal of the CDM is to increase investment in green energy in developing countries by creating an incentive for projects that would qualify for sellable emissions credits. As of 2018, almost 8,000 emissions reduction projects had been initiated. In the early years of the CDM, the largest numbers of credits were issued for projects in China. The majority of CDM-approved projects are still in Asia, but the European Union and the United Nations have made an effort to increase the number in other countries in Asia and in other parts of the developing world. After 2012, China was no longer eligible for the CDM.

With the Paris Agreement, the incentives for developing countries are now a bit different. Under the agreement, each country makes a **nationally determined contribution (NDC)**. NDCs can be achieved however each country chooses. The country might set a greenhouse gas cap, a renewable energy target, or an acreage of forests to be protected. If choosing a greenhouse gas cap, the country may implement a cap-and-trade system and may even link up its system with the European ETS so that its companies can buy and sell credits with other countries.

China is actively developing a domestic cap-and-trade system. Since 2013, the government has run experimental markets in seven cities. On December 9, 2017, China formally launched a nationwide market for carbon emissions. This system is a key Chinese NDC under the Paris Agreement and was also a major point in an agreement that Premier Xi Jinping signed with then U.S. president Barack Obama in 2014. Establishing a national market for emissions trading is a challenge in a huge country with relatively weak regulatory systems. The market is expected to run essentially as an experiment until 2020, by which time government officials hope they will have worked out the kinks in the system.[9]

Once China's system is up and running, it is possible that the government will make agreements with other cap-and-trade systems, including those in Europe and California. Although the details in various national plans differ and are important, all cap-and-trade mechanisms attempt to create property rights in emissions as a way to privatize the right to use the global environment and create incentives to better manage it.

Nationally Determined Contribution (NDC)

The commitment each party to the Paris Agreement makes as to how they will contribute to reducing the threat of global warming.

---

9. Chris Buckley, "Xi Jinping Is Set for a Big Gamble with China's Carbon Trading Market," *New York Times*, June 23, 2017, www.nytimes.com/2017/06/23/world/asia/china-cap-trade-carbon-greenhouse .html?_r=0.

Organizations like the International Whaling Commission, which includes many nonwhaling member countries, may solve collective action problems by creating enforceable regulations.

Regulation The ban on whaling illustrates an alternative model for solving collective action problems related to the environment: a centrally set regulation.[10] Like fisheries in general, whales are a common-pool resource that has been overexploited in the past. To address this issue, the whaling industry voluntarily created the International Whaling Commission (IWC) in 1946. In an attempt to limit annual catches to sustainable yields, each country was assigned an annual quota by the governing council of the IWC. With the council composed almost entirely of representatives of whaling states, and with each member country lobbying to set its quota as high as possible, the IWC set the aggregate quota far above that which would allow the whale population to regenerate itself. As a result, the limits were ineffective and the number of whales plummeted.

Starting in the early 1960s, annual catches fell from approximately 15,000 to less than 5,000 whales per year—not as a result of strict quotas, but because of declining whale populations. Even though the industry recognized that its long-term health required lower quotas and rates of exploitation, the member states were unable to resist their incentives to catch as many whales as quickly as they could.

It is here that the rules of the IWC as an institution became important in finally moving toward effective regulation. Environmentalists became concerned about the whaling issue not from a sustainable catch perspective, but from an interest in protecting whales as a species. Some of their concern was about protecting biodiversity, but much was simply about protecting whales for their beauty and perceived intelligence.

The environmental community eventually figured out a way to use the IWC rules to its advantage by realizing that any country that paid its dues could join the IWC. While there are only a handful of whaling countries, today there are 88 member states in the IWC. Environmentalists have paid the annual membership fees for countries that might not otherwise belong to the organization. With a growing number of anti-whaling members, some "bought" by environmentalists, the IWC finally enacted a complete ban on whaling in 1982, and it took effect in 1985. The efforts of environmentalists were aided by U.S. law, which would not allow countries that whaled to purchase fishing permits within the U.S. exclusive economic zone (EEZ).

The total ban has proved effective. Even on the high seas a ban is much easier to monitor than a numerical limit. Since the 1970s, a number of whale stocks have recovered considerably. Some, like the humpback, are thought to be near their pre-exploitation levels, while others, like the blue whale, have not recovered nearly as well.[11] Scientists are still trying to understand why some species are faring so much better than others.

---

10. M. J. Peterson, "Whalers, Cetologists, Environmentalists, and the International Management of Whaling," *International Organization* 46, no. 1 (Winter 1992): 147–86.

11. https://iwc.int/status (accessed 12/12/17).

In sum, the tragedy of the commons threatens public goods and common-pool resources. The interactions of large numbers of individuals or countries can produce outcomes that are undesirable for society as a whole. Even though we all value the environment, our individual actions have a marginal impact and we free ride on the efforts of others. Problems of collective action apply among individuals and states. Choices that are reasonable for a single actor sometimes create collectively tragic results. Collective action problems are easier to solve under some conditions than others. As in the ETS or the ban on whaling, however, whenever collective action problems are large, society can adopt rules and regulations that change our individual incentives to better protect the local and global environment.

Why Do Polluters Usually Win?

Political struggles over the environment often involve bargaining problems, as well as collective action problems. The failure to mitigate climate change is expected by some to exacerbate underlying political struggles within and between countries, and possibly lead to higher levels of conflict and violence. The evidence to date, however, is far from clear on this prediction (see "How Do We Know?" on p. 556).

At the same time, we know that political struggles over policy can block attempts to mitigate environmental degradation. These bargaining problems typically pit a majority favoring tighter regulations against a minority of special interests that, if not actually advocating environmental degradation, aim to block costly new regulations or to shift the costs of policy change onto others. Even though most may share an interest in the environment, any policy to improve environmental practices will create losers, who will have to give up activities or practices that were previously permitted, and winners, who will enjoy the benefits of a greener world.

The key concept to understand in these bargaining problems is **externalities**, which are costs or benefits resulting from an actor's decision that affect stakeholders other than that actor. When an externality exists, the decision maker does not bear all the costs or reap all the gains from his or her action. If a firm decides to dump waste into a river, others bear the costs of either using contaminated water or purifying it themselves. In this case, the firm has imposed a cost, or negative externality, on others. If a school club cleans a stretch of beach, it is not only its members who benefit from a litter-free and safer swimming area, but also all others who might use the same spot. In this instance, the club has provided benefits, or created a positive externality, for others.

externalities

Costs or benefits for stakeholders other than the actor undertaking an action. When an externality exists, the decision maker does not bear all the costs or reap all the gains from his or her action.

Polluting a river with chemicals is a negative externality because the action harms the health and livelihood of inhabitants downstream who may use the polluted water to farm, bathe, fish, or drink.

Climate Change and Conflict

The idea of climate change as a security threat has been discussed for years, but it became common wisdom after a 2007 report by 11 retired U.S. generals and admirals described climate change as a "threat multiplier."[a] In other words, in any area where conflict might be likely, floods, droughts, rising sea levels, or other changes induced by a warming climate would increase the risk of violence.

Establishing whether climate change leads to increases in conflict is difficult. The arguments presented in the 2007 report and others[b] are supported by numerous "cases" of conflicts that coincided with some major weather event, such as a flood or a drought. But it is easy to think of major natural disasters that have not been associated with an increase in unrest, including the 2004 Asian tsunami, floods in places from China to India to Peru, or even the recent drought in California. What do these examples tell us? Not very much.

Scholarly research into this question is difficult and relatively new. The IPCC noted in 2014 that "collectively the research does not conclude that there is a strong positive relationship between warming and armed conflict."[c] The authors of the report held that climate change would damage "human security because it undermines livelihoods, compromises culture and identity, induces migration that people would rather have avoided, and challenges the ability of states to provide the conditions necessary for human security."[d] However, their review of the available research did not support the hypothesis that climate change would lead to an increase in armed conflict.

In 2012, Nils Petter Gleditsch edited a special issue of the *Journal of Peace Research* that examined the kinds of specific questions that need to be studied to determine whether there is a link. The authors looked at how changes in rainfall, temperature, and the quality of rangeland affected conflict. There was no consensus. Several studies found no link. Some actually found there was more conflict during good years, suggesting that conflict arises when there is something of worth—like fat, valuable cows—to fight over. Other articles, however, did find that conflict increased with the types of weather conditions likely to occur with climate change. Figure A illustrates the problem. Before the mid-1980s, one might be tempted to infer a positive relationship between temperature change and conflict, but more recently the trends have diverged, calling any relationship into question. Still more research is needed.[e]

We cannot know for sure that climate change will not increase conflict. But what seems likely from the research thus far is that any relationship between climate change and armed conflict is likely to be small, since it has been so difficult to detect.

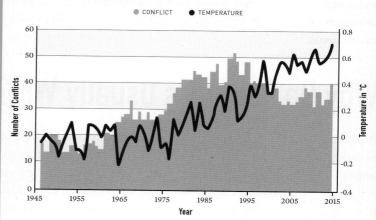

FIGURE A **Global Temperature Deviation and Conflict, 1946–2014**

○ CONFLICT ● TEMPERATURE

Figure source: Halvard Buhaug, PhD, "Globalt Tempuraturavvik Og Konflikt, 1946–2014," in Nils Petter Gleditsch, *Mot en mer fredelig verden?* [Towards a more peaceful world?] (Oslo: Pax, 2016). Reprinted with permission.

Note: Conflict data are from the UCDP/PRIO database; temperature data, from http://data.giss.nasa.gov/histemp. The temperature deviations are measured from the average for the period 1951–80.

a. "National Security and Climate Change," CNA Corporation, 2007, www.cna.org/mab/reports.

b. National Intelligence Council, "Implications for US National Security of Anticipated Climate Change," September 21, 2016, www.dni.gov/files/documents/Newsroom/Reports%20and%20Pubs/Implications_for_US_National_Security_of_Anticipated_Climate_Change.pdf.

c. Quoted in Nils Petter Gleditsch and Ragnhild Nordås, "Conflicting Messages? The IPCC on Conflict and Human Security," *Political Geography* 43 (November 2014): 82–90, https://doi.org/10.1016/j.polgeo.2014.08.007.

d. Gleditsch and Nordås, "Conflicting Messages?"

e. Nils Petter Gleditsch, "Whither the Weather? Climate Change and Conflict," *Journal of Peace Research* 49, no. 1 (2012): 3–9, https://doi.org/10.1177/0022343311431288.

Externalities create a divergence between the individual costs or benefits of action and the broader costs or benefits to society as a whole. Typically, individuals are motivated to act by only their private costs and benefits, and they do not take into account the costs and benefits imposed on others. As a result, from the point of view of society at large, people individually decide to dump too much waste or fail to clean up enough beaches. When externalities exist, the independent decisions of individual actors lead to suboptimal results. Through some form of cooperation, everyone's welfare can be improved, and each individual, in principle, can be made better off.

Externalities create problems of bargaining or redistribution in which one side's gains come as a result of another side's losses. The question is who benefits and who pays the costs of any externality. If the actor gets all the benefits or pays all the costs—if there is no externality—that actor is likely to choose reasonably efficiently how to balance the trade-off. But when the benefits are received by one actor and the costs are imposed on another, the two actors must bargain over the gains and losses and who should pay to mitigate the externality.

The dilemma raises the following questions: Why do those who stand to lose from tighter environmental restrictions so often win? Why do the special interests that oppose environmental regulations tend to succeed in blocking greater controls? To answer these questions, we must examine two sets of winners and losers in international environmental policy.

Domestic Winners and Losers

Almost by definition, "dirty" industries enhance their profits by not paying the full costs of production, which include the harm they impose on others. Industries that create negative externalities benefit from not paying the full cost of production. Firms that can dump waste into a river avoid the expense of treating that waste or otherwise disposing of it in ways that are environmentally safe. This ability to off-load the costs onto others—those who suffer from environmental degradation—increases the profits of the firm, reduces the costs of the goods it sells and makes it more competitive, or both. Firms and industries thus have an interest in opposing stiffer environmental regulations that would compel them to reduce the negative externalities they produce.

Even though they may extract resources or manufacture their products in ways that do not directly degrade the environment, industries also have interests in looser environmental laws. The oil industry, which frequently promotes its clean production methods in glossy magazine ads, has fought attempts to increase support for renewable energy resources that, were they widely available, would compete directly with their main product. Likewise, the auto industry has often opposed efforts to improve gasoline mileage or reduce emissions because the new technologies would raise the price of cars and, at least at the margin, reduce demand.

Competition at home and abroad constrains firms to reduce their costs of production as much as possible. The process of economic globalization heightens this

Firms and industries may not support environmental regulations that would require them to change their manufacturing processes or reduce demand for their products. While some auto companies have started producing electric cars to comply with regulations on gas mileage or emissions, others have resisted.

constraint by bringing domestic firms into competition with foreign manufacturers, which may not face the same pressures for increased environmental regulations in their bases of production. By opposing new environmental regulations—and in some cases, by lobbying to remove existing regulations as competition increases—firms lower their costs of production at the expense of the environment.[12] This competition for regulatory laxity is feared to produce a "race to the bottom" in environmental policy as countries seek to undercut one another in offering business-friendly policies to internationally mobile companies. To date, there is relatively little evidence for such a race. Producing at lower cost, however, benefits not only the firms, but also consumers, who gain from cheaper prices for goods. Indeed, lax environmental regulations may lower the cost of products and thus give consumers incentives to ignore environmental degradation as well.

Nearly every alternative policy for protecting the global environment creates losers and winners who press their governments to change policy in their preferred direction. Nonetheless, the balance of political power typically favors entrenched or vested interests. The industries and groups that would lose from tighter environmental regulations are relatively few, in comparison with the majority that gain from a greener environment, and they suffer direct and immediate costs. In this way, polluters are similar to protectionist industries (discussed in Chapter 7) that gain concentrated benefits from import restrictions and are more motivated to enter the political arena as a result. Oil markets are dominated by just a few major firms, for which the costs of environmental regulations are also highly concentrated. Automobile manufacturers claim that increased mileage standards will require costly new research and development and raise the price of cars, thereby reducing demand. These concentrated costs give the potential losers a stronger incentive to attempt to influence government policy.

As an exception that tests the rule, CFC producers—especially DuPont, the industry leader—dug in their heels on reducing emissions until it became clear that new chemical alternatives would soon be available and might even increase profits. When the costs of change are not large, even politically powerful industries may yield to demands for tighter environmental regulations. Once regulated, moreover,

---

12. Firms may also use disputes over differing international environmental regulations to attempt to restrict international trade and competition. In such cases, concern over the environment can be a form of hidden protectionism. It is no coincidence that environmentalists and labor unions have joined forces against globalization in most developed countries.

firms may then lobby hard to create international agreements that level the playing field by regulating foreign firms as well.[13]

Conversely, the benefits of a cleaner environment are diffuse, and the beneficiaries, as we have seen, suffer from collective action problems. Because the benefits are spread across many individuals or groups, few have strong interests in lobbying their governments to alter current practices. The intensity of the losers' interests in opposing stiffer regulations typically compensates for their smaller numbers relative to the majority.

Moreover, these industries and groups have employees and stockholders who are citizens and voters. Industries can mobilize those workers and stockholders to press their case on elected politicians. Oil companies, for example, have political influence because many voters depend on that industry—or related industries that rely on inexpensive fossil fuels—for their livelihoods. Alternative industries, such as wind or solar power firms, that might blossom if there were a national cap-and-trade program are small and lack the same resources. Their future growth, and the workers and stockholders who might benefit directly from their growth, are mostly promises rather than real-life voters who can reward or punish politicians for the legislation they adopt today.

Over time, however, we can see how this calculus is changing. Today solar power employs more people in the United States than the coal industry does. Oil and gas still are the largest employers, but wind power and biofuels are now also growing. However, different states offer very different pictures. California leads the nation in solar power jobs, and is also the leading state in establishing a cap-and-trade program and expressing support for the Paris Agreement. Wyoming and West Virginia still have many coal jobs, and their residents largely welcomed President Trump's decision to leave the Paris Agreement.[14]

International Winners and Losers

Environmental issues also divide developed and developing countries. Externalities exist not only within countries, creating domestic winners and losers, but also between countries. In this case, the costs of environmental degradation are borne not only by the country releasing pollutants into the atmosphere, for instance, but by neighboring countries or perhaps all countries. This situation creates the vexing question of who gains from lax environmental standards and, more important, which countries should pay for creating a greener world.

Historically, the largest polluters have been rich states in Europe and North America. Since 1850, nearly two-thirds of cumulative carbon emissions have been released by these countries.[15] Even today, the United States uses far more energy and emits far more pollutants per capita than any other country. With 4.5 percent

---

13. On domestic business interests, see Elizabeth R. DeSombre, *Domestic Sources of International Environmental Policy: Industry, Environmentalists, and U.S. Power* (Cambridge, MA: MIT Press, 2000).

14. Nadja Popovich, "Today's Energy Jobs Are in Solar, Not Coal," *New York Times*, April 25, 2017, www.nytimes.com/interactive/2017/04/25/climate/todays-energy-jobs-are-in-solar-not-coal.html.

15. Mengpin Ge, Johannes Friedrich, and Thomas Damassa, "6 Graphs Explain the World's Top 10 Emitters," World Resources Institute, November 25, 2014, https://wri.org/blog/2014/11/6-graphs-explain-world%E2%80%99s-top-10-emitters.

Regions that rely on glacial meltwater, like the Bolivian Andes, stand to suffer greatly from rapidly melting glaciers, even though they may contribute very small amounts of carbon emissions.

of the world's population, the United States emits over 15 percent of the world's carbon. Worldwide, the average individual produces 4.9 metric tons of carbon each year. The average American emits 16.1 tons per year, more than in any other country besides Australia and some of the oil-rich principalities in the Middle East. By contrast, Japan, a state at a comparable level of economic development, averages 9.9 metric tons per person per year.[16] The developed countries have, by far, the largest cumulative and ongoing impact on the environment (see Figure 13.2).

The greatest source of new pollutants in the future, however, will be the developing countries. We have already seen this increase in China, where carbon emissions have grown from 15 percent of the world's total in 2001 to 30 percent today. China's emissions in 2016 totaled 10.7 billion tons, and Chinese citizens now emit 7.7 tons per capita. While that is less than the United States, it is still 13 percent more per person than the European Union average.[17] China continues to rely heavily on coal for 64 percent of its energy needs.[18] But China's carbon emissions now appear to have stabilized. In fact, its emissions decreased by 0.7 percent in 2015 as compared to 2014, largely because of a decline in coal usage.[19] This trend is expected to continue. All this coal brings with it an enormous amount of air pollution, even within China itself. This pollution is an issue that Chinese citizens and, in turn, the government have become increasingly concerned with in recent years.

16. PBL Netherlands Environmental Assessment Agency, "Trends in Global CO2 Emissions: 2016 Report," 2016, http://edgar.jrc.ec.europa.eu/news_docs/jrc-2016-trends-in-global-co2-emissions-2016-report-103425.pdf.

17. PBL Netherlands Environmental Assessment Agency, "Trends in Global CO2 Emissions."

18. "BP Energy Outlook: Country and Regional Insights—China," 2017, www.bp.com/content/dam/bp/pdf/energy-economics/energy-outlook-2017/bp-energy-outlook-2017-country-insight-china.pdf.

19. PBL Netherlands Environmental Assessment Agency, "Trends in Global CO2 Emissions."

FIGURE 13.2 *National Interests and Carbon Emissions*

"Enthusiastic" countries (in green) are willing to spend their own resources to control emissions. "Reluctant" countries (in blue) are usually willing to control emissions only when doing so coincides with other national goals. Most other countries are small emitters (in yellow) that will have relatively little effect on carbon levels, or net carbon exporters (in red) that have little interest in restricting carbon usage. Percentages indicate each country or group's proportion of global carbon emissions.

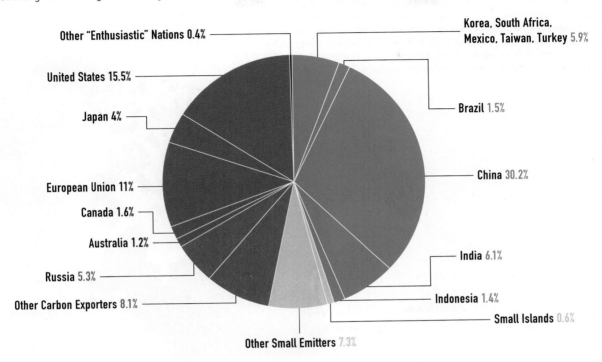

Other "Enthusiastic" Nations 0.4%

United States 15.5%

Japan 4%

European Union 11%

Canada 1.6%

Australia 1.2%

Russia 5.3%

Other Carbon Exporters 8.1%

Other Small Emitters 7.3%

Korea, South Africa, Mexico, Taiwan, Turkey 5.9%

Brazil 1.5%

China 30.2%

India 6.1%

Indonesia 1.4%

Small Islands 0.6%

Since 2005, regulations have expanded significantly.[20] However, pollution in Chinese cities is still far above healthy levels.[21] Although China's large population and growing economy put its environmental practices on the front pages of the world's newspapers, the same story could be told for virtually every other developing country.

Typically, countries increase their pollution until they reach a certain level of development, and then start to increase pollution controls and invest in cleaner technologies.[22] The Yale environmental performance index (EPI) shows that wealthier countries generally have higher environmental performance (see Map 13.1). This index is a composite score of measurements across the full range of environmental issues, from forest and wildlife protection to air and water pollution. While developing countries may have more forests and open space, they usually face real challenges

Figure source: David G. Victor, Global Warming Gridlock: Creating More Effective Strategies for Protecting the Planet (New York: Cambridge University Press, 2011), 10. Figure based on the 2013 data provided by David G. Victor.

20. Jeremy J. Schreifels, Yale Fu, and Elizabeth J. Wilson, "Sulfur Dioxide Control in China: Policy Evolution during the 10th and 11th Five-Year Plans and Lessons for the Future," *Energy Policy* 48 (2012): 779–89.

21. Nickolay A. Krotkov, Chris A. McLinden, Can Li, Lok N. Lamsal, et al., "Aura OMI Observations of Regional SO2 and NO2 Pollution Changes from 2005 to 2015," *Atmospheric Chemistry and Physics* 16 (2016): 4605–29.

22. Gene N. Grossman and Alan B. Krueger, "Economic Growth and the Environment," *Quarterly Journal of Economics* 110, no. 2 (1995): 353–77.

MAP 13.1 *Environmental Performance Index, 2016*

The Center for Environmental Law and Policy at Yale University and the Center for International Earth Science Information Network at Columbia University have developed a composite environmental performance index (EPI) for 180 countries. It provides a common way to measure countries' performance on a range of important environmental issues. The map divides countries into seven categories based on their overall performance. As you can see, the United States and Canada, along with a number of other developed countries, have scores in the top category. On average, sub-Saharan Africa has the lowest scores.

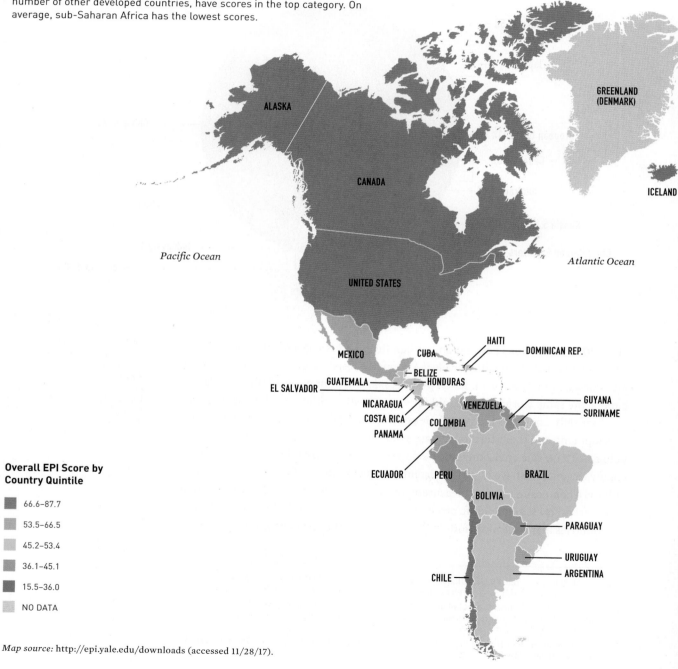

Overall EPI Score by Country Quintile

- 66.6–87.7
- 53.5–66.5
- 45.2–53.4
- 36.1–45.1
- 15.5–36.0
- NO DATA

Map source: http://epi.yale.edu/downloads (accessed 11/28/17).

Arctic Ocean

RUSSIA

NORWAY
UNITED KINGDOM
SWEDEN
FINLAND
GERMANY
IRELAND
BELARUS
FRANCE
UKRAINE
KAZAKHSTAN
MONGOLIA
N. KOREA
S. KOREA
GEORGIA
UZBEKISTAN
KYRGYZSTAN
JAPAN
ITALY
TURKMENISTAN
TAJIKISTAN
CHINA
SPAIN
GREECE
TURKEY
IRAN
NEPAL
BHUTAN
HONG KONG
Pacific Ocean
MOROCCO
ISRAEL
LEB.
SYRIA
IRAQ
KUWAIT
MYANMAR
(BURMA)
ALGERIA
JORDAN
EGYPT
SAUDI ARABIA
UAE
INDIA
TAIWAN
LIBYA
OMAN
PAKISTAN
VIETNAM
MAURITANIA
MALI
NIGER
ERITREA
YEMEN
THAILAND
LAOS
PHILIPPINES
SENEGAL
CHAD
SUDAN
AFGHANISTAN
BANGLADESH
CAMBODIA
GUINEA
NIGERIA
CEN. AFR. REP.
S. SUDAN
ETHIOPIA
SRI LANKA
MALAYSIA
GHANA
CAMEROON
UGANDA
SOMALIA
INDONESIA
PAPUA NEW GUINEA
IVORY COAST
D.R. CONGO
KENYA
Indian Ocean
TANZANIA
SOLOMON ISLANDS
ANGOLA
MALAWI
ZAMBIA
MADAGASCAR
NAMIBIA
MOZAMBIQUE
ZIMBABWE
AUSTRALIA
SOUTH AFRICA
BOTSWANA
NEW ZEALAND

563

in delivering clean air and clean water to their populations, simply because they are still developing.

Exactly when in its development each country chooses to address pollution varies. The Chinese have now taken on this issue, with more than half of the goals in their current "Five-Year Plan" (their major economic planning document) focused on energy and the environment. India is now seeing a rapid rise in air pollution because its coal-fired power plant capacity increased by 93 percent in the past decade without controls on the two main polluting gases.[23] However, the Indian government announced new pollution standards in 2015, with enforcement to begin at the end of 2017.

Some of the easiest steps to prevent further environmental degradation could be taken in the developing world. For some emissions, such as the air pollutants that plague Chinese, Indian, and other developing-world cities, the government could set the kinds of regulations that already exist in the developed world. For other pollutants, especially greenhouse gases, countries that are still building out their infrastructures can limit emissions more easily than a developed country where infrastructure has already been built around fossil fuel–based power.

It is more economically advantageous to build a new wind plant in a developing city with a demand for increased power, for instance, than in a city that already has all the electricity it needs from a natural gas plant that has been bought and paid for. Moreover, because industries in developing countries often use older and less efficient technologies, many energy improvements can be undertaken at relatively low cost and result in significant greenhouse gas savings. The fact that many of the easiest steps to reduce carbon emissions could be taken in the developing world is a key rationale behind the ETS adopted by the European Union, which allows its firms, facing high costs for further reducing their emissions, to buy carbon credits from developing countries, where the costs of reducing an equivalent amount of carbon are much lower.

A similar but distinct issue arises with biodiversity. Most of the world's tropical forests, home to our greatest biodiversity and important carbon sinks, are in developing countries. People concerned about greenhouse gases argue that it is a priority to protect these forests. However, groups in many developing countries note that in the process of developing, North America and Europe engaged in a great deal of deforestation.

As countries develop, land is often converted from forest cover to more economically productive uses like farmland, industry, and cities. The United States has converted an estimated 256 million acres of forest land to other uses during the 400 years since the beginning of European settlement. Most of that conversion occurred during the period of most rapid economic growth in the late nineteenth century, and in fact, U.S. forest cover has remained remarkably stable, at about one-third of the total landmass, since 1912.[24] By contrast, some countries with important tropical forest resources still have over 50 percent forest cover. Two examples are

---

23. Krotkov et al., "Aura OMI Observations."

24. U.S. Department of Agriculture, "U.S. Forest Resource Facts and Trends," 2012, www.fia.fs.fed.us/library/brochures/docs/2012/ForestFacts_1952-2012_English.pdf.

Brazil and India, but both of these countries have seen considerable declines in forested land area over the last 25 years.[25]

Thus the question arises of who should or will pay to leave these forests undeveloped. Their existence creates a positive externality for the global community, and their destruction would create a negative externality. But in the short run, the citizens of developing states might earn a significant national benefit for themselves by exploiting this resource.

The differing interests of the local, national, and international communities create tough bargaining problems in addressing global environmental issues. Even recognizing that they have a disproportionate responsibility for cleaning up the environment, because of both their past practices and their relatively greater present wealth, some developed countries still want to link their efforts to greater contributions by developing countries (see "Controversy" on p. 566).

When industries and environmentalists or rich and poor countries bargain, the result can be political stalemate. Such was the case for the decade after the 1997 Kyoto Protocol. The United States was not willing to join Kyoto, and developing countries were unwilling to make firm commitments to control their emissions. The desire of developed countries was not that developing countries reduce their emissions immediately, because the emissions were quite low (especially in 1997, when the Kyoto Protocol was drafted) and they would need energy to develop. Rather, the issue was that they commit to control emissions and then begin to reduce at a later date.

The impasse was ultimately broken at Copenhagen in 2009. While the Copenhagen Accord was only a one-page document, for the first time it said that all countries, not just developed countries, would make specific commitments to mitigate climate change. Then, two years later in South Africa, countries came together again to agree to the Durban Platform for Enhanced Action, which set out a road map for negotiating a new agreement that would commit the countries of the world to action beyond 2020. They set the deadline for completing that agreement for four years later, 2015 in Paris.

The key to success at Durban was actually a realignment of important developed and developing countries who now saw each other as partners. In Durban, the Europeans teamed up with the countries that emitted the fewest greenhouse gases and stood to suffer most from climate change—namely, the least developed countries and the small island states. They found common interest in pushing the United States and the larger developing countries to commit to do more. The Europeans, after all, had been strictly controlling greenhouse gases under the Kyoto Protocol for a number of years; for competitive reasons, their companies really wanted industries in the United States, as well as in rapidly growing nations like China, to be equally bound.

The United States was very interested in controlling greenhouse gases, but the Obama administration had been unable to push climate legislation through

---

25. Brazil from 65 to 59 percent, and Indonesia from 61 to 50 percent. World Bank data, 1990–2015, http://data.worldbank.org/indicator/AG.LND.FRST.ZS?end=2015&locations=BR&start=1990&year_low_desc=false.

Who Should Bear the Costs of Addressing Global Climate Change?

Nepal is distinguished by snowy ranges, ancient glaciers, deep gorges, and the historic villages of the Sherpa people. It is also home to the rare snow leopard, musk deer, and red panda. But this landscape is fragile; Nepal is warming. In a development that scientists believe to be human-induced climate change, the temperature in this area has been increasing at the rate of 0.06°C per year, faster than the global average,[a] and the majority of glaciers in the Himalayas have been retreating (melting exceeds snowfall) for decades.[b]

Global warming will eventually affect everyone, but it already affects some far more than others. Today, Nepalis face frequent floods as the glaciers melt.[c] If warming trends continue, Nepal will face many more threats. Across the globe, homes, livelihoods, and cultures are at risk; famine and disease will increase; some species will become extinct.

Applying the Concepts

Nepal is an interesting case in which to examine the ethics of global warming. Earlier in this chapter, we noted that countries have relatively similar interests in preventing climate change but suffer from collective action problems that make mitigation difficult. In the case of Nepal, however, its **interests** are more extreme. It does not contribute heavily to global climate change but is more at risk than many countries from its effects. At the same time, as a small and relatively poor country, its **interactions** with others are limited. Indeed, it has little leverage in bargaining with other countries over carbon emissions. If Nepal is to escape from the growing consequences of climate change, it must rely on other countries, a sense of fairness and justice, and the creation of global **institutions** that regulate emissions. What sort of bargain would be fair? Who should bear the costs of change?

For Nepal, one of the main issues in climate negotiations is how to get high-carbon-emitting countries, such as the United States, to reduce their emissions. Though a majority of Americans want the United States to "take aggressive action to slow global warming,"[d] U.S. policy tends to go back and forth, depending on which party controls Washington. Workers for fossil fuel companies tend to be in "red" states, while renewables have blossomed in "blue" states. The U.S. fossil fuel industry, which actively opposes domestic carbon controls, is large and politically well entrenched. In contrast, companies in the renewable sector support such controls, as well as the clean-energy transition of other countries.

The Kyoto Protocol operated on the principle that developed countries like the United States had contributed more to the problem and were wealthier, so they should restrain their emissions first. This was one interpretation of a phrase, "common but differentiated responsibilities," that appeared in the UNFCCC, as well as the other treaties signed at the Rio de Janeiro global conference on sustainable development in 1992.

For many years, the developed countries, particularly the United States, focused on the "common" part of the phrase. Developing countries, however, focused on "differentiated," arguing that they could wait to address greenhouse gases. Even before President George W. Bush pulled out of the Kyoto Protocol, the U.S. Senate signaled that it would not sign on unless large developing countries

a. Arun B. Shrestha and Raju Aryal, "Climate Change in Nepal and Its Impact on Himalayan Glaciers," *Regional Environmental Change* 11, no. 1 (2011): 65–77.

b. Tobias Bolch, A. Kulkarni, A. Kääb, C. Huggel, et al., "The State and Fate of Himalayan Glaciers," *Science* 336, no. 6079 (2012): 310–14.

c. Shaun D. Richardson and John M. Reynolds, "An Overview of Glacial Hazards in the Himalayas," *Quaternary International* 65 (2000): 31–47.

d. Chris Kahn, "Most Americans Want 'Aggressive' Action on Climate Change: Reuters/Ipsos Poll," *Reuters*, June 6, 2017.

also committed to serious greenhouse gas controls. Faced with this resistance from developed countries, developing countries have held together as a group, known as the Group of 77. By Copenhagen, some of the Group of 77—in particular the small island nations at risk of being swamped by sea level rise—chose to be much more forceful than other developing nations.

A new understanding of "common but differentiated responsibilities" has emerged. In the Paris Agreement, each country makes its own "nationally determined contribution" that may conform to the country's own approach to mitigating climate change. Brazil has an economy-wide target, while China has separate targets for energy and forestry. The United States too was able to design its own commitment (indeed, if President Donald Trump had chosen, he could have modified it rather than leaving the agreement entirely).

The Paris Agreement allocates more funding for countries like Nepal, but how much of that money materializes has been thrown into doubt by the United States' withdrawal from the agreement. While the United States will save money by not helping to fund adaptation in the poorest developing countries, many businesses worry that if they don't participate in this global transformation in energy structure, they will lose business opportunities to countries that are more aggressively developing renewable energy technologies.

Although countries have moved toward a new understanding that all have some responsibility for addressing climate change, tough bargaining is still under way over who should bear what cost. President Trump withdrew from the Paris Agreement because he believed that it "disadvantaged" the United States "while imposing no meaningful obligations on the world's leading polluters." While "we're getting out," he said, "we will see if we can make a (new) deal that's fair."[e]

e. White House, Office of the Press Secretary, "Statement by President Trump on the Paris Climate Accord," June 1, 2017, www.whitehouse.gov/the-press-office/2017/06/01/statement-president-trump-paris-climate-accord.

Thinking Analytically

1. What would be a "fair" bargain internationally? Should countries that already emit high levels of carbon have a right to continue to pollute? Should developing countries that have not previously contributed significantly to global emissions be permitted to emit more carbon?

2. Should each person be allocated a quantity of greenhouse gases that he or she can emit annually? Would a Nepali have the same rights to emit a limited quantity of carbon as an American? Or should citizens of developed countries bear a higher cost to make up for their historically higher emissions already in the atmosphere?

3. Depending on your answers to the first two questions, what kind of institution is necessary and appropriate to ensure that the bargain reached is actually implemented?

Congress. By 2014, however, President Obama had come up with a plan to be implemented through executive action (though much of it was subsequently rolled back under the Trump administration). China was also moving along with clean energy under its "Five-Year Plan." As a result, the United States and China were ready to come to the table, first with bilateral agreements and then at the Paris Conference in 2015. Even if the national plans submitted under that agreement do not themselves contain significant cutbacks in carbon emissions by developing countries, the principle that all countries share in the responsibility for reducing emissions has now been firmly established.

Bargaining over the Future Environment

Alternative policy solutions create gains and losses for different groups. Industries prefer that consumers or taxpayers pay to clean up their environmental waste, and developing countries prefer that developed countries restrict their pollutants more severely so that they (the developing countries) can industrialize at lower cost. Even though everyone may gain from cooperation, each actor prefers a different policy outcome. As shown in Figure 2.3 (p. 57), cooperation creates net gains through a movement toward the Pareto frontier, but actors will still bargain over where on the frontier a policy will settle. Cooperation and bargaining occur simultaneously. The political fight is not about the need for protecting the environment, but about who bears the costs of a cleaner environment.

Often, the political battle results in compromise. In the European ETS discussed earlier, economists argued that the most efficient system would be to auction emissions credits equal to total output, thereby allocating the credits to those firms that needed them the most and generating income for the governments involved. Instead, at the insistence of firms, in the first two rounds the credits were given free to existing companies and were based on current emissions levels. This arrangement allowed the firms to pass higher costs along to consumers, while at the same time selling their credits in the ETS. One European NGO has estimated that the companies' windfall profits added up to €24 billion between 2008 and 2014.[26]

While advocacy groups have an agenda that should make us skeptical of any exact estimate, the politics of why the companies would receive a windfall are relatively obvious: they needed to be induced to join the plan and not wield their political influence to block its implementation. In fact, academic research on the European Union's ETS has shown that the cost of the carbon permits was passed through to consumers and that companies' stock market value went up when they were able to charge higher prices.[27]

---

26. Carbon Market Watch, "Industry Windfall Profits from Europe's Carbon Market," March 2016, https://carbonmarketwatch.org/wp-content/uploads/2016/03/Policy-brief_Industry-windfall-profits-from-Europe%E2%80%99s_web_final-1.pdf.

27. Natalia Fabra and Mar Reguant, "Pass-through of Emissions Costs in Electricity Markets," *American Economic Review* 104, no. 9 (2014): 2872–99; James B. Bushnell, Howard Chong, and Erin T. Mansur, "Profiting from Regulation: Evidence from the European Carbon Market," *American Economic Journal: Economic Policy* 5 no. 4 (2013): 78–106.

The "losers" from limits on carbon emissions, in this case, did not actually lose very much. The EU ETS responded to the economic problems caused by free permits, however, by beginning the transition to auctions, and in fact, the majority of permits in the current round are being auctioned. At the beginning, however, the windfall profits for firms were necessary to generate agreement and "buy-in" from the affected industries.

Sometimes, however, the fight between winners and losers from an environmental program is sufficiently intense that it blocks movement toward greater cooperation. Paradoxically, the more we care about the future and about the future environment, the more that is at stake and the more intense this political fight will be.

For the winners from environmental protection, a higher value on the future environment mobilizes supporters into the political arena to change policy. Because they care more about the future, they are willing to exert greater effort today in promoting policies to protect that environment. The longer into the future the winners look, the more likely they are to forgo agreement today in hopes of getting a better agreement that guarantees their preferred policies for a longer period. Each day that passes without significant political progress means that more carbon is accumulating in the atmosphere. But even though the immediate environment might suffer from a lack of cooperation, a better bargain over a longer period might make such a delay worthwhile.

For the losers from tighter environmental regulations, a higher value on the future may also mobilize them into the political arena to try to protect the favorable policies they now enjoy. Policies that greatly reduce carbon emissions, for instance, will reduce profits in industries that depend on fossil fuels not only today, but also in the years ahead. Burning less fossil fuel will reduce not only profits for oil companies, but also the value of the oil reserves they own. Higher costs of production not only lower incomes in developing countries in the present, but also reduce growth and income in the future. The greater the value we place on the future, the more important the environment is to the winners—but the more important the costs of complying with greater regulations are to the losers as well.

Coupled with the problem of bargaining over the future is the equally difficult problem of representing future generations in current decision making. After all, no political system possesses a mechanism that represents the interests of future citizens to the present generation. Given the notoriously short attention spans of politicians, often driven only by the next election, who in any political system represents the interests of future citizens and voters?

We know little about the interests of future generations. Although we can extrapolate from our current preferences, many factors can intervene. We do not know what the future rate of technological change will be, which may make various environmental problems easier or harder to solve than we expect. Assuming that wealth and incomes continue to rise, we do not know how future citizens may evaluate yet more consumption of physical goods, like cars, relative to consumption of intangible goods, like the scenic beauty of an unspoiled coastline or old-growth forest.

Even if we could estimate future interests, there is no one at present to advocate for those future generations in any systematic way. In bargaining between actors at a single moment in time, the winners and losers can choose to be actively involved, or not, in the political process. But there is no realistic way of representing future generations in present political decisions. Environmental TANs often claim that they are representing future generations, but their political clout is still limited. Future generations neither vote now nor pay membership dues to TANs that can, in turn, press governments to change policy. TANs can make normative arguments on behalf of future generations, but this is at best an indirect and significantly weaker form of representation than if the future citizens' votes and voices could be heard today. As a consequence, we are bargaining with ourselves on behalf of future generations—and it is perhaps not surprising that we usually let ourselves win.

How Can Institutions Promote International Environmental Cooperation?

Within countries, governments play an important role in controlling environmental degradation. Producing public goods and regulating the use of common-pool resources are fundamental roles for any government. In all but the so-called failed states, governments tax citizens and use the revenue to provide a variety of public goods, including national defense, police and fire protection, public infrastructure, public health, education, and, of course, environmental protection. Governments also impose restrictions on automobile emissions, the dumping of toxic waste, oil drilling, and so on that aim to improve environmental quality and use scarce resources more efficiently. Government is not a perfect solution. Some governments are too responsive to polluters and fail to enact sufficient environmental protections. But, government's ability to allocate resources authoritatively helps mitigate collective action problems that would otherwise make environmental cooperation even more difficult.

National laws and policies are the primary means for implementing international environmental cooperation. Even if states create international institutions, most of their provisions are enforced authoritatively through national legislation and policy. For instance, the members of the Convention on International Trade in Endangered Species of Wild Fauna and Flora (CITES), one of the earliest and most successful environmental treaties, make decisions at the international level, but national governments must enforce trade restrictions on endangered species, generally through their equivalent of a fish and wildlife service, as well as their customs authority. Transnational environmental problems and solutions still require strong, effective national governments to transform aspirations into practice.

In international relations, there is no higher authority that can compel states to cooperate in mitigating transnational externalities. On global environmental issues, states are limited to voluntary cooperation implemented by laws passed at the national level. Relative to externalities regulated by authoritative governments, international cooperation between sovereign states will always be more difficult and tenuous. States free ride on one another's efforts and overexploit their shared resources. Institutions are not a panacea. In the absence of interests in environmental cooperation and effective bargains between countries, international institutions cannot by themselves create success. Institutions can be only as strong as the interests in cooperation. Nonetheless, as we saw in Chapter 2, international institutions facilitate cooperation among states committed to a cleaner environment by providing information, setting standards, and verifying compliance.

Transnational environmental problems like climate change are primarily combatted by the actions and regulations of individual national governments. Many states have passed laws setting vehicle emissions standards as part of their efforts to fight climate change.

As we discussed in Chapter 11, international agreements can be structured as either hard or soft law. Most environmental treaties, including the most successful, have been structured as soft law. While hard law looks attractive, because it contains penalties for noncompliance, it is often difficult to get countries to agree to it, and if countries do agree, they often make more conservative commitments than they might under soft law. Soft law can often be aspirational—setting goals, such as keeping global warming within 2°C and trying for 1.5°C in the Paris Agreement. What distinguishes an effective treaty like CITES is not enforcement per se, but the precision of its commitments. It has elaborate appendices that give clear limits on the trade in thousands of specific species.

The virtue of aspirational soft law is that it encourages countries to reach for long-term, difficult solutions. It also allows them to take in new information as it arises and adapt their methods and goals. Since most environmental agreements are based on scientific determination of a problem, progress requires constant updating of policy as the science advances. Richard Benedick was the lead U.S. negotiator for the Vienna Convention and the Montreal Protocol. As he said in a speech on the protocol's twentieth anniversary, not only was the agreement about preventive action (negotiations began when the problem was theorized but not proven), but "because of the still evolving science [it was] deliberately designed to be a dynamic and flexible process."[28]

The modern environmental movement began in the 1960s and is often dated from the 1962 publication of Rachel Carson's book *Silent Spring* about toxic chemicals in the environment. It built on the previous century of growing awareness about the

28. Richard E. Benedick, "Science Inspiring Diplomacy: The Improbable Montreal Protocol," in *Twenty Years of Ozone Decline: Proceedings of the Symposium for the 20th Anniversary of the Montreal Protocol*, ed. Christos Zerefos, Georgios Contopoulos, and Gregory Skalkeas, 13–19 (Dordrecht, Netherlands: Springer, 2009).

need for conservation. Organizations to protect birdlife and the first national parks date back to the nineteenth century. The first international agreement, the Ramsar Convention on Wetlands of International Importance, built on this concern about birds and how habitat loss threatened their global migratory patterns. Negotiations began with an international conference that included not just governments, but NGOs, including TANs and other experts. The decision to negotiate an agreement was informed by the advice of the International Waterfowl & Wetlands Research Bureau, a science-oriented TAN now called Wetlands International.[29]

The Ramsar negotiation and its use of scientific information to inform both the decision to draft a convention and the contents of the agreement set the pattern for future environmental agreements. CITES grew out of a similar meeting of the International Union for Conservation of Nature (IUCN). The IUCN has a particularly interesting structure, with national governments, NGOs, and individual scientists as members. Its scientific committees conduct the major research and deliberation in determining which species are threatened, endangered, or extinct. At its 1963 meeting, the IUCN membership agreed to negotiate a treaty on trade in endangered species. The treaty took 10 years to complete and then two more before it came into force in 1975. CITES itself has committees to determine its designations, but much of the scientific work continues to be conducted by IUCN members.

Several later agreements required the formation of new international information bodies to inform the treaty negotiations. In his detailed book on the negotiations for the Vienna and Montreal agreements, Benedick describes the need for finding global scientific consensus, especially because American scientists had taken the lead in the research and were communicating much more closely with the U.S. government. In 1977, UNEP initiated a new body for sharing scientific findings and drawing consensus conclusions, called the Coordinating Committee on the Ozone Layer (CCOL). It was not until 1981 that the UNEP Governing Council authorized the start of negotiations, which began the following year.[30]

A similar approach was taken in addressing climate change. UNEP and the World Meteorological Organization (WMO) established the IPCC in 1988 to bring together scientists from around the world to analyze and evaluate what was known about climate science. The IPCC's first assessment, published in 1990, contributed directly to the negotiations of the UNFCCC, which concluded in 1992. Its second assessment, in 1995, set the stage for the Kyoto Protocol. Each assessment, involving thousands of scientists, has contributed to the negotiations cycle.[31]

Without solid scientific data, including data from the social sciences, which in the IPCC process is included in their reports on mitigation and on impacts and adaptation, it is difficult to know how to adapt to change. Similarly, countries need a well-informed deliberative process to consider how to respond to changing

29. Ramsar, "History of the Ramsar Convention," www.ramsar.org/about/history-of-the-ramsar-convention (accessed 12/13/17); and Wetlands International, "Our History," www.wetlands.org/about-us/our-history (accessed 12/13/17).

30. Richard Elliot Benedick, *Ozone Diplomacy: New Directions in Safeguarding the Planet* (Cambridge, MA: Harvard University Press, 1998).

31. Intergovernmental Panel on Climate Change, "History," www.ipcc.ch/organization/organization_history.shtml (accessed 12/13/17).

conditions. The Paris Agreement continued this approach with a five-year review process. It is widely acknowledged that the first set of country commitments is not sufficient to reach a 2°C target, much less the 1.5°C aspiration set forth in the agreement. The hope of the framers is that, in requiring a scientific review and evaluation every five years, countries, through their repeated interaction, will be encouraged to take on more ambitious goals.[32]

Setting Standards and Verifying Compliance

In addition to setting aspirations and providing information, international environmental institutions can also support cooperation by establishing standards of behavior to which states can be held accountable. Although each issue area and agreement has unique features and histories, countries often negotiate framework conventions that establish general principles to which all states can agree. The Convention on Biological Diversity (CBD), for instance, states that diversity is "a common concern of humankind" that all countries have a duty to protect; the document includes additional principles for the development and use of genetic resources. The UNFCCC, aimed at reducing carbon emissions, has a similar structure.

After establishing such frameworks, states proceed in some issue areas to negotiate more stringent environmental safeguards specifying limits on emissions, banning certain practices, or otherwise defining unacceptable behavior. The CBD has two much more specific protocols, the Cartagena Protocol (on biosafety) and the Nagoya Protocol (on genetic material), and, as we have discussed, the UNFCCC first advanced with the Kyoto Protocol and then the Paris Agreement.[33]

Restrictions on the intentional discharge of crude oil at sea demonstrate how the clarity and transparency of the standard matter in supporting cooperation.[34] After a tanker delivers its cargo of crude oil, an average of 300 tons remains on board, stuck to the cargo tank walls. Before regulations were put into effect, ships would clean their tanks on the return voyage by pumping seawater into the tanks and discharging the slop back into the ocean. With many ships making multiple trips each year, oil tankers were intentionally discharging approximately one million tons of oil into the ocean annually.

The effectiveness of environmental regulations may depend on how easy it is to verify compliance. A change in the rules related to dumping oil at sea made it much easier to check whether ship captains were adhering to the standard, and increased compliance rates to over 98 percent.

32. Joeri Rogelj, Michel den Elzen, Niklas Höhne, Taryn Fransen, et al., "Paris Agreement Climate Proposals Need a Boost to Keep Warming Well below 2 °C," *Nature* 534 no. 7609 (2016): 631–39.

33. A second pattern of negotiations and agreements is simply to establish a procedural regime with a commission that makes annual decisions about regulatory rules. The IWC is an example of this type of organization. On patterns of agreement formation, see Oran R. Young, *International Governance: Protecting the Environment in a Stateless Society* (Ithaca, NY: Cornell University Press, 1994), esp. chap. 4.

34. This case is drawn from Ronald B. Mitchell, "Regime Design Matters: Intentional Oil Pollution and Treaty Compliance," *International Organization* 48, no. 3 (Summer 1994): 425–58.

In the International Convention for the Prevention of Pollution of the Sea by Oil, adopted in 1954, countries first set standards that permitted tankers to continue cleaning their tanks with seawater but mandated that discharges be no more than 100 parts oil per million parts seawater. The standard was subsequently tightened in 1969. Nonetheless, both the looser and the tighter standards were widely ignored. Oil company surveys from the 1970s show that tankers owned by the oil companies themselves averaged discharges of 3 times the legal limit, and that independently owned tankers averaged discharges of 30 times the legal limit.

In 1978, countries adopted new standards that required all tankers to use new but more expensive technologies that minimized discharges by preventing the oil and seawater from coming into contact or by using crude oil itself to wash the tanks. These new technologies were required for all tankers built after 1982, and all existing tankers had to be retrofitted by 1985. Despite the greater cost, compliance rates rose to over 98 percent by 1991.

What explains the difference in compliance with these standards? Since cleaning the tanks with seawater usually took place on the open ocean, far from other observers, ship captains could act with impunity and ignore mandated discharge limits—and it appears that they usually did. The new technologies, in contrast, required the installation of clearly observable equipment on every ship. When a ship entered port, it could easily be verified whether the tanker met with the new standard. The ease of verification forced tanker captains to alter their behavior, virtually ending the intentional discharge of crude oil into the ocean.

For similar reasons, complete bans are easier to verify than restrictions on emissions; this fact helps account for the success of the Vienna Convention and subsequent amendments outlawing CFCs. With CFCs, as with the ban on whaling or on the killing of endangered wildlife, any possession or trade in prohibited substances is sufficient evidence of noncompliance. Enforcement efforts can then focus on tracking down any sales of CFCs (or elephant ivory, rhinoceros horns, and other banned goods). Soon after the major cuts in CFCs went into effect, for instance, the black market grew to about 20 percent of prior consumption. In 1995, the illegal trade in CFCs in the Port of Miami and along the U.S.-Mexican border was second in value only to trade in illegal drugs, prompting a unilateral effort by the United States to block the smuggling. The important point is that the clear rules banning CFCs enabled this crackdown.

Restrictions on carbon emissions are harder to enforce, especially when many independent agents, such as firms, are potentially contributing to the problem. Evidence of some carbon in the atmosphere is not evidence of cheating. To demonstrate that a country is failing to live up to its commitments on global warming requires consistent monitoring of emissions over long periods—a much more daunting task.

In addition to official monitoring and reporting, environmental TANs have been central in verifying compliance with international environmental accords. Most environmental agreements depend on self-reporting of emissions. As we noted in Chapter 2, self-reporting is effective only when reports are subject to external verification. TANs often play the role of fire alarm, sounding the alert when governments violate agreements or fail to report accurately. By calling attention to failures at living up to the letter and, sometimes, the spirit of the agreements, TANs assist member states in identifying and bringing pressure on noncomplying governments. The current dense network of committed environmental activists relieves governments of much of the responsibility for monitoring one another's performance, thereby facilitating and enhancing the prospects for successful cooperation.

One example of TAN monitoring occurred after the IWC instituted a complete ban on whaling in 1982.[35] After phasing out its commercial operations, Japan has continued to engage in scientific whaling, which aims to demonstrate that whale populations are robust enough to permit some commercial whaling. Much of the whale meat nonetheless ends up for sale in Japanese fish markets.

Before the International Court of Justice (ICJ) declared that the country's scientific whaling program was illegal, Japan caught approximately 800 whales per year for self-declared scientific purposes, about the same as Norway's commercial catch (along with Iceland, the only country to defy the ban completely) and all aboriginal whaling catches combined (which are exempt from the ban). Japan has declared that it intends to continue this program even after the ICJ's ruling.

Although it is impossible to police the entire ocean, the limited scope of scientific whaling allows NGOs to track the whaling fleets, observe their operations, often film the killing, and catalog each whale caught. Each season, ships from Greenpeace, an international environmental action group, have shadowed the Japanese fleet, sometimes attempting to disrupt its operations by harassing the factory ships and placing themselves between the hunters and their prey. Countries report their scientific whaling activities to the IWC every year, and as a result of these efforts by the NGOs, relatively accurate independent verification of these self-reports is possible.

Facilitating Decision Making

Effective environmental agreements provide a venue for analytical deliberation and an infrastructure for reaching decisions and then carrying them out. The core decision-making structure of almost all the major environmental agreements, including the CBD, UNFCCC, and Vienna Convention, is a Conference of Parties (COP)—meetings of the member states mostly annually but more often if necessary.

Rule changes, new protocols, and other decisions under these conventions can take place only at a COP. In the run-up to the Paris Agreement, the UNFCCC held preliminary COPs four or five times a year. In addition, complex agreements, like the UNFCCC and the CBD, have numerous smaller groups and subsidiary bodies that deal with policy and technical issues and take their recommendations to the COP. Some treaties have much more specific technical committees, such as CITES, with its species-focused technical bodies and its connection to the IUCN. The existing institution of the UNFCCC was essential to reaching the Paris Agreement;

---

35. Not all opposition to whaling is conducted by international groups. There is, in fact, a steadfast group of Japanese activists who have been opposing Japanese whaling and dolphin hunting (an additional issue that raises international concern) for decades. The Japanese conservationist Sakae Hemmi founded the Elsa Nature Conservancy in Tsukuba, Japan, in 1976 to promote domestic activism aimed at protecting species from whales to elephants. See http://en.elsaenc.net/about-us.

without an existing forum and ongoing negotiations, it is unlikely that states would have been able to make the breakthroughs necessary for this landmark accord.

In addition to the COP, most treaties have a secretariat. UNEP acts as the secretariat for a number of treaties, including the Vienna Convention/Montreal Protocol. The UNFCCC has an independent secretariat, located in Bonn, Germany. A secretariat provides a professional staff to administer the treaties' provisions and prepare for meetings. Some smaller treaties have no permanent staff and operate instead with a coordinating committee. One country will also act as the repository for the treaty and is likely to carry out some coordinating functions in the absence of a secretariat.

The amount of permanent institutional infrastructure in place depends heavily on the complexity of the treaty and agreement among members. Treaties like CITES and the Montreal Protocol have among the most complex and institutionalized infrastructures of any treaties. Simple treaties like the Stockholm Convention rely on decision making at COPs, enforcement by each signatory country, and coordination among national points of contact.

Agreements vary in how rule changes are made and what level of support is needed. Many conventions require consensus, which is generally defined as unanimous support, but even then, conventions may leave themselves some flexibility. The UNFCCC states that "every effort" will be made to make decisions by consensus, but failing that, amendments to the convention can be made by a three-fourths majority. This fail-safe has ensured in recent years that some agreements, including the Copenhagen Accord and the Paris Agreement, were not defeated by one or two holdout countries.

Environmental TANs also provide important policy input for international agreements, creating nearly unique international public-private partnerships on the environment that facilitate cooperation. The UN Conference on Environment and Development in 1992 (the so-called Earth Summit)—which produced conventions on biodiversity, climate change, and desertification—hosted 2,400 NGO participants within the main meeting site, and an additional 17,000 at a parallel conference.

Observer groups have become the norm throughout the UN system. They try to influence negotiations both through direct lobbying of delegates and through side events where they provide information, analysis, and suggested approaches to the questions under debate. They also act as observers, attending formal sessions and reporting on the results. Since Rio, organizations have preferred to be inside the negotiation hall, rather than at the parallel event. This preference led to substantial crowding at Copenhagen, where the 40,000 participants (including government representatives, NGOs, business organizations, and press) exceeded the capacity of the facility.

Since then, the UNFCCC has placed quotas on NGOs (which in UN parlance include TANs and local NGOs, businesses and universities). Nevertheless, there were some 7,000 participants representing over 1,100 UN-defined NGOs at Paris, and many thousands more at the separate parallel event.[36] These groups include the

---

36. "UN Conference on Environment and Development (1992)," May 23, 1997, www.un.org/geninfo/bp/enviro.html; and UNFCCC, "Conference of the Parties, Twenty-First Session, Paris, 30 November to 11 December 2015," December 1, 2015, http://unfccc.int/resource/docs/2015/cop21/eng/misc02p01.pdf.

Accord DePatis c'est fait!

France and other nations celebrated the Paris Agreement as a landmark of international cooperation to combat climate change. However, whether the agreement can successfully compel countries to reduce their emissions remains to be seen.

types of TANs, as well as local environmental NGOs, that we have discussed, but they also include business representatives, who play an important role in representing economic interests to their respective delegations.

Resolving Disputes

A critical aspect of any agreement is providing mechanisms for dealing with conflict. Governing the commons requires countries to come together to find common ground. By anticipating repeated interaction where countries can raise concerns and seek to address them, the structure of meetings provides a venue where conflicts can be addressed over time. As we have seen in this chapter, while some of the simple environmental agreements were negotiated quickly, many have required a decade or even two to arrive at a globally agreed consensus.

International environmental agreements generally lack formal dispute resolution mechanisms. Few such agreements contain autonomous or independent procedures for resolving disputes; rather, most treaties depend on the good faith of countries themselves to work out disagreements within a multilateral setting. The Montreal Protocol to the Vienna Convention, however, was the first global environmental agreement to develop and use a noncompliance response system, located in its Implementation Committee. This mechanism remains focused on facilitating, not enforcing, compliance.

During the 1990s it became clear that several countries from the former Soviet Union (including Belarus, Russia, and Ukraine), as well as some developing countries, were not in full compliance with their emissions obligations. To address the problem, the Implementation Committee urged and finally approved new phaseout plans, with additional financial resources from other industrialized countries, the Global Environmental Facility, and the World Bank facilitating compliance.

The Kyoto Protocol tried to go further with complex enforcement mechanisms, but as we have seen, that approach did not prove popular. At its root, any environmental treaty depends on the consent of the participants. There is no supranational government to enforce decisions on those who choose not to participate. Treaties like the Montreal Protocol have proved successful because the most enthusiastic member states were able to offer sufficient carrots and sticks to the more reluctant ones. The Paris Agreement relies more on normative pressure for all countries to join than on dispute resolution. How effective this approach will be remains to be seen.

Conclusion: Can Global Environmental Cooperation Succeed?

We began this chapter asking why international environmental cooperation is so hard to achieve. To answer that puzzle and tie the threads of our analysis together, we can compare the relative success of international environmental cooperation on ozone depletion and the much slower progress on global climate change. Ozone depletion and global climate change became issues at around the same time. The first convention on ozone depletion was negotiated in 1985, the first on global climate change in 1992.

As described in "What Shaped Our World?" on page 550, concerns about ozone depletion were effectively addressed within a few years, as countries cooperated relatively quickly to curtail the production of CFCs. Efforts to address climate change, in contrast, still face major hurdles today. What accounts for the difference in the two outcomes? How can the analytical tools of interests, interactions, and institutions help us understand why we find successful international cooperation in the first case, and only limited cooperation to date in the second?

At its root, the answer to our puzzle is quite simple. People's daily actions create significant externalities for the environment and one another. These externalities, in turn, produce severe problems of collective action. Individuals and countries would like to benefit from a cleaner environment but would also like others to bear the costs of protecting environmental quality. Both the stratospheric ozone layer and the quantity of greenhouse gases in the atmosphere are global public goods. Although everyone benefits from a thicker ozone layer and fewer greenhouse gases, and everyone is harmed by CFC and carbon emissions, the fact that we all experience these effects may be precisely the problem. Since we all share the benefits of a healthy atmosphere and we all face private costs in changing our behavior, we all attempt to free ride on one another, hoping to reap the benefits of a greener environment without having to give up our current lifestyles. In turn, even when free riding can be overcome, there is still hard bargaining between industries and countries over who should bear the costs of changes in policy.

In the case of ozone depletion, the gains from a ban far exceeded the costs of change. At the time the ban was implemented in 1989, the cost of transitioning to new chemical alternatives was estimated to be $27 billion by 2075, but the Environmental Protection Agency calculated that the reduced skin cancers for Americans alone would save $6.5 trillion in medical costs over the same period.[37] Some of these estimates have since changed, but the important point is that at the time of decision, the expected benefits far outweighed the costs.

In the case of climate change, however, there are large, immediate and continuing costs for reducing carbon emissions, while the benefits are long-term and difficult to calculate. Changes to the global climate are complex, and impacts will vary tremendously by locality. In 2006, the British economist Sir Nicholas Stern published an extensive review of the economics of climate change. It estimated that, without a serious effort at carbon mitigation, climate change would cost the world 5–10 percent of its total gross domestic product (GDP), with the costs being considerably higher in many poor countries. By contrast, the estimate that the Stern team offered was that the transition to clean energy would cost more on the order of 1 percent of global GDP.[38]

If we just look at the numbers, mitigation still looks less expensive than the impacts, but the difference is not quite as stark as the several-hundred-times rate of return that the world achieved by rapidly eliminating ODS from use. In reality, the Montreal Protocol was an amazing bargain, one not likely to be repeated often. Moreover, it touched a very specific part of the economy, and the fear, particularly of skin cancer, was also specific. Climate change touches almost every part of every economy, and the impacts are diverse and diffuse. The costs of climate change are already happening. Scientists know that the probability of droughts and floods and other extreme climate events has already increased. But they are very cautious and can speak in only probabilistic terms about whether climate change "caused" any specific event.

Although both issues involve collective action problems, cooperation in ozone depletion was easier to achieve because of the highly concentrated nature of the CFC industry—in the relatively small number of both firms and countries, with most production and usage occurring in just a handful of developed states. The smaller number of firms and countries involved lowered the costs of collective action and made effective cooperation possible. The United States enjoyed a preeminent position in the industry as both the largest producer and the largest consumer of CFCs. Its leadership on the issue was decisive.

In addition, the problem of collective action is compounded by the distributional consequences of alternative policy solutions, especially in the case of global climate change. Every policy creates winners and losers, but the benefits of eliminating CFCs were clear. In the case of climate change, hydrocarbon fuels have been the lifeblood of modern economies, and the interests that would lose from any significant change in policy are large and politically powerful. As renewables

---

37. Litfin, *Ozone Discourses*, 128.

38. "Stern Review: The Economics of Climate Change: Summary of Conclusions," archived document, http://webarchive.nationalarchives.gov.uk/20100407163608/http://www.hm-treasury.gov.uk/d/Summary_of_Conclusions.pdf (accessed 12/13/17).

producers grow in size and political power in many economies, this is starting to change. Moreover, the International Energy Agency now believes that both the United States and China have decoupled their economies from energy, meaning that they can see economic growth without concomitant growth in energy consumption.[39] Yet, as seen in the calls by President Donald Trump to rescue and preserve jobs in the U.S. coal industry, vested interests continue to play a role in setting environmental policy.

Finally, international institutions have played a role in facilitating and codifying cooperation in both ozone depletion and global climate change. Negotiations have occurred within meetings of global leaders, and the agreements reached at these meetings have been institutionalized into conventions and subsequently amended in various protocols. Accords on both issues began with conventions outlining broad principles of cooperation and then moved on to substantive cuts in subsequent agreements. Greater cooperation on ozone depletion has been helped by relatively clear rules reducing and, later, banning specific chemicals. The rules governing reductions in carbon and other greenhouse gases, in contrast, are less well articulated, perhaps because the underlying issues remain highly contested.

Without doubt, the road from the UNFCCC signing to the accord reached in Paris was very long and exceedingly winding. But despite the much greater complexity, the challenges of collective action, and the potential costs of mitigation, the global community has agreed on a path to reduce greenhouse gases. As of this writing, it is facing one of its greatest challenges, with the U.S. president's announced intention to pull out of the agreement. But the actual impact of that withdrawal may be relatively small. A number of U.S. states, cities, and businesses have stepped up to say they will continue to work to meet the U.S. targets, and the agreement is structured in such a way that it takes four years to withdraw and only 30 days to return.[40]

Moreover, global reaction to the U.S. announcement was not at all like the weakening of commitment in many countries following the U.S. withdrawal from the Kyoto Protocol. Former vice president and Nobel laureate climate activist Al Gore described why he had become more optimistic in the month following the U.S. withdrawal: "The whole rest of the world has redoubled their commitment. And in this country, the governors and the mayors and the business leaders have all said, 'We're still in the agreement, and we're gonna fill the gap. We're gonna meet the U.S. commitment, regardless of what Donald Trump does.'"[41]

The past five decades have seen the development of a complex network of international environmental law and institutions. As we have discussed, these can be relatively easy to negotiate and administer, or they can be among the most

---

39. International Energy Agency, "Decoupling of Global Emissions and Economic Growth Confirmed," March 16, 2016, www.iea.org/newsroom/news/2016/march/decoupling-of-global-emissions-and-economic-growth-confirmed.html.

40. Chelsea Harvey, "Withdrawing from the Paris Deal Takes Four Years. Our Next President Could Join Again in 30 Days," *Washington Post*, June 5, 2017, www.washingtonpost.com/news/energy-environment/wp/2017/06/05/withdrawing-from-the-paris-deal-takes-four-years-our-next-president-could-join-again-in-30-days/?utm_term=.05fcc2436003.

41. John Carucci, "Al Gore Says He's More Optimistic about the Paris Climate Deal," *Associated Press*, July 25, 2017, www.bloomberg.com/news/articles/2017-07-25/al-gore-on-inconvenient-sequel-trump-and-the-environment.

complex and challenging of agreements. They involve the administering of a global commons, resources that we all share and no country or set of countries can control. This process began looking at examples of agreements in other issue areas, but it has developed a pattern of its own, including the heavy reliance on scientific bodies to inform negotiators, and the need for flexible and adaptive agreements.

Most environmental agreements cannot rely on the heavy hand of international government to enforce their rules. Countries must come willingly, perceiving their own interests. That is all the more reason to use adaptive architecture. These interests change over time. As we have started to experience the real cost of climate change and to see the benefits of cleaner energy and greater forest protection, global support for the Paris Agreement has grown. At the same time, we can see real success in other agreements. The ozone hole has begun to heal. Several whale species are now back to their pre-exploitation levels. We will continue to face many environmental challenges in the future, including species loss and the impacts of pollution in our atmosphere, but the lessons of the last fifty years should give us hope that we have institutions that can address them.

Study Tool Kit

Interests, Interactions, and Institutions in Context

- Despite common interests in the quality of the environment, the interactions of individuals, as well as of countries, suffer from problems of collective action and free riding. This is especially true for public goods (global climate) and common-pool resources (fisheries). The result is less overall environmental cooperation than individuals and even countries themselves collectively desire.

- Small groups of actors, one of whom is substantially larger than the others and all of whom interact frequently on multiple issues, are most likely to cooperate effectively on issues relating to the international environment.

- Distributional conflicts within and between countries can impede progress in mitigating harmful environmental practices. Individuals, groups, and states have conflicting interests over who bears the costs of policy change. How environmental policies distribute these costs affects how likely actors are to cooperate successfully on issues relating to the environment.

- International institutions facilitate environmental cooperation primarily by enhancing information and verifying compliance. There is now a wide range of agreements covering many environmental problems. TANs and other NGOs now play an essential role in monitoring compliance with environmental agreements. These accords, however, can be only as effective as the underlying cooperation between countries permits.

Key Terms

global climate change, (p. 543)

United Nations Framework Convention on Climate Change (UNFCCC), (p. 543)

Paris Agreement, (p. 543)

tragedy of the commons, (p. 543)

public goods, (p. 545)

common-pool resources, (p. 545)

nonexcludable goods, (p. 546)

nonrival goods, (p. 546)

Kyoto Protocol, (p. 547)

Vienna Convention, (p. 549)

Montreal Protocol, (p. 549)

cap-and-trade system, (p. 552)

Nationally Determined Contribution (NDC), (p. 553)

externalities, (p. 555)

For Further Reading

Bechtel, Micahel M., Federica Genovese, and Kenneth F. Scheve. "Interests, Norms and Support for the Provision of Global Public Goods: The Case of Climate Co-operation." *British Journal of Political Science* (forthcoming), doi:10.1017/S0007123417000205. Examines individual support by sector of employment for environmental regulation.

Dietz, Thomas, Elinor Ostrom, and Paul C. Stern. "The Struggle to Govern the Commons." *Science* 302, no. 5652 (2003): 1907–12. Lays out a framework for addressing the tragedy of the commons in international agreements.

Gore, Albert. *An Inconvenient Sequel: Truth to Power*. Rodale, 2017. Highlights the dangers of global warming and the technologies to address it.

Green, Jessica. "Transnational Delegation in Global Environmental Governance: When Do Non-state Actors Govern?" *Regulation & Governance* (forthcoming), doi:10.1111/rego.12141. Provides a historical and theoretical overview of when and what governance functions are delegated to private, transnational actors.

Hickmann, Thomas. "The Reconfiguration of Authority in Global Climate Governance." *International Studies Review* 37 (forthcoming), https://doi.org/10.1093/isr/vix037. Reviews alternative governance schemes on the global environment and how they interact at the nonstate, state, and international levels.

Klein, Naomi. *This Changes Everything: Capitalism vs. the Climate*. New York: Simon and Schuster, 2014. Roots the problem of climate change deep in capitalism as an economic system.

Stoett, Peter J. *The International Politics of Whaling*. Toronto: UBC Press, 1997. Discusses the history of the anti-whaling movement, as well as the positions of the key national players involved.

Vaughn, Jacqueline. *Environmental Politics: Domestic and Global Dimensions*. Boston: Wadsworth Cengage Learning, 2011. Provides comprehensive coverage of environmental politics.

Victor, David G. *Global Warming Gridlock: Creating More Effective Strategies for Protecting the Planet*. New York: Cambridge University Press, 2011. Critiques current international environmental strategies and agreements and offers a radical proposal for progress within smaller clubs of like-minded countries.

14

Challenges to the Global Order

THE PUZZLE *In the coming decades, the international system will face challenges from actors seeking weapons of mass destruction, the rise of a new superpower in Asia, and growing opposition to economic globalization. Can political science tell us what the future will hold?*

Above: Supporters of Alternative for Germany (AfD) rally around a banner that reads, "Stop the asylum chaos! It is our country, Mrs. Merkel!" To what degree do populist groups like the AfD pose a threat to our current, globalized world order?

The day after Germany's 2017 federal elections, the leader of Alternative for Germany (Alternative für Deutschland, or AfD) celebrated his party's surprisingly strong showing by hammering home its defining issue: "We don't want to lose Germany to an invasion of foreigners from a different culture."[1] The invasion to which he referred was not an attack by a foreign army; rather, it was a large influx of immigrants and refugees. The long-running civil war in Syria, together with political instability and economic distress in Africa, had created a flow of people seeking safety and opportunity—many of them Muslim, and many of them hoping to settle in Germany and other wealthy European countries.

In its 2017 campaign, the AfD sought to capitalize on the backlash among many Germans against their government's willingness to take in these migrants. In the process, party leaders used language that echoed themes from the country's Nazi past.[2] Though the AfD won only 12.6 percent of the vote, it claimed 94 of the 630 seats in the parliament, making it the third largest party. The 2017 election marked the first time since World War II that a right-wing nationalist party had won any seats in the German legislature.

The success of the AfD in Germany is part of a recent wave of support in developed democracies for "populist" parties and politicians who oppose globalization and international integration. Populist movements come in a variety of forms, but they all claim to speak on behalf of "the people" against corrupt elites both within and outside their country. Contemporary populist movements mobilize voters who feel that they have been harmed by a mixture of economic and cultural changes associated with globalization, such as job losses due to foreign trade, cultural shifts due to the influx of migrants or refugees, and a perceived loss of autonomy to international organizations.

Populist parties direct anger over these developments toward elites who, they allege, have opened borders to foreign goods and people and given away the nation's sovereignty to distant bodies like the European Union (EU) or the United Nations (UN). These concerns played a key role in the British referendum to leave the EU (known as Brexit), the election of right-wing governments in Poland and Hungary, and the 2016 election of President Donald Trump in the United States. Populist politicians have also had recent success in the Philippines, Venezuela, and Turkey.

Seen in a broader context, populist movements are one of several challenges to what has been called the *postwar order*—the institutions and pattern of interactions that emerged after World War II and have fundamentally shaped world politics for the last seven decades. In some respects, this system created significant benefits: large advances in economic development and human well-being, an explosion of cross-border commercial and financial ties, the spread of democratic institutions, and reductions in interstate (though not civil) violence. But, like any set of rules and institutions, the postwar order has favored the interests of some actors over others and created losers as well as winners. Many of the defining challenges of world politics over the next decade are likely to involve conflicts between those countries, groups, and individuals who benefit from the existing system and those who do not.

In this final chapter we explore three sets of challenges that are likely to be central to world politics in the coming decade. The first comes from states and groups whose interests are hostile to those of the United States and its allies and who have sought to resist by developing weapons of mass destruction (WMD)—primarily nuclear, but also chemical or biological weapons. States like North Korea and Iran, and terrorist organizations like Al Qaeda, have tried, with varying degrees of success, to counter the United States' overwhelming military power by acquiring these extraordinarily destructive weapons.

The second challenge comes from the rise of states that might seek to displace the United States as the global leader and alter the rules of the international order in their favor. Foremost among these is China, whose rapid economic growth will soon make it the world's largest economy. In addition to posing a military threat to the United States and its allies in Asia, China represents an economic threat to workers in some sectors of the American economy.

The final challenge comes from the backlash to globalization exemplified by the rise of populist parties like the AfD. There has long been resistance to the economic aspects of globalization from people hurt by exposure to international markets, but the success of populist movements in recent years reflects concerns about threats to national identity and sovereignty. While economic losses can, in principle, be addressed through redistribution, groups who fear cultural changes may be harder to placate without reversing recent international trends.

Thinking Analytically about the Future of World Politics

As we have done throughout this book, we analyze these challenges by thinking in terms of interests, interactions, and institutions. The international institutions and patterns of interaction established after World War II benefit some actors at the expense of others. U.S. military dominance and leadership of global institutions threatens states and groups whose interests are hostile to the United States or who seek greater influence over the rules. Economic institutions that favor open markets threaten the jobs and wages of those who compete with foreign imports and the cultural interests of those who dislike foreign influences.

In each case, conflicting interests give rise to interactions between those seeking to change the system and those that benefit from it. Efforts by states and groups to acquire WMD have brought them into conflict both with the United States and with international regimes designed to limit the spread of these technologies. The rise of China has created tensions with the United States and its allies in the region, leading to a risk of war. The growing strength of parties opposed to globalization has created conflict with other parties, countries, and institutions that favor economic liberalization. How these interactions play out will not only affect important outcomes like war and peace, the spread of nuclear weapons, and the openness of the world's major economies; it will also shape the nature of the international order, if any, that emerges in the coming decades.

1. Jon Stone, "Germany's New Far-Right Party AfD Says It Will Fight an 'Invasion of Foreigners,'" *Independent*, September 25, 2017, www.independent.co.uk/news/world/europe/german-election-results-afd-far-right-merkel-alexander-gauland-2017-coalition-invasion-of-foreigners-a7965886.html.
2. See, for example, "German Election: Just How Right-Wing Is AfD?" *BBC News*, September 25, 2017, www.bbc.com/news/world-europe-37274201.

The Postwar Order and Its Challenges

What we call the *postwar order* is defined by a number of developments that took root in the aftermath of World War II and then expanded with the end of the Cold War. Its primary components were the proliferation of multilateral institutions, the growth of international economic exchange, the spread of democratic institutions, and the emergence of the United States as the leading actor on the world stage.

We have encountered a number of the key postwar institutions throughout this book, including the United Nations, the North Atlantic Treaty Organization (NATO), the General Agreement on Tariffs and Trade (GATT, later renamed the World Trade Organization, or WTO), the International Monetary Fund (IMF), the World Bank, and the European Union. But these well-known organizations are just the tip of the iceberg. Figure 14.1 shows the number of intergovernmental organizations—defined as organizations that have at least three member states—in existence from 1815 to 2014. The explosive growth of these institutions since the end of World War II is particularly pronounced. These organizations deal with an array of issues discussed in this book, including security, trade and finance, development assistance, human rights, and the environment.

The growth and development of these institutions were strongly shaped by interactions among the world's most powerful states. From 1946 to 1991, the competition between the two superpowers—the United States and the Soviet Union—took center stage, leading to the creation of rival alliance blocs: NATO and

Figure sources: Jon C. Pevehouse, Timothy Nordstrom, and Kevin Warnke, "The COW-2 International Organizations Dataset Version 2.0," *Conflict Management and Peace Science* 21, no. 2 (2004): 101–19. Updated to 2014 from data provided by Pevehouse.

FIGURE 14.1 *Number of Intergovernmental Organizations, 1815–2014*

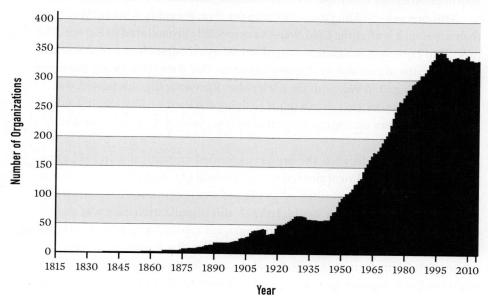

the Warsaw Pact. During this period, U.S.-led economic institutions such as the GATT, IMF, and World Bank were largely confined to the West. The liberalization of trade and financial flows, as well as the disbursement of economic aid to developing states, was not only good for American businesses; it was also part of a strategy by the United States to win allies and increase the economic strength of its bloc.

The superpower competition also affected the United Nations, which found it hard to take effective action on issues that cut across the Cold War divide. Nevertheless, the competing alliance blocs in Europe helped stabilize a continent that had been the site of two world wars earlier in the twentieth century (see Chapter 5), and nuclear weapons helped deter an outbreak of direct conflict between the superpowers (more on this shortly).

With the collapse of the Soviet Union in 1991, the United States emerged as the world's lone superpower. In the ensuing decade, the core institutions of the postwar period expanded in terms of both the number of members and the depth of their activities. Freed from constraints of the Cold War rivalry, the United Nations became much more active in managing both international and civil conflicts, as we saw in Chapter 5.

The WTO and IMF accepted new members from the former communist bloc and developing world. They also took on new functions: world trading rules, which had originally focused on manufactured goods, were broadened to cover other sectors, such as agriculture and services; the IMF, which had been founded to help stabilize exchange rates and international payments, expanded its mandate to monitor all financial issues that affect global stability.

NATO, rather than withering after its mission to contain the Soviet Union was complete, expanded its membership to the east and took on new "out of area" missions (see the "What Shaped Our World?" box in Chapter 5, p. 206). Other regional security organizations, such as the African Union and Association of Southeast Asian Nations (ASEAN), also became more active in managing conflicts.

This process—building institutional order from the ruins of World War II and then expanding it after the Cold War—was especially pronounced in Europe. The process of European integration started in 1951 as a modest effort to cooperate in the production of coal and steel, heavy industries that were strategically important in the emerging Cold War with the Soviet bloc. Economically, this project was intended to promote growth and improve living standards; politically, it would cement the alliance among countries that only six years before had been deadly enemies.

In the ensuing decades, the project expanded dramatically. In 1957, growing economic and political ties led to the creation of a customs union—that is, a union of states with low internal tariffs and a common external tariff when trading with the rest of the world. In 1992, this organization gave way to the European Union, which created a single market among its members, eliminating all barriers to trade. After the end of the Cold War, the European project, like other institutions from this period, took on new members and new roles. The organization has grown from 6 original members to 28, and 16 of these countries

FIGURE 14.2 *The Explosion of World Trade, 1950–2017*

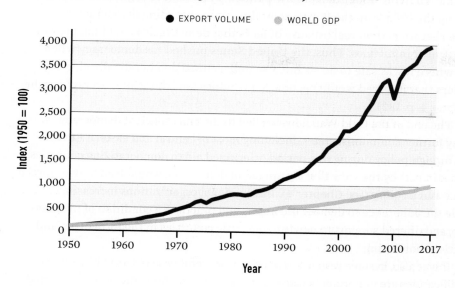

have joined since 1990. In 1995, 26 EU members abolished passport and other border controls, greatly facilitating the movement of people within the region. In 1999, 11 EU members adopted the euro as a common currency and phased out their national currencies; by 2017, 8 additional countries had followed suit. Thus, a century that began with Germany and France fighting two major wars ended with those countries using the same money.

By some key measures, the 70-year period since World War II was quite good for the world. Over this period, the global income per capita grew at its fastest rate in human history (see Figure 1.1 on p. 10). As a result, the percentage of the world's population living in extreme poverty has fallen from over 70 percent in 1950 to about 10 percent today. Life expectancy at birth increased dramatically over this period as well.[3]

World trade exploded during this time, along with a dramatic increase in the flow of capital across borders. Figure 14.2 shows how the volume of world exports has grown dramatically since 1950, faster than the overall world gross domestic product (GDP). Even the global economic downturn in 2009 registers as a onetime blip in this trend. Thanks to the European Union, Europe became the most economically integrated region in the world. About three-fourths of European countries' merchandise exports are bought by other European countries; by comparison, about half of North American or Asian exports stay within their respective regions.[4]

Figure source: Data for 1950–2014 come from World Trade Organization, *International Trade Statistics 2015* (Geneva: WTO, 2015), Table A1a; data for 2015–17, from World Trade Organization, *World Trade Statistical Review 2017* (Geneva: WTO, 2017), Table A1a.

Note: The figure compares the growth of world trade and GDP by setting the values for both in 1950 equal to 100 and measuring subsequent years relative to that baseline. An index value of, say, 500 indicates that the quantity of interest is five times larger than it was in 1950.

---

3. A wealth of data about economic development, poverty, inequality, and living standards is compiled and summarized by Our World in Data, https://ourworldindata.org (accessed 09/29/17).
4. World Trade Organization, *World Trade Report 2010* (Geneva: WTO, 2010), Table I.4.

This period also saw a significant increase in the percentage of the world's population living under democratic political systems (see Figure 4.6 on p. 170). During the Cold War, the West's commitment to spreading democracy was more rhetorical than real because of fears that democracies could fall prey to communist influences. Thus, the United States pushed for democracy when and where it was safe to do so, but also undermined democratically elected leaders that it feared would become Soviet allies (see the "Controversy" box in Chapter 4, p. 182).[5]

The end of the Cold War, however, led to the emergence of democracy in many former communist states, including most of central and eastern Europe. U.S. foreign policy during this period prioritized aid to democratizing countries, driven in part by the view that the spread of democracy would lead to widespread peace and stability (see Chapter 4). International organizations increasingly made the adherence to democratic norms and practices a condition of membership, and offered support to newly democratic countries in the form of aid and election monitoring.[6]

It was also, in some respects, a relatively peaceful time in world history. The qualifications are important because, as we saw in Chapter 6, the post-1945 period saw a large number of long and bloody civil wars, particularly in newly decolonized regions like Africa, Asia, and the Middle East. Many of these conflicts were exacerbated by the Cold War interaction, as these regions became a site of proxy wars between the superpowers. In a more limited sense, however, the period could be considered peaceful. As we saw in Chapter 3, there appears to be a downward trend in interstate wars since 1945. This period is also notable for its absence of wars among great powers, which have historically been the costliest conflicts. And despite the deep ideological hostility between the United States and the Soviet Union, it is remarkable that the superpower rivals never fought each other directly. For this reason, the 45 years following World War II are sometimes referred to as the "Long Peace."[7]

Given that the postwar era was ushered in with the detonation of two atomic bombs over Japan, the fact that the world avoided a feared nuclear holocaust is no small thing. Indeed, early concerns that nuclear technology would spread rapidly around the world turned out to be overly pessimistic, as today only 9 countries (out of 193) have nuclear weapons (see "What Shaped Our World?" on p. 601).

Given all this good news, why are the coming decades likely to be defined by challenges to this system? Although the postwar order created benefits for the world as a whole, the benefits were not evenly distributed: the system created losers

---

5. Tony Smith, *America's Mission: The United States and the Worldwide Struggle for Democracy in the Twentieth Century* (Princeton, NJ: Princeton University Press, 1994).

6. For a summary of democracy promotion efforts during this period, particularly in the context of the spread of election monitoring, see Susan D. Hyde, *The Pseudo-Democrat's Dilemma: Why Election Observation Became an International Norm* (Ithaca, NY: Cornell University Press, 2011), chap. 3.

7. See John Lewis Gaddis, "The Long Peace: Elements of Stability in the Postwar International System," *International Security* 10 (Spring 1986): 99–142.

as well as winners. Like any set of institutions and rules, the postwar order gave some states, particularly the United States and its allies, more influence than others and a larger share of the gains. Some countries, groups, and individuals were left with very little power and therefore see the existing order as indifferent or even hostile to their interests.

In the coming years, the United States may face challenges to its leadership on the world stage from states, like China, that are rapidly growing in economic and military power.

Three sets of actors, in particular, have incentives to challenge the postwar order. The first consists of states and groups whose interests conflict with those of the United States and its allies and who see U.S. military dominance as a core threat to their interests. During the 1990s, the term *rogue states* was coined to refer to a group of countries that were determined to confront the United States and the U.S.-led order: North Korea, Iran, Iraq (before the U.S. invasion in 2003), and Libya (before the ouster of Mu'ammar Qaddafi in 2011). These countries have sought to expand their regional influence at the expense of the United States and its allies, and they see U.S. military power and influence as standing in their way.

Over the last two decades, these states have been joined by a potent set of nonstate actors, most prominently terrorist organizations like Al Qaeda and the Islamic State (IS). Although terrorism long predates September 11, 2001, the attack on that day reflected a major escalation in efforts by some groups to push the United States out of the Middle East and Asia. Groups like Al Qaeda and IS have seen eradicating Western political and cultural influences in those regions as central to their quest to establish an Islamic state, and they use terrorism to circumvent U.S. military power by attacking civilian targets (see the "What Shaped Our World?" box in Chapter 6, p. 282).

Another strategy that dissatisfied actors may use in an effort to neutralize U.S. military dominance, which we consider in detail in this chapter, is the acquisition of weapons of mass destruction—nuclear, chemical, and biological weapons. Since these weapons are both extraordinarily destructive and hard to defend against, possessing them can rapidly increase an actor's ability to impose costs even on the most powerful states. As a result, the proliferation of WMD presents a significant challenge to the United States, its allies, and international agreements designed to slow the spread of these weapons.

A second set of challengers consists of states that were relatively weak when the postwar order was constructed and that now want to use their increasing power to alter existing bargains and institutions. Dramatic economic growth has propelled some previously poor states into the upper ranks of the world economy, and most forecasters predict a significant reshuffling of the largest economies in the coming decades. Figure 14.3 shows the ten largest economies

FIGURE 14.3 *The Ten Largest Economies, 2016 versus 2050*

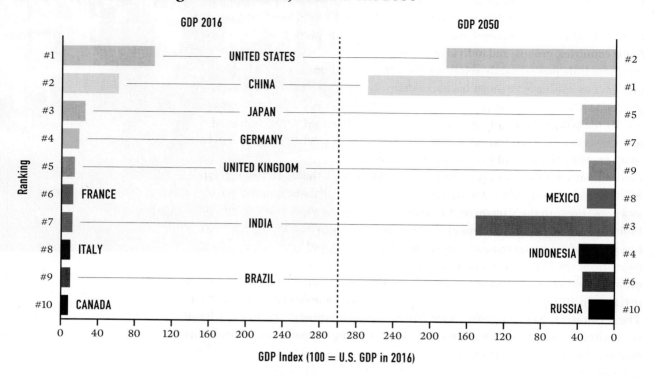

GDP Index (100 = U.S. GDP in 2016)

Figure sources: PwC Global, "The Long View: How Will the Global Economic Order Change by 2050?" February 2017, 68, www.pwc.com/gx/en/world-2050/assets/pwc-the-world-in-2050-full-report-feb-2017.pdf.

Note: GDP is compared using market exchange rates. The size of the U.S. economy in 2016 is fixed at 100, so every other country's economy is measured as a percentage of the United States' current GDP.

in 2016 and compares them to projected rankings for 2050. As indicated, China is expected to overtake the United States as the number one economy within the next decade or two. The center of economic power will also shift from the west and north to the east and south, as India, Indonesia, and Brazil join China in the upper ranks.

These shifts present challenges to the existing order, since countries with increased economic power are now pursuing increased political power. Countries like India and Brazil, for example, have sought greater influence within international institutions. The two are part of an effort—joint with Japan and Germany—to obtain permanent seats on the UN Security Council, thereby breaking the monopoly held by the victors of World War II.[8]

A newly empowered Russia has also challenged the U.S.-led order. After the Soviet Union collapsed, Russia experienced a decade of economic stagnation and internal instability. During this period, Western institutions like the European Union and NATO extended their reach to include former Soviet allies and the former Soviet republics of Latvia, Lithuania, and Estonia. Starting at the turn of the

---

8. For a discussion of UN Security Council reform efforts, in the context of a larger study of whether and how international institutions respond to changes in the power of their members, see Phillip Y. Lipscy, *Renegotiating the World Order: Institutional Change in International Relations* (Cambridge: Cambridge University Press, 2017), esp. chap. 8.

twenty-first century, the Russian economy rebounded primarily because of higher oil prices, and a resurgent Russia, under the leadership of Vladimir Putin, began pushing back against Western institutions. Russian invasions of Georgia in 2008 and Ukraine in 2014 were both motivated by Putin's interest in preventing those states from entering the Western orbit.

Foremost among this set of challenges, though, is the one posed by China's growing economic and military power. As we will discuss later in this chapter, periods when a rising state threatens to surpass the power of the current leader are fraught with uncertainty and have, in some cases, been associated with major wars. The rise of China thus raises the pressing question of whether there will be a struggle over leadership of the international system.

The third and final set of challengers consists of those that see their interests as harmed by globalization, the dramatic expansion of global markets and economic flows encouraged by the United States and Western economic institutions. Although globalization has generated a great deal of wealth overall, its effects are uneven, and for some groups and individuals it has generated both economic and noneconomic costs. We saw in Chapter 10 that many people in poorer countries see the global economic system as a cause of their underdevelopment and have at times sought to shut themselves off from its effects. In the developed world, some workers who have been exposed to global markets have experienced economic insecurity in the form of job losses, downward wage pressure, or greater income volatility. These harmful outcomes have inspired efforts by labor unions and political parties to slow or reverse globalization.

At the same time, economic opposition to globalization has been joined by resistance to the flow of people across borders, including economic migrants and refugees fleeing civil war and instability. In addition to exacerbating domestic concerns about job loss, these flows have sparked opposition from those who see migrants as weakening their country's national identity and sovereignty. Particularly in Europe and the United States, these concerns have fueled the rise of populist parties and politicians whose opposition to foreign influences poses a challenge to the Western postwar order from within the very countries that erected it.

In the next three sections of this chapter we examine some of these challenges more closely to think about how they might play out over the next decade. The purpose is not to make predictions. Not only are political interactions complicated, but many of those discussed in this chapter were developing even as it was being written. Rather, the goal is to use the framework of this book to think carefully about what has happened already and what could happen in the future. In each case, history and theory inform our analysis of how these interactions might play out over time.

Can the Spread of WMD Be Stopped?

On July 28, 2017, North Korea launched a missile from an arms production facility in the north of the country. The missile stayed aloft for about 47 minutes, following a trajectory that took it 2,300 miles into space, before arcing steeply downward and landing in the sea west of Japan, about 620 miles from its launch site. The test was one of several that North Korea conducted in 2017, but it marked an important milestone. From the size and velocity of the missile, experts estimated that it had a maximum range of about 6,000 miles—far enough to hit the western United States, including cities as distant as Chicago. The launch demonstrated for the first time that North Korea had the ability to hit the United States with a missile that could one day carry a nuclear warhead. Just over a month later, North Korea detonated a nuclear explosive much more powerful than anything it had tested before.

The two tests marked North Korea's entry into an exclusive club of states that have the technology to impose enormous costs on the United States in spite of its overwhelming military power. Though not the first U.S. adversary to acquire this capability—Russia and China have had it for decades—North Korea is the most successful of a group of challengers that have sought to develop or acquire WMD in recent years. This group includes a number of states that are or have been hostile to the United States and its allies, particularly Iraq, Iran, North Korea, and Libya, but it also includes nonstate actors like the transnational terrorist groups Al Qaeda and IS. All these actors, although diverse, have two key features in common: interests that put them in conflict with the United States, and an inability to defeat the United States' conventional military power. Thus, these actors have incentives to seek WMD as a relatively easy way to shift the military balance in their favor.

The pursuit of WMD by these actors creates conflict not only with the United States, but also with U.S. allies in Asia, Europe, and the Middle East who might be targeted by these weapons, as well as international institutions that seek to stop the proliferation of these technologies. The interactions between those who want to acquire WMD and those who want to stop the spread of these weapons have presented significant international challenges in recent decades and will continue to be a central feature of world politics in the coming years.

What implications does the spread of such weapons have? What, if anything, can be done to prevent hostile actors from acquiring them?

What Do Theory and History Tell Us?

Stopping the spread of nuclear, chemical, and biological weapons—collectively known as WMD—has been a pressing item on the international agenda for as long as these weapons have existed. At the time of this writing, nine states are known to possess nuclear weapons (the United States, Russia, Great Britain, France, China, India, Pakistan, Israel, and North Korea). Iran has pursued uranium enrichment, raising suspicions that it is seeking nuclear weapons, but those efforts are currently frozen by an international agreement (discussed later in the chapter). In addition, about 20 states possess the technology and knowledge to produce nuclear weapons in a very short time frame if they choose to do so. Fewer states are known to have chemical and/or biological weapons— the production and use of which are outlawed by international treaties—but a handful of states are suspected of having illicit stocks or programs under way to develop them.[9]

Given the horrendous killing power of WMD, it may seem obvious that their spread is undesirable; however, the lessons of theory and history are more complicated. Particularly in the case of nuclear weapons, one can make a strong argument that their overwhelming destructive power has made them a force for peace. This argument hinges on the idea that nuclear war jeopardizes the overriding interest of most actors: survival. Whatever other interests states or individuals may have, those goals are meaningless if attaining them leads to the actor's destruction.[10] Thus, a war involving nuclear weapons threatens to impose costs that far exceed the value of whatever good might be at stake in a dispute.

The massive costs of nuclear war mean that the bargaining range of deals that both sides prefer over war generally includes any possible division of the good; a state should prefer any deal, even one in which it gets nothing, over starting a nuclear war, in which the risk of its complete destruction is high. At the very least, the enormous destructive potential of any war between states with nuclear weapons should encourage caution and a greater willingness to compromise. In short, possession of highly destructive weapons should create a condition of mutual deterrence in which neither side would contemplate an attack on the other, forcing them to resolve their disputes in other ways. During the Cold War, this condition was referred to as one of *mutually assured destruction*, with the colorful acronym MAD.

To work, mutual nuclear deterrence has very few requirements.[11] The first is that each side must possess a survivable second-strike force; that is, each state must possess enough weapons that its arsenal could survive a first strike by the other state and still be formidable enough to cause unacceptable levels of damage for the initiator. Why is this necessary? If one state's nuclear arsenal is relatively easy to destroy with a crippling first strike, then a commitment problem arises that could generate incentives on both sides to initiate preemptive war. In the event of a crisis, the stronger state would be tempted to deliver a knockout blow that would deprive the other state of any ability to retaliate. In the absence of a credible commitment by the stronger state not to strike first, the vulnerable state would face a temptation to "use them or lose them"—to launch its weapons first in order to ensure that they would not be destroyed on the ground. Only when both states have enough weapons to ride out a first strike and still deliver a crippling blow of their own would neither state have a destabilizing temptation to launch preemptively. In practice, this means each side must have not only a large number of weapons, but also a means of protecting them, such as by hardening missile sites against attack or by making the weapons mobile (on vehicles, airplanes, or submarines) so that they are hard to eliminate.

---

9. See, for example, Arms Control Association, "Chemical and Biological Weapons Status at a Glance," September 2017, www.armscontrol.org/factsheets/cbwprolif.

10. Obviously, individuals who engage in suicide terrorism may have different priorities, as we saw in Chapter 6.

11. See Scott D. Sagan and Kenneth N. Waltz, *The Spread of Nuclear Weapons: An Enduring Debate*, 3rd ed. (New York: Norton, 2012), chap. 1.

The second requirement for mutual deterrence to work is that the leaders be rational, at least in the very limited sense that they care about their survival. The deterrent effect of nuclear weapons depends on the assumption that they will inspire caution by making the costs of war loom large relative to the potential benefits. For this to happen, those whose fingers are on the trigger must value their own survival and the survival of their nation enough to consider war unacceptably costly. In addition, the weapons must not be easily subject to accidental launch.

Finally, mutual deterrence assumes that in the event of an attack, each side can reliably verify where that attack originated. Deterrence hinges on the expectation that anyone who initiates an attack will face a devastating counterattack. Hence, the initiator must expect that the target will be able to identify it. If it were impossible to know where the attack originated, then a potential initiator might think it could escape retaliation.

What does the evidence suggest? Although the logic of mutual deterrence may seem overly optimistic, the historical track record is encouraging. There has never been a nuclear war. Indeed, the only actual use of nuclear weapons—the bombings of Hiroshima and Nagasaki, Japan, by the United States in 1945—occurred when a nuclear country attacked a non-nuclear one. This observation suggests that what is dangerous about nuclear weapons is not their spread per se, but their *uneven* spread, which leaves haves and have-nots. Even conventional war between states possessing nuclear weapons is extremely rare; the only such case is the 1999 Kargil War between India and Pakistan (see the "What Shaped Our World?" box in Chapter 4, p. 159).

The deterrent effect of mutually assured destruction is most prominently evident in the absence of war between the United States and the Soviet Union from 1945 to 1990, referred to earlier as the Long Peace.[12] Although several factors contribute to this observation (including the role of the Cold War alliance system discussed in Chapter 5), the fact that both states had enormous nuclear arsenals that gave them second-strike capability induced a level of caution and pragmatism in their relationship that allowed them to avoid direct warfare and to make compromises when necessary.

If the logic and historical track record of nuclear deterrence is so solid, why has there been such an effort to stop the proliferation of nuclear weapons and other WMD? Why might some states have an interest in preventing the spread of these weapons? There are three main reasons. First, even if nuclear weapons may reduce the danger of war in some circumstances, they nonetheless influence the distribution of power among states. A state whose power increases—such as by acquiring a potent new weapon—may seek to revise the status quo in its favor. This development could harm the interests of other states, even if it never leads to war.

For example, if Iran were to acquire nuclear weapons, its power and influence in the Middle East would increase to the detriment of the United States, Israel, Saudi Arabia, and any other country that has disputes with Iran. North Korea's nuclear weapons threaten to make it very costly for the United States or Japan to

---

12. See Gaddis, "The Long Peace."

help South Korea in the event of another war on the Korean peninsula. Hence, states may have an interest in stopping the spread of WMD in order to protect other interests that would be jeopardized by the emergence of an enemy with such capabilities.

Second, the states that have recently obtained, or may soon obtain, these weapons may be unable to meet all the requirements for mutual deterrence noted earlier. Unlike the United States and the Soviet Union during the Cold War, many of these states are relatively poor and domestically unstable. They may not have the resources to build and protect an adequate second-strike force, and they may not have the technology or resources to safeguard their weapons against theft or accidental launch.

The case of Pakistan, which acquired nuclear weapons in the late 1980s, illustrates some of these concerns.[13] As we saw in Chapter 4, Pakistan's military has considerable independence from the civilian leadership, and evidence suggests that the military has handled its nuclear weapons in a risky manner during several crises with India, thereby raising the danger of unintentional use. In addition, influential elements of the regime, particularly the intelligence services, have close ties to militant groups in the region, thereby raising concerns about a transfer of nuclear technology to extremists. Moreover, Pakistan seems to have exercised loose control over its nuclear scientists. A. Q. Khan, the "father" of Pakistan's bomb, is suspected of running a network that sold key technologies to Iran, Libya, and North Korea.[14] If new proliferators resemble Pakistan rather than a more stable state such as, say, Great Britain, then there is reason for concern.

The third concern, and one that has come to the fore since the 9/11 terrorist attacks, is that the spread of WMD may make it more likely that these weapons will fall into the hands of terrorist organizations. This could happen intentionally (such as if a hostile state were to give or sell a weapon to a terrorist) or unintentionally (through theft or the complicity of extremist elements within the state). There is reason to doubt whether the logic of deterrence could prevent the use of WMD by terrorist organizations in the same way that it does with states.

While terrorists may act in rational ways (as we discussed in Chapter 6), at least some have demonstrated their willingness to commit suicide for their cause, suggesting that the threat of retaliation may not dissuade them. Moreover, unlike states, terrorist networks do not constitute a geographically defined target, so it can be especially hard to identify the perpetrators and their base. And even if the responsible organization can be found, it can be difficult to carry out retaliatory

A Pakistani soldier stands guard over missiles that could deliver nuclear weapons. The security of Pakistan's nuclear arsenal is of great concern, since a number of militant groups are active in that country.

---

13. For a discussion of these concerns, see Sagan and Waltz, *Spread of Nuclear Weapons*, chap. 3; and Scott D. Sagan, "How to Keep the Bomb from Iran," *Foreign Affairs* 85 (September–October 2006): 45–59.

14. The status of these allegations is contested. Although the Pakistani government admitted Khan's involvement—and pardoned him after he confessed—Khan later retracted his confession.

strikes without also killing innocent people, since terrorists embed themselves within civilian populations that may or may not share their goals. While it might have been credible during the Cold War for the United States to threaten the Soviet Union with massive retaliation in the event its leaders ordered a nuclear strike, it is harder to make the same threat today against, say, Pakistan for the activities of a small number of terrorists operating within its borders. Hence, a terrorist organization may expect to be able to escape retaliation, and/or it may consider the risks of retaliation acceptable, given terrorists' extreme preferences.

Preventing the Spread of WMD

How can the proliferation of WMD be prevented? The answer depends in part on whether the potential proliferator is a state or a nonstate actor, such as a terrorist group. In general, there are two ways to prevent an actor from acquiring WMD: (1) by altering the actor's incentives so that abstention becomes a better course of action; or (2) by preventing the actor from getting the necessary technology and material, such as the fissile material required to fuel a nuclear explosion. These strategies are not mutually exclusive, but they are likely to meet different levels of success, depending on the actor in question.

As we saw in Chapter 6, terrorists have extreme interests that make them particularly willing to kill and be killed for their cause. Efforts to alter a cost-benefit analysis are less likely to succeed with such actors. It is unclear what promises or threats would induce them to alter their behavior voluntarily. As a result, preventing terrorists from acquiring a WMD capability requires a focus on denying them technology—that is, ensuring that they do not get their hands on highly enriched uranium or plutonium for nuclear weapons, or on chemical or biological agents that can be weaponized. Since nuclear and chemical facilities are large and obvious, most clandestine terrorist organizations cannot pursue this route to developing weapons; they are more likely to buy or steal the components they need. The task of denial therefore primarily entails securing nuclear and laboratory facilities against theft and policing efforts to buy or sell these materials on the black market.

Most states share an interest in preventing nuclear fuel from falling into the wrong hands, so there is a strong basis for international cooperation to secure stockpiles of uranium and plutonium and to police theft and smuggling. Indeed, the United States and Russia, the two largest and most experienced nuclear powers, cooperated extensively in this area in the 25 years after the end of the Cold War. Although these efforts were successful, tensions over Russian support for separatists in Ukraine in 2014, and worsening relations between the two countries since then, have led to a suspension and further unraveling of nuclear security cooperation.[15] Thus, despite states' strong shared interest in preventing nuclear terrorism, joint efforts in this area can fall prey to conflicts over other issues.

---

15. For a summary and time line, see Mariana Budjeryn, Simon Saradzhyan, and William Tobey, "25 Years of Nuclear Security Cooperation by the U.S., Russia and Other Newly Independent States: A Timeline," *Russia Matters*, June 16, 2017, www.russiamatters.org/analysis/25-years-nuclear-security-cooperation-us-russia-and-other-newly-independent-states.

Preventing the spread of WMD to states may also entail denial of nuclear, biological, and chemical ingredients, but given the current diffusion of scientific knowledge and technology, most reasonably advanced states already have the resources to develop a WMD program. As a result, efforts to slow proliferation among states focus primarily on shaping their interests. States that contemplate developing or acquiring WMD do so because they believe there will be some benefit to having them: enhanced security from an outside threat, or greater prestige and influence regionally or globally.[16] Strategies for preventing the spread of WMD must alter these incentives, by increasing either the costs of proliferation or the benefits of abstention.

The main strategies that have been used to this end coincide with the three core concepts of our framework: finding alternative ways to address the security interests of potential proliferators, cooperating through international institutions to establish and enforce rules against proliferation, and engaging in coercive interactions designed to forcibly disarm hostile states.

Guaranteeing the Security Interests of Potential Proliferators

One approach to preventing the spread of nuclear weapons is to address the underlying reason why a state may want such technology in the first place. The most common motive is fear of attack by another nuclear-armed state.[17] This motive is evident from the historical pattern of proliferation. The United States developed nuclear weapons during World War II amid a fear that Nazi Germany would acquire them first. The Soviet Union responded to the onset of the Cold War with a nuclear program of its own, achieving a nuclear capability in 1949. This development sparked concerns in Great Britain and France, which then sought their own nuclear deterrent.

In the early 1960s, a growing rift between the Soviet Union and China led the latter to seek its own nuclear arsenal, which it achieved in the mid-1960s. The Chinese bomb induced fear in neighboring India, which had already had several clashes with China over their disputed border. The Indian nuclear program produced a usable weapon in the 1980s, with the result that India's longtime enemy, Pakistan, embarked on a program of its own. Hence, the spread of nuclear weapons has been driven largely by security concerns, with each new proliferator sparking fears in its rivals and leading them to seek a bomb of their own.

It follows that proliferation can be halted by finding ways to address the security interests that lead states to proliferate. Indeed, the historical record suggests a number of cases in which this strategy has worked—cases in which states that faced stronger and/or nuclear-armed rivals, and had the technological and scientific ability to develop nuclear weapons, nonetheless abstained from doing so. For example, why did China's acquisition of nuclear weapons lead to a response in kind from India, but not from other states in the region that also had reason to fear

---

16. For a discussion of the motives behind nuclear proliferation, see Scott D. Sagan, "Why Do States Build Nuclear Weapons? Three Models in Search of a Bomb," *International Security* 21, no. 3 (Winter 1996–97): 54–86.

17. For a careful analysis of how security interests lead to proliferation, see Alexander Debs and Nuno P. Monteiro, *Nuclear Politics: The Strategic Causes of Proliferation* (New York: Cambridge University Press, 2017).

China (particularly Japan, Taiwan, and South Korea)? The answer lies in the fact that these states found other ways to redress their insecurity. In particular, all three had defensive alliances with the United States, which meant that even though they did not have a nuclear deterrent of their own, they were protected by the "nuclear umbrella" of the United States. Evidence suggests that the Soviet Union induced similar restraint in its ally Syria, which was tempted to develop nuclear weapons in response to Israel.[18] By extending security guarantees to friendly states, the superpowers helped to dampen those states' incentives to seek their own arsenals.

Of course, for such guarantees to work, the promise of protection has to be sufficiently credible that states are willing to entrust their security to another party rather than building their own arsenal. For countries, like North Korea and Iran, that have no nuclear-armed patron willing to defend them, this strategy will not work.[19] Even among close allies, there may be doubts in this regard. Concerns that the United States would not "risk New York to save London or Paris" led Britain and France to acquire nuclear weapons in the 1950s. North Korea's ability to reach U.S. territory with nuclear-armed missiles could induce similar fears in South Korea and Japan. If South Korea believes that the United States will not "risk San Francisco to save Seoul," its government could decide to end its nuclear abstention and acquire its own deterrent against the threat from the north.

International Institutions: The Nuclear Non-Proliferation Treaty

An alternative mechanism for preventing proliferation relies on an international institution to foster cooperation among states with a shared interest in this goal. The primary institutional mechanism for this purpose is embodied in the nuclear Non-Proliferation Treaty (NPT), the origins and main provisions of which are described in "What Shaped Our World?" on page 601. This treaty prohibits all but five states—the United States, Russia, Great Britain, France, and China—from possessing nuclear weapons, and thus provides the legal framework for preventing their further spread.

As with many international institutions, the strength of the NPT lies in setting out standards of acceptable behavior and providing mechanisms for monitoring compliance through the International Atomic Energy Agency (IAEA); the NPT is weaker when it comes to enforcement, which is left to the states themselves. IAEA inspections uncovered evidence of plutonium diversion by North Korea in the early 1990s, and they documented numerous instances of noncompliance by Iran going back several decades. Once cheating is discovered, however, the IAEA has no authority to impose sanctions. Instead, it must submit charges of noncompliance to the UN Security Council, which has the ability to authorize economic or military sanctions. As we saw in Chapter 5, however, the Security Council is not a neutral body; rather, it is dominated by five permanent members (the P5), each of which

---

18. Benjamin Frankel, "The Brooding Shadow: Systemic Incentives and Nuclear Weapons Proliferation," *Security Studies* 2 (Spring–Summer 1993): 47–51.

19. North Korea has a defensive alliance with China, but China has never suggested that it would be willing to extend a nuclear umbrella over North Korea.

The Nuclear Non-Proliferation Treaty

In 1963, U.S. president John F. Kennedy predicted that by 1975, some 20–25 countries might possess nuclear weapons—a prospect that he considered "the greatest possible danger" facing humanity.[a] At the time, only the United States, the Soviet Union, Great Britain, and France had developed a nuclear bomb. China was on the verge, and a number of other countries were exploring the possibility. Yet Kennedy's prediction was far off the mark. By 1975, only two new nuclear states had joined the original five: Israel and India. The next 40 years saw only two more: Pakistan and North Korea. Four states—South Africa, Ukraine, Kazakhstan, and Belarus—possessed nuclear weapons but gave them up, and others have the technology to produce a bomb but have chosen not to.[b]

There are a number of reasons why nuclear weapons have not spread as widely as originally feared. Some of the credit goes to the nuclear Non-Proliferation Treaty (NPT). Concluded in 1968, the treaty has gone from 61 signatories in 1970 to 190 today. How did the NPT come about, and what does it do?

Interests Underlying the NPT was the concern that a world of many nuclear states would be a dangerous place for everyone. In addition to the risk of nuclear war, radioactive fallout from such an event would harm even those not directly involved. Still, this common interest alone was not enough to guarantee a deal. The primary interest of states that already had nuclear weapons was to prevent other countries from eroding their nuclear monopoly.

Most non-nuclear states had two interests at stake. In addition to their security interest in limiting the access of non-nuclear rivals to these weapons, they wanted to protect their ability to develop civilian nuclear energy programs. The fissile material that makes nuclear weapons go bang—plutonium and enriched uranium—is part of the fuel cycle of a nuclear reactor. Restrictions on the ability to possess or produce these fuels could hamper these countries' ability to harness this source of energy. Finally, some states that did not yet have nuclear weapons wanted to hold open the option of getting them and thus had no interest in a treaty.

Interactions The NPT reflects a bargain between the five countries that had tested a bomb by the time the treaty was concluded and everybody else. The former, recognized as nuclear weapons states, promise to refrain from giving non-nuclear states any of their weapons, to make good-faith efforts to reduce and eventually eliminate their own nuclear stockpiles, and to assist non-nuclear states in the development of peaceful nuclear energy programs. In return, the other states promise not to try to develop nuclear weapons, either by purchasing them or diverting nuclear material from their reactors. As we saw in Chapter 2, however, efforts to control arms can give rise to a Prisoner's Dilemma, in which each state fears that its own restraint will be exploited by others. The solution to this problem required not just a deal, but an institution.

Institutions In addition to laying out standards of acceptable behavior, the NPT provided a mechanism for monitoring compliance, in the form of the International Atomic Energy Agency (IAEA).[c] In exchange for assistance, states must sign "safeguard agreements" with the IAEA that impose restrictions on their activities and provide for inspections to ensure that no material is diverted. In the event that a violation of the treaty is detected, enforcement is left to the UN Security Council, which can impose sanctions, as it recently did in the case of Iran.

Instances of cheating by NPT members are rare, but this observation obscures some weaknesses of the institution. Most of the states that developed nuclear weapons after 1968—India, Pakistan, and Israel—never signed the agreement; South Africa signed in 1991 only after it decided to give up its nuclear arsenal. Moreover, the treaty permits states to withdraw with only six months' notice. This is what North Korea did in 2003 after being confronted with evidence that it had been illicitly enriching uranium. There is also no mechanism for enforcing the provision that nuclear states work toward dismantling their arsenals, a promise that they have been slow to fulfill.

---

a. "Text of President Kennedy's News Conference on Foreign and Domestic Affairs," *New York Times*, March 22, 1963.

b. See Scott D. Sagan, "The Causes of Nuclear Weapons Proliferation," *Annual Review of Political Science* 14 (2011): 225–44.

c. The IAEA, in fact, predates the NPT, having been created in 1957.

can veto any enforcement action it does not like. Sanctions against North Korea, for example, have at times been blocked or watered down by China, the country's main trading partner. Hence, enforcement of the NPT requires consensus in the Security Council—something that may not occur if the noncompliant state has backers within that body.

How well has the NPT fared in preventing the spread of nuclear weapons? The track record is mixed. From one perspective, the NPT regime has seen some notable successes. Several countries that previously refused to sign and had active nuclear programs, such as South Africa, Brazil, and Argentina, abandoned their nuclear ambitions and signed the treaty. In the cases of Brazil and Argentina, the NPT played a role in helping these two former rivals shed their nuclear programs in a transparent manner.

The NPT regime also played a productive role in defusing a potential crisis caused by the breakup of the Soviet Union. With the dissolution of that country into 15 new countries, a number of the new states were "born nuclear" because Soviet-era weapons were present in their territory. Since there was general agreement that Russia, the largest of these states, would inherit the former Soviet Union's designation as a nuclear-weapon state, the other three states—Ukraine, Belarus, and Kazakhstan—all came under pressure to give up their weapons and sign the NPT as non-nuclear states.

Because of long-standing fears of Russia, some policy makers in Ukraine thought that the arsenal they had inherited would serve as a useful deterrent against their larger, nuclear-armed neighbor. However, the other nuclear powers insisted that Ukraine could join the NPT only as a non-nuclear state and that the alternative was to be ostracized by the international community, threatening the new country's standing and access to economic aid.[20] Ukraine signed the NPT as a non-nuclear power in 1994; Belarus and Kazakhstan followed suit. In this example, the international institution performed exactly as one would hope: by setting a clear standard for acceptable behavior and raising the expected costs of noncompliance.

The NPT regime has also had notable weaknesses, however. Since the treaty recognizes the right of non-nuclear states to develop civilian nuclear energy programs, there is danger that proliferators will use these programs to conceal illicit activity and evade punishment. Iran, for example, revealed in 2002 that it was enriching uranium and argued, correctly, that it had the right to generate fuel for nuclear reactors (though it did not have the right to conceal those activities from the IAEA). The concern is that the same enrichment process can also be used to make highly enriched uranium for a nuclear weapon.

While IAEA inspections seek to prevent this kind of diversion, several states have managed to cheat on their obligations and escape detection for some time. North Korea, Iraq, Libya, and Iran were all NPT signatories, and all managed to have active or nascent nuclear programs at some point after signing. There is also no mechanism to force states to sign or to prevent them from backing out after they have signed. Hence, the NPT does not provide foolproof protection against determined proliferators.

---

20. Sagan, "Why Do States Build Nuclear Weapons?" 80–82.

約3,700km

今回

約2,700km

先月29日

北朝鮮

北朝鮮

11:02

NHK G

In summer 2017, North Korean tests of ballistic missiles, which could someday be used to carry nuclear weapons, had residents of South Korea and Japan on edge. What can be done to stop or reverse the nuclear programs of hostile actors like North Korea?

Coercive Disarmament What, then, can be done about states like North Korea, Iran, or Iraq under Saddam Hussein—states that have actively sought or, in the case of North Korea, actually acquired nuclear weapons? These states' actions show that they do not fear the international disapproval that comes with being in noncompliance with the NPT. Nor do these states have strong protectors willing to cover them with a nuclear umbrella. Moreover, these states' interests in nuclear weapons may be rooted in more than just insecurity that can be assuaged through security guarantees. Iran has aspirations for greater regional influence, and North Korea has long harbored the goal of unifying the Korean peninsula under its rule.

The ultimate tool for stopping or reversing nuclear proliferation is *coercive disarmament*: the threat or use of military force. A state can issue a compellent threat against a would-be proliferator to dismantle its program or face attack. The United States issued veiled threats to this effect against North Korea during a 1994 crisis over that country's nuclear program, and it made such threats explicit during the crisis that led to the invasion of Iraq in 2003 (though it was later determined that Iraq had already halted its WMD programs).

If threats alone are not enough to induce disarmament, the final option is to use military force to eliminate a foe's nuclear program altogether. A classic example of this strategy is Israel's attack on an Iraqi nuclear reactor in 1981. Without warning, Israeli planes entered Iraqi airspace and bombed a reactor at Osirak that had been part of Iraq's nascent nuclear program. Widely criticized at the time, the attack succeeded in setting back Iraq's program for at least a decade. In September 2007, Israeli planes launched a similar attack on an alleged nuclear site in Syria. Although there is uncertainty about exactly what the Israelis destroyed—and Syria denied that the site was part of a nuclear program—subsequent investigations by the IAEA found evidence consistent with undeclared nuclear activities.[21] During negotiations over Iran's nuclear program, Israel hinted that it might also strike that country's nuclear facilities.

Coercive disarmament faces several major obstacles. First, the threat of force alone is unlikely to work, because disarmament generates a potentially dramatic power shift: the state that gives up its weapons makes itself weaker and, thus, vulnerable to further demands. To frame this point in the language of Chapter 3, coercive disarmament generates a commitment problem: the threatening state must credibly commit that if the target gives in to its demands and disarms, it will not exploit the target's weakness by making further demands. If such a commitment cannot be made credibly, then the target has good reason to resist the threat.

In actual cases that the United States has confronted, a credible commitment along these lines has been hard to achieve because of underlying conflicts of interests. As we noted in Chapter 3, the United States' conflicts with North Korea and Iran were not caused by those countries' nuclear programs. In fact, the causal arrow ran in the opposite direction: the United States has had long-standing conflicts with those countries, and the conflicts contributed to those countries' desire to acquire nuclear weapons. Thus, it would not be unreasonable for Iran and North Korea to fear that if they gave in to U.S. demands to dismantle their weapons programs, they would essentially be making themselves more vulnerable to further demands.

This fear is not hypothetical. In 2003, Libya agreed to a disarmament deal with an assurance that the United States would not seek to oust leader Mu'ammar Qaddafi.[22] Eight years later, the United States intervened in a rebellion against Qaddafi, leading to his ouster, capture, and death (see the "Controversy" box in Chapter 5, p. 226). The North Korean government routinely cites this episode as a reason to oppose any deal with the United States.[23] To enhance the chances that threats of force will succeed, they must be matched with some effort to reassure the target that its newfound weakness will not be exploited. Given the United States' underlying conflicts with these countries, it is not always obvious how to make such a commitment believable.

If threats alone do not work, then force may be the last resort, as in the case of the Israeli attack on the Osirak reactor and the U.S.-led war on Iraq.[24] A central difficulty with replicating the Israeli approach, besides the costs associated with using force, is that states have learned from this example. Proliferators have taken steps to harden and disperse their nuclear sites so that they are less vulnerable to attack.

---

21. IAEA Board of Governors, "Implementation of the NPT Safeguards Agreement in the Syrian Arab Republic: Report by the Director General," November 19, 2008, www.isis-online.org/publications/syria/IAEA_Report_Syria_19Nov2008.pdf.

22. For a discussion of factors leading to this deal, see Bruce W. Jentleson and Christopher A. Whytock, "Who 'Won' Libya?: The Force-Diplomacy Debate and Its Implications for Theory and Policy," *International Security* 30, no. 3 (2005): 47–86.

23. See, for example, Mark McDonald, "North Korea Suggests Libya Should Have Kept Nuclear Program," *New York Times*, March 24, 2011, www.nytimes.com/2011/03/25/world/asia/25korea.html.

24. For a discussion of the effectiveness of military strikes to stop proliferation, see Sarah E. Kreps and Matthew Fuhrmann, "Attacking the Atom: Does Bombing Nuclear Facilities Affect Proliferation?" *Journal of Strategic Studies* 34 (April 2011): 161–87.

North Korea, for example, makes extensive use of tunnels and underground bunkers to hide and protect key elements of its nuclear program. As a result, it is hard to ensure that air attacks will succeed. North Korea also has an enormous arsenal of conventional artillery within range of Seoul and could inflict horrific losses on South Korea in response to an attack. The alternative approach of invading and occupying a country, as in the case of Iraq, increases the chances of verifiably eliminating a program, but the costs associated with such a venture are much higher. Even talking about this possibility has risks. If North Korea feared an invasion and interpreted U.S. military moves as a prelude to an attack, it might decide to launch its weapons preemptively—that is, to use them rather than lose them.

What policy makers are left with in these tough cases is making a decision from among several alternatives, each of which has drawbacks. Military force is costly and of questionable effectiveness, particularly in the long term. Economic sanctions, to be effective, require viable international cooperation, which in some cases is lacking. The international community could, of course, let the state acquire nuclear weapons and rely on deterrence to render those weapons harmless. Deterrence has been the de facto policy toward North Korea since it acquired nuclear weapons a decade ago.[25] This strategy has a good track record historically, but one cost of this approach is that each case of proliferation generates incentives for neighboring states to follow suit. The probable chain reaction increases the risks of accidents or of weapons falling into the wrong hands.

The alternative is for the United States and its allies to strike bargains with states such as North Korea and Iran to address some of the underlying conflicts that led them to seek nuclear weapons in the first place. Such deals would require these states to relinquish their weapons in exchange for economic aid, an end to diplomatic isolation, some kind of security guarantees, and perhaps substantive compromises on some of the regional issues that are the source of hostility. As we saw in the "Controversy" box in Chapter 3 (p. 104), efforts to reach such a deal with North Korea have been frustrating and so far unsuccessful at getting that country to give up its weapons. North Korea is unlikely to bargain away its capability to hit the U.S. mainland, but it might be possible to negotiate limits on its arsenal.

In the case of Iran, negotiations led to a deal in 2015 that sought to restrict that country's nuclear program for 10–15 years in exchange for an easing of economic sanctions and the unfreezing of some assets held in the United States.[26] Although the deal froze the Iranian program and rolled back its enrichment activities, the concessions made so that Iran would agree provoked opposition in the United States, including from President Trump, who called the accord "the worst deal ever

---

25. For an argument that deterrence is the best option with respect to North Korea, see Scott D. Sagan, "The Korean Missile Crisis: Why Deterrence Is Still the Best Option," *Foreign Affairs* 96 (November/ December 2017): 72–82.

26. For a balanced assessment of the deal, see Gary Samore, "The Iran Nuclear Deal: A Definitive Guide," Belfer Center for Science and International Affairs, August 2015, www.belfercenter.org/sites/default/ files/legacy/files/IranDealDefinitiveGuide.pdf.

negotiated."[27] Critics attacked the limited time frame of the freeze, the decision to lift sanctions (thereby relieving pressure on the regime), and the fact that negotiations excluded other issues, such as Iran's ballistic missile program and support for militant groups in the region.[28]

A state is unlikely to voluntarily restrain its activities without provisions to ensure regime survival and prevent further demands. Nonetheless, these kinds of concessions have made the deal vulnerable to criticism from those who prefer a harder line. In October 2017, President Trump announced that he would no longer certify this deal as being in the U.S. national interest, though it remained to be seen how far the United States would go to unravel the agreement. At the time of this writing, the prospect of conflict with both North Korea and Iran testified to the ongoing challenge posed by this issue.

Will China and the United States Fight for Global Leadership?

When representatives of 46 countries gathered in San Francisco in June 1945 to sign the UN Charter, the honor of being the first to sign went to China, in recognition of that country's enormous suffering and efforts during World War II. As the world's most populous country and a major presence in Asia, China was expected to play a significant role in the postwar order, holding one of the coveted permanent seats on the newly created UN Security Council. However, more than a decade of warfare and occupation at the hands of Japan and two decades of civil war had left China in little position to be a world power at the time.

In 1949, when the communists finally prevailed over the nationalists in the civil war, the latter fled to the island of Taiwan, leading to a split between the communist People's Republic of China (PRC) on the mainland and the pro-Western Republic of China (ROC) offshore. At the insistence of the United States, China's seat in the United Nations went to the ROC, and the most populous country in the world no longer had a role in the most important postwar institution. As the United States and its allies built the institutions that govern the global economy—the GATT, the IMF, and the World Bank—the PRC, like other communist countries, was not at the table.

China's exclusion from global institutions lasted two decades. In the early 1970s, a growing rift between China and the Soviet Union created an opportunity for the United States to seek closer relations with the PRC. As part of this process,

---

27. Steve Holland and Yara Bayoumy, "Trump Expected to Decertify Iran Nuclear Deal, Official Says," *Reuters*, October 5, 2017, www.reuters.com/article/us-iran-nuclear-usa/trump-expected-to-decertify-iran-nuclear-deal-official-says-idUSKBN1CA2ID.

28. For a sample of criticism, see Matthew Kroenig, "How to Unwind the Iran Nuclear Deal," *American Interest*, February 11, 2016, www.the-american-interest.com/2016/02/11/how-to-unwind-the-iran-nuclear-deal.

China's growing wealth has translated into increased military power that may eventually match that of the United States. As part of its effort to modernize its military capabilities, China has built aircraft carriers capable of transporting fleets of fighter jets.

the PRC replaced the ROC in most international institutions. In 1971, the PRC took over China's permanent seat on the UN Security Council; in 1980, the PRC replaced Taiwan in the IMF and World Bank.[29] Even so, China had relatively little influence in these institutions, where voting power rested overwhelmingly with the United States, Europe, and Japan. And China would have to wait another two decades before entering the WTO.

China's limited role in the creation of the postwar order is striking in view of projections that it will surpass the United States as the world's largest economy in the next decade. Since it enacted major reforms in 1979, China's economy has grown 11-fold. The country's development has increased not only its wealth, but also its military power. Although figures on China's military spending are uncertain and controversial, it is estimated that the country's defense budget has grown at an average rate of 8.5 percent per year over the last decade.[30]

China has long possessed the largest army in terms of personnel, but its increases in military spending have helped modernize the Chinese military with advanced technology. In the process, China has enhanced its power projection capabilities—that is, its ability to project military force beyond its borders—through investments in aircraft carriers and midair refueling technologies. Moreover, China also possesses a modest arsenal of nuclear weapons: about 270 warheads, with 75–100 intercontinental ballistic missiles capable of hitting Europe or the United States.[31]

29. For a discussion of the process by which China replaced Taiwan in international institutions, see Lipscy, *Renegotiating the World Order*, chap. 9.

30. U.S. Department of Defense, *Annual Report to Congress: Military and Security Developments Involving the People's Republic of China 2017*, 65, www.defense.gov/Portals/1/Documents/pubs/2017_China_Military_Power_Report.PDF (accessed 10/16/17); see also previous issues of this annual report.

31. U.S. Department of Defense, *Annual Report to Congress*, 60.

TABLE 14.1 *Comparing the Military Capabilities of China and the United States*

CAPABILITY	UNITED STATES	CHINA
Total military spending	$605 billion	$145 billion
Percentage of world military spending	39.1%	9.4%
Active military personnel	1,347,300	2,183,000
Nuclear warheads	6,800	270
Intercontinental ballistic missiles	450	75–100
Nuclear submarines	14	4
Aircraft carriers	10	1
Bombers	157	150
Fighter aircraft	3,476	1,913
Main battle tanks	2,831	6,740
Artillery pieces	6,833	13,380

Note: All figures are 2016 estimates.

Sources: International Institute for Strategic Studies, *The Military Balance 2017* (London: Routledge, 2017), chap. 2. Nuclear warhead data from the Stockholm International Peace Research Institute (SIPRI), www.sipri.org/research/armament-and-disarmament/biological-chemical-and-nuclear-weapons/world-nuclear-forces (accessed 10/16/2017).

To be sure, the United States will continue to be the world's dominant military power for some time. In recent years, U.S. defense spending has accounted for 35–40 percent of the world's total. The United States also enjoys a large technological lead, and its nuclear arsenal dwarfs China's many times over (Table 14.1). Nonetheless, although U.S. military power is spread more widely across the globe, including in Europe and the Middle East, the gap between U.S. and Chinese relative military power in Asia is shrinking.

The rise of China is part of a recurring pattern in world politics. Over the long run, the cast of major actors on the world stage is in flux as states and empires rise and fall. The underlying mechanism usually revolves around technology and economic growth.[32] States that discover and adopt new technologies and economic models tend to experience rapid growth in resources and power, thereby extending

32. See, for example, Paul Kennedy, *The Rise and Fall of the Great Powers* (New York: Random House, 1987); and Robert Gilpin, *War and Change in World Politics* (Cambridge: Cambridge University Press, 1981).

their influence in world politics. As other states catch up or make their own innovations, previous leaders can be challenged and even usurped, allowing a new set of players to take center stage. This process not only changes the identity of the main actors in international politics, but also creates dynamics that are themselves important.

What are the implications of China's rise? Will China seek to use its growing power to reshape global institutions from which it was initially excluded? Will conflicts between the United States and China increase the risk of war? To answer these questions, we need to identify how rising power affects the interaction between the rising state and the current world leader. We also need to examine the role that institutions, both international and domestic, might play in containing potential conflict between the two.

What Do Theory and History Tell Us?

Both theory and history tell us that the rise of a new major power is potentially dangerous because of its effect on international bargaining. We saw in Chapter 3 that a large shift in the relative military power of two states has several effects. As a state becomes more powerful, it expects to do better in the event of a war. As a result, it will be more willing to threaten force to change the status quo. Bargains that were acceptable when the state was relatively weak will no longer be satisfactory. Hence, a rising state has an interest in using its newfound power to renegotiate preexisting arrangements. Of course, this development alone does not make war inevitable, since the costs of war ensure that a bargaining range exists. It is possible that the demands of the rising state can be defused peacefully through negotiated changes that reflect the new power distribution. Nonetheless, opportunities for crises will increase, along with the attendant danger of war because of information and commitment problems.

One such problem is particularly dangerous in this context: because the rising state cannot commit *not* to revise deals in the future, the declining state may have an incentive to wage preventive war. As we saw in Chapter 3, the declining state may decide that war now is preferable to some future bargain that favors the rising state. An anticipated decline creates a temporary window of opportunity to try to secure one's military advantage by fighting and defeating the rising challenger. Theory tells us, then, that a change in relative power influences both interests and interactions in a way that makes conflict more likely: the rising state acquires an interest in revising the status quo, and the declining state faces a strategic environment that encourages preventive war.

Does the historical record confirm this fear? The argument that rising power increases the danger of war can be traced to one of the earliest known scholars of war, the Greek historian Thucydides. Writing in the third century B.C.E., Thucydides sought to explain the Peloponnesian Wars between two Greek city-states: Athens and Sparta. In his view, the wars arose because Sparta, which had once dominated the region, sought to contain the growing power and ambition of Athens, which was increasingly challenging Sparta's predominance. Thucydides' oft -quoted conclusion: "What made war inevitable was the growth of Athenian power and the fear which this caused in Sparta."[33]

More recently, scholars have seen echoes of this logic in other major wars; indeed, a recent popular book refers to the risk of war during periods of power transition as "Thucydides' trap."[34] As discussed in Chapter 5, a key dynamic underlying both world wars was the growing ambition of Germany following its unification and rapid industrial and population growth in the late nineteenth century. Before World War I, this assertiveness manifested itself in Germany's drive to acquire more territory, expand its colonial holdings, and wield influence in world politics commensurate with its power. The settlement that followed World War I—which stripped Germany of territory, colonies, and influence—only exacerbated the mismatch between what Germany possessed and what it believed it could possess, given its resources. Although Germany's fanatical, genocidal goals in World War II were due largely to Hitler's extreme ideology, this mismatch ensured that Germany would seek to revise the restrictive terms of the postwar settlement at some point.[35] Hence, the connection between rising power and an assertive foreign policy is borne out in the German case.

It is crucial, however, not to overgeneralize from this case, notwithstanding its obvious importance. There are also cases in which rising power did not lead to war. For example, the United States overtook Great Britain by most measures of power around the dawn of the twentieth century. The transition took place relatively peacefully, with Britain acquiescing to U.S. dominance in the Western Hemisphere in a series of crises over Venezuela and the Alaskan boundary with Canada. The handover of world leadership from Britain to the United States proceeded over the next several decades, aided by their common effort against Germany. By the 1950s, Britain was clearly a junior partner of its former colony.[36]

At that point, the United States faced a strong challenge from the Soviet Union, which built a massive conventional force and attained nuclear parity with the United States by the 1970s. Although the Cold War was a tense and dangerous time, this rivalry also ended without direct warfare between the two superpowers. The combination of American alliances and nuclear weapons helped contain and deter the Soviet threat, and the Soviet Union eventually collapsed as a result of economic exhaustion. Finally, as the Cold War waned, there were concerns about an emerging struggle for power between the United States and either Germany, a powerhouse economy at the center of Europe, or Japan, whose dynamic economic growth in the 1980s led to warnings of a "coming war with Japan."[37] Neither of these predictions

---

33. Thucydides, *History of the Peloponnesian War*, trans. Rex Warner (London: Penguin, 1954), 49.

34. Graham Allison, *Destined for War: Can America and China Escape Thucydides' Trap?* (Boston: Houghton Mifflin Harcourt, 2017). For earlier scholarship suggesting that Thucydides' logic is central to understanding major wars in the modern era, see Robert Gilpin, "The Theory of Hegemonic War," *Journal of Interdisciplinary History* 18 (Spring 1988): 591–613.

35. This case is famously made by A. J. P. Taylor, *The Origins of the Second World War* (New York: Atheneum, 1961), esp. 24.

36. For a discussion of the transition of world leadership from Britain to the United States, see Kori Schake, *Safe Passage: The Transition from British to American Hegemony* (Cambridge, MA: Harvard University Press, 2017).

37. See, for example, George Friedman and Meredith Lebard, *The Coming War with Japan* (New York: St. Martin's, 1991).

came true. Although the United States in some ways accommodated the rising influence of these states, the process was peaceful and never escalated to threats of military conflict.

Why does the interaction between a rising power and the current leader sometimes end peacefully? A large part of the answer lies in the states' interests: how severely their interests conflict and how costly it is to use military power to force change. Consider Figure 14.4, which revisits the simple bargaining framework introduced in Chapter 3. As before, the horizontal bar represents all possible divisions of the good in dispute, and the relative military power of the states involved is captured by the line labeled *War outcome* that divides the bar into shares that each state expects to obtain in the event of a war.

Both the upper and the lower parts of this figure illustrate a power shift in favor of State A. Initially, State B is the stronger state, and the expected war outcome is close to its ideal point (the left end of the bar). We then assume that after a period of relative growth, State A will be stronger, so the war outcome after this power shift will be closer to State A's ideal point (the right end of the bar). The difference between the upper and the lower scenarios is the costs of war for each side. In the upper part, the costs of war are small relative to the shift in power, whereas in the lower part, the costs of war are relatively large.

The situation in the upper scenario of Figure 14.4 is obviously quite dangerous, as we saw in Chapter 3. The declining State B expects to get more through war in the initial period (the portion of the bar to the right of the blue dotted line) than it expects to get from any deal that is in the bargaining range after the power shift; that is, any feasible bargain in the second period is farther from State B's ideal point than what it can achieve by fighting now. Hence, the danger of preventive war is quite real.

This is not the case in the lower scenario, however. Here the bargaining range that will hold after the power shift includes deals that the declining State B prefers over fighting a war now. If the states were to reach a deal at, say, the line labeled *Possible deal*, then State A could credibly commit not to use force to revise the deal in the future. Such a deal gives State A more than it can expect to get through war, even after it has grown stronger. As a result, State B has no incentive to wage a preventive war in the initial period. The danger of war is much lower in this second scenario because the costs of war loom large relative to the shift in power. These costs make it harder for the rising State A to take advantage of its newfound capabilities.

Recall that the costs of war in this model are measured relative to the value of whatever good is in dispute. Hence, the interaction between a rising and a declining state is more likely to look like the lower scenario if either the material costs of war are very high or the value of the good in dispute is low. In short, a power shift is not particularly dangerous if war is too costly to contemplate or if the conflict of interests in the relationship is so small that there is little worth fighting over.

This logic helps explain the relatively peaceful power shifts mentioned earlier. The Cold War challenge by the Soviet Union coincided with an enormous increase in the costs of war due to the advent of nuclear weapons. As we just saw, war was

FIGURE 14.4 *When Are Power Shifts Dangerous?*

Initially, State B is the stronger state, but as power shifts in favor of State A, the expected outcome of war shifts to the right, reducing the value of war for State B. Here, the costs of war are low compared to the size of the power shift, and the best possible deal that State B can get in the future is worse than its value for war now. Hence, the declining State B may have an incentive to wage preventive war.

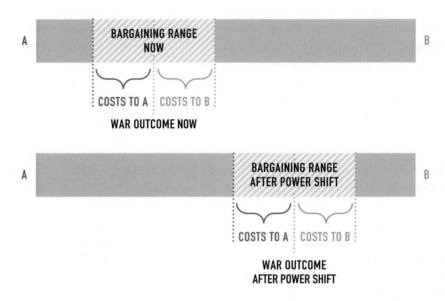

However, if the costs of war are large enough, then a deal may be found that both states prefer over war now and after the power shift. Here, the possible deal gives both states more than their current and future values for war.

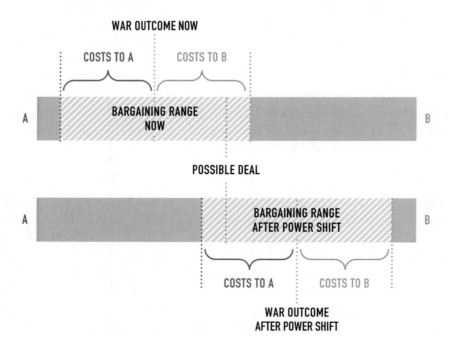

avoided in large part because of the threat of mutually assured destruction in the event of a nuclear exchange. In the case of Germany and Japan in the late twentieth century, there was little threat of a military confrontation with the United States because of the common interests that bound them together—common interests stemming from a shared strategic threat during the Cold War, strong commercial and financial ties, shared democratic values, and a history of beneficial cooperation.

A Coming Showdown or Peaceful Engagement?

We have then three kinds of historical precedents for thinking about the implication of China's rise: (1) the rise of Germany in the first half of the twentieth century witnessed a series of major wars, (2) the Soviet challenge during the Cold War was contained until the country collapsed, and (3) the rise of Germany and Japan in the last decades of the twentieth century was peacefully accommodated. How then is the rise of China in the twenty-first century likely to play out?

One view is that China's rise is inherently dangerous because China was relatively weak as key elements of the postwar order were constructed; thus, it will use its growing power to revise the system in its favor.[38] After World War II the United States built a network of alliances in Asia that enabled it to project power into the region in an effort to contain what was then called "Red" China—the term used to describe the communist PRC. Agreements with Japan, South Korea, Taiwan, and the Philippines led to an extensive U.S. military presence that allowed it to prosecute wars (in Korea and Vietnam, for example) and to patrol vital shipping lanes. American foreign policy shifted away from the containment of communism after the end of the Cold War, but the U.S. alliance network and military presence remained in place, though somewhat diminished in size.

As a result, U.S. military power continues to stand in the way of several Chinese interests in the region. Foremost among these is China's long-standing desire to bring the island of Taiwan back under its rule. China does not recognize Taiwan as an independent country, considering it instead to be a breakaway province. In the 1970s the PRC convinced the United States and other countries to accept this "One China" view; as a result, Taiwan was officially ousted from international institutions, and the U.S. alliance with Taiwan was terminated. Nevertheless, the United States continues to sell arms to the island and has made it clear that it would resist any effort by China to reunify by force (see Chapter 5 for more on the complex strategic interaction here). Thus, although China is much more powerful than Taiwan by any measure, U.S. military power deters China from wielding the threat of force against the island.

The U.S. presence in the region also frustrates other Chinese territorial interests. China has disputes with a number of countries—including key American allies and security partners like Japan, the Philippines, Malaysia, and Vietnam—over their maritime boundaries and small islands in the South and East China Seas (Map 14.1). The disputed waters are rich in fish, oil, and natural gas, and some of the islands

---

38. See, for example, Aaron Friedberg, "The Struggle for Mastery in Asia," *Commentary* 110 (November 2000): 17–26.

MAP 14.1 **Select East Asian Maritime Claims**

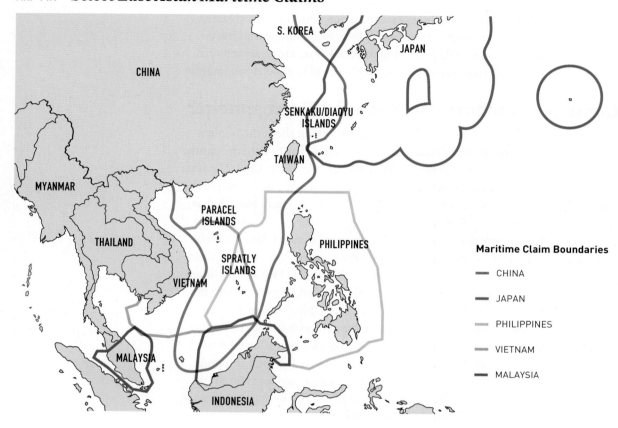

Maritime Claim Boundaries

— CHINA

— JAPAN

— PHILIPPINES

— VIETNAM

— MALAYSIA

Note: This map shows how China's maritime claims have created disputes with its neighbors. To simplify the illustration, some countries' claims are not depicted. For a complete map of maritime claims in East Asia, see Stratfor, "Cooperation as a Means to All Ends in the South China Sea," *RealClearDefense*, September 26, 2016, www.realcleardefense.com/articles/2016/09/27/cooperation_as_a_means_to_all_ends_in_the_south_china_sea_110133.html.

have strategic value for projecting power and controlling shipping lanes. By promising military aid to its partners in the event of a conflict, the United States makes it harder for China to wield its power to obtain a greater share of this valuable territory.

More broadly, the fear of conflict between the United States and China is driven by a concern that China's political and economic systems are incompatible with a U.S.-led international order that values democracy and capitalism. Politically, China is a single-party autocracy (see Map 4.1, p. 172) that does not permit any competitor of the Communist Party and suppresses individual rights to expression, association, and religion. The Chinese regime's strong interest in retaining this system puts it into conflict with the increasing emphasis on democracy and human rights among international institutions and nongovernmental organizations (see Chapter 12). China has resisted pressure to improve its human rights practices, and it has been loath to approve actions by the United Nations to intervene in purely domestic conflicts, arguing that state sovereignty takes precedence. Although China has liberalized its economy in recent decades and embraced many aspects of the liberal international trading system, it has resisted efforts to open key state-dominated sectors to international or domestic competition.

All of these considerations suggest that China has significant conflicts with the existing international order. Therefore, we might expect China to look for opportunities to weaken the U.S. alliance system in Asia, thereby reducing the U.S. presence and influence in the region. It might also seek to weaken institutions and actors that promote democracy or support intervention in domestic conflicts and to sponsor alternative institutions that do not have these priorities.

For example, China supported the creation of the Asian Infrastructure Investment Bank (AIIB) in 2016, which had 56 members and 24 prospective members at the time of this writing.[39] Like the World Bank and other Western-dominated lending institutions, the AIIB provides loans for development projects. Unlike the World Bank, in which the United States holds 16.3 percent of the voting power and China only 4.5 percent, China is the single largest vote holder in the AIIB, with 27.5 percent.[40]

In lieu of cooperation within the existing international order, China may choose to develop and invest in new institutions that operate under its own rules. For example, China spearheaded the development of the Asian Infrastructure Investment Bank in 2016, in which it is the largest vote holder.

Although it is too soon to know how important this new institution will be, in principle the AIIB could serve as an alternative source of loans for borrowers who want to avoid the politically intrusive conditions and governance reforms often demanded by Western institutions.[41]

In this view then, China, unlike Japan, cannot be accommodated in the existing U.S.-led international system, and it will instead seek to overturn that order and institute its own. Just as Germany sought mastery of Europe in the first half of the twentieth century, China will use its new power to seek mastery in Asia, pushing out American influence. If so, the dangers of Chinese assertiveness and the preventive incentives of the United States loom large.

An alternative view is that, even though China wielded little power at the time the postwar order was being built, it currently benefits a great deal from those rules and institutions and therefore has no serious incentive to disrupt them. The openness of the international trading system has been a boon to Chinese exporters and contributed significantly to China's remarkable economic growth in recent decades. China's top export markets in 2016 were the United States, Japan, South Korea, and Germany; the top sources of foreign direct investment into the country

---

39. Information on members, prospective members, and voting power in the AIIB can be found at www.aiib.org/en/about-aiib/governance/members-of-bank/index.html (accessed 10/09/17).

40. Information on voting power in the World Bank comes from http://siteresources.worldbank.org/BODINT/Resources/278027-1215524804501/IBRDCountryVotingTable.pdf (accessed 10/09/17).

41. For a variety of views on the importance of the AIIB, see "Should Washington Fear the AIIB?" *Foreign Affairs*, June 11, 2015, www.foreignaffairs.com/articles/china/2015-06-11/should-washington-fear-aiib.

are Singapore, South Korea, the United States, Taiwan, Japan, and Germany. Thus, China is deeply economically integrated with the United States and U.S. allies in Asia and Europe. As a result, the benefits of the system and the potential costs of conflict are both quite high from China's perspective.

Proponents of this view also put a good deal of faith in the role of institutions, both international and domestic, to peacefully accommodate China's rise and mitigate the risk of war. Already, key international organizations have adjusted to take into account China's growing economy and power. As we saw earlier, this process began in 1971, when the PRC took over China's permanent seat in the UN Security Council from Taiwan. In 1999, China joined the WTO. And reforms to the voting rules in the World Bank and IMF have increased China's clout in those institutions. For example, China's share of voting power in the IMF increased from 2.6 percent in 1990 to 6.1 percent in 2017, making it the third most influential country after the United States and Japan.[42]

In the long run, it is also possible that economic growth will eventually lead to change in China's domestic institutions toward greater political freedom and democracy. The underlying idea is that wealth and trade will give rise to a potent middle class of businesspeople and merchants who will demand greater political liberalization. A vibrant and politically active middle class is generally seen as a key ingredient in the emergence of democracy in western Europe. If prosperity leads to political liberalization, then China's growing power can be rendered harmless through democracy, which will weaken the influence of the Chinese military and sensitize its leaders to the costs of military conflict. In this case, the rise of China could be as benign as the rise of the United States in the late nineteenth century or of western Europe and Japan in the late twentieth century.

What Will the United States Do?

How to respond to the rise of China has been a core question of U.S. foreign policy for much of the last three decades. The terms of the policy debate are framed by the two views summarized in the preceding section. According to those who believe that China will inevitably challenge the U.S.-led international order, the best way to respond is to contain China in the same way that the West contained the Soviet Union during the Cold War.[43]

Such a containment strategy would have two main prongs. The first would be an effort to slow down China's amazing economic growth by denying it access to the large U.S. market. Since a good deal of China's growth is based on exports to the West, advocates of containment argue that allowing these exports to have free access to Western markets serves only to strengthen an inevitable adversary.

---

42. Information on current voting shares in the IMF comes from International Monetary Fund, "IMF Members' Quotas and Voting Power, and IMF Board of Governors," www.imf.org/external/np/sec/memdir/members.aspx (accessed 01/07/18). Information on past shares was provided by Phillip Lipscy; see Lipscy, *Renegotiating the World Order*, chap. 3.

43. See, for example, Gideon Rachman, "Containing China," *Washington Quarterly* 19 (Winter 1996): 1291–40.

The second prong of the containment strategy would be to strengthen and build alliances with China's neighbors in order to create an effective counterweight to its growing power. This would mean maintaining U.S. military bases in the region, particularly in Japan, South Korea, and the Philippines, and strengthening ties with other states that have reason to fear China's growing might, such as India and Vietnam, both of which have territorial conflicts and regional rivalries with China. By adding the power of these countries to that of the United States, such alliances would blunt the impact of China's growth on the balance of military capabilities and increase the costs of war. In short, the containment strategy would seek to prevent China from becoming more aggressive by slowing the rise of its power and making war less attractive.

Supporters of the alternative view advocate a strategy of engagement that seeks to encourage positive institutional changes.[44] At the international level, the engagement strategy involves promoting Chinese membership in a web of institutions dealing with security, trade, and finance. Supporters of engagement successfully pushed for China to (1) be admitted into the WTO; (2) play a larger role in the Association of Southeast Asian Nations (ASEAN), which deals with regional security issues; and (3) have a larger say in the decisions of the IMF and the World Bank.

Such efforts seek to increase the benefits that China derives from the existing set of international institutions and thereby diminish its incentives to upend that order. These reforms not only move the status quo in China's favor but also increase the costs of war relative to the benefits that can be won. The hope is that if China is enmeshed in a web of existing institutions, its leaders will find a belligerent foreign policy—and the threat of exclusion from those institutions—to be too costly.[45]

Before 2017, U.S. policy combined elements of both strategies but prioritized economic engagement. On the military side, the United States maintained its bases in East Asia while pursuing closer partnerships with India and Vietnam. Over the past decade it also spoke of a "pivot to Asia," which means, among other things, a reorientation of military and diplomatic resources away from Europe and the Middle East to Asia.[46] There was, however, no effort to pursue defensive alliances equivalent to an East Asian NATO, nor any serious talk of preventive war.[47]

On the economic side, the United States followed the strategy of engagement, pushing for expanded trade and economic integration. The United States supported

---

44. See, for example, James Shinn, ed., *Weaving the Net: Conditional Engagement with China* (New York: Council on Foreign Relations, 1996); Audrey Cronin and Patrick Cronin, "The Realistic Engagement of China," *Washington Quarterly* 19 (Winter 1996): 141–70; and Kenneth Lieberthal, "A New China Strategy," *Foreign Affairs* 74 (November–December 1995): 35–49.

45. For an argument that membership in security institutions can change the way China's foreign policy makers see their security interests, see Alastair Iain Johnston, *Social States: China in International Institutions, 1980–2000* (Princeton, NJ: Princeton University Press, 2008).

46. Although this process started under the administration of President George W. Bush, the term "pivot to Asia" became popularized under the Obama administration because of the efforts of Secretary of State Hillary Clinton; see Hillary Clinton, "America's Pacific Century," *Foreign Policy*, no. 189 (November 2011): 56–63.

47. Unlike NATO, in which all of the allies are committed to defend one another, U.S. alliances in Asia are bilateral: U.S.–Japan, U.S.–South Korea, and U.S.–Philippines. There are no security commitments between U.S. allies in the region. For a discussion of this difference, see Christopher Hemmer and Peter J. Katzenstein, "Why Is There No NATO in Asia? Collective Identity, Regionalism, and the Origins of Multilateralism," *International Organization* 56 (Summer 2002): 575–607.

Chinese admission into the WTO, guaranteeing favorable treatment of Chinese exports, and promoted China's active participation in a variety of regional and global organizations.

This policy mix—limited military containment plus economic engagement—reflected interests at both the international and domestic levels. Many East Asian countries profit from trade ties with China, and they are reluctant to jeopardize those ties by taking a more confrontational approach. Moreover, the enormous potential costs of a military conflict with China mean that it would be extremely unattractive, and hence unlikely, for the United States to engage China in a preventive war. Although its nuclear arsenal is currently rather small and vulnerable, China is developing more survivable capabilities, including submarine-launched ballistic missiles, which would give it a second-strike force. Thus, nuclear deterrence plays a role in U.S.-China relations similar to the role it played during the Cold War.

In addition to these international considerations, policy toward China is heavily influenced by domestic interests within the United States. China's impressive economic development not only led to concerns about its military power; it also led businesses in the United States and around the world to eagerly contemplate the prospects of selling into the vast Chinese market. As over a billion Chinese consumers became wealthy enough to buy cellular phones and cars, the potential profits were expected to be enormous. American businesses thus lobbied hard to improve relations between the two countries.

For example, President Bill Clinton threatened in 1993 to revoke China's most-favored-nation trading status unless it made concrete improvements in its human rights record. When China refused to comply, American business interests pressured the Clinton administration to drop its threat.[48] The same interests weighed in strongly in 1999 to push for China's admission into the WTO. Hence, export-oriented businesses interested in the potential of the Chinese market influenced policy makers' calculations on how much to confront or accommodate this rising power.

This balance of interests favoring engagement appears to have been upended in 2016 with the election of President Donald Trump. Trump called China an "economic enemy" during his campaign for the presidency and promised to stop China from taking American jobs.[49] The potency of Trump's charge reflected the fact that China has played a much larger role as an exporter of its own products (primarily low-cost clothes, electronics, and toys) than as an importer of U.S. products. Indeed, the United States has consistently run an enormous trade deficit with China, almost $375 billion in 2017. Thus, it is Chinese workers, not Chinese consumers, who are driving China's economic relations with the United States.

Although low-cost imports from China are a boon to American consumers, certain sectors of the American economy have experienced wage and job pressures. Indeed, one study estimated that the dramatic increase in American imports from

48. See David M. Lampton, "America's China Policy in the Age of the Finance Minister: Clinton Ends Linkage," *China Quarterly* 139 (September 1994): 597–621.

49. For a sample of rhetoric that Trump used against China during the campaign, see Veronica Stracqualursi, "10 Times Trump Attacked China and Its Trade Relations with the U.S.," *ABC News*, April 6, 2017, http://abcnews.go.com/Politics/10-times-trump-attacked-china-trade-relations-us/story?id=46572567.

China since 1990 was responsible for about one-quarter of the decline in American manufacturing employment in this period.[50]

U.S. voters who have experienced job and wage losses and trade unions representing workers who compete with Chinese imports have thus been vocal in protesting China's trading practices. Although they are not large in raw numbers, the fact that these voters are concentrated in closely contested states in the Midwest have made their views politically salient. There is evidence that regions of the United States hit hardest by Chinese import competition were more likely to experience a swing of support for Trump in the 2016 election.[51] (See the "Controversy" box in Chapter 7, p. 332.)

At the time of this writing, it was unclear how far the policy of engagement with China would unravel because of these developments. Rhetorically, Trump signaled the end of engagement in his *National Security Strategy of the United States of America*, released in December 2017. Referring to the challenge posed by rising competitors like China, the document declares as "false" the premise "that engagement with rivals and their inclusion in international institutions and global commerce would turn them into benign actors and trustworthy partners."[52] In March 2018, Trump announced that he would impose tariffs on Chinese imports in response to the country's "unfair" trade practices. It remained to be seen whether China would respond by taking action to reduce the trade deficit or by retaliating, leading to a trade war between the world's two largest economies.

There are uncertainties on the security side as well. The Trump administration has taken a hard line against China's efforts to expand its holdings in the South China Sea, while at the same time seeking China's assistance in efforts to disarm North Korea. As noted earlier in this section, the interaction between a rising challenger and a leading state can generate a great deal of uncertainty about the future of the international system; recent shifts in the interests of the leading state have only added to that uncertainty.

Will Globalization Survive the Populist Backlash?

China's impressive economic growth over the past few decades is part of a much larger process that has had important consequences throughout the world: economic globalization. The term *globalization* refers to the spread of activities and

---

50. David Autor, David Dorn, and Gordon Hanson, "The China Syndrome: Local Labor Market Effects of Import Competition in the United States," *American Economic Review* 103 (October 2013): 2121–68.

51. David Autor, David Dorn, Gordon Hanson, and Kaveh Majlesi, "A Note on the Effect of Rising Trade Exposure on the 2016 Presidential Election," unpublished manuscript, January 6, 2017, www.ddorn.net/papers/ADHM-President2016.pdf. For more evidence that trade can affect voting in U.S. presidential elections, see J. Bradford Jensen, Dennis P. Quinn, and Stephen Weymouth, "Winners and Losers in International Trade: The Effects on US Presidential Voting," *International Organization* 71 (2017): 423–57.

52. Office of the President, *National Security Strategy of the United States of America*, December 2017, 3, www.whitehouse.gov/wp-content/uploads/2017/12/NSS-Final-12-18-2017-0905.pdf.

ideas across the globe. As applied to economics, globalization involves increasing integration of national economies through the movement of goods, services, money, and people across borders. This process took off in the last decades of the twentieth century, owing to improvements in technology, particularly transportation, communication, and information technologies. The advent of the Internet, in particular, reduced the effects of distance, making it possible to transmit information anywhere in the world instantaneously.

But globalization was not simply a result of the technological changes that made it possible; it was also a product of decisions made by governments to facilitate the flow of cross-border economic exchanges, as we saw in Chapters 7 and 8. This process has been aided by a series of global and regional trade agreements such as the WTO, the North American Free Trade Agreement (NAFTA), and the European Union. These agreements not only lowered barriers to the movement of goods, capital, and (in the case of the EU) people; they also created mechanisms to outlaw and punish certain kinds of restrictions.

Thus these institutions enshrined the dominance of the liberal economic view that the state should respect private property and that economic exchanges should be determined by the choices of private actors—in short, that markets, rather than governments, should be the primary driver of economic outcomes. While this view has been influential since the eighteenth century, it became the consensus view in the West after World War II. It ascended globally with the end of the Cold War. The result has been an explosion of world trade over the last 50 years and a dramatic increase in the flow of capital across borders (see Figure 14.2).

Although the steady upward slope of the lines in Figure 14.2 suggests an inexorable trend, there are also strong forces pushing in the opposite direction. As we saw in Chapters 7–10, freer flows of trade, capital, and people create losers as well as winners, and the former have interests in slowing or reversing the process. There has long been resistance to globalization among those who see unrestrained trade as endangering their economic livelihoods. More recently, the resistance to globalization in the developed world has been fueled by concerns about immigration, which people see as posing both an economic and a cultural threat. The growing success of populist parties and politicians in Europe and the Americas has shown the power of appeals to reassert national identity and sovereignty against the forces of globalization.

Will globalization continue, pushed forward by the incessant march of technology? Or will the turbulence associated with these changes engender a political backlash significant enough to cause the process of globalization to grind to a halt? Thinking through these questions requires that we understand the interests generated by globalization, how the interaction between the winners and losers will play out, and whether existing institutions can survive this conflict.

What Do Theory and History Tell Us?

Changes in technology influence the way economic actors pursue their interests, particularly their interest in maximizing income. Declining transportation and communication costs create strong incentives to overcome boundaries and increase the scope of markets so that they are global, rather than national or regional. As transportation costs decline, proximity to the consumer becomes less important. A company trying to decide where to build a production facility can focus on different criteria, such as labor costs and tax or regulatory policies. Improved transportation technologies thus allow companies to look around the world to find a location that will allow them to maximize profits.

Declining transportation costs facilitated by technological advances have spurred globalization, as goods can move around the globe more cheaply. Here, a container ship from Liberia navigates through the Panama Canal.

This is true whether the company produces a physical good, such as a toy or an article of clothing, or a service, such as accounting or insurance. Indeed, the decline of communication costs brought about by the Internet has allowed companies to move offshore many services that were traditionally handled domestically, such as customer support services. Some hospitals in the United States have even sent patients' X-rays to India to be read by radiologists there—radiologists who demand a much lower wage than do their American counterparts.[53]

As companies find it profitable to increase the scope of markets, they pressure governments to lower barriers to the movement of goods, services, and money across borders. A company that wants to locate in China but sell its wares to the United States will lobby the United States to allow free entry of Chinese-made products. Otherwise, trade barriers may nullify the advantages of making the goods in China. Multinational companies also have an interest in ensuring that they can move their capital around the globe freely, so that they can transfer profits made in one country to another, or so that they can make direct investment decisions without having to worry about barriers. Furthermore, these companies have an interest in strong protections for their property rights, so that they can open facilities in any country they like without having to fear that their property or profits will be seized. As we have seen, there are a number of reasons why these multinational companies wield substantial influence on government policy and, hence, why they are a potent force in pushing globalization forward.

History also tells us, however, that globalization is neither inevitable nor irreversible. People living in 1913 could look back at similarly impressive trends. In the preceding century, trade had grown from 2 percent of world income to 18 percent. International capital flows were also increasing impressively. Foreign-held assets grew from about 7 percent of world GDP in 1870 to 17.5 percent in 1913. And the movement of people was at a scale that dwarfs migration rates of today: between

---

53. Frank Levy and Kyoung-Hee Yu, "Offshoring Radiology Services to India," Working Paper MIT-IPC-06-005, Industrial Performance Center, Massachusetts Institute of Technology, Cambridge, MA, September 2006.

1870 and 1910, about 10 percent of the world's population relocated permanently from one country to another; the comparable figure for the past three decades is no more than 2 percent.[54]

World War I and the economic dislocations that followed brought this period of globalization crashing to a halt, and during the period between the world wars, new national barriers were erected against the flow of goods and money. Although economic integration is today much wider and deeper than in 1913, this case offers a stark reminder that political conflict can slow or even reverse seemingly inevitable economic processes.

Indeed, globalization in its contemporary form has generated no shortage of conflicts, both among and within states. Globalization generates conflict because it creates losers as well as winners. As we have seen, among the winners are economic actors who can take advantage of increased opportunities to move money and goods throughout the world—particularly, multinational companies and investors. Increased efficiency has also benefited consumers in the form of lower prices on imported goods. Who are the losers?

Economic Costs of Globalization

The main resistance to globalization comes from actors who see the lower barriers to trade and capital flows as threatening to their economic interests. Recall from Chapter 7 that there are two different theories for thinking about who wins and who loses from trade liberalization. The Ricardo-Viner, or specific-factors, model holds that trade interests are determined by the sector one works in: those in sectors that compete with imports want protection, while those in sectors that rely on exports want liberalization. The alternative theory, Stolper-Samuelson, holds that trade interests are determined by the factor of production—capital, labor, or land— that provides one's income. In this view, free trade benefits those factors that are relatively abundant in a country at the expense of those factors that are relatively scarce.

In the developed world, where capital is relatively abundant and labor (particularly, unskilled labor) is scarce, capital wins from free trade, while unskilled labor loses. In the developing world, where unskilled labor is abundant, holders of capital lose from free trade, while labor benefits. It is generally thought that while the predictions of Ricardo-Viner hold in the short term, long-term patterns of conflict follow the predictions of Stolper-Samuelson.[55] In other words, as globalization persists and deepens, conflicts will increasingly crystallize along class lines: capital versus labor, with the positions of each being determined by whether they are in the developing or developed world.

---

54. These figures are from David Dollar and Aart Kraay, "Spreading the Wealth," *Foreign Affairs* 8, no. 1 (January–February 2002): 122–23; and Nicholas Crafts, "Globalisation and Economic Growth: A Historical Perspective," *World Economy* 27, no. 1 (January 2004): 46.

55. Michael Mussa, "Tariffs and the Distribution of Income: The Importance of Factor Specificity, Substitutability, and Intensity in the Short and Long Run," *Journal of Political Economy* 82 (November–December 1974): 1191–203.

Economic Insecurity in the Developed World In developed countries, the group most negatively affected by globalization is workers—especially, unskilled workers. As rich countries become more closely integrated with developing countries, workers in the former face increasing competition from unskilled workers in the latter. A company that makes toys or clothing can find workers willing to accept much lower wages in China or Vietnam than in the United States. As a result, production of labor-intensive goods has moved away from developed countries to the developing world, causing job losses in the former. For example, from 1970 to 2000, the textile and clothing industries in the five richest developed countries shed more than 4 million jobs, over 62 percent of their labor force.[56] Workers in affected sectors who have not lost their jobs have experienced stagnant or falling wages and have suffered from job insecurity.

Given this situation, it is not surprising that labor unions in rich countries have been at the forefront of a backlash against globalization. What may be surprising is how broadly based the opposition to globalization among labor unions has been. Consider, for example, what happened in 1999, when the United States approved a treaty admitting China into the WTO—thereby giving China permanent most-favored-nation trading status. Unions representing textile and clothing workers were in full-throated opposition to the pact, which would increase international competition for this beleaguered sector.

They were joined by some apparently strange bedfellows.[57] For example, the Teamsters Union, which represents truckers, lobbied against the treaty. This stance was curious because at the same time, one of the teamsters' largest employers, United Parcel Service, was lobbying for a coveted new air route for landing cargo planes in China. One U.S. official summed up the contradiction like this: "It seems that the Teamsters want us to have more cargo flights to China, but no cargo." Even stranger was the opposition by the United Auto Workers. Until China's admission into the WTO, virtually no U.S.-made cars could be sold in China; after the treaty passed, U.S. automakers would have freer access to the Chinese market.

Stranger yet was the opposition by a major dockworkers' union, the International Longshore and Warehouse Union. These workers make their living loading and unloading ships that are engaged in international trade. One would think that expanding trade with China should be in their interests. Yet opposition to the pact came not only from workers in sectors that directly compete with Chinese imports, but also from workers in sectors that thrive on exports and might, therefore, have been expected to support the deal.

This kind of class-based, rather than sector-based, opposition is exactly what the Stolper-Samuelson theorem predicts. The insecurities that globalization has created for workers in sectors that compete with imports is rippling outward and

---

56. Organisation for Economic Co-operation and Development, "A New World Map in Textiles and Clothing: Adjusting to Change," Table 3.1, www.oecd.org/dataoecd/29/53/34042484.pdf (accessed 09/21/06).

57. The following is based on Thomas L. Friedman, "America's Labor Pains" *New York Times*, May 9, 2000, A25.

affecting the attitudes of workers in other sectors as well, generating political cleavages along class lines. Their fears are based on a number of concerns that include, but also go beyond, issues of job losses.

One fear is that globalization is exacerbating inequality, with workers increasingly left behind. Indeed, there is evidence of increasing income inequality in many countries, although economists debate how much of this trend is due to international trade. After all, other developments over the last several decades, including the weakening of labor unions and the increasing importance of technology, account for much of the gap. Regardless of the actual role of trade in exacerbating inequality, the perception of a strong effect is widespread and politically potent.

In addition, there is an asymmetry between labor and investment capital that derives from the fact that capital can move around the globe in search of higher profits much more easily than workers can move around looking for jobs and better wages. Companies can threaten to close up shop and move, and this threat gives managers (who represent capital) bargaining leverage over workers to lower wage and benefit demands. It also leads to more job insecurity.

Unions have also expressed concerns about a "race to the bottom" in labor standards. In the developed world, unions fought hard for a number of protections that most people now take for granted: minimum wage laws, prohibitions on child labor, limits on the length of the workweek, and worker safety regulations. These protections either do not exist or are much weaker in developing countries. Unions fear that the increased mobility of investment capital means that companies can move around the world looking for places with fewer worker protections. If countries compete for capital by weakening or resisting demands for these protections, hard-fought gains in labor standards could wither away.

Economic Insecurity in the Developing World

People in poorer countries have also experienced insecurity as a result of globalization. Though the Stolper-Samuelson theorem predicts that in the long run, trade liberalization will raise the incomes of unskilled workers in developing countries, there are several reasons why people in poor countries face globalization with fear and resistance.

One reason has to do with the relatively weak social safety nets that exist in developing countries. In the developed world, growing exposure to international trade after World War II coincided with the expansion of government assistance designed to protect workers from economic hard times, such as unemployment benefits, poverty alleviation programs, and government-subsidized health insurance, that had the effect of cushioning workers from the hard edges of international competition. In poorer countries, however, these safety nets are generally not as strong, so workers face economic dislocations with greater insecurity.

Workers in the developing world may also have less access to institutions that give them clout in political and economic decision making. Representative democracy, for example, is still more common in rich countries than in poor ones. As a result, workers in the latter have a harder time translating their numbers into political power to demand greater redistribution. Similarly, the right to form labor unions is not as strong in many developing states as it is in the developed world. These

Recent populist movements in Europe have been fueled by opposition to the flow of migrants entering the continent from Syria and other countries in the Middle East.

institutions enable workers to pool their efforts and resources and to act collectively in pursuit of wage and benefit demands from employers. Even if globalization creates a larger pie of profits, weak or nonexistent unions make it harder for workers to get a larger slice of that pie.

Finally, increasing capital mobility has exacerbated the volatility of poor economies, since large sums of foreign money can enter or leave at a moment's notice. As we saw in Chapters 8 and 10, countries that lose the faith of international capital markets can suffer a devastating punishment. In a very short time, capital flight can cause inflation and unemployment to spike. And while international institutions like the IMF may come to a country's rescue, their assistance often requires that governments cut back spending and subsidies that benefit the poor. Given all this, it is easy to see why many people in the developing world do not perceive what economic theory tells us is their long-term interest in globalization.

The Rise of the Populists

The backlash against globalization has grown even more potent as opposition based on traditional economic concerns has combined with other, noneconomic sources of resistance. Discontent with economic integration has always rested to some degree on its social and cultural effects: the fear of importing foreign influences and diluting the national identity.[58]

This fear has been exacerbated in recent years not by the movement of goods and capital across borders, but by the movement of people. In Europe, there has for

---

58. Yotam Margalit, "Lost in Globalization: International Economic Integration and the Sources of Popular Discontent," *International Studies Quarterly* 56, no. 3 (September 2012): 484–500.

many years been a steady flow of migrants, primarily from northern Africa and the Middle East, seeking economic opportunity. Starting in 2015, the influx became a flood, as more than a million people arrived in that year alone, either by boat across the Mediterranean Sea or on foot through southeastern Europe. The majority of these newcomers came from Syria, Iraq, and Afghanistan, fleeing long-running civil wars in those countries (see Chapter 6).

In the United States, immigration from Mexico has long been a contentious issue, and deciding what to do about the approximately 11 million people who have come into the country illegally has been politically vexing. In recent years, the salience of the issue increased in both Europe and the United States because of refugees from the civil war in Syria and people fleeing crime in Central America.

Opposition to accepting migrants and refugees stems from a variety of considerations. As we saw in the "How Do We Know?" box in Chapter 8 (p. 380), one factor is economic. For workers in recipient countries, the influx of generally low-skilled labor from abroad is seen as a threat to jobs and wages.[59] There is considerable disagreement among economists about the magnitude of net job losses due to immigration, and the fact that newcomers also purchase goods and services means that there can be positive economic effects as well.[60] Nonetheless, the perception that immigrants are "taking our jobs" has proved to be politically potent.

Opposition to immigrants can also stem from a perception that they are a drain on the country's budget because of their alleged dependence on welfare and unemployment benefits. Once again, there is limited evidence that immigrants disproportionately draw on social spending, and most pay taxes into the system. These facts have not prevented politicians from using the image of lazy immigrants (presumably not the same ones who "took our jobs") who come to their country to live on its generous dole.

Beyond these economic concerns, opposition to accepting foreign migrants can rest on perceptions that they are a cultural threat as well, because they come with different customs, religious beliefs, languages, or skin color. As noted at the start of this chapter, the German AfD party explicitly depicted migration as a foreign invasion and made no secret of the fact that Muslim migrants were the primary target of its opposition. Indeed, studies of attitudes toward immigration show that the religious and ethnic backgrounds of prospective newcomers play a significant role in how willing people in recipient countries are to accept them.[61]

At a minimum, cultural concerns are expressed in terms of assimilation: people may see the perceived unwillingness of migrants to adapt to local customs and speak the local language as a threat to national identity and unity. In more extreme

59. Kenneth F. Scheve and Matthew J. Slaughter, "Labor Market Competition and Individual Preferences over Immigration Policy," *Review of Economics and Statistics* 83, no. 1 (February 2001): 133–45.

60. See, for example, *The Economic and Fiscal Consequences of Immigration* (Washington, DC: National Academies Press, 2017), www.nap.edu/catalog/23550/the-economic-and-fiscal-consequences-of-immigration.

61. For a recent review of the literature, see Jens Hainmueller and Daniel J. Hopkins, "Public Attitudes towards Immigration," *Annual Review of Political Science* 17 (2014): 225–49.

rhetoric, cultural concerns emerge in terms of threats to law and order. In Germany, for example, widely shared (and often wildly overstated or fabricated) stories of Muslim refugees raping Western women epitomize the view that the newcomers are defiling the nation.[62]

To a large extent, flows of people to the United States and Europe are not a result of globalization; nor do they reflect rules or decisions of liberal economic institutions, none of which mandate openness to migration (though there are international agreements that require states to accept people seeking asylum from political threats). Rather, the movement of people is rooted—as it always has been—in persistent underdevelopment, political instability, and civil war. The geographic proximity between wealthy countries, like the United States and Germany, and poor regions, like Central America and northern Africa, makes migration an attractive option for people seeking better circumstances. Nevertheless, opposition to migration intersects with and has given greater potency to opposition to globalization and its institutions by fueling the rise of populism.

As noted at the beginning of this chapter, *populism* describes a broad array of political movements that claim to speak on behalf of "the people" in opposition to corrupt elites, both domestic and foreign.[63] Populism can take a variety of different forms depending on the local context, and it can arise on either the left or the right of the political spectrum. Populists on the left tend to emphasize radical redistribution of wealth, nationalization of property, and anti-imperialism; those on the right tend to stress nationalism, traditional cultural values, and a rejection of foreign influences.

Populist movements have a long history in Latin America, where they tend to be on the left. Recent populist movements in Europe and the United States have been on the right, mobilizing voters opposed to immigration, trade, and international institutions. In doing so, they have drawn support from those who fear wage and job loss because of foreign trade or competition with migrant labor; those who fear cultural and demographic changes because of the influx of people from foreign cultures; and those who resent the influence that international institutions have on national policy making.[64] In short, the populist coalition brings together traditional economic foes of globalization and people motivated by noneconomic interests in protecting cultural identity and national sovereignty.

It is no surprise that this kind of populism has been rising in Europe, where populism had, by 2017, scored electoral victories by the Law and Justice Party in

---

62. See, for example, Melissa Eddy, "Bild Apologizes for False Article on Sexual Assaults in Frankfurt by Migrants," *New York Times*, February 16, 2017, www.nytimes.com/2017/02/16/world/europe/bild-fake-story.html.

63. There is an enormous literature on populism and its rise. An important effort to define populism is Cas Mudde, "The Populist Zeitgeist," *Government and Opposition* 39 (2004): 541–63. For a succinct discussion of the recent rise of populism in Europe, see Anna Grzymala-Busse, "Global Populisms and Their Impact," *Slavic Review* 76 (2017): S3–S8.

64. For some recent studies showing the effects of economic shocks and migration on voting for right-wing, nationalist parties in Europe, see Italo Colantone and Piero Stanig, "The Trade Origins of Economic Nationalism: Import Competition and Voting Behavior in Western Europe," BAFFI CAREFIN Centre Research Paper 2017-49, January 2017; and Sascha O. Becker and Thiemo Fetzer, "Does Migration Cause Extreme Voting?" University of Warwick, Center for Competitive Advantage in the Global Economy, Working Paper 306, October 2016.

FIGURE 14.5 *Share of Votes for Populist Parties in EU Member States, 1945–2017*

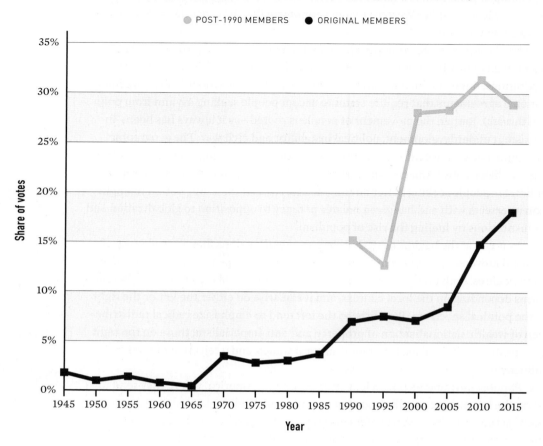

● POST-1990 MEMBERS   ● ORIGINAL MEMBERS

Note: The figure shows the share of votes for populist parties for each five-year period starting in the indicated year. Vote shares are averaged across countries that held an election in the given five-year period. For the purposes of this figure, populist parties were defined as parties whose platform claimed (1) that the party represented the interests of the "people" or "the nation" as opposed to particular groups, classes, or sectors, and (2) that the establishment elite had acted against this popular interest.

Figure source: Anna Grzymala-Busse, "Populist Party Support," Database, Stanford University, 2017.

Poland and the Hungarian Civic Union in Hungary; led to strong showings by the AfD in Germany, the National Front in France, and the Freedom Party of Austria; and fueled the Brexit vote in Great Britain. Figure 14.5 shows vote shares for populist parties in European Union member states in the postwar period. Populist vote shares have been higher in central and eastern European countries that joined the European Union after 1990, but the recent uptick among original EU members in the West is striking.

This trend reflects a combination of factors. One is the building criticism of the European Union and its project of economic and political integration. "Euroskepticism" has long been a factor on the political right, which has opposed the transfer of national policy making to Brussels, the EU capital. That skepticism got a boost in the wake of the 2008 world financial crisis (see Chapter 8), which exposed deep rifts within the union. As countries like Greece, Spain, and Portugal struggled to meet debt payments, a crisis arose over whether and how much other countries should lend financial assistance to prevent them from defaulting on their obligations. This crisis fed a perception in wealthier countries, like Germany, Britain, and France, that the European Union put them on the hook to bail out more profligate members who were not willing to live within their means.

The most consistent predictor of a border wall between two states is the level of income inequality between them: high-income states may build border walls to keep people from adjacent low-income states out. Here, migrants from low-income African countries scale the fence between Morocco and the wealthy Spanish territory of Melilla.

The aforementioned migration crisis further fed right-wing opposition to the European Union. As noted, EU law does not require member countries to accept migrants from outside the union unless they are seeking asylum from war or persecution. But expansion of the European Union into central and eastern Europe after the end of the Cold War created large flows of people from the new member states, which tended to be poorer, into wealthier EU countries. Then, the enormous influx of people into the region starting in 2015 created a new problem that EU institutions struggled to control. Countries on the front lines of the migrant flow, especially Greece, Italy, and Hungary, were unable and unwilling to absorb the influx, and many migrants hoped to move on to wealthier states in northern Europe, such as Germany and Sweden.

Recognizing the need to spread out the burden of absorbing the migrants, the EU developed a resettlement plan whereby each country would commit to accepting a certain number. The plan provoked resistance in a number of countries, particularly those with populist governments or strong populist movements; as of March 2018, Poland and Hungary had not accepted a single individual under the plan. As a result of the crisis, Euroskeptics could add another charge against the institution: it was forcing their countries to take in foreign migrants. Thus, both old and new complaints came together to fuel populist opposition to migration, EU institutions, and the overall project of European integration.

Populism came to the United States with the election of Donald Trump in 2016.[65] Trump's campaign drew heavily on populist themes, including opposition to immigration, free trade, and the ease of international investment, which helps U.S. companies move abroad. As a result, he drew crucial support from voters in areas where the loss of manufacturing jobs was particularly acute. He came into office promising both to build a wall on the border with Mexico—a potent symbol of defending national sovereignty—and to withdraw from or renegotiate prior trade deals, including NAFTA. (For more on the issue of border walls, see "How Do We Know?" on p. 630.)

Trump also took aim at another key institution of the postwar order: NATO. Trump criticized NATO allies for failing to spend enough money on defense (see the "What Shaped Our World?" box in Chapter 5, p. 206). Although this criticism is not new (it was made by Presidents Bush and Obama before him), Trump seemed to

---

65. For evidence of the role of populism in the 2016 U.S. election, see J. Eric Oliver and Wendy M. Rahn, "Rise of the *Trumpenvolk*: Populism in the 2016 Election," *Annals of the American Academy of Political and Social Science* 667, no. 1 (2016): 189–206.

Why Do States Build Border Walls?

On November 9, 1989, thousands of people in Berlin, East Germany, used hammers, picks, and shovels to tear down one of the world's most famous walls: the fortified barrier between East and West Berlin that had solidified the Cold War division of that city. The images of people dancing on the rubble seemed to symbolize the triumph of democracy, liberalism, and open borders.

In retrospect, the period of falling walls ushered in by that event was short-lived. Figure A shows the number of borders around the globe that had a human-made barrier in the period 1945–2016. Within 10 years of the fall of the Berlin Wall, the number of fortified borders started to increase dramatically. The growth is particularly pronounced in the Middle East, northern Africa, and Asia; in Europe, border walls vanished entirely after 1989 but went up again in 2015, at the height of the migration crisis. And on November 8, 2016—almost exactly 27 years after the fall of the Berlin Wall—the United States elected a president whose most prominent campaign promise was to build a wall along the entire U.S.-Mexico border.

Why do states build walls along their borders? The Berlin Wall was built to keep citizens in: to stem the flow of East Berliners trying to flee to the West. More commonly, walls are intended to keep foreigners out—specifically, armies and migrants. This observation suggests two broad interests that motivate wall building: interstate *security concerns* would lead to walls built for defensive purposes, while *opposition to migration* would prompt states to build walls to make it harder for people to cross the border.

To understand the relative importance of these considerations, David Carter and Paul Poast collected data on all human-made border barriers over the last two centuries and examined the factors that determine whether any given pair of neighboring states had a wall.[a] They found that the strongest and most consistent predictor is income inequality: as the difference in GDP between the states increases, so does the likelihood that a wall will be built by the wealthier country. There is also evidence that border walls are more likely to separate democratic from nondemocratic countries. Both of these findings suggest that the main purpose for wall building is to impede the flow of migrants from poorer and less democratic neighbors.

Carter and Poast found less evidence that conventional security concerns lead to walls. Whether the states had a territorial dispute or had recently engaged in a militarized dispute did not appear to have a strong, consistent effect on whether they built a wall. While border fortifications historically served a defensive purpose, modern weaponry has rendered them less effective. Castle walls crumbled with the advent of the cannon. In the 1930s, the French built a series of fortifications and obstacles to prevent a repeat of the German invasion that occurred in World War I, but in World War II, German tanks swept around that line.

This is not to imply that border walls have no security rationale. The surge of wall construction following the 2001 terrorist attacks suggests that fears of infiltration by extremists provided additional justification for barriers. In today's world, walls are built to keep out people, not armies.

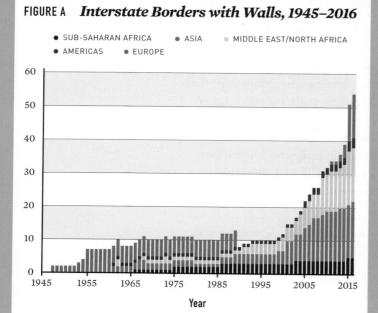

FIGURE A *Interstate Borders with Walls, 1945–2016*

- SUB-SAHARAN AFRICA   ● ASIA   MIDDLE EAST/NORTH AFRICA
- AMERICAS   ● EUROPE

a. David B. Carter and Paul Poast, "Why Do States Build Walls? Political Economy, Security, and Border Stability," *Journal of Conflict Resolution* 61 (2017): 239–70.

Figure source: David B. Carter and Paul Poast, "Why Do States Build Walls? Political Economy, Security, and Border Stability," *Journal of Conflict Resolution* 61 (2017): 239–70. Updated to 2016 with information from Samuel Granados, Zoeann Murphy, Kevin Schaul, Anthony Faiola, et al., "Raising Barriers: A New Age of Walls," *Washington Post*, October 12, 2016, www.washingtonpost.com/graphics/world/border-barriers/global-illegal-immigration-prevention.

imply that the U.S. commitment to defend NATO allies would be contingent on their increasing defense spending—something that no previous president suggested.[66]

As of this writing, it was unclear how much of Trump's populist agenda would actually be carried out. Although the Republican Party won control of Congress in 2016, the party itself is not as populist as the president and still draws significant support from businesses that benefit from globalization, free trade, and low-wage immigrant labor. Most Republicans also continued to support NATO. In the near term, while Trump is in power, this tension may constrain the extent to which U.S. policy changes; in the longer term, the extent to which populism becomes embedded in a political party will determine whether Trump's populism is a temporary anomaly or the start of an enduring trend.

The rise of populism in the West has a transnational dimension that is ironic, given its nationalist orientation:[67] populist parties have given one another support and encouragement, seeing each other as natural allies in their opposition to prevailing institutions. Their rise has also created an opportunity for another adversary of the U.S.-led postwar order: Russia. As noted earlier, Russia has seen its foreign policy interests harmed by the extension of the European Union and NATO into central and eastern Europe. Thus, while Russian president Vladimir Putin is no populist himself, he shares common interests with those in the West who are skeptical of those institutions.[68] As a result, Russia has in recent years given support to populist politicians and parties, including, most prominently, interfering in the 2016 U.S. presidential election by spreading messages online that benefited Trump.[69]

Backlash and the International Trading System

In sum, the last decade has seen the dramatic growth of a broad set of actors motivated by economic, cultural, and foreign policy interests to oppose globalization and the institutions that have propelled it forward. The resulting political backlash has created conflict both within and among states. Just as those who stand to gain from globalization pushed governments to lower barriers to trade and money flows and to construct institutions to facilitate economic integration, those who stand to lose have sought to influence policy in the other direction. The economic losers have an

---

66. See, for example, David E. Sanger and Maggie Haberman, "Donald Trump Sets Conditions for Defending NATO Allies against Attack," *New York Times*, July 20, 2106, www.nytimes.com/2016/07/21/us/politics/donald-trump-issues.html. After Trump became president in 2017, on his first visit to Europe in May he refused to confirm the U.S. commitment to defend NATO allies, though he did later confirm this commitment.

67. For a discussion of the relationship between populism and nationalism, as well as a consideration of populism's transnational aspects, see Benjamin de Cleen, "Populism and Nationalism," in Cristobal Rovira Kaltwasser, Paul Taggart, Paulina Ochoa Espejo, and Pierry Ostiguy, eds., *The Oxford Handbook of Populism*, 342–62, esp. 355–58 (New York: Oxford University Press, 2017).

68. See, for example, Yulia Netesova and Torrey Taussig, "Trump and Putin: Populists of a Feather?" *National Interest*, March 28, 2017, http://nationalinterest.org/feature/trump-putin-populists-feather-19933?page=show.

69. A declassified summary of the U.S. intelligence community's findings with respect to Russian actions can be found in Office of the Director of National Intelligence, "Assessing Russian Activities and Intentions in Recent U.S. Elections," January 6, 2017, www.dni.gov/files/documents/ICA_2017_01.pdf. At the time of this writing, additional investigations by the intelligence community, Congress, and the U.S. Department of Justice continued to explore the extent of Russian interference.

Russia has strategically supported populist movements in Western countries that have shared Russia's interest in reducing the influence of prevailing institutions. Most notably, Russia contributed to the spread of pro-Trump misinformation on social media during the 2016 American presidential election.

incentive to seek protection from foreign competition in the form of trade barriers or restrictions on capital flows.

Economic insecurity has also increased demand for social welfare programs designed to cushion workers from the shocks of competition: unemployment insurance, health insurance, and job retraining programs. As we saw in Chapter 7, free trade generally creates economic benefits that exceed the costs to those whose jobs may be lost. Hence, in principle, everyone could be made better off as long as some of those benefits were redistributed. However, redistribution would naturally come at the expense of the winners, who may or may not accommodate those demands.

Those who see globalization in terms of non-economic costs to cultural identity or national sovereignty have also sought to stem its effects. Unlike economic losses, these losses cannot be compensated through a redistribution of resources; rather, they can propel efforts to elevate the traditional national culture and restrict the expression of foreign cultural influences.

Demands by those who stand to lose from globalization seem likely to prevent further liberalization in the near future. Prospects for further deepening of the WTO have been poor for some time. The WTO's most recent round of global talks, launched in 2001, ended in 2016 after 15 years of fruitless negotiations. The deadlock resulted primarily from the divergent interests of rich and poor countries.

Since World War II, the most dramatic liberalization has taken place in the realm of manufactured goods, the primary producers of which are located in developed countries. Rich countries have also pushed hard to liberalize trade in services, such as banking, accounting, and communications—sectors in which their companies are very competitive. Poorer countries, in contrast, have sought greater liberalization of the agricultural sector, since farming constitutes a significant portion of their economies. Liberalizing trade in agriculture would require rich countries to reduce or eliminate the very generous agricultural subsidies that they pay to their farmers. These subsidies account for about 20 percent of total farm receipts in developed countries, and over 50 percent in some countries, including Japan, South Korea, and Norway.[70]

These government payments support farmers' incomes, allowing the prices of agricultural products to be kept artificially low. In the process, they deprive

---

70. Organisation for Economic Co-operation and Development, *Agricultural Policy Monitoring and Evaluation 2014: OECD Countries* (Paris: OECD Publishing, 2014).

farmers in the developing world of much-needed income. The recent trade talks stalled because of conflict between rich-country governments (which are reluctant to alienate a politically powerful constituency at the same time that they are facing increased import competition from places like China) and poor-country governments (which represent most of the world's farmers).

With global talks stalled, countries still interested in further trade liberalization turned to bilateral and regional agreements. Among these were two ambitious deals: the Trans-Pacific Partnership (TPP), designed to increase trade and investment in the Asia-Pacific region, and the Transatlantic Trade and Investment Partnership (TTIP) between the United States and the European Union. Both have fallen prey to political developments in those countries. Political support for the TPP in the United States withered as soon as it was signed in 2015, and President Trump withdrew from the deal within days of coming into office. Negotiations for the TTIP were halted after Trump's election, and while both sides have expressed a willingness to continue the talks, it appears unlikely that there is sufficient political interest on either side of the Atlantic to conclude a deal.

In the United States, support for free trade was already on the decline in the Democratic Party, which has traditionally represented labor unions. Trump's electoral victory showed that a Republican could win by marrying protectionism with culturally nationalist appeals against immigration. Given Trump's announced intention to withdraw from or renegotiate prior trade deals, the postwar pattern of U.S.-led trade liberalization has at least paused—and may have come to an end.

If so, what comes next? One possibility is that other states will take over the United States' role in sustaining and propelling further liberalization. The TPP may survive the United States' departure, in part because other countries in the Asia-Pacific region, particularly Japan and Canada, are still interested in the deal. The withdrawal of the United States may also create an opening for China to play a larger role in setting trade rules in the region through an alternative agreement known as the Regional Comprehensive Economic Partnership. In Europe, the EU faces immediate challenges from populist governments and parties, as well as the looming departure of its second-largest economy, Great Britain. Will China, Japan, and what remains of the European Union cooperate to lead a global system, or at least maintain economic openness in their respective regions?

The alternative is an unraveling of the global system, which would likely lead to a reduction in international economic activity. In constructing postwar economic institutions, policy makers hoped to avoid a repeat of the 1930s, when the Great Depression led countries to impose tit-for-tat restrictions on trade, exacerbating the economic contraction and increasing political tensions that culminated in world war. The system was successful in many respects, including its ability to contain some of the effects of the 2008 global financial crisis.[71]

Such benefits, however, are abstract and intangible. For those who feel harmed by globalization, the benefit derived from crises that were avoided—or crises that

---

71. See, for example, Daniel W. Drezner, *The System Worked: How the World Stopped Another Great Depression* (Oxford: Oxford University Press, 2014).

happened but were not as bad as they could have been—are immaterial relative to the concrete costs. Weakening political support in the very countries that constructed the system poses the most serious threat to its survival.

Conclusion: Can Common Interests Prevail?

Every case considered in this chapter tells a similar story: the institutions and patterns of interaction that took hold after World War II have created winners and losers. Some states and groups see the current system as hostile to their interests and seek to increase their power by acquiring new weapons. Other states, like China, are growing in power and have an interest in changing current bargains and rules in their favor. Finally, some groups see the process of globalization, and the institutions that have promoted it, as threatening to both economic and noneconomic interests.

The resulting clash of interests will color future interactions, leading to political, economic, and possibly military conflict. The acquisition of WMD by hostile states or terrorist organizations and the growing power of China pose potential threats to the United States and its allies, raising the danger of preventive war. The backlash against globalization and the rise of populism have created political conflict within and between states, undermining political support for the postwar economic system and the institutions that upheld it. At stake is not just the flow of goods and capital across borders, but the ability of people fleeing poverty and violence to find opportunity and security in other countries.

Set against these gloomy observations is the recognition that these challenges also generate common interests. The destructive potential of today's weapons means that the common interest in peace looms large relative to whatever gains could be won through war. As a result, states have an incentive to manage the rise of new powers and the spread of WMD in a peaceful manner. The wealth that can be created by globalization means that everyone can potentially gain, as long as the process is governed in a way that redistributes some of the gain to those actors that stand to lose. The influx of people from different backgrounds can create discomfort and fear, but it can also be a source of vitality and innovation. In short, many of the challenges posed by the changing world can be met if the gains of cooperation can spread in a satisfactory way.

Will this happen? The history of international relations warns us not to be overly optimistic. There are real hatreds in the world, and people do not always act on the basis of an enlightened self-interest. World politics will never be free of conflicting interests or hostile interactions, and institutions will never entirely eliminate these conflicts through rules and redistribution. Some threats cannot be eliminated, only managed.

Yet we have also seen unmistakable signs of progress. Interstate war is not obsolete, but it is less frequent today than in the past. Although many people around the world still live in poverty, there have been tremendous advances in wealth and living standards. Democracy, considered a pernicious and destabilizing political form only two centuries ago, has spread to every continent, giving individuals greater say in the decisions that affect their lives. International cooperation to stop civil conflict and genocide, to protect human rights, and to safeguard the global environment has advanced significantly, even if these efforts fall short of the ideal.

We opened this book with the story of how a lone man defused violence between Arabs and Jews in 1921 by appealing to their shared interest in peace and prosperity. Although the peace of that day did not last, the man's efforts were still worthwhile. Progress is possible, even if perfection is not. Though conflicts will always remain, we have not yet exhausted all the opportunities to recognize and act on humanity's common interests.

Study Tool Kit

Interests, Interactions, and Institutions in Context

- The postwar order—the institutions and pattern of interactions that developed after World War II—generated a number of benefits, including economic development, increased trade and financial flows, the spread of democracy, and the decline of interstate war. Actors that see this order as hostile to their interests or seek greater power within it will pose significant challenges in the coming decade.

- States and terrorist organizations that are hostile to the United States and its allies see weapons of mass destruction—nuclear, chemical, and biological weapons—as a way to counter U.S. military superiority. As a result, there will be growing conflict between actors who want WMD and those who would be harmed by proliferation. Whether the spread of WMD can be slowed depends on whether the latter actors can find a way—through cooperation, coercion, or institutions—to alter the interests of potential proliferators.

- The rise of China as a global power may lead to increased conflict between that country and the current world leader, the United States. Whether this dynamic will lead to war depends on the interests that prevail in both countries and on whether international and domestic institutions can make China a partner, rather than a rival, of the United States.

- Globalization creates winners and losers and increases the potential for political conflict within and among countries. Those who have experienced economic and noneconomic losses from the cross-border movement of goods, capital, and people form a potent opposition to globalization and the economic institutions that have promoted it. The rise of populist resistance in the United States and Europe presents a direct challenge to the postwar order from within the very states that constructed it.

For Further Reading

Debs, Alexander, and Nuno P. Monteiro. *Nuclear Politics: The Strategic Causes of Proliferation.* New York: Cambridge University Press, 2017. Rigorously analyzes how strategic incentives influence whether states decide to acquire nuclear weapons.

Frieden, Jeffry A. *Global Capitalism: Its Fall and Rise in the Twentieth Century.* **New York: Norton, 2006.** Explains the development of the global economy over the last century.

Gilpin, Robert. *War and Change in World Politics.* **Cambridge: Cambridge University Press, 1981.** Develops a general theory of the rise and fall of global leaders and argues that this theory explains major wars over the last several centuries.

Johnston, Alastair Iain. *Social States: China in International Institutions, 1980–2000.* **Princeton, NJ: Princeton University Press, 2008.** Argues that China's increasing engagement with international institutions can change its foreign policy outlook in a way that leads to greater cooperation.

Lipscy, Phillip Y. *Renegotiating the World Order: Institutional Change in International Relations.* **Cambridge: Cambridge University Press, 2017.** Examines whether and how international institutions respond to changes in the relative power of their members.

Milanović, Branko, ed. *Globalization and Inequality.* **Cheltenham, England: Edward Elgar, 2012.** Explores, with a collection of scholarship, how globalization, past and present, affects inequality among and within countries.

Mudde, Cas, and Cristobal Rovira Kaltwasser. *Populism: A Very Short Introduction.* **New York: Oxford University Press, 2017.** Examines the causes and consequences of the success of populist parties around the world.

Sagan, Scott D. "Why Do States Build Nuclear Weapons? Three Models in Search of a Bomb." *International Security* **21, no. 3 (Winter 1996–97): 54–86.** Argues that security needs, domestic politics, and concerns about international status explain why some states try to acquire nuclear weapons while others do not.

Sagan, Scott D., and Kenneth N. Waltz. *The Spread of Nuclear Weapons: An Enduring Debate.* **3rd ed. New York: Norton, 2012.** Presents a debate between two scholars over whether the spread of nuclear weapons is good or bad for the world.

Shirk, Susan. *China: Fragile Superpower.* **New York: Oxford University Press, 2007.** Examines how domestic politics within China will determine whether its rise as a global power takes place peacefully.

Zakaria, Fareed. *The Post-American World: Release 2.0.* **New York: Norton, 2011.** Considers the rising economic and political influence of states like China, India, and Brazil and what these developments mean for the United States and the future of world politics.

Glossary

absolute advantage The ability of a country or firm to produce more of a particular good or service than other countries or firms do with the same amount of effort and resources. Compare *comparative advantage*.

accountability The ability to punish or reward leaders for the decisions they make, as when frequent, fair elections enable voters to hold elected officials responsible for their actions by granting or withholding access to political office.

actors The basic unit for the analysis of international politics; can be either individuals or groups of people with common interests.

adjustable peg A monetary system of fixed but adjustable rates. Governments are expected to keep their currencies fixed for extended periods but are permitted to adjust the exchange rate from time to time as economic conditions change.

agenda setting Actions taken before or during bargaining that make the reversion outcome more favorable for one party.

alliances Institutions that help their members cooperate militarily in the event of a war. Compare *collective security organizations*.

anarchy The absence of a central authority with the ability to make and enforce laws that bind all actors.

appreciate In terms of a currency, to increase in value relative to other currencies. Compare *depreciate*.

asymmetrical warfare Armed conflict between actors with highly unequal military capabilities, such as when rebel groups or terrorists fight strong states.

audience costs Negative repercussions for failing to follow through on a threat or to honor a commitment.

austerity The application of policies to reduce consumption, typically by cutting government spending, raising taxes, and restricting wages.

autocracy A political system in which an individual or small group exercises power with few constraints and no meaningful competition or participation by the general public. Compare *democracy*.

balance of power A situation in which the military capabilities of two states or groups of states are roughly equal.

bandwagoning A strategy in which states join forces with the stronger side in a conflict.

Bank for International Settlements One of the oldest international financial organizations, created in 1930. Its members include the world's principal central banks, and under its auspices they attempt to cooperate in the financial realm.

bargaining An interaction in which two or more actors must choose outcomes that make one better off at the expense of another. Bargaining is redistributive: it involves allocating a fixed sum of value between different actors. Compare *cooperation*.

bargaining range The set of deals that both parties in a bargaining interaction prefer over the reversion outcome. When the reversion outcome is war, the bargaining range is the set of deals that both sides prefer over war.

bilateral investment treaty An agreement between two countries about the conditions for private investment across borders. Most of these treaties include provisions to protect an investment from government discrimination or expropriation without compensation, as well as mechanisms to resolve disputes.

boomerang model A process through which NGOs in one state are able to activate transnational linkages to bring pressure from other states on their own governments.

Bretton Woods monetary system The monetary order negotiated among the World War II Allies in 1944, which lasted until the 1970s and which was based on a U.S. dollar tied to gold. Other currencies were fixed to the dollar but were permitted to adjust their exchange rates.

Bretton Woods System The economic order negotiated among allied nations at Bretton Woods, New Hampshire, in 1944, which led to a series of cooperative arrangements involving a commitment to relatively low barriers to international trade and investment.

brinksmanship A strategy in which adversaries take actions that increase the risk of accidental war, with the hope that the other will "blink" (lose its nerve) first and make concessions.

bureaucracy The collection of organizations—including the military, diplomatic corps, and intelligence agencies—that carry out most tasks of governance within the state.

cap-and-trade system A cap-and-trade system sets limits on emissions, which are then lowered over time to reduce pollutants released into the atmosphere. Firms can sell "credits" when they emit less than their allocation or must buy from others when they emit more than their allocation.

central bank The institution that regulates monetary conditions in an economy, typically by affecting interest rates and the quantity of money in circulation.

civil war A war in which the main participants are within the same state, such as the government and a rebel group. Compare *interstate war* and *terrorism*.

coercion A strategy of imposing or threatening to impose costs on other actors in order to induce a change in their behavior.

coercive diplomacy The use of threats to advance specific demands in a bargaining interaction. See also **crisis bargaining**.

collaboration A type of cooperative interaction in which actors gain from working together but nonetheless have incentives not to comply with any agreement. Compare *coordination*.

collective action problems Obstacles to cooperation that occur when actors have incentives to collaborate but each acts with the expectation that others will pay the costs of cooperation.

collective security organizations Broad-based institutions that promote peace and security among their members. Examples include the League of Nations and the United Nations. Compare *alliances*.

commodity cartels Associations of producers of commodities (raw materials and agricultural products) that restrict world supply and thereby cause the price of the goods to rise.

common-pool resources Goods that are available to everyone, but such that one user's consumption of the good reduces the amount available for others. Common-pool resources are rival but nonexcludable. Compare *public goods*.

comparative advantage The ability of a country or firm to produce a particular good or service more efficiently than the other goods or services that it can produce, such that its resources are most efficiently employed in this activity. The comparison is to the efficiency of other economic activities that the actor might undertake, given all the products it can produce—not to the efficiency of other countries or firms. Compare *absolute advantage*.

compellence An effort to change the status quo through the threat of force. Compare *deterrence*.

cooperation An interaction in which two or more actors adopt policies that make at least one actor better off relative to the status quo without making the others worse off. Compare *bargaining*.

coordination A type of cooperative interaction in which actors benefit from all making the same choices and subsequently have no incentive not to comply. Compare *collaboration*.

credibility Believability. A credible threat is a threat that the recipient believes will be carried out. A credible commitment is a commitment or promise that the recipient believes will be honored.

crisis bargaining A bargaining interaction in which at least one actor threatens to use force in the event that its demands are not met. See also **coercive diplomacy**.

customary international law International law that usually develops slowly, over time, as states recognize practices as appropriate and correct.

decolonization The process of shedding colonial possessions, especially during the rapid end of the European empires in Africa, Asia, and the Caribbean between the 1940s and the 1960s.

default To fail to make payments on a debt.

delegation The degree to which third parties, such as courts, arbitrators, or mediators, are given authority to implement, interpret, and apply international legal rules; to resolve disputes over the rules; and to make additional rules.

democracy A political system in which candidates compete for political office through frequent, fair elections in which a sizable portion of the adult population can vote. Compare *autocracy*.

democratic peace The observation that there are few, if any, clear cases of war between mature democratic states.

depreciate In terms of a currency, to decrease in value relative to other currencies. Compare *appreciate*.

depression A severe downturn in the business cycle, typically associated with a major decline in economic activity, production, and investment; a severe contraction of credit; and sustained high unemployment. Compare *recession*.

deterrence An effort to preserve the status quo through the threat of force. Compare *compellence*.

devalue To reduce the value of one currency relative to other currencies.

diversionary incentive The temptation that state leaders have to start international crises in order to rally public support at home.

entrapment The risk of being dragged into an unwanted war because of the opportunistic actions of an ally.

EOI See **export-oriented industrialization**.

exchange rate The price at which one currency is exchanged for another.

export-oriented industrialization (EOI) A set of policies, originally pursued in the late 1960s by several East Asian countries, to spur manufacturing for export, often through subsidies and incentives for export production. Compare *import-substituting industrialization*.

externalities Costs or benefits for stakeholders other than the actor undertaking an action. When an externality exists, the decision maker does not bear all the costs or reap all the gains from his or her action.

extremists Actors whose interests are not widely shared by others; individuals or groups that are politically weak relative to the demands they make.

FDI See **foreign direct investment**.

first-strike advantage The situation that arises when military technology, military strategies, and/or geography give a significant advantage to whichever state attacks first in a war.

fixed exchange rate An exchange-rate policy under which a government commits itself to keep its currency at or around a specific value relative to another currency or a commodity, such as gold. Compare *floating exchange rate*.

floating exchange rate An exchange-rate policy under which a government permits its currency to be traded on the open market without direct government control or intervention. Compare *fixed exchange rate*.

foreign direct investment (FDI) Investment in a foreign country via the acquisition of a local facility or the establishment of a new facility. Direct investors maintain managerial control of the foreign operation. Compare *portfolio investment*.

free ride To fail to contribute to a public good while benefiting from the contributions of others.

GATT See **General Agreement on Tariffs and Trade**.

General Agreement on Tariffs and Trade (GATT) An international institution created in 1947 in which member countries committed to reduce barriers to trade and to provide similar trading conditions to all other members. In 1995, the GATT was replaced by the WTO. Compare *World Trade Organization*.

genocide Intentional and systematic killing aimed at eliminating an identifiable group of people, such as an ethnic or religious group.

global climate change Human-induced change in the environment, especially from the emissions of greenhouse gases, leading to higher temperatures around the globe.

gold standard The monetary system that prevailed between about 1870 and 1914, in which countries tied their currencies to gold at a legally fixed price.

Group of 77 A coalition of developing countries in the UN, formed in 1964 with 77 members, that seeks changes to the economic order to favor the developing world. It has grown to over 130 members but retains the original name.

Heckscher-Ohlin trade theory The theory that a country will export goods that make intensive use of the factors of production in which it is well endowed. For example, a labor-rich country will export goods that make intensive use of labor.

hegemony The predominance of one nation-state over others.

human rights The rights possessed by all individuals by virtue of being human, regardless of their status as citizens of particular states or members of a group or organization.

humanitarian interventions Interventions designed to relieve humanitarian crises stemming from civil conflicts or large-scale human rights abuses, including genocide.

ICC See **International Criminal Court**.

ICCPR See **International Covenant on Civil and Political Rights**.

ICESCR See **International Covenant on Economic, Social, and Cultural Rights**.

IMF See **International Monetary Fund**.

import-substituting industrialization (ISI) A set of policies, pursued by most developing countries from the 1930s through the 1980s, to reduce imports and encourage domestic manufacturing, often through trade barriers, subsidies to manufacturing, and state ownership of basic industries. Compare *export-oriented industrialization*.

incomplete information A situation in which actors in a strategic interaction lack information about other actors' interests and/or capabilities.

individual petition A right that permits individuals to petition appropriate international legal bodies directly if they believe a state has violated their rights.

indivisible good A good that cannot be divided without diminishing its value.

infrastructure Basic structures necessary for social activity, such as transportation and telecommunications networks, and power and water supply.

institutions Sets of rules (known and shared by the community) that structure interactions in specific ways.

insurgency A military strategy in which small, often lightly armed units engage in hit-and-run attacks against military, government, and civilian targets.

interactions The ways in which the choices of two or more actors combine to produce political outcomes.

interest groups Groups of individuals with common interests that organize to influence public policy in a manner that benefits their members.

interests What actors want to achieve through political action; their preferences over the outcomes that might result from their political choices.

International Bill of Rights The UDHR, ICCPR, and ICESCR collectively. Together, these three agreements form the core of the international human rights regime.

International Covenant on Civil and Political Rights (ICCPR) The agreement, completed in 1966 and in force from 1976, that details the basic civil and political rights of individuals and nations. The ICCPR and ICESCR together are known as the "twin covenants."

International Covenant on Economic, Social, and Cultural Rights (ICESCR) The agreement, completed in 1966 and in force from 1976, that specifies the basic economic, social, and cultural rights of individuals and nations. The ICCPR and ICESCR together are known as the "twin covenants."

International Criminal Court (ICC) A court of last resort for human rights cases that possesses jurisdiction only if the accused is a national of a state party, the crime took place on the territory of a state party, or the UN Security Council has referred the case to the prosecutor.

international law A body of rules that binds states and other agents in world politics and is considered to have the status of law.

International Monetary Fund (IMF) A major international economic institution that was established in 1944 to manage international monetary relations and that has gradually reoriented itself to focus on the international financial system, especially debt and currency crises.

international monetary regime A formal or informal arrangement among governments to govern relations among their currencies; the agreement is shared by most countries in the world economy.

interstate war A war in which the main participants are states. Compare *civil war*.

irredentist An actor that seeks to detach a region from one country and attach it to another, usually because of shared ethnic or religious ties. Compare *separatist*.

ISI See **import-substituting industrialization**.

iteration Repeated interactions with the same partners.

Kyoto Protocol An amendment to the UN Framework Convention on Climate Change, adopted in 1997 and entered into force in 2005, that established specific targets for reducing emissions of carbon and five other greenhouse gases through 2020.

LDCs See **less developed countries**.

League of Nations A collective security organization founded in 1919 after World War I. The League ended in 1946 and was replaced by the *United Nations*.

less developed countries (LDCs) Countries at a relatively low level of economic development.

linkage The linking of cooperation on one issue to interactions on a second issue.

mercantilism An economic doctrine based on a belief that military power and economic influence complemented each other; applied especially to colonial empires in the sixteenth through eighteenth centuries. Mercantilist policies favored the mother country over its colonies and over its competitors.

MFN status See **most-favored nation status**.

military-industrial complex An alliance between military leaders and the industries that benefit from international conflict, such as arms manufacturers.

MNC See **multinational corporation**.

monetary policy An important tool of national governments to influence broad macroeconomic conditions such as unemployment, inflation, and economic growth. Typically, governments alter their monetary policies by changing national interest rates or exchange rates.

Montreal Protocol An international treaty, signed in 1989, that is designed to protect the ozone layer by phasing out the production of a number of CFCs and other chemical compounds.

most-favored nation (MFN) status A status established by most modern trade agreements guaranteeing that the signatories will extend to each other any favorable trading terms offered in agreements with third parties.

multinational corporation (MNC) An enterprise that operates in a number of countries, with production or service facilities outside its country of origin.

national interests Interests attributed to the state itself, usually security and power.

Nationally Determined Contribution (NDC) The commitment each party to the Paris Agreement makes as to how they will contribute to reducing the threat of global warming.

NATO See **North Atlantic Treaty Organization**.

NDC See **Nationally Determined Contribution**.

nonderogable rights Rights that cannot be suspended for any reason, including at times of public emergency.

nonexcludable goods Goods that, if available to be consumed by one actor, cannot be prevented from being consumed by other actors as well. Compare *nonrival goods*.

nonrival goods Goods for which consumption by one actor does not diminish the quantity available for others. Compare *nonexcludable goods*.

nontariff barriers to trade Obstacles to imports other than tariffs (trade taxes). Examples include restrictions on the number of products that can be imported (quantitative restrictions, or quotas); regulations that favor domestic over imported products; and other measures that discriminate against foreign goods or services. "Buy American" laws that govern what state and local governments can buy, for example, are an implicit — but nontariff — obstacle to the purchase of imports.

norms Standards of behavior for actors with a given identity; norms define what actions are "right" or appropriate under particular circumstances.

norms entrepreneurs Individuals or groups that seek to advance principled standards of behavior for states and other actors.

norms life cycle A three-stage model of how norms diffuse within a population and achieve a taken-for-granted status.

North Atlantic Treaty Organization (NATO) An alliance formed in 1949 among the United States, Canada, and most of the states of Western Europe in response to the threat posed by the Soviet Union. The alliance requires the members to consider an attack on any one of them as an attack on all. Compare *Warsaw Pact*.

obligation The degree to which states are legally bound by an international rule. High-obligation rules must be performed in good faith and, if breached, require reparations to the injured party.

oligopoly A situation in which a market or industry is dominated by a few firms.

outbidding A strategy of terrorist attacks designed to demonstrate superior capability and commitment relative to other groups devoted to the same cause.

outside options The alternatives to bargaining with a specific actor.

P5 See **permanent five**.

Paris Agreement An agreement negotiated under the UNFCCC in 2015, signed by 197 countries, and entered into force in 2016. It was the first agreement to require commitments for the control of greenhouse gas emissions from all signatories.

Pax Britannica "British Peace," a century-long period, beginning with Napoleon's defeat at Waterloo in 1815 and ending with the outbreak of World War I in 1914, during which Britain's economic and diplomatic influence contributed to economic openness and relative peace.

peace-enforcement operation A military operation in which force is used to make and/or enforce peace among warring parties that have not agreed to end their fighting. Compare *peacekeeping operation*.

Peace of Westphalia The settlement that ended the Thirty Years' War in 1648; often said to have created the modern state system because it included a general recognition of the principles of sovereignty and nonintervention.

peacekeeping operation An operation in which troops and observers are deployed to monitor a cease-fire or peace agreement. Compare *peace-enforcement operation*.

permanent five (P5) The five permanent members of the UN Security Council: the United States, Great Britain, France, Russia (formerly the Soviet Union), and China.

POCs See **prisoners of conscience**.

portfolio investment Investment in a foreign country via the purchase of stocks (equities), bonds, or other financial instruments. Portfolio investors do not exercise managerial control of the foreign operation. Compare *foreign direct investment*.

power The ability of Actor A to get Actor B to do something that B would otherwise not do; the ability to get the other side to make concessions and to avoid having to make concessions oneself.

precision The degree to which international legal obligations are fully specified. More precise rules narrow the scope for reasonable interpretation.

preemptive war A war fought with the anticipation that an attack by the other side is imminent. Compare *preventive war*.

preventive war A war fought with the intention of preventing an adversary from becoming stronger in the future. Preventive wars arise because a state whose power is increasing cannot commit not to exploit that power in future bargaining interactions. Compare *preemptive war*.

primary products Raw materials and agricultural products, typically unprocessed or only slightly processed. The primary sectors are distinguished from secondary sectors (industry) and tertiary sectors (services).

prisoners of conscience (POCs) Individuals imprisoned solely because of the peaceful expression of their beliefs. The term was coined by the human rights organization Amnesty International.

protectionism The imposition of barriers to restrict imports.

provocation A strategy of terrorist attacks intended to provoke the target government into making a disproportionate response that alienates moderates in the terrorists' home society or in other sympathetic audiences.

proxy wars Conflicts in which two opposing states "fight" by supporting opposite sides in a war, such as the government and rebels in a third state.

public goods Products that are nonexcludable and nonrival in consumption, such as national defense or clean air or water. Compare *common-pool resources*.

quantitative restriction (quota) A limit placed on the amount of a particular good that is allowed to be imported.

quota See **quantitative restriction**.

rally effect The tendency for people to become more supportive of their country's government in response to dramatic international events, such as crises or wars.

recession A sharp slowdown in the rate of economic growth and economic activity. Compare *depression*.

reciprocity In international trade relations, a mutual agreement to lower tariffs and other barriers to trade. Reciprocity involves an implicit or explicit arrangement for one government to exchange trade-policy concessions with another.

regional trade agreements (RTAs) Agreements among three or more countries in a region to reduce barriers to trade among themselves.

resolve The willingness of an actor to endure costs in order to acquire a particular good.

Ricardo-Viner (specific-factors) model A model of trade relations that emphasizes the sector in which factors of production are employed rather than the nature of the factor

itself. This differentiates it from the Heckscher-Ohlin theory, for which the nature of the factor — labor, land, capital — is the principal consideration.

risk-return trade-off In crisis bargaining, the trade-off between trying to get a better deal and trying to avoid a war.

RTAs See **regional trade agreements**.

Security Council See **United Nations Security Council**.

security dilemma A dilemma that arises when efforts that states make to defend themselves cause other states to feel less secure; can lead to arms races and war because of the fear of being attacked.

separatist An actor that seeks to create an independent state on territory carved from an existing state. Compare *irredentist*.

sovereign lending Loans from private financial institutions in one country to sovereign governments in other countries.

sovereignty The expectation that states have legal and political supremacy — or ultimate authority — within their territorial boundaries.

specific-factors model See **Ricardo-Viner model**.

spoiling A strategy of terrorist attacks intended to sabotage a prospective peace between the target and moderate leadership from the terrorists' home society.

state A central authority with the ability to make and enforce laws, rules, and decisions within a specified territory.

Stolper-Samuelson theorem The theorem that protection benefits the scarce factor of production. This view flows from the Heckscher-Ohlin theory: if a country imports goods that make intensive use of its scarce factor, then limiting imports will help that factor. So in a labor-scarce country, labor benefits from protection and loses from trade liberalization.

TAN See **transnational advocacy network**.

tariff A tax imposed on imports. Tariffs raise the domestic price of the imported good and may be applied for the purpose of protecting domestic producers from foreign competition.

terms of trade The relationship between a country's export prices and its import prices.

terrorism The use or threatened use of violence against noncombatant targets by individuals or nonstate groups for political ends. Compare *civil war*.

theory A logically consistent set of statements that explains a phenomenon of interest.

trade barriers Government limitations on the international exchange of goods. Examples include tariffs, quantitative restrictions (quotas), import licenses, requirements that governments buy only domestically produced goods, and health and safety standards that discriminate against foreign goods.

tragedy of the commons A problem that occurs when a resource is open to all, without limit. No one has an incentive to conserve, because others would use the resource in the meantime, so the resource suffers degradation.

transnational advocacy network (TAN) A set of individuals and nongovernmental organizations acting in pursuit of a normative objective.

Treaty of Versailles The peace treaty between the Allies and Germany that formally ended World War I on June 28, 1919.

UDHR See **Universal Declaration of Human Rights**.

UN See **United Nations**.

UNFCCC See **United Nations Framework Convention on Climate Change**.

United Nations (UN) A collective security organization founded in 1945 after World War II. With over 190 members, the UN includes all recognized states. Compare *League of Nations*.

United Nations Framework Convention on Climate Change (UNFCCC) An international agreement enacted in 1992, and entered into force in 1994, that provides an overall framework for intergovernmental efforts on climate change.

United Nations Security Council (UNSC) The main governing body of the UN, which has the authority to identify threats to international peace and security and to prescribe the organization's response, including military and/or economic sanctions.

Universal Declaration of Human Rights (UDHR) A declaration, adopted by the UN General Assembly in 1948, that defines a "common standard of achievement for all peoples" and forms the foundation of modern human rights law.

UNSC See **United Nations Security Council**.

veto power The ability to prevent the passage of a measure through a unilateral act, such as a single negative vote.

Vienna Convention A framework convention adopted in 1985 to regulate activities, especially emissions of CFCs, that damage the ozone layer.

war An event involving the organized use of military force by at least two parties that reaches a minimum threshold of severity.

Warsaw Pact A military alliance formed in 1955 to bring together the Soviet Union and its Cold War allies in Eastern Europe and elsewhere; dissolved on March 31, 1991, as the Cold War ended. Compare *North Atlantic Treaty Organization*.

Washington Consensus An array of policy recommendations generally advocated by developed-country economists and policy makers starting in the 1980s, including trade liberalization, privatization, openness to foreign investment, and restrictive monetary and fiscal policies.

World Bank An important international institution that provides loans at below-market interest rates to developing countries, typically to enable them to carry out development projects.

World Trade Organization (WTO) An institution created in 1995 to succeed the GATT and to govern international trade relations. The WTO encourages and polices the multilateral reduction of barriers to trade, and it oversees the resolution of trade disputes. Compare *General Agreement on Tariffs and Trade*.

WTO See **World Trade Organization**.

Credits

CHAPTER 1   Pages 2–3: Roy Miles Fine Paintings/Bridgeman Images; **p. 6:** North Wind Pictures Archives/Alamy Stock Photo; **p. 9:** North Wind Picture Archives/Alamy Stock Photo; **p. 22:** © Hulton-Deutsch Collection/CORBIS/Corbis via Getty Images; **p. 29:** Swim Ink 2, LLC/CORBIS/Corbis via Getty Images; **p. 31:** Sueddeutsche Zeitung Photo/Alamy Stock Photo; **p. 35:** Michele Tantussi/Getty Images.

CHAPTER 2   Pages 42–43: Martyn Aim/Corbis News/Getty Images; **p. 48:** North Wind Picture Archives/Alamy Stock Photo; **p. 52:** REX/Shutterstock; **p. 61:** Kevin Coombs/REUTERS/Newscom; **p. 66:** Imagine China/Newscom; **p. 71:** UPI/Kazem Ghane/Irna News Agency/Newscom; **p. 76:** AP Photo/Jose Luis Magana.

CHAPTER 3   Pages 88–89: AP Photo/Channi Anand; **p. 95:** Bassam Khabieh/REUTERS/Newscom; **p. 103:** Lucas Jackson/REUTERS/Newscom; **p. 104:** Kyodo via AP Images; **p. 105:** Xinhua/Alamy Stock Photo; **p. 108:** AP Photo/Pavel Golovkin; **p. 114:** © CORBIS/Corbis via Getty Images; **p. 119:** AP Photo/Kyodo News; **p. 126:** Bettmann/Getty Images; **p. 128:** Buddy Mays/Alamy Stock Photo; **p. 133:** Wang Qingqin Xinhua News Agency/Newscom.

CHAPTER 4   Pages 138–139: Press Association via AP Images; **p. 142:** Bettmann/Getty Images; **p. 144:** Doug Wilson/CORBIS/Corbis via Getty Images; **p. 148:** Sven Nackstrand/AFP/Getty Images; **p. 151:** Horacio Villalobos/Corbis via Getty Images; **p. 159:** Arko Datta/AFP/Getty Images; **p. 163:** AP Photo/Tsvangirayi Mukwazhi; **p. 176:** Federico Parra/AFP/Getty Images; **p. 177:** Chris Wattie/REUTERS/Newscom; **p. 182:** AP Photo/Fredrik Persson; **p. 183:** Mohamed Abd El Ghany/REUTERS/Newscom.

CHAPTER 5   Pages 186–187: Deco/Alamy Stock Photo; **p. 191:** AP Photo/Koji Sasahara; **p. 196:** Jung Yeon-Je/AFP/Getty Images; **p. 202:** © Hulton-Deutsch Collection/CORBIS/Corbis via Getty Images; **p. 209:** Pacome Pabandji/AFP/Getty Images; **p. 212:** Kyodo News via Getty Images; **p. 214:** Janine Wiedel Photolibrary/Alamy Stock Photo; **p. 225:** AP Photo/Sayyid Azim; **p. 227:** Collectiva/Alamy Stock Photo.

CHAPTER 6   Pages 236–237: The Asahi Shimbun via Getty Images; **p. 245:** Abdelhak Senna/AFP/Getty Images; **p. 247:** Rana Sajid Hussain/Pacific Press/Newscom; **p. 248:** Mike Goldwater/Alamy Stock Photo; **p. 250:** Fethi Belaid/AFP/Getty Images; **p. 254:** US Army Photo/Alamy Stock Photo; **p. 256:** STRINGER/REUTERS/Newscom; **p. 261:** Scott Nelson/Getty Images; **p. 263:** Abdulmonam Eassa/AFP/Getty Images; **p. 273:** Ratib Al Safadi/Anadolu Agency/Getty Images; **p. 274:** Handout/Alamy Stock Photo; **p. 277:** Belgian Federal Police via AP; **p. 285:** American Photo Archive/Alamy Stock Photo; **p. 287:** Hristo Rusev/NurPhoto/Sipa USA/Newscom.

CHAPTER 7   Pages 294–295: Manan Vatsyayana/AFP/Getty Images; **p. 298:** Bettmann/Getty Images; **p. 300:** Choo Youn-Kong/AFP/Getty Images; **p. 302:** SeongJoon Cho/Bloomberg via Getty Images; **p. 307:** Diego Giudice/Bloomberg via Getty Images; **p. 311:** Yermolov/Shutterstock; **p. 316:** Karol Serewis/Gallo Images Poland/Getty Images; **p. 320:** Kumar Sriskandan/Alamy Stock Photo; **p. 323:** Marcos Brindicci/REUTERS/Newscom; **p. 326:** Fabrice Coffrini/AFP/Getty Images; **p. 332:** Carl Court/Getty Images; **p. 333:** Scott Olson/Getty Images; **p. 335:** Lisa Wiltse/Bloomberg via Getty Images.

CHAPTER 8   Pages 346–347: Alejandro Pagni/AFP/Getty Images; **p. 352:** Matt Cardy/Getty Images; **p. 355:** Ahmed Jallanzo/Epa/REX/Shutterstock; **p. 359:** Patricia De Melo Moreira/AFP/Getty Images; **p. 362:** AP Photo/Charles Dharapak; **p. 364:** Saul Loeb/AFP/Getty Images; **p. 365:** Felipe Amilibia/AFP/Getty Images; **p. 367:** Gerardo C. Lerner/Shutterstock; **p. 369:** Jeff Malet Photography/Newscom; **p. 373:** Voishmel/AFP/Getty Images; **p. 380:** AP Photo/Wisconsin State Journal, Craig Schreiner.

CHAPTER 9   Pages 386–387: John Macdougall/AFP/Getty Images; **p. 392:** Kristoffer Tripplaar/Sipa USA/Newscom; **p. 396:** Xinhua/Alamy Stock Photo; **p. 399:** Kate Holt/Bloomberg via Getty Images; **p. 400:** Kevin LaMarque/REUTERS/Newscom; **p. 401:** Lou-Foto/Alamy Stock Photo; **p. 407:** Everett Collection; **p. 408:** Alfred Eisenstaedt/The LIFE Picture Collection/Getty Images; **p. 414:** STR/REUTERS/Newscom; **p. 419:** Jon Nazca/REUTERS/Newscom.

CHAPTER 10   Pages 424–425: Tom Stoddart/Getty Images; **p. 428:** Mtcurado/iStock Unreleased/Getty Images Plus; **p. 430:** Pacific Press/Alamy Stock Photo; **p. 435:** STR/REUTERS/Newscom; **p. 436:** Sarin Images/GRANGER — All rights reserved; **p. 437:** GRANGER/GRANGER — All rights reserved; **p. 439:** GRANGER/GRANGER — All rights reserved; **p. 441:** De Agostini Picture Library/G. Dagli Orti/Bridgeman Images; **p. 443:** Joerg Boethling/Alamy Stock Photo; **p. 449:** SeongJoon Cho/Bloomberg via Getty Images; **p. 454:** Sia Kambou/AFP/Getty Images; **p. 455:** Renaud Rebardy/Alamy Stock Photo; **p. 456:** Carlos Barria-China Stringer Net/REUTERS/Newscom.

CHAPTER 11   Pages 462–463: AP Photo/Brennan Linsley; **p. 466:** Pierre Crom/Getty Images; **p. 469:** Popperfoto/Getty Images; **p. 471:** Richard Cooke/Alamy Stock Photo; **p. 477:** AP Photo/Juan Carlos Hernandez; **p. 478:** National Archives; **p. 480:** NurPhoto/NurPhoto via Getty Images; **p. 481:** AP Photo/Beatrix Stampfli; **p. 487:** Graeme Robertson/Getty Images; **p. 493:** Bodo Marks/AFP/Getty Images.

CHAPTER 12   Pages 498–499: AP Photo/Ben Curtis; **p. 502:** Jim West/Alamy Stock Photo; **p. 504:** Laurent Fievet/AFP/Getty Images; **p. 508:** Brooks Kraft/CORBIS/Corbis via Getty Images; **p. 510:** Karim Sahib/AFP/Getty Images; **p. 511:** Mikhail Metzel/TASS via Getty Images; **p. 514:** Bettmann/Getty Images; **p. 517:** Zakir Hossain Chowdhury/NurPhoto via Getty Images; **p. 519:** Xinhua/Tim Ireland via Getty Images; **p. 527:** Olga Besnard/Shutterstock; **p. 532:** Mohamed Hammi/SIPA/Newscom; **p. 536:** Jerry Lampen/AFP/GettyImages.

CHAPTER 13   Pages 540–541: Mamunur Rashid/Alamy Stock Photo; **p. 544:** Terry Whittaker/FLPA/ImageBroker/REX/Shutterstock; **p. 547:** Jeremy Sutton-Hibbert/Alamy Stock Photo; **p. 554:** Jure Makovec/AFP/Getty Images; **p. 555:** Wk1003mike/Shutterstock; **p. 558:** REUTERS/Norihiko Shirouzu/Newscom; **p. 560:** Ashley Cooper/Alamy Stock Photo; **p. 566:** Dennis MacDonald/Alamy Stock Photo; **p. 567:** Eye Ubiquitous/UIG via Getty Images; **p. 571:** Luong Thai Linh/EPA/REX/Shutterstock; **p. 573:** Vince Streano/Getty Images; **p. 577:** Geoffroy Van Der Hasselt/Anadolu Agency/Getty Images.

CHAPTER 14   Pages 584–585: Jens Buettner/REX/Shutterstock; **p. 591:** ITAR-TASS Photo Agency/Alamy Stock Photo; **p. 597:** Rizwan Tabassum/AFP/Getty Images; **p. 603:** Kyodo via AP Images; **p. 607:** Li Tang/China News Service/VCG/Getty Images; **p. 615:** Xinhua/Alamy Stock Photo; **p. 621:** John Trax/Alamy Stock Photo; **p. 625:** Craig F. Walker/The Boston Globe via Getty Images; **p. 629:** Jose Palazon/REUTERS/Newscom; **p. 632:** AP Photo/Jon Elswick.

Index

Note: Page numbers in *italics* refer to illustrations.

coercive, xxxiii, 97, 99, 102–3, 603–6
crisis, 97
debt and, 360
definition of, xxix, 55
democracy and, 176–79
duration of interstate wars and, 124, *124*
first-strike advantages and, *123*
foreign investment and, 352, 363
globalization and, 624
between host countries and MNCs, 375
international, 166–68, *167*, 565, 568
international law and, 467, 470
interstate, 194–96
in Iraq War, 55
in Kashmir conflict, 159
norms and, 491
with North Korea, 99, 104–5
outside options and, 66–67
over future environment, 555, 557,
    568–70
as positive-sum game, 55
power and, 63–64, 609–11, *612*, 613
reversion outcome and, 64, 67–68
rising powers and, 609–13
rules and, 76–78
status quo and, *102*
terrorism as failure of, 274–79
war and, 55, 96–101, *100–101*, 102–3,
    118–20, *121*, 135
war as failure of, 78–79, 90, 91, 131,
    257–61
winners and losers at, 63–68
as zero-sum game, 55
bargaining range, 140, 153–54, 166–67,
    167, 595
power shifts and, *121*, 135, 609–13, *612*
rally effect and, *153*
war and, 99
Barings Bank, collapse of, 405
Barnett, Michael N., 64n, 193n
Barringer, William H., 296n
Barsoom, Peter N., 77n, 472n
Basel Convention on the Control of
    Transboundary Movements of
    Hazardous Wastes and Their
    Disposal, 548
Bashir, Omar Hassan al-, 468, 515
Basic Law, Israel (1980), 128–29
Basque separatists, 277, 280
Bates, Robert, 431n
Batista, Fulgencio, 27
Battle of the Sexes game, 85n
Baum, Matthew, 434n
Bayoumy, Yara, 606n
Becker, Sascha O., 627n
Beehner, Lionel, 264n
Beijing, 9

Beijing Conference. *See* United Nations
    Conference on Women (1995)
Belarus, 577, 601, 602
Belgian Congo, 440
Belgium, 398
    terrorist attacks in, 242, *277*
    in Treaty of Lucarno, 202
    in World War I, 19, 126
Ben Ali, Zine al-Abidine, *250*
Benedick, Richard Elliot, 551n, 571, 572n
Benghazi, Libya, 226, *227*
Berger-Levraut, Nancy, 514n
Berlin, 204, 405
Berlin airlift (1949), 26–27
Berlin Brigade, 204
Berlin Crisis (1961), 116
Berlin Wall, 27, *31*, 32, 630
Berman, Eli, 270n, 279n
Bernard, Andrew B., 311n
Betts, Richard K., 158n
Biddle, Stephen, 265n
bilateral investment treaties (BIT), 377
Bill of Rights, U.S., 516
bin Laden, Osama, 34, 90, 103, 256, 272,
    275–76, 289
biodiversity, 549, 564–65, 576
biofuels, 559
biological weapons, 43, 44, 70, 586, 591,
    594, 599
BIS (Bank for International Settlements),
    361
BIT (bilateral investment treaties), 377
Biya, Paul, 526
Black, David, 499n
Blomberg, S. Brock, 398n
blood diamonds, 252, 267
Bloom, David, 427n
Bloom, Mia M., 283n
body of rules, international law as, 465
Boer War (1898–1902), 156
Boko Haram, 242, 252
Bolch, Tobias, 566n
Bolivia, *335*, 457, *560*
Bolton, John R., 535n
boomerang model, 488, *489*, 529–30
border walls, 629, *629*, 630, *630*
Borghard, Erica D., 177n, 178n
Bosco, David, 535n
Bosnia-Herzegovina, 222–24, 231, 233, 254
Bosnian war, 208, 228, 519
    ethnic cleansing in, 222
    peacekeeping operations in, 224
    Srebrenica massacre in, 224
    U.N. peacekeepers in, 223–24
Boston Marathon terrorist attack (2013),
    273
Botswana, 428, *428*, 458

Bowles, Samuel, 517n
Boyer, Mark A., 149n
Brandt, Patrick T., 270n
Braumoeller, Bear F., 130n
Brazil
    agricultural specialization in, 297
    borrowing of, 358
    economic growth in, 28, 592
    effort to obtain permanent seat on
        UNSC, 592
    environmental policies, 567
    financial crisis in, 366, 419
    floating currency, 398
    foreign investment in, 349
    forested land area, 565
    in Group of 20, 452
    gun laws in, 485
    ICC and, 536
    ISI in, 447
    in Mercosur, *323*, 327
    nuclear program of, 602
    political prisoners in, 509
    trade in, 305
    Volkswagen in, 371, 372
Bretton Woods system, 317, 325n, 354, 388,
    402–3, 404, *408*, 421
    Cold War and, 24–25
    collaboration and, 406, 408–9
    definition of, 392
    gold standard and, 392, 402
    IMF established by, 361
brinksmanship, 27n, 113–14, 116–17
Brody, Richard A., 150n
Brooks, Stephen G., 131n, 162n
Brown, David S., 434n
Broz, J. Lawrence, 358n
Brussels airport attack, *277*
Bryan, William Jennings, 406, 407
Buchanan, Patrick, 357
Buckley, Chris, 553n
Budjeryn, Mariana, 598n
Bueno de Mesquita, Bruce, 174n, 175n
Bueno de Mesquita, Ethan, 276n, 280n
Buhaug, Halvard, 243n, 253n
Bulgaria, 18, 411
Bull, Hedley, 465n
Bull, Keith, 548n
Bullock, Allan, 148n
Bumiller, Elizabeth, 97n
"bunker busting" bombs, as alternative to
    nuclear weapons, 477
bureaucracy
    definition of, 146
    military and, 157–58, 160
Burkina Faso, 358, 466
Burnside, Craig, 455n
Burundi, *225*

Tibet and, 94, 187, 188, 213–14, 248
trade specialization and, 300, 301
U.S.-Taiwan relationship and, 115, 199, 434, 606–7, 613
wages in, 374
world trade and, 308, 319, 332, 623, 633
China, Republic of, 22, 158. *See also* Taiwan
Chiozza, Giacomo, 152n
chlorine, ozone and, 550
chlorofluorocarbons (CFCs), 549, 550–51, 557–59, 574, 578, 579
Chong, Howard, 568n
Christensen, Thomas, 201n
Christians and Christianity, 9, 247, 248
CIA. *See* Central Intelligence Agency
Cingranelli, David L., 526n
civil war, 229, 236–68, 290
1816-2016, *244*
2010-2016, *240–41*
in Afghanistan, 95
as bargaining failure, 257–61
casualty threshold for, 239
in Congo (DRC), 244–45
country-level factors in, 252–53
definition of, 91, 239
drugs and, 252
efforts to prevent, 266–68
factors inciting, 245–57
financing, 252, 267
group-level factors in, 250–52
human rights violations in, 513, 519, 520, 521
from indivisibilities, 260–61
international factors in, 254–55, 257
Iraq, 95
irredentism in, 246
length of, 282
peacekeeping missions and, 209
post-1945, 590
refugees from, 593, 626, 627
regime type and, 252–53
in Rwanda, 244–45
separatism as cause of, 246
spillover effects, 243–44
strategies, 261–66
in Syria, 256
terrorism and, 242, 282
Civil War, U.S., 3, 246, 261–62
Clarke, Harold D., 147n
Clean Development Mechanism (CDM), 553
climate, 427
climate change, 64–65, 469, 540–72. *See also* global warming
conflict and, 556, *556*
costs of, 566–67, 579

Earth Summit and, 576
glacial meltwater, *560*, 566
problems of cooperation on, 543–49, 552–55, 578–81
special interests and, 484
Clinton, Bill, and administration, 357, 535, 618
Clinton, Hillary, 617n
CMEA (Council for Mutual Economic Assistance; Comecon), 25
coal industry, 559, 560, 564
cocaine trade, 252
coercion, xxxvi, 65–66, *66*, 279–80
coercive bargaining, xxxiii, 97, 99, 102–3. *See also* crisis bargaining
coercive diplomacy, 97–102, 110–11
coercive disarmament, 603–6
coercive language, war and, 111–17
Cohen, Benjamin J., 165n
COIN (counterinsurgency), 264–65
Colantone, Italo, 627n
Colaresi, Michael, 181n
Cold War, 23–31, 49, 318
alliances in, *26*, 202–5, 596
anticolonialism, *29*
arms race in, 59–60, 70, 71, 492
Berlin airlift in, 26–27
Berlin Crisis (1961), 116
credibility and, 109–10
Cuban missile crisis and, 26, *27*, *114*
decolonization and, 28–30
democracies during, 180
economic interests and, 162, 303, 334, 446
end of, *31*, 31–32, 206
European Union and, 320
human rights and, 506
Korean conflict and, 111–13
Long Peace and, 202–5
military advice in, 158
NATO and, 206, 211
nonaligned movement in, 30
NPT and, 601
nuclear brinksmanship and, 113, 290
nuclear standoff, 129–30
nuclear weapons in, 3, 25–27, 59–60, 284, 595, 598, 599
onset of, 23–24
power and, 64
power shifts from, 613
proxy wars in, 28, 255, 590
rise of Third World in, 30, 427n
superpower blocs in, 24–25, 587–88
thaw in, 30–31
U.N. and, 216–18, *218*
U.S. interventions in Latin America during, 165

U.S. oil interests and, 142
U.S. relations with dictatorships and, 183
U.S.-Soviet rivalry in, 96, 203, 216–18, 302, 610
Cole, Wade M., 512n
collaboration
Bretton Woods system and, 406, 408–9
collective action problems and, 60
cooperation and, 58–59
definition of, 58
in monetary relations, 403, 406, 408–9, 421
public goods problem and, 60
in trade, 321
collective action problems, 145, 238, 251, 262–63, 313–14, 322, 331
collaboration and, 60
collective security organizations and, 210–14
cooperation and, 60, 547–49, 552
environment and, 61, 545–47, 555, 579–80
in foreign policy decisions, 145
group size and, 61, 431, 434, 547–48, 579
collective security organizations, xxx, 188, 205–31. *See also* alliances; United Nations
alliances compared with, 205
bargaining interests and, 209–10
civil war and, 209
collective action problem and, 210–14
commitment problems of, 209
costs of intervention and, 214
definition of, 208
dilemmas of, 210–12
free-rider problem and, 211
institutional responses to challenges of, 212–14
joint decision-making problem and, 210–14
mechanisms of, 208–10
peacekeeping and (*See* peacekeeping operations)
primary purpose of, 208
promoting peace and, 209
threat of intervention and, 208–10
veto power and, 212–13
Collier, Paul, 245n, 253n
Colombia, 252, 289–90
colonialism, 9, 502
colonial possessions (1914), *16–17*
decolonization and, 28–30, 132
development hampered by, 430–31, 439, *439*, 440–42
end of, 4
mercantilism and, 5–8, *6*
Pax Britannica and, 14–15
in Western Hemisphere, 436–37

Ge, Mengpin, 559n
Geely, *352*
GE (General Electric), 372
Gelpi, Christopher, 160n
General Agreement on Tariffs and Trade
    (GATT), 25, 296, 325, 470, 587, 588,
    606
General Confederation of Workers
    (Guatemala), *142*
general deterrence, 103
General Electric, 312
General Motors (GM), 312, 355, 377–78
Geneva Conventions, 463, 464, 467, 513n
    compliance constituencies and, 475
    enforcement limitations of, 471
    high-obligation law and, 469
    norms and, 485
    POWs and, 473–74
Geneva protests against WTO, *326*
genocide, xxvii, 514–15, 518
    Armenian, 468, 514
    convention on, 502–3, 508
    cooperation and, xxxvi, 635
    crimes against humanity and, 468
    in Darfur, *214*, 225, 260, 515, 520
    definition of, 208
    ethnic differences and, 247
    Holocaust as, 23, 514
    humanitarian interventions, 209, 226,
      230, 479
    Rwandan, 34, 224–25, 244, 245, *462–63*,
      464
    Srebrenica massacre, 515
Genocide Convention, 502–3, 508
Georgia, 207, 248, 535n, 593
German Democratic Republic (East
    Germany), 203–5
Germany, Federal Republic of (West
    Germany), 168, 191, 203–5, 320, 410
Germany, Imperial, 120, 126, 195, 610, 613
    colonialism and, 14, 15
    Franco-Russian alliance against, 192
    gold standard and, 405
    loss in World War I, 175
    prelude to World War I and, 199
    rise of, 15, 18, 613
    in Triple Alliance, 200–201
    in World War I, 18, 19
Germany, Nazi, 613
    alliances, 204–5
    economy and, 19, 22
    Holocaust, 23, 468, 501, 502, 514
    in Molotov-Ribbentrop Pact, 189, 196
    nuclear weapons and, 599
    Nuremberg trials and, 468
    in Pact of Steel, 189
    Poland and, 90, 96, 191

Rhineland remilitarized by, 111
    rise of Hitler in, 181, 201
    Soviet Union and, 192–93
    Sudetenland crisis and, 202
    in World War II, 22–23, 168, 180, 201–2
Germany, preunified, 13
Germany, reunified
    anti-immigrant sentiment in, *35*
    BIS and, 361
    effort to obtain permanent seat on
      UNSC, 592
    euro and, 410–11
    fall of Berlin Wall and, 630
    floating rates, 409
    Iraq War opposed by, 206
    Kosovo intervention and, 479
    as lender, 370
    migration to, 378
    NATO and, 206
    populist sentiment in, *584–85*, 585, 586,
      626–27, 628
    post-Cold War, 610–11, 613
    terrorist cells in, 285
    trade barriers of, 335, 613
    trade with China, 615–16
Germany, Weimar, *22*, 213, 324, 406, 416
Gerring, John, *521–23*
Ghana, 30, 336
Ghobarah, Hazem Adam, 290n
Gibler, Douglas M., 189n
Gilpin, Robert, 494n, 608n, 610n
Gintis, Herbert, 517n
Girardin, Luc, 254n
Gizenga, Antoine, *29*
glasnost, 32
Glaspie, April, 110n
Gleditsch, Kristian Skrede, 243n, 247n,
    254n, 255n
Gleditsch, Nils Petter, 89n, 169n, 252n,
    556, *556*
Glennon, Michael J., 472n
global climate change. *See* climate change
Global Environmental Facility, 577
Global Fund to Fight AIDS, Tuberculosis
    and Malaria, *454*, 454–55
global governance, 464
globalization, 4, 13–14, 33, 37–39, 295–96,
    301–2, 305–6, 452–53, *589*, 619–34
    backlash against, 38, 315–16, 332–33,
      364–65, 376, 380, 381, 453, 456–57,
      586, 593, 619–20, 625–34
    challenges to Western economic
      predominance and, 38–39
    China and, 615–16
    conflict and, 622
    decline of war and, 132–33
    defined, 619

development and, 449–50, 453, 456–57,
    622–25
    economic costs of, 622–25
    environmental issues and, 557–58
    financial relations and, 348
    global governance and, 464
    IMF and attitudes toward, 358
    inequality and, xxv–xxvi, 530
    of international finance, 348
    international trade system and, 631–34
    migration and, 378, 382, 621–22
    nationalism and, 131, 625–31
    resistance to, in developed countries,
      623–24
    resistance to, in developing world,
      624–25
    reversibility of, 621–22
    state and, 48
    theory and history of, 609–13
    winners and losers in, 308, 318, 590–91,
      593, 620, 622–25, 632, 634
    world economy and, 531–34, 589, 620
    WTO and, 327, 330
Global South, 427n
global warming, 544–45, *545*. *See also*
    climate change
    science of, 542
    TANs and, 483, 484
Global War on Terror, 285–87, 500, 510, 513
GM (General Motors), 312, 355, 377–78
Goddard, Stacie E., 129n
Goemans, Hein E., 152n, 155n, 175n
Goertz, Gary, 131n
Golan Heights, 93, 210
gold, mining of, 436
Goldblatt, David, 494n
Goldman, Francisco, 514n
gold standard, 13–14, 388, 402–3, 404, 406,
    408–9, 421
    banking and, 406, 408–9
    Barings collapse and, 405
    Bretton Woods agreement and, 392, 402
    costs of, 406
    definition of, 391
    fixed exchange rates and, 391, 392
    France and, 405
    Great Depression and, 406
    history of, 405–6
    Imperial Germany and, 405
    monetary relations and, 405–6
    Nixon's ending of, 409
    opposition to, 393
    stability of, 406
    trade and, 392
    United Kingdom and, 405
    U.S. and, 391, *392*
    U.S. dollar and, 25

misperceptions, war caused by, 92
misrepresentation, war and, 109–11
Mississippi, 358
Mitchell, Ronald B., 573n
Mitchell, Sara McLaughlin, 152n
Mitra, Devashish, 315n
MNCs. *See* multinational corporations
Moene, Karl, 438n
Mohammed, Prophet of Islam, 128
Molina, Mario J., 550n
Molotov-Ribbentrop pact (1939), 189, 196
monarchies, 144
monetary policy, definition of, 391
monetary relations, 386–421. *See also* Bretton
    Woods system; currency; euro
    absence of international system and,
        402, 410, 421
    collaboration and, 403
    commodity standard and, 404
    conflicts of interest and, 399, 402
    cooperation and conflict in, 61, 403,
        420–21
    exchange rates and (*See* exchange rates)
    global nature of, 392
    gold standard and, 405–6
    international monetary regimes and, 404–5
    international order of, 402
    international politics and, 402–11
    national order of, 402
    national paper currency standard and,
        404–5
    Prisoner's Dilemma and, 403
monopolies, 6
Monteiro, Nuno P., 599n
Montreal Protocol (1989), 471, 548, 549,
    550–51, 571, 572, 576, 577, 578, 579
Montzka, Stephen A., 550n
Moravcsik, Andrew, xxxvin, 469n, 515–16
Morgenthau, Hans, xxxii
Morocco, 18, 378, *629*
Morrow, James D., 174n, 175n, 195n,
    473–74, 513n
Morsi, Mohamed, 182, *182*, 183
Morton, David, 485n
most favored nation status (MFN), 325, 618
Mousseau, Michael, 178n
Mozambique, 228
Mubarak, Hosni, 182, 183
Mudde, Cas, 627n
Mueller, John E., 130n, 252n
Mugabe, Robert, *163*
Multilateral Fund, 551
multilateralism, 477, 587–88
multinational corporations (MNCs),
    371–77, 382, 439, 444
    access to local markets and, 372
    conflicts and, 374–76

criticism of, 373
debt crises and, 376
definition of, 371
environment and, 373
expertise and, 373–74
globalization and, 621, 622
host countries' interactions with,
    375–76
host countries' interests in, 373–79
human rights and, 373
labor unions and, 372–73
local politics and, 375
motivation of, 371–73
national sovereignty and, 376
outsourcing and, 372–73
political considerations and, 375
resource location and, 371–72
restrictions on, 376
Mundell-Fleming conditions, 397n
Murdie, Amanda N., 525n
Murphy, Zoeann, 630n
Murray, Williamson, 51n
Musharraf, Pervez, 159
Muslim Brotherhood, 182–83
Muslims, 35, 94, 128–29, 223, 248, 261,
    280–81, 585, 626–27. *See also* Islam
Mussa, Michael, 622n
Mussolini, Benito, 90
Mutua, Makau, 486n
"mutually assured destruction," 132, 595,
    613
Myanmar, 226, *517*
    authoritarianism in, 170
    human rights concerns in, 500

N

NAFTA. *See* North American Free Trade
    Agreement
Nagasaki, 23, *478*, 596
Nagoya Protocol, 573
naming and shaming tactic, 500,
    528, 529
Nanking Massacre, 468
Napoleon I, emperor of the French, 8
Napoleonic Wars (1804–1815), 3, 8
Nash, Eric R., 550n
National Commission on the Disappeared
    (Argentina), 514n
National Front (France), 628
national interests, 47, 49–51, 141–44
nationalism, 14–15, 22, 28, *35*, 36–37, 90,
    126, 131, 147, 181
    populist movements and, *584–85*, 585,
        586, 593, 620, 625–31
    transnational dimensions of, 631
nationally determined contribution
    (NDC), 553

national paper currency standard,
    404–5
National Rifle Association (NRA), 485,
    486
*National Security Strategy for the United
    States of America* (2002), 285, 619
national self-determination, 248–49, 479,
    530
NATO. *See* North Atlantic Treaty
    Organization
natural rights, 501
Nazis. *See* Germany, Nazi
Neate, Rupert, xxvn
negotiation, terrorism and, 289–90
Nepal, 358, 566, 567
Netanyahu, Benjamin, *103*
Netesova, Yulia, 631n
Netherlands, 5, 158, 224
    colonialism and, 15
    euro and, 398
    revolt against Spain, 8
Neumayer, Eric, 525n
New Deal, 504, 506
New England, 7
New International Economic Order
    (NIEO), 30, 451
Newman, Paul A., 550n
New World, 5–7, 13, 14
New York Times, The, 510
New Zealand, 22, 378, 440
NGOs. *See* nongovernmental
    organizations
Nicaragua, 27, 255, 509
Nice truck attack, *236–37*
Nigeria, 242, 252, *435*
Nixon, Richard, 409
Nobel Peace Prize, 482
nonaligned countries, *27*, 30
Non-Aligned Movement, 450–51
nonderogable rights, 508
nonexcludable public goods, 60, 546
nongovernmental organizations (NGOs),
    457
    boomerang model and, 488
    child labor and, 480
    as environmental monitors, 542,
        576–77
    human rights and, 518, 520
nonintervention, principle of, 530
Non-Proliferation Treaty (NPT). *See*
    Treaty on the Non-Proliferation of
    Nuclear Weapons
nonrival in consumption, 60, 546
nonstate actors, 208, 236–91, 598
nontariff barriers, 304
Nordås, Ragnhild, 556n
Nordstrom, Timothy, *587*

Power, Samantha, 224n
POWs (prisoners of war), 473–74
Prasad, Eswar, 348n
Prebisch, Raúl, 442–43, 446, 448
precision, 469–70, 474
preemptive war, 122–23, 125–27, 285–87
press, freedom of, 171, 176
preventive war, 122, 230, 609–10, 618, 634
"price-taker," 343
PRI (Institutional Revolutionary Party, Mexico). *See* Partido Revolucionario Institucional
primary products, 442, 445–46
Prins, Brandon C., 152n
Prisoner's Dilemma, 58–59, 83–84, *84*
    commitment problem and, 118
    cooperation and, 58–59, 68–69, 83–84, 86–87
    in international trade bargaining, 321
    monetary relations and, 403
    tragedy of the commons and, 544
prisoners of conscience (POCs), 509, 512–13
prisoners of war (POWs), 473–74
private goods, 60
privatization, 451, *546*, 620
    environment and, 543–44, 546–47
privileged groups, 61, 322, 549
procedural norms, 476–77
producer surplus, 342–43
production, factors of, 299–302, 380
Progressive, 357
property rights, 429
    cap-and-trade systems, 552–53
Prorok, Alyssa K., 534n
protectionism, 12–13, 75, 298, 304–6, 315–16, 332–33
    agriculture and, 330–31, *331,* 334, 443–45, 632–33
    currency manipulation and, 401
    definition of, 304
    democracy and, 314–15
    development and, 443–44, 447–48
    domestic economy and, 306–18
    environment and, 558
    globalization and, 619
    human rights and, 519
    in India, 318
    Keynes view of, 312
    labor movements and, 309–10
    nationalism and, 633–34
    organization of interests and, 312–14
    quotas and, 304, 307
    redistributive effect and, 307, 586, 632
    Ricardo-Viner model and, 309, 310–11, 622
    specific industries and, 309, 310–11

of steel industry, 295, 308, 310, *311,* 313
    Stolper-Samuelson theorem and, 309–10, 315, 622
    tariffs and, 304–8
Protestants, 247
Protocol 11, 533
provocation (terrorism strategy), 280–81
Proxmire, William, 503
proxy wars, definition of, 255, 590
Prunier, Gerard, 245n
Prussia, 11, 12
pseudodemocracies, 72
public goods, 60–61, 211, 402, 421, 429, 430, 434
    cooperation and, 60
    environment and, 545–47, 550–51, 570, 578
    institutions and, 69
    nonexcludable, 60
    private goods bundled with, 549
    privileged groups and, 61
    types of, 93–96
    undersupply of, 547
Puerto Rico, 517
Putin, Vladimir, *511,* 592, 593, 631
Putnam, Robert D., 141n

Q

Qaddafi, Mu'ammar, 35, 105, 120, 226, 227, 257, 591, 604
Qatar, 326, 451
quantitative restriction, 304
Quinn, Dennis P., 619n
quotas, trade, 304, 307

R

R2P. *See* responsibility to protect (R2P)
Rachman, Gideon, 616n
Rahn, Wendy M., 629n
railroad industry, 9, 13, 373
rain forests, 549, 564–65
rally effect, 150–52, *153*
Ramsar Convention on Wetlands of International Importance, 572
rape, 245. *See also* crimes against humanity
Rasmussen, Chris, 333n
rationality, 269–71, 596
Reagan, Ronald, and administration, 31–32, 70, 551
real effective exchange rate index, 390
realism, xxxi–xxxiv, *xxxii,* xxxvi, 47, 92, 141
rebellion, 245–47. *See also* violence
recession, 356, 367, 393, 413, 416, 419
reciprocity, concept of, 325
reconciliation commissions, 532

Rector, Robert E., 382n
Redding, Stephen J., 311n
redistributive effect, 307, 586, 632
Red Scare (1947–1957), 513
refugee influx, *35,* 244, 378, 381, 519, *584–85,* 585, 593, 629
Regan, Patrick M., 243n
regime change, 95–96, 105, 143, 178, 183
regime types
    civil war and, 253
    global, *172–73*
Regional Comprehensive Economic Partnership, 633
regional trade agreements (RTAs), 32–33, *33,* 327, *328–29,* 330
    human rights and, 519, 536, 537
    international trade and, 326–27
Reguant, Mar, 568n
regulative norms, 477
Reiter, Dan, 65n, 125, 149n, 176n, 268n
religion
    freedom of, 171
    terrorism and, 278–79
    war as caused by, 246, 247
religious freedom, *521*
renewable energy investment, 553, 557, 559, 579–80
renminbi (Chinese currency), 399, 400, 401
Republican Party, U.S., 21, 155, 405, 468, 631, 633
resolve, 66, 107–8, 111–17, 126, 135, 149, 261n
"resource curse," 435, 438
resource location, 371–72
Responsibility to Protect, The (report), 464
responsibility to protect (R2P), 464, 466
    crimes against humanity and, 468
    human rights and, 531
    norms and, xxxvi, 476
    as regulative norm, 477
    soft law and, 471
    sovereignty vs., 479
reversion outcome, 64, 67–68
Revolutionary Armed Forces of Colombia (FARC), 289–90
Reynolds, John M., 566n
Rhineland, 21, 111, 202
Rhodesia. *See* Zimbabwe
Ricardo, David, xxxiv, 340
Ricardo-Viner model (specific factors approach), 309, 310–11, 622
rice industry, 7
Richards, David L., 526n
Richardson, Shaun D., 566n
right to life, 483–84
Riker, James V., 483n